INSPIRE / PLAN / DISCOVER / EXPERIENCE

GERMANY

DK EYEWITNESS

GERMANY

CONTENTS

DISCOVER 6

Welcome to Germany 8
Explore Germany 10
Reasons to Love Germany 12
A Germany Itinerary 16

Germany Your Way 20
A Year in Germany 36
A Brief History 38

EXPERIENCE 46

Eastern Germany   **48**

Berlin 54

Brandenburg 124

Saxony-Anhalt 144

Saxony 162

Thuringia 184

Southern Germany   **202**

Munich 208

Bavaria 242

Baden-Württemberg 288

Western Germany   **328**

Rhineland-Palatinate
and Saarland 334

Hesse 354

North Rhineland-Westphalia ... 380

Northern Germany   **412**

Lower Saxony,
Hamburg and Bremen 418

Schleswig-Holstein 450

Mecklenburg-Vorpommern 464

NEED TO KNOW 484

Before You Go 486
Getting Around 488
Practical Information 492

Index 494
Phrasebook 508
Acknowledgments 511

Left: Gingerbread *(Lebkuchen)* on sale in Munich
Previous page: Bastei rocks, Elbe Sandstone Mountains
Front cover: The Pfarrkirche in Ramsau, Bavaria

DISCOVER

Cologne skyline at sunset

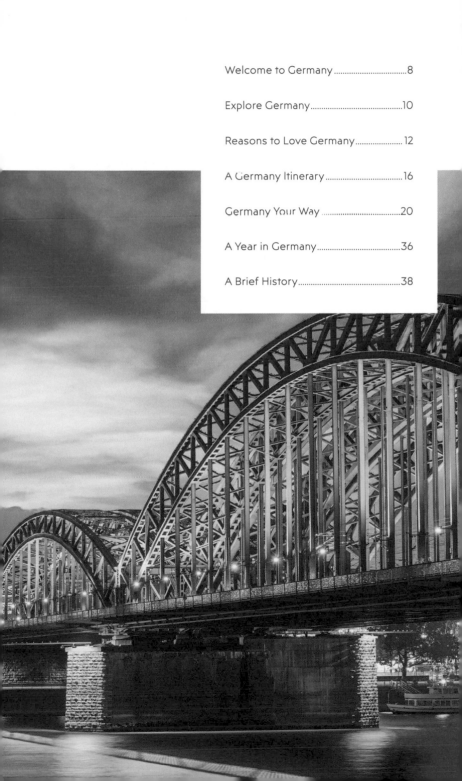

Welcome to Germany 8

Explore Germany 10

Reasons to Love Germany 12

A Germany Itinerary 16

Germany Your Way 20

A Year in Germany 36

A Brief History 38

WELCOME TO
GERMANY

With so many famous sights and hidden gems, Germany offers endless possibilities for adventure, even on a short visit. From breathtaking mountains and stunning valleys to exciting cities and traditional towns, wherever your trip takes you, this DK Eyewitness travel guide is the perfect companion.

1 Boys in traditional Lederhosen hiking in the Bavarian Alps.

2 Christmas shoppers in Heidelberg.

3 The riverside avenue Brühlsche Terrasse, a highlight of Dresden.

In terms of natural beauty, Germany offers windswept beaches and sandy islands along its Baltic coastline, while the south boasts some of Europe's finest lakes as well as deep, mythical forests and the mighty peaks of the Bavarian Alps. In between lie no fewer than 16 national parks, 14 biosphere reserves and close to 100 nature parks. Winding rivers, fairytale castles and medieval churches, plus a network of scenic routes for driving, hiking and cycling, thread them all together.

Germany is also renowned for its prodigious contributions to art, culture and science, which can be experienced through fascinating exhibits at world-class galleries and museums in cities such as Munich, Berlin and Hamburg, as well as smaller, historic towns such as Nürnberg, Dresden and Leipzig. In almost every town visitors will find traces of the country's extraordinary and often turbulent history that spans almost 2,000 years.

It may seem challenging to plan a trip to such a large and varied country, not to mention working out itineraries to fit in all the must-see sights and local secrets. This guidebook breaks down Germany into easily navigable chapters, full of expert local knowledge, ideas for walks and drives, and simple yet comprehensive maps to help you get around. With the Need to Know section providing all the key facts every traveller needs, this Eyewitness guide will help you make the most of all that the country has to offer. Enjoy the book, and enjoy Germany.

EXPLORE
GERMANY

This guide divides Germany into
four distinct regions: Eastern Germany
(p48), Southern Germany *(p202)*,
Western Germany *(p328)* and
Northern Germany *(p412)*.
These regions have been
divided into colour-coded
sightseeing areas, as
shown on this map.

*North
Sea*

Flensburg

Wilhelmshaven

Bremerhaven

Leer

Oldenburg

Bremen

**LOWER SAXONY,
HAMBURG AND BREMEN**
p418

NETHERLANDS

Amsterdam

Osnabrück

Den Haag

Münster

Bielefeld

Rotterdam

Eindhoven

Dortmund

Venlo

Essen

**NORTH RHINE-
WESTPHALIA**
p380

Bruges

Antwerp

Düsseldorf

Leverkusen

Köln

Siegen

HESSE
p354

Brussels

Aachen

Bonn

**WESTERN
GERMANY**

Giessen

BELGIUM

Liège

Lille

Charleroi

Koblenz

Arras

Mainz

Frankfurt
am Main

LUXEM-
BOURG

Trier

**RHINELAND-
PALATINATE AND
SAARLAND**
p334

FRANCE

Mannheim

Heidelberg

Saarbrücken

Heilbronn

Karlsruhe

Stuttgart

Strasbourg

Offenburg

**BADEN-
WÜRTTEMBERG**
p288

Freiburg

Stockach

Mulhouse

Basel

Zurich

SWITZERLAND

EUROPE

*North
Sea*

NORWAY

FINLAND

SWEDEN

DENMARK

*Baltic
Sea*

UNITED
KINGDOM

NETHER-
LANDS

GERMANY

POLAND

BELGIUM

CZECH
REP.

SLOVAKIA

FRANCE

SWITZ.

AUSTRIA

HUNGARY

CROATIA

ROMANIA

SERBIA

BULGARIA

SPAIN

ITALY

GREECE

REASONS TO LOVE
GERMANY

Snow-capped mountains, sandy shores, modern cities and fairytale castles – Germany really does have it all. There are many reasons to visit this beautiful country, but here are the highlights no visitor should miss.

1 ROMANTIC CASTLES

Germany has over 20,000 castles, many of which offer stunning views and glimpses into Germany's past through lavish interiors and historical exhibitions *(p250)*.

REGIONAL DISHES 2

Traditional German food is as diverse as it is delicious. Feast on amazing breads and sausage, and enjoy regional dishes such as *Spätzle, Rote Grütze* and *Handkäs (p30)*.

3 FASCINATING HISTORY

German history spans almost 2,000 years. Take to the streets and you'll find architecture, monuments and whole cityscapes that reveal the traces of its fascinating and multifaceted past.

A SPORTING NATION 4

Germans are justly proud of their successes in a surprisingly broad range of sports, such as football, tennis, handball, basketball, ice hockey and motor racing.

SPAS 5

Spas play an important role in German "wellness" culture, so choose one of the nation's dedicated spa towns or secluded health resorts and soak away your cares (p130).

CULTURAL LEGACY 6

In addition to being a nation of thinkers and poets, Germany brims with artists and has a vibrant network of theatres, film venues and concert halls (p24).

BERLIN 7

The German capital *(p54)* has it all: compelling history, edgy nightlife, green and family-friendly spaces, lively shopping scenes and an endless supply of art and culture.

MEDIEVAL TOWNS 8

With their charming cobbled streets, timber-framed houses and cultural traditions, Germany's well-preserved medieval towns are a delight to explore.

9 BEER AND WINE

Germany is perhaps most famous for its dizzying range of beers *(p216)*, but its wines are an insider secret all visitors should try – particularly crisp, dry Rieslings *(p338)*.

10 SANDY BEACHES
Visitors don't often associate Germany with beaches, but its northern coastline and many inland lakes (such as Wannsee) are peppered with stunning sandy stretches *(p468)*.

MUSICAL HERITAGE 11
Enjoy sublime classical music from Bach, Beethoven and Brahms in concerts and music festivals across the country, or head to Berlin for its alternative club scene *(p67)*.

DIVERSE LANDSCAPES 12
From gently rolling hills and moorlands to craggy mountains and volcanic craters, Germany offers scenic spots for relaxation and lots of opportunities for outdoor adventures *(p32)*.

1

2

3

4

1 Bodensee (Lake Constance), with a view of the Swiss Alps.

2 Enjoying a meal at Munich's Viktualienmarkt.

3 Subway station in Munich.

4 Traditional dumplings.

Germany is a treasure trove of things to see and do. Travelling the length of the country and taking in vibrant cities and the beautiful Bodensee, this itinerary will help you make the most of your trip.

2 WEEKS
In Germany

▌Day 1

Morning Your journey begins in Munich, with a mid-morning snack of Weisswurst at Viktualienmarkt *(p230)*. Next, take in the sights on a leisurely stroll to Marienplatz, with its impressive array of civic monuments.

Afternoon Spend some time in the lovely Englischer Garten *(p238)* and enjoy a relaxing lunch here. Next, admire contemporary art at the Haus der Kunst *(p233)*.

Evening Le Stollberg *(Stollbergstrasse 2)* is a good choice for dinner. It serves refined French food and good wine.

▌Day 2

Morning Escape the busy city streets and head to Schloss Nymphenburg *(p220)*, a Baroque palace with elaborate Italianate gardens and lavish interiors.

Afternoon Once back in Munich, if you want to see more art, lose yourself among the splendid works of the Old Masters at the Alte Pinakothek gallery *(p218)*.

Evening End your day with some classic dumplings at the cheerfully traditional Wirtshaus in der Au *(p232)*.

▌Day 3

Morning It's time to leave Bavaria's capital city behind and catch a train or a coach for a scenic journey to Konstanz *(p304)*. The trip takes almost four hours.

Afternoon Stretch your legs with a walk to the town's pretty harbourfront. Enjoy a leisurely patio lunch at

Wessenberg *(Wessenbergstrasse 41)*, then explore Konstanz's history with a stroll through old town Niederburg.

Evening Enjoy a fish supper and beautiful lake views at the historic Steigenberger Inselhotel's *(Auf der Insel 1)* "Seerestaurant", which used to be a Dominican Monastery.

▌Day 4

Morning Start the day with a ferry ride to Meersburg *(p305)*, which is situated on the opposite shore of Bodensee. Enjoy a wander around the medieval town centre.

Afternoon Visit the Alte Burg – the oldest inhabited castle in Germany – and learn about the fascinating life of poet and composer Annette von Droste-Hülshoff at the nearby Droste Museum.

Evening Sit back with a glass of wine at the rustic Winzerstube Zum Becher *(Höllgasse 4)*, whose extensive list includes wine from its own vineyards.

▌Day 5

Morning Hop on a train to Stuttgart *(p296)*, and make sure you sit next to a window for the two-and-a-half-hour journey through the Bavarian countryside.

Afternoon Stop for lunch at one of the cafés and restaurants that surround Stuttgart's Schlossplatz before hitting the Staatsgalerie *(p298)*, which contains King Wilhelm I's private art collection.

Evening Feast on good-value Swabian dishes at Tauberquelle *(Torstrasse 19)*.

→

Day 6

Morning Have breakfast and coffee at the small restaurant at Stuttgart's Markthalle *(p297)*. Don't miss the building's superb frescoes.

Afternoon Take a trip out to the Mercedes-Benz Museum *(p299)*, whose splendid collection illustrates the development of car production.

Evening Enjoy authentic Persian cuisine at the cosy basement restaurant Nirvan *(Eberhardstrasse 73)*.

Day 7

Morning After breakfast, immerse yourself into Swabian Impressionism at the Kunstmuseum Stuttgart *(p296)*.

Afternoon For lunch, grab some homemade Maultaschen and a Weissbeer at Paulaner am alten Postplatz *(Calwer Strasse 45)* before heading north to Düsseldorf *(p386)*. The train journey takes 2.5 hours.

Evening Explore the beautiful town houses and late-Gothic Rathaus on the city's Altstadt and then dine at Zum Uerige *(Berger Strasse 1)*, a legendary brewpub.

Day 8

Morning View contemporary art at the Kunst im Tunnel gallery, located beneath the Rhine Promenade. Afterwards, stop for an early lunch at a riverside café.

Afternoon Admire the Gothic architecture of the Lambertuskirche before soaking up more art at the prodigious K20 *(p386)*.

Evening Enjoy an evening stroll around the Altstadt, dropping into Galerie am Karlplatz *(Benrather Strasse 6B)* to taste excellent German wines.

Day 9

Morning Catch a train to Bremen *(p424)*, then head straight to the main square to take some great photos of the striking Rathaus and cathedral.

Afternoon Down towards the Weser is Böttcherstrasse *(p427)*, a red-brick street that hosts several interesting museums to explore.

Evening Enjoy regional cuisine at Das Kleine Lokal *(Besselstrasse 40)* and then relax with a cocktail or two at the Blauer Fasan Bar *(Langenstrasse 81)*.

1 The iconic Brandenburger Tor.

2 *Big Torn Campbell's Soup Can (Black Bean)* (1962), by Andy Warhol, in the K20 art gallery, Düsseldorf.

3 Bremen's central station.

4 Harbourfront in Düsseldorf.

5 A classical concert at Berlin's Philharmonie.

6 Lutter & Wegner in Berlin.

Day 10

Morning Explore the medieval houses and lanes around the Schnoorviertel *(p426)* before visiting Kunsthalle *(p424)* for European and international modern art.

Afternoon After lunch head to the Focke-Museum *(p426)* to discover the history of Bremen's art and culture.

Evening Take a stroll in the nearby Rhododendron-Park before heading out to the Meierei im Bürgerpark for an elegant dinner.

Day 11

Morning Take a train to Berlin *(p54)*. Begin your time in the city with a walk through Tiergarten *(p94)*.

Afternoon For a taste of Berlin's edgy art scene, head to Friedrichshain, home to the iconic East Side Gallery – the outdoor graffiti gallery on the remains of the Berlin Wall.

Evening Whether you're looking for bars, clubs, food or concerts, the RAW Gelände complex *(Revaler Strasse)* has everything you need for a good night out.

Day 12

Morning Make your way to Museumsinsel *(p72)*. For a taste of all the island has to offer, the Neues Museum has one of the most wide-ranging and intriguing exhibitions.

Afternoon In the late afternoon, stroll along Unter den Linden *(p77)* ending at the iconic Brandenburger Tor *(p76)*.

Evening Take a tour of the Reichstag in the early evening and watch the sun set from its famous domed rooftop.

Day 13

Morning Start with breakfast at SPHERE, Fernsehturm's *(p81)* rotating restaurant, and enjoy panoramic vistas of the city.

Afternoon Walk along the Spree riverbank to the Nikolaiviertel *(p86)*. Here, explore the alleyways and browse the shops.

Evening Feast on hearty German fare at Zille-Stube *(Spreeufer 3)* on the riverside.

Day 14

For your last day in Germany, select an activity from the Berlin itinerary *(p61)*.

Medieval Romanesque

Spanning from around the 6th to the early 13th century, Romanesque architecture is characterized by Roman-inspired elements such as semicircular arches and groin vaults. The Rhine area, where the style is often referred to as Rhenish Romanesque, is the best place to seek out some of Germany's finest examples: make a beeline for the particularly striking Kaiserdom (*p351*) in Speyer, or the cathedrals in Köln (*p388*) and Worms (*p347*).

Speyer's Romanesque Kaiserdom, a UNESCO World Heritage Site

GERMANY FOR
ARCHITECTURE

Despite the colossal destruction suffered during World War II, Germany is still home to an inspiring collection of buildings that showcase the evolution of European architectural styles, from Romanesque churches in the country's medieval towns to contemporary skyscrapers in the big cities.

Opulent Baroque

Originating in Italy as a way of celebrating the might of the Catholic Church, the fanciful Baroque style became popular throughout Europe following the Thirty Years' War (1618–48). Don't miss the elaborate Schloss Sanssouci in Potsdam (*p137*) – commonly known as the "Versailles of Germany" – or Dresden's Zwinger (*p170*).

Dresden's Frauenkirche, a fine example of the Baroque style

KARL FRIEDRICH SCHINKEL

Renowned architect Schinkel (1781-1841) is responsible for much of modern Berlin, including Neue Wache (*p77*) and the Altes Museum (*p74*). A purveyor of the Neo-Classical and Neo-Gothic, his innovative ideas also influenced the modernist style of the 20th century.

Contemporary Architecture

Germany's division during the Cold War meant that from 1945 to 1989, most Postmodern architecture was built in West Germany, where American and European styles were readily accepted. Reunification brought new opportunities, especially in the reinvigorated Berlin: the contemporary architecture at Potsdamer Platz (p96) includes stunning buildings by Renzo Piano, for example. Beyond the capital, Postmodern fans should head to Hamburg, home to the HafenCity development (p429) and its landmark, the Elbphilharmonie, with its 1,000 curved window panels.

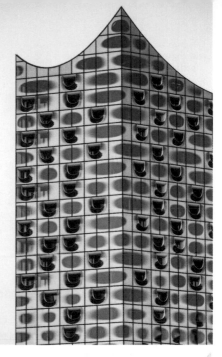

→

The striking façade of the Elbphilharmonie, or Elphi, in Hamburg

Industrial Style

Germany was a forerunner in Europe's Industrial Revolution, which overlapped architecturally in the late 19th century with the Modernist movements of the Deutscher Werkbund and world-famous Bauhaus. Architects such as Peter Behrens began producing buildings in the manner of his immense and streamlined turbine factory for AEG in Berlin.

←

AEG-Turbinenhalle, a textbook example of the industrial style

Traditional Neo-Classical

A reaction against the Baroque style, Classicism became a trend in Germany in the second half of the 18th century. Inspired by the Classical architecture of antiquity, it is most closely associated with Karl Friedrich Schinkel in Berlin and Leo von Klenze in Munich, both of whom drew on Greek influences rather than the French penchant for Roman. While in Berlin, admire Schinkel's Neue Wache (p77), characterized by fine Doric columns, and Carl Gotthard Langhans' Brandenburger Tor (p76); those venturing south to Munich shouldn't miss Klenze's Glyptothek.

→

Schinkel's glorious Neue Wache, a Neo-Classical guardhouse in Berlin

Berchtesgaden village, nestled below the Watzmann massif ↑

GERMANY FOR
NATURAL
WONDERS

The beauty and diversity of Germany's natural landscapes are world famous - and there are plenty of reasons why. From stunning coastline, through alpine mountain scenery to woodlands full of flora and fauna, the country is a haven for those looking to experience the great outdoors.

On the Coast

Germany's coast offers something for everyone: crashing waves for windsurfers, beautiful beaches for families and health resorts for those who want to relax. Mecklenburg-Vorpommern *(p464)* and Schleswig-Holstein *(p450)*, which abut the Baltic coast, are host to a plethora of popular destinations - seek out the islands of Rügen and Usedom, and Jasmund National Park. On the North Sea side, Sylt island is an exceptional area of natural beauty.

→
The white chalk cliffs of Rügen Island, in the Baltic Sea

Climbing a Mountain

Germany's main mountain region is undoubtedly the Bavarian Alps, which form a natural divide along the Austrian border and include the Zugspitze, Germany's highest mountain. The Bavarian Alps are best explored via well-connected tourist hubs such as Garmisch-Partenkirchen, Berchtesgaden, Füssen and Oberstdorf. The neighbouring Berchtesgaden Alps also lay claim to some impressive peaks (most notably, Watzmann and Hochkönig). Want to stay a little closer to earth? Head to smaller mountain ranges such as the Fichtel Mountains and the Sächsische Schweiz (Saxon Switzerland), which are both close to the Czech border, the picturesque Harz mountains in Northern Germany, or the Taunus ranges north of Frankfurt.

TOP 3 CAMPSITES ON LOCATION

Müllerwiese, Black Forest
One of Germany's coolest activity-based campsites can be found in a peaceful location near the Black Forest (www.muellerwiese.de).

Insel-Camp, Fehmarn
Set on the south beach of the island of Fehmarn, right on the Baltic Sea, this five-star campsite offers a spa and sporting activities (www.inselcamp.de).

Camping Resort Zugspitze
This idyllic mountain retreat has a campsite and mountain cabins. Visitors can enjoy an onsite bistro and restaurant plus a range of activities (www.perfect-camping.de).

Skiing down the Watzmann, Berchtesgaden Alps ↑

Lake Constance, bordered by vineyards ↑

Lakes, Rivers and Forests

Threaded by great rivers - the Rhine, Oder, Danube and Main - and speckled with simply stunning lakes - think Bodensee (p304), Chiemsee (p285) or Königsee - Germany is perfect for a holiday on the water. Alternatively, make for a forest retreat; almost a third of the country is covered in forests, many of which offer hiking trails and canopy walkways, plus a chance to spot rare animals such as the Alpine ibex and golden eagle. There are plenty of places to choose from but our pick of the bunch are the Black Forest (p306), Bavarian Forest and Jasmund National Park (p474), which has the world's few surviving primeval beech forests.

↑ Picture gallery in the Goethes Wohnhaus and National Museum

Literary Greats

With a back catalogue featuring the likes of Goethe, Schiller, Thomas Mann, Hermann Hesse and Günter Grass, it's little wonder that German-language authors have won the Nobel Prize in Literature an impressive 13 times. Their reputation grew in the 18th century, with movements like Sturm und Drang and Weimar Classicism, and has continued ever since. Translated editions are readily available, so pack a book to enjoy on the go.

TOP 3 MUSEUMS OF CULTURE

Germanisches Nationalmuseum, Nürnberg
Explore antiquities from the German-speaking world (p256).

Deutsches Museum, Munich
You'll need a full day to see the staggering collection at this technology and science museum (p222).

DDR Museum, Berlin
A fascinating look at daily life in former East Germany (p82).

GERMANY'S CULTURAL LEGACY

As *das Land der Dichter und Denker* – "the country of poets and thinkers" – Germany's cultural prowess is world-renowned. From the classic tomes of Goethe and Schiller to the musical genius of Beethoven and Bach, there's plenty to swot up on before you even start your trip.

Inspiring Artists

Home to some of the leading players of Europe's artistic movements, Germany has myriad galleries and museums to explore. Head to the Albrecht-Dürer-Haus (p255) in Nürnberg to find out about the life of Renaissance painter Dürer, view Otto Dix's Impressionist delights at Stuttgart's Kunstmuseum (p296) or get up close to Max Liebermann at Dresden's Albertinum (p171).

→

The artist's studio at the Brandenburg Gate in Berlin, Max Liebermann (1902)

German Theatre

The theatre has always influenced German culture, and its writers and directors have inspired generations. An example of the strength of this legacy is the *Oberammergauer Passionspiele*: first staged in the Bavarian village in 1634, it is remarkably still staged there every ten years. Of course, heavyweights Lessing, Goethe and Schiller dominate the scene but there is plenty to be enjoyed from later centuries, via such leading lights as Bertolt Brecht. Check out the latest performances at Weimar's Deutsches Nationaltheater *(p193)*.

→

The Deutsches National-
theater fronted by a statue
of Goethe and Schiller

Classical Music

Bach, Beethoven, Brahms: the world of classical music is dominated by German genius. Head to Bonn *(p396)* to explore the life of local boy Beethoven (time your visit with the Beethovenfestival) or visit Wagner's home town, Bayreuth *(p280)*.

←

Portrait of classical music composer
Johann Sebastian Bach (1685–1750)

Film Studios

Germany was a pioneer in the early years of the film industry, with the world's first public film showing held in Berlin in 1895. Visitors can explore this exciting and innovative part of Germany's history at Berlin's Museum für Film und Fernsehen *(p97)*.

→

Poster for Fritz Lang's
1927 Expressionist
film *Metropolis*

Expressionism

Expressionism was an early 20th-century German art movement that favoured the portrayal of emotion over reality. You can see Expressionist masterpieces at Die Brücke Museum, Lenbachhaus *(p238)* and the Pinakothek der Moderne *(p226)*. Expressionist art can also be found in the K20, the Folkwang in Essen and the Kunstmuseum Stuttgart.

$\rightarrow$

The entrance of the Lenbachhaus art gallery, designed by Sir Norman Foster

GERMANY FOR
ART LOVERS

Germany's rich tradition of visual arts spans the Renaissance and Romantic eras right up to German Expressionism and contemporary art. Not only are works of artists, both new and famous, hosted in museums and galleries, they also adorn public spaces in the form of colourful street art and sculpture.

Renaissance

In the 15th and 16th centuries, Germany's Northern Renaissance artists in eschewed overtly religious Catholic-style works. Housed in the Zwinger palace complex *(p172)*, the Gemäldegalerie Alte Meister has an excellent collection from this era. Alte Pinakothek *(p218)* also has a significant set of German Old Masters, such as Stefan Lochner's *Adoration of the Christ Child by the Virgin*.

INSIDER TIP
Gallery Weekend Berlin

For three days at the end of April, around 50 major galleries throughout Berlin open their doors for free to showcase contemporary art. Many new and experimental working galleries also participate in this event.

The Old Masters Gallery at the Zwinger palace complex $\uparrow$

Romanticism

Considered one of the most significant eras in Europe's history and rooted deeply in Germany, Romanticism is celebrated in all its glory at the new Deutsches Romantik-Museum in Frankfurt Am Main *(p364)*. In Berlin, the Alte Nationalgalerie *(p72)* has one of the best collections of works from the early 19th-century German Romantics known as "The Nazarenes", who revived Christian imagery in art, and a Caspar David Friedrich collection that includes the restored masterpieces *Monk by the Sea* and *The Abbey In the Oakwood*. It also features various works by Karl Friedrich Schinkel.

→

Visitors sitting in front of the Alte Nationalgalerie in Berlin.

Modernism

During the late 19th and early 20th centuries, artists departed from traditional art forms and found new ways to represent the changing world around them. German Modernism was influenced by the country's role in WWII, and depicts themes of war and urbanization. Admire Modernist works at the Hamburger Bahnhof *(p100)* and Kunstsammlung Nordrhein-Westfalen *(p386)*.

←

The exterior of Ständehaus am Kaiserteich at Kunstsammlung Nordrhein-Westfalen gallery, Dusseldorf

Street Art

Street art can be found in most large cities in Germany, with dedicated street art museums in Berlin and Munich. Berlin's East Side Gallery *(p110)*, a 1.3-km- (0.8-mile-) long stretch of the Berlin Wall, features various political pieces that perfectly capture the rebellious nature of modern street art.

→

The vividly colourful street art at the East Side Gallery

By the Seaside

Sandy beaches and a wide selection of spas and wellness centres for weary parents – Germany's Baltic coast is ideal for a relaxing break. After something a little more active? Baltic islands like Rügen (p476) have plenty of walking and cycling trails, as do nearby natural parks like Western Pomerania Lagoon Area National Park (p480). Go wildlife spotting, take a ride on a steam train or simply set out on foot on a mini adventure. If it's raining, head a little inland to Schwerin (p472) for a turn around a Disney-esque castle or a museum.

→
Beachlife on Usedom island, in Mecklenburg-Vorpommern

GERMANY FOR
FAMILIES

Planning a family holiday? You'll be spoilt for choice in Germany. Escape to the country for wonderful outdoor adventures, stay close to the cities for a cultural calendar that'll captivate young minds or simply enjoy some sun and sand at the seaside – whatever you do, Germany won't disappoint.

KINDERCAFES IN BERLIN

Berlin's kindercafes, mostly situated in innercity areas popular with young families such as Friedrichshain, Kreuzberg and Prenzlauer Berg, are unique spaces that cater to both children and parents. The former get dedicated play areas, which often include indoor sand pits, ball pools, mazes and the like, while the whole family can tuck into a decent array of coffees, teas, cakes and snacks.

Fun at the Museum

Topping an impressive list of kid-friendly museums is Munich's Deutsches Museum (p222) – head straight for Kid's Kingdom where children can explore the world of science and technology. Berlin has plenty to offer, too: try the Legoland® Discovery Centre, Computer Spiele Museum (perfect for gamers) or the Deutsches Technikmuseum.

→
A demonstration in the Physics exhibition at the Deutsches Museum

Bountiful Bavaria

Home to cultural Munich (p208), and one of the most pictured castles in the world (p266), Alpine retreats and lakeside havens, Bavaria is simply a visitor's paradise. Set up camp in a forest and take your pick from an array of outdoor activities – hiking, climbing, swimming, skiing, the choice is almost endless. Mini princes and princesses can make-believe at spectacular fairytale castles – there are more in Bavaria than in any other German state – or let off steam at a waterpark.

← Heading out on a hike in the beautiful Chiemgau region of Bavaria

TOP 4 THEME PARKS

Europa Park
The largest theme park in Germany (p318).

Legoland® Discovery Centre
◉ D6 ⌂ Günzburg
ⓦ legolandholidays.de
Children can indulge in various Lego-themed activities here.

Playmobil Land
◉ E6 ⌂ Zirndorf
ⓦ playmobil-funpark.de
This park has fun activities and adventures.

Tropical Island
◉ F3 ⌂ Krausnick
ⓦ tropical-islands.de
A tropical rainforest set in an aircraft hangar.

↑ Cross-country skiing in the Schwarzwald (Black Forest)

Down to the Woods

The Schwarzwald (or Black Forest) is a vast expanse of woodland that offers abundant walking trails through and past meadows, lakes, valleys and vineyards (p306). And there's more: activity parks, climbing areas, and kayaking, canoeing and sailing opportunities on the lakes, plus cute towns like Baden Baden, keep all of the family happy. Winter is an ideal time to visit, too: snowy slopes and trails make for excellent downhill and cross-country skiing.

Handkäs mit Musik

With such a pungent aroma, this curdled sour milk cheese (the smell exacerbated by the chopped raw onions served on top) rather divides opinion. Its name comes from the way it is made and shaped by hand. And "mit Musik"? People wryly joke that the music comes later (a nod to the flatulence caused by eating it). If that hasn't put you off, give it a go in Hesse, from where it hails.

→

Handkäs mit Musik served with bread and raw onions

GERMANY FOR
FOODIES

Traditional German cuisine is hearty, warming comfort food. Each region has its own culinary speciality – even the humble sausage takes on a different guise depending on where you go – so there's always something new to try. Here, we round up the dishes you shouldn't miss.

TOP **3** GERMAN SAUSAGES

Bratwurst
A mix of finely minced pork and beef that's usually grilled and served with a bread roll and mustard or ketchup.

Weisswurst
Made from veal and bacon seasoned with parsley, onion, lemon and cardamom. It's usually boiled and eaten skinless, traditionally before noon.

Leberkäse
"Liver cheese" comes from Bavaria and is made from finely minced corned beef, pork and onions. It's baked until a golden crust forms.

Spätzle
From Baden-Württemberg comes *Spätzle*, a soft egg noodle akin to pasta. It's usually served as a side dish, added to soups or doused in sauce, most often cheese (*Käsespätzle*). This comfort food is readily available but try it at a Swabian restaurant, if you can.

→

Tucking into a tasty portion of *Spätzle*

← A Christmas market stall selling *Currywurst*, Berlin's favourite fast food

Currywurst

This ubiquitous dish is a steamed and fried pork sausage that's cut into slices and seasoned with a mix of curry powder and ketchup. Some of the best places to try *Currywurst* are Dönninghaus in Dochum, Konnopke's Imbiss in Berlin and Mö Grill in Hamburg.

HERTA HEUWER

Legend has it that the *Currywurst* was born when Berliner Herta Heuwer, yearning for some variety in her diet shortly after the war, obtained ketchup and curry powder from British soldiers, mixed them together with other spices, and poured the resulting sauce over some grilled pork sausage.

Sauerbraten

A firm family favourite, this meaty pot roast is served up and down the country. A joint of meat is soaked for several days in a marinade (ingredients vary region to region) and then roasted until tender. Enjoy with *Spätzle* or boiled potatoes.

← Roasted *Sauerbraten*, served with potatoes and butter

↑ The simple and elegant *Rote Grütze* dessert from north Germany

Rote Grütze

Translating literally as "red groats", this delicious dessert from Schleswig-Holstein is more appetising than it sounds. Strawberries, raspberries or blackberries (whatever is available) are boiled with sugar to create what is essentially a berry compote. It's served either hot or cold, with cream or vanilla sauce, or without.

Made for Walking

Covered by about 200,000 km (124,275 miles) of accessible trails, this incredible landscape begs to be explored by foot. There's ample choice, but some favourites include the Malerweg in Sächsiche Schweiz (near Dresden) and trails in the Berchtesgadener Land (p258). For the ultimate experience, try hut-hiking, where you can stay overnight in a hut or dairy farm.

→

Hikers following a trail through mountainous terrain in the Alps

GERMANY FOR
ADVENTURERS

Germany is one enormous playground for those in search of an active holiday. Its 16 national parks and undulating landscapes of hills, lakes and forests are untamed yet easily accessible and offer a huge array of outdoor activities, whatever your level of fitness.

SKIING IN BAVARIA

The Bavarian Alps is Germany's premier skiing destination. While the resorts don't have quite the same prestige as those in France or Austria, most are within an hour or two of Munich, making them easily accessible. There's plenty of variety too: from large, busy resorts such as Garmisch Partenkirchen (p278) and Alpsee-Grünten to smaller, quieter towns such as Oberstaufen and family-friendly places like Geisskopf. The region caters for all experience levels and the season usually runs from November to Easter.

Take to the Water

The numerous lakes and rivers sprinkled across the land, plus an oft-overlooked coastline, provide plenty of opportunity to take to the water. Bavaria is your best bet for lakeside activities, while Mecklenburg-Vorpommern provides opportunities to ride the waves. Hire a kayak or surfboard, or simply dive in for a swim – the choice is yours.

A family heads out exploring aboard a kayak ↑

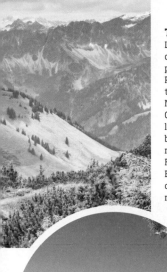

Two Wheels

Looking for a long-distance cycle route? Germany has plenty. Tackle the Elbe Cycle Route, a 1,200-km (745-mile) trail that travels from the North Sea to its source in the Czech Republic, or trace the length of the German-Polish border on the 630-km- (390-mile-) long Oder-Neisse route. For sea views, choose the Baltic Coast Cycle Path, part of the Eurovelo network, or ride along the Kiel Canal, which links the Baltic and North seas. Of course, you needn't cycle the whole distance – pick a section and spend a relaxing day in the saddle.

 ←
Cycling along the Kiel Canal, which connects the Baltic with the North Sea

TOP
3 ADVENTURES FOR THRILL-SEEKERS

Paragliding over the Bavarian Alps
Take a cable car to the top of Rauschberg, take off with a paraglider and enjoy the Alps from a unique perspective.

Racing Cars at Nordschleife
Embrace your inner Michael Schumacher at this motor racing circuit that forms part of Grand Prix track Nürburgring.

Rock Climbing in Berchtesgaden
The Berchtesgadener Land *(p258)* is a rock climber's dream. Scale the Watzmann for the ultimate challenge.

Scale a Mountain

The German landscape is peppered with mighty mountains and heady peaks, making it a mountaineer's paradise. Hardy climbers should scale the Zugspitze; at nearly 3,000 m (9,900 ft), it is the highest peak in Germany. You'll be well-rewarded with stunning views and, in true Bavarian style, a beer garden at the peak. There's also a much-appreciated cable car to take you back down to earth.

↑ A well-equipped and experienced mountaineer scaling a Bavarian mountain cliff face

Peaceful Obersee,
tucked away in a
national park ↑

GERMANY FOR
HIDDEN GEMS

Despite welcoming over 35 million tourists each year, Germany still holds many surprises. The country's size and diversity mean it's capable of constantly rewarding repeat visitors, whether it's a tucked away town or a previously unseen landmark.

A Fairytale Bridge

Nestled in the Kromlauer Park near Gablenz, close to the Polish border, the mesmerising Rakotsbrücke *(p178)* was commissioned in 1860 by a local knight. Known as a "devil's bridge" (due to the belief that no one other than Satan could have created such a thing), it stretches over the Rakotsee, producing with its reflection an almost perfect circle. Visit the park in autumn to see the bridge at its best (though it is enchanting at any time of year). Note that crossing the bridge is strictly prohibited.

→

The enchanting
Rakotzbrücke, framed
by autumn foliage

Calming Waters

The striking Obersee is hidden away in the Berchtesgaden National Park (p258), close to the Austrian border, surrounded by alpine cliffs and forests. There are no villages, just the tiny Fischunkelalm hut, open in summer only. A big part of the lake's charm is its isolation; it can only be reached by first a boat ride across the Königsee and then a short walk. On your way to the lake you'll pass St Bartholomew's church; your driver may also stop in the middle of the lake to sound a tune on his trumpet, which creates a cheery echo around the mountains.

Sailing across the tranquil waters of the Obersee, enjoying picture-perfect views

TOP 3 STORYBOOK TOWNS

Hanau
Little-known hometown of the brothers Grimm and the starting point of the German Fairy Tale Route (p370).

Alsfeld
Packed with half-timbered houses that span several centuries, this is the town that inspired Little Red Riding Hood (p372).

Hofgeismar
Located in the Reinhardswald, this town features an ivy-covered castle (Sababurg) said to be the inspiration for Sleeping Beauty.

GREAT VIEW
Highest Falls

Germany's highest waterfall can be found in the Obersee. After taking a turn around the lake, set off on an hour's hike (note the trail is often slippery after rain) for splendid views of this tumbling torrent of water.

Pretty half-timber homes in the town of Meersburg ↑

Make Your Way to Meersburg

Meersburg is one of the most alluring destinations along the shores of the Bodensee (p304). Comprising a pedestrianised lower and upper town, connected by stairways and a steep street, its main architectural highlights are its scenic Old Castle (the oldest inhabited castle in Germany) and a neighbouring New Castle built by famed baroque architect Balthasar Neumann. A handsome promenade lined with cafés and restaurants makes a delightful spot to watch the world go by.

A YEAR IN
GERMANY

Colourful carnivals to welcome the spring, a plethora of outdoor events in the heady heat of summer, beer festivals to see in the autumn, and cinammon-scented Christmas markets to ease the winter chill. Germany's cultural calendar is brimming all year round.

Spring

As warm sunshine finally breaks the chill of winter and flowers and trees burst into bloom across the country, Germany's towns and cities wake from their slumber and spring to life. The season of forest strolls and rural bike rides, spring also brings a wave of popular cultural events such as the famous Karneval in Köln, the International Dixieland Festival in Dresden, the Bach Festival in Thuringia and Hamburg's famous Reeperbahn Festival.

1. A woman cycling through the meadows of the Oytal Valley

Summer

German summers are synonymous with sun-soaked beer gardens and the great outdoors. This is the season to explore the country's vast and wild expanses – forests, mountains,

KIELWEEK

Running since 1882, Kieler Woche is one of the largest sailing events in the world. Taking place in Kiel during the last week of June, it draws some 5,000 sailors, 2,000 ships and around three million visitors. An impressive fireworks display marks the end of the festival.

lakes and rivers – as well as its picture-book villages and vibrant cities, where open-air events like the Rhein in Flammen in Koblenz and Munich Opera Festival take centre stage.

2. Summer afternoon in Munich's Englischer Garten

Autumn

Mellowing temperatures, bright, clear skies and the burnished hues of changing leaves signal the end of summer, but locals tend to make the most of the outdoors until mid-November. Unmissable events include Oktoberfest in Munich, Beethovenfest in Bonn and Cannstatter Volksfest in Stuttgart. Autumn is also a great time to explore Germany's many wine regions.

3. Swing carousel at Cannstatter Volksfest in Stuttgart

Winter

As the nights draw in, Germans switch to hibernation mode. However, outdoor activities don't stop completely, as families take to the ice rinks for skating, forests become popular with winter hikers, and cultural spaces provide entertainment as well as warmth. Dustings of snow add a layer of fairytale charm, as do the Christmas markets that pop up across the country. Meanwhile the capital hosts major winter events such as the beloved Berlinale, Transmediale and Berlin Fashion Week.

4. A German Christmas market with, (inset), gingerbread hearts

TOP 3 CHRISTMAS MARKETS

Nürnberg
The oldest and most famous Christmas market in the world offers traditional handmade decorations and sweet treats.

Köln
Set in front of the city's historic cathedral, this sprawling festive market has plenty of musical cheer, including festive choirs and swingtime jazz.

Berlin
The most romantic of Berlin's markets is held at the Baroque palace of Schloss Charlottenburg, where quaint wooden huts serve *glühwein* and plenty of sweet treats. There's also a funfair for children.

A BRIEF
HISTORY

For hundreds of years, the area that is now Germany was made up of many smaller states. It wasn't until the late 19th century that the country was unified into one nation, and the differences in culture, language and traditions of these former separate states still exist today.

Germanic Tribes

By the second century BC, Germanic tribes had spread south from Scandinavia and settled in the basins of the Rhine, Danube and Main rivers, displacing the original Celtic tribes who lived there. The area was called Germania by the Romans, who had two provinces in the southern region. Under Emperor Augustus, Roman legions waged wars with the Germanic tribes, continuing to conquer territories in Germania until they were defeated under Arminius. After the decline of the Roman Empire in the 4th century, the area between the Rhine and the Elbe was ruled by the Franks, a West Germanic tribe.

1 Map of Schleswig-Holstein during the Holy Roman Empire. ↑

2 Charlemagne, King of the Franks.

3 Roman-Germanic Wars.

4 Sarcophagus showing the battle between Romans and Germanics in the Marcomannic Wars.

Timeline of events

9 AD
Germanus defeats the Roman armies

c 300–500
The Migration Period. Many tribes, particularly Germans, travel through Europe and settle in new areas, contributing to the decline of the Roman Empire

476
Overthrow of Romulus Augustulus, the last Roman emperor, by Odovacar

774
Frankish king Charlemagne conquers Lombardy at their capital of Pavia in 774

The Carolingian Dynasty

Charlemagne was crowned King of the Franks in 768, and spent several decades expanding his realm, until it included much of present-day Germany, France and northern Italy. His family, the Carolingian dynasty, had close ties to the Papacy, and when the Eastern Roman Empire sought a male leader (giving no credence to the self-declared Empress Irene), the Pope crowned Charlemagne as Emperor. After his death, internal conflict began to plague the Carolingian dynasty, until their territories were split, creating present-day France and Germany. By the late 9th century, the Carolingian rule was over.

Birth of the Holy Roman Empire

Otto I, crowned King of Germany in 936, saw himself as the successor of Charlemagne. He consolidated his powers and gained support by ending civil wars, defending his territories against invasion, as well as strategically appointing family members into duchies throughout the kingdom. His territories grew to include Italy, and in 962 he was crowned ruler of the Holy Roman Empire.

↑ Bust of Emperor Augustus, born Gaius Octavius Thurinus in 63 BC

800

Charlemagne crowned Holy Roman Emperor by Pope Leo III on Christmas Day

843

Treaty of Verdun divides Carolingian Empire among Charlemagne's grandsons

911–18

Conrad I (Conrad of Franconia) elected German king

962

German King Otto I crowned Roman emperor after gaining control of northern Italy; beginning of Holy Roman Empire

1

2

Crisis in the Middle Ages

Prosperity and growth in Germany and throughout Europe were shattered by a series of disasters in the 14th century. Chief among them were the Great Famine – brought about by bad weather and poor harvests between 1315 and 1317 – and the Black Death in 1348. This was a plague carried by rat fleas, which purportedly travelled along the Silk Road from Asia and then spread via merchant ships. Religious and political upheavals were led by these disasters, and the population throughout Germany was decimated – in some areas, it is thought that 40 per cent of the population was wiped out.

The Reformation

Recovering from these crises, the Holy Roman Empire continued as a major power in Europe. However, the rise of theologian Martin Luther – who challenged the church in his 1517 work, the *Ninety-Five Theses or Disputation on the Power of Indulgences* – set in motion the Reformation, which ultimately led to the division of Germany into a northern Protestant part and a Catholic south.

THE HANSEATIC LEAGUE

Civil war broke out between the houses of Hohenstaufen and Welf, each vying to lead the Holy Roman Empire. The eventual fall of the Hohenstaufens during the Middle Ages marked the end of the old imperial system and gave rise to the Hanseatic League, an alliance of merchant guilds and market towns.

Timeline of events

1027

Coronation of Konrad II begins the Salian dynasty, which provides four Holy Roman Emperors and lasts until 1125

1138

Coronation of Konrad III, the first King of Germany of the Hohenstaufen dynasty

1250

Death of Emperor Frederick II Hohenstaufen begins the Great Interregnum, a period with no emperor

1517

Martin Luther writes *Ninety-Five Theses*

The Thirty Years' War

The influence of the Counter-Reformation in the early 17th century ended the relative stability that had reigned for several decades, and played a role in the beginning of the Thirty Years' War (1618–48). This conflict between the Holy Roman Empire and multiple adversaries across central Europe resulted in massive fatalities in Germany, the decline of the Holy Roman Empire, bankruptcy of many of the combatants, and the splintering of Germany into various independent states.

The Rise of Prussia

From the mid-17th- to the late 18th century, Germany became a loose federation of small states. The rising star of all these territories was Brandenburg, ruled by the house of Hohenzollern, which, from 1657, also ruled the duchy of Prussia. In 1701 the Elector Friedrich III crowned himself "King in Prussia" (becoming Friedrich I), and the name "Prussia" was then applied to all areas ruled by Hohenzollern. Under the later king, Friedrich II – known as Frederick the Great – the Prussian capital of Berlin became a centre of the Enlightenment.

⓵ Frederick the Great with Emperor Joseph II. ↑

⓶ Swedish King Gustav II Adolf dies at the Battle of Lützen during the Thirty Years War.

⓷ Depiction of the plague as a demon.

Did You Know?

Frederick the Great is buried at Potsdam's Sanssouci, which was his favourite residence.

1618–48
Thirty Years' War. Failure of Habsburg emperors' attempt to restore Catholic dominance

1648
Treaty of Westphalia confirms near-total independence of territorial states

1555
Peace of Augsburg, after which Catholicism and Lutheranism are formally recognized in Germany, and each prince given the right to decide which is to be practised in his territory

1740–86
Frederick II (Frederick the Great) reforms his country as an enlightened despot

The German Empire

From 1803 to 1815, the Napoleonic Wars pitted the French Empire against European alliances. Napoleon defeated Prussia at Jena in 1806, and the country was occupied by France – but after Napoleon's final defeat at Waterloo in 1815, Prussia was restored to its position of power. Nationalism grew, and uniting Germany became the goal of the Prussian premier Otto von Bismarck. After a successful campaign, the German Empire was pronounced in 1871. The economy flourished due to a boom in industry, and, by the 20th century, Germany was a powerful state with overseas colonies. However, imperialist tendencies began to grow, and tensions in European politics led to war.

World War I

German generals had hoped for a quick victory upon entering World War I in 1914, but the war dragged on for the next four years, devastating Europe and ending in Germany's defeat. The Allied offensive in the summer of 1918 forced Germany to the negotiating table, and within days the state monarchs were toppled from power and Kaiser Wilhelm II abdicated.

1 German soldiers during World War I.

2 Battle of Leipzig.

3 Meeting to discuss the Treaty of Versailles.

4 An Allied soldier writes his name in the Reichstag after Germany's defeat.

132
—
billion gold marks had to be paid by Germany in reparations after World War I.

Timeline of events

1794–1815
The French Period, during which most of Northern Europe, including Prussia, is controlled by Republican or Napoleonic France

1813
Prussia, Austria and Russia defeat Napoleon at the Battle of Leipzig

1871
Otto von Bismarck achieves unification of Germany

1914–18
World War I devastates Europe; Allied victory leads the German Empire to fall

4

The Weimar Years

A new constitution was signed in the town of Weimar in 1919, and throughout the subsequent "Weimar years" (1919–33) Germany struggled with political and economic instability. The world stock-market crash of 1929 and the ensuing Depression put the German government under even greater pressure, paving the way for extremist politicians and the appointment of Adolf Hitler as Chancellor in 1933. The Reichstag fire in February of that year was used as a pretext to arrest communist and liberal opponents and, by March 1933, Hitler's Nazi (National Socialist German Workers) Party was in control.

World War II

Hitler's invasion of Poland in 1939 signalled the start of World War II, and in January 1942 the Nazi's systematic extermination of all European Jews began. After years of bitter warfare across the globe, the tide began to turn against the Germans. In April 1945 more than 1.5 million Soviet soldiers invaded Berlin and found the populace starving and the city lying in ruins. Hitler committed suicide shortly after, and Germany conceded defeat.

1919

Signing of the Treaty of Versailles on 28 June. Germany loses colonies and land to neighbours

1933

Adolf Hitler becomes Chancellor, proclaiming the Third Reich a year later

1945

Germany is defeated, Hitler commits suicide, and the Allies divide Germany

1939

Hitler's invasion of Poland triggers the start of World War II

A Nation Divided

At the Potsdam Conference of 1945, Germany was divided into four sectors, occupied by Soviet, US, British and French troops. Unfortunately, tensions increased between the Western powers and the Soviet Union, rapidly escalating into the "Cold War" (1947–91). In May 1949 the Federal Republic of Germany was established in the western zones, with its capital in Bonn. Later that year the German Democratic Republic (GDR) was set up in the Soviet zone. East Berlin became the capital of the GDR, and West Berlin remained a separate enclave of western Germany. As the westernmost outpost of the Eastern Bloc, the GDR was subject to restrictions, and an exodus to the West began. On 13 August 1961, construction began on the Berlin Wall, and the Stasi secret police began to watch over citizens' activities.

Reunification

The division of Germany continued for another 28 years. Change was made possible thanks to a number of democratic changes going on in Eastern Europe. The Berlin Wall finally fell on 9 November 1989, and the country was officially reunified

↑ The former inner German border between the east and the west

Timeline of events

1949
The Federal Republic of Germany and the German Democratic Republic are founded

1961
Construction of the Berlin Wall ends the flight of people from East to West

1968
East Germany begins to decriminalize homosexuality, followed by West Germany the following year

1989
Protests bring an end to Communist rule. Germans from East and West tear down the Berlin Wall

3

on 3 October 1990. On the surface, reunification took place with impressive speed and with few major problems. However, on closer inspection, East and West Germany continue to show great differences in terms of factors such as economy, education, health, migration, productivity and consumption – with the advantages tipped almost exclusively towards the West.

Germany Today

In the 21st century, Germany has become not only one of the world's great economic powers but a cultural stronghold too. It plays a key role in technology and industry as well as within the global realms of art and sport. Its population – the largest of any European country at 82 million – is, on the whole, well-educated, cosmopolitan and enjoys a high standard of living. Multicultural communities are growing as the country recently became home to over a million refugees from Africa and the Middle East, alongside an influx of other nationalities. Germany also enjoys a prominent position in the European Union. Following the rise of far-right populism throughout the West, some consider Germany to be "the leader of the free world".

1 Children playing by the sector boundary sign in Berlin in 1953. ↑

2 Residents climbing on the Berlin Wall at the Bradenburg Gate.

3 Berlin's glitzy Potsdamer Platz.

Did You Know?

Germany has pledged to replace all its nuclear power sources with renewable energies by 2022.

1990
East Germans elect pro-unification parliament; the state is merged into a Federal Republic

2005
Angela Merkel becomes the first female Chancellor in a "Grand Coalition" government

2015
Germany pledges to welcome one million refugees into the country

2017
The Bundestag legalizes same-sex marriage

EXPERIENCE

Old Town in Rothenburg ob der Tauber

Eastern Germany..48

Southern Germany...................................202

Western Germany....................................328

Northern Germany....................................412

EASTERN GERMANY

Berlin 54

Brandenburg 124

Saxony-Anhalt 144

Saxony 162

Thuringia 184

Rakotzbrücke in Rhododendronpark, Saxoy

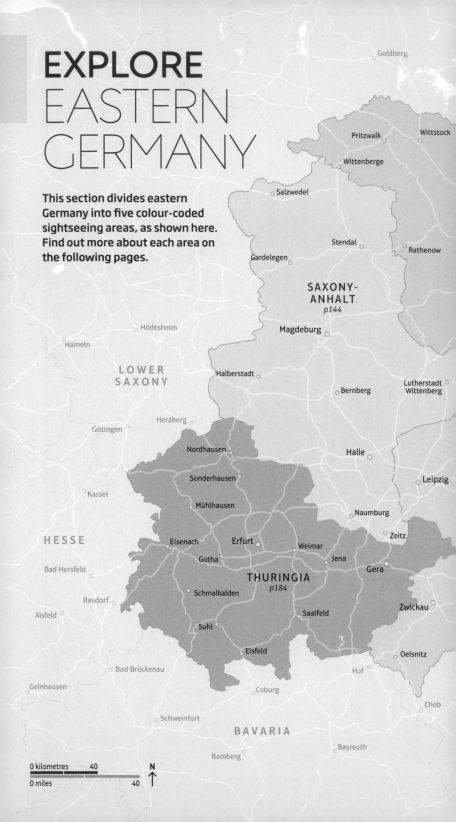

EXPLORE
EASTERN
GERMANY

This section divides eastern
Germany into five colour-coded
sightseeing areas, as shown here.
Find out more about each area on
the following pages.

Goldberg

Pritzwalk

Wittstock

Wittenberge

Salzwedel

Stendal

Rathenow

Gardelegen

**SAXONY-
ANHALT**
p144

Magdeburg

Hildesheim

**LOWER
SAXONY**

Hameln

Halberstadt

Bernberg

Lutherstadt
Wittenberg

Herzberg

Götingen

Nordhausen

Halle

Leipzig

Sonderhausen

Kassel

Mühlhausen

Naumburg

Zeitz

HESSE

Eisenach

Erfurt

Weimar

Jena

Gera

Bad Hersfeld

Gotha

THURINGIA
p184

Rasdorf

Schmalkalden

Alsfeld

Zwickau

Suhl

Saalfeld

Oelsnitz

Gelnhausen

Eisfeld

Hof

Bad Brückenau

Coburg

Cheb

BAVARIA

Schweinfurt

Bayreuth

Bamberg

0 kilometres 40

0 miles 40

N
↑

MECKLENBURG-
VORPOMMERN

Neubrandenburg

Szczecin

Drawsko
Pomorskie

Stargard

Walcz

Prenzlau

Templin

Schwedt

Choszczno

Neuruppin

Myślibórz

Bad
Freienwalde

Oranienburg

Gorzów
Wielkopolski

Międzychód

BERLIN
p54

Seelow

POLAND

Potsdam

Frankfurt
an der Oder

BRANDENBURG
p124

Swiebodzin

Besskow

Jüterbog

Guben

Zielona Gora

Lübbenau

Cottbus

Herzberg

Żary

Torgau

Zagan

Hoyerswerda

SAXONY
p162

Görlitz

Legnica

Döbeln

Bautzen

Dresden

Zittau

Freiberg

Chemnitz

GERMANY

Teplice

Chomutov

CZECH
REPUBLIC

Žatec

Chodová
Planá

Pilsen

GETTING TO KNOW
EASTERN GERMANY

The eastern region of Germany is rich in dramatic scenery as well as fascinating cultural sights, including Baroque palaces and traditional towns. The region is also home to the nation's capital: the exciting city-state of Berlin *(p54)*.

PAGE 122

BRANDENBURG

The jewel in Brandenburg's crown is its stunning capital of Potsdam, with its abundant Prussian castles and gardens. Beyond the city, the region is characterised by a peaceful network of nature reserves and flat, open landscapes punctuated with lakes.

Best for
Palaces and green spaces

Home to
Potsdam

Experience
Canoeing in the Spreewald

PAGE 144

SAXONY-ANHALT

A land of beautiful countryside woven with hiking and cycling trails, this is the birthplace of Martin Luther and the Bauhaus movement, and reminders of the state's rich past are everywhere.

Best for
Green spaces, history and cycling

Home to
Wörlitzer Park, Lutherstadt Wittenberg and Naumburg Dom

Experience
Take a gondola ride along Wörlitzer Park canals

SAXONY

PAGE 162

Saxony's alluring architecture and rich cultural treasures can be explored and admired in the lively town of Leipzig and the regional capital Dresden. Both offer museums, galleries and theatres galore for visitors who want to experience first hand Germany's rich heritage as a country of music and art. But Saxony offers even more beyond the town centres. The countryside is dotted with fine castles and fortresses, and is home to enchanting mountain ranges such as the Erzgebirge and Sächsische Schweiz (Saxon Switzerland).

Best for
Culture and hiking

Home to
Leipzig and Dresden

Experience
Hiking amidst the scenic rocks and hills of the Sächsische Schweiz region, making sure to enjoy the sweeping views from its famous Bastei Bridge

THURINGIA

PAGE 184

Hikers, campers and cyclists are drawn to Thuringia for its dense southern forest, but its charms are more subtle and varied than one might think. The region is peppered with medieval castles such as the dramatic Wartburg and historic towns and cities including the vibrant capital Erfurt, and Weimar – once home to intellectual heavyweights Goethe and Schiller. The region also offers many great spa and health resorts, which are open all year.

Best for
Spas and culture

Home to
Erfurt, Weimar and Eisenach-Wartburg

Experience
Hiking to the high-altitude Rennsteig through the Thuringian Forest and sampling a Thuringian Bratwurst on the way

BERLIN

Berlin: Eastern Centre 68

Berlin: Western Centre 88

Berlin: Beyond the Centre 104

Sun peeking through the Brandenburger Tor on Pariser Platz

EXPLORE
BERLIN

This section divides Berlin
into two sightseeing areas, as
shown here, and an area beyond
the city centre. Get to know each
area on the following pages.

WEDDING

MOABIT

Fritz-Schloss-
Park

Schlosspark

Schloss
Charlottenburg

Bröhan-
Museum

Spree

Englischer
Garten

**BERLIN:
WESTERN CENTRE**
p88

Grosser
Stern

Spree

Tiergarten

Kunstgewerbemuseum
Gemäldegalerie

DIPLOMATEN-
VIERTEL

Ernst-Reuter-
Platz

Sophie-
Charlotte-
Platz

CHARLOTTENBURG

Zoo Berlin

Breitscheid-
platz

Lutzow-
platz

Kaiser-Wilhelm-
Gedächtnis-Kirche

Adenauer-
platz

Wittenberg-
platz

Nollendorf-
platz

Winterfeldt-
platz

Fehrbelliner
Platz

WILMERSDORF

Rathaus
Schöneberg

Volkspark
Wilmersdorf

SCHÖNEBERG

SCHMARGENDORF

0 kilometres   1

0 miles   1

N

FRIEDENAU

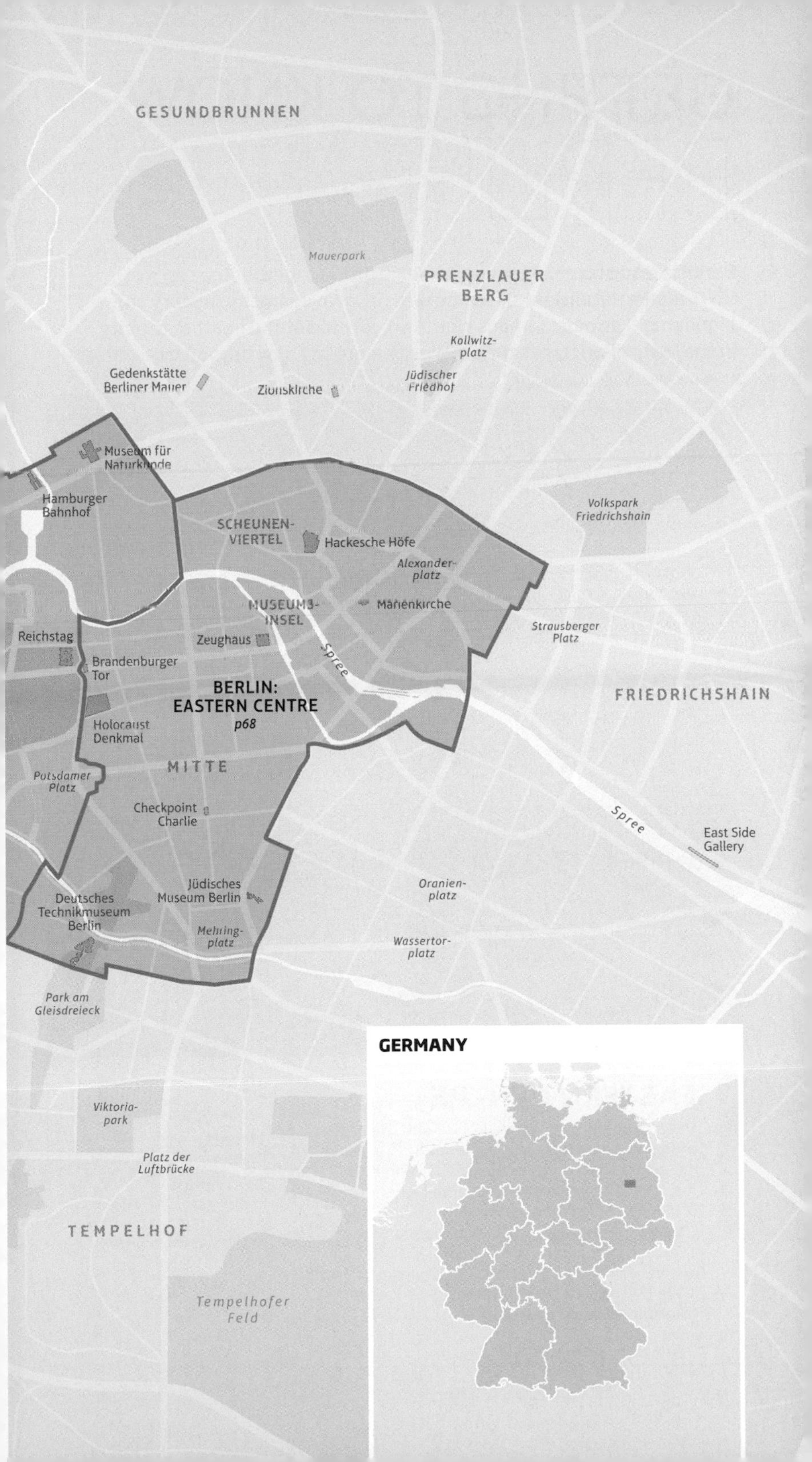

GESUNDBRUNNEN

Mauerpark

PRENZLAUER
BERG

Kollwitz-
platz

Gedenkstätte
Berliner Mauer

Zionskirche

Jüdischer
Friedhof

Museum für
Naturkunde

Hamburger
Bahnhof

SCHEUNEN-
VIERTEL

Hackesche Höfe

Volkspark
Friedrichshain

Alexander-
platz

MUSEUMS-
INSEL

Marienkirche

Reichstag

Zeughaus

Spree

Strausberger
Platz

Brandenburger
Tor

BERLIN:
EASTERN CENTRE
p68

FRIEDRICHSHAIN

Holocaust
Denkmal

MITTE

Potsdamer
Platz

Checkpoint
Charlie

Spree

East Side
Gallery

Jüdisches
Museum Berlin

Oranien-
platz

Deutsches
Technikmuseum
Berlin

Mehring-
platz

Wassertor-
platz

Park am
Gleisdreieck

GERMANY

Viktoria-
park

Platz der
Luftbrücke

TEMPELHOF

Tempelhofer
Feld

GETTING TO KNOW
BERLIN

Berlin is made up of 12 boroughs which group together the city's 96 *Ortsteile* (localities), each one with its own character, history and highlights. The most famous sights are located at the heart of the city in the Mitte district, yet there's plenty more to enjoy beyond the centre.

EASTERN CENTRE

PAGE 68

This area boasts Berlin's most iconic sights. Here you'll find the UNESCO listed Museumsinsel, a unique museum district on the northern end of Spreeinsel. Take a stroll down the tree-lined Unter den Linden boulevard, with its procession of baroque and Neo-Classical buildings, and you'll reach the imposing Brandenburger Tor. Near the historic heart of the city where the original settlement of Berlin was established in the 13th century, the reconstructed old town of Nikolaiviertel brings medieval Berlin back to life.

Best for
Sightseeing and culture

Home to
Museumsinsel

Experience
Shopping at the Alexa Mall on Alexanderplatz and checking out its family-friendly miniature Berlin, Loxx am Berlin

PAGE 88

WESTERN CENTRE

Decades on from reunification, western Berlin still has a distinctly different feel to the eastern part of the city. Development around the Zoologischer Garten has transformed the area into a hub of hotels, restaurants and shopping complexes. These now rival the ever popular Ku'damm boulevard and its bisecting streets, jam-packed with high-end shops, cafés and restaurants. For a one-stop shop of entertainment, venture into the marvel of modern architecture that is Potsdamer Platz.

Best for
Entertainment, dining and shopping

Home to
The Reichstag

Experience
Stroll the Ku'damm and browse its endless high-end fashion shops and theatres

PAGE 104

BEYOND THE CENTRE

There are lots of rewards awaiting those who venture outside the city centre. All it takes is a short S-Bahn or bicycle ride and you'll discover the beautiful palace of Charlottenburg to the west. To the north, Prenzlauer Berg offers leafy streets lined with boutiques and cafés, while further east visitors can explore the legacy of the GDR at the Stasi Museum. Southwest of the centre is the glittering Wannsee lake, the idiosyncratic Pfaueninsel, and the vast Grunewald forest.

Best for
Green spaces and lakes

Home to
Schloss Charlottenburg and East Side Gallery

Experience
Take a bike ride through the Grunewald forest

←

1 Inside the Sony Centre.

2 The Gemäldegalerie.

3 The old belfry of Kaiser-Wilhelm-Gedächtnis-Kirche.

4 Ending the evening at one of the city's traditional pubs.

2 DAYS

In Berlin

Day 1

Morning Start the day in style with breakfast and impressive views of the city at Panoramapunkt on the 25th floor of Kollhoff-Tower *(Potsdamer Platz 1)*. From here you can explore the exciting area of Potsdamer Platz *(p96)* with its many museums, shops and fascinating sights, from modern art installations to original sections of the Berlin Wall outside the S-Bahn entrance. For a quick and healthy lunch, try Weiland's Wellfood *(Marlene-Dietrich-Platz 1)*; for something grander, visit POTS *(Potsdamer Platz 3)* in the Ritz Carlton Hotel.

Afternoon After lunch, walk across to the Kulturforum *(p102)*. One of the most comprehensive museums is the Gemäldegalerie *(p96)*, which is well worth a couple of hours to explore. The adjacent Kunstgewerbemuseum *(p98)* has lots to interest design fans, while over on nearby Leipziger Platz *(p97)*, adults and kids alike can enjoy the multimedia Spy Museum, which includes a laser maze.

Evening To experience the sophisticated side of Berlin, book dinner at the Michelin-starred FACIL *(Potsdamer Strasse 3)* before attending a concert at the Philharmonie *(p98)*. An evening stroll through the Tiergarten *(p94)* is a wonderful after-concert activity, or you can continue down Potsdamer Strasse for some classy cocktails at Victoria Bar *(Potsdamer Strasse 102)*.

Day 2

Morning Grab a casual breakfast at one of the hip cafés in the Bikinihaus Mall, after which you can browse the local fashion and design boutiques. You'll soon see that Bikinihaus *(Budapester Strasse 38–50)* is not your average shopping centre: the ground floor houses 70 wooden pop-up shops that independent stores can rent for up to a year, which keeps things fresh and exciting. When you're done, cross the street to explore the interiors of the unique and moving Kaiser-Wilhelm-Gedächtnis-Kirche *(p99)*.

Afternoon Head down the elegant Fasanenstrasse to enjoy a classic villa-style lunch at the Café am Literaturhaus *(Fasanenstrasse 23)*. Next, catch a bus or underground train to the unmissable Schloss Charlottenburg *(p108)*. There are stunning interiors and artwork to see inside the palace, but make sure you leave enough time to explore the gorgeous palace grounds. Pause in between for a restorative coffee and cake at the Orangerie *(Spandauer Damm 20)*.

Evening If you have some time left, explore one or more of the palace's nearby museums, which include the Sammlung Berggruen *(p112)*, the Scharf-Gerstenberg and the Schlossstrasse Villas. End your day as the locals do at the Brauhaus Lemke am Schloss *(Luisenplatz 1)*, which offers a traditional German menu.

Costumed participants holding signs at the 41st CSD celebration in Berlin ↑

BERLIN FOR
LGBT+
CULTURE

Berlin's prominent LGBT+ scene sprung into life in the 19th century, and was immortalized during the Weimar era. Today, the city has the most active gay scene in Germany, with citywide infrastructure, regular events and a distinctive community hub in the scintillating "gaybourhood" of Schöneberg.

Community History

Berlin's LGBT+ legacy extends back to at least 1897, when the world's first gay magazine, Der Eigine, was published and the Scientific-Humanitarian Committee – the very first gay and lesbian organization in the world – was founded by Magnus Hirschfield. By the Weimar era, Berlin was known as the Gay Capital of Europe and was home to icons such as actress and cabaret star Marlene Dietrich and English author Christopher Isherwood. A more recent spokesperson for Berlin's gay community was former mayor Klaus Wowereit (2001–2014). Despite the city's liberal history, same-sex marriage wasn't legalized in Germany until 2017.

↑ Green party members celebrating the vote to legalize same-sex marriage in Parliament

Berlin Pride

Berlin Pride - also referred to as Christopher Street Day (CSD) - comprises many offshoot events that run parallel to the main, month-long Pride festival, which usually starts at the end of May. These events include a CSD Gala, Kreuzberg Pride, Gay Night at the Zoo, Dyke March, Libertarian CSD and Radical Queer March. Other LGBT+ events in the city include Folsom Europe, Hustlaball, Spreewieso Berlin and the Yo!Sissy Queer Music Festival.

> INSIDER TIP
> ### MonGay Movie Nights
>
> Since 1997, the Kino International cinema has been playing films with gay and lesbian content every Monday for its MonGay series, all shown in their original version with German subtitles.

↑ People wave the rainbow flag at the Berlin Pride parade

Schöneberg

Berlin has many gay districts, but Schöneberg is something special. Just as in the Weimar era, the vibrant centre point of the area is Nollendorfplatz. The local cafés and bars - Café Berio, Osbili, Romeo and Romeo and Prinzknecht - have long-catered to the gay clientele that congregate there. The world's first gay museum, the Schwules Museum, which opened in 1985, is also here, and showcases the history of the gay rights movement in Germany and Europe. The district also hosts regular events like Folsom Europe and major parts of Pride Week.

↑ The dome of the Nollendorfplatz U-Bahn station lit in rainbow colours

The Story of Berlin

For an overview of the city's 800-year history, head to the Berlin Story Bunker. Another must-visit is the Jewish Museum *(p83)*, which documents the integration and eventual destruction of the city's Jewish population. The Märkisches Museum *(p81)* is also worth a visit for its collection of local artifacts.

The interactive Family Album collection at the Jewish Museum

BERLIN FOR
HISTORY BUFFS

Home to Prussian palaces, Soviet architecture, monuments, and of course the infamous wall that once divided the East and West, Berlin continues to draw visitors back time and time again. Nowhere else seems to offer such an insight into the events of the past.

GDR History

Traces of the GDR (German Democratic Republic) can be seen everywhere in the city. The DDR Museum *(p82)* offers a look at East German life, with exhibits spanning the methods of the secret police, a prison cell and a reconstructed apartment. To see the Berlin Wall, visit the East Side Gallery *(p110)*, which features murals from 118 artists. Also worth a visit is the Berlin Wall Memorial *(p123)*, which is packed with installations and stories of daring escapes and tragic deaths.

Prussian Capital

The Hohenzollerns ruled Berlin, Prussia and eventually Germany for over 500 years until the end of World War I and transformed Berlin from a humble backwater to a cosmopolitan European capital. They created many of the city's grand sights and cultural institutions, such as Unter den Linden, Tiergarten and Schloss Charlottenburg. They also built most of Museumsinsel, the Berliner Dom, the Rotes Rathaus and the Reichstag, among others. The most famous Hohenzollern building is the Stadtschloss (City Palace), a reconstruction of which is set to open in 2021.

→

Visitors at Schloss
Charlottenburg, a
Berlin landmark

THE BERLIN WALL TRAIL

Construction of the Mauerweg (Berlin Wall Trail) began in 2002 and was completed in 2006. It traces the course of the former GDR border fortifications encircling West Berlin for around 160 km (99 miles). This trail can be hiked or cycled, either in its totality, or by choosing one or more of its 14 sections. Along the way there are stretches of natural beauty, memorials to those who perished at the Wall and information points with other interesting facts. The path also runs across Mauerpark, which was originally part of the Berlin Wall.

↑ More than 100 graffiti
paintings (inset) cover
the East Side Gallery

Berlin by Bike

Berlin is one of Europe's great cycling cities, with more than 900 km (550 miles) of bike routes. The inner city is criss-crossed with bike lanes *(fahrradwege)*, making it ideal for sightseeing on two wheels. Outside the centre, there are marked routes that run along the Panke river, around the Tegeler See, through the Grunewald and even along the former Berlin Wall *(p110)*. Highly recommended is the 28-km (17-mile) Wannsee route RR1, one of the longest and most scenic cycling trails in Berlin. Starting at Schlossplatz, it winds through the city's south-eastern suburbs, ending at the historic Gleinicker Brücke, or the "Bridge of Spies".

BERLIN FOR
OUTDOOR
ACTIVITIES

Although Berlin is known for its vibrant cultural scene, it's also a great place to enjoy the outdoors. From fun and frivolous to downright quirky, the city offers an impressive spread of outdoor pursuits to get your adrenaline pumping.

On the Water

Berlin's lakes, such as Wannsee *(p120)* in the west and Müggelsee in the east, are ideal for watersports, with options to sail yachts, rent motorboats or try water-skiing. Insel der Jugend has pedalo and rowing boats for hire, while StandUpClub Berlin *(www.standupclub.de)* offers SUP lessons. Wannsee's Water Sports Center Berlin *(www.segelschule-wannsee.de)* also has various courses.

Sailing boats by the Grunewaldturm, on the scenic Wannsee

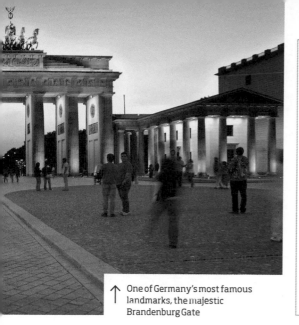

One of Germany's most famous
landmarks, the majestic
Brandenburg Gate

TOP 3 CYCLE RENTAL COMPANIES

**Fat Tire Bike
Rentals**
Reserve a bike online,
pick it up and off you go.
W fattiretours.
com/berlin

Berlin on Bike
Choose from a range
of themed tours, or
hire a bike and explore
on your own.
W berlinonbike.de

**Berlin Take
a Bike**
Conveniently located
on the Wall Cycle Path.
W takeabike.de

Hiking Trails

Strike out in pretty much any direction
and within an hour you'll be in the rural
environs of Brandenburg. Here, the
Wuhletal hiking trail winds its way
south from Eichepark to Köpenick
S-Bahn station via the Wuhle river
valley and various pleasant meadows
and parks. The Havel Heights Trail
(Havelhöhenweg) runs along the
Havel from Pichelsberg through
Grunewald to the Strandbad Wannsee.
The Panke Hiking trail starts at Bernau
in Brandenburg and ends in the city
centre, taking in Alt-Lübars (the oldest
village in Berlin), Schloss Tegel *(p115)*
and the Lübarser Felder nature reserve,
where you can see water buffaloes.

→ The beautiful canopy
walkway near Beelitz, on
the outskirts of Berlin

Daredevil Pursuits

Berlin is a playground for visitors of all ages
and abilities seeking adventurous pursuits.
Options include base flying, taking a ride over
Berlin in the iconic Die Welt helium balloon,
one of the world's biggest, or partaking in a
high-rope course either in the city or the
more rural Jungfernheide forest.

→ Base flying from the top of the
Park Inn hotel on Alexanderplatz

Berlin-Alexanderplatz station and the Fernsehturm

BERLIN:
EASTERN CENTRE

This part of Berlin is the historic centre of
the city, and includes the Mitte district and
parts of Kreuzberg. Its beginnings date back
to the 13th century, when two settlements were
established on the banks of the River Spree.
One was the former Cölln, situated on an island,
and the other its twin settlement, Berlin. Berlin's
first church, the Nikolaikirche, survives to this
day in the city's reconstructed old town of
Nikolaiviertel. This part of the city is home to
most of its historic buildings, which are located
mainly along Unter den Linden. It also includes
the Museumsinsel, the location of the vast
Berliner Dom and the impressive collection
of museums that gives the island its name.

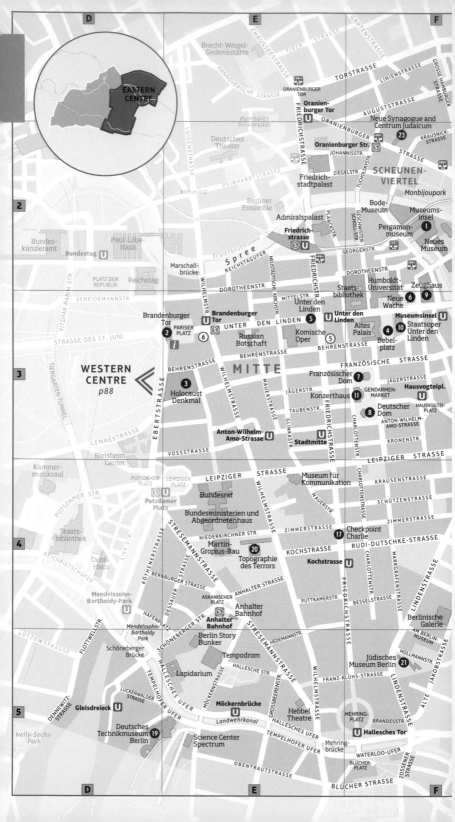

BERLIN: EASTERN CENTRE

Must See
1. Museumsinsel

Experience More
2. Brandenburger Tor
3. Holocaust Denkmal
4. Bebelplatz
5. Unter den Linden
6. Neue Wache
7. Französischer Dom
8. Deutscher Dom
9. Zeughaus
10. Staatsoper Unter den Linden
11. Konzerthaus
12. Marienkirche
13. Rotes Rathaus
14. Märkisches Museum
15. Fernsehturm
16. Alexanderplatz
17. Checkpoint Charlie
18. DDR Museum
19. Deutsches Technikmuseum Berlin
20. Topographie des Terrors
21. Jüdisches Museum Berlin
22. Haus Schwarzenburg Museums
23. Neue Synagoge and Centrum Judaicum
24. Hackesche Höfe

Eat
1. Zum Nussbaum
2. Gaststätte Zur letzten Instanz

Drink
3. Zille Stube
4. Schankhalle Pfefferberg

Stay
5. Clipper City Home
6. Hotel Adlon

❶
MUSEUMSINSEL

📍 F2

At the eastern end of Unter den Linden lies Museum Island, which is home to some of the world's greatest museums, including the Bode-Museum, the Altes Museum and the splendid Pergamonmuseum. Housing a staggering collection of art and artifacts from two millennia of civilization, it is an absolute must for any visitor to Berlin.

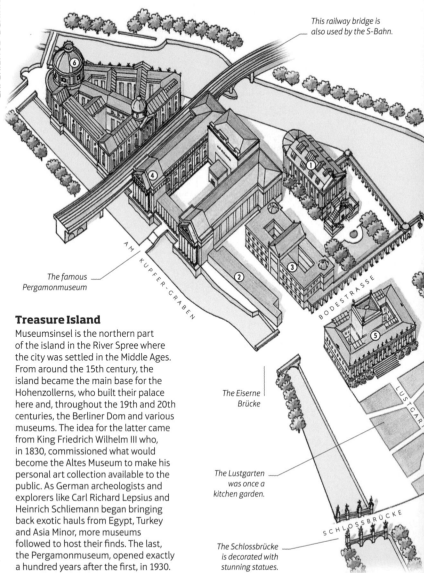

This railway bridge is also used by the S-Bahn.

The famous Pergamonmuseum

The Eiserne Brücke

The Lustgarten was once a kitchen garden.

The Schlossbrücke is decorated with stunning statues.

Treasure Island

Museumsinsel is the northern part of the island in the River Spree where the city was settled in the Middle Ages. From around the 15th century, the island became the main base for the Hohenzollerns, who built their palace here and, throughout the 19th and 20th centuries, the Berliner Dom and various museums. The idea for the latter came from King Friedrich Wilhelm III who, in 1830, commissioned what would become the Altes Museum to make his personal art collection available to the public. As German archeologists and explorers like Carl Richard Lepsius and Heinrich Schliemann began bringing back exotic hauls from Egypt, Turkey and Asia Minor, more museums followed to host their finds. The last, the Pergamonmuseum, opened exactly a hundred years after the first, in 1930.

→
The Alte
Nationalgalerie's
beautiful courtyard

Alte Nationalgalerie

⌂ Bodestrasse 1-3
Ⓢ Hackescher Markt,
Friedrichstrasse 🚌100,
300 🚋12, M1, M4, M5
🕐10am-6pm Tue-Sun (to
8pm Thu) 🌐smb.museum

Originally intended to
house the collection of
modern art of the Akademie
der Künste (Art Academy),
the Old Nationalgalerie
building was designed by
Friedrich August Stüler and
erected between 1866 and
1876. The collection features
paintings and sculptures that
were created in the century
of its foundation. Highlights
include works by Caspar
David Friedrich, Johann
Gottfeid Schadow, Carl
Blechen and Adolph
Menzel, as well as
pieces by French
Impressionists
Edouard
Manet
and Paul
Cézanne.

② James-Simon-Galerie

⌂ Bodestrasse 10178
Ⓢ Hackescher Markt,
Friedrichstrasse 🚌100,
300 🚋 M1, M4, M5, M6, M12
🕐Noon-6pm Tue-Wed &
Fri-Sun (to 8pm Thu)
🌐smb.museum

Named in honour of James
Simon (1851–1932), a patron
of the Berlin State Museums,
this building, completed in
1919, was designed by David
Chipperfield and serves as a

←
Map of
Museumsinsel
showing six
of its most
important
sights on the
northern end
of Spreeinsel

KARL-
LIEBKNECHT

SCHLOSSPLATZ

*The new Humboldt
(2021) Forum will
resurrect the
old Stadtschloss
(City Palace).*

central reception area for
the visitors of the various
museums of the island.

③ Neues Museum

⌂ Bodestrasse 1-3
Ⓢ Hackescher Markt,
Friedrichstrasse 🚌100,
300 🚋12, M1, M4, M5
🕐10am-6pm daily (to 8pm
Thu) 🌐smb.museum

The New Museum was
completed in 1855 to a design
by Friedrich August Stüler.
The building was closed to
the public at the start of
World War II, and was badly
damaged by Allied bombs in
1945. The museum remained
closed for decades, but reopened in 2009 after a long
reconstruction project led
by British architect David
Chipperfield. Now the
building once again houses
the Egyptian Museum as
well as the Museum of
Prehistory and Early History.
Many sculptures, sarcophagi,
murals and architectural
fragments of various eras
are on display.

→

Visitors near a section of the Pergamon Altar, Pergamonmuseum

④ Pergamonmuseum

🏛 Am Kupfergraben 5
Ⓢ Hackescher Markt,
Friedrichstrasse 🚌 100, 300
🚊 12, M1 🕐 10am–6pm daily
(to 8pm Thu) W smb.museum

The Pergamonmuseum was completed in 1930 to a design by Alfred Messels and Ludwig Hoffmann. It houses one of the most prestigious collections of antiquities in Europe, the result of archaeological excavations by German expeditions to the Near and Middle East. Major renovation until after 2025 means a selection of treasures are shown in the south wing, while most of the Museum of Antiquities' pieces are on display in the Altes Museum. While the Pergamon Altar in the main hall is closed until 2024, a temporary exhibition space nearby, "Pergamonmuseum, Das Panorama", holds a 3D simulation of it and a panorama of the ancient metropolis of Pergamon.

⑤ Altes Museum

🏛 Am Lustgarten
(Bodestrasse 1-3)
Ⓢ Hackescher Markt
🚌 100, 300 🕐 10am–6pm
Tue–Sun (to 8pm Thu)
W smb.museum

Designed by Karl Friedrich Schinkel, this museum building is one of the world's most beautiful Neo-Classical structures, with an impressive

The Altes Museum's grand façade and stunning park ↓

Did You Know?

The Pergamonmuseum takes its name from its main attraction, the altar of Zeus from Pergamon.

Museum Highlights

Neues Museum

△ The famous bust of Queen Nefertiti dates back to 1350 BC and is one of Museum Island's biggest draws.

87-m- (285-ft-) high portico supported by 18 Ionic columns. Officially opened in 1830, the museum was purpose-built to house the royal collection of art and antiquities.

Following World War II, the building was used only for temporary exhibitions. It now houses the Antikensammlung, with a magnificent collection of Greek, Roman and Etruscan antiquities.

⑥

Bode-Museum

🚇 Monbijoubrücke (Bodestrasse 1-3)
Ⓢ Hackescher Markt, Friedrichstrasse 🚌 100, 147, 300 🚊 M1, M4, M5, M6
🕐 10am–6pm daily (to 8pm Thu) 🌐 smb.museum

Constructed between 1897 and 1904, the Bode-Museum was designed by Ernst von Ihne to fit the wedge-shaped northwestern end of Museumsinsel. The interior was designed with the help of Wilhelm von Bode, who was the director of the Berlin state museums at the time.

The museum displayed a rather mixed collection that included some old masters. Its original name, Kaiser Friedrich Museum, was changed after World War II. Following the reassembling of the Berlin collections, all the paintings were rehoused in the Kultur-forum *(p102)*, while the Egyptian art and the papyrus collection were moved to the Neues Museum *(p73)*.

The building houses over 50,000 coins, plus medals and Byzantine art. It is also home to an extensive collection of sculptures, including the works of Donatello, Tilman Riemenschneider and Antonio Canova. A copy of the

magnificent equestrian statue of the Great Elector, Friedrich Wilhelm, by Andreas Schlüter, is also on show in the old hall.

⑦

Berliner Dom

🚇 Am Lustgarten
Ⓢ Hackescher Markt 🚌 100, 200, 300 🕐 Times vary, check website 🌐 berlinerdom.de

The original Berlin Cathedral was completed in 1750, based on a modest Baroque design by Johann Boumann. The present Neo-Baroque structure is the work of Julius Raschdor and dates from 1894. The central copper dome is some 98-m- (321-ft-) high. Following severe World War II damage, the cathedral has been restored in a simplified form but still contains some original features like the pulpit and altar, and beautiful reconstructed mosaics.

Pergamon-museum

▽ The Processional Way leading up to the monumental Ishtar Gate of Babylon boasts ceramic tiles featuring 60 lions.

Alte National-galerie

▽ Adolph Menzel's oil painting, *Torchlight Procession of Students* (1859), is an atmospheric highlight.

Altes Museum

△ Attributed to the painter Pistoxenos, this attic red kylix with javelin throwers (c 465 BC) is one of many antiquities housed here.

Bode-Museum

△ Dating from around 1520, this reliquary bust of a holy bishop is part of the Bode-Museum's Sculpture Collection.

EXPERIENCE MORE

2

Brandenburger Tor

📍E3 🏛Pariser Platz
Ⓢ&Ⓤ Brandenburger Tor
🚌100, 300

The Brandenburg Gate is the quintessential symbol of Berlin. A magnificent Neo-Classical structure, based on the entrance to the Acropolis, it was built between 1788 and 1791, with its sculptured decorations added in 1795. A pair of pavilions, once used by guards and customs officers, frames its powerful Doric colonnade and entablature. The bas-reliefs depict scenes from Greek mythology, and the whole structure is crowned by Johann Gottfried Schadow's grand sculpture, *Quadriga*. In 1806, during the French occupation, Napoleon had the sculpture dismantled and taken to Paris. On its triumphal return in 1814, it was declared a symbol of victory, and the goddess received a staff bearing the Prussian eagle and an iron cross with a laurel wreath.

The gate has witnessed many of Berlin's important events. Located in East Berlin, it was restored between 1956 and 1958, when the damaged *Quadriga* was rebuilt in West Berlin. Over the next 40 years it watched over the divided city, until 1989, when the first section of the Berlin Wall fell.

In 2016 a museum opened next to the gate. Open Monday through to Friday for

↑ The Holocaust Denkmal, a memorial to the Jews killed by the Nazis

groups only, and weekends for all visitors, it offers a multimedia excursion through Berlin's history.

3

Holocaust Denkmal

📍E3 Ⓢ&Ⓤ Brandenburger Tor 🚌200, 300, M41, M48, M85

Germany's national Holocaust memorial was designed by American architect Peter Eisenman. Completed in 2005, it is made up of a large field with dark grey steles of various heights that symbolize the six million Jews and others

murdered by the Nazis in concentration camps between 1933 and 1945.

Visitors can walk their own route, and there is an information centre underneath the memorial. There are also memorials in the nearby Tiergarten *(p94)* to LGBT, Sinti and Roma people murdered during World War II.

4

Bebelplatz

📍F3 Ⓢ&Ⓤ Friedrich-strasse 🚌100, 300

Bebelplatz was intended to be the focal point of the Forum Fridericianum – an area designed to mirror the grandeur of ancient Rome. Although the plans were only partly implemented, many important buildings were eventually erected here.

In 1933 the square was the scene of the notorious

book-burning act organized by the Nazis. Some 25,000 books, written by authors considered to be enemies of the Third Reich, were burned. Today, a monument in the square commemorates this dramatic event.

Unter den Linden

◘E3 ⑤&Ⓤ Brandenburger Tor, Unter den Linden ■100, 300

One of Berlin's most famous streets, Unter den Linden starts at Schlossplatz and runs down to Pariser Platz and the Brandenburger Tor. It was once the route to the royal hunting grounds, which were later transformed into the Tiergarten.

In the 17th century the street was planted with lime trees, to which it owes its name. Although the original trees were removed around 1658, four rows of limes were planted in 1820.

During the 18th century Unter den Linden became the main street of the westward-growing city and gradually came to be lined with prestigious buildings, which were restored in the years following World War II.

After the reunification of Germany in 1990, Unter den Linden acquired several cafés and restaurants, as well as many smart shops. The street has also become the venue for a wide range of interesting outdoor events. It is usually crowded with tourists and students browsing the bookstalls located around the Humboldt Universität and the Staatsbibliothek (State Library).

Neue Wache

◘F3 ◨Unter den Linden 4 ⑤Hackescher Markt ■100, 300 ◷10am–6pm daily

Designed by Karl Friedrich Schinkel and completed in 1818, the new Guardhouse is considered one of the finest examples of Neo-Classical architecture in Berlin. The front is dominated by a huge Doric portico with a frieze of bas-reliefs depicting goddesses of victory.

In 1930–31 the building was turned into a monument to soldiers killed in World War I. Following its restoration in 1960, Neue Wache became the Memorial to the Victims of Fascism and Militarism. It was rededicated in 1993 to the memory of all victims of war and dictatorship. Inside is an eternal flame and a granite slab over the ashes of an unknown soldier, a resistance fighter and a concentration camp prisoner. In the roof opening is a copy of the sculpture *Mother with her Dead Son,* by Berlin artist Käthe Kollwitz.

←

The iconic and imposing Brandenburger Tor, a historic gateway to the city

←

The Französischer Dom and statue of Friedrich Schiller

8

Deutscher Dom

📍 F3 ⌂ Gendarmenmarkt 1
☎ (030) 22 73 04 31
Ⓤ Stadtmitte or
Hausvogteiplatz
🕐 May-Sep: 10am-7pm
Tue-Sun; Oct-Apr: 10am-
6pm Tue-Sun

The German cathedral at the southern end of the square is an old German Protestant-Reformed church. Based on a five-petal shape, it was designed by Martin Grünberg and built in 1708 by Giovanni Simonetti. In 1785 it acquired a dome-topped tower that is identical to that of the French cathedral.

Burned down in 1945, it was rebuilt in 1993, with its interior adapted as exhibition space. On display is the exhibition "Milestones – Setbacks – Sidetracks". Over five floors, it traces the historical development of the parliamentary system in Germany.

9

Zeughaus

📍 F3 ⌂ Unter den Linden 2
☎ (030) 20 30 40
Ⓢ Hackescher Markt
🚌 100, 300 🕐 New wing:
10am-6pm daily

This former arsenal was built in the Baroque style in 1706 under the guidance of Johann

€400,000,000

The cost of the refurbishment of the Staatsoper: almost double the original estimate.

7

Französischer Dom

📍 F3 ⌂ Gendarmenmarkt 5
☎ (030) 20 64 99 22/3
Ⓤ Stadtmitte or
Hausvogteiplatz
🕐 Museum: 10am-6pm
Tue-Sun; Church: noon-
5pm Tue-Sun

Although the two churches standing on opposite sides of the Konzerthaus seem identical, their only common feature is their matching front towers. The French cathedral was built for the Huguenot community, who found refuge in protestant Berlin following their expulsion from France after the revocation of the Edict of Nantes in 1598. The modest church, built between 1701 and 1705 by Louis Cayart

and Abraham Quesnay, was modelled on the Huguenot church in Charenton, France, which was destroyed in 1688. The interior features a late-Baroque organ from 1754.

The structure is dominated by a massive, cylindrical tower, encircled by Corinthian porticos at its base. The tower and porticos were designed by Carl von Gontard and added around 1785. It houses the Huguenot Museum, which charts the history of the Huguenot community in France and Brandenburg.

A viewing platform 40 m (131 ft) above the ground is one of the city's highest historic observation platforms. It is open every day between 10:30am and 7pm, and offers stunning views of the skyline.

Arnold Nering, Martin Grünberg, Andreas Schlüter and Jean de Bodt. A magnificent structure, its wings flank an inner courtyard and its exterior is decorated with Schlüter's sculptures, including masks of dying warriors. Home to the Museum für Deutsche Geschichte of the GDR since 1952, it became the Deutsches Historisches Museum (DHM) in 1990, housing an extensive exhibition on German history. A modern glass and steel building designed by architect I M Pei was added in 2003 and hosts a wide range of temporary exhibits. The DHM will be closed from mid-2021 until 2025, while the Pei building will remain open to the public.

Staatsoper Unter den Linden

📍F3 🚇Unter den Linden 7 Ⓢ Friedrichstrasse Ⓤ Unter den Linden 🚌100, 300 🕐Times vary; see website 🌐staatsoper-berlin.de

The early Neo-Classical façade of the State Opera House is one of the most beautiful sights on Unter den Linden. Built by the painter and architect Georg Wenzeslaus von Knobelsdor between 1741 and 1743, it has been reworked and restored several times. The building is home to the Berlin State Opera and has played host to many international singers, musicians and conductors.

Konzerthaus

📍F3 🚇Gendarmenmarkt 2 Ⓤ Stadtmitte 🌐konzert haus.de

A late Neo-Classical jewel, this magnificent concert hall is one of the greatest achievements of Berlin's best-known architect, Karl Friedrich Schinkel (p77). It was built between 1818 and 1821 around the ruins of Langhans' National Theatre, destroyed by fire in 1817. The portico columns were retained in the new design. Following bomb damage in World War II, it was reconstructed as a concert hall, and the exterior was restored to its former glory. The Konzerthaus is now home to the Konzerthausorchester Berlin.

The whole building is decorated with sculptures alluding to drama and music. The façade, which includes a huge Ionic portico with a set of stairs, is crowned with a sculpture of Apollo riding a chariot pulled by griffins.

In front of the theatre stands a shining white marble statue of Friedrich Schiller, sculpted by Reinhold Begas and erected in 1869. Removed by the Nazis, it was returned to its rightful place in 1988.

Johann Strauss's operetta *Die Fledermaus*, staged at Staatsoper Unter den Linden ↓

← The striking red Marienkirche, a medieval relic in the heart of modern Berlin

13 Rotes Rathaus

🅟 G2 🏠 Rathausstrasse 15 🅢 Alexanderplatz 🆄 Rotes Rathaus 🆄 Klosterstrasse 🚌 248, TXL

The Red Town Hall is an impressive structure that functions as Berlin's main town hall. Its predecessor was a more modest structure that, by the end of the 19th century, was inadequate to meet the needs of the growing metropolis.

The present building was designed by Hermann Friedrich Waesemann, and the construction lasted from 1861 until 1869. The walls are made from red brick, and it was this, rather than the mayors' political orientation, that gave the town hall its name.

The Rotes Rathaus was severely damaged during World War II, but after its reconstruction in the 1950s, it became the seat of the East Berlin authorities. The West Berlin magistrate was housed in Schöneberg town hall (p119). Following the reunification of Germany in 1990, the Rotes Rathaus became the centre of

12 Marienkirche

🅟 G2 🏠 Karl-Liebknecht-Strasse 8 ☎ (030) 24 75 95 10 🅢 Alexanderplatz 🆄 Rotes Rathaus 🚌 100, 200 🕐 Apr-Dec: 10am-6pm daily (Jan-Mar: to 4pm)

St Mary's Church, or the Marienkirche, was first established as a parish church in the second half of the 13th century. Started around 1280, construction was completed early in the 14th century. During reconstruction works in 1380, following a fire, the church was altered slightly, but its overall shape changed only in the 15th century, when it acquired the front tower. In 1790 the tower was crowned with a dome, designed by Carl Gotthard Langhans, which includes both Baroque and Neo-Gothic elements.

The Marienkirche was once hemmed in by buildings, but today it stands alone in the shadow of the Fernsehturm (Television Tower). The early

Gothic hall design and the lavish decorative touches make this church one of the most interesting in Berlin. An alabaster pulpit by Andreas Schlüter, dating from 1703, is decorated with bas-reliefs of St John the Baptist and the personifications of the Virtues.

The Baroque main altar was designed by Andreas Krüger around 1762. The paintings with which it is adorned include three works by Christian Bernhard Rode.

A Gothic font, dating from 1437, is supported by three black dragons and decorated with the figures of Jesus Christ, Mary and the Apostles.

→ The Berlin skyline, dominated by the Fernsehturm TV tower

authority, housing the offices of the mayor and the Berlin cabinet.

Märkisches Museum

📍 G3 🏛 Am Köllnischen Park 5 📞 (030) 24 00 21 62 Ⓢ Jannowitzbrücke Ⓤ Märkisches Museum 🚌 147, 265 🕙 10am-6pm Tue-Sun

Built between 1901 and 1908, this complex of red brick buildings was inspired by the brick-Gothic style popular in the Brandenburg region. The museum, founded in 1874, is dedicated to the cultural history of Berlin from the first settlements to today. The art department "Berliner Kunst", for example, presents a remarkable collection of paintings, sculpture, textiles, faience, glass and porcelain. One of the galleries houses some historical mechanical musical instruments.

Fernsehturm

📍 G2 🏛 Panoramastrasse 1A Ⓢ & Ⓤ Alexanderplatz 🚌 100, 200, 300 🚋 M2, M4, M5, M6 🕙 9am-midnight daily (Nov-Feb: from 10am) 🌐 tv-turm.de

The television tower, called by the locals *Telespargel* (asparagus), or toothpick, remains the city's tallest structure at 368 m (1,207 ft). It is also the second-tallest structure in Europe. The tower was built in 1969 to a design by a team of architects including Fritz Dieter and Günter Franke, with the help of Swedish experts. However, the idea for the tower originated much earlier from Hermann Henselmann (creator of the Karl-Marx-Allee development) in the Socialist-Realist style.

Alexanderplatz

📍 G2 Ⓢ & Ⓤ Alexanderplatz 🚌 100, 200

Alexanderplatz has a long history, although it would be hard now to find any visible traces of the past. Once known as Ochsenmarkt (oxen market), it was the site of a cattle and wool market. It was later renamed after Tsar Alexander I, who visited Berlin

GREAT VIEW
Fernsehturm

By far the best view of Berlin is from the viewing gantry of the TV Tower. It's Europe's highest publicly accessible building and provides views of the German capital in its entirety.

---

in 1805. At that time, the square boasted a magnificent monumental colonnade designed by Carl von Gontard.

In time, houses and shops sprang up around the square, and a market hall and urban train line were built nearby. "Alex" became one of the city's busiest spots. Its frenzied atmosphere was captured by Alfred Döblin (1878–1957) in his novel *Berlin Alexanderplatz*.

In 1929 attempts were made to develop the square, though only two office buildings were added – the Alexanderhaus and the Berolinahaus, both designed by Peter Behrens.

World War II erased most of the square's buildings and they were replaced by 1960s edifices, including the Park Inn Hotel and the Fernsehturm. The area now has several shopping plazas and cinemas, as well as open-air markets during the holidays.

⑰ Checkpoint Charlie

⦿ E4 ⬛ Friedrichstrasse 43-45 ☎ (030) 253 72 50 Ⓤ Kochstrasse 🚌 M29

The name of this notorious border crossing between the American and Soviet sectors comes from the word used for the letter C in the international phonetic alphabet.

Between 1961 and 1990 Checkpoint Charlie was the only crossing for foreigners between East and West Berlin. It became a symbol of both freedom and separation for the many East Germans trying to escape Soviet communism.

Today, a single watchtower is all that remains. Next to it, the Haus am Checkpoint Charlie museum details the years of the Cold War in Berlin.

⑱

DDR Museum

⦿ F2 ⬛ Karl-Liebknecht-Strasse 1 Ⓢ & Ⓤ Alexanderplatz 🚌 100, 200, 300 🕐 10am-8pm Mon-Sun (to 10pm Sat) 🖥 ddr-museum.de

This privately run museum provides an interactive look at daily life in the former East Germany. Visit a reconstructed flat and take a simulated ride in an old Trabant car through a concrete housing estate.

⑲

Deutsches Technikmuseum Berlin

⦿ D5 ⬛ Trebbiner Strasse 9 Ⓤ Gleisdreieck 🚌 140, M29 🕐 9am-5:30pm Tue-Fri, 10am-6pm Sat & Sun 🖥 sdtb.de/stiftung/startseite

The German Museum of Technology was established in 1982 to bring more than 100 smaller, specialized collections

↑ Planes suspended from the ceiling in the Deutsches Technikmuseum Berlin

under one roof. The current collection is arranged on the site of the former freight depot, the size of which allows exhibits such as locomotives, water towers and ships to be displayed full-size and in their original condition.

Of particular interest are the dozens of locomotives and railway carriages from different eras, as well as large aviation and shipping exhibitions. Further exhibits explore the history of road transport, the internet, paper manufacturing, printing, weaving, telecommunications and computer technology. There are also two windmills, a brewery and an old forge. The section called Spectrum is popular with children for its hands-on experiments.

A special attraction here is the Historical Brewery. The

building was once used by the brewery Tucher Bräu for storing beer, but it was destroyed in World War II. Decades later, the brewery was rebuilt on four levels. Some visitors claim they can smell roasted malt. From the top of the brewery building, there is a spectacular view over Berlin.

⑳

Topographie des Terrors

⦿ E4 ⬛ Niederkirchnerstrasse Ⓢ & Ⓤ Potsdamer Platz, Anhalter Bahnhof 🚌 M29 🕐 10am-8pm daily 🖥 topographie.de

During the Third Reich, Prinz-Albrecht-Strasse (Niederkirchnerstrasse) was probably the most frightening address in Berlin: here, three of the most terrifying Nazi political departments had their headquarters. The Neo-Classical Prinz-Albrecht palace, at Wilhelmstrasse 102, became the HQ of Reinhard Heydrich and the Third Reich's security service. Prinz-Albrecht-Strasse 8 housed the head of the Gestapo, Heinrich Müller, while the Hotel Prinz Albrecht at No. 9 became HQ of the Schutzstaffel or SS.

After World War II, the bomb-damaged buildings were pulled down and, in 1987, a temporary hall was built to house an exhibition on the history of the site. Today the museum houses the permanent "Topography of Terror" exhibition and multiple changing temporary exhibitions, a library, event spaces and education programmes.

Jüdisches Museum Berlin

F5 **Lindenstrasse 14** **Hallesches Tor, Kochstrasse** **M29, M41, 248** **10am-10pm Mon, 10am-8pm Tue-Sun** **jmberlin.de**

The building housing the city's Jewish Museum is an exciting and imaginative example of 20th-century architecture. Designed by a Polish-Jewish architect based in the United States, Daniel Libeskind, the plan, shape, style and interior and exterior arrangement of the building are all part of a profoundly complicated philosophical programme. The museum's architecture itself is intended to convey something of the tragic history of the millions of Jews killed in the Holocaust.

The interior arrangement is dominated by a gigantic empty crack, which cuts a swathe through the building. Several corridors lead to a windowless Holocaust tower.

The collection focuses on Jewish history and art, with an emphasis on portraying stories through related objects. The thousands of historical exhibits include artifacts that were once part of everyday Jewish life in Berlin.

The museum is accessible only through an underground passageway located in the former Berlin-Museum building next door.

EAT & DRINK

Zille Stube
In the middle of the historic quarter of Nicolaiviertel, this quaint and cosy pub serves classic drinks and German cuisine.

G3 **Spreeufer 3** **zillestube-nikolaiviertel.de**

Schankhalle Pfefferberg
This friendly inn has a beer garden and sits atop a little hill in a former brewery complex. It offers beer and hearty meals.

G1 **Schönhauser Allee 176** **schankhalle-pfefferberg.de**

→
The stark metal façade of the Jüdisches Museum Berlin

Haus Schwarzenberg Museums

QF2 **A**Rosenthaler Strasse 39 **S**Hackesher Markt **U**Weinmeister-strasse **N2, N5, N42** **M1, M5** **W**haus-schwarzenberg.org

This complex is a cool and grungy hangover from the early 1990s. Its crumbling, postwar façades are splashed with colourful street art, some by local artists such as El Bocho and Miss Van. Its courtyard eschews high-end boutiques and cafés in favour of an edgy bar, a street-art shop and gallery, and the **Monsterkabinett** – a collection of moving mechanical monsters built by the owners, a non-profit artist collective.

The complex also hosts a trio of notable small museums that explore local resistance

EAT

Zum Nussbaum
A reconstruction of a 16th-century pub which used to exist nearby, serving traditional Berlin cuisine including rollmops, meatballs and vegetable pancakes.

QG3 **A**Am Nussbaum 3 **C**(030) 242 30 95

€€€

Gaststätte Zur letzten Instanz
The oldest pub in Berlin offers classic German fare in a wood-panelled room.

QG3 **A**Waisenstrasse 14-16 **W**zur-letzteninstanz.com

€€€

to the Nazis. The **Gedenk stätte Stille Helden** (Silent Heroes Memorial Centre) commemorates people who risked their lives to hide or rescue persecuted Jews. One such man was Otto Weidt, a German entrepreneur who saved a number of his blind Jewish employees at his workshop, which is now the **Museum Blindenwerkstatt Otto Weidt** (Museum Otto Weidt's Workshop for the Blind). It displays photographs and back-stories of Weidt, his family and his workers, and visitors can still see the room where Jewish families were hidden. The third museum, the **Anne-Frank-Zentrum**, offers an engaging and eclectic look at the famous teenager's life.

Monsterkabinett
 CTimes vary; see website **W**monsterkabinett.de

Gedenkstätte Stille Helden
 C10am-8pm daily **W**gedenkstaette-stille-helden.de

Museum Blinden-werkstatt Otto Weidt
C10am-8pm daily **W**museum-blindenwerkstatt.de

Anne-Frank-Zentrum
C10am-6pm Tue-Sun **W**annefrank.de

Neue Synagoge and Centrum Judaicum

QF2 **A**Oranienburger Strasse 30 **S**Oranien-burger Strasse **M1, M6** **C**Daily **W**centrum judaicum.de

Construction of the synagogue, begun in 1859 by architect Eduard Knoblauch,

↑ Beer garden and dining area in one of the courtyards of Hackesche Höfe

was finished in 1866. The design was a response to the asymmetrical plot of land, with a narrow façade flanked by a pair of towers and crowned with a gilded dome.

This was Berlin's largest synagogue until it was partially destroyed during the infamous *Kristallnacht* in 1938. It was further damaged by Allied bombing in 1943 and was eventually demolished in 1958. Reconstruction began in 1988, and the stunning new building was completed with due ceremony in 1995.

Adjoining the Neue Synagoge, the Centrum Judaicum (Jewish Centre) occupies the former premises of the Jewish community council, and contains archives, a library and a research centre devoted to the history and cultural heritage of the Jews of Berlin. The Centre also uses restored rooms of the Neue Synagoge to exhibit various materials relating to the local Jewish community, which included one of the greatest of all Jewish thinkers and social activists, Moses Mendelssohn (1729–86). Be aware that security is strict at both the synagogue and the Centrum Judaicum.

24

Hackesche Höfe

9 F2 **A** Rosenthaler Strasse 40–41
S Hackescher Markt
U Weinmeisterstrasse
M M1, M4, M5, M6

Running from Oranienburger Strasse and Rosenthaler up as far as Sophienstrasse, Hackesche Höfe (*Höfe* means "courtyards") is a huge, early 20th-century complex. It is made up of an intricate series of nine interconnecting courtyards surrounded by tall and beautifully proportioned buildings. The development dates from 1906 and was designed by Kurt Berendt and August Endell, both outstanding exponents of the German Secession style. Damaged during World War II, Hackesche Höfe has since been restored to its original splendour. The first courtyard is especially attractive, featuring glazed facings with geometric designs in fabulous colours. A range of restaurants, bars, art galleries, shops and restaurants can be found here, as well as offices and apartments on the upper floors. The complex also has a small theatre, the Chamäleon, specializing in contemporary circus shows. For many Berliners the Hackesche Höfe has become something of a cult spot.

A SHORT WALK
NIKOLAIVIERTEL

Distance 1 km (0.5 miles) **Time** 15 minutes
Nearest U-Bahn station Märkisches Museum

St Nicholas' Quarter, or the Nikolaiviertel, owes
its name to the parish church whose spires rise
above the small buildings in this part of town.
The Nikolaiviertel is full of narrow alleys crammed
with popular restaurants, tiny souvenir shops and
small museums. The district retains the features
of long-destroyed Alt-Berlin (Old Berlin) and is
usually filled with tourists looking for a place to
rest after an exhausting day of sightseeing –
particularly in the summer. Almost every other
house is occupied by a restaurant, inn, pub or
café, so the area is quite lively until late at night.

Did You Know?

Many Berlin artists,
such as Ibsen, Lessing,
Kleist and Hauptmann,
once lived in the
Nikolaivertel.

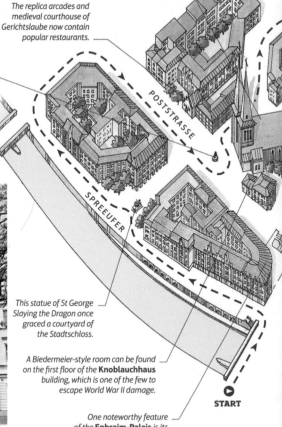

The **Nikolaikirche**
is now a museum, with
its original furnishings
incorporated into
the exhibition.

The replica arcades and
medieval courthouse of
Gerichtslaube now contain
popular restaurants.

A statue of a bear holds
Berlin's city shield at
the **Wappenbrunnen**
(Coat of Arms Fountain).

POSTSTRASSE

SPREEUFER

0 metres   75
0 yards   75

N ↑

This statue of St George
Slaying the Dragon once
graced a courtyard of
the Stadtschloss.

A Biedermeier-style room can be found
on the first floor of the **Knoblauchhaus**
building, which is one of the few to
escape World War II damage.

▶
START

One noteworthy feature
of the **Ephraim-Palais** is its
elegant façade. Inside there is
also an impressive spiral
staircase and balustrade.

↑ A bear, the symbol of
Berlin, inside a fountain
in front of Nikolaikiche

Locator Map
For more detail see p70

↑ The towering Rotes Rathaus, housing
the offices of the mayor of Berlin

The monumental **Rotes Rathaus**
*(Red Town Hall; p80), which once
stood in a densely built-up area,
rises from an empty square.*

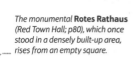

○ **FINISH**

SPANDAUER STRASSE

MÜHLENDAMM

JÜDENSTRASSE

The **Stadthaus**, *built
in 1911 by Ludwig
Hoffmann houses
several departments
of the Town Hall.*

STRALAUER STRASSE

MÜHLENDAMM

NEUE JÜDENSTRASSE

The small but fascinating
Hanfmuseum *(Hemp
Museum) specializes
in all aspects of the
hemp plant.*

The façade of **Palais Schwerin
and Münze** *is decorated with a
Neo-Classical frieze by Johann
Gottfried Schadow, depicting
the development of metal-
processing and coin-minting.*

ROLANDUFER

*Canal locks
on the Spree*

Inside the Reichstag dome

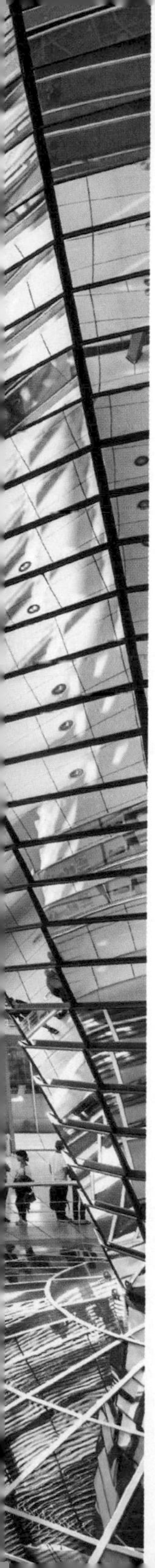

BERLIN: WESTERN CENTRE

This part of Berlin includes the areas of Tiergarten, Charlottenburg and parts of Kreuzberg, as well as a small section of Mitte. To the south of Tiergarten is the Kulturforum – a large complex of museums and other cultural establishments, which was created after World War II. The neighbouring area of Potsdamer Platz is now an ultra-modern and stylish development, built on the wasteland that formerly divided East and West Berlin.

Although the eastern part of Charlottenburg does not have a great number of historic buildings, it is one of the city's most attractive districts, which, after World War II, became the commercial and cultural centre of West Berlin.

BERLIN: WESTERN CENTRE

Must See
1. Reichstag

Experience More
2. Kurfürstendamm
3. Zoo Berlin
4. Tiergarten
5. Siegessäule
6. Bauhaus-Archiv
7. Bendlerblock
8. Gemäldegalerie
9. Potsdamer Platz
10. Leipziger Platz
11. Neue Nationalgalerie
12. Kunstgewerbemuseum
13. Philharmonie und Kammermusikaal
14. Kaiser-Wilhelm-Gedächtnis-Kirche
15. Musikinstrumenten-Museum
16. Regierungsviertel
17. Hamburger Bahnhof
18. Museum für Naturkunde
19. Haus der Kulturen der Welt
20. Brecht-Weigel-Gedenkstätte

Eat
① Dachgarten-Restaurant

Stay
② Hotel Zoo
③ 25hours Hotel Bikini
④ Das Stue
⑤ Waldorf Astoria

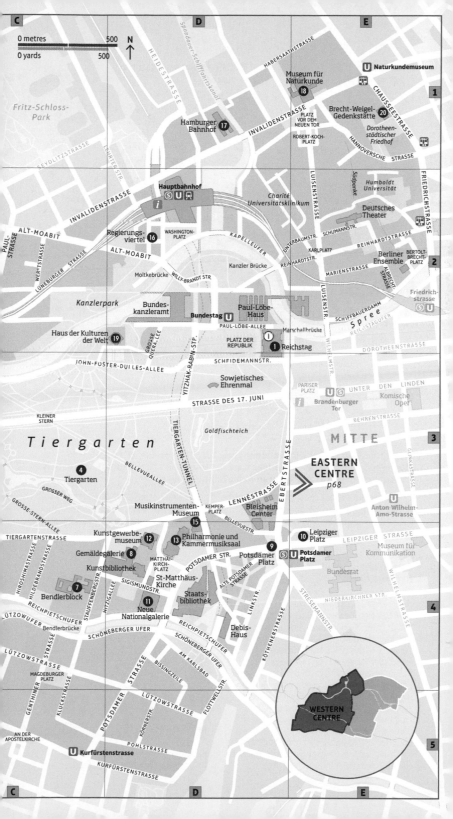

The historic Reichstag topped with a modern glass dome ↑

THE REICHSTAG

♀D2 **☐Platz der Republik** **⑤Brandenburger Tor** **Ⓤ Bundestag** **🚌100, 245, M85**
⏰8am-midnight daily; bookings for a time slot to visit or for a restaurant reservation are required at least a few days in advance **ⓦbundestag.de**

One of Berlin's most recognizable landmarks, the Reichstag, seat of Germany's parliament, has survived fascism and fire – not to mention bombardment and being wrapped in fireproof polypropylene fabric by artists – to become a symbol of a modern, politically transparent Germany.

Construction and Restoration

Constructed to house the German parliament, the Reichstag was built between 1884 and 1894 to a Neo-Renaissance design by Paul Wallot. In 1933 a fire destroyed the main hall, and World War II delayed rebuilding for years. In the 1960s, the structure underwent a partial restoration that included the controversial removal of most of the ornamentation on the façade. After German reunification in 1990, the Reichstag once again became the home of the German parliament. The magnificent rooftop glass dome was added in 1999 by British architect Lord Norman Foster. It is a highlight of the Reichstag, with its photogenic curves, mirrored columns and stellar views across the city.

↑ A Reichstag tour group, viewing graffiti left by Red Army troops

EAT

Dachgarten-Restaurant
The only government building restaurant in the world with public access offers gourmet German cuisine and fine views of eastern Berlin.

🏠 Platz der Republik 1
🌐 feinkost-kaefer.de/berlin

€€€

GREAT VIEW
Festival of Lights

For ten days in October, the annual Festival of Lights transforms some of Berlin's most striking landmarks, including the Reichstag, into washes of abstract colour and light via projections and video art. Walking routes and LightSeeing tours are available.

↑ The Reichstag dome, offering stunning views inside and out

27 February 1933
▽ Fire destroys the Reichstag. Many believe this was ordered by the Nazis to obtain emergency powers

19 April 1999
▽ The building receives a spectacular new glass dome, which was designed by Lord Norman Foster

Timeline

5 December 1894
△ Designed by Paul Wallot, the Reichstag is dedicated, the final stone being laid by Kaiser Wilhelm II

7 July 1995
Artists wrap the Reichstag in plastic

EXPERIENCE MORE

2

Kurfürstendamm

 A4 Kurfürstendamm
🚌 109, 110, M19, M29, M46, X10

The eastern area of the Charlottenburg region, around the boulevard known as Kurfürstendamm (the Ku'damm), was developed in the 19th century. Luxurious buildings were constructed along the Ku'damm, while the areas of Breitscheidplatz and Wittenbergplatz filled up with hotels and department stores. After World War II, with the old centre

(Mitte) situated in East Berlin, Charlottenburg became the centre of West Berlin, with dozens of new company headquarters and trade centres being built. Kurfürstendamm is now Berlin's main shopping street.

3

Zoo Berlin

📍 B4 🏛 Hardenbergplatz 8/ Budapester Strasse 34
Ⓢ & Ⓤ Zoologischer Garten
🚌 100, 109, 149, 200, 245, 249, M46, X10, X34
🕐 Spring & summer: 9am–6:30pm daily; autumn: 9am–5:30pm daily; winter: 9am–4:30pm daily 🌐 zoo-berlin.de

This zoological garden is actually part of the Tiergarten and dates from 1844, making it one of Germany's oldest zoos. In addition to exotic animals such as kiwis and axolotls, the zoo is home to many endangered species as well as rare domestic animal breeds. A monkey house contains a family of gorillas, orangutans and mandrills,

↑ Visitors enjoying the sun by the lake in the Tiergarten

and there is a darkened pavilion for viewing nocturnal animals. A glazed wall in the hippopotamus pool enables visitors to observe these enormous animals in the water. The large aquarium contains sharks, piranhas and unusual coral reef species. There is also a huge terrarium with an overgrown jungle that is home to some crocodiles.

4

Tiergarten

📍 C3 Ⓢ Tiergarten, Bellevue 🚌 100, 187, 200

Once a forest used as the Elector's hunting reserve, the Tiergarten was transformed into a landscaped park by Peter Joseph Lenné in the 1830s. A Triumphal Avenue, lined with statues of the country's rulers and statesmen, was built in the eastern section at the end of the 19th century.

World War II inflicted huge damage, but replanting has restored the Tiergarten, and its avenues are bordered with statues of figures such as Johann Wolfgang von Goethe and Richard Wagner.

Near the lake and the Landwehrkanal are memorials to Karl Liebknecht and Rosa Luxemburg, the leaders of the Spartakus movement who were assassinated in 1918.

Siegessäule

Q B3 **A** Grosser Stern **S** Bellevue **U** Hansaplatz **🚌** 100, 106, 187 **🕐** Apr–Oct: 9:30am–6:30pm Mon–Fri (to 7pm Sat & Sun); Nov–Mar: 10am–5pm Mon–Fri (to 5:30pm Sat & Sun)

This triumphal column, based on a design by Johann Heinrich Strack, was built to commemorate victory in the Prusso-Danish war of 1864. After further Prussian victories in wars against Austria (1866) and France (1871), a gilded figure representing Victory,

known as the "Goldelse", was added to the top. It originally stood in front of the Reichstag building but was moved to its present location by the Nazi government in 1938. The base is decorated with bas-reliefs honouring battles, while higher up a mosaic frieze depicts the founding of the German Empire in 1871. A terrace offers magnificent views.

Bauhaus-Archiv

Q C4 **A** Klingelhöfer-strasse 14 **U** Nollendorf-platz **🚌** 100, 187, M29 **🕐** For renovation work until 2022 **W** bauhaus.de

The Bauhaus school of art, started by Walter Gropius in 1919, was one of the most influential art institutions of the 20th century. Originally based in Weimar, it inspired many artists and architects. Staff and students included Mies van der Rohe, Paul Klee and Wassily Kandinsky. The school moved to Berlin in 1932 from Dessau, but was closed by the Nazis in 1933.

After the war, the Bauhaus-Archiv was relocated to Darmstadt. In 1964 Walter Gropius designed a building to house the collection but, in 1971, the archive was moved to Berlin and the design was adapted to the new site. As Gropius had died in 1969, Yugoslav-American architect Alexander Cvijanovic took over the project. Built between 1976 and 1979, the gleaming white building, with its glass-panelled gables, houses the archive, library and exhibition halls.

←

The Goldelse standing atop the magnificent Siegessäule column

STAY

Hotel Zoo
Right on Kurfürstendamm boulevard, this former mansion became an upscale hotel in 1911. It houses a grand living room and also features a lovely rooftop terrace.

Q A4 **A** Kurfürstendamm 25 **W** hotelzoo.de

25hours Hotel Bikini
This trendsetting hotel has rooms that overlook the adjacent zoo, plus a buzzing top-floor bar and restaurant.

Q B4 **A** Budapester Strasse 40 **W** 25hours-hotels.com

Das Stue
Located inside the former Danish embassy, Das Stue ("living room" in Danish), has a plush and playful Nordic-style interior that houses a Michelin-starred restaurant, Susanne Kaufmann Spa and a cool cocktail bar.

Q B4 **A** Drakestrasse 1 **W** das-stue.com

Waldorf Astoria
A slick five-star hotel with luxurious rooms and glamorous spa, as well as an American-themed cocktail bar and fine dining restaurant.

Q A4 **A** Hardenbergstrasse 28 **W** waldorfastoriaberlin.de

❼

Bendlerblock (Gedenkstätte Deutscher Widerstand)

📍C4 🏠Stauffenbergstrasse 13-14 Ⓤ Mendelssohn-Bartholdy-Park 🚌M29, M48 🕐9am-6pm Mon-Wed & Fri, 9am-8pm Thu, 10am-6pm Sat & Sun 🌐gdw-berlin.de

The collection of buildings known as the Bendlerblock was built during the Third Reich as an extension to the German State Naval Offices. During World War II they were the headquarters of the Wehrmacht (German Army). It was here that a group of officers planned their assassination attempt on Hitler on 20 July 1944. When the attempt led by Claus Schenk von Stauffenberg failed, he and his fellow conspirators were arrested and sentenced to death. Stauffenberg, Friedrich Olbricht, Werner von Haeften, and Ritter Mertz von Quirnheim were shot in the Bendlerblock courtyard. A monument commemorating this event, designed by Richard Scheibe in 1953, stands where the executions were carried out. On the upper floor of the building there is an interesting exhibition which documents the history of the German anti-Nazi movements.

---

❽

Gemäldegalerie

📍D4 🏠Matthäikirchplatz 4-6 🚇&Ⓤ Potsdamer Platz Ⓤ Mendelssohn-Bartholdy-Park 🚌200, 300, M29, M41, M48, M85 🕐10am-6pm Tue-Sun (to 8pm Thu) 🌐smb.museum

The paintings in the Picture Gallery collection have been carefully chosen by specialists who, from the beginning of the 19th century, systematically acquired pictures to ensure that all the major European schools of painting were represented. After the division of the city in 1945, the collection was split over several sites in East and West Berlin. Following reunification, with the construction of a new home as part of the Kulturforum development, this unique set of paintings was united again. The building was designed by Heinz Hilmer and Christoph Sattler, and the pictures are gently lit by the diffused daylight that streams in from above. The vast hall in the centre of the building allows the visitor to take a break from sightseeing at any time. With a futuristic sculpture by Walter de Maria set in a water-filled pool, it is ideal for moments of quiet contemplation and rest.

---

❾

Potsdamer Platz

📍D4 🏠Potsdamer Platz 🚌200, 300, M41, M48, M85, N2 🌐potsdamerplatz.de

To experience the vibrant energy of Berlin, there is no better place to visit than Potsdamer Platz. The square evolved into a major traffic hub with the construction of a railway station, where the city's first ever train made its maiden journey. During the Roaring Twenties it was Europe's busiest plaza and a bustling entertainment centre, frequented by famous artists and authors. The square was almost destroyed during World War II and was left as a derelict wasteland for decades. Redevelopment began in 1992, with a total investment of $25 billion. Now the city's old hub is once again a dynamic centre, boasting an array of entertainment, shopping and dining opportunities in splendid

↑ Artworks at the Gemäldegalerie in the Kulturform complex

The bright night-time neon illuminations of Potsdamer Platz →

Panoramapunkt

Potsdamer Platz 1
Times vary; check website
panoramapunkt.de

10

Leipziger Platz

E4 Potsdamer Platz
Potsdamer Platz 200,
M41, M48, M85, N2

This small square just east of Potsdamer Platz is fast becoming an exciting hub of its own. The Mall of Berlin now occupies the site of the former Wertheim department store, which was once the largest in Europe. It contains shops and restaurants of every variety, as well as a hotel, a running club and the XXL slide, which winds from the second floor all the way to the ground floor.

At the southern end of Leipziger Platz is the **Dalí Museum**, exhibiting works by the renowned Surrealist artist. A few doors down is the **German Spy Museum**, a multimedia museum that explores the history of the secret services around the world, with an emphasis on espionage in Cold War-era Berlin. The museum exhibits collections of authentic and replica espionage equipment.

Dalí Museum

Leipziger Platz 7 Times vary; check website daliberlin.de

German Spy Museum

Leipziger Platz 9
10am–8pm daily
deutsches-spionage museum.de

modern buildings designed by architects such as Renzo Piano, Helmut Jahn and Arata Isozaki.

The Sony Center is one of Berlin's most exciting architectural complexes, a glitzy steel-and-glass construction covering 4,013 sq m (43,195 sq ft). It is home to the offices of Sony's European headquarters, apartment complexes, restaurants, cafés, shops, a huge multiplex cinema and an integrated IMAX cinema. One of the main attractions in the Sony Center is the **Museum für Film und Fernsehen** (Museum of Film and Television), which gives visitors a backstage glimpse of Hollywood and the historic UFA (Universal-Film-AG) film studios (p134).

One of the highlights of this avenue is the Kohloff Tower skyscraper, which is topped by a 96-m- (315-ft-) high observation platform called **Panoramapunkt** (Panorama Point). It offers a breathtaking view of the city and can be reached via Europe's fastest elevator.

Situated in a square dedicated to the famous Berlin-born actress Marlene Dietrich, the city's largest musical stage is housed in the Theater am Potsdamer Platz, designed by Renzo Piano. It has staged a mix of local musical productions and German versions of Broadway hits. The exclusive Adagio nightclub is located in the basement of this building, and Berlin's most popular casino, Spielbank Berlin, can also be found here.

Museum für Film und Fernsehen

Potsdamer Strasse 4 10am–6pm Tue, Wed & Fri–Sun (to 8pm Thu) deutsche-kinemathek.de

Did You Know?

Between 1961 and 1989 Potsdamer Platz was divided in two by the Berlin Wall.

11

Neue Nationalgalerie

D4 ⌂Potsdamer Strasse 50 S&U Potsdamer Platz U Mendelssohn-Bartholdy-Park 🚌200, M29, M41, M48, M85 For renovation until 2021

After World War II, when this magnificent collection of modern art ended up in West Berlin, the commission to design a suitable building to house it was given to the elder statesman of modern architecture, the 75-year-old Mies van der Rohe. The result is a striking, minimalist building with a flat steel roof over a glass hall, which appears to float in mid-air and is supported only by six slender interior struts.

The collection comprises largely 20th-century art, but begins with artists of the late 19th century, such as Edvard Munch. German art is well represented: as well as the Bauhaus movement, the gallery shows works by exponents of a crass realism, such as Otto Dix. Celebrated artists of other European countries are also included – Pablo Picasso, Salvador Dalí and René Magritte. Post-World War II art is represented by Barnett Newman, Frank Stella and

 INSIDER TIP
Grand Reopening

In 2021 the Neue Nationalgalerie will reopen its doors after a renovation project lasting four years. The redesign has been put in the hands of London's David Chipperfield Architects.

many others. The sculpture garden houses important works, both figurative and abstract.

12

Kunstgewerbe-museum

D4 ⌂Matthäikirchplatz S&U Potsdamer Platz U Mendelssohn-Bartholdy-Park 🚌200, 300, M29, M41, M85 10am–6pm Tue–Fri, 11am–6pm Sat & Sun �smb.museum

The Museum of Decorative Arts holds a rich collection embracing many genres from the early Middle Ages to the modern day. Goldwork is especially well represented, as are metal items from the Middle Ages. Among the most valuable exhibits is

a collection of medieval goldwork from the church treasures of Enger and the Guelph treasury from Brunswick. The museum also takes great pride in its collection of late Gothic and Renaissance silver from the civic treasury in the town of Lüneburg. In addition, there are fine examples of Italian majolica, and 18th- and 19th-century German, French and Italian glass, porcelain and furniture. The collection also includes historical fashion.

13

Philharmonie and Kammermusiksaal

D4 ⌂Herbert-von-Karajan-Strasse 1 S&U Potsdamer Platz U Mendelssohn-Bartholdy-Park 🚌200, M29, M41 �berliner-philharmoniker.de

Home to one of the most renowned orchestras in Europe, the unusual Philharmonic and Chamber Music Hall building is among the finest postwar architectural achievements in Europe. Built between

Exteriors of the striking Philharmonie *(right)* and Kammermusiksaal buildings ↑

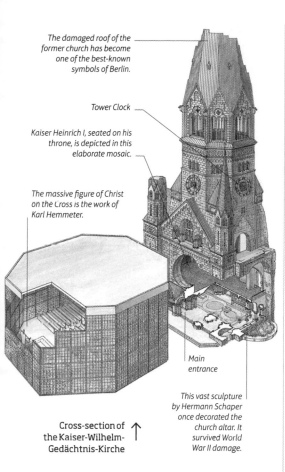

The damaged roof of the former church has become one of the best-known symbols of Berlin.

Tower Clock

Kaiser Heinrich I, seated on his throne, is depicted in this elaborate mosaic.

The massive figure of Christ on the Cross is the work of Karl Hemmeter.

Main entrance

This vast sculpture by Hermann Schaper once decorated the church altar. It survived World War II damage.

Cross-section of the Kaiser-Wilhelm-Gedächtnis-Kirche ↑

church was designed by Franz Schwechten and consecrated in 1895. It was almost completely destroyed by Allied bombs in 1943, and after World War II the ruins were removed, leaving only the massive front tower at the base of which the Gedenkhalle (Memorial Hall) is situated. The damaged tower is a symbol of peace and the city's determination to rebuild after World War II. The hall documents the church's history and contains some original ceiling mosaics, marble reliefs and a collection of interesting liturgical objects. In 1961 Egon Eiermann designed an octagonal church in blue glass, as well as a new freestanding bell tower.

15

Musikinstrumenten-Museum

**◉ D3 ☐ Tiergartenstrasse 1
Ⓢ & Ⓤ Potsdamer Platz
🚌 200, M41, M48, M85
⏰ 9am–5pm Tue–Wed &
Fri, 9am–8pm Thu, 10am–
5pm Sat & Sun ⓦ sim.spk-
berlin.de**

Nestled behind the Philharmonie, in a small building designed by Edgar Wisniewski and Hans Scharoun between 1979 and 1984, the fascinating Museum of Musical Instruments houses over 750 exhibits dating from 1888. Intriguing displays enable you to trace each instrument's development, from the 16th century to the present day. You can marvel at the harpsichord of Jean Marius, once owned by Frederick the Great, and the violins made by Amati and Stradivarius. Most spectacular of all is the silent-film-era cinema organ, a working Wurlitzer dating from 1929.

1960 and 1963 to a design by Hans Scharoun, the Philharmonie pioneered a new concept for concert hall interiors, with a podium occupying the central section of the pentagonal hall, around which are galleries for the public. The exterior is reminiscent of a circus tent. The gilded exterior was added between 1978 and 1981.

Between 1984 and 1987 the Kammermusiksaal, which was designed by Edgar Wisniewski on the basis of sketches by Scharoun, was added to the Philharmonie. This building consolidates the aesthetics of the earlier structure by featuring a central multi-sided space covered by a fanciful tent-like roof.

14

Kaiser-Wilhelm-Gedächtnis-Kirche

**◉ A4 ☐ Breitscheidplatz,
Ⓢ & Ⓩ Zoologischer Garten
Ⓤ Kurfürstendamm
🚌 100, 200 ⏰ 9am–7pm
daily ⓦ gedaechtniskirche-
berlin.de**

The Kaiser Wilhelm Memorial Church is one of Berlin's most famous landmarks, and is surrounded by a lively crowd of street traders and buskers. The vast Neo-Romanesque

> **The Kaiser Wilhelm Memorial Church is one of Berlin's most famous landmarks, and is surrounded by a lively crowd of street traders and buskers.**

Mao (1972), a portrait
by Andy Warhol in the
Hamburger Bahnhof

containing over 30 million
exhibits. Despite several
extensions and renovations,
it has maintained its unique
old-fashioned atmosphere.

The museum's highlights
are the world's largest
dinosaur skeleton – the
Brachiosaurus – housed in
the glass-covered courtyard,
and the original skeleton of
a *Tyrannosaurus rex* called
Tristan Otto. The Brachiosaurus measures 23 m (75 ft)
long and 12 m (39 ft) high.

The adjacent rooms feature
collections of fish, birds and
mammals. Favourites with
children include Bobby the
Gorilla, who lived in Berlin Zoo
(p94) from 1928 until 1935,
and the famous polar bear
Knut. The museum also has
an impressive collection of
minerals and meteorites.

Regierungsviertel

◉ D2 ⑤ Brandenburger
Tor Ⓤ Bundestag
🚌 100, M41, M85

This bold concept for a
government district was
the winning design in a
competition held in 1992.
Located in the bend of the
River Spree, the new government quarter was built to
accommodate the relocation
of the German government
from Bonn *(p396)* in 1999.

Most of the buildings offer
limited public access, but
several exhibitions are open
daily, and art and architecture
tours run at weekends.

Hamburger Bahnhof

◉ D1 ⬛ Invalidenstrasse
50/51 ⑤ & Ⓤ Haupt-
bahnhof Ⓤ Zinnowitzer-
strasse 🚌 120, 123, 147,
245, M41 🚊 12, M6, M8
🕐 10am–6pm Tue–Sun (to
8pm Thu) 🖥 smb.museum

This museum is situated in a
Neo-Renaissance building,
formerly the Hamburg
Railway station, which dates

from 1847. It stood vacant
after World War II but,
following refurbishment
by Josef Paul Kleihues, it
was opened to the public in
1996. The neon installation
surrounding the façade is
the work of Dan Flavin.
The museum houses a
magnificent collection of
contemporary art, including
the work of Erich Marx and,
from 2004, the world-
renowned Flick collection.
The result is one of the best
modern art museums to
be found in Europe, which
features not only art, but also
film, video, music and design.

Museum für
Naturkunde

◉ E1 ⬛ Invalidenstrasse 43
Ⓤ Naturkundemuseum
🚌 147, 245 🚊 12, M6, M8
🕐 9:30am–6pm Tue–Fri,
10am–6pm Sat & Sun
🖥 museumfuer
naturkunde.berlin

Occupying a purpose-built
Neo-Renaissance building
built between 1883 and 1889,
this is one of the biggest
natural history museums
in the world, with a collection

Haus der Kulturen der Welt

⊙ D2 ⊙ John-Foster-Dulles-Allee 10 ⊙ Hauptbahnhof ⊙ Bundestag ⊟ 100 ⊙ 10am–7pm daily ⊙ hkw.de

The House of World Cultures, designed by the American architect Hugh Stubbins, was intended as the American entry in the international "Interbau 1957" architecture competition. It soon became a symbol of freedom and modernity in West Berlin during the Cold War, particularly when compared to the GDR-era architecture of Karl-Marx-Allee (p116) in East Berlin. Unfortunately, its roof failed to withstand the test of time, and the building partially collapsed in 1980. After reconstruction it was reopened in 1989, with a change of purpose: to bring world cultures to a wider German audience via events, exhibitions and performances.

Standing nearby is the black tower of the Carillon, built in 1987 to commemorate the 750th anniversary of Berlin. Suspended in the tower is the largest carillon in Europe, comprising 67 bells. Twice daily, at noon and 6pm, the bells give a brief computer-controlled concert.

Brecht-Weigel-Gedenkstätte

⊙ E1 ⊙ Chausseestrasse 125 ⊙ (030) 200 57 18 44 ⊙ Naturkundemuseum, Oranienburger Tor ⊟ 142 ⊟ 12, M5, M6, M8 ⊙ 10am–3:30pm Tue & Sat, 10–11am Wed & Fri, 10am–6:30pm Thu, 11am–6pm Sun

The house where Bertolt Brecht and his wife, the actress Helene Weigel, lived and worked is now a memorial. Brecht, one of the greatest playwrights of the 20th century, was associated with Berlin from 1920, but emigrated in 1933. After the war, his left-wing views made him an attractive potential resident of the newly created German socialist state. Lured by the promise of his own theatre, he returned to Berlin in 1948 with Weigel.

He lived in the first-floor apartment here from 1953 until he died in 1956. Weigel lived in the second-floor apartment, and after Brecht's death moved to the ground floor. She also founded an archive of Brecht's works, which is located on the second floor of the building.

Did You Know?

The T-rex skeleton at the Museum für Naturkunde is named Tristan Otto after the owner's sons.

↑ The colossal Brachiosaurus skeleton - the world's largest - in the Museum für Naturkunde

A SHORT WALK
AROUND THE KULTURFORUM

Distance 1 km (0.5 miles) **Time** 15 minutes
Nearest S-Bahn station Potsdamer Platz

The idea of creating a new cultural centre in West Berlin was put forward in 1956. The first building to go up was the Berlin Philharmonic concert hall, built to an innovative design by Hans Scharoun in 1961. Most of the plans for the various other components of the Kulturforum were realized between 1961 and 1987, and came from such architects as Ludwig Mies van der Rohe. The area is now a major cultural centre with fascinating museums and stunning architecture to enjoy as you explore.

The **Kunstgewerbemuseum**
*(Museum of Arts and Crafts)
contains a unique collection of
items including fashion and
furniture, dating from the Middle
Ages to the present day (p98).*

The **Kupferstichkabinett**
*(Gallery of Prints and
Drawings)*

The **Kunstbibliothek** *(Art Library) has a
rich collection of books, graphic art and
drawings, many of which are displayed
in its exhibition halls.*

*Important works by Old Masters
such as Jan van Eyck and Jan
Vermeer are exhibited in the*
Gemäldegalerie *(p96).*

↑ Gallery of fashion at the
Kunstgewerbemuseum

REICHPIETSCHUFER

LANDWEHRKANAL

Covered in a layer of golden aluminium, the **Philharmonie and Kammermusiksaal** *(p98) is known all over the world for its superb acoustics.*

Locator Map
For more detail see p90

The **Musikinstrumenten-Museum** *(Museum of Musical Instruments; p99) contains a unique collection of instruments dating from the 16th to the 20th centuries.*

St-Matthäus-Kirche *is a 19th-century church that stands out among the modern buildings of the Kulturforum.*

Hans Scharoun designed the public lending and research **Staatsbibliothek** *(State Library) in 1978.*

SCHAROUNSTRÄSSE

MATTHÄI-KIRCH PLATZ

SIGISMUNDSTRASSE

POTSDAMER STRASSE

FINISH

START

| 0 metres | 100 | N |
| 0 yards | 100 | ↑ |

Sculptures by Henry Moore and Alexander Calder stand outside the streamlined building of the **Neue Nationalgalerie** *(p98), designed by Ludwig Mies van der Rohe.*

→
The striking exterior of St-Matthäus-Kirche

BERLIN: BEYOND THE CENTRE

In 1920, as part of great administrative reform, seven towns, 59 parishes and 27 country estates were incorporated into the city, thus creating an entirely new city covering nearly 900 sq km (350 sq miles). This metropolis extended to small towns of medieval origin, such as Spandau, as well as to private manor houses and palaces, towns and smart suburban districts – each of which had been evolving independently for many years. Although the 20th century changed the face of many of these places, their unique characters have remained undiminished.

Thanks to this diversity, a stay in Berlin can simultaneously equate to visiting several cities. A short journey by S-Bahn enables you to travel from the cosmopolitan city centre of the 21st century to the vast forests of the Grunewald or the beach at Wannsee lake. You can explore everything from Charlottenburg's tranquil streets and palace park, to Spandau's Renaissance citadel, cobbled lanes and vast Gothic church of St-Nikolai-Kirche – all just half an hour away from the centre and well worth a visit.

BERLIN: BEYOND THE CENTRE

Must Sees

1 Schloss Charlottenburg
2 East Side Gallery

Experience More

3 Bröhan-Museum
4 Sammlung Berggruen
5 Schlosspark
6 Langhansbau
7 Messegelände
8 Olympiastadion
9 Spandau
10 Gedenkstätte Plötzensee
11 Schloss Tegel
12 Tempelhof Flughafen and Tempelhofer Feld
13 Karl-Marx-Allee
14 Prenzlauer Berg
15 Stasi-Prison
16 Stasi-Museum
17 Treptower Park
18 Köpenick
19 Viktoriapark
20 Rathaus Schöneberg
21 Museum Europäischer Kulturen
22 Jagdschloss Grunewald
23 Strandbad Wannsee
24 Brücke-Museum
25 Pfaueninsel
26 Nikolskoe
27 Klein Glienicke
28 Neukölln
29 Gedenkstätte Berliner Mauer

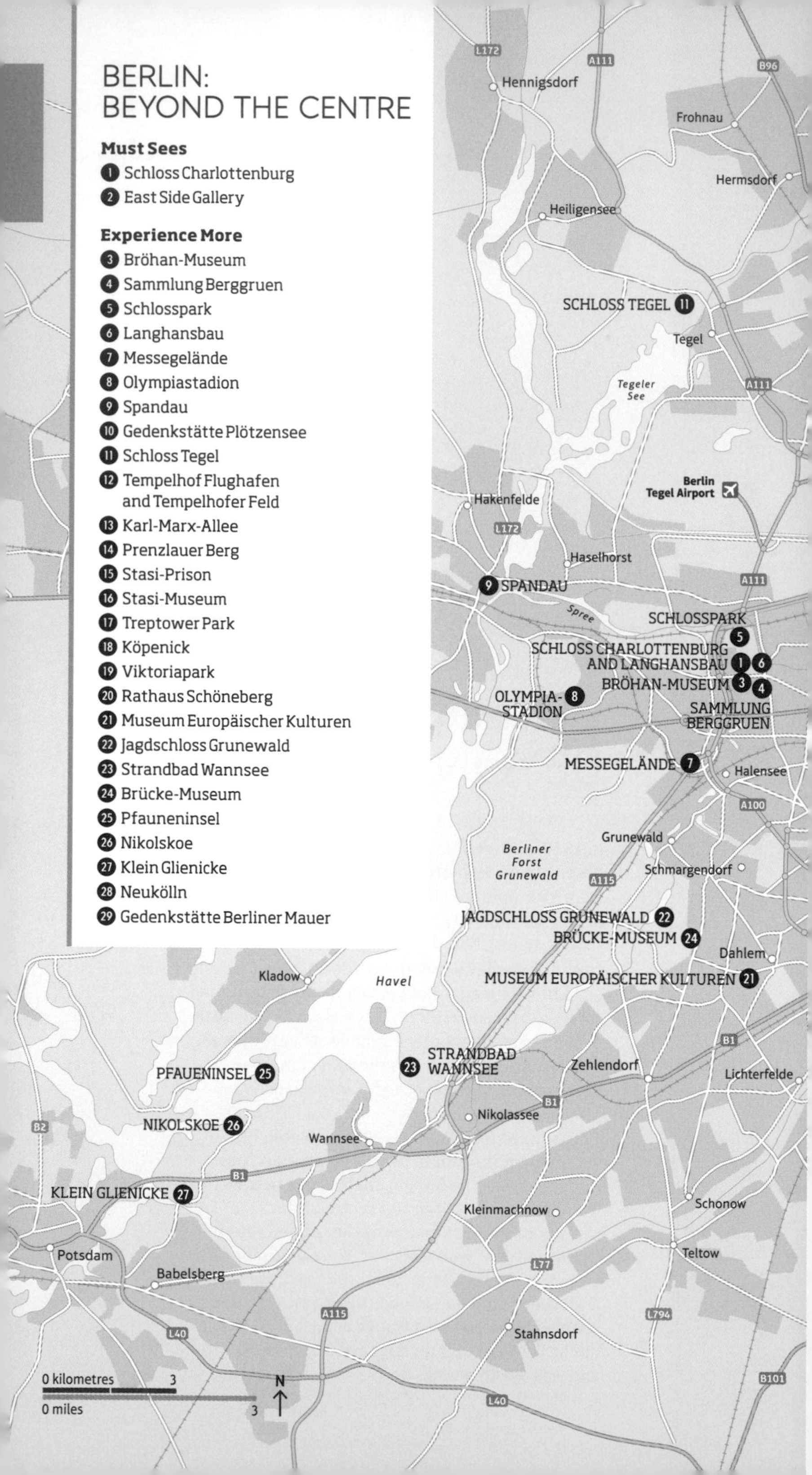

L172 A111 B96
Hennigsdorf
Frohnau
Hermsdorf
Heiligensee
SCHLOSS TEGEL 11
Tegel
A111
Tegeler See
Berlin Tegel Airport
Hakenfelde
L172
Haselhorst
A111
9 SPANDAU
Spree
SCHLOSSPARK
5
SCHLOSS CHARLOTTENBURG AND LANGHANSBAU 1 6
BRÖHAN-MUSEUM 3 4
OLYMPIA-STADION 8
SAMMLUNG BERGGRUEN
MESSEGELÄNDE 7
Halensee
A100
Grunewald
Berliner Forst Grunewald
Schmargendorf
A115
JAGDSCHLOSS GRUNEWALD 22
BRÜCKE-MUSEUM 24
Dahlem
MUSEUM EUROPÄISCHER KULTUREN 21
Kladow
Havel
B1
STRANDBAD WANNSEE
Zehlendorf
Lichterfelde
PFAUENINSEL 25
23 STRANDBAD WANNSEE
B1
Nikolassee
NIKOLSKOE 26
Wannsee
B2
KLEIN GLIENICKE 27
Kleinmachnow
Schonow
Potsdam
Teltow
Babelsberg
L77
A115
L794
Stahnsdorf
L40
B101
L40

0 kilometres 3
0 miles 3
N

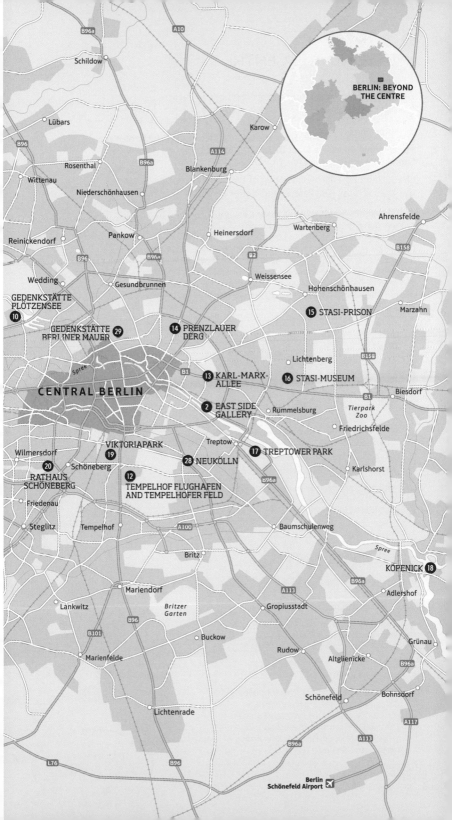

Schildow

B96a

A10

B96

Lübars

Karow

Rosenthal

B96a

Blankenburg

A114

Wittenau

Niederschönhausen

Reinickendorf

Pankow

Heinersdorf

Wartenberg

Ahrensfelde

B158

B96

Wedding

Gesundbrunnen

B96a

Weissensee

Hohenschönhausen

Marzahn

10 GEDENKSTÄTTE
PLÖTZENSEE

29 GEDENKSTÄTTE
BERLINER MAUER

14 PRENZLAUER
BERG

15 STASI-PRISON

Spree

B1

13 KARL-MARX-
ALLEE

Lichtenberg

B158

Biesdorf

B1

CENTRAL BERLIN

16 STASI-MUSEUM

2 EAST SIDE
GALLERY

Rummelsburg

*Tierpark
Zoo*

Friedrichsfelde

Wilmersdorf

19 VIKTORIAPARK

Schöneberg

Treptow

17 TREPTOWER PARK

20

28 NEUKÖLLN

Karlshorst

**RATHAUS
SCHÖNEBERG**

12

TEMPELHOF FLUGHAFEN
AND TEMPELHOFER FELD

B96a

Friedenau

Steglitz

Tempelhof

A100

Baumschulenweg

Spree

KÖPENICK **18**

Mariendorf

Adlershof

Lankwitz

*Britzer
Garten*

A113

Gropiusstadt

B96

Grünau

Buckow

B101

Rudow

Altglienicke

B96a

Marienfelde

Bohnsdorf

Schönefeld

A117

Lichtenrade

B96

A113

B96a

Berlin
Schönefeld Airport

1 🖼️ 🖼️

SCHLOSS CHARLOTTENBURG

🏠 Spandauer Damm 20-24 🚇 Jungfernheide & Westend Ⓤ Richard-Wagner-Platz, Sophie-Charlotte-Platz 🚌 109, 309, M45 🕐 Apr-Oct: 10am-6pm Tue-Sun; Nov-Mar: 10am-5pm Tue-Sun 🌐 spsg.de

Charlottenburg Palace is made up of two magnificent buildings: the Altes Schloss (Old Palace) and Neuer Flügel (New Wing).

Built in 1695, the palace in Charlottenburg was intended as a summer home for Sophie Charlotte, the wife of Elector Friedrich III. Johann Eosander Göthe enlarged the palace between 1701 and 1713, crowning it with a cupola and adding the orangery wing. This section of the palace is now known as the Altes Schloss. The Neuer Flügel extension was undertaken by Frederick the Great (Friedrich II), and designed by Georg Wenzeslaus von Knobelsdor in the mid-18th century. The palace was restored to its former elegance after World War II and its richly decorated interiors are unequalled in Berlin.

↑ Schlosspark, a favourite weekend spot for locals

↑ The Goldene Galerie, a Rococo garden ballroom, dating from 1746

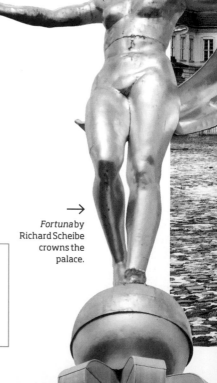

This sculpture replaced the original destroyed in World War II.

→ *Fortuna* by Richard Scheibe crowns the palace.

GALLERY GUIDE

The ground floor of Altes Schloss houses the opulent chambers of Friedrich III, a portrait gallery and the Porcelain Cabinet. The upper floors include the apartment of Friedrich Wilhelm IV and a silver and tableware collection.

INSIDER TIP
Neuer Flügel

The New Wing has a separate entrance from the main section of the palace, and requires a separate ticket. It holds the elegant apartments and exquisite furniture of Friedrich Wilhelm II, and hosts art and history exhibitions.

↑ The central section of the Altes Schloss, designed by Johann Arnold Nering

② ⊗ ⊗

EAST SIDE GALLERY

◩ Mühlenstrasse 78-80 ⑤ & Ⓤ Warschauer Strasse Ⓤ Schlesisches Tor 🚌 300 🕐 10am-7pm daily 🌐 eastsidegallery-berlin.com

Running alongside the River Spree, the East Side Gallery is the longest surviving stretch of the Berlin Wall – as well as the most colourful, thanks to the numerous paintings that have adorned its surface since 1990. More than 100 artists have contributed to the gallery, and millions of visitors to the city come here every year to enjoy their work.

Unique Historical Legacy

Although it's not the city's official Berlin Wall memorial (*p123*), this 1.3-km (0.8-mile) stretch is the longest section of the wall that still exists today. Located in the former East Berlin district of Friedrichshain, the wall was protected by border guards and watchtowers until the collapse of the GDR in 1989. Soon after, dozens of artists began using it as a political canvas, decorating it with murals, slogans and paintings.

Official Art Gallery

The improvised gallery was appointed an official one in 1990 and given protected memorial status the following year. The gallery was repainted for its 20th anniversary in 2009, with some original artists refusing to repaint or retouch their artworks for reasons of authenticity. In 2016 a multimedia museum opened at the south end of the East Side Gallery, giving an overview of the Berlin Wall era through screens, interactive displays, original newsreel footage and filmed interviews with Berliners who lived through it.

↑ The exterior of East Side Gallery, covered in graffiti

Timeline

15 August 1961

▽ While on border patrol duty, East German soldier Conrad Schumann leaps over the barbed wire fencing and defects to West Germany

24 August 1961

Günter Litfin is the first person to be shot and killed by East German border patrol whilst trying to escape East Berlin

13 August, 1961

The border between East and West Berlin is closed, and the first barriers are installed

1962

△ A second fence is erected 100 m (110 yd) behind the first. The buildings between the two fences are demolished and the space becomes known as the "death zone"

↑ *My God, Help Me to Survive This Deadly Love* (1989), by Dmitri Vrubel

STRUCTURE OF THE BERLIN WALL

Initially the border consisted simply of rolls of barbed wire, but these were replaced by a 4-m- (13-ft-) high wall and a second wall topped with a thick pipe to prevent people reaching the top with their fingers. Alongside ran what was known as a "death zone", controlled by guards with dogs, with 293 watchtowers, 57 bunkers and alarms.

1975

Reinforced concrete is used to construct the fourth iteration of the wall. This is the version of the Berlin Wall that can be seen in existing remains today

31 December 1989

▽ David Hasselhoff performs live on top of the Berlin Wall

9 November 1989

A miscommunication televised across East and West Berlin leads to the opening of the borders and people flooding through the Berlin Wall checkpoints

13 June 1990

△ The government begins tearing down the wall, aided by "wall-pickers" who have been chipping away at it since November

EXPERIENCE MORE

Bröhan-Museum

⌂ Schlossstrasse 1a
Ⓢ Westend Ⓤ Richard-
Wagner-Platz, Sophie-
Charlotte-Platz 🚌 109,
309, M45 🕙 10am-6pm
Tue-Sun 🚫 Public hols
🌐 broehan-museum.de

Located in a late-Neo-Classical
building is this small and
interesting museum
dedicated to the decorative
arts. The collection was
amassed by Karl H Bröhan,
who, from 1966, collected
works of art from the Art
Nouveau (Jugendstil or
Secessionist) and Art Deco
styles. The paintings of artists
who were connected with the
Berlin Secessionist movement
are especially well represented. Alongside the paintings
are fine examples of other
media and crafts, including
ceramics, glassware,
silverwork and textiles.

There is also a display of
furniture by Hector Guimard,
Eugène Gaillard, Henri van de
Velde and Joseph Hoffmann,
glasswork by Emile Gallé, and
porcelain from the best
European manufacturers.

→
An amphora vase, dating
from around 1905, in the
Bröhan-Museum

Sammlung Berggruen

⌂ Schlossstrasse 1
Ⓢ Westend Ⓤ Richard-
Wagner-Platz, Sophie-
Charlotte-Platz 🚌 109,
309, M45 🕙 10am-6pm
Tue-Sun 🌐 smb.museum

Heinz Berggruen assembled
this collection of art dating
from the late 19th and first
half of the 20th century. Born
and educated in Berlin, he
emigrated to the US in 1936,
spent most of his life in Paris,
but finally entrusted his
collection "Picasso and his
Time" to the city of his birth.
The museum opened in what
was once the west pavilion of
the barracks. The exhibition
halls were modified according
to the designs of Hilmer and
Sattler, who also designed the
layout of the Gemäldegalerie.

The Sammlung Berggruen
is well known for its large
collection of works by Pablo
Picasso. In addition, the
museum has more than 20
pieces by Paul Klee; paintings
by Matisse and Cézanne; and
sculptures by Henri Laurens
and Alberto Giacometti.

---

⑤

Schlosspark

⌂ Luisenplatz (Schloss
Charlottenburg)
Ⓢ Westend Ⓤ Richard-
Wagner-Platz, Sophie-
Charlotte-Platz 🚌 109,
309, M45

The extensive Palace Park
around Schloss Charlottenburg,
a favourite place for Berliners

→
The Mausoleum
situated among the trees
in the Schlosspark

to stroll, is largely the result of work carried out after World War II, when 18th-century prints were used to help reconstruct the layout of the original grounds. Just behind the palace is a French-style Baroque garden, created to a strict geometrical design with a vibrant patchwork of flower beds, shrubs and ornate fountains. Beyond the curved carp lake is a less formal English-style land-scaped park, originally laid out between 1819 and 1828 under the direction of the renowned royal gardener Peter Joseph Lenné.

Designed by Karl Friedrich Schinkel and completed in 1825, the Neo-Classical **Neuer Pavillon** is a charming two-storey building with rooms around a central staircase. A cast-iron balcony encircles the structure. Destroyed in World War II, parts of the building were rebuilt in 1970. Since then it has housed Romantic paintings, including master-pieces by Caspar David Friedrich and Schinkel himself.

The **Mausoleum** in which Queen Luise, wife of Friedrich Wilhelm III, was laid to rest was designed by Heinrich Genz in the style of a Doric portico-fronted temple. After the king's death in 1840, the

 Façade of Langhansbau pavilion in the grounds of Schloss Charlottenburg ↑

mausoleum was refurbished to house his tomb. The tombs of the king's second wife and those of Kaiser Wilhelm I and his wife were added later.

Built as a summerhouse for Friedrich Wilhelm II, with Baroque and Neo-Classical elements, the **Belvedere** now houses the Royal Porcelain Collection, with pieces from the Rococo period onward.

Neuer Pavillon
📞 (030) 32 09 17 43 🕐 Apr-Oct: 10am–5:30pm Tue-Sun; Nov-Mar: noon–6pm Tue-Sun

Mausoleum
🕐 Apr-Oct: 10am–5:30pm Tue-Sun

Belvedere
📞 (030) 32 09 17 45 🕐 Apr-Oct: 10am–5:30pm Tue-Sun

6
Langhansbau

🏛 Luisenplatz (Schloss Charlottenburg) 📞 (030) 32 09 10 🚇 Richard-Wagner-Platz 🚌 109, 309, M45 🕐 For temporary exhibitions only

This Neo-Classical pavilion was designed by Carl Gotthard Langhans and added to the orangery wing of the Schloss Charlottenburg *(p108)* between 1787 and 1791.

Currently housed in a villa on Fasanenstrasse, the private Käthe Kollwitz Museum will be moved into the Langhansbau in summer 2022. Kollwitz (1867–1945) is considered one of Germany's most important early 20th-century artists. Her drawings and sculptures portrayed the social problems of the poor, as well as human tragedy and suffering.

7
Messegelände

🏛 Hammarskjöldplatz 🚉 Messe Nord/ICC 🚇 Kaiserdamm 🚌 139, 218, X49

The pavilions of the vast exhibition and trade halls south of Hammarskjöldplatz cover more than 160,000 sq m (1.7 million sq ft). The original exhibition halls were built before World War I, but nothing of these buildings remains. The oldest part is the **Funkturm** (Radio Tower) and the pavilions surrounding it.

Funkturm
🏛 Hammarskjöldplatz 🚉 Messe Nord/ICC 🚇 Kaiserdamm 🚌 104, 218, 349, X34 🕐 Times vary, check website 🌐 funkturm-messeberlin.de

Olympiastadion

🅰 Olympischer Platz 🆂 &
Ⓤ Olympiastadion Ⓒ Late
Mar-May: 9am-7pm daily;
Jun-mid-Sep: 9am-8pm
daily; mid-Sep-Oct: 9-7pm
daily; Nov-late Mar: 9am-
4pm daily 🆆 olympia
stadion-berlin.de

Olympiastadion, originally
known as Reichssportfeld,
was built for the 1936 Olympic
Games in Berlin. Inspired by
the architecture of ancient
Rome, it was designed by
Werner March in the Nazi
architectural style. To the west
of the stadium lie the Maifeld
and what is now called the
Waldbühne. The former is an
enormous assembly ground
surrounded by grandstands
and fronted by the Glocken-
turm, a 77 m (250 ft) bell
tower, while the latter is
an open-air amphitheatre.

> 📷 PICTURE PERFECT
> ### Tempelhof Airport
>
> The austere design of
> Berlin's now defunct
> Tempelhof Airport is
> great for photographers
> looking for unusual
> shots of some of Berlin's
> iconic architecture.

↑ Exhibition of statues
that once stood at
the Zitadelle Spandau
(inset)

After modernization in 2004,
it now features a sweeping,
illuminated roof.

Spandau

Ⓤ Altstadt Spandau,
Zitadelle 🚌 X33

Spandau is one of the oldest
towns in the area of greater
Berlin. Although the town
was only granted a charter in
1232, evidence of the earliest
settlement here dates back
to the 8th century.

The area was spared the
worst of the World War II
bombing, so there are still
some interesting sights. The
heart of the town is a network
of medieval streets with a
picturesque market square
and a number of the original
timber-framed houses. In the
north of Spandau, sections of
the town wall dating from the
15th century are still standing.
In the town centre is the
magnificent Gothic St-Nikolai-
Kirche, dating from the 1400s.
The church holds many ecclesiastical furnishings, such as a
splendid Renaissance stone

altar from the end of the 16th
century, a Baroque pulpit from
around 1700 that came from
a royal palace in Potsdam
(p132), and many epitaphs.

A castle was first built
on the site of the **Zitadelle
Spandau** (citadel) in the
12th century, but today only
the 36 m (120 ft) Juliusturm
(tower) remains. In 1560
the building of a fort was
begun here, to a design by
Francesco Chiaramella da
Gandino. It took 30 years to
complete and most of the
work was supervised by
architect Rochus Graf von
Lynar. Although the citadel
had a jail, the town's most
infamous resident, Rudolf
Hess, was incarcerated a
short distance away in a
military prison after the 1946
Nuremberg trials. In 1987,
when the former deputy
leader of the Nazi party died,
the prison was torn down.

Zitadelle Spandau

♿🚻🎫 🅰 Juliusturm 64
Ⓒ 10am-5pm daily
🆆 zitadelle-berlin.de

Gedenkstätte Plötzensee

⌂ Hüttigpfad 16 Ⓤ Jakob-Kaiser-Platz, then 🚌 123, 126 🕐 Mar-Oct: 9am-5pm daily (Nov-Feb: to 4pm) 🌐 gedenkstaette-ploetzensee.de

A narrow street leads from Saatwinkler Damm to the site where nearly 2,500 people convicted of crimes against the Third Reich were hanged. The simple Plötzensee Memorial is housed in a brick hut that still retains the iron hooks from which the victims were suspended.

Claus Schenk von Stauffenberg and the other main figures in the assassination attempt against Hitler on 20 July 1944 were executed in the Bendlerblock (p96), but the rest of the conspirators were executed here at the Plötzensee prison.

Count Helmut James von Moltke, one of the leaders of the German resistance movement, was also killed here. He was responsible for organizing the Kreisauer Kreis, a political movement that gathered and united German opposition to Hitler.

Schloss Tegel

⌂ Adelheidallee 19-21 📞 (030) 434 31 56 Ⓤ Alt Tegel 🚌 124, 133, 222 🕐 May-Sep: 10am-4pm Mon

Schloss Tegel is one of the most interesting palace complexes in Berlin. The site was occupied in the 16th century by a manor house. In the second half of the 17th century, this was rebuilt into a hunting lodge for the Elector Friedrich Wilhelm. In 1766 ownership passed to the Humboldt family, and in the 1820s Karl Friedrich Schinkel thoroughly rebuilt the palace, giving it its current style.

Decorating the elevations on the top floor of the towers are tiled bas-reliefs designed by Christian Daniel Rauch, depicting the ancient wind gods. Some of Schinkel's marvellous interiors have survived, along with several items from what was once a large collection of sculptures. The palace is still privately owned by descendants of the Humboldt family, but it opens on Mondays for guided tours.

It is also worth visiting the park in which the palace stands. On the western limits of the park lies the Humboldt family tomb, also designed by Schinkel. The granite column here is topped by a copy of Bertel Thorwaldsen's splendid sculpture *Hope*; the original stands inside the Schloss Tegel.

Flughafen Tempelhof and Tempelhofer Feld

⌂ Platz der Luftbrücke Ⓤ Platz der Luftbrücke 🚌 104, 166, 184, 248 🌐 thf-berlin.de

Tempelhof was once Germany's largest airport. Built in 1923, it is typical of Third Reich architecture. Additions to the original structure were completed in 1939. In 1951 a monument was added in front of the airport to commemorate the airlifts of the Berlin Blockade.

Decommissioned as an airport in 2000, it is now a park that is popular with cyclists, skateboarders and in-line skaters who come here to enjoy the unobstructed airport runways.

Novelty kites being flown at a kite festival hosted at Tempelhofer Feld park

⑬
Karl-Marx-Allee

Ⓤ **Strausberger Platz, Weberwiese**

The almost 2 km (1 mile) section of Karl-Marx-Allee between Strausberger Platz and Frankfurter Tor is effectively a huge open-air museum of Socialist Realist architecture. The route to the east was named Stalinallee in 1949 and chosen as the site for the showpiece of the new German Democratic Republic. The avenue was widened to 90 m (300 ft) and, over the next ten years, huge residential tower blocks and a row of shops were built. The designers, led by German architect Hermann Henselmann, succeeded in combining three sets of architectural guidelines. They used the Soviet wedding cake style according to the precept: "nationalistic in form but socialist in content", and linked the whole work to Berlin's own traditions. Hence there are motifs taken from famous Berlin architects Schinkel and Gontard, as well as from the renowned Meissen porcelain.

↑ Outdoor seating at a café on Weinbergsweg, in Prenzlauer Berg

The buildings on this street, renamed Karl-Marx-Allee in 1961, are now considered historic monuments.

---

⑭
Prenzlauer Berg

Ⓤ **Eberswalder Strasse** 🚊 **12, M1, M10**

Towards the end of the 19th century, this was one of the most impoverished, densely populated districts of Berlin, which became a centre for anti-Communist opposition.

After 1989, however, artists, professionals and students began to arrive from all parts of Germany and Europe, creating a vibrant community.

Schönhauser Allee is the main thoroughfare. A former old brewery was transformed into the **Kulturbrauerei**, a centre for cultural events. It also houses the Museum in der Kulturbrauerei with a permanent exhibition "Alltag in der DDR" (Everyday Life in the GDR) showcasing everyday items used in former East Germany.

Heading up Sredzkistrasse you reach Husemannstrasse. This beautiful street with shops and inns gives the impression of Berlin around the year 1900. Amid the greenery around Belforter Strasse is a water tower built in the mid-19th century. Nearby, on Schönhauser Allee, there is an old Jewish cemetery dating from 1827. Among those buried here is the renowned painter Max Liebermann.

91,000
The number of employees the Stasi had in 1989, 2 per cent of the East German population.

Kulturbrauerei

📍 Schönhauser Allee 36-39
🕐 10am-6pm Tue-Sun (to 8pm Thu)
🌐 kulturbrauerei.de

15

Stasi-Prison

📍 Genslerstrasse 66
🚇 Landsberger Allee, then 🚊 M5, M6 🚌 256 🕐 9am-6pm daily 🌐 stiftung-hsh.de

This museum was established in 1995 within the former Stasi (GDR secret service) detention centre. The building was part of a huge complex built in 1938. In May 1945, the occupying Russian authorities created a special transit camp here, in which they interned war criminals and anyone under political suspicion. From 1946 the buildings were refashioned into the custody area for the KGB; in 1951 it was given over to the Stasi, who turned the cellars into the "submarine" – a series of cells without daylight. It was replaced by a new prison building in 1960.

The prisoners' cells and the interrogation rooms are also on view, two of which have no windows and are lined with rubber.

16

Stasi-Museum

📍 Ruschestrasse 103 (Haus 1) 🚇 Magdalenenstrasse 🕐 10am-6pm Mon-Fri, 11am-6pm Sat-Sun 🌐 stasimuseum.de

Under the German Democratic Republic, this huge complex of buildings at Ruschestrasse housed the Ministry of the Interior. It was here that the notorious Stasi (State Security Service) had its headquarters. The Stasi's "achievements" in infiltrating its own community were without equal in the Eastern bloc.

Since 1990 one of the buildings has housed a Stasi museum. Refurbished in 2016, the three-floor exhibition documents the genesis, evolution and activities of the Stasi through interesting artifacts, photographs and documents. Exhibits include miniature cameras and bugging devices. You can also walk around the office of infamous Stasi chief Erich Mielke.

← Frankfurter Tor, at the junction of Karl-Marx-Allee and Frankfurter Allee

↑ The Treptower Park memorial to the soldiers killed in World War II

17

Treptower Park

📍 Archenhold-Sternwarte, Alt-Treptow 🚇 Treptower Park 🚌 166, 165, 265

The vast park in Treptow was laid out in the 1860s to a design by Johann Gustav Meyer. In 1919 revolutionaries Karl Liebknecht, Wilhelm Pieck and Rosa Luxemburg assembled 150,000 striking workers here.

The park is best known for the colossal monument to the Red Army. Built between 1946 and 1949, it stands on the grave of 5,000 Soviet soldiers killed in the battle for Berlin in 1945.

In the farthest part of the park is the oldest and largest public observatory in Germany, the **Archenhold Sternwarte**, built in 1896. Given a permanent site in 1909, it was used by Albert Einstein for a lecture on the Theory of Relativity in 1915. It is also home to the world's longest reflecting telescope and a small planetarium.

Archenhold Sternwarte
🎦 📍 Alt-Treptow 1
🕐 2-4:30pm Wed-Sun (for guided tours only)
🌐 planetarium-berlin.de

⑱ Köpenick

Ⓢ Spindlersfeld, then 🚌 167 or Ⓢ Köpenick, then 🚌 164, 167 🚋 27, 60, 61, 62, 68

Köpenick is much older than Berlin. In the 9th century AD, a fortified settlement known as Kopanica, inhabited by Slavs, occupied a small island in the River Dahme. From the late 12th century Köpenick belonged to the Margrave of Brandenburg. In about 1240 a castle was built on the island, around which a town began to evolve. Crafts-men arrived here and, after 1685, a large colony of Huguenots also settled.

In the 19th century Köpenick recreated itself as an industrial town. Despite wartime devastation it has retained its historic character and, though there are no longer any 13th-century churches, it is worth strolling around the old town. By the old market square and in the neighbouring streets, modest houses have survived that recall the 18th century, alongside buildings from the end of the 19th century.

At Alt-Köpenick No. 21 is a vast brick town hall built in the style of the Brandenburg Neo-Renaissance. In 1906 a famous swindle took place here. Wilhelm Voigt dressed himself in a Prussian officer's uniform, "arrested" the mayor, and emptied the city treasury. The event inspired a popular comedy by Carl Zuckmayer, *The Captain from Köpenick*.

Köpenick's greatest attraction is **Schloss Köpenick**: a three-storey Baroque palace, built between 1677 and 1681 for the heir to the throne Friedrich (later King Friedrich I), to a design by the Dutch architect Rutger van Langevelt. In 2003 the Kunstgewerbemuseum opened a suite of Renaissance and Baroque rooms to the public in the Köpenick Palace.

Schloss Köpenick

 🏛 Schlossinsel 1 🕐 10am–5pm Thu–Sun 🌐 smb.museum

⑲ Viktoriapark

Ⓤ Platz der Luftbrücke 🚌 104, 140

This rambling park, with several artificial waterfalls, short trails and a small hill, was designed by Hermann Mächtig and built between 1884 and 1894. The Neo-Gothic Memorial to the Wars of Liberation at the summit of the hill is the work of Karl Friedrich Schinkel and was constructed between 1817 and 1821. The monument commemorates the Prussian victory against Napoleon's army in 1813. The monument's cast-iron tower is well ornamented. In the niches of the lower section of the memorial are statues of 12 allegorical figures by Christian Daniel Rauch, Friedrich Tieck and Ludwig

←

One of the artificial waterfalls in the grounds of Viktoriapark

Wichmann. Each figure symbolizes a battle and is linked to a historic person. These people tend to be either a military leader or a member of the royal family.

 20

Rathaus Schöneberg

 John-F-Kennedy-Platz
 Rathaus Schöneberg

The Schöneberg town hall is a gigantic building with an imposing tower, which was built between 1911 and 1914. From 1948 to 1990 it was used as the main town hall of West Berlin, and it was outside here, on 26 June 1963, that US President John F Kennedy gave his famous speech. More than 300,000 Berliners assembled at the Rathaus to hear the young president say "*Ich bin ein Berliner*" – "I am a Berliner" – intended as an expression of solidarity from the democratic world to a city defending its right to freedom. (An urban myth has since claimed that the phrase actually means "I am a small doughnut", but this is incorrect – although there is, indeed, a small doughnut in Germany known as a *Berliner*.)

21

Museum Europäischer Kulturen

Arnimallee 25 Dahlem Dorf 110, X11, X83
10am–5pm Tue–Fri, 11am–6pm Sat & Sun
smb.museum

Of the three museums that were once housed in the town of Dahlem – the Ethnologisches

↑ An elaborate dress on display in the Museum Europäischer Kulturen

Museum, which focused on pre-industrial societies from around the world; the Museum für Asiatische Kunst, one of the largest museums of Asian art in the world; and the Museum Europäischer Kulturen – only the latter remains. The collections from the other two museums are scheduled to be rehomed in the Humboldt Forum in 2021.

The Museum of European Cultures houses 280,000 items that represent everyday life and culture in Europe from the 18th century to the present day. The museum is organized according to material groups (textiles, graphic art, photography) and themes (from youth culture to religion) and includes objects from ethnic minorities across Europe. There are also regular special exhibitions on topics such as migration and spirituality.

EAT

Stilbruch
Located in a traditional half-timbered house, this charming culinary hotspot offers a romantic, candle-lit interior, a menu of regional German classics and dreamy views out to the Havel river - a perfect way to spend a relaxing afternoon or evening.
Eiswerder-strasse 22 stilbruch-restaurant.de

Frühsammers
Set inside a villa in the Grunewald tennis club is a couple-run fine-dining restaurant. It offers tasting menus with wine pairings, as well as cheaper and simpler contemporary cuisine when the owners are not in the kitchen.
Flinsberger Platz 8
fruehsammers.de

Ratskeller Köpenick
Despite the traditional name and a staunch commitment to German cuisine, the fresh presentation and innovative fish, meat and vegetable dishes here look and taste modern.
Alt-Köpenick 21
ratskeller-koepenick.de

> The Museum of European Cultures houses 280,000 items that represent everyday life and culture in Europe from the 18th century to the present day.

 ←

Berliners sunbathing on the beautiful sandy beach of Strandbad Wannsee

to the town of Dahlem in 1964. In addition to other works of art contemporary to the Brücke, there are paintings from the later creative periods of the Brücke artists.

25

Pfaueninsel

🏠 Pfaueninsel 📞 (030) 80 58 68 30 🚆 Wannsee, then 🚌 218, then 🚢 Schloss Pfaueninsel 🕐 Apr–Oct: 10am–5:30pm Tue–Sun

This picturesque island, named for the peacocks that inhabit it, is now a

22

Jagdschloss Grunewald

🏠 Hüttenweg 100 🚌 115, X10 🕐 Apr–Oct: 10am–6pm Tue–Sun; Nov–Dec & Mar: 10am–4pm Sat & Sun 🌐 spsg.de

One of the oldest surviving civic buildings in Berlin, this royal hunting lodge was built for the Elector Joachim II on the edge of the Grunewaldsee in 1542. It was rebuilt around 1700 in a Baroque style.

Inside is Berlin's only surviving Renaissance hall, which currently houses a collection of paintings that includes the biggest collection of canvases by Cranach the Elder and the Younger, among others.

On the ground floor you can see a collection of illustrations depicting forest life and the history of forestry. Opposite the Jagdschloss,

a hunting museum (Jagd-zeugmagazin) houses historic weapons and equipment.

23

Strandbad Wannsee

🏠 Wannseebadweg 🚆 Nikolassee 🚌 112, 218

The vast lake Wannsee, on the edge of Grunewald, is a popular destination for Berliners seeking recreation. The southeastern corner has yachting marinas and harbours. Farther north is one of the largest inland beaches in Europe, Strandbad Wannsee, developed between 1929 and 1930 by the construction of shops, cafés and changing rooms on man-made terraces. It is also pleasant to walk around Schwanenwerder island, with its many elegant villas.

24

Brücke-Museum

🏠 Bussardsteig 9, Dahlem 🚌 115 🕐 11am–5pm Wed–Mon 🌐 bruecke-museum.de

This elegant Functionalist building hosts a collection of German Expressionist painting linked to the Brücke (Bridge) group. It is based on almost 80 works by Schmidt-Rottluff bequeathed

---

 PICTURE PERFECT
Pfaueninsel

This is a great place to take your camera. The resident peacocks are not usually shy about putting on a display, but if they happen to be feeling modest, there is still plenty of intriguing architecture to shoot.

---

nature reserve, reached by ferry across the Havel river. It was laid out in 1795 according to a design by Johann August Eyserbeck. Its final form, which you see today, is the work of the landscape architect Peter Joseph Lenné.

One of the most interesting sights on the island is the small romantic palace of Schloss Pfaueninsel. Dating from 1794, it was designed by Johann Gottlieb Brendel for Friedrich Wilhelm II and his mistress Wilhelmine Encke (the future Countess Lichtenau) to use in the summer. The palace was constructed out of wood, with a façade fashioned in the form of a ruined medieval castle. The cast-iron bridge that links the towers was built in 1807. The palace is usually open to the public in the summer months, when visitors can see the splendid 18th- and 19th-century furnishings on display. However, it is currently closed for renovation until 2024.

Other sights worth visiting include Jakobsbrunnen (Jacob's Well), which was built to resemble an ancient ruin. Towards the northeast corner of the island is the Luisen-tempel in the form of a Greek temple. Its sandstone portico was relocated to the island from the mausoleum in Schlosspark Charlottenburg (p112) in 1829. Nearby is a stone commemorating Johannes Kunckel, an alchemist who lived on Pfaueninsel in the 17th century. During his quest to discover how to make gold, he discovered a method of producing ruby-coloured glass. Near the Aviary, home to multicoloured parrots and pheasants, is a tall fountain that was designed by Martin Friedrich Rabe In 1824.

DRINK

Alte Krug

This wood-panelled pub-restaurant has a vast beer garden that comfortably seats up to 500 people.

🏠 Königin-Luise-Strasse 52 🌐 alterkrug-berlin. de

Inselcafé

In summer there are deckchairs set out right by the river at this café on the Insel der Jugend.

🏠 Insel der Jugend 🌐 inselberlin.de

↑ The faux-medieval elegance of Schloss Pfaueninsel, on an island in the Havel river

↑ The terrace of the Blockhaus Nikolskoe restaurant, in Nikolskoe

26 Nikolskoe

 Nikolskoer Weg
Ⓢ Wannsee, then take 🚌 316

Across the river from Pfaueninsel (Peacock Island) is Nikolskoe. Here you'll find the Blockhaus Nikolskoe, a Russian-style *dacha* (country house) that was built in 1819 for the future Tsar Nicholas I and his wife, the daughter of King Friedrich Wilhelm III. The house was built by the German military architect Captain Snethlage, who was also responsible for the Alexandrowka estate in Potsdam (*p132*). Following a fire in 1985, the *dacha* was reconstructed. It currently houses a restaurant.

Close by is the church of St Peter and Paul, which was built between 1834 and 1837, to a design by Friedrich August Stüler. The body of the church is completed by a tower crowned by an onion-shaped dome, reflecting the style of Russian Orthodox sacral architecture.

27   Klein Glienicke

🏠 Königstrasse 36 🚌 316
📞 (030) 805 86 75 10
🕐 Apr–Oct: 10am–6pm Tue–Sun; Nov–Dec & Mar: 10am–5pm Sat & Sun

The palace in the palace-park of Klein Glienicke was built in 1825–7 to a design by Karl Friedrich Schinkel for Prince Karl of Prussia. The charming park in which it is located was created by Peter Joseph Lenné. Beyond, the Neo-Classical palace consists of an irregular cluster of buildings, grouped around a courtyard, including a pergola, a stable and a tower. Passing by the palace, you approach the Coach House, also by Schinkel and now housing a restaurant. Nearby are an orangery and greenhouses designed by Ludwig Persius. The Klosterhof, thought to be by Ferdinand von Arnim, is a mock monastery with a cloister and two chambers and many Byzantine and Romanesque architectural elements from Italy. Towards the lake is the Grosse Neugierde, a circular pavilion based on the Athenian monument to Lysikrates from the 4th century BC. From here there are beautiful views across the Havel river and Glienicker Brücke (known under the East German regime as the bridge of unity). The border with

→ Classical statuary in the grounds of the palace of Klein Glienicke

West Berlin ran across this bridge where, during the Cold War, the exchange of spies was conducted.

Neukölln

171, 194, M29, M41, N7, N9, N94

This thriving neighbourhood has become home to a large population of people from all around the world, as students, young professionals and creatives flock here, drawn by the inexpensive rents and cool atmosphere. Characterized by a vibrant mixture of international expats, Neukölln is one of the city's fastest-growing – and fastest-gentrifying – districts. Some tourists would ignore the neighbourhood after seeing traffic-heavy drags like Sonnennallee and the bleak main square, Hermannplatz; however, those willing to explore further will soon understand why Neukölln is so popular with the locals. The areas around Schillerstrasse and Weserstrasse – not to mention Kreuzkölln – are lined with bistros, galleries and boutiques. While there

$\rightarrow$
Photos of people killed while trying to flee East Berlin at the Gedenkstätte Berliner Mauer

aren't many major sights in the area, there are still a few places worth visiting, including the pretty Körnerpark, the Kindl Centre for Contemporary Art, Schloss Britz, Britzer Garten and Neukölln's historic centre, Alt-Rixdorf.

Gedenkstätte Berliner Mauer

Bernauer Strasse 119
Nordbahnhof
Bernauer Strasse M8, M10, 245, 247 Times vary, check website
berliner-mauer-gedenkstaette.de

The Berlin Wall Memorial on Bernauer Strasse is dedicated to the men, women and children who were killed by the Eastern border guards while attempting to escape into West Berlin. Only small fragments of the Berlin Wall have survived to this day. One of these, along Bernauer Strasse, is now an official place of remembrance. The location of the memorial is particularly poignant since in 1961 this street was cut in two, resulting in people jumping into West Berlin from upper-floor buildings that stood right on the dividing line, while border guards were bricking up doors and windows facing west.

Today the memorial is a grim, sombre reminder of the hardship the division inflicted on the city. It includes a museum and a number of installations along 2 km (1 mile) of the former border.

BRANDENBURG

Ruled first by Albrecht der Bär (Albert the Bear),
the province of Brandenburg grew in importance
in the 15th century thanks to the rise of the
Hohenzollern dynasty. The region became
entangled in the Thirty Years' War and suffered
devastating losses; depopulated and plundered,
it took Brandenburg many years to recover, but
it finally rose again in the early 18th century as
part of the Kingdom of Prussia.

Encircling both the German capital of Berlin and
its own regional capital – Potsdam – the province
of Brandenburg is a peaceful, attractive lowland
region that offers a multitude of activities and
attractions, including grand palaces, thermal spas
and stunning churches and monasteries. Officially
the German federal state with the most inland
waterways, its landscapes are crisscrossed by a
dense network of rivers and canals and studded
with more than 3,000 lakes. Northeast of Berlin
lie the forests, open moorlands and valleys of the
Schorfheide region, which offers lots of activity
opportunities for cyclists and hikers, as well as
the popular Werbellin Lake.

BRANDENBURG

Must See
1. Potsdam

Experience More
2. Elbtalaue
3. Brodowin
4. Brandenburg an der Havel
5. Neuruppin
6. Kloster Chorin
7. Frankfurt an der Oder
8. Cottbus
9. Oranienburg
10. Jüterbog
11. Spreewald

Neubrandenburg

Stargard

Pasewalk

Lychen

Templin

Schorfheide

Zehdenick

Liebenwalde

Sachsenhausen

ORANIENBURG

Hennigsdorf

Berlin Tegel
Airport

Berlin
see p54

Berlin Schönefeld
Airport

Ludwigsfelde

Luckenwalde

Dahme

Schlieben

Herzberg

Elsterwerda

Riesa

Prenzlau

Uckermark

Strom

Welse

Schwedt

Angermünde

Oder

KLOSTER
CHORIN 6

BRODOWIN

Oderberg

Eberswalde

Bad Freienwalde

Wriezen

Bernau

Strausberg

Müncheberg

Fürstenwalde

Königs
Wusterhausen

BRANDENBURG

Markisch
Buchholz

Beeskow

Schwielochsee

Lübben

SPREEWALD

Lübbenau

Lehde

Luckau

Vetschau

Finsterwalde

Niederlausitz

Doberlug-
Kirchhain

Grossräschen

Lauchhammer

Senftenberg

Ruhland

Grossenhain

Kamenz

Chojna

Myślibórz

Barlinek

Debno

Gorzów
Wielkopolski

POLAND

Sulecin

Oderbruch

Alte Oder

Seelow

Lebus

FRANKFURT AN
DER ODER 7

Boczów

Torzym

Oder-Spree-Kanal

Cybinka

Eisenhüttenstadt

Neuzelle

Krosno
Odrzanskie

Lieberose

Guben

Peitz

COTTBUS 8

Forst

Lubsko

Żary

Rusocice

Bad Muskau

Neisse

Spremberg

SAXONY
p162

0 kilometres   20
0 miles   20

N

BRANDENBURG

Löcknitz

Nuthe

Spree

Spree

Schliela

$\rightarrow$

1 Schloss Cecilienhof.

2 Kayaking in Spreewald.

3 Schloss Sanssouci.

4 Edvard Munch's *Girls on the Bridge* in Potsdam's Museum Barberini.

2 DAYS
In Brandenburg

Day 1

Morning To get acquainted with the state capital of Potsdam *(p132)*, start with a stroll around the Alter Markt *(p135)*. The square is surrounding by fine reproductions of legendary buildings, including the Brandenburg parliament at Neuer Landtag *(p132)* and the Museum Barberini *(p133)*.

Afternoon Grab a slice of cake at Café Haider *(Friedrich-Ebert-Strasse 29)*, which has been serving great German food since 1878, and then head to the magical Schloss Sanssouci *(p137)*, one of the most beautiful palace complexes in Europe. Explore the riches within the palace as well as the expansive gardens that surround it. If you still have time, check out the large gardens of Schloss Cecilienhof *(p134)*, designed by Paul Schultze-Naumburg in the style of an English country manor.

Evening Wander round the picturesque streets and wooden log cabins of the Russian colony, Alexandrowka *(p132)*, and its Dutch counterpart of Holländisches Viertel *(p135)*, with its gabled red-brick houses, coffee houses and restaurants. Enjoy an elegant, French-inspired dinner at Restaurant Juliette *(Jägerstrasse 39)*.

Day 2

Morning A leisurely train ride (about an hour and a half) will take you from Potsdam to Lübben. Head straight for the centre of town around Hauptstrasse, where you'll be well placed to find a late breakfast or brunch. Lübben is just a quick stop on your travels today, but if you're with kids you can take a stroll around the Castle Island area to stretch your legs and enjoy the playgrounds. Then it's time to move on with a boat trip or a bike ride down to Lübbenau.

Afternoon In Lübbenau check out the Baroque church and Neo-Classical house of the von Lynar family, but make sure you leave time for the real highlight of the area: the picturesque forest trails and waterways of the Spreewald. This UNESCO-listed biosphere reserve is known for its canals and is best explored in canoes or punts.

Evening Return to Lübbenau to sample regional cuisine at Cafe Fontane *(Ehm-Welk-Strasse 42)*, which has a welcoming interior, friendly service and a variety of fish, pasta and meat dishes. Afterwards, take a stroll around the small but attractive town centre, which has a fairly lively port area and historic architecture.

Medicinal Mineral Spas

Mineral spas use the chemical properties of natural mineral springs - sulphur, calcium and magnesium to name a few - as therapy for everything from arthritis and rheumatism to depression. This kind of therapy was especially popular in the 19th century, when wealthy people began heading to scenic mountain regions to "take the waters". The invention of penicillin and other antibiotics set the trend back, but today mineral spas are in vogue again, though more for fun than the health benefits. Popular mineral spas include Fontane Therme in Neuruppin (p138) and Bad Belzig's SteinTherme (www.steintherme.de).

→

Mist over the waters of the Fontane Therm resort in Neuruppin

BRANDENBURG FOR
A SPA BREAK

With one of the most comprehensive spa cultures in Europe, Germany is big on relaxation. Packed with health retreats (look out for towns with Bad in front of their name) and countless *Therme* (wellness and beauty spas), Brandenburg is the perfect place to come for a spot of pampering.

TOP 3
THERME RESORTS IN BRANDENBURG

Saarow Therme
🅰 Bad Saarow
Using the waters of the Catharine Spring, the salty thermal pools here are as relaxing as they are beautiful.

Spreewald Therme
🅰 Spreewald
Water from deep below the Spreewald fills the ten pools at this resort located deep within the biosphere reserve.

Kritsalltherme
🅰 Bad Wilsnack
Mediterranean decor accompanies a partially-domed, salt-water lake.

The Kneipp Cure

Kneipp therapy is named after the Bavarian priest Sebastian Kneipp (1821-97), who developed his hydrotherapeutic healing methods in the 1800s while seeking relief from tuberculosis. Also known as "Kneipping" or the "Kneipp Cure", the principle of Kneipp therapy is based around various water-based cures – showers, wraps, baths and especially cold-water treatments, including ice baths, and walking barefoot in the snow. One of Brandenburg's best Kneipp resorts is Strandhotel in Buckow, surrounded by lakes and beautiful countryside only an hour outside Berlin.

→

A woman enjoying the traditional Kneipp cure of walking in cold water

GERMANY: BIRTHPLACE OF HOMEOPATHY

Homeopathy – the "like cures like" method of alternative medicine – was founded in Germany by Dr Samuel Hahnemann. His ideas became popular in the 19th century – at first among the upper classes, but soon throughout all of German society. Homeopathy was revived in the 1970s and began to spread internationally, though critics have denounced it as a pseudoscience. Even so, homeopathy enjoys privileged legal status in Germany, and in some cases is supported by the federal health care system.

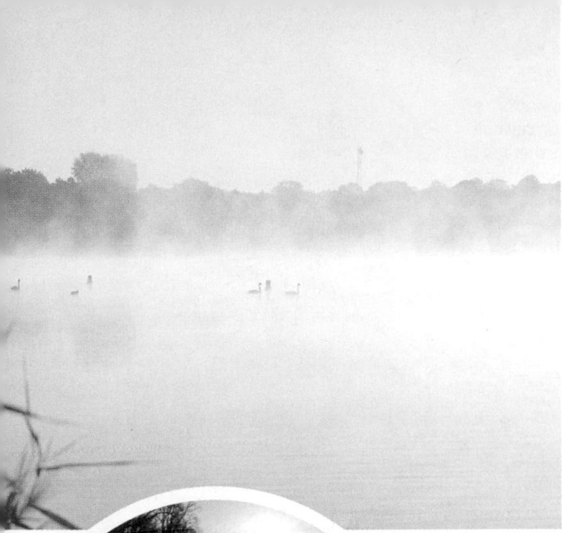

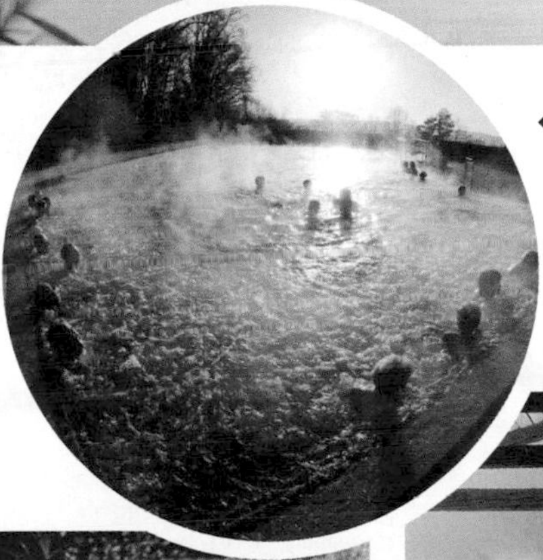

← Bathers enjoying the warm waters of a steamy outdoor Therme pool

↑ The beautiful interior of Bleiche Resort & Spa in Burg im Spreewald

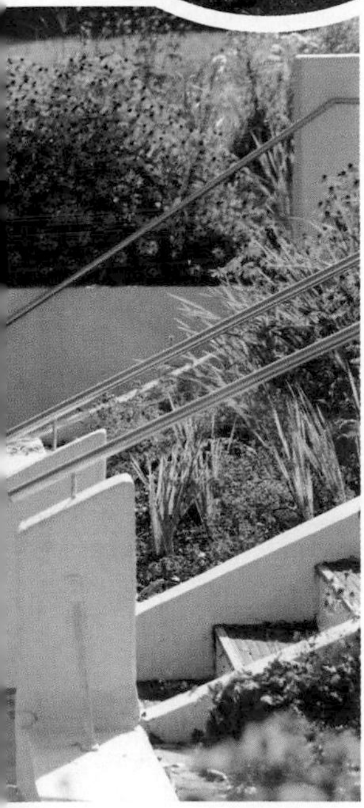

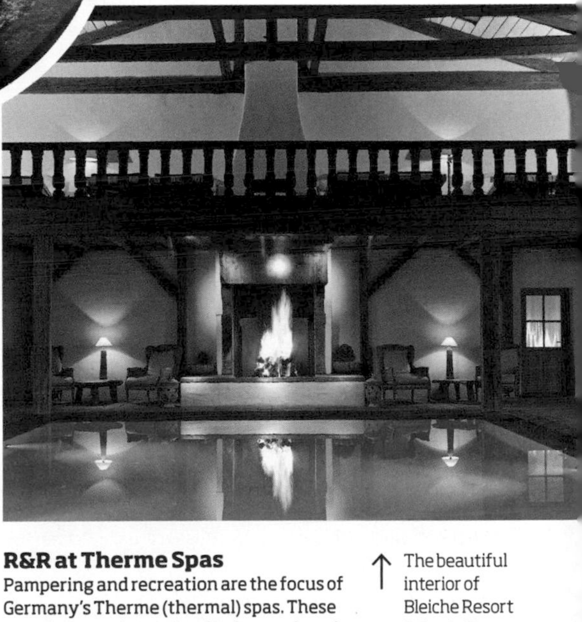

R&R at Therme Spas

Pampering and recreation are the focus of Germany's Therme (thermal) spas. These usually comprise a mix of indoor and outdoor pools, saunas and steam baths, and a selection of beauty treatments such as massages, manicures, pedicures and body wraps. A great choice for a luxury spa holiday is Bleiche Resort & Spa *(www.bleiche.de)*.

❶

POTSDAM

F3 **Park Sanssouci, Charlottenhof, Potsdam Hauptbahnhof** 605, 606, 610, 631, N14, X5, X15 91, 94, 98 **Luisenplatz; open 9:30am-6pm Mon-Sat, 10am-4pm Sun & hols; www.potsdam-tourism.com**

Potsdam is one of Germany's most attractive towns. Tourists flock to see the magnificent royal summer residence, Schloss Sanssouci, to visit the old city centre and the Russian colony of Alexandrowka, and to stroll around the parks of Schloss Babelsberg.

An independent city close to Berlin, Potsdam – with over 150,000 inhabitants – is also the capital of Brandenburg. The first documented reference to Potsdam dates back to AD 993; it was later granted municipal rights in 1317. The town blossomed under Friedrich Wilhelm, the Great Elector (1620–88), and then again in the 18th century. However, Potsdam suffered very badly during World War II, particularly on the night of 14–15 April 1945 when Allied planes bombed the town centre. It is now a flourishing town with serene spots and impressive sights.

①

Marble House

Am Neuen Garten 10 603 **Times vary, check website** spsg.de

The small Marble House on the edge of Heiliger See is a beautiful example of early Neo-Classical architecture. Its name comes from the Silesian marble used on its façade. The main part was built in 1787–1793 by Carl von Gontard to a design and under the direction of Carl Gotthard Langhans, on the initiative of King Friedrich Wilhelm II (1786–97).

②

Alexandrowka

Russische Kolonie Allee/ Puschkinallee 92, 96 638 alexandrowka.de

A visit to Alexandrowka takes the visitor into the world of Pushkin's fairy tales. Wooden log cabins with intricate carvings, set in their own gardens, create a charming and serene residential estate. They were constructed in 1826 under the direction of the German architect Snethlage, for 12 singers of a Russian choir that was established in 1812.

———

③

Neuer Landtag

Alter Markt 1 8am-6pm Mon-Fri; courtyard: 8am-8pm daily landtag.brandenburg.de

Replicating the old city palace with its Knobelsdorff staircase, the new Brandenburg parliament building opened in 2014. The courtyard, foyer and restaurant are all open to the public.

←
Potsdam's modern residential buildings iluminated at night

(4) Marstall

📍Breitestrasse 1a 🚌606 🚊91, 92, 96 ⏰10am-6pm Tue-Sun 🌐filmmuseum-potsdam.de

This long Baroque pavilion, built in 1685 and once used as royal stables, is the only remaining building of a royal residence. Today it houses a film museum devoted to the amazing Babelsberg Film Studio nearby. A cinema offers several screenings per day – a great way to spend an afternoon in Potsdam if the weather isn't on your side.

(5) Museum Barberini

📍Alter Markt, Humboldt-strasse 5-6 🚉Potsdam Hauptbahnhof 🚌603, 605, 606, 609, 614 🚊631, 638, 650 v91, 92, 93, 96, 98, 99 ⏰10am-7pm Mon & Wed-Sun 🌐museum-barberini.de

Located inside a reconstruction of Frederick the Great's 18th-century Barberini Palace on the Alter Markt, this three-floor museum offers glamorous exhibition halls as well as events and educational programmes. The permanent collection is built around the philanthropist Hasso Plattner's collection of French Impressionist landscape paintings, but there are also several temporary exhibitions per year that range from Old Masters to contemporary art.

DRINK

Gleis 6
An atmospheric bistro with vintage decor, a decent cocktail menu of Caipirinhas and Mojitos, offering a simple food menu of soups, salads and burgers until late. Good starting point for a night out.

📍Karl-Liebknecht-Strasse 4 📞(0331) 74 82 429 ⏰11:30am-2pm & 5pm-1am Mon-Fri, 5pm-2am Sat, 5-11pm Sun

€€€

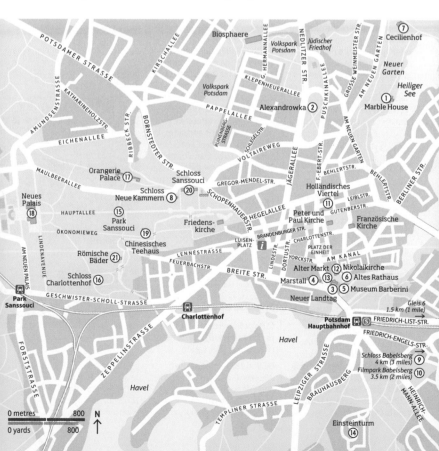

The English country manor style of Cecilienhof palace and its elegant courtyard

irregular building with many towers and bay windows, built in the spirit of English Neo-Gothic, with allusions to Windsor Castle and Tudor style, it now holds the Museum of Pre-History.

Filmpark Babelsberg

🏠 **Grossbeerenstrasse** 🕐 **Apr–Oct: 10am–6pm daily** 🌐 **filmpark.de**

This amazing film park was laid out on the site where Germany's first films were produced in 1912. From 1917 the studio belonged to Universum-Film-AG (UFA), which produced some of the most famous films of the silent era, including Fritz

Altes Rathaus

🏠 **Am Alten Markt 9**
📞 **(0331) 28 96 868**
🕐 **10am–5pm Tue, Wed & Fri; 10am–7pm Thu; 10am–6pm Sat & Sun**

The roof tower of the old town hall features a 4-m- (13-ft-) high gilded figure of Atlas carrying a globe. It was built in 1753 to a design by Johann Boumann the Elder and rebuilt under the GDR. It is currently used as a museum.

Cecilienhof

🏠 **Im Neuen Garten 11**
📞 **(0331) 96 94 244** 🚌 **603**
🕐 **Apr–Oct: 10am–6pm Tue–Sun; Nov–Mar: 10am–5pm Tue–Sun**

The Cecilienhof played an important role as the venue for the 1945 Potsdam Conference. Completed in 1917, the palace is the most recent of all Hohenzollern dynasty buildings. Designed by Paul Schultze-Naumburg, it is a timber-frame building with inner courtyards. Today it is a hotel, but the large park remains open to the public even when the Potsdam Conference rooms are closed to visitors.

Schloss Neue Kammern

🏠 **Park Sanssouci** 🕐 **Apr: 10am–6pm Wed–Mon; May–Oct: 10am–6pm Tue–Sun** 🌐 **spsg.de**

The New Chambers adjoin Schloss Sanssouci in the west, like the Bildergalerie (picture gallery) in the east. As part of this ensemble it was originally built in 1747 as an orangery, to a design by Georg Wenzeslaus von Knobelsdorff. The building has an attractive roof with sloping ends and sides. In 1768 Frederick the Great ordered it to be transformed into guest accommodation. The architect, Georg Christian Unger, left the exterior of the orangery largely untouched but converted the interior into sumptuous suites and four elegant halls. The Rococo decor has been maintained.

Schloss Babelsberg

🏠 **Park Babelsberg 10** 🕐 **For restoration with no date for reopening** 🌐 **spsg.de**

Built in 1833–5 for Prince Wilhelm (Kaiser Wilhelm I), by Karl Friedrich Schinkel, this extravagant castle ranks as one of his finest works. An

THE POTSDAM CONFERENCE

On 17 July 1945 the heads of government of Great Britain, the United States and the Soviet Union met in Schloss Cecilienhof to confirm the decisions made earlier that year at Yalta. They decided to abolish the Nazi Party, to limit the size of the German militia, and also to punish war criminals and establish reparations. The conference played a major part in establishing a political balance of power in Europe.

Lang's *Metropolis* and some films with Greta Garbo, Marlene Dietrich and Heinz Rühmann. *The Blue Angel*, starring Marlene Dietrich, was also shot at Babelsberg, but subsequently, the studios were used to film Nazi propaganda. The studio is still operational today, and part of it is open to visitors, with professionals such as set-builders, makeup artists and animal handlers on site to demonstrate their behind-the-scenes skills.

Holländisches Viertel

📍 Friedrich-Ebert-Strasse, Kurfürstenstrasse, Hebbelstrasse, Gutenbergstrasse 🚌 603, 638 🚊 92, 96

A stroll through the four blocks of the Dutch Quarter is a cosy affair. The 134 gabled red-brick houses with shuttered windows were built in 1733–42 by Friedrich Wilhelm I for Dutch settlers.

Nikolaikirche

📍 Alter Markt 📞 (0331) 27 08 602 🕐 9:30am–7:30pm daily (from 11:30am Sun)

This imposing Neo-Classical church was designed in 1828–30 by Karl Friedrich Schinkel and the building work was supervised by Ludwig Persius.

Alter Markt

After World War II the town centre was an inhospitable traffic junction, but it now features fine reproductions of remarkable buildings.

Einsteinturm

📍 Albert-Einstein-Strasse 📞 (0331) 29 17 41 🕐 Oct–Mar: visits daily by arrangement, call ahead 🚌 691

The Einstein Tower, an observatory built in 1920–21 by Erich Mendelssohn, is a fine example of German Expressionist architecture. Its fantasy forms demonstrate the qualities of reinforced concrete to spectacular effect. However, the cost of formwork limited the use of the material to the first storey, while the upper floors are plastered brickwork.

↑ Restaurants lining the streets of the beautiful Dutch Quarter

⑮

Park Sanssouci

🏠 Schopenhauerstrasse/ Zur Historischen Mühle 🚌 612, 614, 695 🕐 8am–dusk daily 🌐 spsg.de

This enormous park, which occupies an area of nearly 3 sq km (1 sq mile), is one of the most glorious palace complexes in Europe. The first building to be constructed on the site was Schloss Sanssouci, built as the summer palace, of Frederick the Great (1712–86). Over the years, Park Sanssouci was expanded considerably and other palaces and pavilions were added. Now the range of different garden styles makes a simple stroll through this park particularly pleasant. There are also a large number of sculptures, columns, obelisks and grottoes for the visitor to explore, and the vistas and perspectives that suddenly open up across the park are breathtaking.

Shrubbery-lined avenue ↑ leading up to the grand Neues Palais

⑯

Schloss Charlottenhof

🏠 Geschwister-Scholl-Strasse 34a 🚌 605, 606 🚊 91 🕐 May–Oct: 10am–5pm Tue–Sun 🌐 spsg.de

This small Neo-Classical palace stands at the southern end of Park Sanssouci, known as Park Charlottenhof. Built in 1826–9 for the heir to the throne, the future King Friedrich Wilhelm IV, this single-storey building was designed by Karl Friedrich Schinkel in the style of a Roman villa. Some wall paintings are still in place, as well as a collection of Italian engravings. The most interesting part is the Humboldt Room. The palace is encircled by a beautiful landscaped park designed by Peter Joseph Lenné.

→ Sculpture fronting the grand Orangerie-schloss

⑰

Orangerie Palace

🏠 Maulbeerallee (Nordischer Garten) 🚌 695 🕐 Apr–Oct: 10am–5pm Wed–Mon; Nov–Mar: 10am–6pm Wed–Mon 🌐 spsg.de

Above the park towers the Orangerie, designed in Italian Renaissance style and crowned by a colonnade. The central section of this three-winged palace complex encompasses the impressive Raphael Hall, with its interesting collection of more than 50 19th-century copies of paintings by Raphael, including well-known works such as the *Sistine Madonna* and the *Transfiguration*.

⑱

Neues Palais

🏠 Am Neuen Palais 🚌 605, 606, 695 🕐 Apr–Oct: 10am–6pm Wed–Mon; Nov–Mar: 10am–5pm Wed–Mon 🌐 spsg.de

One of Germany's most impressive palaces, the imposing Baroque New Palace, on the main avenue in Park Sanssouci, was built for Frederick the Great to initial plans by Georg Wenzeslaus von Knobelsdorff in 1750. Its

Did You Know?

The Neues Palais was rarely used as a royal residence, but instead hosted guests for celebrations.

construction, to designs by Johan Gottfried Büring, Jean Laurent Le Geay and Carl von Gontard, was delayed until 1763–9, after the Seven Years' War. The vast, three-wing structure comprises over 200 richly adorned rooms and has many interesting sculptures. The south wing houses the king's quarters.

(19)

Chinesisches Teehaus

🏛 Ökonomieweg (Rehgarten) 🚌 606, 695 🚋 91, 94 🕐 May-Oct: 10am-5:30pm Tue-Sun 🌐 spsg.de

The lustrous, gilded pavilion that can be seen glistening between the trees from a distance is the Chinese Teahouse. Chinese art was very popular during the Rococo period – people wore

Chinese silk, wallpapered their rooms with Chinese designs, lacquered their furniture, drank tea from Chinese porcelain and built Chinese pavilions in their gardens. The one in Sanssouci was built in 1754–6 to a design by Johann Gottfried Büring. Circular in shape, it has a centrally located main hall surrounded by three studies. Between these are pretty trompe l'oeil porticos. The structure is covered with a tent roof and topped with a lantern. Gilded ornaments, columns and Chinese figures surround the pavilion. Originally a tea room and summer dining house, it today houses a collection of 18th-century porcelain.

(20)

Schloss Sanssouci

🏛 Maulbeerallee 🚌 X15 🕐 Apr-Oct: 10am-5:30pm Tue-Sun; Nov-Mar: 10am-4:30pm Tue-Sun 🌐 spsg.de

This Rococo palace was built in 1745–7 by Georg Wenzes-laus von Knobelsdorff. Sanssouci ("carefree") was the perfect name for the enchanting castle. The Damenflügel,

the west wing added in 1840, the private rooms of Freidrich the Great and the guestrooms are open to visitors.

(21)

Römische Bäder

🏛 Lenné-Strasse (Park Charlottenhof) 🚌 606 🚋 91 🕐 May-Oct: 10am-5:30pm Tue-Sun 🌐 spsg.de

The Roman Baths form a picturesque group of pavilions which served as accommodation for the king's guests. They were designed in 1829–40 by Karl Friedrich Schinkel, with the help of Ludwig Persius. The gardener's house at the front stands next to a low, asymmetrical tower, built in the style of an Italian Renaissance villa. In the background, to the left, extends the former bathing pavilion, which is currently used for temporary exhibitions. The pavilions are grouped around a garden planted with colourful shrubs and vegetables.

→ Grand steps leading up to the picturesque Schloss Sanssouci

EXPERIENCE MORE

 2

Elbtalaue

🅰E2 🚇 to Wittenberge or Bad Wilsnack 🚉Bahnhof 1, Bad Wilsnack; www. elbtalaue.de

The Elbe valley in the western part of Prignitz is an area of gentle rolling hills and unspoiled nature. Storks, increasingly rare in Germany, still nest here. When travelling around this parkland it is worth stopping at Pritzwalk to admire the late-Gothic Nikolaikirche (St Nicholas church). Another place of interest is Perleberg with its picturesque market square, featuring an original 1515 timber-frame building, a sandstone statue of the knight Roland

(1546), now standing by the 1850 Town Hall, and the town's star attraction – the 15th-century Gothic Jakobskirche (church of St Jacob).

Bad Wilsnack owes its fame to the discovery of the therapeutic properties of the iron oxide-rich mud found in the surrounding marshes. Already known in medieval times, the town was an important place of pilgrimage. After a church fire, in 1384, three hosts displaying the blood of Christ were found untouched on the altar. The Gothic Nikolaikirche (church of St Nicholas), which survives to this day, was built soon after for the pilgrims.

← Statue of the knight Roland in the market square of Perleberg, a town in the Elbtalaue

Plattenburg castle, in a scenic situation on an island, is also worth a visit. Combining late-Gothic and Renaissance architecture, it is used as a venue for concerts.

3

Brodowin

🅰F2 🚇🚌 🌐brodowin.de

Located in the Schorfheide-Chorin biosphere reserve, and close to Plagefenn nature reserve, this small village was founded by Dutch and German farmers several centuries ago. It is known for its tight-knit community and commitment to top-quality organic produce. It is particularly well known for its milk products, which are sold all over Brandenburg.

The area is full of beautiful woodlands and heaths to explore as well as interesting sights like the Parsteiner See, Kloster Chorin (p140) and the Niederfinow ship lift.

The village itself is a lively place with a large commitment not only to farming, but also to

 The Gothic church of Neuruppin, one of the city's oldest buildings

local conservation projects and educational activities for its children. Such great initiatives include the annual village festival and a *Hoffest* (farm festival), where visitors can get insights into the village's eco-friendly agricultural undertakings.

4

Brandenburg an der Havel

🅰E3 🚉🚌 *i* Neustädtischer Markt 3; www.stadt-brandenburg.de

Brandenburg is the oldest town of the region. It was settled by Slavs as early as the mid-8th-century, and a mission episcopate was established here in 948. Scenically sited on the Havel river, it has preserved historic centres on three islands, despite wartime destruction.

The oldest island is the Dominsel, with its Romanesque Dom St Peter und St Paul. This cathedral was constructed from 1165 to the mid-13th century. In the 14th century it was raised and given new vaultings. It contains numerous valuable

Gothic objects, including the "Czech" altar (around 1375), the present main altar (from Lehnin, 1518) and the sacrarium of the same year. The most valuable treasures are found in the **Dommuseum**.

Other sights worth visiting are the huge, late-14th-century Katharinenkirche built by Hinrich Brunsberg, the Gotthardtkirche, in the Altstadt (old town), with its Romanesque façade and Gothic interior, the Gothic Rathaus (Town Hall), with a statue of Roland from 1474, and the **Stadtmuseum**, a museum of local history.

The small town of Werder offers a Neo-Gothic church built by August Stüler, an historic windmill and a charming ensemble of 18th-century fishermen's houses. It is most famous for the annual Blossom Festival in May, when some 750,000 people gather to enjoy fruit wines and folk music.

Dommuseum

♿ 🏠 Burghof 10 ⏰ Times vary, check website 🌐 dom-brandenburg.de

Stadtmuseum

♿ 🏠 Ritterstrasse 96 ⏰ 1pm–5pm Tue–Sun 🌐 stadtmuseum-brandenburg.de

---

5

Neuruppin

🅰E2 🚌 *i* Karl-Marx-Strasse 1; www.neuruppin.de

The town of Neuruppin, in a scenic location on the

shores of a large lake – the Ruppiner See – is mainly Neo-Classical in style, having been rebuilt to the design of Bernhard Matthias Brasch after the great fire of 1787. The only older buildings are the Gothic post-Dominican church and two small hospital chapels. Neuruppin is the birthplace of the architect Karl Friedrich Schinkel (p77) and the novelist Theodor Fontane.

The town's modern spa resort, **Fontane Therme**, is attached to a hotel and situated on the town's lake. It offers several pools (indoor and outdoor), saunas and options for massages and other spa treatments.

Fontane Therme

♿ 🕐 🏠 An der Seepromenade 21 🌐 resort-mark-brandenburg.de

Approaching the Cistercian abbey at Chorin, now a classical music venue ↑

and can now be seen in St Gertraud (church of St Gertrude), which dates back to 1368. The main altar from 1489 and the huge, 5-m- (16-ft-) tall candelabrum from 1376 are particularly valuable. Another Gothic church, built in 1270, has been transformed into the CPE Bach Konzerthalle (concert hall), named after Carl Philipp Emmanuel Bach, son of German composer Johann Sebastian.

Nearby is Eisenhüttenstadt, the GDR's first "socialist city". Originally named Stalinstadt (Stalin City), it adopted its current name (Iron Works City) following the de-Stalinization era, and was an industrial boomtown until the Wall fell. The **Dokumentationszentrum Alltag der DDR** showcases objects and narratives from everyday life in the city and wider East Germany.

Dokumentationszentrum Alltag der DDR

⊘ ◻ Erich-Weinert-Allee 3, Eisenhüttenstadt
◷ 11am–5pm Tue–Sun
🖥 alltagskultur-ddr.de

6

Kloster Chorin

◻ F2 ◻ Amt Chorin 11A 🚆 Chorin ◷ Apr–Oct: 9am–6pm daily (Nov–Mar: to 4pm) 🖥 kloster-chorin.org

On the edge of the Schorfheide forest, listed as a World Biosphere Reserve by UNESCO, stands one of Brandenburg's most beautiful Gothic buildings – the Cistercian Kloster of Chorin. The Cistercians arrived here in 1258, but work on the present Gothic abbey did not start until 1270. The church is a triple-nave, transeptial basilica, with a magnificent façade. Preserved today are two wings of the monastic quarters plus several domestic buildings. Following the dissolution of the monastery in 1542, the entire complex fell into disrepair. Today the abbey, deprived of its traditional furnishings, is used for classical concerts as well as historical and contemporary art exhibitions. The park established by Peter Joseph Lenné is a pleasant place for a stroll.

7

Frankfurt an der Oder

◻ F3 🚆 🚌 ◻ Grosse Oderstrasse 29; www.frankfurt-oder.de

After being destroyed in World War II, Frankfurt an der Oder was split into two parts – one of them now the Polish town of Słubice. Germany's "Other Frankfurt" offers riverside charm and Eastern Bloc architecture.

Its most famous son is playwright and writer Heinrich von Kleist (1777–1811); the Kleist-Museum, devoted to his life and work, is in the former garrison school. The Gothic Rathaus (town hall) in the centre escaped destruction in World War II and now houses an art gallery. The main church, Marienkirche (church of St Mary), has stood in ruins since 1945. Its stained glass originates from around 1367 and illustrates Christ's Life and Suffering, the Creation of the World and the Legend of the Antichrist. Some Gothic furnishings were rescued

> The Documentation Centre of Everyday Culture of the GDR showcases objects and narratives from everyday life in the city and wider East Germany.

8

Cottbus

F3 Bahnhofstrasse Berliner Platz 6; www.cottbus-tourismus.de

Tourists rarely visit Cottbus, despite its many attractions. The enchanting town square is surrounded by Baroque buildings. At No. 24 is the quaint Löwenapotheke (lion's pharmacy), which houses a small pharmaceutical museum, the **Brandenburgisches Apothekenmuseum**, with displays of historical interiors. Nearby, the Gothic Oberkirche St Nikolai features an original late-Gothic mesh vaulting. Another Gothic structure is the Wendenkirche (Sorbian church), a former Franciscan church built in the 14th and 15th centuries.

Perhaps the most attractive building in Cottbus is the Staatstheater (state theatre), designed in Jugendstil (Art Nouveau style) by Bernhard Sehring and built in 1908. The **Wendisches Museum** is devoted to the culture of the Sorbs, which is experiencing a revival (p181).

Schloss Branitz is a late-Baroque palace, built in the 1700s, at the southeastern edge of town. It became the residence of Prince Hermann von Pückler-Muskau in 1845, who had its interior redesigned by Gottfried Semper. Today the palace houses the **Fürst-Pückler-Museum**, which exhibits paintings by Karl Blechen, a local artist from Cottbus. The star attraction of the palace is its Park, designed by the prince himself. This vast landscaped garden includes a lake with an island on which stands a grass-covered mock-Egyptian earth pyramid containing the tomb of the extravagant and eccentric Prince.

Brandenburgisches Apothekenmuseum

Altmark 24 (0355) 239 97 Visits possible with guide 11am–2pm Tue–Fri; 2pm & 3pm Sat & Sun

Wendisches Museum

Mühlenstrasse 12 (0355) 79 49 30 10am–5pm Tue–Fri, 1–5pm Sat, Sun & public hols

Schloss Branitz and Fürst-Pückler-Museum

Kastanienalle 11 (0355) 751 50 Apr–Oct: 10am–6pm daily; Nov–Mar: 11am–4pm Tue–Sun

Schloss Branitz, on the outskirts of Cottbus, and its stylish interior (inset) ↓

⑨ Oranienburg

🅰F3 🚗🚌 *ℹ*Schlossplatz 1; www.oranienburg-erleben.de

The star attraction of the town is **Schloss Oranienburg,** the Baroque residence built for Louisa Henrietta von Nassau-Oranien, wife of the Great Elector Friedrich Wilhelm. Designed by Johann Gregor Memhardt and Michael Matthias Smids, it was built in 1651–5 and later extended to its present H-shape.

Built by the Nazis in 1936, the concentration camp at **Sachsenhausen**, northeast of Oranienburg, was liberated in 1945 by the Russians. Up to 200,000 people were incarcerated in this camp, and it is estimated that over 30,000 died here, killed by mass extermination, hunger or disease. Sachsenhausen is now a memorial and museum. Each area of the camp hosts an exhibit – for example, the one in the former infirmary focuses on medicine and racism under the Nazi regime.

Schloss Oranienburg

⊗ 🏠Schlossplatz 1
📞(03301) 53 74 37
🕐10am–4pm Tue–Fri 🕐Mon

Sachsenhausen

⊗ 🏠Strasse der Nationen 22 🚉 Oranienburg, then 🚌804, 821 🕐8:30am–6pm Tue–Sun (mid-Oct–mid-Mar: to 4:30pm)
🌐sachsenhausen-sbg.de

⑩ Jüterbog

🅰F3 🚗🚌
*ℹ*Mönchenkirchplatz 4; (03372) 46 31 13

Jüterbog is a small, picturesque town featuring many Gothic structures including some well-preserved sections of three city walls with gates and

↑ Jüterbog's Dammtor gateway and imposing fortifications

towers, dating back to the 15th century. It also boasts a beautiful town hall with arcades and three churches. Nikolaikirche (church of St Nicholas), the largest of them, is a magnificent hall church, with a twin-tower façade, built in several stages. The so-called New Sacristy houses a set of medieval wall paintings, while the naves contain many Gothic furnishings.

⑪ Spreewald

🅰F3 🚉Lübben
*ℹ*Raddusch, Lindenstrasse 1;Lübbenau, Ehm-Welk-Strasse 15; www.spreewald.de

Designated as a World Biosphere Reserve, this marshy region, criss-crossed by hundreds of small rivers and canals, attracts large numbers of tourists each year. An all-day trip by *Kahn* (boat) or canoe, which is best started in Lübben or Lübbenau, can prove to be an unforgettable experience. The splendour of nature, numerous water birds and the endless chain of small restaurants that serve meals straight from the jetty,

ensure an exciting day for the visitor. Do not miss the local speciality, pickled gherkins.

Lübben has an original Gothic church and a Baroque palace, rebuilt in the 19th century. Lübbenau features a small Baroque church and the Neo-Classical house of the von Lynar family.

In Lehde the private collection of the Bauernhaus-und Gurkenmuseum – the only gherkin museum in Germany – are highly recommended. And nearby Luckau has a lovely town square and Baroque houses.

↑ Paddling a canoe on a
canal near Lübbenau,
in the Spreewald

Christmas market in the state capital, Magdeburg

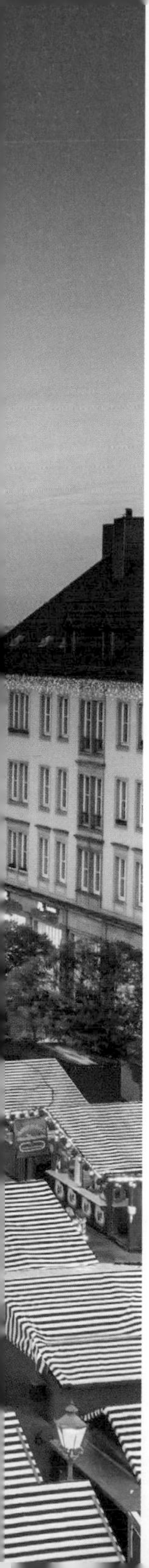

SAXONY-ANHALT

After World War II Saxony-Anhalt was occupied by the Soviets, and in 1949 it was incorporated into the GDR. It underwent major industrial development, mainly due to lignite mining. The state of Saxony-Anhalt was first created in 1947, only to be abolished five years later. It was finally re-established as a federal state in 1990, with Magdeburg as its capital.

The scenic Harz mountains, a popular recreation area with fascinating rock formations and pleasant walks, are the best known attraction of Saxony-Anhalt. Yet this state also boasts no fewer than four UNESCO heritage sites and a number of interesting towns steeped in history and blessed with magnificent historic remains.

The landscape in this region is highly varied. Its northern part, the Altmark, is a largely flat area of farmland and heath, which once formed Hanseatic trade routes and is today popular with walkers and horse riders. The eastern part of the region is more industrialized and includes two very important towns: the small town of Wittenberg, where Martin Luther proclaimed his theses in 1517, thus launching the Reformation, and Dessau, the seat of the Bauhaus Art School and today part of the Garden Kingdom of Dessau-Wörlitz.

SAXONY-ANHALT

Must Sees

1 Wörlitzer Park
2 Lutherstadt Wittenberg
3 Naumburg Dom

Experience More

4 Naumburg
5 Halberstadt
6 Wernigerode
7 Lutherstadt Eisleben
8 Quedlinburg
9 Bernburg
10 Querfurt
11 Merseburg
12 Halle
13 Dessau
14 Tangermünde
15 Magdeburg
16 Ballenstedt

LOWER SAXONY, HAMBURG AND BREMEN
p418

THURINGIA
p184

SAXONY-ANHALT

WÖRLITZER PARK

A E3 **☐ Förstergasse 26, Oranienbaum** **◯ Apr & Oct: 10am–6pm daily; Nov–Mar: 10am–4pm Mon–Fri** **ⓦ welterbe-gartenreich.de**

Part of the Garden Kingdom of Dessau-Wörlitz – a UNESCO World Heritage site since 2000 – Wörlitzer Park is one of the first English-style landscaped gardens to appear in continental Europe, located close to Lutherstadt Wittenberg and the Bauhaus city Dessau.

Wörlitzer Park was established in stages, commencing in 1764, for Prince Leopold III Friedrich Franz of Anhalt-Dessau. Many famous gardeners worked in Wörlitz, including Johann Christian Neumark, as well as architect Friedrich Wilhelm von Erdmannsdorff. Showcasing the religious tolerance espoused by the French Enlightenment, the garden features an Italian-influenced synagogue as well as a Neo-Gothic church (St Peter's). Schloss Wörlitz, built between 1769 and 1773, was the first building in the Classical style in Germany and houses a valuable collection of sculpture, furniture and paintings. Visitors can also explore the Gotisches Haus (Gothic House) that served as the prince's private hideaway, and the Gotisches Haus, whose collection includes Swiss glass pictures. The only way to see all of the sights in the garden is via a guided tour, which can be either on foot or via a pleasant gondola ride.

Did You Know?

Wörlitzer Park is a highlight of the Garden Dreams route, which links 43 parks and gardens in Sachsen-Anhalt.

Wörlitzer Park Throughout the Seasons

CLASSICAL CONCERTS

The park's artificial lake (Wörlitz Lake) is home to the small but charming Stone Island, and features a copy of Mount Vesuvius, providing a charming Italianate setting for classical concerts, held here on summer evenings. If bad weather does strike, the concerts are moved to the beautiful St Petri Church. Tickets can be bought in advance and the serene experience usually lasts three hours.

Spring

▷ Visitors taking a tour of the park in spring will have the best chance of seeing the park's stunning buildings – such as the Gotisches Haus (Gothic House) – surrounded in blooming trees and flowers.

Summer

▽ In summer the park comes alive with the sounds of theatre, concerts and operas. It's also the perfect season for rowing on the lake to visit the many islands and canals twisting through the park.

Autumn

◁ Visitors can admire the red leaves contrasting against the blue waterways and stunning park structures, such as the white Weisse Brücke.

Winter

▽ Trading in its colourful flowers and verdant trees for a blanket of white snow in particularly cold years, the park is still a beautiful and perhaps even more magical place in the winter. Seasonal events include a Christmas market, festive plays and falconry.

← The Weisse Brücke (White Bridge) and Schloss Wörlitz *(inset)*

↑ Colourful houses lining the market square in Lutherstadt Wittenberg

②

LUTHERSTADT WITTENBERG

🅰E3 **ℹ**Schlossplatz 2; 03491-49 86 10; www.lutherstadt-wittenberg.de

This small town, named after its most famous resident, Martin Luther, enjoys a scenic position on the banks of the Elbe river. Its main development took place during the 16th century, when it became the capital of the Reformation, and as such it still attracts many visitors.

①
Wittenberg Castle

🏠Schlossplatz **☎**(03491) 43 34 920 ⏰9am-5pm Tue-Sun

Built for the Elector Friedrich the Wise (best known for his early defence of Martin Luther), in 1489–1525, Wittenberg Castle was greatly altered during reconstruction following fire and wartime damage.

Accessed via the visitor centre, the Christian Art Foundation Wittenberg offers a superb collection of original graphic works on religious and existential themes by internationally renowned artists.

②
Schlosskirche

🏠Schlossplatz **☎**(03491) 40 25 85 ⏰Times vary, check website 🌐schloss-kirche-wittenberg.de

Built after 1497, this church is renowned as the site where Martin Luther allegedly posted his Theses in 1517. The original door no longer exists, but the church contains many interesting tombs – including that of Friedrich the Wise, which was created in 1527 in the workshop of Hans Vischer – as well as the modest tombs of Martin Luther and Philipp Melanchthon.

③
Cranachhaus

🏠Markt 4 **☎**(03491) 420 19 11 ⏰10am-3:30pm Mon-Sat

This 16th-century house once belonged to Lucas Cranach the Elder, and his son, Cranach the Younger, was born here. His studio was at Schlossstrasse 1.

④
Rathaus

🏠Markt 26 ⏰10am-5pm Tue-Sun

The Renaissance town hall was built in 1523–35, and twice

↑ The ornate ceiling of Schlosskirche Wittenberg

The Life of Martin Luther

September 1508

▽ Luther moves to Lutherstadt Wittenberg to study and lecture at the local university

1821

▽ A commemorative statue by Johann Gottfried Schadow erected in the town

10 November 1483

△ Martin Luther is born to Hans and Margerethe Luther in Lutherstadt Eisleben

31 October 1517

△ Luther posts his 95 Theses to the church doors, sparking the Reformation

---

extended in the 16th century. In its forecourt are two 19th-century monuments. To Martin Luther by Gottfried Schadow and to Philipp Melanchthon by Friedrich Drake.

---

⑤
Marienkirche

🏛 Kirchplatz 📞 (03491) 40 44 15 🕐 10am–5pm Tue-Sat, noon–5pm Sun ✖ Mon

The Gothic church of St Mary with its twin-tower façade was built between the 13th and 15th centuries. Luther was married to Katharina von Bora in this church, where he also

preached, and six of their children were baptised. Inside is a magnificent Reformation altar (constructed in 1547), the work of father and son Cranach, as well as interesting tombs and epitaphs.

---

⑥
Melanchthonhaus

🏛 Collegienstrasse 60 📞 (03491) 40 32 79 🕐 Apr-Oct: 10am–6pm daily; Nov-Mar: 10am–5pm Tue-Sun

This museum is devoted to Luther's closest ally, Philipp Schwarzerd, generally known as Melanchthon.

⑦
Lutherhaus

🏛 Collegienstrasse 54 📞 (03491) 42 030 🕐 Apr-Oct: 10am–6pm daily; Nov-Mar: 10am–5pm Tue-Sun

Originally an Augustinian monastery, this building later became the residence of Martin Luther and his family. It now houses the largest Reformation museum in the world, and is a UNESCO World Heritage Site. It has a large number of documents relating to the Reformation and Luther's translation of the Bible. The museum also chronicles the work of Lucas Cranach the Elder.

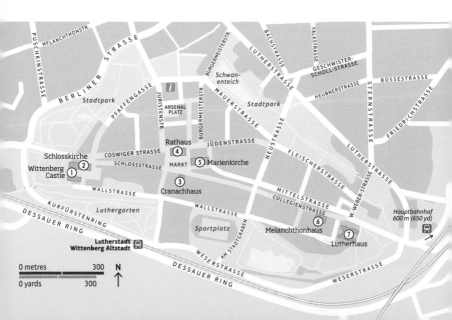

0 metres 300
0 yards 300
N

NAUMBURG DOM

🅰 E4 🏠 Domplatz 16-17 📞 (03445) 230 11 33 🕒 Mar-Oct: 9am-6pm Mon-Sat, 11am-6pm Sun; Nov-Feb: 10am-4pm Mon-Sat, noon-4pm Sun

One of the finest examples of Gothic architecture in Germany, the Naumburg Cathedral of Saints Peter and Paul is a highlight along the Romanesque route.

The present cathedral is the second to be built on the same site; only a section of the eastern crypt survived of the earlier Romanesque church. Construction started before 1213, with the earliest parts including the main body and the late-Romanesque east choir. Among the most celebrated aspects of the interior are the sculptural works of the Naumburg Master, which include Uta of Naumburg, and St. Elisabeth; the chapel window paintings by contemporary artist Neo Rauch; and the striking altar wings by Lucas Cranach the Elder.

West Choir

The stained-glass windows depict scenes of the apostles of virtue and sin. Some sections are original 13th-century work, but two were completed in the 19th century.

The statues of Margrave Ekkehard and his wife, Uta, are true masterpieces – the artist succeeded marvellously in capturing the beauty and sensitivity of his subjects.

The Gothic twin portal depicts the Crucifixion, a moving and highly expressive group sculpture by the brilliant "Naumburger Meister" whose identity remains unknown.

THE NAUMBURG MASTER

The works of a German architect and sculptor, simply known as "the Naumburg Master", have been preserved for posterity. Inspired by French Gothic style, the Master arrived in Naumburg in the mid-1200s and contributed architecture, statues and glass paintings to the cathedral.

This late-Gothic triptych (around 1510) depicts the Virgin Mary with the Infant.

EXPERIENCE Saxony-Anhalt

Illustration of the ornate cathedral, Naumburg Dom

The richly ornamented pulpit basket, from 1466, and the adjoining stairs have been renovated.

Sarcophagus of Bishop Dietrich II

East Choir

The main altar, built in the mid-14th century, is a stone retable depicting the Crucifixion with the saints.

EXPERIENCE MORE

4

Naumburg

E4 Markt 6; www.naumburg.de

Along with the town's star attraction, Naumburg also boasts a late-Gothic Rathaus (town hall) restored in Renaissance style and a main square surrounded by quaint houses. Further Naumburg attractions include the Marientor gate – which dates from 1445 and is the last standing of five gates that once secured the city – and the Gothic **Stadtkirche St Wenzel**. The latter stands in the market square, and its steeple is the tallest tower in the city. Inside there are two paintings by Lucas Cranach the Elder, as well as the 18th-century organ that Johann Sebastian Bach played on. The philosopher, Friedrich Nietzsche spent his childhood at No 18 Weingarten, now a small museum.

Stadtkirche St Wenzel

Topfmarkt 18 (03445) 201516 Apr & Nov: 1–3pm Mon-Sat; May-Oct: 10am–5pm Mon-Sat

↑ Naumburg's picturesque town square, hung with floral baskets

STAY

Zur Alten Schmiede
The best place to stay in Naumburg is this historical hotel in the centre of town

E4 Lindenring 36-37 ck-domstadt-hotels.de

€€€

Zur Henne
Just out of Naumburg to the north in Henne, this prominent brick guesthouse has rooms done out in leather and wood, very welcoming hosts and bicycle hire.

E4 Henne 1 gasthaus-zur-henne.de

€€€

Pension Onkel Ernst
Right in the centre of Naumburg, Uncle Ernst's place is a much-loved retreat with bright and breezy rooms, each sporting its own hip design.

E4 Marienstrasse 19 onkel-ernst.de

€€€

Gasthof Zufriedenheit
The name of this hotel translates to "Satisfaction," which is pretty much guaranteed at this contemporary hotel and its snazzy restaurant.

E4 Steinweg 26, Naumburg gasthof-zufriedenheit.de

€€€

A steam train running along the Brockenbahn, in Harz National Park ↑

 5

Halberstadt

D3 🚗🚌 **i** Holzmarkt 1; www.halberstadt-tourismus.de

Halberstadt enjoys a picturesque location in the foothills of the Harz Mountains. Its history goes back to the 9th century, when it became a seat of a mission episcopate.

HARZ MOUNTAIN TRAIL

A tourist trail across the Harz Mountains leads through historic towns and villages, such as Harzgerode, known for its many timber-frame houses. Other regional attractions include the Rübeland Caves, with their fascinating rock formations, and the Hexentanzplatz, a platform suspended above a cliff, from where witches fly to celebrations on Walpurgis Night (30 April).

Once an important town, Halberstadt had 80 per cent of its buildings destroyed during World War II. Fortunately, many of its beautiful historic buildings have been restored to their former glory.

The vast St Stephans Dom is the fourth successive church built on the same site. Construction began in the 13th century and the church was consecrated in 1491. The two-tower transeptial basilica ranks as one of the most beautiful pure Gothic forms in Germany. Its oldest part is the 12th-century font. Also notable are the Romanesque Crucifixion group (around 1220), set above the choir screen, and several examples of Gothic sculpture. Stained-glass windows from around 1330 have survived in the Marian Chapel, and 15th-century windows can be found along the cloisters and in the presbytery.

The adjoining chapter buildings contain one of Germany's richest cathedral treasures – the **Domschatz**, with precious 12th-century tapestries, many sculptures and liturgical vessels.

Other churches in the old town district include the Romanesque Liebfrauen-kirche (Church of our Lady) and the Gothic Marktkirche St Martini (market church of St Martin). Timber-frame houses extend over many streets; look out for the Vogtei, Bakenstraße, Rosenwinkel and Graue Hof.

Domschatz

⊗ 🕐 Apr-Oct: 10am-5:30pm Mon-Sat, 11am-5:30pm Sun; Nov-Mar: 10am-4pm Tue-Sun 🌐 dom-und-domschatz.de

---

 6

Wernigerode

D3 🚗🚌 **i** Marktplatz 10; www.wernigerode-tourismus.de

Wernigerode is situated at a confluence of two rivers: the Holtemme and the Zillierbach. Timber-frame houses lean across its winding streets, and a castle rises above the town. The Harzquerbahn, a narrow-gauge railway that links the towns and villages in the Harz Mountains, between Werni-gerode and Nordhausen,

provides another popular attraction. The Brockenbahn runs between Wernigerode and the Brocken mountain.

Strolling around the Old Town, it is worth stepping into St John's church (St Johannis). It contains some late-Gothic features, including the font and the altar. The variety of ornaments adorning the houses in Wernigerode is truly staggering. Particularly interesting are the houses along Breite Strasse, the town's main shopping street, which is closed to traffic.

The fairytale castle of **Schloss Wernigerode**, spiked with turrets, was built on the site of an older fortress. Now a museum, it houses the Stolberg-Wernigerode family art collection. The castle ramparts afford a fantastic view of the town and the nearby Harz mountains.

The small town of Osterwieck, 22 km (14 miles) to the north, has over 400 timber-frame buildings, dating mainly from the 16th and 17th centuries.

Schloss Wernigerode

⊛⊛ 🚗 Am Schloss 1
🕐 May-Oct: 10am-6pm daily;
Nov-Apr: 10am-5pm Tue-Fri,
10am-6pm Sat & Sun 🆆
schloss-wernigerode.de

Lutherstadt Eisleben

🄰E4 🚗🚌 ℹ Markt 22;
www.lutherstaedte-
eisleben-mansfeld.de

Martin Luther was born in Eiseleben in 1483 and eventually returned and died here in 1546. Now called Lutherstadt Eisleben, this charming hub features an ensemble of UNESCO World Heritage sites that are linked to the religious reformer and explain his life and the Reformation.

Did You Know?

Martin Luther only journeyed outside of German-speaking lands once in his lifetime.

As well as preaching at the city's multiple (and still extant) churches, Luther promoted the construction of one of the region's first Protestant churches. A reconstruction of his birth house includes a permanent exhibition about him and his life in the city, and features a few original artifacts like his baptismal font (1518). The house where Luther died – also a reconstruction – focuses on the history of the Reformation as well as Luther's final years, and also showcases historic exhibits like furniture, documents and the original cloth that covered his coffin.

All of these sites are linked by the Luther Trail, which also passes through the town's medieval market square.

> **The variety of ornaments adorning the houses in Wernigerode is truly staggering. Particularly interesting are the houses along Breite Strasse.**

↑ Traditional half-timbered houses lining the cobbled streets of Quedlinburg

8

Quedlinburg

🅐 E3 🚗🚌 🛈 Markt 4; (03946) 90 56 24 and 63 88 990

The rise of the small town of Quedlinburg was closely connected with its convent, established in 936 by Emperor Otto I and his mother, St Mathilde. On the hill above the town stands the vast Romanesque structure of the Stiftskirche St Servatius (Collegiate Church of St Servatius), built between 1017 and 1129. Its old crypt, the Huysburg, is adorned with Romanesque wall paintings and contains tombs of the prioresses and of the Emperor Heinrich I

(Henry the Fowler) and his wife Mathilde. An exhibition of treasures is shown in the arms of the transept, including the Romanesque reliquary of St Servatius and the remaining fragments of the 12th-century Knüpfteppich (tapestry). The Quedlinburg Schloss, a Renaissance palace surrounded by gardens, occupies the other side of the hill.

Both the old and new Town of Quedlinburg have valuable examples of timber-frame architecture. The buildings date from various times – the modest house at Wordgasse 3, from around 1400, is the oldest surviving timber-frame building in Germany. Also noteworthy are the numerous churches, including the 10th-century Norbertinenkirche, the Wippertikirche with its early-Romanesque crypt, and the 15th century, late-Gothic Marktkirche St Benedicti.

Did You Know?

The castle, collegiate church and old town in Quedlinburg are on the UNESCO World Heritage List.

9

Bernburg

🅐 E3 🚗🚌 🛈 Lindenplatz 9; www.bernburg.de

Once the capital of one of Anhalt's duchies, Bernburg enjoys a picturesque location on the banks of the Saale river. It has a Bergstadt (upper town) and a Talstadt (lower town), and its attractions include the

→ The distinctive silhouette of the Bernburg Schloss, overlooking the River Saale

Gothic parish churches and the town square with its Baroque buildings. The most important historic building is the Bernburg Schloss, built on a rock. The castle owes its present look to refurbishments (1540–70), yet many features are much older, including the 12th-century Romanesque chapels and Gothic towers.

---

⑩

Querfurt

🅰 E4 🚌 **ℹ** Markt 14; www.querfurt.de

The narrow streets of Querfurt are crammed with timber-frame houses, and the giant Schloss towers over the town square with its Renaissance town hall. The castle's present form is the result of Renaissance refurbishments, but it maintains many beautiful Romanesque features, such as the 11th-century donjon (keep), known as Dicker Heinrich (Fat Henry) and a 12th-century church. Also worth seeing are the burial chapel, the Baroque Fürstenhaus (ducal house) and a small museum, situated in the former armoury and granary.

↑ Crucifix hanging over the central nave in the cathedral at Merseburg

⑪

Merseburg

🅰 E4 🚃🚌 **ℹ** Burgstrasse 5; www.merseburg.de

The first thing visitors see as they arrive in Merseburg is the Domburg – a vast complex of buildings spiked with towers, consisting of a cathedral and residences. The cathedral is not uniform in style; it includes some Romanesque elements (the eastern section and twin towers in the west) erected in the 11th and 12th centuries, and the late-Gothic triple-nave main body, which was built in 1510–17. All

that remains of the older, early-Romanesque structure is the crypt, underneath the presbytery. The cathedral contains remarkable Gothic and Renaissance features, as well as numerous sarcophagi of bishops, such as that of Thilo von Troth (1470). The chapter buildings house a library with precious manuscripts, including the Merseburg Bible (from around 1200). Adjacent to the cathedral is a three-wing Renaissance-style Schloss. Magnificent portals and an attractive oriel in the castle's west wing are noteworthy.

⑫ Halle

🅰E4 🚌🚋 🅸 Marktplatz 13; www.halle.de

Halle is an old town with a rich history in commerce and trade. Its wealth was founded on the production and sale of salt ("white gold"), and it later became a centre for the chemical industry.

Halle has preserved most of its historic heritage. On the Marktplatz (town square) stands an interesting church, Unser Lieben Frauen (Our Lady), whose late-Gothic main body (1530–54) was positioned between two pairs of towers that had remained intact from previous Romanesque churches. The house at Nikolaistrasse 5, the birthplace of Georg Friedrich Händel, now houses a small museum, the Händel-Haus. In Domplatz stands the early-Gothic Cathedral, built between 1280 and 1331 and restored between 1525 and 1530 in Renaissance style. Other medieval churches include the late-Gothic Moritzkirche, built in the latter part of the 14th century. It is also worth visiting the **Kunstmuseum Moritzburg Halle**, housed in the refurbished Citadel

building known as Moritzburg and built in 1484–1503. On the outskirts of town stands Burg Giebichenstein, the former castle residence of the Magdeburg bishops. The upper part of the castle remains in ruins, while the lower part houses an Arts and Crafts College.

The **Landesmuseum für Vorgeschichte** (State Museum of Prehistory) has more than 11 million exhibits. Its centre-piece is the Nebra Sky Disc, a 3,600-year-old bronze disc recognized by UNESCO as the earliest known image of the night sky.

For something a little more contemporary, the **Beatles Museum** offers an overview of the Fab Four via record covers, photos and paraphernalia.

Kunstmuseum Moritzburg Halle

⊗ 🅰 Friedemann-Bach-Platz 5 📞 (0345) 21 25 90 🕙 10am–6pm Tue–Sun

Landesmuseum für Vorgeschichte

⊗ 🅰 Richard-Wagner-Strasse 9 📞 (0345) 52 47 30 🕙 9am–5pm Tue–Fri, 10am–6pm Sat, Sun & public hols

Beatles Museum

⊗⊗🕙🖱 🅰 Alter Markt 12 🕙 10am–6pm Tue–Sun 🌐 beatlesmuseum.net

↑ The Walter Gropius-designed Bauhaus complex in Dessau

⑬ Dessau

🅰E3 🚌🚋 🅸 Zerbster Strasse 2c; www.visitdessau.com

Dessau, once a magnificent city and the capital of the duchy of Anhalt-Dessau, is less attractive today, yet it has some excellent historic sights. In the town centre are some interesting Baroque churches and the Johannbau, the remains of a Renaissance ducal residence.

Dessau is mostly known for the Bauhaus. The famous art school flourished here after the move from Weimar in 1925. Today, more than 300 buildings from that era still exist. The iconic Bauhaus building and the Master's Houses, both UNESCO World Heritage sites, are open to the public.

In 2019, a new museum, the **Bauhaus Museum Dessau**, opened its doors. It contains the world's second-largest collection of Bauhaus items.

On the banks of the River Elbe, the Kornhaus is another Bauhaus icon. This striking building, now a restaurant, combines Bauhaus architecture with the river landscapes of the Middle Elbe Biosphere Reserve.

Many splendid residences set in landscaped gardens were built in 18th- and 19th-century Dessau. In the town centre stands a Neo-Classical palace, **Schloss Georgium**, built in 1780. Today it houses the Anhalt Picture Gallery, a collection of old masters, including works by Rubens, Hals and Cranach the Elder.

Haldeburg, on the outskirts of Dessau, has a Neo-Gothic hunting lodge built in 1782–3, while Mosigkau boasts **Schloss Mosigkau**, Princess Anna Wilhelmina's Baroque residence, designed by Christian Friedrich Damm. It contains excellent examples of 17th-century paintings.

In Oranienbaum, 12 km (7 miles) east of Dessau, stands a late-17th-century palace that was built for Princess Henrietta Katharine of Orange by the Dutch architect Cornelius Ryckwaert.

Bauhaus Museum Dessau
⊗ 🅐 Mies-van-der-Rohe-Platz 1 🕐 10am-6pm Tue-Sun 🅦 bauhaus-dessau.de

Schloss Georgium
⊗ 🅐 Puschkinallee 100 📞 (0340) 61 38 74 🕐 10am-5pm Tue-Sun

Schloss Mosigkau
⊗ ⊗ 🅐 Knobelsdorffallee 2 📞 (0340) 50 25 57 21 🕐 Apr & Oct: 10am-5pm Sat & Sun; May-Sep: 10am-6pm Tue-Sun

←

View across the Göbel fountain of Halle's Unser Lieben Frauen church

Cobbled streets and timbered houses in the town of Tangermünde ↑

⑭
Tangermünde

🅐 E3 🅐🚌 ℹ Markt 2; www.tourismus-tangermuende.de

Situated at the confluence of the Tanger and Elbe rivers, this town grew rapidly during medieval times. For centuries it remained the seat of the Brandenburg margraves, and King Karl IV chose it as his second residence. The town joined the Hanseatic League, and grew in status thanks to its trade links.

The Gothic **Rathaus** (town hall) has timber-frame architecture. The east wing dates back to 1430 and is the work of Heinrich Brunsberg, while the west wing, with its arcades, was added around 1480. The Rathaus contains the municipal museum.

Tangermünde has retained some remains of the city walls, dating from around 1300 and including a magnificent late-Gothic gate, the Neustädter Tor, whose tall, cylindrical tower has intricate, lacy ceramic ornaments.

The Romanesque abbey in Jerichow, 10 km (6 miles) north of Tangermünde, is the earliest brick structure of the region. It was built in the 1150s for Norbertine monks. The west towers were completed during the 15th century. Its austere, triple-nave vaulted interior is impressive.

Rathaus (Stadtge-schichtliches Museum)
🅐 Am Markt 📞 (039322) 421 53 🕐 1-5pm Tue-Sun

55

The number of years the Bauhaus College was closed (from 1931 to 1986).

⑮

Magdeburg

🅰E3 ☒☒ 𝒊Breiter Weg 22;
www.visitmagdeburg.de

The large-scale development of Magdeburg, today the capital of Saxony-Anhalt and a port on the River Elbe, began in the 10th century when Emperor Otto I established his main residence here. In medieval times the town became a political and cultural centre. After the abolition of the arch-bishopric and the destruction wrought by the Thirty Years' War, it lost its political importance. About 80 per cent was destroyed during World War II, but it is still worth a visit.

Dom St Mauritius und St Katharina, the vast Magdeburg cathedral, is one of the most important Gothic churches in Germany. Its construction, which started in 1209 on the site of an earlier Romanesque church,

↑ Magdeburg's cathedral, on the River Elbe, and a detail *(inset)* of its elegant Gothic statuary

was completed in 1520. The result is a lofty, aisled basilica with transept, cloisters, a ring of chapels surrounding the presbytery and a vast twin-tower façade. The cathedral has several original sculptures. Other notable features include the tomb of Emperor Otto I, as well as the 12th-century bronze tomb plaques of archbishops Friedrich von Wettin and Wichmann. The memorial for the dead of World War I is the work of Ernst Barlach, dating from 1929.

The **Kulturhistorisches Museum** contains works of art, archaeological finds and historic documents of the town. Its most valuable exhibit is the Magdeburger Reiter (Magdeburg Rider), a sculpture dating from around 1240 of an unknown ruler (probably Otto I) on a horse.

The austere Romanesque church of **Kloster Unser Lieben Frauen** (of Our Lady), Magdeburg's oldest building, was built for the Norbertine order during the second half of the 11th and the early 12th

centuries. The adjacent Romanesque abbey is a museum with medieval and modern sculptures.

The **Dommuseum Ottonianum Magdeburg** tells the stories of Emperor Otto the Great and his wife, Queen Edith, accompanied by finds from archaeological excavations around the cathedral and a virtual interactive model. The present Baroque Rathaus (town hall), built in 1691–8 on the site of an earlier, late-Romanesque town hall, was restored after World War II.

ROMANESQUE ROUTE

Stretching over 1,200 km (746 miles), the Romanesque Route runs through 65 towns and villages, linking more than 80 examples of Romanesque architecture, including churches, abbeys, palaces and castles. Highlights include the cathedral treasures in Halberstadt, Merseburg and Naumburg, plus the collegiate church in Quedlinburg.

89

The percentage of buildings that burned down in the Sack of Magdeburg during the Thirty Years' War.

Near the market square is the Gothic **Pfarrkirche St Johannis** (church of St John), destroyed during World War II and later rebuilt. In 1524 Martin Luther preached here. Today it is used as a concert hall.

Dom St Mauritius und St Katharina

🅐 Domplatz 🄲 (0391) 541 04 36 🄳 Apr & Oct: 10am–5pm Mon–Sat; May–Sep: 10am–6pm Mon–Sat; Nov–Mar: 10am–4pm Mon–Sat (from 11:30am Sun)

Kulturhistorisches Museum

🅐 Otto-von-Guericke-Strasse 68–73 🄲 (0391) 540 35 30 🄳 10am–5pm Tue–Fri, 10am–6pm Sat & Sun

Kloster Unser Lieben Frauen

🅐 Regierungsstrasse 4–6 Kunstmuseum 🄲 (0391) 56 50 20 🄳 10am–6pm Sat & Sun

Dommuseum Ottonianum Magdeburg

🅐 Domplatz 15, Magdeburg 🄳 10am–5pm Tue–Sun 🅦 dommuseum-ottonianum.de

Pfarrkirche St Johannis

🅐 Am Johannisberg 1 🄲 (0391) 59 34 50 🄳 Mar–Oct: 10am–6pm Tue–Sun; Nov–Feb: 10–5pm Tue–Sun

---

16

Ballenstedt

🅐 E4 🚆🚌 ℹ Anhaltiner Pl. 11; www.ballenstedt.de

On the edge of the Harz Mountains is the town of Ballenstedt, a worthwhile stop on the Romanesque Route. Once the domain of the von Anhalt-Bemburg family, it is famous for its Baroque castle and surrounding complex, which features a park designed by landscape architect Peter Joseph Lenné, and the grave of Albert the Bear, the first Margrave of Brandenburg.

The town also offers the Castle Theatre Ballenstedt, which dates back to 1788 and was once the workplace of Franz Liszt.

Nearby lie the Gegensteine, two free-standing rock peaks that form part of Gegensteine-Schierberg nature reserve.

TOP 4 HISTORIC SIGHTS IN NORTHERN SAXONY-ANHALT

St Nikolai, Stendal
This cathedral from the mid-15th century is renowned for the stained-glass windows in the presbytery and transept.

Dom St Marien, Havelberg
Dating back to 1150, this cathedral has preserved its Romanesque style after a redesign in the early 14th century.

Stephanskirche, Tangermünde
Built for Augustinian monks, this late-Gothic hall church contains beautiful historic features, such as its organ, pulpit and font.

Neustädter Tor, Tangermünde
Tangermünde's city walls date from around 1300 and include this gate, whose tall tower has intricate, lacy ceramic ornaments.

↑ One of the two Gegensteine rock peacks near Ballenstedt

The dramatic Bastei rock formation in the Elbe Sandstone Mountains

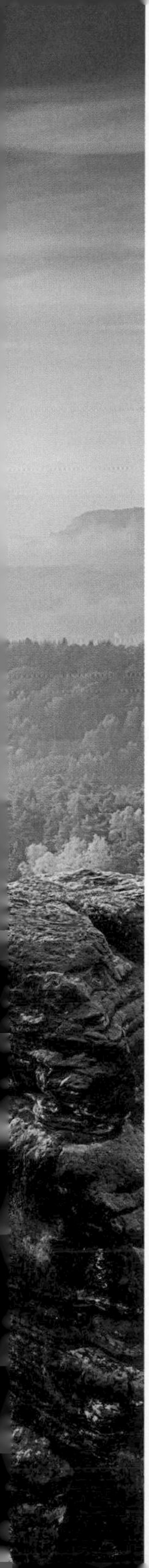

SAXONY

Lying between Berlin and Prague, Saxony has a long history spanning some of the most significant events that shaped Europe, including the Reformation, the Napoleonic Wars and the fall of the Iron Curtain. From 1697 until 1763 Saxony was united with Poland, and the Saxon Great Electors were also kings of Poland. During this period Saxony flourished, and Dresden became a major centre of the arts and culture until the Seven Years' War (1756–63) put an end to the region's prosperity. In 1806 Saxony declared itself on the side of Napoleon, and the Great Elector acquired the title of King. But Saxony paid a heavy price for supporting Napoleon – following the Congress of Vienna (1815), the kingdom lost the northern half of its territory to Prussia, and in 1871 it was incorporated into the German Empire.

With such an eventful past, Saxony is rich in historic sites, and its capital city, Dresden, ranks among the most beautiful and interesting towns in Germany, despite the devastation it suffered during World War II. The region also boasts the enchanting Erzgebirge mountains and the glorious scenery of "Saxon Switzerland", where the mighty Elbe river runs amid fantastic rock formations.

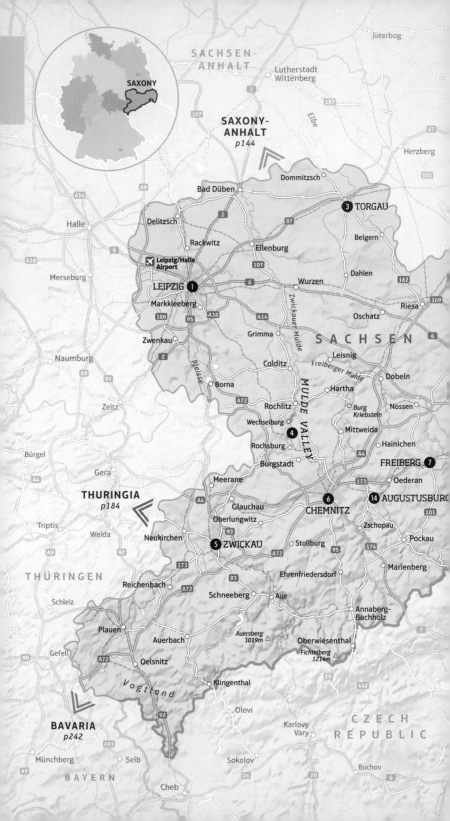

SAXONY

Must Sees
1 Leipzig
2 Dresden

Experience More
3 Torgau
4 Mulde Valley
5 Zwickau
6 Chemnitz
7 Freiberg
8 Meissen

9 Moritzburg
10 Bautzen
11 Bad Muskau
12 Zittau
13 Görlitz
14 Augustusburg
15 Pirna
16 Kamenz
17 Oybin

↑ Leipzig's magnificent Renaissance town hall and market square

①

LEIPZIG

🅰E4 **✈Flughafen Leipzig-Halle** **🅿** **ℹKatharinenstrasse 8 & Augustplatz 9; www.leipzig.travel/de**

Best known for its significant role in East German protests that led to the downfall of the GDR in the late 1980s, Leipzig is a vibrant city today. Nicknamed "Little Berlin" due to its thriving art and music scene, it is an important centre for the German book trade.

**① **

Deutsches Buch- und Schriftmuseum

🄰Deutscher Platz 1
📞(0341) 22 71 324
🕙10am-6pm Tue-Sun

This museum is devoted to the history of German printing, publishing and book production. It contains rare manuscripts and old prints.

---

② 

Grassimuseum

🄰Johannisplatz 5-11
🕙10am-6pm Tue-Sun
🌐grassimuseum.de

The Grassimuseum is one of Germany's greatest museum complexes, housing three fascinating collections: the Museum für Völkerkunde (ethnography); the Museum für Musikinstrumente (musical instruments); and the Museum für Angewandte Kunst (decorative arts).

**③ **

Nikolaikirche

🄰Nikolaikirchehof 3
🕙11:30am-6:30pm Mon-Sat (to 1:30pm Sun)
🌐nikolaikirche.de

In Nikolaikirchhof stands the Nikolaikirche (church of St Nicholas). The present church was built during the 16th century, although the lower sections of its north tower date from the 12th century. It has Neo-Classical furnishings.

**④ **

Völkerschlachtdenkmal

🄰Strasse des 18 Oktober 100 📞(0341) 24 16 870
🕙10am-6pm daily (Nov-Mar: to 4pm)

This giant, Teutonic-style monument is the work of German architect Bruno Schmitz. It was completed for the centenary of the 1813 Battle of the Nations, also known as the Battle of Leipzig, where the combined Prussian, Austrian and Russian armies defeated Napoleon. It now houses a small museum.

↑ Impressive Neo-Classical interior of the Nikolaikirche

⑤

Altes Rathaus

📍 Markt 1 📞 (0341) 26 17 760 🕐 Stadtgeschicht-liches Museum: 10am-6pm Tue-Sun

The grand Renaissance town hall, built in 1556 to a design by Hieronymus Lotter, is now the home of the municipal museum. One room is devoted to Felix Mendelssohn-Bartholdy, who conducted the symphony orchestra from 1835 until his death in 1847.

⑥

Museum der Bildenden Künste

📍 Katharinenstrasse 10 🕐 10am-6pm Tue & Thu-Sun, noon-8pm Wed 🌐 mdbk.de

Leipzig's Museum of Fine Arts has an excellent collection of German masters, including Lucas Cranach the Elder,

as well as other magnificent European paintings, canvases by Jan van Eyck and Tintoretto and sculptures by Balthasar Permoser and Auguste Rodin.

⑦

Bach Archiv und Bach Museum

📍 Thomaskirchhof 15-16 🕐 10am-6pm Tue-Sun 🌐 bachmuseumleipzig.de

The Bach Archive and Museum houses a large permanent exhibition, artifacts and documents relating to the life and works of the composer Johann Sebastian Bach.

⑧

Russische Kirche

📍 Philipp-Rosenthal-Strasse 51a 📞 (0341) 87 81 453 🕐 10am-5pm daily (winter: to 4pm)

The Russian Orthodox Church of St Alexius was completed in

TOP 3 MUSIC VENUES

Neues Gewandhaus
Completed in 1981 on Augustusplatz, this is the third concert hall to bear this name.

Opernhaus
The current home of the Leipzig Opera on Augustusplatz was completed in 1960.

Alte Handelsbörse
The old stock exchange was reconstructed after World War II and is now a concert hall.

1913 to commemorate the 22,000 Russian soldiers who died in 1813 in the Battle of the Nations. The Russian architect, Vladimir Pokrowski, based his design on the beautiful churches of Novgorod in Russia.

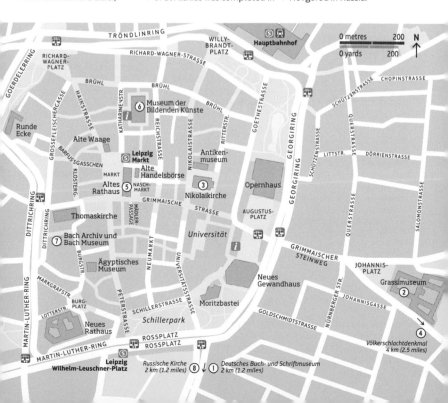

↑ Theaterplatz, with Hofkirche and Residenzschloss

DRESDEN

A E4 **✈** Dresden-Klotzsche 15 km (9 miles) from centre
🚊🚌 *i* Neumarkt 2 (beside Frauenkirche); Wiener Platz 4
(in the railway station); www.dresden.de/tourism

The beautiful city of Dresden is a cultural centre filled with historic monuments, impressive architecture, and inspiring museums. Since 2002, meticulous work has been undertaken to renew the city after damage caused by flooding.

Dresden first gained its pre-eminence in 1485, when the Albertine Wettins established their residence here. The town acquired magnificent buildings during the 18th century, although most of these were destroyed on the 13/14 February 1945, when British and American air forces mounted a carpet-bombing raid on the city. Restoration is still in progress to return Dresden to its former glory.

① Neues Rathaus

A Dr-Külz-Ring

The giant Neo-Renaissance new town hall, in the southwest of the old town, was erected in 1905–1910. Its round tower (70 m/230 ft), crowned with a gilded statue of Hercules, offers a good view of the old city centre.

② Sächsische Staatsoper

A Theaterplatz 2
w semperoper.de

The Neo-Renaissance confection that is the Saxon State Opera is one of Dresden's landmarks. It is also known as Semperoper after its creator, Gottfried Semper, who designed it twice: the first building, constructed in 1838–41, burned down in 1869; the second was erected in 1878. Reconstruction after World War II lasted until 1985. The opera house held many world premieres, including works by Wagner and Strauss.

③ Hofkirche

A Theaterplatz (entrance on Schlossplatz) **©** Daily

This monumental Baroque royal church has served as the Catholic Dom (cathedral church) of the Dresden-Meissen diocese since 1980. The church was designed by Gaetano Chiaveri and built in 1738–51.

The interior has two-tier passageways that run from the main nave to the side naves. It also features a magnificent Rococo pulpit by Balthasar Permoser and a vast organ – Gottfried Silbermann's last work.

④ Fürstenzug

A Augustusstrasse

Langer Gang (Long Walk) is a long building, dating from 1586–91, which connects the castle with the Johanneum.

The elegant façade facing the courtyard is decorated with sgraffito and provided an excellent backdrop for tourn-aments and parades. The wall facing the street is adorned with the Fürstenzug (procession of dukes) – a magnificent, 102-m- (335-ft-) long frieze depicting the procession of many Saxon rulers. The frieze was originally created by Wilhelm Walther in 1872–6 using the sgraffito technique, but it was replaced in 1907 by 24,000 Meissen porcelain tiles.

⑤
Kreuzkirche

🏠 An der Kreuzkirche 6
☎ (0351) 439 39 20
🕐 Summer: 10am-6pm Mon-Fri; winter: 10am-4pm Mon-Fri; Tower: 10am-5pm daily

This Baroque/Neo-Classical church was built in 1764–92 to a design by Johann Georg Schmidt. To commemorate the shelling in World War II, the interior has not been fully restored. The Cross of Nails from the ruins of Coventry Cathedral in England creates a powerful symbolic link between the two countries.

⑥
Verkehrsmuseum

🏠 Augustusstrasse 1
🕐 10am-5pm Tue-Sun
🌐 verkehrsmuseum-dresden.de

This Renaissance building, originally designed as royal stables by German architect Paul Buchner, was refurbished in the mid-18th century and housed first a gallery of paintings, later an armoury and a porcelain collection. Since 1956 it has been a museum of transport, with old trams, locomotives and vintage cars.

> 🔍 HIDDEN GEM
> ### Goldener Reiter
> The Neustadt (new town), on the right bank of the Elbe, offers visitors a glistening, gilded equestrian statue of Augustus the Strong – the work of Jean Joseph Vinache, court sculptor to Augustus.

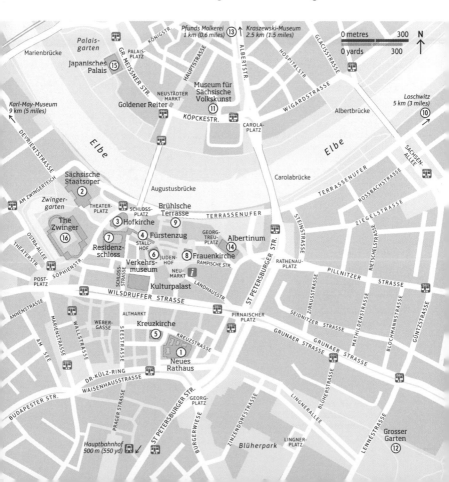

↑ Stunning interior of the impressive Residenzschloss

 7

Residenzschloss

⌂ Taschenberg 2
🕒 10am-6pm Wed-Mon
🌐 skd.museum

This former residence of the Wettin family was built in stages from the late 15th to the 17th centuries. It houses some of the most beautiful art collections in East Germany, including the world-famous Grünes Gewölbe (Green Vaults), a vast collection of royal jewels, gems and table decorations. Book in advance for the ground-floor "vault". The Hausmannsturm tower affords a great view of the Dresden skyline.

 8

Frauenkirche

⌂ An der Frauenkirche
🕒 10am-noon, 1-6pm daily
🌐 frauenkirche-dresden.de

The giant Church of Our Lady, designed by Georg Bähr and built in 1726–43, has been restored to its former glory. Destroyed in 1945 by Allied bombing, its shell survived intact, only to collapse later. Notable features include an elegant cupola and, inside, a colourful dome.

9

Brühlsche Terrasse

⌂ Brühlsche Terrasse

Once part of the town's fortifications, this attractive terrace was transformed into magnificent gardens by the diplomat and patron of arts Heinrich von Brühl, after whom it is named. Offering splendid views over the River Elbe, it was known as "the balcony of Europe". There are several great buildings on the terraces – the first one, seen from Schlossplatz, is the Neo-Renaissance Landtag (parliament building); next to it is a small Neo-Baroque building, the Secundogenitur library, now a popular café; this is followed by the Kunst-akademie (Art Academy), known as Zitronenpresse (lemon squeezer) because of its ribbed glass dome. The terrace features works by the sculptor Ernst Rietschel and architect Gottfried Semper.

 10

Loschwitz

⌂ Loschwitz/Blasewitzer Brücke

The suspension bridge which spans the River Elbe in the eastern part of the town is painted blue, hence its nickname "Blaus Wunder"

→ Striking Frauenkirche dominating the city's skyline

Kraszewski-Museum
This small museum on Nordstrasse is devoted to the life of the Polish writer Józef Ignacy Kraszewski.

Karl-May-Museum
This Radebuhl museum explores the life and work of Karl May, creator of Winnetou, a fictional American Indian chief.

Slaughterhouse-Five
The titular slaughter-house from Kurt Vonnegut's book still stands on Messering.

("Blue Wonder"). The bridge leads to Loschwitz, a neighbourhood in a picturesque location amidst hills, which has many attractive villas and small palaces.

 Museum für Sächsische Volkskunst (Jägerhof)

🏠 Köpckestrasse 1
🕐 10am-6pm Tue-Sun
🌐 volkskunst.skd.museum

This Renaissance hunting lodge on the north bank of the Elbe was built between 1568 and 1613. Its west wing – the only part that escaped destruction – now houses a folk art museum with collections of Saxon culture and traditions, especially from the Erzgebirge mountains.

 Grosser Garten

🏠 City centre 🌐 grosser-garten-dresden.de

The history of this great garden goes back to the 17th century, although it has been redesigned several times since. At the centre stands an early Baroque palace built in 1678–83. A miniature railway takes visitors to Carolasee, a boating lake. It also stops at the botanical gardens in the northwest section of the park. The Mosaikbrunnen (Mosaic Fountain) nearby was designed by Hans Poelzig.

⑬ **Pfunds Molkerei**

🏠 Bautzner Strasse 79
🕐 10am-6pm Mon-Sat, 10am-3pm Sun
🌐 pfunds.de

In the 19th-century part of the Neustadt, with its many bars, galleries, pubs and fringe theatres, stands this old dairy founded by Paul Pfund. Its interior is lined with dazzling, multi-coloured tiles, showing Neo-Renaissance motifs relating to the dairy's products. Today there is a shop that offers hundreds of dairy products, as well as a small bar where visitors can sample the specialities.

 Albertinum

🏠 Brühlsche Terrasse
🕐 Galerie Neue Meister: 10am-6pm Tue-Sun
🌐 skd.museum

Originally a royal arsenal, the Albertinum was rebuilt in its current Neo-Renaissance style in the 1880s by Carl Adolf Canzler. Forty years earlier, Bernhard von Lindenau had donated his considerable fortune to the city to set up a collection of contemporary art, which was then displayed in the Albertinum. Today, the building houses two magnificent collections. The Galerie Neue Meister contains paintings from the 19th and 20th centuries, including works by the German Impressionists Lovis Corinth and Max Liebermann, canvases by the Nazarine group of painters and works by European masters such as Edgar Degas, Vincent van Gogh and Claude Monet.

The Albertinum's other collection, the Skulpturen-sammlung, is a small assortment of sculptures, including remarkable late-Baroque and early-Rococo works by Balthasar Permoser.

⑮ **Japanisches Palais**

🏠 Palaisplatz II 📞 (0351) 81 44 08 41 🕐 Times vary. call ahead

Originally the Dutch Palais, this three-wing structure was built in 1715. It was extended in 1729–31, by Zacharias Longuelune, for Augustus the Strong's Japanese porcelain collection, at which time the palace changed its name. Today it holds spectacular exhibitions.

↑ Carl Lohse's *Ludwig Renn* on display at the Albertinum art museum

(16) ⊘ Ⓜ Ⓨ Ⓓ

THE ZWINGER

🏠 Theaterplatz 1 ⏰ 10am–8pm Tue-Sun ⓦ skd.museum

The Zwinger is one of the most significant landmarks in Dresden and a striking example of Baroque architecture that once formed part of a protective fortress but today hosts a museum complex.

Built in the space between the former town fortifications, the Zwinger was originally a wall fortification commissioned by Augustus the Strong, and constructed in 1709–32 to a design by Matthäus Daniel Pöppelmann, with the help of the sculptor Balthasar Permoser. Its spacious courtyard, once used to stage tournaments, festivals and firework displays, is completely surrounded by galleries into which are set pavilions and gates. Today it houses several art collections, incuding the Gemäldegalerie Alte Meister (Dresden Gallery of Old Masters contains) which is considered to be one of Europe's finest art collections. Other sites of interest on the grounds include the Crown Gate at the entrance and the Nymphs' Bath by Permoser.

A valuable collection of scientific instruments, clocks, sextants and globes reside in the Mathematisch-Physikalischer Salon.

The Kronentor gate (Crown Gate) owes its name to the crown positioned on its dome.

Allegorical figures crown the balustrades

→
The Zwinger, the most famous building in Dresden

Glockenspielpavillon, formerly known as Stadtpavillon (Town Pavilion)

The porcelain collection holds Japanese and Chinese pieces but its centrepiece is a collection of Meissen porcelain.

←
Works by Old Masters at the Gemäldegalerie Alte Meister

Did You Know?

Augustus II, king of Poland and elector of Saxony, commissioned the Zwinger for royal festivities.

A stunning marriage of architecture and sculpture, the Wallpavilion is a masterpiece crowned by a statue of Hercules, symbolizing the Elector, Augustus the Strong.

The Nymphenbad fountain features tritons, nymphs and grottoes – popular in the Baroque era.

The Gemäldegalerie Alte Meister (Gallery of Old Masters) occupies the wing that was added by Gottfried Semper.

Courtyard

INSIDER TIP
Grand Reopening

After years of renovations, the Semper Gallery in the Zwinger reopened in February 2020. More than 20 of the collection's masterpieces were restored, and now sit alongside state-of-the-art multimedia displays.

Gemäldegalerie Alte Meister Guide

Ground Floor

▽ As well as the tapestry room, highlights on this floor also include Giorgione's *Sleeping Venus* and Raphael's enchanting *Sistine Madonna* (c 1512; below), which owes its name to St Sixtuss church in Piacenza, for which Pope Julius II had commissioned it.

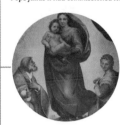

First Floor

▽ This floor explores 15th to 16th-century German painting and 17th-century French, Dutch and Flemish painting. Don't miss Titian's *Tribute Money (below)*.

Second Floor

▽ One of the most impressive of the German, Czech, Austrian, English and Swiss paintings displayed here is Jan Vermeer van Delft's *Girl Reading a Letter* (c 1695; below).

EXPERIENCE MORE

Torgau

F4 🚉🚌 **ℹ** Markt 1;
www.tic-torgau.de

This small town, with its scenic location on the Elbe, was once the favourite residence of the Saxon Electors. Its main square is surrounded by attractive houses of various styles, in particular Renaissance. The Renaissance Rathaus (town hall), built in 1561–77, has a lovely semicircular oriel.

📷 **PICTURE PERFECT**
Karl Marx Monument

One of Chemnitz's most photographed sights is its 13-m- (42-ft-) tall Karl Marx monument, which dates back to the GDR era. How about a selfie with the father of communism?

Other old town attractions include the Marienkirche, a late-Gothic church with an extended Romanesque west section. The interior has many original features, including a painting by Lucas Cranach the Elder, *The Fourteen Helpers*, and the tomb of Luther's wife, Katharina von Bora, who died in Torgau.

The main historic building in Torgau is the Renaissance Schloss Hartenfels, built on the site of a 10th-century castle. Its courtyard is surrounded by clusters of residential wings, including the late-Gothic Albrechtspalast, built in 1470–85, the Johann-Friedrich-Bau (1533–6), with its beautiful external spiral staircase and early-Baroque west wing (1616–23). The Schlosskapelle (castle chapel), which was consecrated by Martin Luther in 1544, is considered to be one of the oldest churches built for Protestants.

Mulde Valley

F4

Several magnificent old castles nestle in the scenic hills at the confluence of two rivers – the Zwickauer Mulde and the Freiberger Mulde. In the small town of Colditz, with its timber-frame houses, lovely Renaissance town hall and Gothic church of St Egidien, stands a huge Gothic castle built in 1578–91 on the site of an 11th-century castle. During World War II it was a prisoner-of-war camp known as Oflag IVC.

In Rochlitz, 11 km (7 miles) south of Colditz, stands another large castle, built in stages from the 12th to the 16th centuries. Travelling farther south you will encounter other castles: the Wechselburg, a reconstructed Baroque castle featuring a late-Romanesque collegiate church, as well as the

↑ The imposing hulk of the Renaissance Schloss Hartenfels in Torgau

 Zwickau's neighbouring concert hall and Rathaus in the town centre

Renaissance castle in Rochsburg. In the neighbouring Zschopau valley stands the magnificent, oval Burg Kriebstein, built in stages and completed in the late 14th century. This fortress houses a small museum and concert hall, and medieval music concerts are held here during the summer.

5

Zwickau

🅐E4 🚉🚌 𝒊Hauptstrasse 6; www.zwickautourist.de

An old commercial town, Zwickau flourished in the 15th and 16th centuries. Today it is known for the Trabant cars that were produced here during the GDR era. Almost all the town's attractions can be found in the old town, on the banks of the Zwickauer Mulde river. The most important historic building in the town is the Dom St Marien (cathedral of St Mary), a magnificent late-Gothic hall-church built in 1453–1537. Preserved to this day are its original main altar, dating from 1479, the work of

Michael Wolgemut; the grand architectural Holy Tomb of Michael Heuffner, dating from 1507; and the Renaissance font and a pulpit of 1538, both by Paul Speck.

Also worth visiting in the old town are the 15th-century Dünnebierhaus, the Schumann-Haus, the composer's birthplace (1810), and the Renaissance Gewandhaus (cloth house), once the seat of the Drapers' Guild and now a theatre and museum.

6

Chemnitz

🅐F4 🚉Georgstrasse 🚌Markt 𝒊Markt 1; www.chemnitz-tourismus.de

After World War II, when 90 per cent of its buildings had been reduced to rubble, the town was rebuilt in the Socialist-Realist style and renamed Karl-Marx-Stadt. Only a handful of historic buildings escaped destruction. The most interesting is the Schlosskirche, the former Benedictine abbey church St Maria, built at the turn of the 15th and 16th centuries.

Sights in the town centre include the reconstructed Altes Rathaus (old town hall),

the Gothic Roter Turm (Red Tower) and remains of fortifications. In the main square is the reconstructed Baroque Siegertsches Haus, originally built in 1737–41 to a design by Johann Christoph Naumann. The new town centre is dominated by the vast Stadthalle (city hall) with Lew Kerbel's 1971 monument to Karl Marx. The **Kunstsammlungen Chemnitz** has a museum of natural history and a fine arts collection, including works by Karl Schmidt-Rottluff.

Kunstsammlungen Chemnitz

♿ 🚪Theaterplatz 1
🕐Times vary, check website
🌐kunstsammlungen-chemnitz.de

 Chemnitz's monument to Karl Marx, sculpted by Lew Kerbel

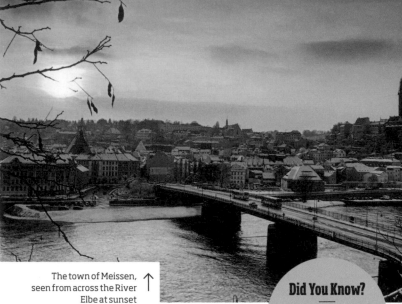

The town of Meissen, seen from across the River Elbe at sunset ↑

Freiberg

 **F4** 🚗🚌 ℹ Schloßplatz 6; www.freiberg.de

Development of this mining town was due to the discovery of silver deposits, and Freiberg was granted town status in 1168. It escaped World War II with remarkably little damage.

Today Freiberg's attractions include the reconstructed old town and many historic buildings, the gem among them being the **Dom St Marien** (cathedral of St Mary). This late-Gothic hall-church, erected at the end of the 15th century, features a stunning main portal, the Goldene Pforte, dating from 1225–30.

> Today Freiberg's attractions include the reconstructed old town and many historic buildings, the gem among them being the Dom St Marien (cathedral).

Inside are many original items, such as a tulip-shaped pulpit (1505) and two Baroque organs by Gottfried Silbermann. Organ recitals take place on Thursdays at 8pm, May through to October.

When visiting nearby Untermarkt (lower market), it is worth going to the **Stadt- und Bergbaumuseum** (Municipal and Mining Museum), which explains the history of mining in the area, as well as the collection of minerals at the **Mineralien- und Lagerstättensammlung der Bergakademie**. A stroll along the winding streets will take visitors to Obermarkt (upper market), where a fountain with the statue of the town's founder can be seen.

Dom St Marien

Ⓢ 🏠 Untermarkt 1. Goldene Pforte: 📞 (03731) 225 98 🕐 Times vary, check website

Stadt- und Bergbaumuseum

🎟 🏠 Am Dom 1 📞 (03731) 202 50 🕐 10am–5pm Tue–Sun

Mineralien- und Lagerstättensammlung der Bergakademie

🏠 Brennhausgasse 14
📞 (03731) 39 22 64
🕐 9am–noon & 1–4pm Wed–Fri, 9am–4pm Sat

Meissen

 F4 🚗🚌 ℹ Markt 3; www.stadt-meissen.de

Meissen's history began in AD 929, when Heinrich I made it the bridgehead for his expansion to the east, into Slav territories. In 966 Meissen became the capital of the newly established Meissen margravate, and in 968 a bishopric.

The town has retained much of its charm. In the market square are the late-Gothic Rathaus (town hall), built in 1472–8, some beautiful Renaissance houses and the Frauenkirche, a

Gothic, 15th-century church boasting the world's oldest porcelain carillon, which was hung here in 1929. It is also worth visiting St Afra's church, built in the 13th century for the Augustinian monks.

The **Albrechtsburg** is a vast, fortified hilltop complex with a cathedral and an elector's palace. The latter was built in 1471–89 for the Wettin brothers, Ernst and Albrecht. Designed by Arnold von Westfalen, its special feature is the magnificent external spiral staircase. From 1710 the palace was used as a porcelain factory, but was restored to its former glory in 1864. Huge wall paintings of this period, showing historical scenes, are the work of Wilhelm Römann. The Meissner Dom (cathedral church of St John and St Donatus), built from the mid-13th century to the early 15th century, has some splendid early-Gothic sculptures, an altar by Lucas Cranach the Elder in the Georgskapelle

→

Schloss Moritzburg, originally built as a hunting lodge

(St George's chapel) and ducal tombs in the Fürstenkapelle (prince's chapel).

Meissen is famous for its porcelain manufacture. The first porcelain factory in Europe, the **Staatliche Porzellan-Manufaktur**, was set up in 1710 in the castle and moved to its present premises in 1865. Documents relating to the history of the factory and many examples of its products are on display in the exhibition rooms. Guided tours and demonstrations take the visitor through all the stages of the porcelain manufacturing process.

Albrechtsburg

 ⌂ Domplatz 1 📞 (03521) 470 70 ⏰ Mar-Oct: 10am-6pm daily (Nov-Feb: to 5pm daily)

Staatliche Porzellan-Manufaktur

♿✕📷 ⌂ Talstrasse ⏰ May-Oct: 9am-6pm daily; Nov-Apr: 9am-5pm daily 🌐 meissen.com

---

❾
Moritzburg

🅰F4 🅿 🛈 Schlossallee 3b; (035207) 85 40

The first hunting lodge in this marshy region was built in the mid-16th century, for Moritz of Saxony. The present **Schloss**

Moritzburg is the result of extensive alterations ordered by Augustus the Strong, directed by Matthäus Daniel Pöppelmann, and carried out in 1723–6. The result is a square building, with four cylindrical corner towers. Much of the interior has survived, including period furnishings and hunting trophies.

Also open to visitors is the 17th-century castle chapel, decorated with splendid stucco ornaments. Augustus the Strong ordered the marshes to be drained, and the newly available land to be transformed into landscaped gardens and lakes. The **Fasanenschlösschen** (Little Pheasant Castle) in the eastern part of the gardens features several interesting Rococo interiors, and also houses a zoological exhibition.

At the end of World War II, the German artist Käthe Kollwitz spent the last years of her life in Moritzburg. The house in which she lived and worked is now the Käthe-Kollwitz-Gedenkstätte.

Schloss Moritzburg

 ⏰ Feb-Mar: 10am-4pm Sat & Sun; Apr-Oct: 10am-5:30pm daily; Nov-Dec: 10am-4pm Tue-Sun 🌐 schloss-moritzburg.de

Fasanenschlösschen

 ⏰ As above

Bautzen

🅰F4 🏛🚌 **ℹ Hauptmarkt 1; www.bautzen.de**

This town is scenically situated on a high rock overhanging the Spree river valley. Known mainly for its top-security jail for political prisoners during the GDR era, today it enchants visitors with its beautifully reconstructed old town. Many signs are bilingual, German and Sorbian, reflecting the fact that Bautzen is the cultural capital of the Sorbs (*p181*). The winding streets with their original houses, the city walls, the crooked Reichenturm tower and the Baroque town hall in the town square form a very attractive complex. It is also worth climbing the 15th-century Alte Wasserkunst (Old Water-works), a tower that pumped Spree water up to the town, for splendid views.

The cathedral Dom St Peter is now used jointly by Catholics (choir) and Protestants (nave). The late-Gothic castle Schloss Ortenburg houses the **Sorbisches Museum**, devoted to Sorbian history and culture.

Sorbisches Museum

🅰 Ortenburg 3 🕑 10am–6pm Tue–Sun sorbisches-museum.de

Bad Muskau

🅰G4 🚌 **ℹ Schlossstrasse 6; www.badmuskau.de**

Bad Muskau, a small town and spa, boasts one of Saxony's most beautiful parks, which has been included in the UNESCO Heritage list. It was created between 1815 and 1845 by Prince Hermann von Pückler-Muskau. The Neo-Renaissance **Schloss Muskau** palace at its centre was destroyed in World War II and

HIDDEN GEM
Rakotzbrücke

In Rhododendronpark Kromlau near Bad Muskau is this stunning bridge (*p34*). There are other "devil's bridges" in Europe, each with a devil-related legend.

reopened after reconstruction in 2013. An exhibition reveals the life, work and travel of Prince Pückler-Muskau and the tower offers a wonderful view over the English-style landscaped park; a nature reserve since 1952. Its main part, on the northern shores of the Lusatian Neisse river, is in Poland. A joint Polish-German programme has opened the entire area to visitors from both sides of the border.

Schloss Muskau

♿ 🅰 Schlossstrasse 📞(035771) 631 00 🕑 Apr-Oct: 10am–6pm Tue–Sun

→ The pretty, café-lined Obermarkt, in the border town of Görlitz

 Zittau

 🏠 G4 🚗🚌 🛈 Markt 1; www.zittau.eu

The city of Zittau is an excellent starting point for excursions into the Zittau Mountains, a paradise for rock-climbers, walkers and nature lovers. The town itself is splendidly preserved, with many historic buildings, such as the beautiful Baroque Noacksches Haus. The Neo-Renaissance Rathaus (town hall) was completed in 1845, to a design by Carl Augustus Schramm. Next to the Rathaus, Johanniskirche, built by Karl Friedrich Schinkel, combines elements of Neo-Classical and Neo-Gothic styles.

 Görlitz

🏠 G4 🚗🚌 🛈 Obermarkt 32; www.visit-goerlitz.com

This border town, whose eastern part – Zgorzelec – has belonged to Poland since 1945, has a history dating back to 1071. The town flourished in the 15th and 16th centuries, and in 1990 an extensive restoration plan was begun, so that visitors could see its historic buildings in their former glory. Görlitz's old buildings have made it a popular spot for national and international film productions (including *The Grand Budapest Hotel*), lending it the nickname "Görliwood".

The charming houses in Obermarkt (upper market),

 ← The dreamy Neo-Renaissance palace in the park of Bad Muskau

the Renaissance portals and decorations on houses in Brüderstrasse and the Untermarkt (lower market), with its vast town hall complex, enchant everyone. The older wing of the town hall, the work of Wendel Roskopf, has a staircase with Renaissance ornaments that winds around the statue of Justice.

One of the most remarkable churches is the imposing five-nave, 15th-century Pfarrkirche (parish church) of St Peter und St Paul, whose Baroque furnishings are among the finest in Saxony. One of Görlitz's curiosities is the Heiliges Grab (Holy Tomb), completed in 1504, a group of three chapels that are replicas of churches in Jerusalem. Görlitz still has remains of its medieval town fortifications with original towers and gates, including the Kaisertrutz, a 15th-century barbican, which is now home to the town's art collection.

Just outside the town, the local Berzdorfer See is a good spot for swimming, sailing and cycling. The small town of Ostritz, 16 km (10 miles) to the south, has a Cistercian abbey, St Marienthal (1230). Its red-and-white buildings are inhabited by nuns, who show visitors around and serve food and beer.

EAT

Am Schlossbrunnen
This family-run restaurant inside a hotel offers dishes made with local produce, including fish from the nearby lakes. The homemade ice creams are a particular highlight.

🏠 G4 🔘 Köbelner Strasse 68, Bad Muskau ⏰ D Mon-Sat, L Sun 🌐 schlossbrunnen.de

€ € €

Bar & Restaurant Salü
Salü serves decently priced and delicious German, Italian and international dishes. The bar also offers a surprisingly good selection of whiskies, gins and rums.

🏠 G4 🔘 Schwarze Strass 7, Görlitz 🌐 salue-goerlitz.de

€ € €

EXPERIENCE Saxony

⑭ Augustusburg

🏰F4 🚌 🛈 Marienberger Strasse 24; www.augustusburg.de

The small town is insignificant compared with its vast **Schloss Augustusburg** palace complex. This Renaissance hunting palace was built for the Elector Augustus in 1567–72, on the site of the former Schloss Schellenberg. Constructed under Hieronymus Lotter and Erhard van der Meer, today it houses several museums devoted to motorcycles and hunting.

Schloss Augustusburg

🚶 🕐 Apr–Oct: 9:30am–6pm daily (Nov–Mar: 10am–5pm) 🌐 schloesserland-sachsen.de

⑮ Pirna

🏰F4 🚇🚌 🛈 Am Markt 7; www.pirna.de

In the old town, on the banks of the River Elbe, Pirna has preserved an amazingly

↓ The striking exterior of the imposing Schloss Augustusburg complex

↑ Lush palms in the Palmenhaus at the Baroque Schloss Pillnitz

regular, chequerboard pattern of streets. Its greatest attraction is the Marienkirche, a late-Gothic hall-church with fanciful vaulting designed by Peter Ulrich von Pirna and painted by Jobst Dorndorff, in 1545–6. Inside, an original late-Gothic font and a Renaissance main altar can be seen.

Other interesting buildings are the mid-16th-century Rathaus (town hall) with its Gothic portals, the beautiful houses in the town square and the ex-Dominican Gothic church of St Heinrich. The palace of Schloss Sonnenstein, extended during the 17th and 18th centuries, towers above the old town.

About 10 km (6 miles) southwest of Pirna is the picturesque **Schloss Weesenstein**, much altered from its Gothic origins until the 19th century. It houses a small museum with a lovely collection of wallpapers.

The charming **Schloss Pillnitz**, a summer residence on the banks of the Elbe, was built in 1720–23 by Augustus the Strong and designed by Matthäus Daniel Pöppelmann. There are two parallel palaces: the Bergpalais (Mountain Palace) and the Wasserpalais (Water Palace); the latter can be reached by stairs directly from the river jetty. Between 1818 and 1826 the two palaces were joined by a third, the Neues Palais (New Palace). Today the Bergpalais houses a museum of decorative art. The main attraction, however, is the park, laid out in English and Chinese styles.

Schloss Weesenstein

🚶🚻 🏰 Am Schlossberg 1, Müglitztal 🕐 Apr–Oct: 10am–6pm; Nov–Mar: 10am–4pm Tue–Sun 🌐 schloss-weesenstein.de

Schloss Pillnitz

🚶🚻🏠 🏰 August-Böckstiegel-Strasse 2, Pillnitzh 🕐 Times vary, check website 🌐 schloss pillnitz.de

180

↑ Gothic abbey ruins peeking through the trees on the cliffs above Oybin

 16

Kamenz

⚠F4 🚉🚌 ℹSchulplatz 5; www.kamenz.de

The best time to visit Kamenz is the end of April or June, when the rhododendrons that cover the Hutberg mountain (294 m/965 ft high) are in bloom. The poet Gotthold Ephraim Lessing was born in Kamenz in 1729. Although his house no longer exists, the **Lessingmuseum**, founded in 1929, is devoted to his work.

A great fire destroyed much of the town in 1842, but it spared the late-Gothic St Marien church, a four-nave

15th-century structure with Gothic altars and other interesting features. Equally noteworthy for their furnishings are the Gothic ex-Franciscan St Annen church – now a museum for sacred art – and the hall-church Katechismuskirche. The old cemetery and the funereal church Begräbniskirche St Just are also worth a visit, as is the Museum der Westlausitz, a museum of the local region. Swing by the market square and admire its distinctive red-coloured townhall.

Lessingmuseum

🏠Lessingplatz 1–3 📞(03578) 380 50 🕐9am–5pm Tue–Fri, 1pm–5pm Sat & Sun

 17

Oybin

⚠F4 🚉🚌 ℹHaus des Gastes, Hauptstrasse 15; www.oybin.com

The charming spa town of Oybin, 9 km (6 miles) south of Zittau, can be reached by narrow-gauge railway. Its attractions include the hilltop ruins of a Gothic abbey, immortalized by artist Caspar David Friedrich. It is worth timing your visit for a Saturday evening in summer, when you can witness the procession of torch-bearing monks or listen to a concert.

THE SORBS

The Sorbs, also known as the Lusatians or Wends, are an indigenous Slav minority who live in the eastern regions of Saxony and Brandenburg. Their ancestors, the Lusatian Slavs, were conquered by Germans during the 10th century. Although condemned to extermination by the Nazis, today they enjoy complete cultural autonomy. The revival of their language and traditions is apparent in the bilingual signs in towns.

A DRIVING TOUR
SÄCHSISCHE SCHWEIZ

INSIDER TIP
Ways to Explore

Some of the highlights of Sächsische Schweiz require an uphill walk – particularly the Bastei and Lilienstein rock. If you don't fancy the climb, you can still see the sights from a relaxing boat trip on the Elbe (book ahead at www.saechsische-dampfschiffahrt.de). The area also has lots of trails for avid hikers.

Distance 41 km (25 miles) **Stopping off points** Don't miss out on a detour to the Bastei, or the Lilienstein rock for a lesser-known attraction

Saxon Switzerland, the wonderfully wild region around the gorge cut into the Lusatian mountains by the River Elbe, features stunningly bizarre rock formations and several formidable castles. You can drive this route and admire the scenery from you car, but to experience the real natural beauty of the region you'll need to get out and explore some of these places on foot.

1850
The year the Bastei Bridge – the first tourist building in Europe – was built.

Grosssedlitz – a vast Baroque park, established after 1719 – is where this walk starts. The park continues to delight visitors to this day with its flower beds and numerous sculptures.

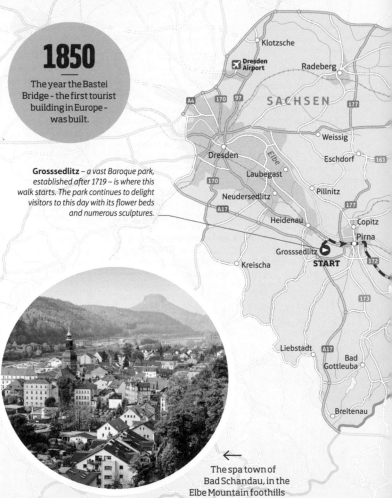

← The spa town of Bad Schandau, in the Elbe Mountain foothills

Locator Map
For more detail see p164

↑ Bastei Bridge and the jagged peaks of the ancient Bastei rock formation

Atop the craggy Schlossberg hill is **Burg Stolpen***, a medieval castle where Countess Cosel – one of Augustus II the Strong's mistresses – was imprisoned for 49 years.*

Hauswalde

Gross-röhrsdorf

Bischofswerda

Grossharthau

Putzkau

Berthelsdorf

Stolpen
FINISH

Heselicht

Neustadt

Lohmen

Hohnstein

Sebnitz

Elbe Bastei △

Porschdorf

Lilienstein

Bad Schandau

Festung Königstein

König-stein

Elbe

Bielatal

Rosenthal

The medieval castle of **Burg Hohnstein** *is now a youth hostel – another great base for those who want to stay and hike the area.*

The **Bastei** *(bastion) comprises so-called inselbergs – bizarre, tall rock formations that rise abruptly. Connected by foot-bridges, they offer splendid views.*

Bad Schandau *has a small spa that is popular as a base for walking tours into the surrounding mountains. A small railway, the Kirnitzschtalbahn, takes visitors to a scenic waterfall, the Lichtenhainer.*

Climbing up the tall **Lilienstein rock** *rewards visitors with splendid views over the Elbe of Festung Königstein.*

The powerful fortress of **Festung Königstein** *was built in the 16th century on the site of a medieval castle, and altered in subsequent centuries. Spectacular views have made it a popular tourist destination.*

| 0 kilometres | 10 |
| 0 miles | 10 |

N ↑

Winter in the Thüringer Wald mountain range

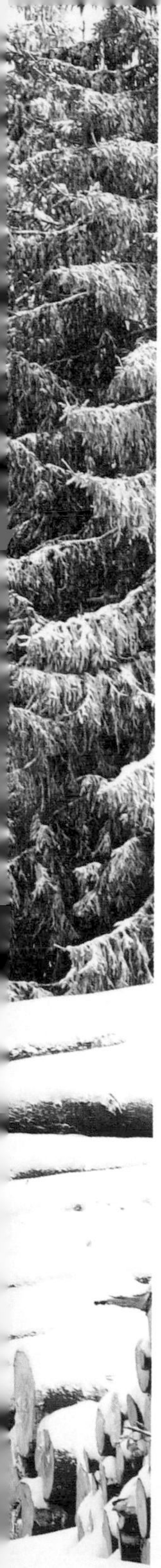

THURINGIA

After the Thuringian War of Secession ended in 1264, the region was split into several smaller principalities and lost its original political might. However, driven by the ambitions of many of its rulers, magnificent castles, churches and abbeys were built everywhere and, thanks to enlightened royal sponsors, many towns became important cultural centres, such as 18th-century Weimar, known for its central role in the German Enlightenment. After World War II, Thuringia was initially occupied by the US Army, but it soon passed into the Soviet sphere of influence, and in 1949 it became part of the GDR. In 1952 Thuringia lost its status as a federal state, but this was restored in 1990 in the reunited Federal Republic of Germany.

The majority of tourist attractions can be found in the southern part of the state. The Thuringian Forest has many popular health resorts and wintersport centres. This highland area, cut with deep river gullies, is littered with medieval castles built on steep crags. Many of these are now no more than picturesque ruins, but others, such as the Wartburg, have been completely restored to their former glory, and today delight visitors with their magnificent interiors.

LOWER SAXONY,
HAMBURG
AND BREMEN
p418

HESSE
p354

BAVARIA
p242

THURINGIA

Must Sees
1 Erfurt
2 Weimar
3 Wartburg

Experience More
4 Eisenach
5 Heiligenstadt
6 Kyffhäuser Mountains
7 Sondershausen
8 Gotha
9 Gera
10 Jena
11 Schloss Heidecksburg
12 Saalfeld
13 Altenburg

SAXONY-ANHALT p144

SAXONY p162

THURINGIA

↑ A snow-dusted Christmas market in Erfurt's central Domplatz

❶

ERFURT

🗺 D4 ✈ Erfurt-Weimar 🚉🚌 ℹ️ Benediktsplatz 1; www. erfurt-tourismus.de

The Thuringian capital, Erfurt, is one of the oldest towns in the region. As an important trading post between east and west, the town grew quickly. Erfurt University was founded in 1392 and became a stronghold for radical thought (Martin Luther was one of its pupils). In the 18th century the town became a horticultural centre, a legacy that lives on in the beautiful egapark.

①

Dom St Marien

🏛 Domstufen 📞 (0361) 64 61 265 🕐 May-Oct: 9:30am-6pm Mon-Sat, 1-6pm Sun; Nov-Apr: 9:30am-5pm Mon-Sat, 1-5pm Sun

The wide stairs leading from Domplatz to the main entrance of the cathedral provide a good view over the 14th-century Gothic presbytery, which is supported by a massive vaulted substructure, known as the Kavaten. The main body of the cathedral dates from the 15th century, but its huge towers are the remains of an earlier Romanesque building. The church interior has lovingly preserved Gothic decorations and rich furnishings.

②

St Severi-Kirche

🏛 Domstufen 📞 (0361) 57 69 60 🕐 May-Oct: 9:30am-6pm Mon-Sat, 1-6pm Sun; Nov-Apr: 9:30am-5pm Mon-Sat, 1-5pm Sun

This five-nave Gothic hall-church, next to the cathedral, dates from the late 13th and early 14th century. Inside it has the Gothic sarcophagus of St Severus, from about 1365, a huge font of 1467 and interesting Gothic altars.

③

Fischmarkt

This market square, with its Neo-Gothic town hall (1870–74), is surrounded by Renaissance houses. Nearby are three Gothic churches: Michaeliskirche, opposite the ruins of the late-Gothic university buildings, the Allerheiligenkirche, and the Predigerkirche.

④

Krämerbrücke

The "merchant's bridge" which spans the River Gera is one of Erfurt's most interesting structures. The present stone bridge was built around 1325. It is lined with houses and shops, dating mainly from the 17th to 19th centuries.

⑤

Augustinerkloster-Augustinerkirche

🏛 Augustinerstrasse 10 📞 (0361) 57 66 00 🕐 8am-6pm Mon-Fri (to 4pm Sat & Sun)

This early Gothic church was built for Augustinian monks at

→ Erfurt's Neo-Gothic town hall dominates the Fischmarkt

the end of the 13th century. Noteworthy are its original Gothic stained-glass windows. In the neighbouring monastery is the reconstructed cell where Martin Luther lived.

⑥
Stadtmuseum

🏠 Johannesstrasse 169
📞 (0361) 65 55 644
🕐 10am–6pm Tue–Sun

Erfurt's history museum is housed in an unusual, late-Renaissance building called Zum Stockfisch, built in 1607.

⑦
Anger

This market square is Erfurt's main shopping area. It is lined with handsome mansions, Gothic churches and Renaissance buildings.

⑧
Angermuseum

🏠 Anger 18 🕐 10am–6pm Tue–Sun 🌐 kunstmuseen.erfurt.de

This museum has a collection of decorative and sacred arts and 19th- and 20th-century German works. One of its rooms is decorated with Expressionist murals (1923–4) by Erich Heckel. The medieval section is in the presbytery of the Barfüsserkirche, a former Franciscan church that was destroyed during World War II.

⑨
egapark

🏠 Cyriaksburg, Gothaer Strasse 38 🕐 Mar–Oct: 9am–6pm daily; Nov–Feb: 10am–4pm 🌐 egapark-erfurt.de

On the hill around Erfurt's ruined fort are the grounds of the Erfurter Gartenausstellung – or "egapark" – a park and leisure complex. It contains exhibition halls, gardens, and a museum of horticulture and beekeeping.

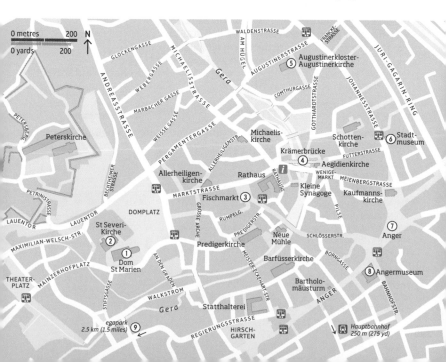

↑ The Rathaus on Marktplatz, the main square in Weimar's old town

2

WEIMAR

 **E4** **Markt 10; www.weimar.de/tourismus**

Weimar was a significant centre for German culture during a period which became known as the Golden Age, from 1758 to 1832. It continued to play a part in the lives of many influential artists and thinkers, and it was where the Bauhaus School was founded in 1919. The city also gave its name to the Weimar Republic, the democratic German State which lasted from World War I to 1933.

3

Kirms-Krackow-Haus

Jakobstrasse 10 **(03643) 54 54 01** **Apr-Oct: 1-5pm Fri, 11am-5pm Sat & Sun**

This Renaissance house, which was extended in the late 18th century, illustrates how people lived in Goethe's time.

4

St Peter und St Paul

Herderplatz **Times vary, check website** **ek-weimar.de**

This church has belonged to a Lutheran parish since the time of the Protestant Reformation. The late-Gothic hall building

1

Neues Museum Weimar

Jorge-Semprún-Platz 5 **10am-6pm Wed-Mon** **klassik-stiftung.de**

The New Museum is an important sight in the Weimar Modernism Quarter, which was developed to celebrate the 100th anniversary of the Bauhaus movement in 2019. The museum also hosts a series of themed interactive handicraft workshops.

2

Stadtmuseum

Karl-Liebknecht-Strasse 5-9 **10am-5pm Tue-Sun** **stadtmuseum.weimar.de**

The City Museum is devoted to the history of Weimar, but it also hosts temporary exhibitions and a natural history section. It is housed in a Neo-Classical house, which was built in the late 18th century for the publisher Justin Bertuch, one of the most influential businessmen of Weimar's Golden Age.

Did You Know?

Duchess Anna Amalia was a gifted composer as well as the regent of several German states.

HIDDEN GEM
Artists' Church

Jakobskirchhof is the oldest extant burial ground in the city, dating back to the 12th century. Its mausoleum holds the remains of several artists including Cranach the Elder and Friedrich Schiller.

has Baroque furnishings and an original altar painted by the Cranachs. It is also known as the Herderkirche, after the poet who preached here.

The church forms part of the UNESCO site named "Classical Weimar", a selection of buildings that relate to Weimar's Golden Age.

⑤
Wittumspalais

🏠 Theaterplatz ⏰ Apr-Oct: 10am-6pm Wed-Mon (Nov-Mar: to 4pm) 🌐 klassik-stiftung.de

This Baroque palace was the home of Dowager Duchess Anna Amalia (1739-1807). Acting as regent for her son Karl August from 1758–85, she was one of the few female leaders in Germany during the long history of the Holy Roman Empire.

Anna Amalia acquired the Wittumspalais at the end of her regency and had the interior redesigned, adding beautiful frescoes designed by the director of the Leipzig Academy of Drawing.

⑥
Stadtschloss

🏠 Burgplatz 4 Schloss-museum 📞 (03643) 54 59 60 🚫 For renovations until 2023

This vast ducal castle was rebuilt in the Neo-Classical style for Duke Karl August

(1757–1858), the son of Anna Amalia. He inherited several German states and later became the Grand Duke of Saxe-Weimar-Eisenach, reigning until his death.

His castle has original interiors and fine paintings from the Weimar Art School

⑦
Schillerhaus

🏠 Schillerstrasse 12 ⏰ Apr-Oct: 9:30am-6pm Tue-Sun; Nov-Mar: 9:30am-4pm Tue-Sun. 🌐 klassik-stiftung.de

This museum is in the house where Friedrich Schiller lived when he wrote *Wilhelm Tell* (1804), and the period interiors provide a glimpse into the writer's life.

The bell tower of the Stadtschloss

EAT

Erbenhof

This elegant restaurant serves regional cuisine based on Thuringian recipes, made with local ingredients.

🏠 Brauhausgasse 10-14 🌐 erbenhof.de

€€€

Lava Soul Kitchen

The décor and menu here are casual but the quality of food is high.

🏠 Karl-Liebknecht-Strasse 10 🌐 lava-weimar.de

€€€

Shiva

This classic Indian restaurant offers great traditional dishes like lamb rogan josh and dal.

🏠 Carl-August-Allee 17A 🌐 shiva-restaurant-weimar.jimdo.com

€€€

---

 ⑧

Liszt Museum

🏠 Marienstrasse 17 🕐 Apr-Oct: 10am-6pm Tue-Sun (Nov-Mar: to 4pm) 🌐 klassik-stiftung.de

Hungarian composer and musician Franz Liszt lived here from 1869 to 1886, while he composed the *Hungarian Rhapsody*. His apartment has been preserved to this day, and visitors can enjoy his music in an exhibition on the ground floor.

---

⑨

Bauhaus Museum Weimar

🏠 Stéphane-Hessel-Platz 1 🕐 10am-2:30pm Mon 10am-6pm Tue-Sun 🕐 Until April 2019 🌐 bauhausmuseum weimar.de

This museum is devoted to the art school founded here in 1919 by Walter Gropius. Bauhaus aimed to blend different forms of art and was one of the most influential artistic movements of the 20th century.

---

⑩

Schloss Belvedere

🏠 Belvedere Park 🕐 Apr-Oct: 11am-5pm Tue-Sun 🌐 klassik-stiftung.de

This ducal summer residence, which was built between 1724 and 1732 in Belvedere Park, has a fine collection of decorative art from the Rococo period and a wonderful park.

---

⑪

Goethes Gartenhaus

🏠 Park an der Ilm 🕐 10am-6pm Wed-Mon (Nov-Mar: to 4pm)

Goethe's first home in Weimar, this small villa is in the pleasant park – which Goethe helped design – alongside the River Ilm.

---

⑫

Herzogin-Anna-Amalia Bibliothek

🏠 Platz der Demokratie 4 📞 (03643) 54 52 00 🕐 9:30am-2:30pm Tue-Sun

This former Mannerist palace, also known as Grünes Schloss (Green Palace), became the library of Duchess Anna Amalia in 1761. Its oval Rococo interior,

The Rococo Hall at the Herzogin-Anna-Amalia-Bibliothek

 ←

A painting of
Schloss Belvedere by
Curt Herrmann (1912)

Goethe and Schiller, whose
statues – by sculptor Ernst
Rietschel – stand outside.

---

 ⑮

Buchenwald

⊙ Apr-Oct: 10am-6pm Tue-
Sun (Nov-Mar: to 4pm Tue-
Sun) ⓦ buchenwald.de

Buchenwald, 8 km (5 miles)
north of Weimar, was the site
of a concentration camp set
up by the Nazis. During the
period 1937 to 1945, over
54,000 people were killed
here. It is now a museum and
a documentation centre.

one of the finest of its type in
Europe, now contains a public
research library for literary and
cultural history, specialising in
German literature from 1800.

---

 ⑬

Goethes Wohnhaus and National Museum

⊙ Frauenplan 1 ⊙ 9:30am-
6pm (Nov-Mar: to 4pm)
ⓦ klassic-stiftung.de

This house was presented to
Goethe by Duke Karl August.
Here the writer wrote his most
famous work, *Faust* (1808). The
museum shows items asso-
ciated with Goethe, including
some of his private art and
natural scientific collections,
as well as his personal library.

---

⑭

Deutsches Nationaltheater

⊙ Theaterplatz 2 ⓦ national
theater-weimar.de

The present Neo-Classical
building, completed in 1907
is the third theatre to stand
on this site. Well-known
conductors who worked here
include Franz Liszt and Richard
Strauss, and it was also the
venue for the world premiere

of Wagner's *Lohengrin*. In 1919
the National Congress sat
in the Nationaltheater and
passed the new constitution
for the Weimar Republic. The
Deutsches Nationaltheater is
home to the Staatskapelle
Weimar, one of the world's
oldest orchestras, and is
closely associated with

→

Goethe and Schiller
statue at the Deutsches
Nationaltheater

↑ The hilltop castle of Wartburg, surrounded by forest

3 ⊘ Ⓜ ⓨ 🛍

WARTBURG

🅐D4 🅒(03691) 25 00 🚇🚍 🕓Apr–Oct: 8.30am–8pm daily (tours to 5pm); Nov–Mar: 9am–5pm daily (tours to 3:30pm) 🅦wartburg.de

Looming impressively over the town of Eisenach, Wartburg was the first German castle to achieve UNESCO World Heritage status. Dating back to the 11th century, it offers art and architecture that span 1,000 years of German history.

This mighty fortress was probably founded by Ludwig the Jumper, and was reputedly the setting for a singing contest immortalized by Wagner in his opera *Tannhäuser*. Between 1211 and 1228 the castle was home to St Elisabeth of Thuringia, and from 4 May 1521 until March 1522 Martin Luther found refuge here while he translated the New Testament into German. Major reconstruction in the 19th century gave the castle its old-time romantic character, with areas like the Romanesque 12th-century great hall, in which a series of concerts is held every summer. The castle is also home to an extensive art collection – created on the recommendation of Goethe nearly 200 years ago – which includes sculptures by Tilman Riemenschneider, paintings by Lucas Cranach the Elder and assorted Renaissance artworks.

Bergfried, a vast, square tower crowned with a cross

The impressive and ornate festival hall

Landgrafenzimmer (the Landgraves' Chambers), in the oldest part of the castle

---

LUTHERHAUS EISENACH

One of the oldest (and most charming) half-timbered houses in Thuringia, Lutherhaus Eisenach is the house Luther is said to have lived in between 1498 to 1501. Alongside the permanent multimedia exhibition, "Luther and the Bible", visitors can find examples of medieval art, paintings by Cranach and more.

The buildings of ↑ Wartburg, enclosed within wide stone walls

EXPERIENCE MORE

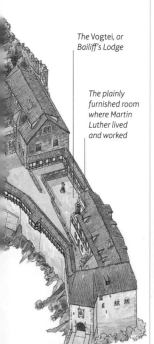

↑ A painting of St Elisabeth, on display in the castle

Did You Know?

Many historians argue that Martin Luther's nailing of his Theses to a church door is simply a legend.

The Vogtei, *or Bailiff's Lodge*

The plainly furnished room where Martin Luther lived and worked

❹
Eisenach

🅰D4 🚉🚌 🛈 Markt 24 (Stadtschloss); www. eisenach.info

At the foot of the castle hill, Eisenach was founded in the middle of the 12th century and played an important political role in medieval times. There are interesting remains of fortifications, dating from the late 12th century, which include a Romanesque gate, the Nikolaitor. The Nikolaikirche nearby, also Romanesque in style, once belonged to the Benedictine Sisters. In the market square is a 16th-century town hall, and in Lutherplatz stands the house where Martin Luther once lived; it is now a modern museum of his work.

The **Predigerkirche**, built in honour of Elisabeth von Thüringen shortly after she had been canonized, is part of the Thüringer Museum and has been used for changing exhibitions since 1899. It also houses a permanent exhibition, "Medieval Art in Thuringia".

Automobile Welt Eisenach is a museum that celebrates the local car manufacturing industry. Its collection includes old BMWs and Wartburgs.

Johann Sebastian Bach was born in Eisenach in 1685. His birthplace is now demolished, but the **Bachhaus** museum is devoted to his life and work.

Predigerkirche

♦ 🅰 Predigerplatz 4
📞 (03691) 78 46 78 🕐 10am–1pm Wed–Sun

Automobile Welt Eisenach

🅰 F Naumanstrasse 10
📞 (03691) 77 212 🕐 Apr–Oct: 10am–6pm Tue–Sun; Nov–Mar: 11am–5pm Tue–Sun

Bachhaus

♦ 🅰 Frauenplan 21
🕐 10am–6pm daily
🌐 bachhaus.de

The pretty market square in Eisenach ↑

The enormous Barbarossa monument *(inset)* in the Kyffhäuser Mountains

A small health resort, Bad Frankenhausen, nestles at the foot of the mountains. It has a number of Gothic churches, including Oberkirche, famed for its leaning tower, and a Renaissance palace, now home to a small museum. Nearby, on the Schlachtberg (Slaughter Mountain), the decisive battle in the Peasants' War took place. The Pavilion Museum there holds a vast panoramic picture of the battle, painted in 1971–5.

crypt and an amusing Gothic pulpit, made in the shape of a book-holding chorister.

6
Kyffhäuser Mountains

🅐D4 *i* Anger 14, Bad Frankenhausen; (034671) 717 17

This small mountain range along the border between Thuringia and Saxony-Anhalt is not only picturesque but is also shrouded in legends and associated with important historic events.

According to one legend, Emperor Friedrich I Barbarossa found his final resting place in one of the caves. Allegedly, he did not drown during the Crusades, as history would have us believe, but is waiting here, with six knights. As soon as his beard is long enough to wind three times around the table where he is sitting, he will return to save Germany from oppression. On the site of the former imperial palace now stands a monument with a figure of Barbarossa and an equestrian statue of Emperor Wilhelm I – the work of Bruno Schmitz, erected in 1891–6.

5
Heiligenstadt

🅐D4 🚊🚌 *i* Wilhelm-strasse 50; www.heilbad-heiligenstadt.de

This pleasant spa and health resort, well placed for the gardens of Eichsfeld, is worth a visit. It is the birthplace of Tilman Riemenschneider, an outstanding sculptor of the Gothic era; it is also the place where the poet and writer Heinrich Heine was baptized in 1825, at the age of 28.

Heiligenstadt has several churches worth visiting, including the Gothic Pfarr-kirche St Marien, with wall paintings dating from around 1500. Not far from the church stands the Friedhofskapelle St Annen, an octagonal Gothic cemetery chapel. The town's most interesting church, however, is the Stiftskirche St Martin, dating back to the 14th–15th centuries. It has a well-preserved Romanesque

7
Sondershausen

🅐E4 🚌 *i* Markt 9; www.sondershausen.de

Sondershausen was the capital city of the small principality of Schwarzburg-Sondershausen. The town's main attraction is the Schloss (ducal palace), a sprawling building built in stages from the 16th to the 19th century. The palace has some interesting original interiors. Particularly noteworthy are the Am Wendelstein rooms, decorated with 17th-century stucco ornaments, as well as the Neo-Classical Liebhaber-theater (Connoisseurs' Theatre of around 1835) and the Baroque Riesensaal (Giants' Hall), a ballroom with 16 large statues of ancient gods. When strolling around the palace gardens it is worth looking at the Achteckhaus, an octagonal building dating from 1700.

The most interesting Neo-Classical building complex in town can be found around the Marktplatz (market square).

The opulent ballroom of Gotha's Gothic Schloss Friedenstein

In the Hainleite hills, 4.5 km (3 miles) south of Sondershausen, stands the Jagdschloss Zum Possen, once an 18th-century hunting lodge, now an inn. The timber-frame observation tower nearby affords beautiful views of the district. Nordhausen, situated 20 km (12 miles) to the north, is worth visiting for its attractive timber-frame houses and its 14th-century cathedral, Dom zum Heiligen Kreuz (Holy Cross), with a Romanesque crypt.

 8

Gotha

AD4 **🚉🚌** **i**Hauptmarkt 33; www.gotha.de

From 1640 the old commercial town of Gotha was the capital of Saxe-Gotha and later of Saxe-Coburg-Gotha Duchy, the dynasty from which Prince Albert, Queen Victoria's husband, descended. The vast ducal palace, **Schloss Friedenstein**, towers above the city and was the first Baroque building in Thuringia. Particularly noteworthy are

the ballroom, the palace chapel with the ducal sarcophagi in the crypt and the court theatre, built in 1683. The palace museum houses an art collection including works by eminent artists such as Peter Paul Rubens, Anton van Dyck, Frans Hals and Jan van Goyen. To the south of the palace stands a Neo-Renaissance building, which was purpose-built for the ducal art collection. Now it houses the Museum der Natur, a natural history museum. The Renaissance town hall (1567–77) located in the old town is surrounded by a number of interesting houses.

Gotha played an important role in the German workers' movement: the Socialist Workers' Party (today's SPD), was founded here in 1875. The conference hall has been reconstructed and houses the **Gedenkstätte der Deutschen Arbeiterbewegung** (Memorial to the German Workers' Movement).

Schloss Friedenstein

🎨🏛 **A**Schlossplatz I **🕙**10am–5pm Tue–Sun (Nov–Apr: to 4pm) **w**stiftung friedenstein.de

Gedenkstätte der Deutschen Arbeiterbewegung

AAm Tivoli 3 **C**(03621) 70 41 27 **🕙**By prior arrangement

 9

Gera

AD4 **🚉🚌** **i**Markt 1a; www.gera.de

The second largest town in Thuringia, Gera has many attractions, including a Rathaus (town hall) whose oldest, Renaissance part dates from 1573–6. Near the market square, in Nikolaiberg, you will find the Salvatorkirche. This Baroque church got its Secession-style interior in 1903, after a fire. The theatre (1900–02) was designed in the same style, by Heinrich Seeling. The Küchengarten (kitchen garden) surrounds the ruins of Schloss Osterstein, of which only the Baroque orangery remains. It now houses the **Kunstsammlung**, which shows changing special exhibitions in the south wing and, in the north wing, works from Otto Dix dating between 1944 and 1969. Otto Dix, a leading artist of the *Neue Sachlichkeit* (New Objectivity), was born in Gera, in what is now the **Otto-Dix-Haus**.

Kunstsammlung

AOrangerieplatz 1 **🕙**11am–5pm Tue–Sun **w**museen-gera.de

Otto-Dix-Haus

AMohrenplatz 4 **C**(0365) 832 49 27 **🕙**11am–5pm Tue–Sun

Snow-dusted buildings in Gera's Untermhaus district

Did You Know?

At 149 m (488 ft), Jena's JenTower is the highest building in Eastern Germany.

10

Jena

D4 Markt 16; www.visit-jena.de

Jena is famous for the Carl-Zeiss-Jena Optical Works and its university, founded in 1558. One of the most important schools in Germany, its former tutors included Schiller, Fichte and Hegel. The oldest university building is the Collegium Jenense. The main building was built by Theodor Fischer in 1905–8. The complex includes a 145-m- (475-ft-) high cylindrical tower block, built in 1972 and known as the "phallus Jenensis".

In the town's main square, Marktplatz, stands the late-Gothic Rathaus (town hall), dating from the early 15th century. Once every hour, a figure known as the Schnapphans tries to catch a ball, a symbol of the human soul. The Gothic church of St Michael nearby was built in the 15th and the 16th centuries. The Stadtmusem Alte Göhre has an interesting collection of regional history. In Unterer Markt (lower market) the Romantikerhaus is worth a visit; formerly the home of Johann Gottlieb Fichte, it now houses a museum devoted to the Romantic period.

A few miles from Jena lie the Dornburg Palaces, a trio of palaces in varying styles: Old Palace, Renaissance Palace (aka Goethe Palace), and the Rococo Palace. Their gardens and delightful views have earned them the nickname "Thuringia's balcony".

11

Schloss Heidecksburg

E4 Schlossbezirk 1 10am-6pm Tue-Sun (Nov-Mar: to 5pm) heidecksburg.de

Although the town of Rudolstadt has the Gothic-Renaissance St Andreas church, a fascinating 16th-century town hall and some historic houses, tourists come here mainly to see majestic Schloss Heidecksburg, a vast palace perched on a hill. Its present form is mainly the result of the reconstruction work that was carried out in the mid-18th century by Johann Christoph Knöffel and Gottfried Heinrich Krone. Inside are some beautifully arranged Rococo state rooms. The museum also has a splendid porcelain collection, a gallery of paintings and the so-called Schiller's Room. From the castle there are fantastic views of the Schwarza valley.

12

Saalfeld

E4 Am Markt 6; www.saalfeld-tourismus.de

Saalfeld flourished in the 14th–16th centuries. From 1680 it was the seat of the Duchy of Sachsen-Saalfeld, and its magnificent Baroque Residential Palace, built between 1676 and 1720, dates from this period. The former palace chapel, now used as a concert hall, is particularly note-worthy. Also worth visiting is the Johanniskirche, a late-Gothic hall-church with

A decorative fountain in the courtyard of Schloss Heidecksburg ↑

interesting furnishings, a valuable Gothic Holy Tomb and the sculpted life-size figure of John the Baptist, carved by Hans Gottwalt, a student of sculptor Tilman Riemenschneider.

Another interesting building in Saalfeld is the early-Renaissance Rathaus (town hall), built in 1529–37. The town also has well-preserved medieval town fortifications with gates and towers. In the southern part of the town stands the Hoher Schwarm, ruins of a 13th-century Gothic castle. In Garnsdorf, on the outskirts of Saalfeld, are the **Feengrotten** (fairy grottoes), created by both natural and human activity. From the mid-16th century until 1846, alum slate was mined here, called "Jeremiasglück" (Jeremiah's good fortune). The mine was finally closed due to humidity, but the dripping water has created some astonishingly colourful stalagmites and stalactites.

From Saalfeld it is also worth taking a trip to the Hohenwarte-Talsperre, an artificial lake and paradise for watersports enthusiasts. Burg Ranis, a scenic hill-top castle,

was probably built in the 11th century for an emperor. Later it became the seat of the Thuringian landgraves, Meissen margraves and the counts of Schwarzburg. Now it houses a museum of the region's natural history.

Feengrotten Grottoneum
⊛ ⓘ ☺ ⊛ ⬛ Feengrotten-weg 2 ⬛ May–Oct: 10am–5pm daily; Nov–Apr: 11am–3:30pm daily ⬛ feengrotten.de

---

⑬
Altenburg

⬛ E4 ⬛ ⬛ ⬛ An der Baderei 1; www.altenburger-originale.de

In Germany Altenburg is known as "Skatstadt", the town of skat, a traditional and very popular card game. Altenburg also has some fascinating historic remains. The **Schloss** (ducal castle), which towers over the old town, has a 10th-century tower, reconstructed mainly in the Baroque style. Today the castle houses the **Spielkartenmuseum** (museum of playing cards).

→
Altenburg's fountain decorated with skat players

The late-Gothic castle church is also worth seeing. It has rich Baroque furnishings and an organ that was played by the composer Bach. Next to the castle gardens, the **Lindenau-Museum** houses Augustus von Lindenau's collection of 16th–20th century paintings and sculptures, including works by Botticelli, Fra Angelico and Auguste Rodin. The old town, at the foot of the hill, has a beautiful Renaissance town hall with an enormous octagonal tower. In Brühl Platz is a fountain and the figures of skat players, as well as the Baroque Seckendorffsche Palais and the Renaissance chancellery.

Schloss und Spielkartenmuseum
⊛ ⬛ Schloss 2–4 ⬛ (03447) 51 27 12 ⬛ 10am–5pm Tue–Sun

Lindenau-Museum
⊛ ⬛ Gabelentzstrasse 5 ⬛ (03447) 895 53 ⬛ Noon–6pm Tue–Sun

SOUTHERN GERMANY

Munich	208
Bavaria	242
Baden-Württemberg	288

Kloster St Trudpert (St Trudpert's Abbey) in the Black Forest

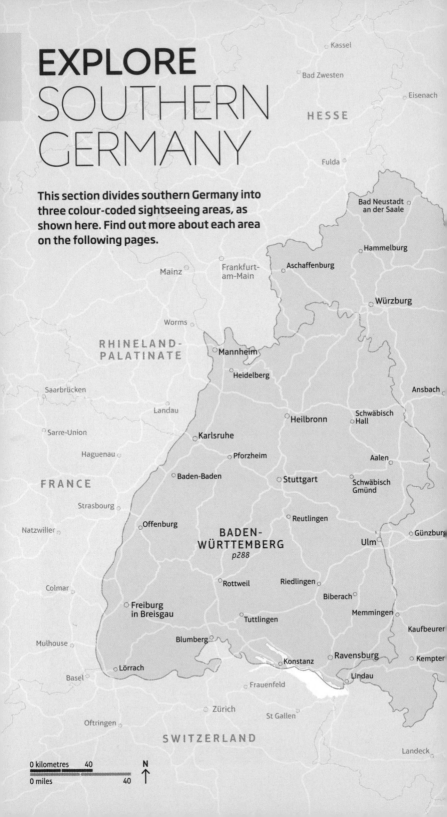

EXPLORE
SOUTHERN
GERMANY

This section divides southern Germany into three colour-coded sightseeing areas, as shown here. Find out more about each area on the following pages.

Kassel

Bad Zwesten

Eisenach

HESSE

Fulda

Bad Neustadt an der Saale

Hammelburg

Mainz

Frankfurt-am-Main

Aschaffenburg

Würzburg

Worms

RHINELAND-PALATINATE

Mannheim

Heidelberg

Ansbach

Saarbrücken

Landau

Heilbronn

Schwäbisch Hall

Sarre-Union

Karlsruhe

Pforzheim

Aalen

Haguenau

FRANCE

Baden-Baden

Stuttgart

Schwäbisch Gmünd

Strasbourg

Offenburg

Reutlingen

Natzwiller

BADEN-WÜRTTEMBERG
p288

Ulm

Günzburg

Colmar

Rottweil

Riedlingen

Biberach

Freiburg in Breisgau

Tuttlingen

Memmingen

Kaufbeuren

Blumberg

Mulhouse

Ravensburg

Kempten

Lörrach

Konstanz

Lindau

Basel

Frauenfeld

Zürich

St Gallen

SWITZERLAND

Oftringen

Landeck

0 kilometres 40
0 miles   40

N
↑

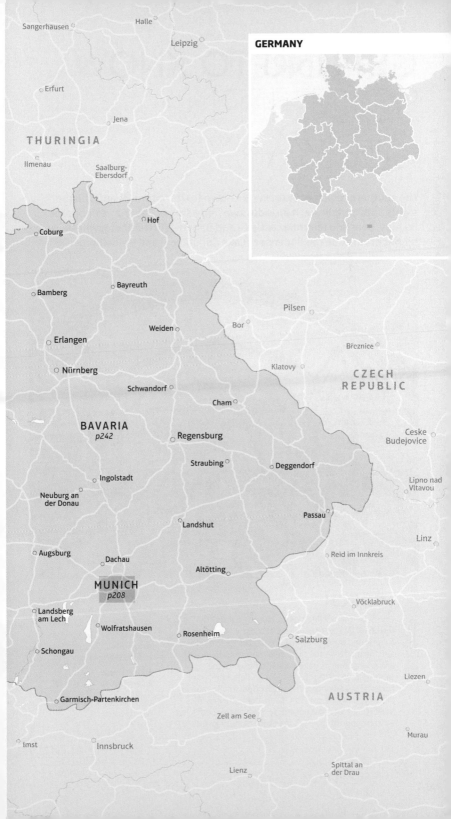

GETTING TO KNOW
SOUTHERN
GERMANY

The southern region of Germany is known for its natural beauty, historic sights and folk culture. It includes two large states: Bavaria - famous for its Alps, beer and fairytale castles - and Baden-Württemberg, whose highlights include the Bodensee (Lake Constance) and Heidelberg.

MUNICH

PAGE 208

One of Germany's finest cities, Munich is also the beating heart of Bavaria. Effortlessly straddling the cultural and the commercial – as well as the traditional and the modern – the city offers museums, theatres and art institutions galore. It's also home to the world-renowned Oktoberfest, an endless number of convivial beer gardens, and retail opportunities aplenty. If the busy city life gets too much, there are lots of quiet places for some downtime, such as the Englischer Garten or one of the city's many churches or galleries.

Best for
Culture and shopping

Home to
Alte Pinakothek, Schloss Nymphenburg, Deutsches Museum and Residenz

Experience
Enjoy the artistic treasures on display at the Alte Pinakothek before relaxing in the Englischer Garten

PAGE 242

BAVARIA

The largest federal state in Germany also happens to be one of the most scenic. Its beautiful lakes attract lovers of watersports, while the mountainous regions of the Bavarian Forest offer vast expanses of unspoiled nature. The Alps, with their charming mountain hostels and numerous ski-lifts, provide endless possibilities for enjoyment. Towns and villages including Rothenburg ob der Tauber and Nürnberg feature magnificent historic sights and perfectly preserved regional architecture, especially in their old town centres.

Best for
Mountains, lakes and castles

Home to
Bamberg, Nürnberg, Berchtesgadener Land, Würzburg, Rothenburg ob der Tauber und Schloss Neuschwanstein

Experience
Head to the Berchtesgadener Land for hiking trails through fantastic scenery

PAGE 288

BADEN-WÜRTTEMBERG

Another of Germany's most celebrated and traditional regions, Baden-Württemberg has a similar allure to its neighbour Bavaria. With its beautiful towns, luxurious resorts and stunning natural scenery, Baden-Württemberg is an ideal destination for relaxation and adventure.

Best for
Lakes, forests and historic towns

Home to
Residenzschloss Ludwigsburg, Stuttgart, Schwäbische Alb, Bodensee, Schwarzwald and Heidelberg Castle

Experience
Venture through the mythical Schwarzwald and try the region's eponymous gateaux

MUNICH

The capital of Bavaria is sometimes called "Germany's secret capital". Lying right at the heart of Europe, the city rapidly overshadowed once powerful neighbours to become southern Germany's main metropolis. With its vibrant cosmopolitan atmosphere, fine buildings, museums and shops, Munich is one of Europe's most elegant cities.

The citizens of Munich have been known for centuries for their love of the arts, and the masterpieces that were created here during the Baroque and Rococo periods were equal to Italian and French works. In the 19th century the town's development continued along Neo-Classical lines, gaining for it the name of "Athens on the Isar". But it is not only art that gives Munich its unique charm. The country's biggest folk festival, the Oktoberfest, is held each year in Theresienwiese, and visitors can be sure that the city's shops are equal to those of Paris and Milan.

In contrast to its traditional image of lederhosen and beer steins, Munich is also one of Germany's main centres for the high-tech and media industries, with many TV stations, film studios and book and newspaper publishers based here.

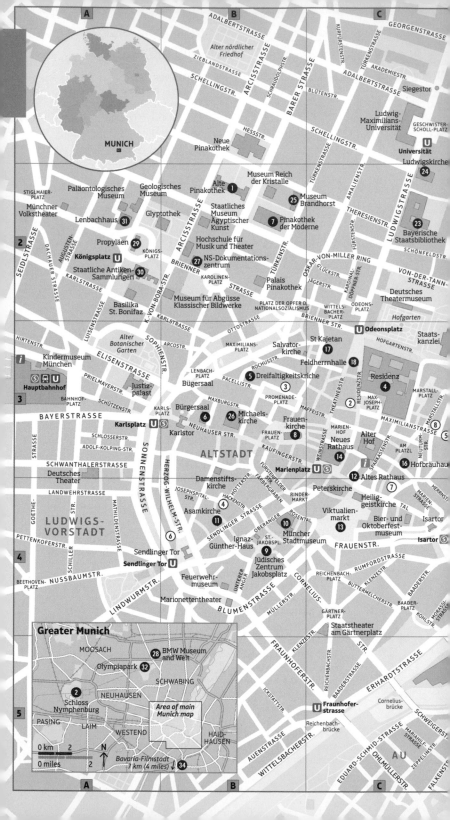

MUNICH

Must Sees

1. Alte Pinakothek
2. Schloss Nymphenburg
3. Deutsches Museum
4. Residenz

Experience More

5. Dreifaltigkeitskirche
6. Bürgersaal
7. Pinakothek der Moderne
8. Frauenkirche
9. Jüdisches Centrum Jakobsplatz
10. Münchner Stadtmuseum
11. Asamkirche
12. Altes Rathaus
13. Viktualienmarkt
14. Neues Rathaus
15. Museum Fünf Kontinente
16. Hofbräuhaus
17. St Kajetan
18. Feldherrnhalle
19. Haus der Kunst
20. Bayerisches Nationalmuseum
21. Sammlung Schack
22. Archäologische Staatssammlung
23. Bayerische Staatsbibliothek
24. Ludwigskirche
25. Museum Brandhorst
26. Michaelskirche
27. NS-Dokumentationszentrum
28. BMW Museum and Welt
29. Propyläen
30. Staatliche Antiken-Sammlungen
31. Lenbachhaus
32. Olympiapark
33. Englischer Garten
34. Bavaria-Filmstadt

Eat

1. Wirtshaus in der Au
2. Spatenhaus an der Oper
3. Trader Vic's

Shop

4. servus.heimat
5. Maximilianstrasse

Stay

6. Motel One München Sendlinger Tor
7. Cortiina
8. Vier Jahreszeiten

1 The impressive Neues Rathaus on Marienplatz.

2 Munich's Westfriedhof U-Bahn station.

3 The convivial Hofbrauhaus.

4 Contemporary designs at the Pinakothek der Moderne.

1 DAY

In Munich

Morning

Set yourself up with a stately breakfast at the Spatenhaus an der Oper *(Residenz-strasse 12)*, which has a wonderful outdoor terrace. Once you're ready to set out for your next stop, make sure to head up Residenzstrasse, so you can pause to admire the stunning Residenz *(p224)* – the former seat of Bavarian kings. A few minutes away is the Pinakothek der Moderne *(p226)*, containing several different museums and collections devoted to modern art, from exemplary works of Pop Art and Cubism to modern design and graphic art exhibits.

Afternoon

Walk from Königsplatz to Marienplatz *(p240)*, where more wonderful architecture awaits in the shape of the faux-Gothic Neues Rathaus *(p230)*, with its Glockenspiel (which plays at 11am and 5pm daily, and also at noon in summer), and the authentically Gothic Altes Rathaus *(p230)*, which houses a toy museum. There are several fine churches in the immediate area that are worth exploring, including the Frauenkirche

(p228), with its domed spires, the Heiliggeistkirche, and the Peterskirche *(p230)*, whose tower offers stellar views of the surrounding city. After wandering the endless food stalls of the Viktualienmarkt *(p230)*, stop off for a beer at the Hofbräuhaus *(Platzl 9)*, a beer hall and restaurant dating back to the 16th century, when it was founded as the royal brewery to the Residenz.

Evening

Time for some retail therapy. It's mere steps from the Hofbräuhaus to the city's most fashionable street, Maximilian-strasse *(p228)*, which offers high-end fashion boutiques, as well as galleries and several good restaurants and cafés. After some fine Italian food at the welcoming Brenner Operngrill *(Maximilianstrasse 15)*, head back towards the city centre in time to round the day off with some opera at the National Theatre *(www.staatsoper.de)*.

Admiring grand paintings ↑
in Munich's magnificent
Alte Pinakothek gallery

MUNICH FOR
CULTURE
LOVERS

While it is well-known for its traditional values, Munich has much to offer besides Bavarian beer halls. Shaped as a capital of science and art in the 19th century, Munich has a thriving cultural scene and an impressive roster of world-class museums and top-notch arts venues.

Make for the Museums

Featuring some 80 museums, Munich has something to suit almost every interest. The Stadtmuseum *(p229)* offers exhibits all about the city, making it a great place to start your time in Munich. Planes, trains and robotics are star attractions at the impressive Deutsches Museum *(p222)*, while automobiles take pride of place at BMW Museum + Welt *(p237)*. Fans of the arts should make a beeline for the Residenz *(p224)*, Germany's largest city palace and now a museum. Note that most museums close on Mondays and some open their doors for just €1 on Sundays.

→
Planes on display
at the innovative
Deutsches Museum

Accessible Art

Munich has an admirable collection of historic art, with the Alte Pinakothek *(p218)* being a particular highlight for classical art lovers. But fans of modern artists and innovative styles will also find that the city has an impressive contemporary art scene. One of the biggest and most dynamic spaces is the Kunsthalle München *(www.kunsthalle-muc.de)*, which organises three high-profile exhibitions of international artists annually. Smaller galleries focusing on emerging and local artists include the Friday Gallery *(Frauenstrasse 18)* and Nir Altman *(www.niraltman. com)*, while niche venues such as Galerie Hegemann *(www. galerie-hegemann.de)* lean towards street and urban art.

Saint Joseph and Saint Joachim (c 1503) by Albrecht Dürer ↑

Milky Chance, a German folk group, performing at Muffatwerke ↑

Musical Munich

From elegant classical music concerts in the stately Gasteig Philharmonic Hall to underground hip hop or drum and bass in industrial hotspots like Muffatwerke and the Freiheizhalle, Munich has music for everyone. Jazz fans usually get their buzz at the legendary Unterfahrt, while Backstage is the place for alternative rock aficionados. Milla is the place for up and coming bands, both local and international. For something more experimental and cultural, the Hochschule für Musik has a consistently good programme, while international DJs play at dedicated electronic music clubs such as Pacha *(pacha-muenchen.de)*.

FOR THE LOVE OF BEER

Beer is unquestionably Germany's favourite alcoholic drink. Germans drink an average of 100 litres of beer annually and during Munich's Oktoberfest a staggering 7 million litres are served. The country's oldest brewery, established in 1040, is the Weihenstephan Benedictine monastery in Freising, believed to be the oldest working brewery in the world. And the tradition continues: Bavaria is home to over 700 breweries, producing around 40 different types of beer.

WHERE TO DRINK

For a local brew, head to a *Bierkeller* (beer cellar) or *Bierstube* (pub) or – if the weather's good – a *Biergarten* (beer garden). Bavaria has plenty of each, including Munich's Hirschgarten, which can cater for up to 8,000 patrons, and the hugely popular Hofbräuhaus *(p232)*.

THE ULTIMATE BEER FESTIVAL

Attracting millions of visitors every year, Oktoberfest is one of the biggest folk festivals in the world. A celebration of all things beer and Bavaria, the event runs in Munich from the end of September to early October, and sees dirndl- and lederhosen-clad crowds partake in raucous revelry.

$\longrightarrow$

The exterior of Munich's crowd-pleasing Hofbräuhaus

TYPES OF BEER

1 **Dunkel** (dark) beer ranges from dark amber to red-brown in colour, and from malty to chocolatey in taste. Bavarian *dunkelbiers* are more full-bodied due to a special Munich malt and a brewing technique known as decoction mashing.

2 **Helles**, the most popular of Munich's beers, was introduced in 1894, ostensibly as a competitor to the popular Czech Pilsner. A lager by definition, its warm and attractive gold colour is matched to a light and pleasant, medium-bodied taste.

3 **Eisbock** is a strong beer named for the process of freezing the beer (a *bock*) to separate the water content from its alcohol and sugars. The ice is removed to reveal a unique beer with a hoppy character and sweet to fruity taste.

4 **Weissbier** is a translucent lager whose specialized yeast content gives it a sweet flavour.

5 **Maibock** has a creamy head and a toasty or even spicy taste due to the kind of hops used; usually Pilsner and/or Vienna malt, with Munich malt, Noble hops and lager yeast.

↑ Inside the Hacker-Festhalle during Munich's much-celebrated Oktoberfest

① ⟨⟩ Ⓜ ▭ 🏛

ALTE PINAKOTHEK

📍B2 🏠Barer Strasse 27 Ⓤ Königsplatz
🚌100,🚋27 🕐10am–8pm Thu–Sun
(to 8:30pm Tue & Wed) 🌐pinakothek.de

With over 700 beautifully displayed artworks from the 14th to 18th centuries, the Old Pinakothek is a treasure trove showcasing the golden ages of European painting. Exploring the Neo-Classical hallways of this elegant gallery is a must for any art-lover.

The Three Pinakotheks

The Alte Pinakothek is named after the pinacotheca galleries of ancient Greece and Rome. There are also two other Pinakotheks in Munich: the Neue Pinakothek (currently closed for renovations) which focuses on 19th century artworks, and the Pinakothek der Moderne (p226) which houses contemporary art.

The Alte Pinakothek houses an art collection which was started when Wilhelm IV the Steadfast (ruled 1508–50) decided to adorn his residence with historic paintings. The Wittelsbach collection grew with acquisitions and commissions, and by the 18th century an outstanding collection of paintings had been amassed. King Ludwig I ordered the construction of a gallery to showcase the collection, and now visitors can enjoy works by Old Masters and exemplary paintings showing the evolution of European art styles from the Middle Ages to the late-Rococo period.

GALLERY GUIDE

On the ground floor, the East Wing showcases Early German paintings, as well as splendid German altar pieces from the regions of Swabia, Franconia, Old Bavaria and South Tyrol. The west wing is dedicated to various special exhibitions, while the first floor galleries contain works by Dutch, Flemish, French, German, Italian and Spanish artists.

Gallery Highlights

c 1455

▽ *Adoration of the Magi*, the centre panel of Rogier van der Weyden's stunning Saint Columba Altarpiece

1505–1506

▽ With its peaceful ambiance and calm figures, Raphael's *The Canigiani Holy Family* is a masterpiece of serenity

c 1450

△ *Saint Luke Drawing the Virgin*, by Rogier van der Weyden, also known as Roger de la Pasture

1478–1480

△ Also known as *Madonna with Child*, the *Virgin and Child* is one of Leonardo da Vinci's most famous paintings

Did You Know?
___

The museum hosts the second largest collection of Rubens paintings after the Prado Museum.

↑ *The Last Judgement* (c 1617), with other works by Rubens, and the museum's façade *(inset)*

1529

▽ The *Battle of Alexander at Issus*, by Albrecht Altdorfer, depicts Alexander the Great's battle with Persian King Darius III

1826

▽ The gallery itself is a beautiful Italian Renaissance building designed by Leo von Klenze and completed in 1836

1526

△ The *Four Apostles*, one of many works by German Renaissance master, Albrecht Dürer, on display at the Alte Pinakothek

1548

△ *Portrait* depicting Holy Roman Empreror Charles V (ruled 1519-56), by Lambert Sustris

② ⊘ 🍴 🖥

SCHLOSS NYMPHENBURG

📍 **A5** 🚇 **Rotkreuzplatz** 🚊 **12, 17** 🕐 **Apr–15 Oct: 9am–6pm daily; 16 Oct–Mar: 10am–4pm daily** 🌐 **schloss-nymphenburg.de**

Munich's impressive Nymphenburg Palace lies just north of the Altstadt. Built as a summer residence for the Wittelsbach in 1664, it offers a wealth of wonderful architecture, furnishings, gardens and museum collections.

One of Europe's most beautiful palaces, Schloss Nymphenburg grew up around an Italianate villa originally built for the Electress Henriette-Adelaide, to a design by Agostino Barelli. The palace was dedicated to the pastoral goddess Flora and her nymphs, hence its name. Several additions were made over the years, including four pavilions. These were designed by Joseph Effner and Enrico Zuccalli, who directed works from 1715. Built to the side of the original villa, they were connected by arcaded passageways. Within the building and grounds visitors can admire a range of architectural styles, from Baroque to Neo-Classical.

The Gallery of Beauties, where portraits of royal favourites are hung.

An ornate collection of carriages is housed in the former stables here, referred to as the Marstallmuseum.

→ The palace and its beautiful landscaped gardens

🏔 PICTURE PERFECT
Wildlife Watch

The palace's 198-ha (490-acre) park was initially Italian in design, but was transformed into a classical English landscape by Friedrich Ludwig von Sckell at the start of the 19th century. Alongside gushing waterfalls and spouting geysers, the park is also home to a range of wildlife; have your camera ready to capture rabbits, deer, swans and foxes.

The porcelain factory, which was transferred to Nymphenburg in 1761, is one of the oldest such factories in Europe.

Did You Know?

King Ludwig II (of Neuschwanstein fame) was born in the palace in 1845.

Amalienburg, a superb Rococo-style hunting lodge by François de Cuvilliés.

The striking façade of Schloss Nymphenburg's main building ↑

Magdalenenklause, a hermitage commissioned by Maximilian Emanuel in which to pray and meditate.

The Botanical Garden features many rare plants.

The original Italianate villa containing the Festsaal, a vast Rococo ballroom.

→
The Gallery of Beauties, in which hangs a series of female portraits

③ 🗺 Ⓜ 🍴 🖥 🏧

DEUTSCHES MUSEUM

📍D5 🚇Museumsinsel 1 🚉Isartor
Ⓤ Fraunhoferstr 🚌132 🚊17, 18
🕐9am–5pm daily (some exhibits
may be closed during renovations)
🌐deutsches-museum.de

Munich's German Museum is one of the oldest and most frequently visited science and technology museums in the world. It's also one of the largest – you could easily while away an entire day here.

Founded in 1903 by engineer Oskar von Miller the museum's exhibits cover the greatest technological achievements from the Stone Age to the present day. Visitors can see an astonishing variety of aircraft, vintage machinery, sailing ships and vehicles, and explore interactive exhibits on nanotechnology and robotics. Highlights include the first motor-propelled aircraft, constructed by the Wright brothers. The museum's collection is so vast that it spans three locations: Museum Island, the Flugwerft Schleissheim hangar (Ferdinand-Schulz-Allee) and the Verkehrszentrum (Am Bavariapark 5). Tickets for each site can be purchased separately, or there's a discounted combo ticket available too.

→

The Bicycle Wall, featuring cycles from the first generation of German "low bicycles"

MODERNIZING THE MUSEUM

Despite being open since 1925, the Deutsches Museum is currently undergoing its very first comprehensive overhaul, one that will make it one of the world's most modern science and technology museums. By 2021, some sections will be fully restored with new technology, while others will have a completely new design by 2028.

Must See

Kinderreich

▽ Young children (3–8 years) can learn about science and technology in fun, imaginative ways in Kid's Kingdom. Exhibits include a giant guitar, a Lego building site, and an electric light cinema.

Flugwerft Schleissheim

▽ This hangar, the site of one of Bavaria's first airfields, contains 70 historic aircraft. Workshops allow visitors to watch old planes being restored.

Verkehrszentrum

▽ Vintage car enthusiasts will find beautiful models to admire in the Road Transport section. The collection also includes impressive motorcycles, utility vehicles and a selection of antique bicycles.

↑ The 65-m- (213-ft-) high tower of the museum, soaring above the city

RESIDENZ

📍C3 🏛Residenzstrasse 1 Ⓤ Odeonsplatz 🕐 Apr-15 Oct: 9am-6pm daily;
16 Oct-Mar: 10am-5pm daily 🌐 residenz-muenchen.de

The largest city palace in Germany, this former residence of Bavarian kings has housed a museum since 1920. Today, it is one of the most eminent palace museums in Europe and its attractions include a beautiful Renaissance facade, a splendid banqueting hall and a range of gold and silver treasures.

The Munich Residenz was a centre of power in Bavaria from 1508 to 1918, when it was opened to the public as a significant interior decoration museum. Over the years, the sprawling complex, owned by the Wittelsbach dynasty, was gradually extended. Major work in the 17th century included new surroundings for the Brunnenhof (Fountain Court) and the construction of buildings around the imperial courtyard, Hofkapelle (Court Chapel) and Reiche Kapelle (Rich Chapel), while Königsbau and Festsaalbau were added in the first half of the 19th century. The Renaissance façade includes two magnificent portals and features a statue of the Holy Virgin as Patroness of Bavaria (Patrona Boiariae).

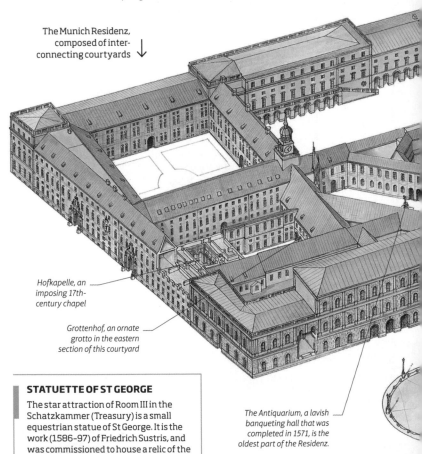

The Munich Residenz, composed of inter-connecting courtyards

Hofkapelle, an imposing 17th-century chapel

Grottenhof, an ornate grotto in the eastern section of this courtyard

The Antiquarium, a lavish banqueting hall that was completed in 1571, is the oldest part of the Residenz.

STATUETTE OF ST GEORGE

The star attraction of Room III in the Schatzkammer (Treasury) is a small equestrian statue of St George. It is the work (1586-97) of Friedrich Sustris, and was commissioned to house a relic of the saint. In the 17th century it was displayed in the Residenz on important feast days.

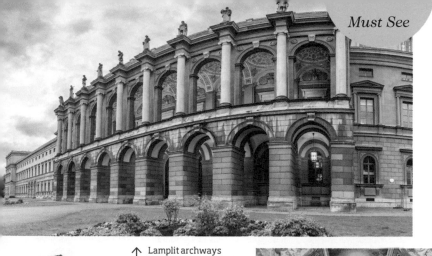

↑ Lamplit archways forming a curved wall of the Residenz

Cuvilliés-Theater, which opened in 1753, is considered to be Europe's finest surviving Rococo theatre.

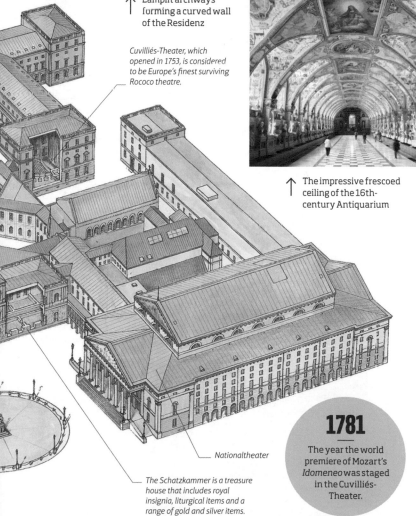

↑ The impressive frescoed ceiling of the 16th-century Antiquarium

Nationaltheater

The Schatzkammer is a treasure house that includes royal insignia, liturgical items and a range of gold and silver items.

1781

The year the world premiere of Mozart's *Idomeneo* was staged in the Cuvilliés-Theater.

EXPERIENCE MORE

 Dreifaltigkeitskirche

📍B3 🏠Pacellistrasse 6
🚋19 🕐7:30am-7pm daily

The Baroque church of the Holy Trinity is one of the few historic buildings in the city that avoided bomb damage in World War II. The church was built as a votive gift from the city's aristocracy and clergy in the hope of averting the dangers threatened by the War of the Spanish Succession (1702–14). The foundation stone was laid in 1711 and the church was consecrated seven years later. The royal architect, Giovanni Antonio Viscardi, assisted by Enrico Zucalli and Johann Georg Ettenhofer, created a building that is one of the most beautiful examples of Italian Baroque in Munich. The church's original features include the dome fresco by Cosmas Damian Asam, *The Adoration of the Trinity*.

⑥ Bürgersaal

📍B3 🏠Neuhauser Strasse 14 📞(089) 219 97 20
Ⓢ&Ⓤ Karlsplatz 🚋18, 19, 20, 21, 27 🕐Lower church hall: 8am-7pm daily; upper church hall: 10:30am-noon daily

This church belonging to the Marian congregation was designed by Giovanni Antonio Viscardi and built by Johann Georg Ettenhofer in 1709–10. (The Marian congregation, founded in 1563, is linked to the Jesuit order.)

The church was damaged during World War II, but still has some original frescoes. In the oratory is a figure of the *Guardian Angel* by Ignaz Günther (1770), a fine example of south-Bavarian Rococo. Rupert Mayer, parish priest during World War II and Munich's leading opponent of Nazism, is buried in the crypt.

 HIDDEN GEM
Auer Mühlbach

Escape the city hustle for this bucolic stream that runs through Au and Haidhausen. It creates attractive scenes as it flows through residential areas – Mondstrasse is even known as Klein Venedig (Little Venice).

⑦

Pinakothek der Moderne

📍B2 🏠Barer Strasse 40
Ⓤ Königsplatz 🚌53 🚋27
🕐10am-6pm Tue-Wed & Fri-Sun, 10am-8pm Thu
🌐pinakothek.de

Designed by German architect Stephan Braunfels and built in 1995–2002, this gallery complements the collections in the nearby Alte and Neue Pinakotheks, bringing the worlds of art, design, graphics, jewellery and architecture together under one roof.

The collections are laid out over three floors. The basement level is home to the outstanding International Design Museum (Die Neue Sammlung). The ground floor contains exhibition rooms for architecture and works on paper. A leading collection of painting, sculpture and new media is on the first floor.

Highlights include Cubist works by Picasso and Georges Braque, and paintings by Matisse, Giorgio De Chirico and Max Beckmann. Pop Art, Minimal Art and photorealism are also represented.

←

Façade of the Bürgersaal, a church designed by Giovanni Antonio Viscardi

↑ Exhibition at the Design
Museum of Pinakothek
der Moderne

⑧
Frauenkirche

📍 B3 🏠 Frauenplatz 1
📞 (089) 290 08 20
Ⓢ & Ⓤ Karlsplatz,
Marienplatz 🚋 19
🕐 8am–5pm Mon–Sat
(from 9:30am Sun)

The site of the Church of Our Lady was originally occupied by a Marian chapel, built in the 13th century. Some 200 years later, Prince Sigismund ordered a new, much bigger church to be built on the site. Its architects were Jörg von Halspach and Lukas Rottaler. The Frauenkirche was completed in 1488, though the distinctive copper oniondomes were not added to its towers until 1525. The church is one of southern Germany's biggest Gothic structures, which can accommodate a congregation of about 2,000.

A triple-nave hall with no transept features rows of side chapels, a gallery surrounding the choir and a monumental western tower. The whole huge structure measures over 100 m (330 ft) in length and almost 40 m (130 ft) wide.

The church treasures that escaped destruction during World War II include a Marian painting, dating from around 1500, by Jan Polak; the altar of St Andrew in St Sebastian's chapel, with statues by Meister von Rabenden and paintings by Polak, dating from 1510; and the monumental tomb of Emperor Ludwig IV of Bavaria, the work of Hans Krumpper (1619–22).

---

⑨
Jüdisches Zentrum Jakobsplatz

📍 B4 🏠 St Jakobsplatz 16
Ⓢ & Ⓤ Marienplatz 🕐 Jewish
Museum: 10am–6pm Tue–Sun 🌐 juedisches-museum-muenchen.de

The Jewish Museum, the Jewish Community Centre of Munich and Upper Bavaria, and the main synagogue, Ohel Jakob, together constitute a prestigious modern centre for Munich's Jewish community.

The museum is housed in a cube-shaped building. Three floors of exhibitions, plus a library and a learning centre, all provide extensive

↑ Ohel Jakob synagogue, part of the Jüdisches Zentrum Jakobsplatz

---

SHOP

servus.heimat
A life-saving store for anyone looking for Bavarian-themed gifts and souvenirs. Goods here range from the kitsch to the unique and customized, but they are always top quality.

📍 B4 🏠 Brunnstrasse 3
Ⓦ servusheimat.com

Maximilianstrasse
This long, glamorous street runs through the middle of the city and is lined either side with plush boutiques and luxury stores, often tucked away inside showy 19th-century buildings.

📍 C3
🏠 Maximilianstrasse

information on Jewish culture and history, and highlight important aspects of contemporary Jewish life. The synagogue is crowned by a light-flooded roof. The community centre contains the administrative department, the rabbinate and conference rooms, as well as a kindergarten, a public full-time school, a youth and arts centre and a kosher restaurant.

10 Münchner Stadtmuseum

📍 B4 🏛 St Jakobsplatz 1
Ⓢ & Ⓤ Marienplatz
Ⓤ Sendlinger Tor
🕐 10am–6pm Tue–Sun
🌐 muenchner-stadtmuseum.de

A few steps away from the Viktualienmarkt (p230), on St Jakobsplatz, stands the Münchner Stadtmuseum. Its rich collection has been housed since 1888 in the former arsenal building, which was built in 1491–96 by Lukas Rottaler. It is one of Munich's most fascinating museums,

with exhibits such as "Typisch München!" ("Typical Munich!") illustrating the everyday lives of the city's citizens from the Middle Ages to the present day.

Among the Stadtmuseum's greatest treasures are the famous ten *Morris Dancers* by Erasmus Grasser (1480), carved in lime wood and originally numbering 16.

Other displays include furniture (in styles ranging from Baroque to Art Deco), photographs, film and musical instruments. There is also the Puppet Theater/Fairground Attraction collection, which includes original puppets, and a variety of paintings and prints.

The museum regularly stages special exhibitions. A cinema, the Filmmuseum, puts on nightly showings of films in their original language with subtitles.

11 Asamkirche

📍 B4 🏛 Sendlinger Strasse 32 Ⓤ Sendlinger Tor
🚋 16, 17, 18, 27 🚌 52, 152
🕐 9am–6pm daily

Officially known as St Johann-Nepomuk, this gem of Rococo architecture stands in Sendlingerstrasse and is part of a complex built by the Asam brothers in the mid-18th century. In 1729–30, the sculptor and stuccoist Egid Quirin Asam acquired two properties that he intended to convert into a family home. He subsequently acquired a plot adjacent to these properties, where he wished to build a church devoted to the newly canonized St Nepomuk, a Bohemian monk who had drowned in the Vltava river in Prague. Above the entrance to the church is a statue of the saint.

At the same time, Cosmas Damian, his brother, bought a plot on which he built the presbytery. The church building adjoins the residential house of Egid Quirin. The two buildings were joined by a corridor and from one of his bedroom windows the artist could see the main altar.

In this small but unique church, the Asam brothers achieved a rare and striking unity of style. In the dimly lit interior, with its dynamically shaped single nave, no surface is left unembellished. The eye is drawn to the altar, which features a sculpted group of the Holy Trinity.

←

The richly decorated interior of the Rococo Asamkirche, dedicated to St Nepomuk

↑ Astronomical clock on the tower of Munich's Altes Rathaus

12

Altes Rathaus

 C3 ⌂ Marienplatz 15
Ⓢ & Ⓤ Marienplatz
🕐 To the public

Munich's old town hall stands in the eastern part of Marienplatz, immediately next to the new town hall. The original building, which has been remodelled several times, was built in 1470–75 by Jörg von Halspach, who also designed the Marian church.

The building's present Neo-Gothic look is the result of remodelling work carried out between 1877 and 1934, when the nearby ring road was being built.

The interior of the building, which was restored following World War II bomb damage, has a Dance Hall with a wooden cradle vault ceiling. It is adorned with an old frieze featuring 87 (originally 99) heraldic arms painted by Ulrich Füetrer in 1478, and a further seven carved by Erasmus Grasser in 1477. The figures standing by the walls are copies of the famous dancing Moors, whose originals by Erasmus Grasser (1480) are kept in the City

Museum. The lofty tower rising above the old city gate (Talbrucktor) was remade in 1975 based on pictures dating from 1493. Since 1983, the tower has housed the toy collection of the **Spielzeugmuseum**.

Spielzeugmuseum
♿ 🕿 (089) 29 40 01
🕐 10am–5:30pm daily

13

Viktualienmarkt

 C4 ⌂ Peterplatz-Frauenstrasse
Ⓢ & Ⓤ Marienplatz 🚌 52

Right at the heart of the city is the Viktualienmarkt, a large square that has been the city's main marketplace for more than 200 years. Apart from stalls selling vegetables and fruit brought in daily from suburban orchards and village gardens, the local beer garden provides a welcome retreat for a beer or snack.

One of the features of the square is a statue of Munich actor and comedian Karl Valentin (1882–1948), also commemorated in the nearby Valentin Karlstadt Musäum.

An impressive view over the market can be enjoyed from the tower of Peterskirche (St Peter's church), alongside the square.

14 🍴 🍹

Neues Rathaus

 C3 ⌂ Marienplatz 8
🕿 (089) 233 00
Ⓢ & Ⓤ Marienplatz 🕐 May–Oct: 10am–7pm daily; Nov–Apr: 10am–5pm Mon–Fri

The Neo-Gothic new town hall in Marienplatz was built by Georg Hauberrisser between 1867 and 1909. Its 100-m-(330-ft-) high façade is decorated with a fascinating set of

→ People enjoying a sunny day in the beer garden of the Viktualienmarkt

statues depicting Bavarian dukes, kings and electors, saints, mythical and allegorical figures as well as a variety of gargoyles inspired by medieval bestiaries.

The central façade features an 80-m- (260-ft-) high clock tower. Each day, at 11am, noon and 5pm in summer, and noon and 5pm in winter, the bells ring out a carillon, while mechanical knights fight a tournament and a crowd dances. The latter is a re-enactment of the first coopers' dance, which was held in 1517 to boost the morale of citizens when the town was beset by the plague. Other mechanical figures appear in the windows on the seventh floor in the evenings (9:30pm in summer, 7:30pm in winter). These are flanked by figures of the town guardsman carrying a lantern and the Guardian Angel blessing a Munich child, the "Münchner Kindl".

Visitors can climb the Neues Rathaus tower to a viewing gallery above the clock, offering great views over Marienplatz and even of the Alps on a clear day.

15

Museum Fünf Kontinente

📍 **D3** 🏛 **Maximilianstrasse 42** 🚊 **19** 🕐 **9:30am–5:30pm Tue-Sun** 🌐 **museum-fuenf-kontinente.de**

On the opposite side of the ring road from the Maximilianeum (the Upper Bavaria government building) is the Bavarian museum of ethnography. Built between 1858 and 1865 and designed by E Riedel, the façade is decorated with eight figures personifying the virtues of the Bavarian people: patriotism, diligence, magnanimity, piety, loyalty, justice, courage and wisdom.

Originally intended to house the Bavarian National Museum (now in Prinzregenten-strasse, *p234*), the building has been home to the ethnography museum since 1925. It is the second largest such museum in Germany after Berlin.

The origins of the museum's collection go back to 1782, when curios taken from the

↑ The Neues Rathaus in Marienplatz, with the Frauenkirche to the left

treasures of various Bavarian rulers were exhibited in a gallery in the gardens of the residence. Attention began to focus on ethnography after expansion of the collection in 1868. The museum currently houses some 300,000 exhibits ranging from religious artifacts to everyday items, allowing visitors to explore the art and culture of non-European nations, with a particular emphasis on China, Japan, South America and East and Central Africa. The collection is presented in a series of changing exhibitions.

Did You Know?

The Viktualienmarkt beer garden is the only place in Munich that serves beer from all the city's breweries.

16
Hofbräuhaus

📍 C3 🏛 Platzl 9
Ⓢ & Ⓤ Marienplatz
🕐 9am–midnight daily
🌐 hofbraeuhaus.de

The Hofbräuhaus is the most popular beer hall in Munich and a great tourist attraction. Established as a court brewery in 1589 by Wilhelm V, it was originally housed in Alter Hof, but moved to Platzl in 1654. In 1830 permission was granted to build an inn where beer could be sold to the public.

The Neo-Renaissance form of the building dates from 1896. The Schwemme, on the ground floor, is a large hall with painted ceiling and room for about 1,000 guests. The Festsaal, on the first floor, has a barrel-shaped vault and can accommodate 600 guests.

In a courtyard, surrounded by chestnut trees, is the beer garden, which is always very popular during the summer.

17
St Kajetan

📍 C3 🏛 Salvatorplatz 2a
Ⓢ & Ⓤ Marienplatz 🚋 19
🕐 7am–8pm daily
🌐 theatinerkirche.de

In Odeonsplatz, next to Feldherrnhalle, stands one of the most magnificent churches in the city, St Cajetan. When Henrietta Adelaide of Savoy presented the Elector Ferdinand with his long-awaited heir, Maximilian, the happy parents vowed to build an abbey in commemoration. The project was given to an Italian architect, Agostino Baralli, who based his design on the church of St Andrea della Valle, in Rome.

Although construction work on the church ended in 1690, the façade – designed by François de Cuvilliés – was

↓ The airy, frescoed Hofbräuhaus beer hall, and a decorative wooden panel (inset)

EAT

Wirtshaus in der Au
Waitresses at this inn wear Dirndl dresses. Try the spinach and beetroot dumplings.

📍 D5 🏛 Lilienstrasse 51
🌐 wirtshausinderau.de

Spatenhaus an der Oper
This elegant restaurant in the heart of Old Town offers traditional Bavarian dishes in a relaxed setting.

📍 C3 🏛 Residenzstrasse 12 🌐 kuffler.de

Trader Vic's
Creative Polynesian food and cocktails in the cellar-bar of the plush Hotel Bayerischer Hof.

📍 B3
🏛 Promenadenplatz 2-6
🌐 bayerischerhof.de

→ The steps of the Feldherrnhalle, with St Kajetan behind

not completed until 1765–8. The interior of the church is adorned with stuccos by Giovanni Antonio Viscardi and furnished in rich Baroque style. St Cajetan's twin towers and copper dome are dominant features on the Munich skyline.

 18

Feldherrnhalle

**C3 Odeonsplatz
Odeonsplatz 100
19 Daily**

Until 1817–18, the site of the monumental Field Marshals' House was occupied by a Gothic town gate. In the early 19th century, however, when Kings Maximilian I Joseph and Ludwig I decided to expand Munich northwards and westwards, their chief architect, Leo von Klenze, ordered the gate to be pulled down, as it stood in the way of the prestigious thoroughfare (Ludwigstrasse) that he intended to build.

HITLER AND THE FELDERRNHALLE

On the evening of 8 November 1923, Adolf Hitler announced the start of the "people's revolution" and ordered the takeover of the central districts of Munich. The following day, a march of some 2,000 people acting on his orders was stopped by a police cordon outside the Feldherrnhalle. The marchers were dispersed, and Hitler managed to flee but was later arrested.

Built in 1841–4, the Feldherrnhalle was designed by Friedrich von Gärtner, who modelled it on the Loggia dei Lanzi in Florence. Intended as a monument to the heroes of Bavaria, the interior contains statues of two great military leaders, Johann Tilly and Karl Philipp von Wrede, by Ludwig Schwanthaler.

The central carved composition devoted to the heroes of the 1870–71 Franco-Prussian War is newer, dating from 1882. It was designed by Ferdinand von Miller.

In 1923 the Feldherrnhalle was the scene of Hitler's unsuccessful "Beer-Hall Putsch", after which he was arrested. This resulted in the loggia acquiring a certain cult status in Nazi propaganda.

 19

Haus der Kunst

D2 Prinzregenten-strasse 1 100 10am–8pm Fri-Wed, 10am–10pm Thu hausderkunst.de

Erected between 1933 and 1937, the Neo-Classical House of Art is the work of a Nazi architect, Paul Ludwig Troost. It opened its doors in 1937 with a display of propaganda art, which was proclaimed by the

Nazis as "truly German". Since 1945 the building has become a dynamic centre of modern art that is noted for its temporary exhibitions. Its central hall, the former Ehrenhalle (Hall of Honour) – which was subdivided into smaller spaces – was reopened in stages, each one accompanied by a special exhibition.

In 2006 the hall once again became the centre of the building and is used as a space for events and temporary installations. In the foyer is a permanent exhibition documenting the history of the building. The museum's Golden Bar serves as a daytime café with a rotating menu.

↑ A colourful modern art exhibit at Haus Der Kunst

20

Bayerisches Nationalmuseum

📍 D3 🏛 Prinzregenten-strasse 3 🚌 100 🚊 17 🕐 10am–5pm Tue–Wed & Fri–Sun, 10am–8pm Thu 🌐 bayerisches-nationalmuseum.de

The Bavarian National Museum was founded in 1855 by King Maximilian II. Between 1894 and 1900 it acquired a new building in Prinzregentenstrasse,

designed by Gabriel von Seidel; this building alone is worth a closer look. The complex structure consists of wings representing various architectural styles, while the ground floor features halls that are built in styles that are appropriate to their exhibits. This means that the visitor can see Romanesque and Gothic art displayed in fitting Neo-Romanesque and Neo-Gothic rooms, Renaissance art in Neo-Renaissance rooms. The individual rooms have been arranged in subject groups, with paintings and sculptures supplemented by superb collections of decorative art and everyday objects, including furniture. The exhibits include a beautiful sculpture of Mary Magdalene by Tilman Riemenschneider.

The first-floor collections are arranged thematically and include German porcelain,

Delicate Meissen porcelain in the Bayerisches Nationalmuseum

clocks, ivory carvings, textiles and gold items. Particularly interesting is a collection of small oil sketches, painted by artists when designing some large-scale compositions, such as an altar or a ceiling painting.

A special annexe houses the Bollert Collection, which contains sculptures from the late-Gothic period.

21 🎨

Sammlung Schack

📍 E3 🏛 Prinzregenten-strasse 9 🚌 100 🚊 17 🕐 10am–6pm Wed–Sun (1st & 3rd Wed of month: to 8pm) 🌐 pinakothek.de

The German paintings on display in the Schack Gallery come from the private collection of Adolf Friedrich von Schack, a 19th-century German poet. They are housed in this elegant museum, built in 1907 by Max Littmann for use by the Prussian Legation.

As Schack's main interest was in 19th-century painting, the collection features works that represent the Romantic period, including Leo von Klenze and Carl Spitzweg, as well as witty, fairytale works by Moritz von Schwind. Particularly notable are his *Morning*, *In the Woods* and *Rübezahl* – in which the mythical Guardian of the Riesengebirge Mountains wanders through an enchanted forest. Late-19th-century painters are represented by Franz von Lenbach, Anselm Feuerbach and, above all, by Arnold Bocklin. Bocklin's Romantic works, which are full of symbolism, include *Villa on the Coast* and *Man Scaring a Deer*. The gallery has a large collection of landscapes, including Italian scenes by German masters, and a valuable collection of paintings on historic themes.

Archäologische Staatssammlung

 E2 Lerchenfeld-strasse 2 100 17
 For restoration until 2023
 archaeologie-bayern.de

Immediately adjacent to the Bavarian National Museum is the Prehistory Museum, which was founded in 1885 by King Ludwig II. Since 1976 this spacious building has housed a rich collection of artifacts from various parts of Bavaria. The oldest items in the collection date from the Palaeolithic era, while later exhibits illustrate the region's early history. The collection includes Bronze Age, Roman and early medieval treasures.

→

The tall twin bell towers of the 19th-century Ludwigskirche

Bayerische Staatsbibliothek

 C2 Ludwigstrasse 16
 Odeonsplatz, Universität
 Times vary; check website
 bsb-muenchen.de

The monumental Bavarian State Library was designed by Friedrich von Gärtner, who took over from Leo von Klenze as the architect on the prestigious Ludwigstrasse project, commissioned by King Ludwig I. Gärtner was also responsible for the Feldherrnhalle, Siegestor, St Ludwig's Church and the university building.

This massive structure, in a style reminiscent of the Italian Renaissance, was erected between 1832 and 1843. Its external staircase is adorned with the seated figures of Thucydides, Hippocrates, Homer and Aristotle. Equally impressive are the stairs leading to the main rooms, which are modelled on the Scala dei Gianti of the Doge's Palace in Venice. With its collection of 34 million media units, the library is one of the biggest in Germany.

Ludwigskirche

 C2 Ludwigstrasse 20
 Universität 8am–8pm daily (to 8:45pm Tue, to 7pm Sat)

Inspired by the Romanesque churches of Lombardy, Friedrich von Gärtner built the vast St Ludwig's church between 1829 and 1844.

The interior has magnificent frescoes designed by the main exponent of the Nazarene style, Peter von Cornelius, and painted by his associates. Von Cornelius himself painted the massive choir fresco, *The Last Judgement*, which rivals in size Michelangelo's *Last Judgement*.

25

Museum Brandhorst

B2 **Theresienstrasse 35a** **Köningsplatz** 100, 154 27 10am-6pm Tue-Sun (to 8pm Thu) **museum-brandhorst.de**

Set in a striking building, this museum houses the Udo and Anette Brandhorst collection. It has over 700 modern and contemporary artworks, including the largest collection of works by Andy Warhol in Europe. It also focuses on Cy Twombly's oeuvre; his "Lepanto" cycle (2001) is on permanent display here. Other artists represented include Joseph Beuys, Damien Hirst, Jean-Michel Basquiat, Sigmar Polke and Mike Kelley.

26

Michaelskirche

B3 **Neuhauser Strasse 6** & **Karlsplatz** 18, 19, 20, 21, 27 10am-7pm Mon & Fri; 8am-8:15pm Tue; 8am-7pm Wed, Thu & Sat; 7am-10:15pm Sun

The monumental St Michael's church was built by Duke

4,000

The amount of steel in tons it took to build BMW Welt.

Wilhelm V for the Jesuits who arrived here in 1559. The foundation stone was laid in 1585 and initial building work on the first church, which was smaller than the present one, commenced in 1588. However, the tower in front of the presbytery collapsed, demolishing a large part of the building. A transept and new presbytery were added to the remaining part of the building and the church – which was the first Jesuit church in northern Europe – was consecrated in 1597.

The interior of the Michaelskirche is awe-inspiring, with its wide, well-proportioned nave, three pairs of shallow chapels on either side, a short transept and an elongated presbytery.

It is not certain who was the architect of the project, but it is believed that Wolfgang Müller created the main body of the church and Wendel Dietrich the Mannerist façade. Later extensions are thought to be the work of a Dutch architect, Friedrich Sustris.

However, the main highlight of the church lurks in the **crypt**, which is open to the public and holds the tombs of many members of the Wittelsbach dynasty, including King Ludwig II.

Crypt

9:30am-4:30pm Mon-Fri, 9:30am-2:30pm Sat & Sun

27

NS-Dokumentations-szentrum

B2 **Max-Mannheimer-Platz 1** **Königsplatz** 10am-7pm Tue-Sun **ns-dokumentation szentrum-muenchen.de**

The NS–Documentation Centre for the History of National Socialism, in a six-storey white cube, is a prominent reminder of Munich's role in the rise

The striking, stark exterior of Museum Brandhorst

of Nazi ideology. Built on the site of the so-called Braunes Haus (Brown House), the former party headquarters of the Nazi Party, the centre has excellent permanent and temporary exhibitions, a learning centre and an educational programme.

28

BMW Museum and Welt

Q A5 **Ⓐ** Am Olympiapark 1 & 2 **Ⓞ** Times vary; check website **Ⓦ** bmw-welt.com

This vast ensemble, close to the city's Olympiapark, houses three different areas that chart the history and development of auto-industry giant BMW, showcasing some of the company's most successful designs and demonstrating how its cars are put together.

The curvaceous, silver-grey main museum, designed by Viennese architect Karl Schwanzer in the 1970s, highlights the company's founding and its progress through the decades. The BMW World showroom, which can be visited independently and free of charge, has more than 100 examples of not just BMWs but associated vehicles like Minis and Rolls-Royces, plus concept cars, motorbikes and a vast vending machine

that potential owners can use to help choose their cars. The BMW Group Plant provides insights into how these elegant vehicles are manufactured. There are also a couple of shops selling BMW related products.

29

Propyläen

Q A2 **Ⓐ** Königsplatz **Ⓤ** Königsplatz

Derived from the Propylaea (gateway) to the Athenian Acropolis, this magnificent Neo-Classical structure stands at the end of Brienner Strasse and is visible from as far as Karolinenplatz. Built by Leo von Klenze in 1846–62, its austere form, featuring Doric porticos, provides an excellent final touch to the composition of Königsplatz by linking together the National Collection of Antiquities and the Glyptotheca.

The Propyläen is also a symbolic gateway to the new parts of the city. It was funded by the private foundation of King Ludwig I, although built after his abdication.

The carved decorations by Ludwig Michael Schwanthaler depict scenes from the Greek War of Liberation against Turkey (1821–9), led by King Otto I, son of Ludwig I.

↑ Children studying the design of a car at the BMW Museum

30

Staatliche Antikensammlungen

Q A2 **Ⓐ** Königsplatz 1 **Ⓤ** Königsplatz **Ⓞ** For renovation until 2021 **Ⓦ** antike-am-koenigsplatz. mwn.de

The National Collection of Antiquities is housed in a building on the south side of the Königsplatz, designed by Georg Friedrich Ziebland. In addition to one of the world's finest collections of antique vases, there are many other masterpieces of Greek, Roman and Etruscan ornamental art, jewellery and small statues. Among the famous exhibits is a golden Greek necklace from the 4th century BC.

> 💬 INSIDER TIP
> **Museenlinie Bus 100**
>
> The most useful bus for visitors, the 100 bus route runs from the Ostbahnhof to the Hauptbahnhof via many of Munich's major museums and galleries.

fireworks displays and regular open-air rock and pop concerts in the summer months. Next to the park are the BMW Museum and BMW Welt, one of the city's top attractions (*p237*).

Englischer Garten

Q D2 **U** Giselastrasse
🚌 54

The idea of creating this garden, which would be open to all the inhabitants of Munich and not only to its aristocracy, came from Count von Rumford, an American-born chemist and physicist who lived in Bavaria from 1784. As the region's Minister of War, he was responsible for reorganizing the Bavarian army. His idea of creating a garden of this size – covering an area of 5 sq km (2 sq miles) – right in the centre of a large city, was quite unique in Germany. In 1789, taking advantage of his influential position, he persuaded Karl Theodor to put his plans into action.

The project leader was German landscape gardener Friedrich Ludwig von Sckell. He was brought to Munich from Schwetzingen by the elector to create the garden on an area of former marshland. Opened in 1808, the Karl-Theodor-Park is today known simply as the Englischer Garten (English Garden). It is a popular place for long walks, jogging or just lying on the grass in the cool shade of a spreading old tree.

Lenbachhaus

Q A2 **O** Luisenstrasse 33
U Königsplatz
W lenbachhaus.de

This Italian-style villa was built between 1887 and 1891 by Gabriel von Seidl for painter Franz von Lenbach.

Since 1929, it has housed the Municipal Art Gallery. As well as masterpieces such as *Portrait of a Man* by Jan Polak (around 1500), it also boasts the world's biggest collection of works by Der Blaue Reiter (The Blue Rider) artists. Kandinsky was a leading proponent of this movement.

The **Kunstbau**, part of Lenbachhaus, is in a subway station under Königsplatz and holds temporary exhibitions.

Kunstbau
🕐 10am–6pm Tue–Sun (to 8pm Tue)

Olympiapark

Q A5 **U** Olympiazentrum
🚌 173 **🚃** 20, 21
W olympiapark.de

Built for the 1972 Olympic Games, this vast sports

↑ The colourful interior of the Lenbachhaus, built in the late 19th century

stadium has become a Munich landmark, as it is the location of a 290-m- (950-ft-) high television tower, the Olympiaturm. At the top of the tower there is a viewing platform (open 9am–midnight daily) with amazing views and a restaurant.

The stadium has three main facilities: the Olympic Stadium, which seats 62,000 spectators; the Olympic Hall; and the Swimming Hall. In what is one of the most original constructions of 20th-century German architecture, all three are covered by a vast transparent canopy, stretched between a series of tall masts to form an irregular tent.

The stadium includes many other facilities, such as an indoor skating rink, a cycle racing track and tennis courts. The sports complex is located beside the park's artificial lake.

Apart from sporting events, the Olympiapark hosts many popular events, including

There are some interesting old buildings in the park, such as the Monopteros, a Neo-Classical temple by Leo von Klenze (1837), and the Chinese Tower (1789–90), which is similar to the pagoda in London's Kew Gardens. The Tower stands in one of the park's beer gardens.

It is worth trying to time your visit to allow you to see the Japanese Teahouse, where the gentle art of tea brewing is demonstrated. It is open just one weekend each month.

Bavaria-Filmstadt

 B5 Bavariafilmplatz 7 25 Times vary; check website filmstadt.de

Commonly nicknamed "Hollywood on the Isar", this vast site covers an area of over 3.5 sq km (1.4 sq miles). Since 1919 the world's greatest cinema stars have worked here, including Orson Welles and Billy Wilder. The British film director Alfred Hitchcock

made his first films here (*The Pleasure Garden*, 1925 and *The Mountain Eagle*, 1926). Elizabeth Taylor, Gina Lollobrigida and Romy Schneider have all stood in front of the cameras here.

Visitors to the site will come across some well-known characters who have appeared in films such as *E.T.* or *The NeverEnding Story*, which were filmed here. The sets of other films made here – including *Enemy Mine* and *Cabaret* – can be seen, and you can also peep into the submarine that was reconstructed for Wolfgang Petersen's classic film *Das Boot* (1981), which follows the voyage of a submarine during World War II. The Bullyversum (named after "Bully" Herbig, a German comedian, actor and director) is an interactive 3D adventure.

VIP tours of the Filmstadt include fascinating demonstrations of many technical filmmaking tricks and techniques. A special attraction is the cinema called Showscan, whose seats move according to the story on the screen, giving visitors the sensation of a trip through the universe or of flying through the tunnels of an old silver mine.

STAY

Motel One München Sendlinger Tor

This reliable budget chain offers value rooms with bright features. There is also a great café-bar and lounge on site.

B4 Herzog-Wilhelm-Strasse 28 motel-one.com

Cortiina

Just a five-minute walk from Marienplatz, this elegant hotel has individually decorated rooms, a swish cocktail bar and a restaurant.

C4 Ledererstrasse 8 cortiina.com

Vier Jahreszeiten

A prestigious hotel with boutique style rooms and a range of five-star facilities, as well as a lounge and sauna.

C3 Maximilianstrasse 17 kempinski.com

← The Olympiapark grounds, with the iconic television tower

A SHORT WALK
AROUND MARIENPLATZ

Distance 1 km (0.5 miles) **Time** 15 minutes
Nearest U-Bahn station Karlsplatz

Strolling around Marienplatz is a great way to get a sense of its medieval layout. The square was once the city's salt- and corn-market. The origins of Munich itself lie with a handful of monks who built their abbey here, giving the place its name (from the word for 'monks'). In 1175 town status was officially bestowed on Munich and in 1180 the town was allocated to the Wittelsbachs, who soon established a residence here. During the Reformation, Munich became a bastion of Catholicism and an important centre of the Counter-Reformation. Its magnificent churches, Altes Rathaus (Old Town Hall) and the Residenz all bear witness to that era.

*Known as the **Karlstor** (Karl's Gate), the west entrance to the old town was part of the medieval fortifications. It was given its present name in 1791, in honour of Elector Karl Theodore.*

KARLS PLATZ

START

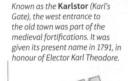
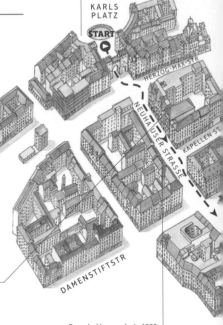

HERZOG-MAX-STR
NEUHAUSER STRASSE
KAPELLEN ST
DAMENSTIFTSTR

Bürgersaal (p226) was built in 1710 for a Marian congregation (followers of the Virgin Mary) as a place of meeting and worship. It includes an upper and lower church. Rupert Mayer, an opponent of Nazism, is buried in the crypt. He was beatified in 1987.

*Founded by monks in 1328, **Augustiner-Bräu** is the oldest and most celebrated brewery in Munich. It currently occupies two 19th-century houses with picturesque façades. Augustiner's tent and tower are one of the most popular traditions of Oktoberfest (p216).*

Did You Know?
Augustiner-Bräu's most popular beer is a pale lager called Augustiner Helles.

 Bürgersaal's Upper Church designed by Giovanni Antonio Viscardi

↑ Visitors gathering to see the mechnical dolls dance on the Neues Rathaus's clock tower

Locator Map
For more detail see p210

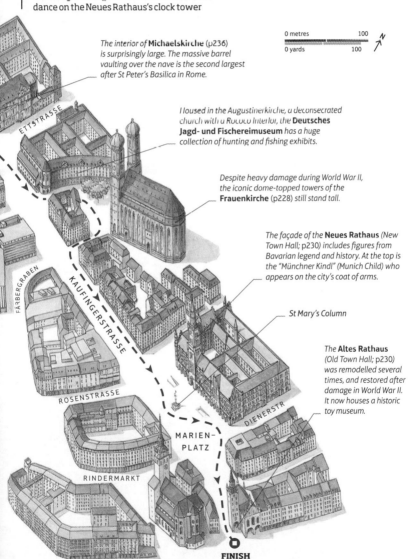

The interior of **Michaelskirche** *(p236) is surprisingly large. The massive barrel vaulting over the nave is the second largest after St Peter's Basilica in Rome.*

0 metres	100
0 yards	100

Housed in the Augustinerkirche, a deconsecrated church with a Rococo interior, the **Deutsches Jagd- und Fischereimuseum** *has a huge collection of hunting and fishing exhibits.*

Despite heavy damage during World War II, the iconic dome-topped towers of the **Frauenkirche** *(p228) still stand tall.*

The façade of the **Neues Rathaus** *(New Town Hall; p230) includes figures from Bavarian legend and history. At the top is the "Münchner Kindl" (Munich Child) who appears on the city's coat of arms.*

St Mary's Column

The **Altes Rathaus** *(Old Town Hall; p230) was remodelled several times, and restored after damage in World War II. It now houses a historic toy museum.*

ETTSTRASSE

FÄRBERGRABEN

KAUFINGERSTRASSE

ROSENSTRASSE

DIENERSTR

MARIEN-PLATZ

RINDERMARKT

FINISH

Canoeing on the Eibsee at the base of the Zugspitze

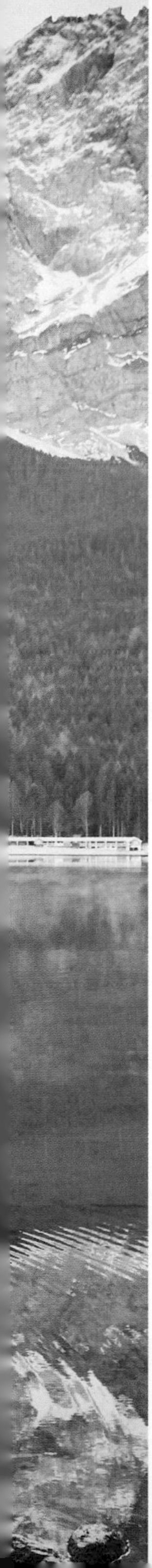

BAVARIA

During the 16th and 17th centuries the duchy of Bavaria was the bulwark of Roman Catholicism within the Holy Roman Empire and, during the reign of Maximilian I, Bavaria fought against the Protestant Union in the Thirty Years' War (1618–48). Following the fall of the Holy Roman Empire, Bavaria became a kingdom and remained as such until 1918.

Bavaria's turbulent history has left behind a rich architectural and cultural legacy, spanning some 100,000 architectural monuments, over a thousand museums and art collections and world-famous castles like Neuschwanstein. In addition to Roman antiquities, Baroque fortresses and fairytale castles, the region also has more than its share of glorious Alpine scenery, beer halls and colourful festivals, all of which make this one of the most popular parts of Germany for tourists.

BAVARIA

Must Sees

1 Bamberg
2 Nürnberg (Nuremberg)
3 Berchtesgadener Land
4 Würzburg
5 Rothenburg ob der Tauber
6 Schloss Neuschwanstein

Experience More

7 Hohenschwangau
8 Oberstdorf
9 Füssen
10 Kempten
11 Aschaffenburg
12 Pommersfelden
13 Coburg
14 Wallhalla
15 Vierzehnheiligen
16 Fränkische Schweiz
17 Straubing
18 Dachau
19 Schleissheim
20 Fünfseenland
21 Ingolstadt
22 Landshut
23 Neuburg an der Donau
24 Freising
25 Andechs
26 Landsberg am Lech
27 Altötting
28 Burghausen
29 Garmisch-Partenkirchen
30 Oberammergau
31 Ottobeuren
32 Bayreuth
33 Regensburg
34 Lindau
35 Augsburg
36 Schloss Linderhof
37 Passau
38 Chiemsee

7 DAYS
In Bavaria

Day 1

Morning Arrive in Oberammergau and enjoy a breakfast of regional food at Ammergauer Maxbräu *(Ettaler Strasse 5)*.

Afternoon Take a bus ride to Ludwig II's Schloss Neuschwanstein *(p266)*, the iconic embodiment of fairytale Germany.

Evening Return to Oberammergau and settle in for traditional German cuisine at the rustic Zauberstub'n *(Ettaler Strasse 58)*.

Day 2

Morning Take the train to Garmisch-Partenkirchen *(p278)* and explore the town's Alte Pfarrkirche St Martin, which features some well-preserved Gothic wall paintings and net vaulting.

Afternoon Grab lunch at Gasthof Fraundorfer *(Ludwigstrasse 24)*, which offers regional food as well as occasional yodeling performances, before taking the cable car to Germany's highest peak, the Zugspitze.

Evening Return to Garmisch-Partenkirchen and tuck into traditional Italian pizza at La Toscana *(Sonnenstrasse 3)*.

Day 3

Morning Eat a filling breakfast before catching the fast train to your next stop, Berchtesgaden *(p258)*, a journey of just under five hours.

Afternoon Visit the beautiful Schloss Berchtesgaden to admire the stunning architecture and collection of artistic treasures there.

Evening Take a trip up to the Kehlsteinhaus *(p259)* – Hitler's former mountain-top base – where you'll find a restaurant with stellar views.

Day 4

Morning Enjoy a boat trip on the Königsee *(p259)* to take pictures of the scenic and photogenic Sankt Bartholomä church.

Afternoon On returning from the lake, head to Sophie's Café *(Maximilianstrasse 9)* for a casual lunch, then take a leisurely hike through the Zauberwald.

Evening Head to Gasthaus Grafihöhe Windbeutel *(Scharitzkehlstrasse 8)* for Alpine cuisine and memorable views.

1. Schloss Neuschwanstein.
2. German National Museum.
3. Christmas market in Nürnberg.
4. Sunset in Passau.
5. Zugspitze Cable Car.
6. St Stephen's Cathedral, Passau.

Day 5

Morning After breakfast, take the scenic four-hour train journey to Passau (p285).

Afternoon Hop on a cruise to the spa town of Bad Füssing, home to Europe's biggest spa world.

Evening Take an evening stroll to admire the architecture around Passau's historic centre before hitting Café Museum (Bräugasse 17) for dinner and jazz.

Day 6

Morning Breakfast at Mr. Crêpes (Unterer Sand 7) before hopping on the train and enjoying the views en route to Nürnberg (p254).

Afternoon Get a panoramic overview of the city from the top of the 12th-century Sinwellturm. Then visit the Albrecht-Dürer-Haus (p255), where the renowned artist and engraver lived from 1509 until his death in 1528.

Evening Dine at Weinstuben Heilig-Geist-Spital (Spitalgasse 16), which offers traditional German cuisine and a scenic riverside location.

Day 7

Morning Head to Nürnberg's main square to see the Schöner Brunnen fountain in Hauptmarkt (p257), a replica of the 14th-century original but outstanding just the same – as are the Gothic Frauenkirche and the Rathaus (p256). For a late breakfast, try some Bratwürste, ordered as three in a bun ("Drei im Weckla") from the square's food stalls.

Afternoon Stroll through Nürnberg's old town, which is home to the impressive 14th-century Marthakirche, the Frauentor (p254) and St Lorenz-Kirche. Grab a coffee on Lorenzer Platz (p254) and watch the locals go about their business and then get an overview of German art and culture at the Germanisches Nationalmuseum (p256).

Evening Take a break from German food with a thin-crust pizza at Padelle d'Italia (Theatergasse 17). Afterwards, enjoy a performance at the Staatstheater Nürnberg (www.staatstheater-nuernberg.de), which hosts operas, concerts and plays, or catch some cabaret at the Loni-Übler-Haus (Marthastrasse 60).

Lakeside Delights

Germany is dotted with beautiful lakes, and Bavaria is no exception. Chiemsee *(p285)* is the largest lake in the region and is often referred to as the "Bavarian sea". Boasting 64 km (40 miles) of shoreline, it offers the obvious watersports and lake cruises as well as a string of lakeside towns and villages, and car-free islands, some of which are entirely uninhabited. Take a boat tour to see the lake at its best.

← Cruising across the serene waters of the Chiemsee

BAVARIA FOR
NATURAL
WONDERS

Verdant valleys, snow-capped Alpine peaks, ancient woodlands and sparkling lakes, the region of Bavaria is a feast for the eyes wherever you look. Make your way to this stunning area of Germany for spectacular scenes and an abundance of activities.

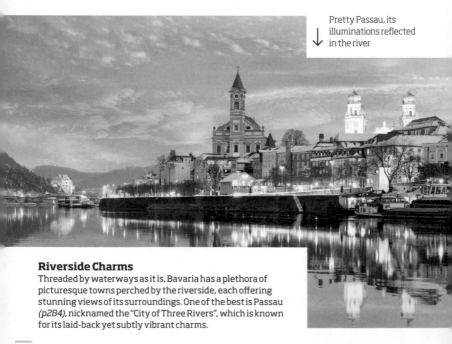

↓ Pretty Passau, its illuminations reflected in the river

Riverside Charms

Threaded by waterways as it is, Bavaria has a plethora of picturesque towns perched by the riverside, each offering stunning views of its surroundings. One of the best is Passau *(p284)*, nicknamed the "City of Three Rivers", which is known for its laid-back yet subtly vibrant charms.

Alpine Adventures

Stretching from Bavaria's southeastern corner to the Allgäu region, and nestled on the Austrian border, the Bavarian Alps are an impressive natural highlight. The rocky peaks not only make for fabulous photography, but also offer world-class hiking, climbing and skiing possibilities.

←

Out on a hike in the superlative Bavarian Alps

KING LUDWIG PATH

This scenic 120-km (75-mile) hike through impressive Alpine terrain to the Allgäu region is rewarded by soaring views of the fairytale Schloss Neuschwanstein *(p266)* as well as epic scenery.

Wonderful Wald

The Bavarian Forest (Bayerischer Wald) is the oldest National Park in Germany and offers an array of recreational opportunities. While not the largest forest in the land, it is particularly scenic, with a mix of ancient woodlands, majestic peaks and one of the longest treetop trails in the world, the 44-m (144-ft) "Baumei".

→

The Bayerischer Wald and a footbridge through it *(inset)*

A City Palace

Built with impressive speed, Residenz Würzburg *(p262)* was inspired by a mix of architectural styles from Italian Baroque to French Château, making for a fascinating ensemble of Western architecture. The building's interior was brought to life via artists such as famed fresco painter Giovanni Battista Tiepolo.

→

The ornate façade of Residenz Würzburg, in the city of Würzburg

BAVARIA FOR
CAPTIVATING CASTLES

With its spectacular landscapes and centres of culture, it's no surprise that royalty built some of their greatest castles in Bavaria. From enchanting fairytale towers to ornate city palaces, here we round up some of the region's highlights.

Fit for a Fairytale

Perhaps one of the most famous castles in the world, Schloss Neuschwanstein *(p266)* enjoys a dramatically scenic setting. Built for King Ludwig II in 1869–86 in the 13th-century Romanesque style, some of its interior murals are based on themes from Wagner's operas such as "Tannhäuser" and "Lohengrin".

GRAND DESIGNS

One of the principal motivations for King Ludwg II to build his fairytale palace was to restore a sense of royal privilege after losing his sovereign power to the Prussian Empire. The castle was intended as a place where he could escape and feel like a king despite the political reality of his situation.

As if from the pages of a fairytale: Schloss Neuschwanstein

Glorious Gardens

The only palace Ludwig II actually completed in his lifetime, Schloss Linderhof *(p285)* is influenced by French architecture (18th-century summer palaces, specifically) and blends a Baroque façade with a Rococo interior that nods to the Louis XV-era in France. The rooms show workmanship of an incomparable artistic quality and the showpiece gardens combine English landscape aesthetics with Renaissance and Baroque elements.

→

Schloss Linderhof, surrounded by beautiful green gardens

Typical Turrets

Schloss Hohenschwangau *(p268)* looks as if it has jumped straight out a picturebook. Flanked by angular towers, it was rebuilt in the Gothic style in the 19th century and used as a summer and hunting residence by royalty. The castle grants stunning views from every corner.

←

Schloss Hohenschwangau, with its corner turrets

A Medieval Masterpiece

One of the most intact medieval castles in Europe, Burghausen *(p278)* dates back to 1025. Its fascinating history includes thwarting invasion by the Turkish Ottoman Empire in the 15th and 16th centuries, and playing a role in the Thirty Years' War. The main Gothic structure has a chapel, several museums and even some modern apartments.

→

The Gothic Burghausen, perched on a ridge above town

↑ Bamberg's splendid Altes Rathaus on the River Regnitz

❶

BAMBERG

🅐 D5 ✈ Nürnberg, 60 km (37 miles) south of town
ℹ Geyerswörthstrasse 5; www.bamberg.info

A UNESCO World Heritage site since 1993, Bamberg is situated on seven hills like ancient Rome and features a splendidly preserved medieval old town, encircled by the branches of the River Regnitz. The town is known for its excellent beer, produced by the nine breweries that operate here.

①

Dom

🅐 Domplatz 5 🕐 Times vary, check website
🆆 bamberger-dom.de

Bamberg's skyline is dominated by the cathedral of St Peter and St George, a mix of late Romanesque and early French-Gothic styles. It was founded in 1004 and consecrated in 1012, and again in 1237 after being demolished by fire and subsequently rebuilt. This is a triple-nave basilica with two choirs, whose apses are flanked by two pairs of towers. The cloisters were built between 1399 and 1457, while the monumental sculptures adorning the portals date from the 13th century.

The western choir holds the only papal grave in Germany, that of Pope Clement II, who had been the local bishop.

②

World Heritage Visitor Centre

🅐 Untere Mühlbrücke 5 🕐 Apr-Oct: 10am-6pm daily; Nov-Mar: 11am-6pm daily 🆆 welterbe.bamberg.de

Spanning around 220 sq m (2,368 sq ft) of space, this exhibition is dedicated to explaining the city's UNESCO World Heritage status. In addition to model buildings that illustrate medieval and Baroque architecture, visitors can find audio stations, films and an interactive model of the old town of Bamberg.

③

Alte Hofhaltung Historisches Museum

🅐 Domplatz 7 🕐 May-Oct: 10am-5pm Tue-Sun
🆆 museum.bamberg.de

On the west side of Domplatz stands a magnificent portal, graced with statues of the imperial couple Heinrich II and Kunigunde. This is the gate to the former bishop's residence, built on the site of the former palace of emperor Heinrich II. Within the building's wings is a pleasant courtyard. Inside is an engaging museum that focuses on the history of the region, using fascinating paintings and artifacts.

④

Wasserschloss Concordia

🅐 Concordiastrasse 🕐 To the public

This magnificent Baroque palace, which enjoys a scenic position on the water's edge, was built for Counsellor

Böttinger between 1716 and 1722 to a design by Johann Dientzenhofer. The building now houses an art institute.

---

⑤
Altes Rathaus

The Baroque lower bridge, Untere Brücke, provides a magnificent view over the upper bridge, Obere Brücke, with its fabulous town hall. This originally Gothic seat of the municipal authorities was remodelled in 1744–56 by Jakob Michael Küchel. The half-timbered structure of the Rottmeisterhaus, which seems to be gliding over the waves of the River Regnitz, was added in 1688.

---

⑥
Klein-Venedig

"Little Venice" is a district of fishermen's cottages, their

picturesque façades adorned with pots of geraniums. Visitors come here for a glass of *Rauchbier* – a local beer with a smoky flavour – while they enjoy the view.

---

⑦
Neue Residenz und Staatsgalerie

🏠 **Domplatz 8** 🕐 **Apr–Sep: 9am–6pm daily; Oct–Mar: 10am–4pm daily** 🌐 **schloesser-bayern.de**

The New Residence, of the Bamberg prince-bishops, with its richly decorated apartments and the Imperial Hall, was built between 1695 and 1704 and is the work of Johann Leonhard Dientzenhofer. Its walls are adorned with magnificent tapestries and frescoes painted by the Tyrolean artist Melchior Steidl. The walls and pillars of the Imperial Hall feature the Habsburg family tree, while 16 statues represent Emperors of the Holy Roman

Empire. The palace houses a collection of old German masters, including *The Flood* by Hans Baldung Grien and three fine canvases by Lucas Cranach the Elder.

---

⑧
Grüner Markt

With its historic houses and adjacent Maximilianplatz, the Green Market lies at the heart of the old town. It features the magnificent Baroque St Martin's church, built in 1686–91 by the Dientzenhofer brothers. Also notable is the late-Baroque St Catherine hospital and seminary, built by Balthasar Neumann, which now serves as the town hall.

---

⑨
Kloster Michelsberg

🏠 **Michelsberg** 🕐 **Apr–Oct: 1–5pm Wed–Fri, 11am–5pm Sat, Sun & hols** 🌐 **brauerei museum.de**

The Benedictine abbey that stood on this site was founded in 1015. The surviving church was built after 1121 and remodelled in the 16th and 17th centuries. The abbey's Baroque buildings, by the Dientzenhofer brothers, date from the 17th and 18th centuries. The abbey's tower brewery houses a museum.

---

⑩
Schloss Seehof

🏠 **Memmelsdorf** 🕐 **Apr–Oct: 9am–6pm Tue–Sun** 🌐 **schloesser-bayern.de**

Built and designed by Antonio Petrini in 1686, this palace was originally the summer residence of the prince-bishops of Bamberg. The nine state rooms are magnificent.

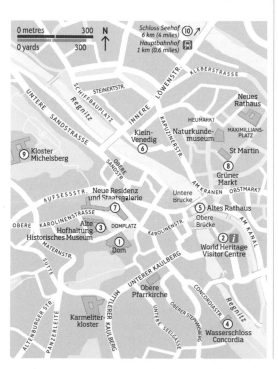

↑ Sunset over the rooftops of Nürnberg's old town

2

NÜRNBERG

🅰 E6 ✈ On the northeast outskirts of town Ⓤ🚉
ℹ Hauptmarkt 18; www.tourismus.nuernberg.de

Situated on the River Pegnitz, this town (known as Nuremberg in English) is loved for its delicious gingerbread and sausages. Nürnberg is also the symbol of Germany's fascinating history, with its earliest records dating from 1050, when the town was a trading settlement.

①

Frauentor

 Frauentorgraben

The Frauentor (Ladies' Tower) is one of the most attractive gates into the old town. It is installed in the massive city walls that were constructed during the 15th and 16th centuries. The vast tower, Dicker Turm (Fat Tower), was erected nearby in the 15th century. Königstor (King's Tower), a magnificent gate that once stood to the right of Dicker Turm, was dismantled in the 19th century. Beyond Frauentor are a number of alleys with half-timbered houses, shops and cafés.

②

Mauthalle

 Hallplatz 2

The massive structure that dominates Königstrasse is a Gothic granary built in 1498–1502 by German architect Hans Beheim the Elder. It originally housed the town's municipal scales and the customs office. In the 19th century the building was converted into a department store and continues in that role today, following post-war reconstruction.

③

Lorenzer Platz

Overlooked by the church of St Lorenz, Lorenzer Platz is a popular meeting place for the citizens of Nürnberg and visitors alike. Outside the church is the Fountain of the Virtues, Tugendbrunnen (1589), with water cascading from the breasts of its seven Virtues. Nearby is a statue of St Lorenz, which is a copy of the 1350 Gothic original. Diagonally across the square is the Nassauer Haus, a Gothic mansion whose lower storeys were built in the 13th century. The upper floors were added in the 15th century.

A short distance from the square, in Karolinenstrasse, is a fine sculpture (*Large Totem Head*, 1968) by Henry Moore.

> **Overlooked by the church of St Lorenz, Lorenzer Platz is a popular meeting place for the citizens of Nürnberg and visitors alike.**

4
Heilig-Geist-Spital

🏠 Spitalgasse 16
🕐 Restaurant: 11:30am–
11pm daily 🌐 heilig-geist-
spital.de

In the centre of town, on the banks of the River Pegnitz, stands the Hospital of the Holy Spirit. Founded in 1332, this is one of the largest hospitals built in the Middle Ages and features a lovely inner courtyard with wooden galleries. The wing that spans the river was built in 1488–1527. Lepers were kept at some distance from the other patients, in a separate half-timbered building that was specially erected for the purpose. From 1424 until 1796 the insignia of the Holy Roman Empire were kept here rather than in the castle.

The Heilig-Geist-Spital now houses a retirement home and a restaurant. The entrance to the building is on the northern side of the river.

5
Albrecht-Dürer-Haus

🏠 Albrecht-Dürer-Strasse
39 🕐 Times vary, check
website 🌐 museen.
nuernberg.de

Having spent much of his childhood in a house on the corner of Burgstrasse and Obere Schmiedgasse, the renowned German artist and engraver Albrecht Dürer later lived in this half-timbered house from 1509

until his death in 1528. It stands as Germany's first artist's memorial site.

On the 300th anniversary of his death, the building was bought by the town and many rooms have since been reconstructed. The third-floor room now contains a printing press dating from Dürer's time. Copies of his pictures provide a useful insight into the work of this distinguished Nürnberg citizen.

ALBRECHT DÜRER

One of the most outstanding painters of the Renaissance era, Dürer began his career as a goldsmith in his father's workshop. He achieved fame not only as a skilled painter, but also as a brilliant engraver and respected theoretician.

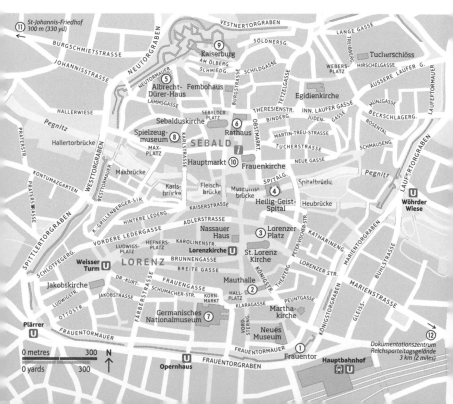

⑥
Rathaus

▢ Rathausplatz

The present town hall consists of several sections. Facing the Rathausplatz is the oldest, Gothic part, built in 1332–40 and remodelled in the early 15th century. Behind, facing Hauptmarkt, is the Renaissance part, built in 1616–22 by Jakob Wolff. Its magnificent portals are decorated with heraldic motifs. The courtyard features a fountain dating from 1557.

⑦
Germanisches Nationalmuseum

▢ Kartäusergasse 1
◷ 10am–6pm Tue–Sun (to 8:30pm Wed) ⌨ gnm.de

This museum, which was officially opened in 1852, was founded by a Franconian aristocrat named Hans von Aufsess. It houses a unique collection of antiquities from the German-speaking world, including religious relics, artworks and old scientific equipment. In 1945, towards the end of World War II, parts of the buildings that had originally housed the museum were bombed. The architecture of the modern building, which

was completed in 1993, cleverly incorporates the remaining fragments of a former Carthusian abbey. Among the most valuable items in the museum's collection are works by Tilman Riemenschneider, Konrad Witz, Lucas Cranach the Elder, Albrecht Altdorfer, Albrecht Dürer and Hans Baldung Grien.

⑧
Spielzeugmuseum

▢ Karlstrasse 13–15
☏ (0911) 231 31 64
◷ 10am–5pm Tue–Fri, 10am–6pm Sat & Sun

This enchanting toy museum, established in 1971, houses a magnificent collection of tin soldiers and a huge collection of dolls and puppets. Its greatest attraction, however, is a collection of antique dolls houses, filled with miniature furniture and equipment.

⑨
Kaiserburg

▢ Innerer Burghof ◷ Apr–Oct: 9am–6pm daily; Oct–Mar: 10am–4pm daily
⌨ kaiserburg-nuernberg.de

The three castles that tower over Nürnberg comprise the central burgraves' castle, with

Did You Know?

The Hauptmarkt hosts a weekly food market, as well as an annual flea market and an Easter market.

the Free Reich's buildings to the east, and the imperial castle (whose origins go back to the 12th century) to the west. When climbing up the Burgstrasse you will first reach the Fünfeckturm (Pentagonal Tower), which dates from 1040. The oldest building in town, it is an architectural relic of the von Zollern burgraves' castle. At its foot are the Kaiserstallung (emperor's stables), which now house a youth hostel. A further climb will bring you to the courtyard of the imperial palace, which features

←
Gallery of artworks, Germanisches Nationalmuseum

↑ Hauptmarkt's Christmas market illuminated by festive lights

THE CHURCHES OF NÜRNBERG

As a town brimming with historical sights, Nürnberg is home to many beautiful churches, each with its own character and treasures. The small hospital church of St Martha dates from the 14th century, and though almost devoid of furnishing, it has some magnificent Gothic stained-glass windows. Completed in 1273, Sebalduskirche is the oldest in town, and houses many beautiful relics, including the bronze tomb of St Sebald. Frauenkirche contains a clock that displays a procession of electors paying homage to the emperor every day at noon.

a round tower (Sinwellturm) dating from the 12th century, and a deep well – the Tiefe Brunnen. Passing through the inner gate of the castle you will finally reach its heart, the residential building.

Hauptmarkt

Each year the Hauptmarkt provides a picturesque setting for the town's festive Christkindlesmarkt. Throughout Advent you can buy gingerbread, enjoy the taste of German sausages, warm yourself with a glass of mulled wine spiced with cloves and buy locally made souvenirs.

Nürnberg's star attraction is the Gothic Schöner Brunnen (Beautiful Fountain), which was erected around 1385 but

replaced in the early 20th century with a replica. It consists of a 19-m- (62-ft-) high, finely carved spire standing at the centre of an octagonal pool. The pool is surrounded by a Renaissance grille that includes a famous golden ring: the local tradition is that if you turn the ring three times, your wishes will come true.

St-Johannis-Friedhof

🏛 Am Johannisfriedhof

The St John's cemetery is one of the best preserved and most important in Europe. Established in 1518, it has provided a resting place for many illustrious citizens, including the painter Albrecht Dürer (No. 649), the sculptor Veit Stoss (No. 268),

the goldsmith Wenzel Jamnitzer (No. 664) and the painter Anselm Feuerbach (No. 715). The cemetery also contains a rich array of tombs from the 16th, 17th and 18th centuries.

Dokumentationszentrum Reichsparteitagsgelände

🏛 Bayernstrasse 110
🕐 9am-6pm Mon-Fri, 10am-6pm Sat & Sun
🌐 museen.nuernberg. de/dokuzentrum

This vast, unfinished building complex in the southern part of town dates from the Nazi era, built for National Party gatherings. The building now houses a historical exhibition and archive, reminding and educating visitors of its horrifying past.

↑ The Pfarrkirche beside the mountain-fed Ramsau Ache river

 ③

BERCHTESGADENER LAND

⛰F7 🏠Berchtesgaden ℹ️Königsseer Strasse 2, Berchtesgaden; (0865) 28 96 70

Berchtesgadener Land is one of the most beautiful regions in the whole of Europe. It occupies the area of the Berchtesgadener Alps, whose boundaries are defined by the River Saalach to the west, the River Salzach to the east, the Steinernes Meer (Stony Sea) to the south and, to the north, Untersberg, which is 1,972 m (7,500 ft) above sea level. To the south of Berchtesgaden village lies the National Park (Nationalpark Berchtesgaden).

① Berchtesgaden

Encircled by mountains – the Watzmann, the Kehlstein and the Untersberg – the eponymous capital of the Berchtesgaden region offers a rich selection of attractions. The castle, formerly an Augustinian priory, houses the art collection of Crown Prince Ruprecht, the local salt mine has a fascinating exhibition, and there's also a comprehensive swimming complex in town with indoor and outdoor thermal pools as well as a sauna.

② Dokumentations-zentrum Obersalzberg

🏠Salzbergstr 41, Berchtesgaden
🚍Berchtesgaden 🚌838
🕐9am–5pm Mon–Sun
🌐obersalzberg.de

This documentation centre offers an impressive overview of the history of Obersalzberg. It specifically focuses on National Socialism and the ways that the region and Nazi ideology intertwined. The permanent exhibition explores themes such as the site's history, the National Socialist Community, Hitler and his foreign policy, and the persecution of the Jews. The building's bunker area contains regular special exhibitions, lectures and events supplement the main exhibition.

③ Wallfahrtskirche Maria Gern

🏠Gerner Strasse, Berchtesgaden

One of the loveliest baroque buildings in the region, the pilgrimage church of Maria Gern was built in 1709 in this idyllic location, atop a small hill known as the Reitbichl. As well as a an attractive exterior, the elliptical interior features articulated vaults, a decorated high altar made of walnut, and a series of votive images from the 17th to the 20th century. The ceiling is a wonderful mix of stucco and frescoes that depict the life of Mary.

---

 ④

Königsee

🛈 Schönau am Königsee; www.schloesser. bayern.de

Germany's largest and cleanest lake serves as the focal point of the Berchtesgadener Land. Lying 600 m (2,000 ft) above sea level, it covers 5.5 sq km (2 sq miles). For environmental reasons, only electric boats and rowing boats are allowed on the lake. Tours pass the photogenic St Bartholomä church, and the sheer mountain walls which, when the boatman blows his trumpet, bounce the sound back impressively.

 ⑤

Ramsau an der Ache

🛈 Im Tal 2; www.ramsau.de

Set in an enchanting location in the Ramsau valley, this popular village has been associated with mountaineering for many decades, thanks especially to mountaineer Johann Grill, who first scaled the Watzmann's east wall in 14 hours, and whose statue is in front of the town hall. Spectacular views of the mountains can be enjoyed from the small parish church, and the Zauberwald forest and the Hintersee lake are also nearby.

---

⑥

Hintersee

🛈 Ramsau; www. berchtesgaden.de/ hintersee

This scenic lake has given its name to a picturesque hamlet nearby. It's small enough to be walked around in an hour and

KEHLSTEINHAUS

Standing on the summit of Kehlstein, this stone building was given to Hitler as a birthday present in 1939 by one of his closest allies, Martin Bormann. It houses a popular restaurant with spectacular views over part of the Alps.

ferry trips are available. If walking, look out for the themed trail, which has information boards about the 19th century painters who created many works of art here. In winter, the frozen lake is a popular place for ice-skating.

Wallfahrtskirche Maria Gern in Berchtesgadener Land

↑ The Alte Mainbrücke bridge, leading to Würzburg's old town

4

WÜRZBURG

🅐 D5 ✈ Frankfurt, 120 km (75 miles) west of town
🚌 ℹ Falkenhaus, Marktplatz 9; www.wuerzburg.de

The bombing raid on Würzburg on 16 March 1945 lasted for about 20 minutes and destroyed over 80 per cent of the town's buildings. However, Würzburg has risen from the ashes to enchant visitors with its picturesque position on the banks of the River Main and its rich cultural heritage.

①

Residenz Würzburg

🏛 Residenzplatz 2
🕐 Apr-Oct: 9am-6pm daily; Nov-Mar: 10am-4:30pm daily 🌐 residenz-wuerzburg.de

This vast palace complex on UNESCO's World Heritage list was commissioned by two prince-bishops, the brothers Johann Philipp Franz and Friedrich Karl von Schönborn. Its construction between 1720 and 1744 was supervised by several architects, but, the Residenz is mainly associated with the architect Balthasar Neumann, who was responsible for the overall design. Inside, visitors will find a stunning selection of elaborate and richly decorated rooms, including thre Treppenhaus where the world's largest fresco adorns the vault of the staircase.

②

Dom St Kilian

🏛 Domplatz 📞 (0931) 38 66 29 00 🕐 Times vary, check website

After the great cathedral churches of Mainz, Speyer and Worms, this is Germany's fourth-largest Romanesque church. The impressive Dom St Kilian was built between 1045 and 1188, its patron saint an Irish monk who came to Würzburg in AD 686. The three-nave basilica has a transept and a twin-tower façade. Inside, the Romanesque main nave with its flat roof contrasts sharply with the Baroque stucco embellishments of the choir.The north nave houses a group of bishops' tombs, two of which are the work of Tilman Riemenschneider. At the end of the north transept is a chapel, built by Balthasar Neumann for the bishops of the House of Schönborn.

③

Neumünster

🏛 St-Kilians-Platz

Just north of the cathedral, the Neumünster church was built in the 11th-century

> **The interior of the Käppele (Little Chapel) is lavishly decorated with beautiful wall paintings.**

at the burial site of St Kilian and his fellow Irish martyrs, St Kolonat and St Totnan.

The church's imposing Baroque dome and its red sandstone façade date from the 18th century. Adorning the interior are numerous works of art, including a late 15th-century Madonna by the 15th-century German sculptor Tilman Riemenschneider. The north door leads to a lovely small courtyard; the remains of the cloister date from the Hohenstauf period. Under a lime tree is the resting place of a famous medieval minstrel, Walther von der Vogelweide.

A procession is held each year on St Kilian's feast day (8 July) during which the skulls of the martyrs are carried in a transparent box from the west crypt to the cathedral, where they are put on public display.

④ Festung Marienberg

🏛 **Festung Marienberg**
🕐 **Apr-Sep: 9am-6pm Tue-Sun; Oct-Mar: 10am-4:30pm Tue-Sun**
🌐 **schloesser.bayern.de**

Built on the site of an old Celtic stronghold, the Marienberg Fortress towers above the town on the hill that gives the fortress its name. In AD 707 a church was built here and, in 1201, work began on a fortress that served as the residence of the prince-bishops until 1719. Within its fortifications stands the first original donjon church, dating from the 13th century, and the Renaissance-Baroque palace.

Tours of the fortress run regularly from mid-March to October. Festung Marienberg also houses two very worthwhile museums:

↑ The glorious Baroque façade of Wurzburg's Neumünster church

the Fürstenbaumuseum's exhibits illustrate the 1,200-year history of the town, while the Museum für Franken (Franconian Museum), in the former arsenal, contains a valuable collection of sculptures by local sculptor Tilman Riemenschneider.

Due to ongoing renovations (due to end 2026), some areas of the fortress may be closed.

---

⑤ Käppele

🏛 **Mergentheimer Strasse**

Standing at the top of a hill at the southwestern end of the city, this twin-towered Baroque chapel is the work of Balthasar Neumann. The fairy-tale feel of the façade is complemented by the interior of the Käppele (Little Chapel) which is lavishly decorated with wall paintings by Matthias Günther.

---

⑥ Alte Mainbrücke

Connecting the old town and Festung Marienberg, this beautiful bridge was built in 1473–1543. It is the oldest bridge over the Main.

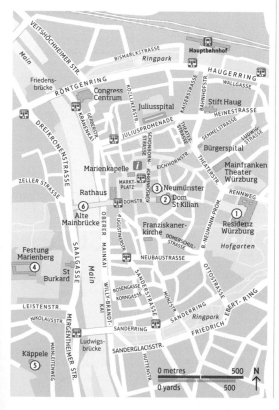

including stained-glass windows that are over 700 years old.

⑤

ROTHENBURG OB DER TAUBER

 D6 🚌 ℹ️ Marktplatz 2; rothenburg-tourismus.de

A major highlight along Bavaria's Romantic Road, Rothenburg has a captivating medieval charm. Dating back to the 10th century, its small centre offers treats such as the Gothic church of St Jakob, the Rothenburg Museum and the Rödertor city gate.

①
Rathaus

📍 Marktplatz 1 🕐 Times vary, check website 🌐 rothenburg.de

The town hall, designed and built by Leonhard Weidmann, consists of the surviving Gothic section with a tower, and the later Renaissance structure added in 1681.

②
Burggarten

📍 Alte Burg 🕐 Daily

The castle garden is reached through Burgtor, the tallest of the town's gates. The garden – which, during the Middle Ages, was the site of Schloss Hohenstaufen – provides a magnificent view of the town.

③
St Jakob's Kirche

📍 Klostergasse 15 🕐 Times vary, check website 🌐 rothenburg tauber-evangelisch.de/ jakobskirche

One of Germany's most notable medieval churches, St Jacob's grand Gothic towers are a unique aspect of the town's skyline. The interior contains several major relics,

④
Weihnachtsmuseum

📍 Herrngasse 1 🕐 Times vary, check website 🌐 weihnachtsmuseum.de

Every day feels like Christmas thanks to this museum. The main exhibition shows how this religious celebration and its rituals (such as tree decorations) have developed over the years. Kids of all ages will love the 150-strong historic Santa Claus collection.

SHOP

Käthe Wohlfahrt Weihnachtsdorf
This Christmas shop brand has a store and "Christmas village" near the museum.

📍 Herrngasse 1 🌐 kaethe-wohlfahrt. com

← Rödergasse, with its charming fountain and Markusturm clock tower

⑤ Rödertor

🏠 Rödertor/Rödergasse

The best preserved segments of the old city wall are around the 14th century Rödertor gate. The Röderturm tower has great views of the Altstadt (Old Town).

⑥ Rothenburg Museum

🏠 Klosterhof 5 🕐 Nov-Mar: 1-4pm; Apr-Oct: 9:30am-5:30pm 🌐 rothenburg museum.de

The former Dominican abbey has since 1935 housed the Imperial Town Museum devoted to the town's history. The abbey kitchen – the oldest surviving kitchen in Germany – is also open to visitors.

⑦ Mittelalterliches Kriminalmuseum

🏠 Burggasse 3-5 🕐 Apr-Oct: 10am-6pm; Nov-Mar: 1-4pm 🌐 kriminal museum.eu

Many blood-curdling exhibits are on display here, as well as a collection of instruments of torture and punishment that stretch back 1,000 years.

⑧ Historiengewölbe

🏠 Marktplatz 1 🕐 Times vary, check website 🌐 meister trunk.de

These historic vaults contain dungeons, a guardhouse and a prison, and provide an overview of life in town during the Thirty Years' War (1618–48).

↑ A shame mask displayed at the Kriminalmuseum

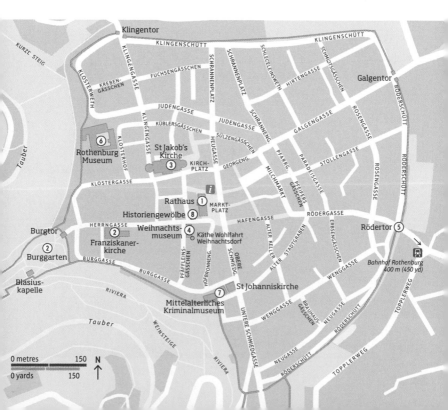

Schloss Neuschwanstein, home of the eccentric "Swan King", Ludwig II ↑

6 ⬡ ⬡ ⬡ ⬡

SCHLOSS NEUSCHWANSTEIN

Ⓐ D7 🏠 Neuschwansteinstrasse 20, Hohenschwangau ⏰ Apr-15 Oct: 9am-6pm daily; 16 Oct-Mar: 10am-4pm daily 🛈 Ticket centre in Hohenschwangau 🌐 neuschwanstein.de

Built by King Ludwig II as a retreat from public life, the idiosyncratic Neuschwanstein Castle is today one of the most popular palaces in Europe, enticing around 1.5 million visitors per year to make the steep 30-minute walk up from the village of Hohenschwangau.

Set in magnificent mountain scenery high above the lakes of Forggensee, Alpsee and Schwansee, this fairytale castle was built in 1869–86 for the Bavarian king Ludwig II, to plans by the theatre designer Christian Jank. The king was undoubtedly inspired by Wartburg castle in Thuringia (p194), which he visited in 1867, as well as the Baroque commissions of the Bourbon king of France. The pale grey limestone castle offers superb views, and among its highlights are Ludwig's personal apartments (his dressing room has a spectacular painted ceiling), the state rooms, the grotto, Sängersaal (Singers' Hall) and a multimedia exhibition.

↑ Visitors on the Marienbrücke to see a stunning view of the castle

King Ludwig II

Notoriously shy and enigmatic, Ludwig II possessed few attributes of a royal ruler, preferring fairytales, building castles and watching plays to constitutional duties. After his kingdom began to fall apart, his government declared him insane and a year later he was deposed. The following day he died in mysterious circumstances at Lake Starnberg.

↑ Singers' Hall, a tribute to medieval knights and the Holy Grail legend

Life of King Ludwig II

25 August 1845

▲ Born in Schloss Nymphenburg, the elder son of Maximilian II (above) and Princess Marie of Prussia

10 March 1864

▽ Acceded to the throne at the age of 18, with no experience of politics

1866

Prussia conquered Austria and Bavaria in the "German War", which made Ludwig a vassal of his Prussian uncle

13 June 1886

Died under mysterious circumstances at Lake Starnberg

↑ The ornate interior of Schloss Hohenschwangau

EXPERIENCE MORE

7

Hohenschwangau

AD7 **Q**Schwangau 3, 818
i Münchener Strasse 2,
Shwangau; www.
schwangau.de

The skyline of Schwangau is dominated by two castles, Schloss Neuschwanstein *(p266)* and the majestic **Schloss Hohenschwangau**. The fortified castle that occupied this site in the Middle Ages was remodelled in 1538–47 and, in 1567, it passed into the hands of the Wittelsbach family. It was destroyed during the Tyrolean War but in 1832 the heir to the throne (later Maximilian II) ordered the ruins to be rebuilt in Neo-Gothic style. The plans were prepared by Domenico Quaglio; after his death, work on the castle was continued by Georg Friedrich Ziebland and Joseph Daniel Ohlmüller.

This four-storey building, standing on medieval foundations, is flanked by angular towers. The wall paintings that decorate the rooms of the castle date from 1835–36. Their iconographic content, which is based on old Germanic sagas, is the work of Moritz von Schwind. A walk around the castle provides an excellent opportunity to study the Wittelsbach family history and to see the mid-19th-century furnishings. There are magnificent views of the surroundings from the castle's lovely terraced gardens.

Schloss Hohenschwangau
⊗⊗⊜ **O**Apr–mid-Oct:
8am–5pm daily; mid-Oct–
Mar: 9am–3pm daily
whohenschwangau.de

8

Oberstdorf

AD7 **Q** **i**Prinzregenten-
Platz 1; (08322) 70 00

Oberstdorf lies in the valley of the River Iller. The ideal skiing conditions and the mild all-year-round climate make this one of the most popular health resorts in Germany. Nearby is the skiing stadium (Schattenberg-Skistadion) with its famous ski-jump, where the annual "four ski-jump" tournament starts each year.

Although the fire of 1865 destroyed large sections of the settlement here, some of the most important historic buildings escaped. These include Seelenkapelle (souls chapel), whose façade is decorated with a 16th-century wall painting typical of the region, and two chapels, Lorettokapelle and Joseph-skapelle, which were joined together in 1707. Just to the east of Oberstdorf is the 2,224-m (7,300-ft) Mount Nebelhorn, whose summit can be reached in a few minutes by cable car. This offers a spectacular view over the majestic Allgäuer Alps as well as providing an excellent starting point for mountain hiking.

Füssen

🅐 D7 🚌 ℹ️ Kaiser-Maximilian-Platz 1; www.fuessen.de

Situated conveniently on an important trade route, Füssen experienced its most rapid growth in the l ate Middle Ages, as witnessed by many of the buildings in Reichenstrasse and the remains of the town forti-fications, which include Sebastiantor (Sebastian gate) and sections of the walls with five turrets.

Perched on a rock, high above the town, stands the palace of the Augsburg prince-bishops. Started in 1291 by the Bavarian Prince Ludwig the Severe, construction was continued from 1490 to 1503 by the Augsburg bishops. The residential buildings of the palace range around a courtyard whose walls are decorated with trompe l'oeil door and window frames.

> Oberstdorf lies in the valley of the River Iller. The ideal skiing conditions and the mild all-year-round climate make this one of the most popular health resorts.

The eastern crypt and the church tower of St Mang are the remains of the medieval monastery complex. The late 10th-century crypt shows the remains of wall paintings.

Kempten

🅐 D7 🚌 ℹ️ Rathausplatz 24; www.kempten-tourismus.de

Kempten lies at the centre of one of Germany's most appealing tourist regions, the Allgäu, which stretches from Bodensee (Lake Constance) to the west and the River Lech to the east. The town, which boasts a history of over 2,000 years, was first mentioned by the Greek geographer and historian Strabo as a Celtic settlement, Kambodunon. Later, the Romans established Cambodunum on the right bank of the river Iller. Along with Augusta Vindelicorum (Augsburg) and Castra Regina (Regensburg), this was one of the most important towns in the Roman province of Raetia.

Medieval Kempten grew around a Benedictine abbey, founded in 752. In the north-western part of town is the church of St Lorenz. A triple-nave, galleried basilica with a twin-tower façade, this is the work of Michael Beer and Johann Serro. The town's parish church of St Mang dates from the 15th century and in the Rathausplatz is an attractive town hall dating from 1474. The **Kempten Residenz** is a historic property in beautiful grounds. On the right bank of the River Iller is the **Archäologischer Park Cambodunum**, with excavated remains of Roman Cambodunum. The 13th-century Erasmuskapelle chapel is also worth visiting.

Kempten Residenz

♦♦ 🏛️ Residenzplatz 4-6 🕐 Apr-Sep: 9am-4pm Tue-Sun; Oct: 10am-4pm Tue-Sun; Nov & Jan-Mar: 10am-4pm Sat & Sun; Dec: 12:15-4pm daily 🌐 schloesser.bayern.de

Archäologischer Park Cambodunum

♦♦♦ 🏛️ Cambodunumweg 3 📞 (0831) 2525 7777 🕐 Mar-Nov: 10am-5pm 🌐 apc-kempten.de

←

Remains of the Kleine Thermen (little baths) at the Archäologischer Park

Aschaffenburg

C5 🚉 🛈 Schlossplatz 2;
(06021) 39 58 00

Situated in northwest Bavaria, Aschaffenburg enjoys a scenic position on the hilly right bank of the River Main. The town was the second residence of the electoral archbishops for more than 800 years.

The northwest part of the old town features a majestic, red sandstone riverside castle, **Schloss Johannisburg**, which along with its chapel is a unique masterpiece of 17th-century architecture.

The palace tour includes the world's largest collection of cork architectural models of famous buildings in Rome, and the State Gallery, with one of the most important collections of Lucas Cranach the Elder's paintings. Also worth seeing is the famous Lucas Cranach's *Altar of St Magdalene* in the Stiftsmuseum and Matthias Gruenewald's *Lamentation of Christ* in the Basilica of St Peter and Alexander.

Located just above a vineyard a short distance to the northwest of the castle is Pompejanum, an idealized Roman villa. King Ludwig I of Bavaria was inspired by the excavations at Pompeii and commissioned this unique villa for art lovers and students of ancient culture.

Schloss Johannisburg
Schlossplatz 4
Apr-Sep: 9am-6pm Tue-Sun; Oct-Mar: 10am-4pm Tue-Sun schloesser.bayern.de

---

Pommersfelden

D5 🛈 Hauptstrasse 11;
(09548) 922 00

On the edge of the Steigerwald – a popular hiking area – is the small village of Pommersfelden, which is dominated by its magnificent Baroque palace, **Schloss Weissenstein**. The palace was commissioned by the Mainz Archbishop and Elector and the Prince-Bishop of Bamberg, Lothar Franz von Schönborn. It was built, in only five years (1711–18), to a design by the architect Johann Dientzenhofer.

This masterpiece of secular Baroque architecture is worth visiting. Particularly interesting is the three-storey-high ornamental ceiling by Johann Rudolf Byss and Giovanni Francesco Marchini. The most spectacular room in the well-preserved interior is the Marble Hall, which features a fresco by Michael Rottmayr. Other attractions include a gallery, a library, and a valuable collection of furniture. After visiting the palace, you can stroll around its gardens, which were created by Maximilian von Welsch in 1715, in what was the then fashionable, geometric French style. It is now laid out in English-garden style.

Schloss Weissenstein
Times vary, check website schoenborn.de

Coburg

D5 🚉 🛈 Herrngasse 4;
(09561) 89 80 00

Former residence of the Wettin family, Coburg is situated on the bank of the River Itz. It is dominated by a massive fortress, the **Veste Coburg**, which is one of the largest in Germany. Coburg's origins go back to the 11th century, but its present-day appearance is mainly the result of remodelling that was carried out in the 16th and the 17th centuries.

The fortress consists of a number of buildings clustered around several courtyards and surrounded by a triple line of walls. The complex is now a museum, housing various collections, including prints and drawings, arms and armour.

In 1530 the fortress provided refuge to Martin Luther who, as an outlaw, hid here from April until October. The room in which he hid is filled with antique furniture and features a portrait of Luther, painted by Lucas Cranach the Younger.

Schloss Johannisburg in Aschaffenburg, seen from across the River Main

↑ Busts of comrades
in Ludwig I's Walhalla
memorial and *(inset)* the
monument's exterior

Among the most important
buildings in the old town are
the late-Gothic church of
St Maurice and a beautiful
Renaissance college building
that was founded by Prince
Johann Casimir in 1605. On the
opposite side of the market
square is the town hall, built in
1577–9 and remodelled in the
18th century.

Farther along is the town
castle, **Schloss Ehrenburg**,
which was built in the
16th century on the site
of a dissolved Franciscan
monastery. The original castle
building burned down in 1693
and was subsequently rebuilt.
The façade facing the square
was remodelled by Karl
Friedrich Schinkel in
Neo-Gothic style.

The castle has some fine
interiors, including the
Baroque Riesensaal (Giants'
Hall) and Weisser Saal (White
Hall), and a chapel with rich
stucco decorations.

Veste Coburg

🏛️🎭🏰 🕐 Apr-Oct: 9:30am-
5pm daily; Nov-Mar: 1-4pm
Tue-Sun 🌐 kunstsamm
lungen-coburg.de

Schloss Ehrenburg

🏛️🏛️🏰 🏠 Schlossplatz 1
🕐 Apr-Sep: 9am-6pm Tue-
Sun; Oct-Mar: 10am-4pm
Tue-Sun 🌐 schloesser.
bayern.de

---

⑭ 🏛️

Walhalla

🅰️E6 🏠 Donaustauf
🕐 Apr-Oct: 9am-6pm; Nov-
Mar: 10am-noon, 1-4pm
daily 🌐 schloesser.
bayern.de

Completed in 1842 by Leo
von Klenze, this enormous
monument to the national
glory stands imperiously
above the River Danube. The
building has the form of a
Neo-Classical temple and
is adorned with 131 marble
busts of artists and scientists.

MEDIEVAL TOWNS IN CENTRAL BAVARIA

Medieval history is still
palpable in some of the
towns in Bavaria. In the
west lies Dinkelsbühl,
an old Franconian town
with one of the best-
preserved medieval
urban complexes in
Germany. The
residential district
consists mainly of
timber-frame houses.
In the centre of the
state is Berching: a
charming little town
in the valley of the
River Sulz, boasting a
history that goes back
to the 9th century. To
this day it retains the
complete enclosure of
its medieval city walls,
including towers and
gates with oak doors.
Farther north is
Amberg, on the River
Vils. This well-preserved
old town is encircled by
medieval walls. The
arches of the iconic
Stadtbrille bridge reflect
in the river to resemble
a pair of glasses.

↑ The Baroque interior of the church of the Vierzehnheiligen

 15

Vierzehnheiligen

🅐 D5 🅐 Bad Staffelstein
🕙 May–Sep: 6:30am–8pm daily; Oct–Apr: 7:30am–5pm daily 🔲 vierzehn heiligen.de

High above the River Main is Banz Abbey, a Benedictine monastery built in 1695 by brothers Johann Leonhard and Leonhard Dientzenhofer. Opposite is the pilgrimage church of the Fourteen Saints of Intercession. The first two chapels, built in the 15th and 16th centuries, became too small to accommodate the growing numbers of pilgrims so, in 1741, the foundation stone was laid for the monumental new church, designed by Balthasar Neumann. Built in 1743–72, this is one of the most famous masterpieces of South German Baroque, with magnificent Rococo furnishings. The building is cross-shaped, with a twin-tower façade.

The interior has an exceptionally dynamic style, achieved by combining the longitudinal and central planes: the three ovals laid along the main axis join with the two circles of the transept. The centrepiece of the nave is the Altar of Mercy, which stands at the spot where, according to a 1446 legend, a shepherd had visions of the infant Christ with the Saints of Intercession. The altar features statues of the 14 saints, and are the work of J M and F X Feuchtmayr (1763). The rich stucco decorations and frescoes were crafted by Giuseppe Appiani.

 16

Fränkische Schweiz

🅐 D/E5 🛈 Oberes Tor 1, Ebermannstadt; (09191) 86 10 54

The area popularly known as Franconian Switzerland covers the area between Nürnberg, Bamberg and Bayreuth. One of Germany's most beautiful tourist regions, it offers green meadows, magnificent highlands covered with cornfields, lovely castles perched on top of high outcrops, fabulous rocks and deep caves with stalactites. Its towns and villages, with their charming inns and timber-frame houses, look like a setting for *Snow White and the Seven Dwarfs*. The main routes across the area run alongside its rivers – the Wiesent, Leinleiter, Püttlach and Trubach. The Wiesent, which is ideal for canoeing, cuts across the region from east to west, joining the River Regnitz near Forchheim. The town has many timber-frame houses, including the old town hall, dating from the 14th to the 16th century. Near Forchheim, in Ebermannstadt, is a Marian church with a fine Madonna. The federal route B470 leads to the picturesque village of Tüchersfeld, which is built into the rocks.

A good base for exploring this area is the village of Pottenstein. St Elisabeth of Thuringia is said to have stayed here in 1227. The town is overlooked by an 11th-century castle, and nearby is a cave with impressive rock formations.

Straubing

E6 ⊞ ⓘFraunhoferstrasse 27; (09421) 94 46 01 99

This market town enjoys a picturesque setting on the river Danube. The 600-m- (1,970-ft-) long market square is arranged into two sections, Theresienplatz and Ludwigplatz, and is part of the former trade route that led to Prague. The area is lined with buildings in Baroque, Neo-Classical and Secession styles.

At the centre of the market square stands the landmark 14th-century municipal tower, which offers a splendid view over the towns of the Bavarian Forest. At Ludwigplatz 23 is the "Lion's Pharmacy", where the Biedermeier painter Karl Spitzweg worked as an apprentice in 1828–30.

Upon turning from colourful Theresienplatz and into Seminargasse or Jakobsgasse, you will reach the monumental brick structure of the parish church of St Jakob (1400–1590). This triple-nave hall-church, crowned with a network vault, retains many original features, including stained-glass windows in the chapels of Maria-Hilf-Kapelle (1420) and St Bartholomew. The so-called Moses' Window in the Chapel of St Joseph was made in 1490 in Nürnberg, based on a sketch provided by Wilhelm Playdenwurff. In the Cobbler's Chapel (Schusterkapelle) hangs a painting of *Madonna and Child*, by Hans Holbein (around 1500). Overlooking the Danube is a 14th- to 15th-century ducal residence, formerly a ducal residence. The Agnes-Bernauer Festival, held every four years, takes place in the courtyard of the castle. The Gäubodenvolksfest is the second largest folk festival in Bavaria after the Munich Oktoberfest. The **Gäuboden-museum** has a magnificent collection of Roman artifacts.

In the tiny village of Aufhausen, 21 km (12 miles) to the west, is the beautiful late-Baroque pilgrimage church of Maria Schnee. Built by Johann Michael Fischer in 1736–51, it includes magnificent wall paintings by the Asam brothers and a statue of the Madonna. Commissioned by Duke Wilhelm V of Bavaria, the Gnadenmadonna is believed to pardon sins.

In Oberalteich, some 10 km (6 miles) to the east, is the beautiful church of St Peter and St Paul built in the early 17th century for the Benedictine order. Inside, an unusual hanging staircase leads to the galleries, while the vestibule is decorated with stucco ornaments depicting bird motifs.

In Windberg, 22 km (14 miles) east of Oberalteich, is a Romanesque Marian church whose main portal (around 1220) features an image of the Madonna in the tympanum.

Gäubodenmuseum

⊘ ⬀Fraunhoferstrasse 23
🕐 10am–4pm Tue–Sun
🌐 gaeubodenmuseum.de

 The summer sun over the green Fränkische Schweiz landscape

18

Dachau

A E7 🚆 ℹ Konrad-Adenauer-Strasse 1; www.dachau.de

For most people the name Dachau is inextricably linked with the concentration camp that was built here by the Nazis in 1933. Since 1965, the whole site has been designated as a memorial, **KZ-Gedenkstätte Dachau**, to over 40,000 prisoners who were murdered there, with a permanent exhibition in the former domestic quarters of the camp.

Dachau itself is a beautiful town with many historic buildings. On the southwestern edge of the old town stands **Schloss Dachau**, summer residence of the Wittelsbachs. The palace of today was created in the 18th century from the western wing of an earlier castle, the work of Joseph Effner.

In the early 20th century the area surrounding the castle housed a colony of artists who had tired of city life, known as Malschule Neu-Dachau (new Dachau Art School). Many of their paintings, inspired by the local scenery, can be seen in the **Dachauer Gemäldegalerie** (Painting Gallery).

KZ-Gedenkstätte Dachau
◎ ⓐ 🚗 Alte Römerstrasse 75
🕘 9am–5pm daily 🌐 kz-gedenkstaette-dachau.de

Schloss Dachau
⊛ ⓘ 🚗 Schlossstrasse 2
🕘 Apr–Sep: 9am–6pm Tue–Sun; Oct–Mar: 10am–4pm Tue–Sun 🌐 schloesse.bayern.de

Dachauer Gemäldegalerie
⊛ 🚗 Konrad-Adenauer-Strasse 3 🕘 11am–5pm Tue–Fri, 1–5pm Sat & Sun 🌐 dachauer-galerien-museen.de

---

19

Schleissheim

A E7 🚗 Oberschleissheim
📞 (089) 375 589 58

Schleissheim is situated barely 14 km (9 miles) from Munich, making it easy to visit its Baroque palace and park.

Now somewhat neglected, the park was established in the 17th and 18th centuries and includes three palaces. The modest **Altes Schloss** was built in 1623 for Prince Wilhelm V and houses an exhibition of religious folk art.

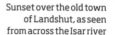

→

Sunset over the old town of Landshut, as seen from across the Isar river

Schloss Lustheim is a small, Baroque, hermitage-type palace, built in 1684–7 by Enrico Zucalli for the Elector Max Emanuel. It has beautiful interiors and a magnificent collection of Meissen porcelain.

The newest building is the **Neues Schloss** (New Palace), designed by Enrico Zucalli. Work began in 1701 but was not completed until the second half of the 18th century. It now houses exhibits belonging to the Bavarian State Museum.

**Altes Schloss,
Schloss Lustheim and
Neues Schloss**
⊛ 🚗 Apr–Sep: 9am–6pm Tue–Sun; Oct–Mar: 10am–4pm Tue–Sun 🌐 schloesser-schleissheim.de

---

20

Fünfseenland

A E7 🚆🚌 ℹ Hauptstrasse 1, Starnberg; www.fuenfseenland.de

Upper Bavaria's Fünfseenland consists of, as the name suggests, five lakes set in a glacial plain: the big

←

The Great Gallery, on the first floor of the Neues Schloss, in Schleissheim

Starnberger See and Ammersee, plus Pilsensee, Wörthsee and Wesslinger See. The lakes were once used exclusively by royalty, but nowadays draw tourists who come to swim, sail and windsurf at the lakes, as well as hike and cycle the countryside trails between them. The area is also dotted with interesting towns and villages offering lovely restaurants, cafés and beer gardens.

Ingolstadt

A E6 R i Moritzstrasse 19; (0841) 305 30 30

The River Danube flows through this former seat of the Wittelsbach family, and the town features many important historic buildings dating from the Middle Ages and the Renaissance and Baroque periods. Among the most outstanding architecture is the church of the Virgin Mary, a triple-nave hall structure. Its Gothic-Renaissance main altar dates from 1572.

Another notable building is the Neues Schloss, which was built between the 15th and 18th centuries and features stately rooms and a Gothic chapel. It now houses the **Bayerisches Armeemuseum** (Bavarian Army Museum).

A true gem of Bavarian architecture is the church of St Maria Victoria, the work of Cosmas Damian Asam.

The **Deutsches Medizinhistorisches Museum** exhibits medical instruments and has a beautiful formal garden of medicinal plants.

Bayerisches Armeemuseum

⊕ ⊓ Neues Schloss, Paradeplatz 4 ⊙ 9am–5:30pm Tue–Fri, 10am–5:30pm Sat & Sun W armeemuseum.de

Deutsches Medizin-historisches Museum

⊕ ⊓ Anatomiestrasse 18–20 ⊙ 10am–5pm Tue–Sun W dmm-ingolstadt.de

Landshut

A E6 R i Altstadt 315; (0871) 92 20 50

The earliest records of Landshut date from 1150. One hundred years later it was a town and the main centre of power of the Dukes of Lower Bavaria. In 1475 it was the scene of the lavish wedding of Duke Georg of the House of Wittelsbach and the Polish Princess Hedwig Jagiellonica.

Landshut has preserved its medieval urban layout, with two wide parallel streets,

Altstadt and Neustadt, and clusters of historic 15th- to 16th- century buildings. Opposite the town hall in Alstadt is the **Stadtresidenz**, a town house modelled on the Palazzo del Tè in Mantua. It was the first Renaissance palace to be built in Germany.

The vast brick basilica of St Martin (1385–1500) is a narrow hall-church featuring network vaults (1459) and the world's tallest brick steeple.

Landshut is dominated by the 13th- to 16th- century **Burg Trausnitz**, with its medieval tower, a Renaissance palace (1568–78) and the **Kunst- und Wunderkammer** (Room of Arts and Wonder), a branch of the Bayerisches Nationalmuseum (p234).

From Landshut, take a trip to Moosburg, 14 km (9 miles) west, home of the early 13th-century church of St Castulus.

Stadtresidenz

⊕ ⊕ ⊓ Altstadt 79 C (0871) 251 42 ⊙ Apr–Sep: 9am–6pm Tue–Sun; Oct–Mar: 10am–4pm Tue–Sun

Burg Trausnitz & Kunst-und Wunderkammer

⊕ ⊙ Apr–Sep: 9am–6pm daily (Oct–Mar: to 4pm) W burg-trausnitz.de

23

Neuburg an der Donau

AE6 **R** *i*Ottheinrichplatz 118; (08431) 552 40

Perched on a promontory overlooking the Danube, Neuburg is one of Bavaria's loveliest towns. During the Middle Ages, it changed hands frequently but was eventually ruled by the Wittelsbach Court Ottheinrich, under whom the town grew and prospered on an unprecedented scale. He was the founder of **Schloss Neuburg**, built between 1534 and 1665, whose massive round towers still dominate the town. Its earliest part is the east wing. The courtyard, surrounded by arcades, has beautiful frescoes by Hans Schroer. In the tower is a staircase adorned with paintings. The castle chapel, completed in 1543, is one of Germany's oldest, purpose-built Protestant churches.

In Amalienstrasse stands the former Jesuits' College and the court church (Hofkirche).

Work on the church began in the late 16th century and was completed in 1627. It was intended to be a Protestant church, but the ruling family converted back to Catholicism during its construction and it was taken over by the Jesuits, who turned it into a counter-reformation Marian church. The triple-nave hall structure has an exquisite interior in gold, white and grey.

Among many old buildings that survive in the town centre are the Graf-Veri-Haus and the Baron-von-Hartman-Haus in Herrenstrasse. To the east of town stands the Grünau Castle (Jagdschloss), built for Ottheinrich in 1530–55.

Just 18 km (11 miles) to the south, Schrobenhausen is the birthplace of the painter Franz von Lenbach, who was born in 1836. A museum in Ulrich-Peisser-Gasse honours him.

Schloss Neuburg

⊛ ⊚ **A**Residenzstrasse 2 **O**Apr–Sep: 9am–6pm Tue–Sun; Oct–Mar: 10am–4pm Tue–Sun **w**schloesser. bayern.de

↑ Elaborate altarpiece in the Baroque-style cathedral of Freising

24

Freising

AE6 **R** *i*Rindermarkt 20; (08161) 544 41 11

Situated on the banks of the River Isar, just 20 minutes by train from Munich, is the old town of Freising. Its history is closely connected with St Korbinian, who founded the bishopric here in the early

8th century. Korbinian died around AD 725 and his remains still lie in the crypt of the Dom – the cathedral church of the Birth of the Virgin Mary and St Korbinian (1159–1205). This is a five-nave basilica, without transept, with an elongated choir and a massive twin-tower western façade. Its interior was remodelled in Baroque style by the Asam brothers in 1724–5. The four-nave Romanesque crypt features a famous column (Bestiensäule), which is decorated with carvings of fantastic animals. Nearby is the **Diözesanmuseum,** whose vast ecclesiastical collection includes two paintings by Rubens.

At the southwestern end of the old town is a former monastery, Weihenstephan, home to the world's longest-established brewery and a botanical garden.

Diözesanmuseum
⊗ 🏠 Domberg 21
📞 (08161) 487 90
🕑 For renovation

Andechs

🅰 E7 🛈 Andechser Strasse 16; www.andechs.de

The village of Andechs, located at the summit of the 700-m- (2,300-ft-) high Holy Mountain of the same name, is well known as the destination of pilgrimages to the local church. But it is also the target of many less spiritual trips to the *Bräustüberl* (beer room), where visitors can refresh themselves with the excellent beer that is brewed here by the local monks.

The present triple-nave Gothic hall-church was built over a six-year period, between 1420 and 1425. Its Rococo interior dates from 1755. The lower tier of the main altar contains the orante *Miraculous Statue of the Mother of God* (1468), while the upper tier features the *Assumpta* by Hans Degler (1609). On selected feast days, holy relics are displayed on the altar gallery.

 INSIDER TIP
Herrsching to Andechs Hike

This 4-km- (2.5-mile-) long walk will take you from the bustle of Munich to bucolic Bavaria. Reward yourself at the end with the monks' beer at the monastery in Andechs.

Landsberg am Lech

🅰 D7 🚉 🛈 Hauptplatz 152; (08191) 12 82 46

The history of Landsberg goes back to 1160, when Heinrich der Löwe (Henry the Lion) built his castle here, on the right bank of the River Lech. During the 13th century, the surrounding settlement grew into a town, which soon became a major trading centre. Religious conflicts, culminating in the Thirty Years' War, put an end to developments, but in the late 1600s the town once again became a commercial and cultural hub.

At the heart of Landsberg is the Hauptplatz (main square), with its Baroque town hall and the intricately carved 14th-century tower, Schmalztor.

In Ludwigstrasse is the late-Gothic parish church, Mariä Himmelfahrt, whose interior features a statue of the *Madonna and Child* by Hans Multscher. Bayertor, the original town gate, is in the eastern part of the old town.

The **Neues Stadtmuseum** is a useful source of information on local history.

Neues Stadtmuseum
⊗ 🏠 Von-Helfenstein-Gasse 426 📞 (08191) 12 83 60
🕑 For renovation until 2024

←

View of Schloss Neuburg across the River Danube, in Neuburg an der Donau

27
Altötting

⚑E7 🚉 ℹ️Kapellplatz 2a; www.altoetting.de

Altötting is renowned as the earliest destination of pilgrimages to the "Miraculous Statue" of the Virgin Mary (1330). The statue stands in the Wallfahrtskapelle St Maria, which consists of two parts. The central Gnadenkapelle (Grace Chapel, around AD 750) was once the baptistery. The external chapel was built in 1494 and the ambulatory in 1517. It also houses the so-called "Silver Prince", representing the miraculously cured son of the Prince-Elector Karl Albrecht. Many Bavarian royals wished to be buried here.

Nearby is the Romanesque-Gothic church of St Philip and St Jacob (1228–30 and 1499–1520), which contains many tombstones.

The Schatzkammer (treasury) was housed in the former sacristy, but after Pope Benedict XVI turned it into a chapel in 2006 the **Neue Schatzkammer and Wallfahrtsmuseum** (Pilgrimage Museum) were built. Exhibits include an exquisite example

of French enamel and gold art, the *Goldenes Rössl* (*Golden Steed*; around 1400). Despite its name, its theme is the Adoration of the Magi.

Neue Schatzkammer and Wallfahrtsmuseum

Kapellplatz 4 🕐Mar-Nov: 10am-4pm Tue-Sun; Dec: 1pm-6pm Mon-Fri, 10am-6pm Sat & Sun 🌐neueschatzkammer.de

---

28
Burghausen

⚑F7 🚉 ℹ️Stadtplatz 99; (08677) 88 71 40

Picturesque Burghausen is situated on the River Salzach. Towering over it all is **Burg Burghausen**, the world's longest castle, built on a high ridge stretching for 1,050 m (1,150 yds). Work on the castle started in 1253, but most of the buildings were erected during the reign of Duke Georg der Reiche (George the Rich) and have late-Gothic forms. The duke's wife, Hedwig Jagiellonica, whom he married in Landshut *(p275),* was later rejected by him and she spent her final days in this fortress.

The castle consists of two main parts: the castle itself, with tower, residential quarters, courtyard and domestic buildings; and the approach (Vorburg). The residential building has some fine 15th-and 16th-century paintings. A special door links the Prince's quarters with the "internal" chapel of St Elisabeth.

The castle approach has five courtyards (Vorhöfe). In the fourth courtyard is the "external" chapel of St Jadwiga (Aussere Burgkapelle St Hedwig) – the work of Wolfgang Wiesinger, a native of Salzburg (1489). This has numerous original buildings, including the town hall, which was created by combining three burgher houses from the 14th and 15th centuries.

Burg Burghausen

** 🕐Apr-Sep: 9am-6pm daily; Oct-Mar: 10am-4pm daily 🌐burg-burghausen.de**

29
Garmisch-Partenkirchen

⚑E7 🚉 ℹ️Richard-Strauss-Platz 2; www.gapa.de

Lying in the valley of the River Loisach, Garmisch-Partenkirchen is the best-known resort in the Bavarian Alps, offering ideal skiing conditions. In 1936 it hosted the Winter Olympic

←

A candlelight procession passes by the Gnadenkapelle in Altötting

↑ A hockey game on the frozen lake below Burghausen Castle

> **Burghausen is situated on the River Salzach. Towering over it all is Burg Burghausen, the world's longest castle.**

Games and, in 1978, the World Skiing Championships. From Garmisch-Partenkirchen, Germany's highest peak, Zugspitze (2,962 m/9,718 ft), can be reached by taking the narrow-gauge railway to Zugspitzplatt or a cable car, which reaches the summit in a few minutes. Garmisch-Partenkirchen's parish church of St Martin (Alte Pfarrkirche St Martin) is worth a visit. It was built in the 13th century and extended in the 15th century and features some well-preserved Gothic wall paintings and net vaulting. The **Werdenfels Museum** shows how people in this region lived in the past, with a collection of furniture, clothing and room reconstructions.

Werdenfels Museum
⊗ ⌂ Ludwigstrasse 47
🕒 10am–5pm Tue–Sun
Ⓦ werdenfels-museum.de

Oberammergau

🅰D7 🚉 ℹ Eugen-Papst-Strasse 9A; www.ammergauer-alpen.de

Situated some 20 km (12 miles) north of Garmisch-Partenkirchen, on the site of a 9th-century Welfs' fort, Oberammergau is world famous for its folk art and passion plays. The Thirty Years' War (1618–48) and the plague of 1632 came close to wiping out the entire population of the village. Its surviving inhabitants pledged that if they were saved from extinction they would stage for evermore a play about Christ's Passion. No further deaths occurred and, to this day, the villagers have kept their pledge. Every ten years, some 2,500 people take part in the six-hour-long spectacle, in which they transform themselves from Bavarians into Jews and Romans from the time of Christ. About one hundred performances are staged between mid-May and mid-October in the huge Passionsspielhaus (Passion Play Theatre).

Worth seeing in the village are the Rococo church of Saint Peter and Saint Paul (1735–40) and the Pilatushaus, with its illusionist painting of Christ before Pilate on the façade. The **Oberammergau Museum** has a notable collection of wooden cribs.

Oberammergau Museum
⊗ ⌂ Dorfstrasse 8 🕒 10am–5pm Tue–Sun 🚫 Feb, Mar, Nov Ⓦ oberammergau museum.de

Ottobeuren

Ⓐ D7 **ⓘ** Marktplatz 6;
(08332) 921 90

Situated 13 km (8 miles) from Memmingen, the small health resort of Ottobeuren is the site of one of Germany's most famous Benedictine abbeys. Founded in 764, the abbey is still a place of prayer and work for the monks who live here. In the 18th century the abbey was remodelled by Abbot Rupert II. The new buildings were completed in 1731, and the richly decorated interiors, with stuccoes by Andrea Maini, still survive. A new abbey church was built between 1737 and 1766, with construction supervised initially by Simpert Kramer. In 1748 this was taken over by Johann Michael Fischer, who was responsible for its final appearance.

The interior of the church has a magnificent unity of style: Rococo stuccoes by Johann Michael Feuchtmayr are in perfect harmony with the vault frescoes by Johann Jakob Zeiller as well as the splendid altars and stalls by Martin Hörmann and Johann

RICHARD WAGNER (1813-1883)

The German composer is inseparable from Bayreuth, where he enjoyed his greatest triumphs. His career began in Magdeburg, Königsberg and Riga. From there he fled to Paris to evade creditors. His reputation was established by performances of his romantic operas *The Flying Dutchman* (1843) and *Tannhäuser* (1845) in Dresden. Wagner's long-time sponsor was the eccentric Bavarian king Ludwig II. From 1872 Wagner lived in Bayreuth, where the Festspielhaus was built specifically for his operas.

Zeiller's brother Franz Anton. The abbey's three beautiful organs can be heard at regularly held recitals.

Bayreuth

Ⓐ E5 **✖ Ⓡ**
ⓘ Opernstrasse 22; www.
bayreuth.de

Lovers of German music associate this town with the composer Richard Wagner

(1813–83), who took up residence here in 1872. Established in 1231, Bayreuth originally belonged to the family of Count von Andechs-Meran; in 1248 it passed to the margraves of Nürnberg (von Zollern) and, since 1806, Franconian Bayreuth has belonged to Bavaria. The town flourished during the 17th and 18th centuries when it was the residence of the margraves, particularly during the time of Margravine Wilhelmine,

sister of the Prussian King Frederick the Great and wife of Margrave Friedrich.

Bayreuth's cultural legacy is evident in the Markgräfliches Opernhaus – one of the finest theatres in Europe – and the Frank-Liszt-Museum honouring the Hungarian composer.

The **Neues Schloss** (New Palace) was commissioned by Margravine Wilhelmine and built by Joseph Saint-Pierre. The elongated, three-storey structure combines classical lines with a rustic ground floor. The Italian wing was added in 1759. Nearly all the rooms still have their original Baroque and Rococo decor, while the park is arranged in a typically English style.

The villa that is now the **Richard Wagner Museum**, dedicated to the composer, was originally built for Wagner by Carl Wölfel. It was destroyed during World War II but restored in the 1970s. Each July and August, Wagner festivals are held at the Festspielhaus (Festival Theatre). The world premiere of *The Ring of the Nibelung* played here in 1876.

In 1715–18, following the example of the French king Louis XIV and the fashion among the nobility for playing at asceticism, Margrave Georg Wilhelm ordered the building of the **Eremitage** complex as a retreat. With its horseshoe-shaped orangery, the hermitage (or Altes Schloss, Old Palace) was given as a gift to Margravine Wilhelmine in 1732, who transformed it into a pleasure palace.

Approximately 20 km (12 miles) to the northwest of Bayreuth is Kulmbach. Well known for its breweries, the town hosts a big beer festival each year, in July and August. Its town hall has a beautiful Rococo façade dating from 1752. From here you can walk to the castle hill to visit the vast Plassenburg fortress, which has belonged to the Hohenzollern family since 1340. Until 1604 this was the seat of the von Brandenburg-Kulmbach margraves. Built in 1560–70, the gem in its crown is the Renaissance courtyard with arcades (Schöner Hof). The castle houses a huge collection of tin figurines.

Around 25 km (16 miles) from Bayreuth, in Sanspareil Park near Hollfeld, is the Felsentheater – an unusual 80-seat theatre set in a natural grotto.

↑ The Festspielhaus, specially designed for the Wagner Festival

Neues Schloss
⊕⊗⊜ 🏠 Ludwigstrasse 21
🕐 Apr-Sep: 9am-6pm daily;
Oct-Mar: 10am-4pm daily
🌐 schloesse.bayern.de

Richard Wagner Museum
⊕⊗⊜ 🏠 Villa Wahnfried, Richard-Wagner-Strasse 48
🕐 Jul-Aug: 10am-6pm daily;
Sep-Jun: 10am-5pm Tue-Sun
🌐 wagnermuseum.de

Eremitage
⊕⊗⊜ 🏠 Eremitage 4
🕐 Castle: Apr-Sep: 9am-6pm daily; 1-15 Oct: 10am-4pm; Park: daily; tours every 45 minutes in German only
🌐 schloesse.bayern.de

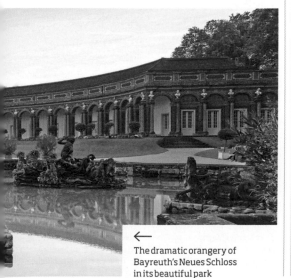

← The dramatic orangery of Bayreuth's Neues Schloss in its beautiful park

The sumptuous stuccoed interior of the Alte Kapelle, Regensburg

 33

Regensburg

E6 **Rathauspl 4; www.tourismus. regensburg.de**

Regensburg was once a Celtic settlement and later a garrison of the Roman legions. The outline of the Roman camp is still visible around St Peter's Cathedral. In the early 6th century, Regensburg was the seat of the Agilolfa ruling family, and in AD 739, a monk named Boniface established a bishopric here. From AD 843, Regensburg was the seat of

> **INSIDER TIP**
> ### Regensburg's Wurstküche
>
> This sausage kitchen is said to be one of the oldest restaurants in the world, and still serves customers to this day. About 40,000 sausages are sold here every week, in fact.

the Eastern Frankish ruler Ludwig der Deutsche (the German). From 1245 it was a free town of the Holy Roman Empire and, throughout the Middle Ages, remained South Germany's fastest growing commercial and cultural centre. The city centre is a UNESCO World Heritage site.

The Steinerne Brücke (Stone Bridge) is an outstanding example of medieval engineering. This 339 m (1,112 ft) long bridge over the Danube was built in 1135–46 and provides the best panoramic view of Regensburg. Near the bridge gate, Brückentor, stands an enormous salt warehouse (Salzstadel) topped with a vast five-storey roof. Immediately behind this is the **Historische Wurstküche** (sausage kitchen), which has probably occupied this site since as early as the 12th century and may have served as a canteen for the bridge-builders. Its Regensburger sausages are definitely worth trying.

In Rathausplatz stands the 13th-century **Altes Rathaus** (old town hall), where the Perpetual Imperial Diet (the first parliament of the Holy Roman Empire) sat between 1663 and 1806. Benches in the chamber were coloured to indicate who could sit where – for example, red benches for electors. The adjoining new town hall dates from the late 17th to early 18th century.

Towering above the city, on the site of the former Roman camp, is the brick cathedral, Dom St Peter built between 1275 and 1525. Its western towers were added only in 1859–69. The **Domschatz-museum** has a collection of ecclesiastical vestments.

The Alte Kapelle (old chapel) is really a Marian collegiate church on the foundations of a Romanesque chapel. The building has been remodelled several times and contains beautiful Rococo stuccoes.

In the south of the town are the buildings and churches of the former St Emmeram Abbey, tastefully incorporated into the ducal complex **Schloss Thurn und Taxis**.

Regensburg has many unique ancestral palaces dating from the 14th and 15th centuries, with high towers modelled on northern Italian architecture. Some 20 of the original 60 towers have survived. One of the most beautiful is the residential tower Baumburger Turm. Nearby, at Watmarkt 5, stands the equally beautiful Goliathhaus, where Oskar Schindler lived for a time in 1945. A commemorative plaque has been placed at the rear of the building.

Designed by the Wörner Traxler Richer architect trio, the ultramodern **Museum der Bayerischen Geschichte** on the banks of the Danube illustrates the timeline of Bavarian history and the events that made it what it is today. There are also regular temporary exhibitions.

Historische Wurstküche

🏠 Thundorferstrasse 3
🕐 9am-7pm daily
🌐 wurstkuchl.de

Altes Rathaus

🕥 🏠 Rathausplatz Reichstagsmuseum 📞 (0941) 507 34 40 🕐 Times vary; call ahead

Domschatzmuseum

🕥🕥 🏠 Krauterermarkt 3
🕐 Dec-Oct: 11am-5pm Tue-Sat, noon-5pm Sun
🌐 domschatz-regensburg.de

Schloss Thurn und Taxis

🕥🕥🕥 🏠 Emmeramsplatz 5
📞 (0941) 504 82 42 🕐 Apr-Oct: 11am-5pm Mon-Fri, 10am-5pm Sat & Sun; Nov-Mar: 10am-3:30pm weekends and hols only
🌐 thurnundtaxis.de

Museum der Bayerischen Geschichte

🕥 🏠 Donaumarkt 1
🕐 9am-6pm Tue-Sun
🕐 Mon 🌐 museum.bayern/museum.html

> **Picturesque Maximilianstrasse is lined with the houses of rich patricians; their shady arcades (*Brodlauben*) are typical of Lindau architecture.**

34 Lindau

🗺 D7 🚉 ℹ️ Alfred-Nobel-Platz 1; (08382) 26 00 30

In Roman times Lindau was a fishing settlement lying over three islands in Lake Constance. The first historic records of the town date from AD 882. On the south side of the old-town island is the harbour, with its 13th-century lighthouse (Mangturm). The New Lighthouse (Neuer Leuchtturm), built in 1856, is on the neighbouring pier. The marble Lion of Bavaria opposite is the symbol of Lindau.

The old town features many historic buildings, and picturesque Maximilianstrasse is lined with the houses of rich patricians; their shady arcades (*Brodlauben*) are typical of Lindau architecture.

In Schrannenplatz, in the northwest, is the church of St Peter. Since 1928 this has been a memorial to those killed in World War I. Its eastern part dates from the mid-12th century, while the bigger western section was built between 1425 and 1480. Inside are many wall paintings, including some by Hans Holbein the Elder. Nearby is the Diebsturm (Thief's Tower) of 1380. The **Stadtmuseum** (town museum) is housed in Haus zum Cavazzen (1729) in Marktplatz, which also features a lovely Neptune fountain.

South of the Market Square is the 12th-century Protestant Church of St Stephen.

Stadtmuseum

🏠 Marktplatz 6 📞 (08382) 94 40 73 🕐 For renovation until 2022

→ Lindau harbour, with the Lion of Bavaria statue, and the New Lighthouse *(inset)*

35
Augsburg

🅐D6 🚆🚌 ⓘRathausplatz 1; www.augsburg-tourismus.de

Situated at the confluence of the Lech and Wertach rivers, Augsburg is the third largest town in Bavaria and one of the oldest in Germany. As early as 15 BC this was the site of a Roman camp, which later became a town known as Augusta Vindelicorum. Until the end of the 13th century, the town was ruled by powerful bishops. From 1316, as a Free Imperial City of the Holy Roman Empire, Augsburg grew to become one of the richest and most powerful cities in Germany. The Thirty Years' War (1618–48), however, put an end to the town's prosperity.

One of the town's highlights is the **Dom Unserer Lieben Frau** (Cathedral of the Holy Virgin). Originally a Romanesque twin-choir, pillared basilica with crypt, western transept and two towers dating from 994–1065,

the cathedral was remodelled between 1331 and 1431 along Gothic lines. It was given two further side aisles, a choir with an ambulatory and a French-style ring of chapels. Original features include the richly carved portals and a replica of the Romanesque bronze door with 35 panels depicting allegorical figures. There are some unique stained-glass windows, dating from 1140.

The Fuggerei, in Augsburg's Jakobervorstadt (Jacob's Suburb), is Europe's oldest social housing estate. It was founded in 1516 by Jacob Fugger, a member of what was then the richest family in Europe. The intention was to provide homes for the town's poorest citizens, particularly families with children. Today, however, it has evolved into a home for retired citizens. The 52 houses in Fuggerei were built in 1516–25 and line six streets. They are surrounded by gardens. One of the buildings houses the **Fuggerei-Museum**, devoted to the history of the estate and with a fascinating shop, the Himmlisches Fuggereilädle.

→
The town of Passau at dusk, with boats lining the Danube

Dom Unserer Lieben Frau
🕘 🅐Frauentorstrasse 1
🕒7am–6pm daily

Fuggerei-Museum
🅐Mittlere Gasse 14 📞(0821) 31 98 81 14 🕒Apr–Sep: 9am–8pm daily; Oct–Mar: 9am–6pm daily

36
Passau

🅐F6 🚉 ⓘRathausplatz 3 & Bahnhofstrasse 28; www.tourism.passau.de

Passau, whose long history goes back to Roman times, lies on a peninsula between the rivers Danube and Inn, near the Austrian border. During the second half of the 5th century, St Severinus established a monastery in Passau as well as several more nearby. In 739 an Irish monk called Boniface, known

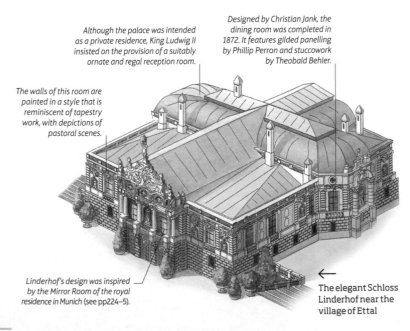

Although the palace was intended as a private residence, King Ludwig II insisted on the provision of a suitably ornate and regal reception room.

Designed by Christian Jank, the dining room was completed in 1872. It features gilded panelling by Phillip Perron and stuccowork by Theobald Behler.

The walls of this room are painted in a style that is reminiscent of tapestry work, with depictions of pastoral scenes.

Linderhof's design was inspired by the Mirror Room of the royal residence in Munich (see pp224–5).

←
The elegant Schloss Linderhof near the village of Ettal

as "Germany's Apostle", founded a bishopric here, and for many years this was the largest diocese of the Holy Roman Empire. Large parts of the town were destroyed by fires in 1662 and 1680. Reconstruction was then carried out by Italian artists, who gave the town its exquisite Baroque, Rococo and Neo-Classical façades. However, Passau retains a medieval feel in its narrow alleys and archways.

   37

Schloss Linderhof

🅰 D7 🅰 Linderhof 12, Ettal ⏰ Apr-15 Oct: 9am-6pm daily; 16 Oct-Mar: 10am-4:30pm daily 🇼 schloss linderhof.de

In the early 1850s, Schloss Linderhof was bought by the Bavarian king Maximilian II. The surrounding remote mountain district had great appeal to the young heir to the throne, Ludwig, later to become the eccentric King Ludwig II. In 1874 work started on remodelling the existing Königshäuschen (Royal Cottage) in the Neo-Rococo style.

The palace is surrounded by a delightful garden which is dotted with romantic little buildings, including the Schwanenweiher (Swan Lake), Venusgrotte (Venus Grotto) and the Marokkanisches Haus (Moroccan House).

 38

Chiemsee

🅰 E7 🚉 🛈 Tourismusverband Chiemsee, Felden 10, Bernau am Chiemsee; www.chiemsee-alpenland.de

Bavaria's largest lake, Chiemsee, is a real paradise for water sports enthusiasts, with sailors, water-skiers, swimmers and divers all enjoying the opportunities it offers. The circular path around the lake and several hiking trails in the vicinity prove enjoyable for the pedestrians too. Chiemsee is set amid magnificent Alpine scenery in the region known as the Chiemgau, which stretches eastwards from Rosenheim to the border with Austria along the River Salzach.

Chiemsee is surrounded by numerous small towns and villages and dotted with islands, some of which feature fascinating historic buildings. Excellent land, water and rail transport facilities ensure trouble-free travel to all destinations in the area.

 PICTURE PERFECT
Colours of Passau

The three rivers that meet in Passau provide an unusual multi-coloured spectacle. When seen from the hills above, the waters of the Ilz, Danube and Inn appear black, brown and light green respectively, forming a watery tricolour as they flow out of town.

A SHORT WALK
AUGSBURG

Distance 1 km (0.5 mile) **Time** 15 minutes
Nearest tram stop Rathausplatz

Once a Roman camp and later a Free Imperial City of the Holy Roman Empire, Augsburg (*p284*) is one of the oldest and most interesting towns in Germany. Its ancient streets are bursting with beautiful and interesting sights, from its handsome 11th-century cathedral to its fascinating 16th-century Fuggerhaüser housing complex – all of which can turn a short stroll into a fascinating open-air history tour. Associated with Brecht and Mozart, the town's cultural attractions include the Rococo Schaezler Palace, the absorbing Maximilian Museum and a puppet theatre museum.

*Featuring a bronze statue of Emperor Augustus, the **Augustusbrunnen** (Augustus Fountain) was created in the workshop of Dutchman Hubert Gerhard in 1594.*

START

PHIL.-WELSER-STRASSE

*Set in a Renaissance patrician mansion, the **Maximilianmuseum** has a splendid collection of work by local gold- and silversmiths.*

*The star attraction of the unassuming, ex-Carmelite **St Anna-Kirche** is the Renaissance memorial chapel endowed by the brothers Ulrich and Jacob Fugger in 1509.*

ANNASTRASSE

BGM.-FISCHER-STRASSE

*A bronze group by Hans Reichle, St Michael Overcoming Satan (1607), adorns the façade of the former **Zeughaus** (arsenal) by Elias Holl, an important early Baroque architect.*

ZEUC
PLAT

WALLSTRASSE

KÖNIGS-
PLATZ

 ←

A tram travelling down Maximilianstrasse in Augsburg's old town

→ The Perlach Tower *(left)* and town hall *(right)*

The **Rathaus** *(Town Hall)*, built by Elias Holl in 1615–20, is widely considered the most significant secular Renaissance building north of the Alps.

St Moritz Kirche

Augsburg's ancient main thoroughfare, **Maximilianstrasse**, features a trio of fountains built in honour of the town's 1600th birthday.

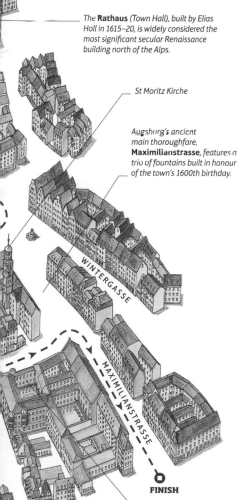

WINTERGASSE

MAXIMILIANSTRASSE

FINISH

↑ The beautifully minimalist interior of Moritzkirche, redesigned in 2010

Did You Know?

After World War II, the Fuggerhäuser was rebuilt in 1951 by Carl Fürst Fugger-Babenhausen.

0 metres 75
0 yards 75
N ↑

Commissioned by Jacob II Fugger (1459–1525) for himself and his family, the Italian-style **Fuggerhäuser** building was built in 1512–15.

BADEN-WÜRTTEMBERG

This southwestern area of Germany was the cradle of two great dynasties that played a significant part in German and European history and culture. The Hohenstaufen dynasty produced kings and emperors who ruled during the most magnificent period of the German Middle Ages (1138–1254). The Hohenzollern family produced Brandenburg dukes, Prussian kings and German emperors from 1871 to 1918.

Its turbulent history has given the province its cultural and religious diversity, which, along with its areas of stunning natural beauty, has made Baden-Württemberg one of the country's most popular tourist destinations. Its charming old university towns, such as Tübingen and Heidelberg, historic castles, luxurious resorts and the magnificent recreation areas of the Schwarzwald (Black Forest) and Bodensee (Lake Constance) guarantee enjoyable and memorable holidays. Visitors will also find an array of interesting museums showcasing everything from cuckoo clocks to cars (both invented here), a wealth of opera houses and theatres, and several major theme parks, including Europa Park, which claims to be the country's biggest.

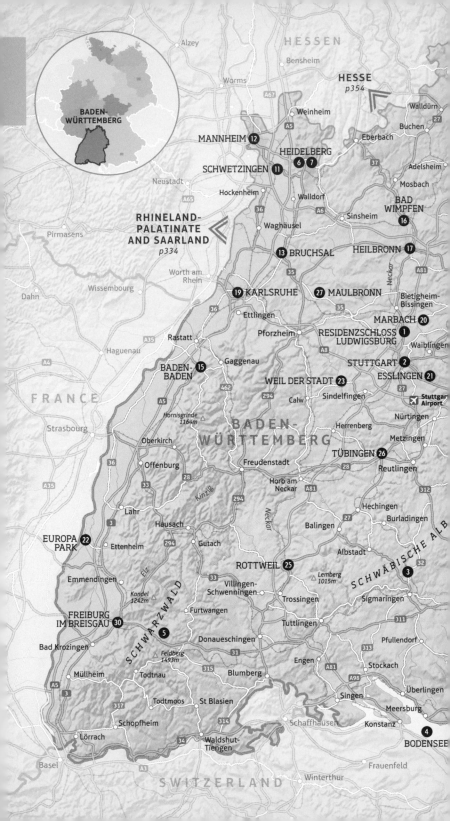

BADEN-WÜRTTEMBERG

Must Sees

1. Residenzschloss Ludwigsburg
2. Stuttgart
3. Schwäbische Alb
4. Bodensee
5. Schwarzwald
6. Heidelberg Castle

Experience More

7. Heidelberg
8. Wertheim
9. Tauberbischofsheim
10. Bad Mergentheim
11. Schwetzingen
12. Mannheim
13. Bruchsal
14. Schwäbisch Hall
15. Baden-Baden
16. Bad Wimpfen
17. Heilbronn
18. Schwäbisch Gmünd
19. Karlsruhe
20. Marbach
21. Esslingen
22. Europa Park
23. Weil der Stadt
24. Weikersheim
25. Rottweil
26. Tübingen
27. Maulbronn
28. Ulm
29. Ravensburg
30. Freiburg im Breisgau

←

1 Heidelberg Castle amidst autumn foliage.

2 Tins containing the Studentenkuss in Cáfe Knösel, Heidelberg.

3 The Philosopher's Path, a beatiful walk in the hills overlooking Heidelberg.

4 Residenzschloss Ludwigsburg, known as the "Swabian Versailles".

3 DAYS
In Baden-Württemberg

Day 1

Morning After arriving in Heidelberg *(p309)*, grab breakfast at the charming and popular Café Rossi *(Rohrbacher Strasse 4)*. Head for the nearby hills to find the historic treasures of the breathtaking ruins of Heidelberg Castle *(p308)* – the funicular railway is an option, if you don't want to tackle the short, steep walk.

Afternoon Around Marktplatz you can admire the Neptune Fountain and the landmark Heiliggeistkirche, which has fabulous architecture, a glamorous interior and a viewing platform. A grand lunch can be found few minutes away at the Restaurant Romer *(Grabengasse 7)*, but be sure to pick up a Studentenkuss (students' kiss) – a chocolate praline made in Cáfe Knösel *(Haspelgasse 20)* – for an after-lunch treat.

Evening Stroll the Philosopher's Path, which was founded by university professors and poets, and whose charms include memorable views over the town, scenic vineyards and a botanical garden. Cross the Neckar river via the Alte Brücke and enjoy seasonal German fare at Kulturbrauerei *(Leyergasse 6)*.

Day 2

Morning Spend the morning walking in the Odenwald Mountains, where you can enjoy walking trails such as the Via Naturae and the Forest Adventure Trail, as well as admire more great views from the summit of Königstuhl.

Afternoon After a picnic lunch in the hills, head back down into Heidelberg to catch a train to Ludwigsburg *(p294)*.

Evening Explore Ludwigsburg centre, whose highlights include attractive historic buildings and charming, winding alleyways. Enjoy excellent Greek food and warm service at Restaurant Elefanten *(Osterholzallee 31)*.

Day 3

Morning Head to the city's grandiose Residenzschloss Ludwigsburg *(p294)*, which blends Baroque, Rococo and Neo-Classical architectural styles.

Afternoon Spend the afternoon exploring the palace's many highlights, including the Queen's Library, the Western Gallery, the Marble Hall and the Northern Garden. There are also several museums on site, including a fashion and ceramics museum and an interactive museum for kids.

Evening Head to Gutsschenke Restaurant *(Domäne Monrepos 22)*, located in a hotel surrounded by a lovely park.

Did You Know?

The palace grounds host the "Baroque in Bloom" show from March to November each year.

RESIDENZSCHLOSS LUDWIGSBURG

⚑ C6 ⚐ E Schlosstrasse 30 ⏰ Times vary, check website 🌐 schloss-ludwigsburg.de

One of the finest examples of Baroque architecture in Germany, this "Swabian Versailles" has an impressive 452 rooms spread over 18 buildings, blending magnificent architectural styles and showcasing stunning period decor.

Situated near Stuttgart, Ludwigsburg was founded in 1704 on the initiative of Eberhard Ludwig, Duke of Württemberg. Originally he intended to build only a hunting lodge here, but in 1718 the duke made Ludwigsburg – rather than Stuttgart – his principal residence, and began the work of transforming it into a world-class palace complex. Construction was completed in 1733, and involved many outstanding architects and interior decorators, including Philipp Jenisch, Johann Nette, Donato Frisoni and Diego Carlone. Between them, they created a sumptuous building in a wide variety of styles, from Baroque and Rococo to Neo-Classical, and filled it with period furnishings, ornate frescos, and various museum-worthy collections (porcelain, fashion) and artworks throughout the endless rooms. The Palace Theatre, which still has its original stage machinery, is a definite highlight, as are the Duke's Rococo-heavy private apartments.

North Garden

This magnificent park was laid out in 1963 for the palace's 250th anniversary.

Western Gallery

▽ The gallery features opulent stucco ornaments by Ricardo Retti and Diego Carlone (1712-15).

↑ The North Garden, maintained in Baroque style and a highlight of the palace complex

Emichsburg

This romantic castle, built in 1798-1802, was named after the founder of the Würtemberg dynasty.

Marmorsaal

▷ The vast Marble Hall in the new wing was remodelled in 1816, when it was given a grand and elegant design inspired by Classical art and architecture.

EUROPE'S HISTORIC THEATRE ROUTE

The European Route of Historic Theatres is a joint project with 16 partners across a dozen countries. The route connects 120 of the continent's best-preserved old theatres, which can be visited via a series of week-long journeys across Europe. Germany has 15 of the theatres (including the Palace Theatre at Residenzschloss Ludwigsburg), some associated with famous names like Wagner and Goethe and others built for monarchs or the clergy.

Schloss Favorite

◁ The "Favorite" hunting lodge was built in 1716-23. It was later converted into a wildlife park.

Märchengarten

▷ The landscaped section of the park includes the "Fairytale Garden", which contains models, statues and scenes from German fairytales.

↑ Sunrise over the charming Neues Schloss on Schlossplatz

2

STUTTGART

🅰C6 ✈South of town 🅿 ℹ️Königstrasse 1A; www.stuttgart-tourist.de

The capital of Baden-Württemberg, Stuttgart grew from a 10th-century stud farm to become the ducal and later the royal capital of Württemberg. Beautifully situated among picturesque hills, the town is a major industrial attraction and also a well-known publishing and cultural centre.

1

Altes Schloss

🅰Schillerplatz 6 ⏱10am-5pm Tue-Sat, 10am-6pm Sun 🌐landesmuseum-stuttgart.de

When Württemberg castle burned down in 1311, it was decided to move the family seat to Stuttgart. In 1325 the existing small castle was extended, creating Drnitzbau. This wing has survived and can be seen from Karlsplatz. A large-scale Renaissance remodelling project, designed by Aberlin Tretsch and carried out in 1553–78, gave the castle its square layout, with three-storey arcaded cloisters encircling the inner courtyard. The southwestern wing contains the Schlosskapelle (chapel), the first sacral

building in Stuttgart built especially for the Protestants. The palace now houses the Landesmuseum Württemberg, which includes vast collections of decorative art, including those displaying the ducal and royal insignia of Württemberg. The prehistory section includes jewellery from the Frankish period and the preserved tomb of a Celtic nobleman from Hochdorf.

2

Schlossplatz

This is the largest square in Stuttgart. At its centre stands the Jubiläumssäule – a column erected in 1841–6 to celebrate the 25-year reign of Wilhelm I. On the east side of the square is a huge palace complex,

Neues Schloss, built in 1746–1807, while on the opposite side stands Königsbau Passagen, a 19th century Neo-Classical structure housing shops and cafés.

3

Kunstmuseum Stuttgart

🅰Kleiner Schlossplatz 1 ⏱10am-6pm Tue-Sun (to 9pm Fri) 🌐kunstmuseum-stuttgart.de

The spectacular glass cube of the Stuttgart Art Museum was designed by the Berlin architects Hascher & Jehle and completed in 2005. It houses the municipal art collection, which includes works by such artists as Adolf Hölzel, Joseph Kosuth, Dieter Krieg, Dieter Roth and the Swabian Impressionists, and has an outstanding collection of Otto Dix's work.

Did You Know?

Stuttgart is credited as the birthplace of the petrol powered motorcar.

④
Schlossgarten

The magnificent gardens stretching north of the Neues Schloss were established in the early 19th century. They have maintained much of their original charm, with neat avenues and interesting sculptures. Other attractions include the Carl-Zeiss-Planetarium, and a vast Neo-Classical theatre building – the Württembergisches Staatstheater – completed in 1912 by Max Littmann. In 1982–3 it was given a new, dome-covered wing, the Theaterpavilion, designed by Gottfried Böhm.

⑤
Schloss Solitude

🏛 Solitude 1 🕐 For tours only; times vary, check website 🌐 schloss-solitude.de

This exquisite small palace, standing on the slopes of a

hill, was built for Prince Karl Eugen in 1763–67. The Prince not only commissioned the residence, but also took an active part in its design, which is the work of Pierre Louis Philippe de la Guêpière, who introduced the Louis XVI-style to Germany. Following its full restoration in 1990, and the provision of 45 residential studio apartments, the palace now serves art students on scholarships.

⑥
Markthalle

🏛 Dorotheenstrasse 4 🕐 7:30am-6:30pm Mon-Fri, 7am-5pm Sat

Stuttgart's market hall, built in 1912–14 on the site of an earlier vegetable market, is one of the finest in Europe. Designed in the Art Nouveau style, it features magnificent frescoes. It was initially set up as a food exchange, and still sells fresh fruit and vegetables to the general public today. It also houses a few restaurants.

DRINK

Biergarten im Schlossgarten
A welcoming spot with German beers and great Swabian dishes.

🏛 Am Schlossgarten 🌐 biergarten-schlossgarten.de

Paulaner am alten Postplatz
Set up in 1747, this venue offers Bavarian cuisine and Paulaner beer, among other drinks.

🏛 Calwer Strasse 45 🌐 paulaner-stuttgart.de

Palast der Republik
Once a public toilet block, this is now a staple for after-work beers.

🏛 Friedrichstrasse 27 🌐 (0711) 226 48 87

↑ A unique lithograph on purple paper of Munch's *The Scream* (1895)

⑦ Staatsgalerie

📍 Konrad-Adenauer-Strasse 30-32 🕐 10am-5pm Tue-Sun (to 8pm Thu) 🌐 staatsgalerie.de

The State Gallery grew from the museum of fine arts founded by King Wilhelm I in 1843 and containing the king's private collection. Now it ranks among the finest of German galleries. As well as its own magnificent collection of old masters and modern artists, the gallery has an extensive collection of graphics. In 1984 the art gallery acquired an extension designed by British architect James Stirling.

⑧ Stiftskirche (Heiliger Kreuz)

📍 Stiftstrasse 12

From the south side of Schillerplatz there is a view of the presbytery of the collegiate church of the Holy Cross. This Gothic church, the work of Hänslin and Aberlin Jörg, was built in the 15th century and incorporated the walls of the previous, early-Gothic church. Despite World War II damage, this renovated church still has the original stone gallery of the

🏔 GREAT VIEW
Fernsehturm

This television tower is 217 m (712 ft) high and stands on a wooded hilltop, Hoher Bopser. Its observation platform provides splendid views over Schwäbische Alb, the Black Forest and, on a clear day, the Alps.

dukes of Württemberg, built in 1576–84 by Simon Schlör to a design by Johann Steiner, as well as Gothic furnishings.

⑨ Hegel-Haus

📍 Eberhardstrasse 53 🕐 10am-1pm & 2-6pm Mon-Sun 🌐 hegel-haus.de

Georg Wilhelm Friedrich Hegel – the creator of one of the most important modern philosophical systems – was born in this house on 27 August 1770.

The house is now a small museum, which contains an interesting exhibition devoted to the life and work of the influential philosopher. Be sure to explore the Escape Room here, which offers an immersive experience by recreating Hegel's time at Jena University.

⑩ Liederhalle

📍 Berliner Platz 1

A must for all lovers of modern architecture, the Liederhalle, in the centre of Stuttgart, is a successful synthesis of tradition and modernism. Built in 1955–6 by Adolf Abel and Rolf Gutbrod, this fine cultural and congress centre, with three concert halls clustered around an irregular hall, is still impressive today.

⑪ Schillerplatz

This is undoubtedly one of Stuttgart's most beautiful areas. It is here that the stud farm that gave Stuttgart its name is said to have stood. Today, a pensive statue of Friedrich Schiller occupies the centre of the square. Schillerplatz is surrounded by historic buildings: the Old Chancellery, built in 1542–4, which now houses a restaurant; the Prinzenbau (1605–78); and the attractive Stiftsfruchtkasten, a gabled granary, now home to a museum of musical instruments.

The Schiller statue by Bertel Thorwaldsen in Schillerplatz ↑

↑ A sandstone carving of Vishnu (c 8th century) at the Linden-Museum

Linden-Museum

🏛 Hegelplatz 1 🕐 10am–5pm Tue-Sat, 10am–6pm Sun 🌐 lindenmuseum.de

This is one of Germany's finest ethnology museums. It was founded by Count Karl von Linden, who was also its director from 1889 until 1910. The museum contains many fascinating exhibits from all over the world, including a Tibetan sand mandala, masks from Cameroon, Chinese burial pottery and a full-size reproduction of an Islamic bazaar.

Mercedes-Benz Museum

🏛 Mercedesstrasse 100 🕐 9am-6pm Tue-Sun 🌐 mercedes-benz.com

To the east of the town centre is the glitzy Mercedes-Benz Museum – a must-visit for all automobile enthusiasts. Its outstanding collection illustrates the development of motorcar production, from the earliest models to today's state-of-the-art, computerized products. Set up to celebrate the centenary of Mercedes-Benz's inventions, the museum features more than 70 historic vehicles. The collection includes the world's two oldest automobiles, Gottlieb Daimler's horseless carriage and Carl Benz's three-wheeled automobile dating from 1886. Also on display is a hand-made limousine that was built in the 1930s for the emperor of Japan, and the first "Popemobile", which was designed for Pope Paul VI.

Another interesting exhibit is the iconic 1950s racing car Silberpfeil (Silver Arrow), as well as models that were built for attempts on world speed records. Visitors can also learn the history of the automotive corporation Daimler-Benz AG, which was created by the merger in 1926 of Daimler-Motoren-Gesellschaft and Benz & Cie, Rhein.

Bad Cannstatt

Once an independent health resort, Bad Cannstatt is now the most populous district of Stuttgart. One of its main attractions is the Neo-Classical Schloss Rosenstein, which was built in 1824–9 at the request of King Wilhelm I, and based on amended designs by John Papworth. The king was also the initiator of the beautiful "Wilhelm's complex". This includes a Moorish-style villa located in a symmetrically laid-out landscaped park and garden, with many Oriental-style pavilions, fountains, terraces and other decorative elements. Completed in the 1840s, its main designer was Karl Ludwig Wilhelm von Zanth. The park has now been transformed into a wonderful botanical-zoological garden.

Bad Canstatt is also famous for the lively Cannstatter Volksfest, a beer festival and funfair held annually from late-September to early October every year.

> Schillerplatz is undoubtedly one of Stuttgart's most beautiful areas. It is here that the stud farm that gave Stuttgart its name is said to have stood.

Stuttgart's open-plan and inviting Stadtbibliothek (Public Library)

3

SCHWÄBISCHE ALB

🗺 C7   ℹ️ Bismarck Strasse 21, Bad Urach
🌐 schwaebischealb.de

The Swabian Jura mountain range extends 220 km (137 miles) long and 40 km (25 miles) across. Beech woods and scented juniper shrubs dominate the mellow landscape, whose system of stalagmitic caves was carved from the sedimentary limestone rocks.

1

Burg Hohenzollern

🏠 Bisingen ⏰ Times vary, check website 🌐 burg-hohenzollern.com

The ancestral seat of the Hohenzollern family was remodelled in 1850–67, and only the 15th-century St Michaelkapelle survives from the original fortress. Guided tours take visitors through the revamped royal chambers (which can also be visited without guides on certain days). The castle also has a restaurant, Zollernstüble, that serves lunch and snacks.

2

Schloss Sigmaringen

🏠 Karl-Anton-Platz 8 ⏰ Mar-Dec: 9am-6pm daily (Mar, Nov & Dec: to 5pm) 🌐 hohenzollern-schloss.de

Sigmaringen's skyline is dominated by its castle, which was reconstructed following a fire in 1893. Home of the Swabian branch of the Hohenzollern family since 1535, its 450 rooms document the House of Hohenzollern and also house one of the most important and impressive private collections of armouries in Europe.

The town of Sigmaringen itself has a unique and rather unexpected place in 20th century history, as it became the city-state of the exiled government of Vichy France in the closing months of World War II.

3

Hechingen

Located 40 miles (64 km) south of Stuttgart, the highlight of this small town is an open-air museum based on the excavation of a 1st–3rd-century AD Roman villa.

4

Haigerloch

🏠 Pfluggasse 5 ⏰ Times vary, check website 🌐 haigerloch.de

In the vaults of Haigerloch is a vast bunker that was once used as an atomic research laboratory towards the end

← The hilltop castle of Burg Hohenzollern, Bisingen

of World War II. Other sights in the town include a Jewish cemetery and a synagogue, and a Roman tower.

---

 ⑤
Beuron

The small village of Beuron has several castles in the near vicinity (Hausen and Werenwag), mostly strung out along the river, as well as some significant religious architecture, including the baroque abbey church of St Martin and St Mary, and the chapel of St Maurus.

Burg Lichtenstein

🏰 Lichtenstein ⏰ Times vary, check website 🌐 schloss-lichtenstein.de

Immortalized by Wilhelm Hauff's novel *Lichtenstein*, this castle was built in the 19th century by Count Wilhelm of Württemberg. Located at the edge of the Schwäbische Alb, 817 m (680 ft) above sea level, its

↑ Bridge leading into the beautiful Burg Lichtenstein

architecture and interior are romantic in style. Visitors can find an armoury, painted rooms, a wood-panelled knight's hall and plenty of artworks. Outside lie a chapel, garden and courtyard.

---

⑦
Donaubergland

The Donaubergland comprises a landscape of majestic peaks and alpine valleys that has been dubbed the "Grand Canyon" of the Schwäbische Alb. The best way to explore it is via the Donaubergland trail, which traverses 60 kilometres (37 miles) of stunning scenery, from the highest peaks in the region to caves, castles, ruins and historic towns.

 ⑧
Hohenneuffen

🏰 Neuffen 📞 (07025) 22 06 ⏰ 9am–5pm daily

This massive castle, the most impressive ruin in the Schwäbische Alb, dominates the tiny town of Neuffen. Looming above the Alb escarpment, the original castle was built in the 12th century, and was turned into a fortress between the 14th and 16th centuries.

> **The massive castle of Hohenneuffen is the most impressive ruin in the Schwäbische Alb region.**

4

BODENSEE

🅐C7 ⓘHafenstraße 6, Konstanz
ⓦbodensee.eu

Known as Lake Constance in English, the Bodensee lies on the border of Germany, Switzerland and Austria. The area surrounding the lake is one of the most attractive in Germany, in terms of both natural beauty and cultural heritage. Towns and villages around the shores have countless reminders of past times and cultures. The best time for a visit is summer, when local fishermen stage colourful fairs and water-sports are possible.

 Konstanz

ⓘBahnhofplatz 43
ⓦkonstanz-info.com

Situated on the northwestern shore of the Bodensee, Konstanz is the largest town in the region, and also particularly lively thanks to its large student population. Its main attraction is the magnificent 11th-century Romanesque cathedral, but the cobbled harbour promenade is also a delight to stroll around in good weather.

 Wasserburg

ⓘMarienplatz 2
ⓦwasserburg.de

Wasserburg's name can be translated as "water castle". It was founded in 784 on what was then an island which became a peninsula in 1720

when it was linked to the mainland by a causeway. Some of the old causeway's sandstone columns still remain. A steamship pier was built in 1872, the first railway station in 1899, and electric lighting was introduced in 1911–12. Sights here today include a 14th-century church, the eponymous castle, and the law courts, which now serve as a museum.

 Reichenau

ⓘPirminstrasse 145
ⓦreichenau-tourismus.de

The greatest attraction of this island is the Benedictine abbey, which was founded in 724 and grew famous during the era of Otto the Great (10th century) for its illuminated manuscripts. It also has a beautiful Romanesque Gothic church and an intoxicating herb garden.

> Situated on the northwestern shore of the Bodensee, Konstanz is the largest town in the region, and also particularly lively thanks to its student population.

↑ Church of St George in Wasserburg, backed by snow-covered Swiss Alps

④
Meersburg

🛈 Kirchstrasse 4
ⓦ meersburg.de

Located directly across the lake from Konstanz, the exquisite Baroque town of Meersburg has two historic residences – the 18th-century Baroque Neues Schloss and the Altes Schloss (New and Old Palaces). The latter is a 16th-century structure built on top of a hill, and contains an old Carolingian palace.

Meersburg's romantic medieval center, ringed by vineyards, makes for some wonderful casual exploration, as do the Vineum Bodensee, the Zeppelin Museum and Tapestry Art Museum.

⑤
Mainau

ⓦ mainau.de

Mainau, situated just off the shore of the Bodensee, is known as the island of flowers. The most beautiful displays are in the park surrounding the 18th-century Baroque palace, which contains a palm house and the largest butterfly pavilion in Germany. Other attractions in Mainau include the Schlosskirche (Palace Church), and an Italian rose garden created for Grand Duke Friedrich I of Baden. Flower shows and festivals take place on the island round the year.

⑥
Lake Dwelling Museum

🅰 Strandpromenade 6, Uhldingen-Mühlhofen
🕘 Times vary, check website
ⓦ pfahlbauten.com

This museum consists of over a hundred lake dwelling settlements that mostly date back to the Stone and Bronze Age, and reconstructed scenes from the Neolithic period.

↑ Relaxing in a blooming garden on the island of Mainau

Did You Know?

Cuckoo clocks have been produced in the Black Forest since the 18th century.

Snow-dusted ↑
hills of the vast
Schwarzwald

⑤

SCHWARZWALD

🅐 B7　🛈 Wehratalstrasse 19, Todtmoos　ⓦ todtmoos.de; schwarzwald-tourismus.info

This expansive forest, named the Black Forest for its dense woodland canopies, stretches from the spa town of Baden-Baden as far as the Swiss border, and contains scenic valleys, great mountain heights and sprawling meadows, not to mention beautiful lakes and hiking trails aplenty.

Covered with tall fir trees and spruces, the Schwarzwald is one of Germany's most picturesque regions. Located in the southwest corner of Baden-Württemberg, the area is famous not just for its unspoilt landscapes, cuckoo clocks, *Kirschwasser* (schnapps) and *Schwarzwälder Kirschtorte* (Black Forest gâteau); in the past, Celts and Romans came to appreciate the therapeutic qualities of the local spring waters. (The sources of the rivers Danube and Neckar are here). The area, especially in and around the national park that was formed inside the region in 2014, is also a paradise for skiers, kayakers, climbers, hang-glider pilots and sailors – not to mention the 32,800 km (18,000 miles) of trails available for hikers and cyclists. If time is limited, take a drive along the scenic Schwarzwald-Hochstrasse route.

→
Cuckoo clocks, a renowned local product

←
The world's largest cuckoo clock, Triberg im Schwarzwald

BLACK FOREST RAILWAY

The Black Forest Railway is one of Europe's most scenic train journeys. Running between Offenburg and Singen, the 149-km (93-mile) route passes through dense pine forests, over mountains and past fairytale villages, at times running alongside rivers such as the Kinzig and the Brigach, and crossing high viaducts. A Eurail Pass valid for travel within Germany can also be used for a journey on this line.

↑ Hikers passing a tumbling mountain stream near Todtnau

↑ Schloss Heidelberg clinging to a hillside, surrounded by forest

HEIDELBERG CASTLE

🅐C6 🅐Schlossberg 🅒8am–6pm daily 🆆schloss-heidelberg.de

The atmospheric ruins of this old castle rise romantically over the university town of Heidelberg. Despite its dilapidated state, the complex still manages to capture the grandiose aura of the Wittelsbach dynasty, drawing an estimated one million visitors every year who come to see this regional landmark and breathe in its history.

This majestic castle is really a vast residential complex that was built and repeatedly extended between the 13th and 17th centuries. Originally a supremely well-fortified Gothic castle, this was the seat of the House of Wittelsbach palatines. After remodelling in the 16th century, it became one of Germany's most beautiful Renaissance residences. However, its splendour was extinguished by the Thirty Years' War and the 1689 war with France, during which most of the structure was destroyed and never rebuilt.

Ottheinrichsbau houses the Deutsches Apothekenmuseum.

Friedrichsbau (Friedrich's Palace) is one of the latest parts of the castle, dating from 1601–07.

🔺 GREAT VIEW
Terrace Treat

The castle gardens – created by architect Salomon de Caus in tribute to Heidelberg's natural surroundings – feature a Great Terrace, which offers panoramic views over the city and the Neckar river.

Castle moat

The grand ↑ Heidelberg castle complex

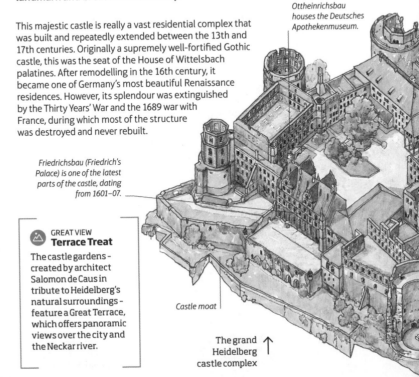

EXPERIENCE MORE

FRIEDRICHSBAU FIGURES

Ornate figures adorn the façade of Friedrichsbau. The bottom row depicts Wittelsbach rulers, including Friedrich IV, who commissioned the figures. The sculptures are actually copies; the originals are inside the building itself.

Ruprechtsbau, built around 1400, is the oldest surviving part of the castle.

Main entrance

Heidelberg

🅰C6 🚉 🛈 Willy-Brandt-Platz 1 (Hauptbahnhof); www.heidelberg.de

Heidelberg is the home of Germany's oldest university, which was founded in the 14th century. One of its most beautiful buildings, the Alte Universität (Old University) can be found in Heidelberg's old town. The name is a little misleading: the building was completed in 1735, its previous incarnation destroyed during the Palatine War of Succession in 1693. Inside the Old University you will find the Alte Aula, a representation hall, whose north wall and ceiling feature allegorical paintings by Ferdinand Keller. In front of the Old University is a fountain crowned by a sculpture in the form of the heraldic Palatinate lion. The Alte Universität is now mainly used for events, and also hosts the **Universitäts-museum,** which documents the history of the university.

Another important building is the Heiliggeistkirche. This collegiate church, whose Baroque dome is a city landmark, was completed in 1515. The canons of the college were also university scholars and therefore the church aisle has special galleries for the vast collections of library books. The Universitätsbibliothek (university library) building, designed by Joseph Durm of Karlsruhe, was completed in 1905. With more than 3 million volumes, this is one of the largest libraries in Germany. The exhibition rooms hold many precious manuscripts and old prints, including the Codex Manesse, illustrated with 137 beautiful miniatures.

The **Kurpfälzisches Museum** is another Heidelberg attraction. The French count Charles de Graimberg spent the bulk of his considerable fortune on an extensive collection of fine art, arms and various curios associated with the history of the Palatinate and the castle of Heidelberg. In 1879, his collection became the property of the town and forms the core of this very interesting museum, which also includes a fascinating archaeology section.

Universitätsmuseum

⊘ 🏠Grabengasse 1 🕐Apr-Sep: 10am–6pm Tue–Sun; Oct–Mar: 10am–4pm Tue–Sat 🖥uni-heidelberg.de

Kurpfälzisches Museum

⊘ 🏠Hauptstrasse 97 🕐10am–6pm Tue–Sun 🖥museum-heidelberg.de

↑ The light-filled interior of the Universitätsbibliothek

8

Wertheim

AD5 **R** **i** Gerbergasse 16;
www.tourismus-
wertheim.com

The rivers Tauber and Main meet at Wertheim, which historic records date back to 1183. A gunpowder explosion in 1619, plus the destruction caused by the Thirty Years' War, turned the Wertheimer Burg into a romantic ruin. Its tall watchtower offers great views.

Not far from Wertheim's market square is a Baroque Protestant church, dating from the 15th–18th centuries. It is home to tombs of the von Wertheim family; the most spectacular is of Count Ludwig II von Löwenstein-Wertheim and his wife.

Also worth visiting in town are the **Glasmuseum**, where exhibits range from fragrance bottles and Christmas tree decorations to jewellery and scientific instruments, and **Grafschaftsmuseum Wertheim**, which houses a collection of folkloric exhibits. The **Museum Schlösschen im Hofgarten** (Little Castle in the Courtyard) in a charming Rococo palace, houses Romantic and Impressionist paintings and Parisian porcelain.

Glasmuseum

⊗ **A** Mühlenstrasse 24
O 10am-5pm Tue-Sat,
1-5pm Sun & hols
w glasmuseum-
wertheim.de

Grafschaftsmuseum Wertheim

⊗ ⊕ **A** Rathausgasse 6-10
C (09342) 30 15 11
O 10am-noon & 2:30-4:30pm
Tue-Fri, 2:30-4:30pm Sat,
2-5pm Sun

Museum Schlösschen im Hofgarten

A Würzburger Strasse 30
O Mar-Oct: 2-5pm Tue-Sat,
noon-6pm Sun & hols;
Nov-Feb: 2-5pm Fri & Sat,
noon-6pm Sun **w** schloess
chen-wertheim.de

9

Tauberbischofsheim

AD5 **R** **i** Marktplatz 8;
(09341) 803 33

Boniface, the Anglo-Saxon missionary to the German tribes, established Germany's first nunnery in AD 735. Its first prioress, Lioba, who was related to Boniface, gave her name to the Baroque church that stands in Tauberbischofs-heim's market square.

The town, which enjoys a picturesque location in the valley of the River Tauber, still has a group of original half-timbered houses. On the market square is the Baroque Rehhof (1702) and the old "Star Pharmacy" in a house

---

TEUTONIC ORDER

The Order of the Hospital of St Mary of the German House in Jerusalem was officially founded in Acre (Akkon) in 1190. Its aim was to care for sick pilgrims or Crusaders. In 1231-83 the Teutonic Knights took over all of Prussia and, in 1308-09 all Eastern Pomerania around Danzig, and they moved their headquarters to Marienburg. In 1525 the Grand Master, Albrecht von Hohenzollern-Ansbach, converted to Lutheranism and secularized Teutonic Prussia. However, the order remained in existence in the Holy Roman Empire: its German Master, Walter von Cronberg, who resided in Mergentheim, became de facto Grand Master. Napoleon abolished the Order in 1809, but it still exists today, with its headquarters in Vienna.

The castle ruins of the charming Wertheimer Burg, above the River Main

once occupied by Georg Michael Franck, grandfather of the Romantic poets Clemens and Bettina Brentano.

In the eastern section of Hauptstrasse stands Haus Mackert – a Baroque mansion built in 1744 for a wealthy wine merchant. In Schlossplatz is the Kurmainzisches Schloss, an imposing palace built in the 15th–16th centuries, which now houses the **Landschafts-museum** with exhibits from the early history of the region.

Landschaftsmuseum

⊗ 🄰Schlossplatz 6
📞(09341) 37 60
🄲Palm Sunday-Oct:
2-4:30pm Tue-Sat, 10am-noon & 2-4:30pm Sun

---

⑩
Bad Mergentheim

🄰D5 🄰 🄸Marktplatz 1;
(07931) 57 48 15

Lying in a charming spot on the River Tauber, Bad Mergentheim was, from 1525 until 1809, the seat of the Grand Masters of the religious order of the Hospital of St Mary of the German House in Jerusalem, more commonly known as the Teutonic Knights. When three Hohenlohe brothers entered the order in 1220, they contributed to it their share of their father's estate. This laid the foundations for one of the most powerful Teutonic commands at the heart of the Holy Roman Empire. From 1244 until 1249 Heinrich von Hohenlohe held the office of Grand Master. The former Hohenlohe's castle,

constructed in the 12th–13th centuries, was remodelled in Renaissance style between 1565 and 1628 by Michael Bronner and Blasius Berwart. They gave the castle its winding stairs and the opulent decor of the stair-case. The Baroque-Rococo Schlosskirche (castle church) dominates the complex. Its interior was designed by François de Cuvilliés, while the ceiling fresco *(The Victorious Cross)* is the work of Nicolaus Stuber. The residential palace now houses the **Deutschordens-museum**, with exhibits on a variety of themes relating to the region.

Many of the town's historic buildings survive to this day, including the 13th-century church of the Knights of St John of Jerusalem and St Mary's church constructed by the Dominican Order and containing the epitaph of the Grand Master Walther von Cronberg. The **Pfarrkirche** (parish church) in the Stuppach district contains a masterpiece by Grünewald (1519), known as the *Madonna of Stuppach*.

Deutschordensmuseum

⊗ 🄰Schloss 16
🄲Apr-Oct: 10:30am-5pm Wed-Sun; Nov-Mar: 2-5pm Tue-Sat, 10:30am-5pm Sun
🅆schloss-mergentheim.de

Pfarrkirche

⊗ 🄰Grünewald Strasse 45
📞(07931) 26 05
🄲8:30am-6:30pm daily

EAT

Zum Ochsen
In a former theatre, this restaurant serves a wide range of beers, along with classic German fare like *Knodelsuppe* and *Bratwurst*.

🄰D5 🄰Marktplatz 7, Wertheim 🅆facebook.com/zum.ochsen

€€€

→
Decorative fountain in the market square of Bad Mergentheim

Manicured gardens in front
of the pastel-coloured
Schloss Schwetzingen ↑

Schwetzingen

🅰C6 🇮Dreikönigstrasse 3;
(06202) 87 400

Built during the reign of the
electors Johann Wilhelm,
Karl II Philip and Karl Theodor
as their summer residence,
Schloss Schwetzingen is a
Baroque-Renaissance palace
which is open to the public for
guided tours. Erected on the
site of a medieval castle, it is
one of the best-known palace
complexes of 18th-century
Europe. The conversion of the
16th-century hunting lodge
was carried out by J A Breuning
and the side wings were built
by Alessandro Galli da Bibiena.
The magnificent Rococo
theatre, designed by Nicolas
de Pigage, was built in 1752,
while the palace garden is the
work of Johann Ludwig Petri,
who designed it in the French
style. The garden includes a
mosque with two minarets
and a bathhouse. In 1776
Friedrich Ludwig von Sckell
converted it into an
English-style garden.

Schloss Schwetzingen

🚻🅟🎫🍴 🏠Schloss
Mittelbau, 68723 ⏰Apr–Oct:
9am–8pm daily; Nov–Mar:
9am–5pm daily 🌐schloss-
schwetzingen.de

Mannheim

🅰C5 🚉 🇮Willy-Brandt-
Platz 5; www.visit-
mannheim.de

Mannheim existed as a fishing
hamlet as far back as AD 766.
In 1606 Elector Friedrich IV the
Righteous ordered a fortress
to be built on the site, at the
junction of the rivers Rhine
and Neckar. A trading settlement sprang up nearby and
was soon granted town status.
Having been repeatedly
destroyed through the years,
the town was finally rebuilt in
Baroque style during the reign
of the Elector Johann Wilhelm.

The town-centre layout
follows the regular Baroque
pattern of the early 18th
century, when the town was
divided into 136 regular
squares. In 1720, when Elector
Karl III Philip decided to move
his residence from Heidelberg
to Mannheim, the foundation
stone for a Baroque palace
was laid in the grounds of a
former citadel.

With over 400 rooms, this
became one of the largest and
most opulent of all German
palaces. Like the residences of
many European rulers at that
time, it was modelled on
Versailles. The main palace
has a horseshoe layout, and
its symmetry is emphasized
by a central projecting
entrance. Building work was
done by Johann Clemens
Froimont, Alessandro Galli
da Bibiena, Nicolas de Pigage
and Guillaume d'Hauberat.

The third largest town of
the region after Stuttgart,
Mannheim boasts many other
historic buildings, including
the Jesuit church of St Ignatius
and St Francis Xavier, designed
by Alessandro Galli da Bibiena
and built in 1733–60. Original
wall paintings by Egid Quirin
Asam no longer exist, but the
altars have survived to this
day, as has JI Saler's sculpture
Silver Madonna in Radiant Glory
(1747). Also worth visiting are
the Baroque Altes Rathaus
(old town hall, 1701–23) and
Secessionist buildings in
Friedrichsplatz such as the
Kunsthalle (art museum) and
Wasserturm (water tower) –
the symbol of Mannheim.

The town has several
interesting museums: the
Kunsthalle Mannheim has a
large collection of 19th- and
20th-century art, including
Francis Bacon's *Study After
Velasquez's Portrait of Pope
Innocent X*. The **Reiss-
Engelhorn-Museen** have
a fine collection of 18th-
century Dutch paintings and
sections devoted to early
history and ethnography.

The **TECHNOSEUM** (Museum
of Technology and Labour)
houses a collection of historic
machinery. Mannheim saw the
first official demonstration of
many inventions that have
now become part of everyday

life. In 1817 Baron Karl
Friedrich von Sauerbronn
demonstrated his first bicycle
in the town and, in 1886, Carl
Friedrich Benz unveiled his
first automobile, produced
at the nearby factory.

Kunsthalle Mannheim

🎨🕐📷 ⬛Friedrichsplatz
4 🕐10am–6pm Tue–Sun (to
10pm first Wed of the month,
to 8pm Thu) 🌐kuma.art

Reiss-Engelhorn-Museen

🎨🕐📷 ⬛Quadrat D5 and C5
🕐11am–6pm Tue–Sun
🌐rem-mannheim.de

TECHNOSEUM

🎨🕐📷 ⬛Museumsstrasse
1 🕐9am–5pm daily
🌐en.technoseum.de

 13

Bruchsal

⬛C6 🚃 🏛Am Alten
Schloss 2; (07251) 50 59 461

Bruchsal belonged to the
bishops of Speyer from 1056
until 1803, since when it has
been part of Baden. The town
rose to prominence in the
17th century, when the Prince-
Bishop of Speyer, Damian
Hugo von Schönborn, moved
his residence from Speyer to
Bruchsal. He not only initiated
the town's development but
ordered a palace to be built
for himself and his court. The
foundation stone of **Schloss
Bruchsal** was laid in 1722
and the building works were
carried out by Maximilian von
Welsch, who was responsible

for the right wing, and
Michael Rohrer, who built
the left wing between 1723
and 1728. The main body,
preceded by a ceremonial
courtyard, was designed by
Baron Anselm von Grünstein.
The central part of the palace
is occupied by a magnificent
staircase built by the great
Balthasar Neumann, with
stuccowork by Johann Michael
Feuchtmayr and paintings by
Johann and Januarius Zick.
The palace suffered severe
bomb damage in 1945, but its
major part was reconstructed
between 1964 and 1975.

St Peter's church was built
in 1740–49 by Johann Georg
to Balthasar Neumann's 1736
design. The church features
magnificent Baroque tombs
of Schönborn and his successor,
Cardinal Franz Christoph von
Hutten. The palace garden
was designed in the French
style by Johann Scheer.

This former residence of
prince-bishops now houses a
section of the Karlsruhe
Museum, which features
Germany's largest collection
of Flemish and French
tapestries. It is also home to
the **Deutsches Musik-
automaten Museum**,
which includes 500
mechanical musical
instruments. Short
demonstrations
are given on these
throughout the day.

Schloss Bruchsal

🎨🕐 ⬛Schönbornstrasse 2
🕐10am–5pm Tue–Sun & hols
🌐schloss-bruchsal.de

Deutsches Musikautomaten Museum

🎨🕐 ⬛Schönbornstrasse 2
🕐10am–5pm Tue–Sun & hols
🌐dmm-bruchsal.de

→
Statue in
the grounds
of Schloss
Bruchsal

14

Schwäbisch Hall

⬛D6 🚃 🏛Am Markt 9;
www.schwaebischhall.de

Archaeological excavations
in 1939 proved the existence
of a Celtic settlement on this
site as early as 500 BC. The
town features a great number
of historic buildings from
various periods, including
many half-timbered 15th- to
16th-century houses, Baroque
town houses, and a Rococo
town hall and town palace
(Keckenburg). The most
interesting building is the
hall-church of St Michael,
whose Gothic main body
was built in 1427–56. The
Romanesque tower on the
western façade, however,
dates from the 12th century.
The late-Gothic hall-choir
(1495–1527) has highly
decorative net vaults.
Original furnishings include
the main altar, the stalls and
the Holy Sepulchre.

15

Baden-Baden

🅰 C6 ✈ Baden Airport
🚉 ℹ Schwarzwaldstrasse
52 & "i-Punkt" in der
Trinkhalle; www.baden-
baden.de

Known as the "summer capital of Europe", the elegant spa resort of Baden-Baden is one of the oldest towns in Germany and was once the favourite destination of European aristocracy from Russia to Portugal. Even before the Romans built their camp here around AD 80, the site was occupied by a Celtic settlement of the Latenian period.

During the days of the Roman Empire, the area was already known in Italy for the therapeutic properties of its

> **During the days of the Roman Empire, the Baden-Baden area was already known in Italy for the therapeutic properties of its waters.**

waters. Romans named the town *Civitas Aurelia Aquensis*, often shortened to Aquae. In the 3rd century AD, Aquae was conquered by the Germanic tribe of Alemanni and in the 6th century AD by the Franks, who built a fortress in the town. The margrave, Hermann II, known as Marchio de Baduon, was the first important ruler of Baden.

During the horrific Black Death, the qualities of the local waters were once again recognized as beneficial to health. During the Palatinate War of Succession, Baden-Baden was almost totally destroyed but, by the end of the 18th century, it had become one of Europe's most fashionable resorts.

The old town of Baden-Baden lies at the foot of the Schlossberg (castle hill). The oldest surviving building in the town is

the Gothic collegiate church, built during the 13th–15th centuries and then remodelled in the 18th century. To the south of the church is the bathing hall – Friedrichsbad – which was built in Neo-Renaissance style in 1877. Nearby stands the magnificent New Palace, which was the residence of margraves from the 15th century onwards. It was remodelled along German Renaissance lines in the 16th century by Kaspar Weinhart. The interiors are decorated with paintings by Tobias Stimmer.

Most of the spa buildings are the work of Friedrich Weinbrenner. His elegant Kurhaus (spa house) in Werderstrasse has been used as a casino since 1838. The most famous gamester at the casino was the Russian author Fyodor Dostoevsky, who was not

always lucky at roulette. His novel *The Gambler* (1866) is supposedly set in Baden-Baden. Nearby is the Trinkhalle (pump room), with its mineral water fountains. Built in 1839–42, it is decorated with wall paintings illustrating Schwarzwald (Black Forest) legends.

Rising behind the town is the last project completed by the German architect Leo von Klenze before his death – the Orthodox burial chapel of a Romanian aristocratic family, the Stourdza Mausoleum. In Schillerstrasse is the villa built in 1867 for the Russian writer Ivan Turgenev, who lived here until 1872, while the exhibition displayed in the **Brahmshaus** is devoted to the life and works of the German composer Johannes Brahms (1833–97), who lived here from 1865 until 1874.

On the outskirts of town is **Kloster Lichtenthal**, a Cistercian nuns' abbey with a church dating from the 14th–15th centuries. Its ducal chapel contains

many epitaphs of the Baden margraves. The abbey also has an interesting museum.

The **Staatliche Kunsthalle Baden-Baden** is an interesting gallery that opened in 1909, and now hosts ever-changing exhibitions dedicated to individual artists or focusing on important cultural themes. The **Stadtmuseum** (town museum) next door includes sections on glass, porcelain and paintings, as well as some old gambling equipment.

Brahmshaus
⊛ ⬜ Maximilianstrasse 85 📞 (07221) 711 72 ⏰ 3–5pm Mon, Wed, Fri; 10am–1pm Sun (10am–4pm daily during Brahmstage, late Oct)

Kloster Lichtenthal
⊛⊛ ⬜ Hauptstrasse 40 📞 (07221) 50 49 10 ⏰ 3pm Wed, Sat, Sun

Staatliche Kunsthalle Baden-Baden
⊛⊛⊛⬜ ⬜ Lichtentaler Allee 8a ⏰ 10am–6pm Tue–Sun ⬜ kunsthalle-baden-baden.de

Stadtmuseum
⬜ Lichtentaler Allee 10 📞 (07221) 93 22 72 ⏰ 11am–6pm Tue–Sun

←

Baden-Baden's colonnaded Trinkhalle *(inset)*, decorated with murals

↑ Charming, centuries-old half-timbered houses in Bad Wimpfen

16 Bad Wimpfen
⬜ C6 🏛 ℹ Hauptstrasse 45; www.badwimpfen.de

This town was created out of two settlements, Bad Wimpfen am Berg (on the hill) and Bad Wimpfen im Tal (in the valley), which remain distinct to this day. The settlement on top of the hill grew around the Hohenstauf family palace, whose chapel and arcade windows, resting on pairs of decorated columns, can still be seen. Built at the order of Friedrich I Barbarossa in 1165–75, this was the main imperial palace (Kaiserpfalz) of the Holy Roman Empire. One of the surviving towers offers views over the Neckar valley.

Bad Wimpfen im Tal is built around the former collegiate church of St Peter and St Paul. This is a triple-nave basilica with transept, two eastern towers and cloister, dating from the 13th–15th centuries. The south façade of the transept and the portal are richly decorated with carvings, which are probably the work of Erwin von Steinbach, one of the builders of Strasbourg Cathedral. The church interior features many original carved statues and stalls.

The imposing Gothic structure of the church of St Kilian, Heilbronn

 Karlsruhe

C6 🚉 🛈 Bahnhofsplatz 6; www.karlsruhe-tourismus.de

Karlsruhe flourished during the 19th century as a centre for science and art. In 1945 it lost its status as a regional capital, but is now the seat of the Bundesverfassungsgericht, the highest courts of the Federal Republic.

The town originated in 1715 when the margrave of Baden, Karl Wilhelm von Baden-Durlach, ordered a lodge to be built in his favourite hunting grounds. Karl liked the area and the lodge so much that he decided to move his residence here and live the remainder of his days in peace – hence the town's name, meaning "Karl's rest". The original Baroque-style design was expanded during the reign of his successor, Karl Friedrich.

The palace, which forms the hub of 32 streets, was designed by Leopoldo Retti, Mauritio Pedetti, Balthasar Neumann, Philippe de la Guêpière and others, and built in 1749–81. The town is based on a fan-like plan, spreading from a base formed by the palace's open-sided wings. The rest of the circle, whose centre is marked by the octagonal palace tower (1715), is filled with green areas, including the palace garden. In the early 19th century, the town was remodelled along

> **Karl liked the area and the lodge so much that he decided to move his residence here and live the remainder of his days in peace.**

Heilbronn

C6 🚉 🛈 Kaiserstrasse 17; (07131) 56 22 70

Heilbronn's earliest records date from the 8th century, when the town was known as Heli-brunna. By the late 19th century, Heilbronn had become Württemberg's main industrial centre, with a large port on the River Neckar. The town suffered major destruction during World War II, but amongst the surviving buildings is the church of St Kilian, a Gothic basilica dating from the 13th century, with a triple-nave hall-choir flanked by two towers. The western tower was built in 1508–29. The magnificent altarpiece is an original late-Gothic polyptych (1498), the work of Hans Seyffer. Near the 15th–16th-century Rathaus (town hall) is a house reputed to have been the home of Käthchen, a character in Heinrich von Kleist's play *Das Käthchen von Heilbronn*. Close to the rebuilt church of St Peter and St Paul stands the former Teutonic convent – the Deutschhof.

Heilbronn is also one of Germany's largest and oldest wine-producing towns, and is well-known for its red wines, wine festivals and seasonal wine taverns.

Schwäbisch Gmünd

D6 🚉 🛈 Marktplatz 37/1; (07171) 60 34 250

This town – the birthplace of the architect Peter Parler and painters Hans Baldung Grien and Jörg Ratgeb – was once renowned throughout Europe for the magnificent goods produced by its goldsmiths. It has many great historic buildings, mainly churches, such as the late-Romanesque church of St John, which dates from around 1220, but was subsequently remodelled. The church of St Cross is known not only for being the first Gothic hall-church in southern Germany, but also the first major work of the illustrious family of architects – the Parlers. This triple-nave hall with a hall-choir, featuring an ambulatory and a ring of side chapels, was built in several stages between 1320 and 1521. Its western façade has a high triangular top with blind windows. Inside the church are many valuable historic relics, such as the Holy Sepulchre (1400), the stalls, which date from around 1550, and the organ gallery (1688). Other interesting structures in the town include the town fortifications and several half-timbered houses.

INSIDER TIP
Medieval Spectaculum

Every August, the Medieval Spectaculum festival enlivens Karlsruhe with jugglers, acrobats and live music. Visitors can taste mead, try archery and even eat medieval cuisine.

Neo-Classical lines. The main architect of this project was Friedrich Weinbrenner. The equilateral market square is positioned along the palace axis. It is filled with similar but not identical buildings and features a central pyramid containing Karl Wilhelm's tomb. South of Marktplatz is the circular Rondellplatz. Weinbrenner's other works include the monumental town hall (1811–25), the Protestant town church and the Catholic parish church of St Stephan.

Karlsruhe has interesting museums. The Badisches Landesmuseum in the castle houses antiquities, decorative arts, sculpture, porcelain and furniture, from the Middle Ages to the present day. In a Neo-Renaissance building (1843–46) is the **Staatliche Kunsthalle**, with its collection of mainly German and Dutch paintings from the 16th–19th centuries. These include the *Crucifixion* by Grünewald (1523).

Entirely different in character are the collections of the **Zentrum für Kunst und Medien (ZKM)**, which occupies a former ammunitions factory in the western part of the town. In its work, the ZKM combines research and production, exhibitions and performances, collections and archives focusing on the development of the art and media of the 20th and 21st centuries. The **Stadtmuseum im Prinz-Max-Palais** contains the local history museum.

Staatliche Kunsthalle

🖼️🖼️ 🏠Hans-Thoma-Strasse 2–6 🕙10am–6pm Tue–Sun (to 9pm Thu) 🌐kunsthalle-karlsruhe.de

Zentrum für Kunst und Medien (ZKM)

🏠Lorenzstrasse 19 🕙10am–6pm Wed–Fri, 2–6pm Sat, 11am–6pm Sun 🌐zkm.de

Stadtmuseum im Prinz-Max-Palais

🏠Karlstrasse 10 📞(0721) 133 42 31 🕙10am–6pm Tue & Fri, 10am–7pm Thu, 2–6pm Sat, 11am–6pm Sun

STAY

Goldener Adler
This upmarket hotel offers old-world decor and contemporary flair. There's a decent restaurant, too.

🗺️D6 🏠Am Markt 11, Schwäbisch Hall 🌐hotelgoldeneradler.de

€€€

Villa Hirzel
Overlooking the river, this hotel has nine rooms with antiques and four-poster beds.

🗺️D6 🏠Remspark 2, Schwäbisch Gmünd 🌐villa-hirzel.de

€€€

Insel-Hotel
This hotel on an island in the Neckar boasts an indoor pool.

🗺️C6 🏠Willy-Mayer-Brücke 1, Heilbronn 🌐insel-hotel.de

€€€

↑ Fascinating exhibits at the Zentrum für Kunst und Medien (ZKM) in Karlsruhe

⑳ Marbach

ⒶC6 🚉 🛈 Marktstrasse 23;
www.schillerstadt-
marbach.de

This small town would probably never merit an entry in any guidebook were it not for the fact that in 1759 the great writer Friedrich Schiller was born here. The modest, half-timbered house in which the poet spent his childhood has survived, and is now a small museum – the **Schiller-Geburtshaus**. The town also possesses a vast museum of literature (**Schiller-Nationalmuseum**), which is housed in a Neo-Baroque palace. Its collection is not limited to the life and work of Schiller, but also includes many documents relating to German literature.

Other attractions in Marbach include some of the original half-timbered houses and the remains of the town walls and gates in the old town. The late-Gothic Alexanderkirche is also worth a visit. Built in the second half of the 12th century by Aberlin Jörg, the church features interesting network vaulting covered with paintings.

↑ Bust of the writer Friedrich Schiller, born in Marbach

Schiller-Geburtshaus
♿♿ 🅿 Niklastorstrasse 31
🕐 Apr–Oct: 9am–5pm daily;
Nov–Mar: 10am–4pm daily
🌐 schillersgeburtshaus.de

Schiller-Nationalmuseum
♿ 🅿 Schillerhöhe 8–10
📞 (07144) 84 80
🕐 10am–6pm Tue–Sun

㉑ Esslingen

ⒶC6 🛈 Rathausplatz 2;
(0711) 35 120

Set among vineyards on the banks of the River Neckar, the beautiful town of Esslingen produces excellent sparkling wines. The town's historic buildings were fortunate in surviving intact the ravages of World War II. A walk through the winding streets and narrow alleys of the old centre will yield many interesting sights, while a climb to the top of the hill affords a splendid view of the town and the Neckar valley, as well as the amazing Innere Brücke, a 14th-century bridge. From there visitors can descend towards the market square, stopping on the way to visit Frauenkirche, a Gothic hall-church dating from the 14th century. Its front tower, the work of Ulrich and Matthäus von Ensingen, was added later.

In the market square is the Stadtkirche St Dionysius, the oldest church in town, built in the 13th century on the site of an earlier, 8th-century building. Inside are some magnificent early-Gothic stained-glass windows and late-15th-century Gothic furnishings, including the choir partition, the sacrarium and the font. The nearby church of St Paul, built in the mid-13th century for the Dominicans, is the oldest surviving Dominican church in Germany. In neighbouring Rathausplatz stands the half-timbered old town

hall, Altes Rathaus, with its beautiful Renaissance façade, and the Baroque Neues Rathaus. Designed as a palace for Gottlieb von Palm by Gottlieb David Kandlers, the new town hall was built between 1748 and 1751.

㉒
Europa Park

ⒶB7 🅿 Europa-Park-
Strasse 2, Rust
🚉 Ringsheim, then bus
7231 🕐 Times vary; check
website for details
🌐 europapark.de

Located between Freiburg and Strasbourg, in the small town of Rust, this sprawling theme park occupying 95 ha

↑ View over the rooftops and vineyards of the town of Esslingen

(235 acres) is the largest in Germany and the second most popular in Europe after Disneyland Paris. Thrill-seekers will find plenty of adrenaline-fuelled roller-coasters, including the Silver Star (one of the highest in Europe), the WODAN-Timburcoaster – which gathers speeds of up to 100 km (62 miles) per hour – a water roller-coaster and a loop-the-loop ride. There are also a number of themed play-grounds for younger children.

The park is divided into 15 areas, each themed to a different European country. There's a flying theatre and ice-skating shows; a 4D cinema; rides for smaller children and a vintage cars section; craft workshops and water balloon catapults. It's possible to book a hotel on site as well as camp, and there are abundant options for food and drinks, too. Unlike most major theme parks, Europa Park is family owned.

㉓
Weil der Stadt

🅐C6 🛈Marktplatz 5; www.weil-der-stadt.de

The town of Weil der Stadt is best known as the birthplace of the astronomer and mathematician Johannes Kepler (1571–1630) and the religious reformer Johannes Brenz (1499–1570).

The town's late-Gothic church of St Peter and St Paul was completed in 1492. Inside is a beautiful Renaissance sacrarium, dating from 1611. The Marktplatz, with a statue of Kepler at its centre, has a Renaissance town hall (1582). Nearby stands the house in which the astronomer was born and which now houses a small museum, the **Kepler-Museum**.

Kepler-Museum

🌐 🏠Keplergasse 2 🕐10am-noon & 2-4pm Thu-Fri, 2-4pm Sat, 2-5pm Sun 🌐kepler-museum.de

JOHANNES KEPLER

This outstanding astronomer studied theology in Tübingen, where he encountered the work of Nicolaus Copernicus, becoming a fervent advocate of his theory. Forced to flee in 1600, Kepler went to Prague, where he worked with Tycho Brahe. Many years of research led him to formulate three laws of planetary motion.

24

Weikersheim

🅐D5 🛈Marktplatz 2;
(07934) 10 255

Lying 11 km (7 miles) east of
Bad Mergentheim is the
picturesque little town
of Weikersheim. A Rococo
fountain from 1768 is at the
centre of the market square,
while the late-Gothic parish
church is on the north side.
The latter is a triple-nave hall-
church with a single-tower
western façade and two
towers by the choir. Inside
are many tombs of the von
Hohenlohe family. Also on the
market square stands the
Tauberländer Dorfmuseum,
which charts the history of
rural life in Franconia. In the
western part of town stands
the well-preserved **Schloss
Weikersheim**, the palace
complex of the Counts von
Hohenlohe, which dates from
the 16th–18th centuries. Its
highlight is undoubtedly the
enormous Rittersaal, a
sumptuous banqueting hall
measuring 35-m- (115-ft-)
long by 12-m- (39-ft-) wide.

The counts and their
aristocratic guests used to
enter this room on horseback.
Its original furnishings include
paintings and reliefs depicting
hunting scenes.

A true rarity is the original
Baroque Hofgarten (palace
garden), designed by Daniel
Matthieu and built in 1709.

Tauberländer Dorfmuseum

🔲 🏠Marktplatz 🕻(07934)
12 09 🕐Apr-Oct: 1.30-5pm
Fri-Sun

Schloss Weikersheim

🔲🔲 🕻(07934) 99 29 50
🕐Apr-Oct: 9am-6pm daily;
Nov-Mar: 10am-noon &
1-5pm daily

25

Rottweil

🅐C7 🚉🛈Hauptstrasse 21;
www.rottweil.de

On the banks of the River
Neckar, Rottweil is Baden-
Württemberg's oldest town. It
grew from a Roman settlement
that was established on a hill

Did You Know?

The Rottweiler dog
breed is named after
the town of Rottweil.

top here in AD 73. In 1234
Rottweil was granted town
status, and by 1401 it had
become a free town of the
Holy Roman Empire. Between
1463 and 1802 it belonged to
the Swiss Confederation,
which was founded in 1291 by
the cantons of Uri, Schwyz
and Unterwalden. In 1802 the
town passed into the rule of
the dukes of Württemberg.

Rottweil has many historic
remains, including sections of
the fortified city walls, with
several well-preserved turrets.
The parish church of St Cross
(Heilig-Kreuz-Münster) dates
back to the 12th century, and
has a triple-nave basilica with
stellar and network vaults.
Late-Gothic altars, including
St Bartholomew's, by Michael

Wolgemut, and a crucifix attributed to Veit Stoss, are among its features.

To the south of the church stands the late-Gothic Rathaus (town hall) built in 1521. On the opposite side of the street, at Hauptstrasse 20, the **Stadtmuseum** has a rich collection of items from the town's history, and costumes from Rottweil's popular carnival (Fasnet, or Fasching), a tradition that goes back to the Middle Ages.

The **Dominikanermuseum** has Roman relics, such as the Orpheus mosaic, dating from the AD 186, and an outstanding collection of late-Gothic sculpture.

The Hauptstrasse is lined with burghers' houses, displaying characteristic oriel windows.

> **Between 1463 and 1802 Rottweil belonged to the Swiss Confederation, which was founded in 1291 by the cantons of Uri, Schwyz and Unterwalden.**

Nearby is one of the most beautiful historic buildings in Rottweil, the Kapellenkirche, built in 1332. Its 70-m (230-ft) tower and three portals are adorned with carved ornaments reminiscent of the French Gothic style. The Baroque interior features frescoes by Josef Fiertmayer. The Gothic Dominican church, built in 1266–82 and remodelled in the 18th century, has frescoes by Joseph Wannenmacher (1755).

↑ Masked figures during the Fasnet carnival procession in Rottweil

The **Puppen- und Spielzeugmuseum** is home to a fine collection of historic dolls and toys. For some top-notch views of the area, take the **Thyssenkrupp** panoramic elevator.

Stadtmuseum
⊗ ⌂ Hauptstrasse 20
☎ (0741) 76 62 ⊙ 2–4pm
Tue–Sun

Dominikanermuseum
⊗ ⌂ Kriegsdamm 4
☎ (0741) 76 62 ⊙ 10am–5pm
Tue–Sun

Puppen- und Spielzeugmuseum
⊗ ⌂ Hauptstrasse 49
⊙ 10am–12:30pm, 2–5:30pm
Wed–Fri, 10am–12:30pm Sat,
2–5pm Sun Ⓦ
puppenmuseum.de

Thyssenkrupp
⊗ ⓜ ⌂ Berner Feld 60
⊙ Times vary, check website
Ⓦ testturm.thyssenkrupp-elevator.com

← The 18th-century Baroque gardens of Schloss Weikersheim

26
Tübingen

🅰C6 🅿 🛈 An der
Neckarbrücke 1; www.
tuebingen-info.de

Along with Heidelberg and
Freiburg im Breisgau, Tübingen
is the home of one of southern
Germany's three top universi-
ties. It was founded in 1477 by
Count Eberhard the Bearded.

The first records of the
fortress that later gave rise to
a settlement on this site date
from 1078. By around 1231
the settlement had become a
town. In 1342 Tübingen passed
to the counts of Württemberg,
having previously belonged to
the counts Palatinate.

Schloss Hohentübingen,
which towers over the town,
has a magnificent gateway
(Unteres Tor). Built in 1606, it is
adorned with the coat of arms
of the House of Württemberg.
The walled castle complex,
with its central courtyard and
long approach, was built in
stages during the periods
1507–15, 1534–42 and 1606.
A walk along the Burgsteige
takes you to the old town.

Here, at the centre of
Marktplatz, is the Neptune
Fountain, created by Heinrich
Schickhard in 1617. In the
western corner of the square
is a Renaissance town hall,
built in 1435 and extended in
the 16th century. It features
an astronomical clock (1511).
Sgraffiti on the western façade
dates from 1876; that on the
elevations facing Haaggasse
is from the 16th century.

The collegiate church of
St George (**Stiftskirche St
Georg**), built in 1440–1529,
is a triple-nave hall with side
chapels, galleries and a tower.
Of particular note are the
ducal tombs, the late-Gothic
reading room and the 15th-
century stained-glass
windows of the choir. Fine
stalls, adorned with carved
figures of the Prophets, date
from the late 15th century.

The bookstore in Holzmarkt
(Buchhandlung Heckenhauer)
is where Hermann Hesse once
served as an apprentice book-
seller. On the banks of the
Neckar is the **Hölderlinturm**,
in which the German poet
Friedrich Hölderlin lived from
1807 until his death. Nearby is

↑ A punt on the River
Neckar, with Tübingen
in the background

the Alte Burse building, which
was constructed in 1478–80
and later remodelled in 1803–
1805. It was formerly used to
accommodate students and
also served as a lecture hall.
Martin Luther's close associate
Philipp Melanchthon lectured
here between 1514 and 1518.

The Protestant seminary
in Neckarhalde was founded
by Prince Ulrich in 1536. Its
graduates include the poets
Hölderlin, Eduard Mörike and

🅰 GREAT VIEW
Neckar Island

Picture-perfect views
of Tübingen can be
enjoyed from Neckar
Island. This scenic
man-made island was
constructed in 1910,
and is renowned for
its spectacular avenue
of plane trees, some of
which are more than
200 years old.

Friedrich Schiller, as well as philosophers Georg Hegel and Friedrich Schelling.

The **Kunsthalle** (art gallery) is famous in Germany not only for its temporary exhibitions, but also for its fine collection of modern art. Other popular attractions in Tübingen include the **Stadtmuseum**, which is devoted to the town's history, as well as the superb **Auto- und Spielzeugmuseum**, which combines exhibits on cars and toys.

Schloss Hohentübingen
⊛ 🏠 Burgsteige 11
📞 (07071) 297 73 84
🕙 10am–5pm Wed–Sun

Stiftskirche St Georg
⊛ 🏠 Holzmarkt 1 📞 (07071) 525 83 🕙 9am–4pm daily (to 5pm Easter–Thanksgiving)

Hölderlinturm
⊛ 🏠 Bursagasse 6
📞 (07071) 25 42 45 🕙 10am–2pm & 3–5pm Tue–Fri; 2–5pm Sat & Sun

Kunsthalle
📧 🎦 🏠 Philosophenweg 76
🕙 11am–6pm Tue, Wed & Fri–Sun; 11am–7pm Thu
🌐 kunsthalle-tuebingen.de

Stadtmuseum
⊛ 🏠 Kornhausstrasse 10
📞 (07071) 20 41 711 or (07071) 94 54 60 🕙 11am–5pm Tue–Sun

Auto- und Spielzeugmuseum
⊛ 🏠 Brunnenstrasse 18
🕙 10am–noon & 2–5pm Wed–Fri; 10am–5pm Sat, Sun & public hols 🌐 boxenstop-tuebingen.de

---

㉗
Maulbronn
🅰 C6 🚹 Klosterhof 31; (07045) 10 30

Maulbronn grew up around a Cistercian monastery, **Kloster Maulbronn**, founded in 1147 in the valley of the

River Salzach by monks who came here from Alsace. The church, built in 1147–78, is an elongated, triple-nave basilica with a transept and a chancel. The early Gothic porch in front of the church was added in 1220.

Originally the church had a wooden ceiling. In 1424 it was replaced with a network vault, in stark contrast to the plain walls. In the Middle Ages monks meditated as they walked around the cloisters. Talking was strictly forbidden.

Outside the enclosure are domestic buildings, such as a former mill, a forge, a bakery and a guest house. Defence walls with turrets and a gate tower encircle the entire complex, which is a UNESCO World Heritage site.

Kloster Maulbronn
📧 🕙 🏠 Klosterhof 5
🕙 Mar–Oct: 9:30am–5:30pm daily; Nov–Feb: 9:30am–5pm Tue–Sun
🌐 kloster-maulbronn.de

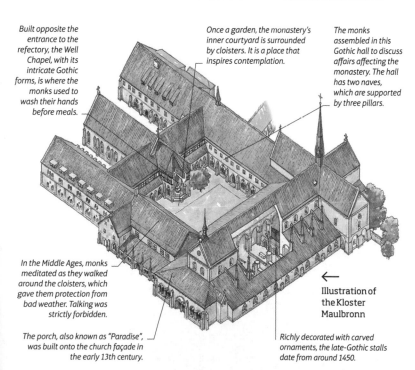

Built opposite the entrance to the refectory, the Well Chapel, with its intricate Gothic forms, is where the monks used to wash their hands before meals.

Once a garden, the monastery's inner courtyard is surrounded by cloisters. It is a place that inspires contemplation.

The monks assembled in this Gothic hall to discuss affairs affecting the monastery. The hall has two naves, which are supported by three pillars.

In the Middle Ages, monks meditated as they walked around the cloisters, which gave them protection from bad weather. Talking was strictly forbidden.

← Illustration of the Kloster Maulbronn

The porch, also known as "Paradise", was built onto the church façade in the early 13th century.

Richly decorated with carved ornaments, the late-Gothic stalls date from around 1450.

Ulm

A D6 🚉 ℹ️ Münsterplatz 50; www.tourismus.ulm.de

Lying on the River Danube, Ulm dates back to AD 854. It became a town in 1165 then, in 1274, a free town of the Holy Roman Empire. During the 15th century Ulm was one of the richest towns in Europe but the Thirty Years' War put an end to its rapid development. In 1810 Ulm came under the rule of the Württemberg kings. The town is renowned as the birthplace of Albert Einstein in 1879. During World War II, most of the old town was destroyed during bombing raids.

Fortunately the Münster (minster), a true masterpiece of European Gothic architecture, survived unscathed. A vast, five-nave basilica, its 161-m- (530-ft-) high west tower is the highest church tower in the world. The cathedral's construction, from 1377 until 1545, was overseen by the greatest

Did You Know?

Ulm is home to the world's largest church steeple.

builders of the German Gothic – Heinrich and Michael Parler, Ulrich von Ensingen, Hans Kun and Matthäus Böblinger. The unfinished cathedral was extended in 1844–90, based on the original medieval design. The interior contains many great features, including the altar by Hans Multscher (1443), the famous stalls with figures of poets, philosophers, prophets and apostles carved by Jörg Syrlin the Elder, 15th-century stained-glass windows, and the font, by Jörg Syrlin the Younger.

The town has other fine historic buildings that survived the war, including the Gothic-Renaissance town

hall, which is decorated with brightly coloured frescoes and features an astronomical clock. Other sights in Marktplatz include the Gothic fountain Fischkasten (Fish Crate), dating from 1482, and the Reichenauer Hof, which dates from 1370–1535.

The **Museum Ulm**, which is housed in a number of historic 16th- and 17th-century buildings, has a collection of art spanning a period from the Middle Ages up to the present day. The collection includes the work of local artists, such as Hans Multscher. The **Museum Brot und Kunst** specializes in artifacts related to bread and bread-making, including items depicting bread in art and graphic designs.

Museum Ulm
♿ Marktplatz 9 ⏰ 11am–5pm Tue–Fri (to 6pm Sat & Sun) 🌐 museumulm.de

Museum Brot und Kunst
♿ 🚉 Salzstadelgasse 10 ⏰ 10am–3pm Mon, 10am–5pm Tue, Thu & Sun, 10am–7pm Wed 🌐 museumbrotundkunst.de

Ravensburg

A D7 🚉 ℹ️ Marienplatz 35; www.ravensburg.de

The first historic records of the Ravenspurc fortress date from 1088, when it was one of the seats of the Welf family. It is believed to be the birthplace of Henry the Lion, the powerful Duke of Saxony and Bavaria, born in 1129. The settlement that sprang up at the foot of the castle became a free imperial city in 1276. From 1395 paper was produced here and, during

←

The imposing interior of the Gothic, five-nave Ulm Münster

Martinstor (St Martin's Gate), originally part of Freiburg's fortifications

the 15th century, the town became one of the richest in Germany from its involvement in the linen trade.

Standing in Kirchstrasse is the 14th-century Liebfrauenkirche (parish church), which retains original 15th-century features, including the main altar and some fine stained-glass windows.

In Marienplatz stands the late-Gothic town hall (14th–15th century), with its lovely Renaissance bay window. Also in Marienplatz is the Waaghaus (1498), which housed the weigh house and mint on the ground floor, with a trading hall upstairs, when Ravensburg was engaged in coin production. The watchtower (Blaserturm) is crowned by a Renaissance octagon that has become the symbol of the town. Another attractive building here is the Lederhaus (leather workers' house), which dates from 1513–14. Near the town hall is the old 14th- to 15th-century granary (Kornhaus).

Marktstrasse features many old burgher houses. No. 59, the oldest house in town, dates from 1179. The neighbouring house was built in 1446. The tall white cylindrical tower that can be

seen from here is known as the "sack of flour" (Mehlsack). It was erected in the 16th century. A magnificent view of the town can be obtained from Veitsburg, which occupies the site of the original Welf castle.

30
Freiburg im Breisgau

🅰B7 🚉 🛈Rathausplatz 2-4; www.visit.freiburg.de

The dukes of Zähringen first established Freiburg in 1120. The town, which later belonged to the Counts von Urach, became so rich over the years that, in 1368, it bought its freedom and voluntarily placed itself under the protection of the Habsburgs. Marshal Vauban fortified the town in the 17th century, when Freiburg briefly belonged to France. Since 1805 it has been part of Baden. Situated between Kaiserstuhl and Feldberg, it is a natural gateway to the southern Schwarzwald (Black Forest).

The town centre is a pleasant place for a stroll and will reveal architectural highlights, including the

varied houses around Münsterplatz, Freiburg University – which occupies a Baroque Jesuit complex – and the Haus zum Walfisch (Whale House) in Franziskanergasse, the lovely bay window of which is a magnificent example of late-Gothic style.

In picturesque Münsterplatz you will find the cathedral, which started as a Romanesque basilica around 1200 and was completed by 1513 in the French Gothic style. Inside is the original main altar by Hans Baldung Grien. The square is also still used as a marketplace.

Completed in 1520, with ground-floor arcades and richly adorned gables, the Kaufhaus ("merchant's hall") was used by the city administration as a market and a customs and financial centre.

The town centre is a pleasant place for a stroll and will reveal architectural highlights, including the varied houses around Münsterplatz and Freiburg University.

A SHORT WALK
HEIDELBERG

Distance 1km (0.5 mile) **Time** 15 minutes
Nearest bus stop On Alte Brücke or Am Hackteufel

The area around Haupstrasse is a great place to explore on foot as it takes visitors into the heart of old town Heidelberg (p309). For centuries it was a centre of political power, with a lively and influential cultural life. In 1386, Germany's first university was established here by the Elector Ruprecht I (ruled 1356–90). The building of Heidelberg's castle (p308) also began during his reign, continuing until the mid-17th century. However, in the late 17th century, French incursions totally destroyed medieval Heidelberg, including the castle. The town was subsequently rebuilt in the early 18th century in Baroque style, while the castle has been kept as a historic ruin.

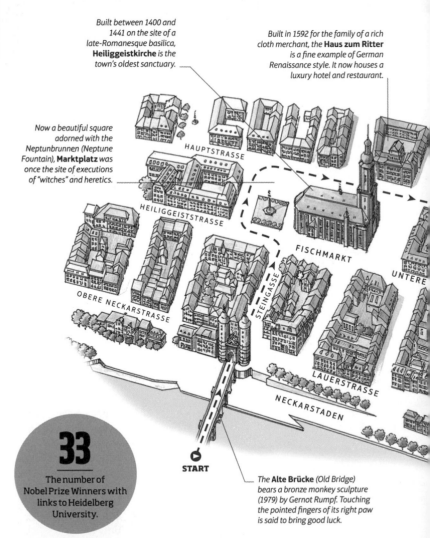

Built between 1400 and 1441 on the site of a late-Romanesque basilica, **Heiliggeistkirche** is the town's oldest sanctuary.

Built in 1592 for the family of a rich cloth merchant, the **Haus zum Ritter** is a fine example of German Renaissance style. It now houses a luxury hotel and restaurant.

Now a beautiful square adorned with the Neptunbrunnen (Neptune Fountain), **Marktplatz** was once the site of executions of "witches" and heretics.

HAUPTSTRASSE

HEILIGGEISTSTRASSE

FISCHMARKT

UNTERE

OBERE NECKARSTRASSE

STEINGASSE

LAUERSTRASSE

NECKARSTADEN

START

33
The number of Nobel Prize Winners with links to Heidelberg University.

The **Alte Brücke** (Old Bridge) bears a bronze monkey sculpture (1979) by Gernot Rumpf. Touching the pointed fingers of its right paw is said to bring good luck.

⌖ GREAT VIEW
Philosophers' Walk

On the slopes of Heiligenberg hill, at an altitude of approximately 200 m (650 ft), the Philosophenweg (Philosophers' Walk) offers magnificent views of Heidelberg.

↑ Sunset over Heidelberg's Altstadt (old town) and the Neckar river

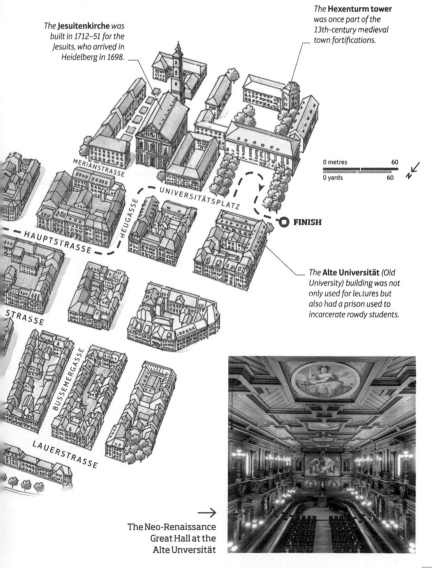

*The **Jesuitenkirche** was built in 1712–51 for the Jesuits, who arrived in Heidelberg in 1698.*

*The **Hexenturm tower** was once part of the 13th-century medieval town fortifications.*

MERIANSTRASSE

UNIVERSITÄTSPLATZ

HEUGASSE

HAUPTSTRASSE

STRASSE

BUSSEMERGASSE

LAUERSTRASSE

| 0 metres | 60 |
| 0 yards | 60 |

🅞 FINISH

*The **Alte Universität** (Old University) building was not only used for lectures but also had a prison used to incarcerate rowdy students.*

→ The Neo-Renaissance Great Hall at the Alte Unversität

WESTERN GERMANY

Rhineland-Palatinate
and Saarland................................... 334

Hesse.. 354

North Rhine-Westphalia 380

Skyscrapers in Frankfurt am Main

EXPLORE WESTERN GERMANY

This section divides western Germany into three colour-coded sightseeing areas, as shown here. Find out more about each area on the following pages.

NETHERLANDS

Lingen

Enschede

Gronau

Coesfeld

Münster

Kleve

NORTH RHINE-WESTPHALIA
p380

Wesel

Essen

Dortmund

Duisburg

Mulheim

Hagen

Düsseldorf

Wuppertal

Antwerp

Roermond

Dormagen

Solingen

Brussels

Hasselt

Maastricht

Köln

Waremme

Aachen

Hennef

Liège

Verviers

Bonn

Namur

Charleroi

BELGIUM

St Vith

Adenau

Koblenz

Houffalize

Prüm

RHINELAND-PALATINATE & SAARLAND
p334

Wittlich

RHINELAND-PALATINATE

Neufchâteau

LUXEMBOURG

Trier

Morbach

Charleville-Mézières

Luxembourg City

Nohfelden

Marville

SAARLAND

Kaiserslautern

Thionville

Homborg

FRANCE

Saarbrücken

Pirmasens

Verdun

Metz

Saint-Avold

Pannes

Sarre-Union

Delme

0 kilometres 40

0 miles 40

N

GETTING TO KNOW
WESTERN GERMANY

Famed for its excellent wines and the festivities of Köln's annual carnival, western Germany is the country's wealthiest and most heavily industrialized region. The region is also rich in tourist attractions: romantic castles, impressive cathedrals and fascinating, historic cities.

PAGE 334

RHINELAND-PALATINATE AND SAARLAND

This romantic region is renowned for its wines as well as its gently seductive landscapes, which include the volcanic Eifel area, the Westerwald and the Mosel and Rhine valleys lined with medieval fortresses and vineyards. These valleys are best experienced via a slow river cruise. Historic cities such as Trier and Worms showcase Romanesque architecture, while Völklingen highlights the region's industrial legacy.

Best for
Castles, historic towns and vineyards

Home to
The Westerwald and Trier

Experience
Enjoy a leisurely river cruise between Koblenz and Bingen that will take you past vineyards, castles and scenic cliffs

HESSE

PAGE 354

Located in the heart of Germany, Hesse is famous for its urban highlight, Frankfurt am Main, whose reputation as a banking centre belies its picturesque charms and cultural prowess. Beyond the big city lies architecture ranging from Romanesque churches to Gothic cathedrals, university towns including Marburg, Darmstadt and burgeoning art hub Kassel, as well as the wild landscapes of the Waldecker Land.

Best for
Wine, dining, countryside

Home to
Kassel, Waldecker Land and Frankfurt am Main

Experience
Take a stroll around Frankfurt's Römer and the River Main, enjoying the city's wealth of culture

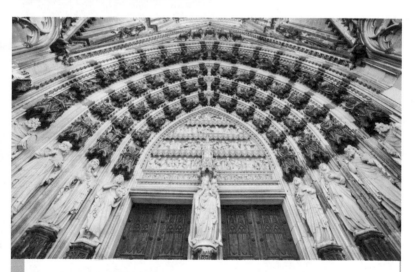

NORTH RHINE-WESTPHALIA

PAGE 382

Formerly a heavy industrial centre, today's North Rhine-Westphalia is a mixed bag of cultural and architectural highlights found in cities including Köln, Düsseldorf and Münster, and rural delights such as the Teutoburg Forest, the mountains of the Northern Eifel and the lake-dotted Sauerland. The industrial Ruhr valley has now been transformed into a cultural hub.

Best for
Museums, architecture and culture

Home to
Düsseldorf, Köln and Bonn

Experience
Explore the Industrial Heritage Trail, stopping off to explore cultural highlights in cities such as Essen and Duisburg

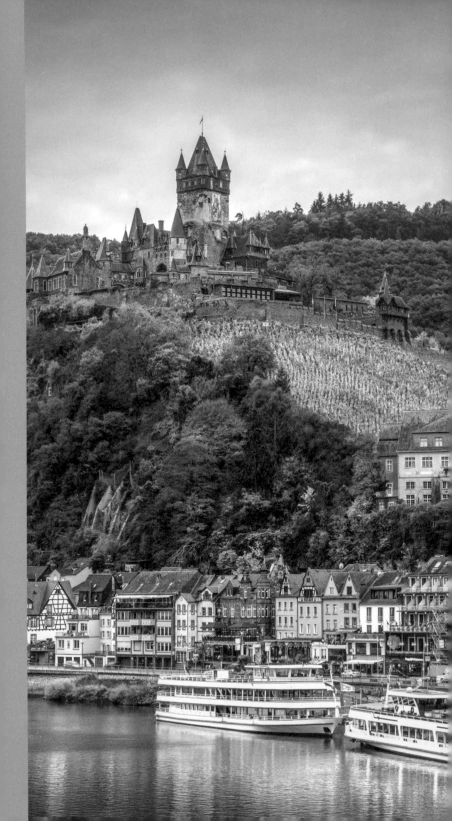

RHINELAND-PALATINATE AND SAARLAND

These two states did not emerge in their present form until after World War II. The Rhineland-Palatinate was created from the previously independent Bavarian Palatinate and the southern part of the Central Rhineland, making it a true jigsaw puzzle of territories. The Saarland was under French rule until 1956 and today forms a bridge between France and Germany, the two driving forces of European unity.

Together the states make up one of Germany's most romantic regions. The picturesque Mosel valley is lined with grand medieval fortresses, such as Burg Eltz, while Worms on the Rhine is the setting for most of the Nibelungen legend as well as the residence of the mythical king of Burgundy, Gunther. The Deutsches Eck ("German Corner") in Koblenz is the strategic spot where the Mosel flows into the Rhine, and Koblenz also marks the beginning of the romantic Rhine valley. A boat trip upriver, justifiably popular with visitors, will pass some spectacular rocky scenery, including the Lorelei Rock and countless castles set among vineyards on either side of the river.

RHINELAND-PALATINATE AND SAARLAND

Must Sees

1 The Westerwald
2 Trier

Experience More

3 Saarbrücken
4 Völklingen
5 Homburg
6 Ottweiler
7 Worms
8 Oppenheim
9 Koblenz
10 Maria Laach
11 Mainz
12 Speyer

HESSE
p354

BADEN-WÜRTTEMBERG
p288

▽ Ahr

Set along the River Ahr, just south of Bonn, the Ahr wine region is one of Germany's northernmost. The vineyards are perched on steep, rugged cliffs, and produce mostly red wines, such as Spätburgunder, but also whites. The valley can be explored via the Ahrsteig trail or the Ahr Cycle Route.

SUCCESS WITH RED

Germany will probably always be best known for its white wines but, despite the country's lack of Mediterranean climate, its red wines have been revolutionized in recent decades. Spätburgunder, a Pinot Noir, is a particular success story and now accounts for about a third of German wine production. The country is today the world's third-largest Pinot Noir producer, just behind France and the USA.

RHINELAND-PALATINATE AND SAARLAND
RAISE A GLASS

A major producer of wines – especially whites – Germany has abundant vineyards, particularly in West Germany. Head here to sample some of the best Rieslings on the market, full-bodied Silvaner and increasingly excellent Pinot Noirs.

△ Mittelrhein

The Mittelrhein, also referred to as "the Rhine Gorge", is located along the River Rhine. The 95-km- (60-mile-) long stretch is especially scenic, its vineyards peppered with medieval castles and rocky peaks. Some 65 percent of the area produces white wines, mostly Riesling.

▽ Mosel

The Mosel Valley region has hundreds of vineyards, many of them located on the steep banks of the Mosel River and its two smaller tributaries, the Saar and the Ruwer. These vineyards produce predominantly Riesling, but also Müller-Thurgau, Kerner and other grapes. With only around a third of the wine from here exported, a visit is very rewarding.

△ Nahe

To the south of the Hunsrück mountains, between the Rhine and Mosel valleys, the Nahe region is a tranquil area of orchards, meadows and vineyards. It is named after the Nahe River, on whose banks lie most of the region's vineyards. Though this is one of the smaller wine regions, the diverse soil types here make for a varied selection of grapes.

◁ Rheinhessen

Germany's largest wine region, Rheinhessen occupies an attractive landscape of gently rolling hills. Situated in the Rhine Valley, it is bordered by the Nahe on the west and the Rhine to the north and east. Its varied terrain and decent climate mean it can grow several grape varieties, including white wine favourites Silvaner, Scheurebe and Siegerrebe.

◁ Palatinate (Pfalz)

Bordered by Rheinhessen to the north and France to the south and west, the idyllic Palatinate or Pfalz region, peppered with castles, orchards and charming villages, is one of the warmest wine-growing regions in Germany, with approximately 1,800 hours of sunshine each year. It produces full-bodied white wines, mostly from the Riesling and Müller-Thurgau grapes, but is also one of the main red-wine regions, with around 40 percent of the growing area producing strong and complex reds.

TOP 5 GERMAN WINES

Spätburgunder
A Pinot Noir, light in colour and body.

Weissburgunder
A Pinot Blanc, elegant with a subdued taste.

Grauburgunder
A Pinot Grigio, ranging from dry to rich.

Riesling
Can range from dry to very sweet.

Müller-Thurgau
A straw-yellow colour and fresh, fruity taste.

THE WESTERWALD

A C4 **A** **i** Kirchstrasse 48a, Montabaur; (02602) 30 01 0

This mountainous region offers a wealth of attractive landscapes, from forests and valleys to romantic villages. It is also peppered with farms and industrial sites, such as ironmines and clay quarries, that offer new sights and adventures down every road.

The low mountain range known as the Westerwald lies between Köln and Frankfurt, and borders the Rhine, Sieg and Lahn rivers. Known primarily for its gently rolling hills, historic towns and verdant forests, it is also dotted with a slew of interesting and varied sights. Bad Marienberg, a medieval spa town, and Hachenburg, with its impressive castle and half-timbered buildings, make good bases to explore the region and are interesting in their own right.

Exploring the Westerwald

Picturesque places to explore include the extinct volcano Fuchskaute, the scenic Holzbachschlucht gorge, and the Kroppacher Schweiz conservation area. The Limes Museum in Bad Hönningen is a fascinating place to explore the days of the Roman Empire. Another fine way to experience the region is to join the 235-km (146-mile) Westerwald Trail, which runs through the Westerwald Lake District to the Birkenhof distillery, where you can watch schnapps being made.

↑ The historic Schloss in Montabaur, now a hotel

Bad Marienberg, a medieval spa town, and Hachenburg, with its impressive castle and half-timbered buildings, make good bases to explore the region.

↑ Brightly coloured houses in the central market square of Hachenburg

KANNENBÄCKER

Kannenbäcker means "potter", an apt name for an area that has had a strong connection with ceramics since the discovery of one of the largest clay deposit regions in Europe was made here in the 16th century. Pottery continues to be produced here to this day, and the history of the industry is portrayed in a ceramics museum in Höhr-Grenzhausen. For visitors interested in making a purchase, there are also two international ceramics markets in the region each year – one in Höhr-Grenzhausen and the other in Ransbach-Baumbach, both of which draw thousands of visitors eager to peruse the region's distinctive creations and artworks.

656 m

The height of the Westerwald's highest mountain, Fuchskaute. (2,152 ft)

↑ Idyllic countryside and mist-shrouded hills of the Westerwald in early autumn

↑ The Hauptmarkt, arguably Germany's most attractive square

2

TRIER

 **B5** ℹ️ **An der Porta Nigra** 🌐 **trier-info.de**

One of Germany's oldest towns, Trier was founded in 17 BC as Augusta Treverorum, supposedly by Emperor Augustus himself. As well as preserving impressive Roman antiquities, Trier attracts a vast number of visitors for its wine, and pleasing river views. It is also the birthplace of Karl Marx.

①

Hauptmarkt

Trier's main market square, one of the most attractive in Germany, dates back to the 10th century. The Marktkreuz (market cross) erected around the same time symbolized the town's right to hold markets. Today a copy of the original cross is mounted on a granite Roman column, with a relief of the Lamb of God. On the southeastern side of the square is the Petrusbrunnen (St Peter's fountain), from 1595, with sculptures of St Peter and the Four Virtues. On the southwestern side stands the 15th-century Steipe, with a steep gabled roof. Originally it was used by the town councillors as a guest house and banqueting hall. The Baroque Rotes Haus (Red House) next door dates from 1683. Löwenapotheke, in a 17th-century building on the southeastern side of the square, is Germany's oldest pharmacy, its records dating back to the 13th century.

②

Museum am Dom Trier

🏛️ **Bischof-Stein-Platz 1**
🕙 **10am–6pm Tue–Sun**
🌐 **bistum-trier.de**

A 19th-century former Prussian prison near the cathedral now houses the art collection of the Diocese, including early Christian works of art. Its most prized possession is a 4th-century ceiling painting from the imperial palace that once stood on the site of the cathedral. Rediscovered in 1945, the fresco was painstakingly restored over the following decades. Another exhibit is the reconstructed crypt of the Benedictine church of St Maximin, which has 9th-century Carolingian wall paintings.

③

Aula Palatina (Konstantin-Basilika)

🏛️ **Konstantinplatz**
📞 **(0651) 42 570** 🕙 **Apr–Oct: 10am–6pm Mon–Sat, 1–6pm Sun; Nov–Mar: 10am–noon & 2–4pm Tue–Sun**

Another UNESCO World Heritage site, the Aula Palatina (Palatinate Hall) dates from AD 310. An enormous elongated, rectangular brick building with a vast semi-circular apse, it served as the throne hall of the Roman emperor or his representative. Following the town's sacking by Germanic tribes, the building was reduced to rubble. In the 12th century the apse was converted into a tower, to accommodate the archbishop. In the 17th century the Aula

Palatina was integrated into the newly built palace and its eastern wall was partly demolished. The hall served as army barracks during Napoleonic and Prussian times, but the Prussian king Friedrich Wilhelm IV eventually ordered its reconstruction. From 1856 it has served as the Protestant church of St Saviour. It was restored after bombing in 1944.

④
Rheinisches Landesmuseum

🏠 Weimarer Allee 1
🕐 10am–5pm Tue–Sun
🌐 landesmuseum-trier.de

Only a few steps separate the electoral palace from the Rhine Regional Museum founded in 1077. Its collections are grouped into four sections: prehistoric, Roman, Franconian-Merovingian and medieval to contemporary. The largest space is devoted to Roman relics. Among the star exhibits are a magnificent mosaic depicting Bacchus, and a superb statuette of a nymph, undoubtedly the work of a major artist. Also on display is Trier's gold hoard, the largest hoard of Roman imperial gold coins ever discovered.

⑤
Stadtbibliothek

🏠 Weberbach 25 🕐 Times vary, check website
🌐 stadtbibliothek-weberbach.de

The municipal library contains a number of important collections that were assembled in the early 19th century, when many monastic libraries closed down. Among its treasures are 74 full-page miniatures of the famous Trier Apocalypse (from around AD 800), and one of the few surviving copies of the first Bible printed by Gutenberg.

TRIER CHURCHES

Trier has an exceptional ensemble of churches. The Dom St Peter on Liebfrauenstrasse is a UNESCO World Heritage site which incorporates the remains of an older 4th-century church. The oldest cathedral in Germany, it was constructed in stages from the early 11th century to the 14th century. Its furnishings include several outstanding objects, such as the tomb of the papal envoy Ivo (1144). Next to the cathedral stands the Liebfrauenkirche, built in 1235–60. It is also a UNESCO World Heritage site and one of the earliest known examples of German Gothic architecture.

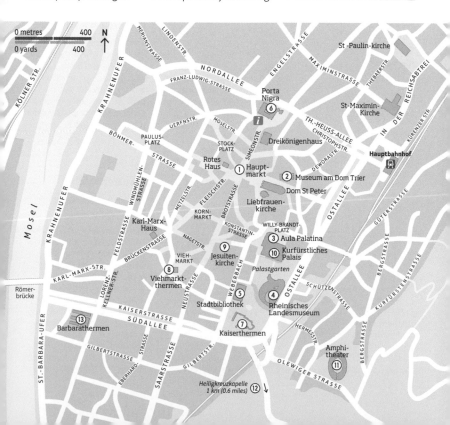

Porta Nigra

⚐ Simeonstrasse 60
🕐 9am–6pm daily (Mar & Oct: to 5pm; Nov–Feb: to 4pm)
🌐 zentrum-der-antike.de

This town gate, named Porta Nigra (Black Gate) in the Middle Ages because of the colour of its weathered stone, was erected in the 2nd century, and is now a UNESCO World Heritage Site. A similar gate would have stood at the town's southern entrance. The oldest German defensive structure, it still impresses with its colossal size. Two gateways lead onto a small inner courtyard, and there are two tiers of defence galleries with large open windows. It is flanked by the four-storey western tower and the three-storey unfinished eastern tower.

In the 12th century the building was transformed into the two-storey church of St Simeon and served as such until the early 19th century.

Porta Nigra, the oldest defensive structure in Germany ↑

Kaiserthermen

⚐ Weimarer Allee/Kaiserstrasse 🕐 Apr–Sep: 9am–6pm daily (Oct & Mar: to 5pm; Nov–Feb: to 4pm)
🌐 zentrum-der-antike.de

Not far from the Rheinisches Landesmuseum are the remains of the vast imperial baths. Built in the early 4th century, during the reign of Constantine, they were the third largest bathing complex in the Roman world. The remaining sections of the walls and foundations indicate the former layout. Best preserved are the walls of the caldarium, the room with the hot water pool. Next to it is the round tepidarium, the warm baths. The spacious frigidarium was used for cold baths. Considerable room was given to the palaestra, which was an outdoor exercise area. Visitors can also explore the bath's former supply tunnels.

Viehmarktthermen

⚐ Viehmarktplatz
🕐 9am–5pm Tue–Sun
🌐 zentrum-der-antike.de

Following excavations completed in 1994, the remains of these Roman baths, along with those of medieval refuse pits and the cellars of a Capucin monastery, are now on display to the public under a large glass canopy.

Jesuitenkirche

⚐ Jesuitenstrasse 13
🕐 9am–5pm daily

The Gothic Church of the Holy Trinity was built for Franciscan friars, who settled in Trier before 1238. The surviving church, from the late 13th century, went to the Jesuits in 1570. It houses the tomb of Friedrich von Spee (1591–1635).

The college (1610–14) was transferred to the university following the dissolution of the Jesuit Order. It now houses a theological seminary.

KARL MARX

Revolutionary socialist Karl Marx (1818-83) was born into a well-to-do Jewish family in Trier. After being exiled for his articles as a political journalist, he moved to London and collaborated with Friedrich Engels on a radical new theory of social organization: Communism.

Kurfürstliches Palais

⬛ Konstantinplatz
🕐 By appointment only; occasional tours and concerts (ask at tourist information)

The Electoral Palace is considered to be one of the most beautiful Rococo palaces in the world. It has undergone several transformations over the centuries and remains of the earlier buildings can still be seen. The present building was designed by Johannes Seiz and built in 1756–62 for Archbishop Johann Philipp von Walderdorff. The sculptures were created by Ferdinand Tietz. The central tympanum shows Pomona, Venus, Apollo and a group of angels. The stairs, which lead from the garden to the inner staircase, were designed in the 18th century, but not built until 1981. They have beautiful

→

The grand Rococo exterior of Kurfürstliches Palais, designed by Johannes Seiz

handrails with typical Rococo motifs. The gardens are equally lovely and include a miniature garden, a landscape garden and a mother-and-child area.

Amphitheater

⬛ Petrisberg 🕐 9am–6pm daily (Mar & Oct: to 5pm; Nov–Feb: to 4pm)
🌐 zentrum-der-antike.de

Near the imperial baths are the ruins of the Roman amphitheatre, dating from the 1st century AD. This was the scene of gladiatorial fights and animal contests. The entire structure, consisting of an elliptical arena and a stepped auditorium, was surrounded by a high wall, divided into individual storeys by colonnaded arcades. The complex was designed to seat up to 20,000 people.

Heiligkreuzkapelle

⬛ Arnulfstrasse/ Rotbachstrasse

The chapel of the Holy Cross is one of Trier's more interesting historic buildings. Built in the Romanesque style in the second half of the 11th century, it is a small building with a ground plan in the shape of the Greek cross, with an octagonal tower. It suffered serious damage in World War II, but was carefully restored to its original state in the years 1957–8.

Barbarathermen

⬛ Südallee 🕐 9am–6pm daily (Mar & Oct: to 5pm; Nov–Feb: to 4pm)
🌐 zentrum-der-antike.de

Not far from the Roman bridge across the Mosel river are the ruins of the Barbara baths (2nd century AD). Although not much has been preserved above ground, the extensive system of underground heating channels, the hypocaust, clearly demonstrates the original size of this public bath complex. In the Middle Ages, patrician and aristocratic families transformed the baths into their residences. In the 17th century Jesuit monks dismantled the remaining structures and used the recovered building materials to construct their own college.

EXPERIENCE MORE

Saarbrücken

🅐B6 🚊 ℹ️ Rathaus St Johann, Rathausplatz 1; www.saarbruecken.de

The capital of Saarland, Saarbrücken was originally the Franconian fortress of Sarabrucca. The town, on the Saar River, flourished in the 17th and 18th centuries under Duke Wilhelm Heinrich von Nassau-Saarbrücken.

The churches and other prestigious buildings are largely the work of Friedrich Joachim Stengel, court architect to the von Nassau-Saarbrücken family. He designed the Catholic Basilika St Johann (1754–8) in the market square, as well as the monumental Schloss, the palace on the opposite bank of the Saar (1739–48).

Opposite the Schloss stands the Altes Rathaus (old town hall), which today houses a museum of ethnography. The Protestant Ludwigskirche (1762–75) is one of the last works by Stengel and is laid out in the shape of a Greek cross. The Stiftskirche (collegiate church) St Arnual, in the southwestern part of the town, contains the Gothic and Renaissance tombs of the von Nassau-Saarbrücken family. Since 1960 it has also featured a "German-French Garden". One of the garden's entrances leads to Gulliver-Miniwelt (Gulliver's Mini World), with small versions of the world's most famous buildings.

Völklingen

🅐B6 ℹ️ Im Neuen Bahnhof, Rathausstrasse 55; (06898) 13 28 00

About 10 km (6 miles) west of Saarbrücken lies industrial Völklingen, which was granted town status in 1937. In 1881 Saarbrücken native Carl Röchling bought a small steel mill, the Völklinger Hütte, which became the heart of his family's industrial empire. The steel mill still exists and is a UNESCO World Heritage site.

Homburg

🅐B6 ℹ️ Talstrasse 57A; (06841) 10 18 20

This town grew up around the Hohenburg castle (later Homburg castle), now just a picturesque ruin. In nearby Schlossberg remains were found of a fortress that was built in 1680–92 by Sébastien Le Preste Vauban on the orders of the French king Louis XIV. The greatest attraction of Homburg, however, is its Schlossberg caves, the largest man-made caves in Europe, cut into the red sandstone.

↑ Daniel in the lion's den on a stained-glass window in Dom St Peter, Worms

Ottweiler

🅐B5 ℹ️ Rathausplatz 5; (06824) 35 11

The small picturesque town of Ottweiler has a beautifully preserved old town. The Alter Turm (Old Tower), which in the 15th century formed part of the town's fortifications, now

→ View of Oppenheim with its spectacular red Katharinenkirche

serves as a belfry to the parish church, whose origins go back to the 15th century.

Rathausplatz is a beautiful complex of historic houses, dating from the 17th and 18th centuries. In Schlossplatz is the Renaissance Hesse Haus (around 1590).

Worms

 C5 🚉 ℹ Neumarkt 14; (06241) 85 37 306

Worms is one of the oldest towns in Germany. In the Middle Ages it was the home of the Reich's Parliament, hosting more than 100 sessions. The Dom St Peter is one of the largest late-Romanesque cathedrals in Germany. It was built in 1171–1230 as a two-choir basilica, with eastern transept, four towers and two domes. Its northern nave includes five beautiful sandstone reliefs from a Gothic cloister, which no longer exists. The interior furnishings date mainly from

modern times. Particularly noteworthy is the high altar designed in the 18th century by Balthasar Neumann, and the stalls dating from 1760.

In nearby Marktplatz is the Dreifaltigkeitskirche (church of the Holy Trinity) from 1709–25. Northeast of the square is the Stiftskirche St Paul (collegiate church of St Paul), built in the 11th–12th centuries and finished in the 18th century. Not far from here is the only surviving Renaissance residential building in Worms, the Rotes Haus (Red House).

In the west of the old town is the Heiliger Sand (Holy Sands), the oldest Jewish cemetery in Europe, with tombstones dating back as far as the 11th century. Also worth a visit is the 14th-century Liebfrauen-kirche (church of Our Dear Lady). The most noteworthy feature of the 11th- to 12th-

century Magnuskirche (St Magnus church) is its crypt, from around AD 800, while the Stiftskirche St Martin (collegiate church of St Martin), from the late 11th century, has some interesting portals.

Oppenheim

 C5 🚉 ℹ Merianstrasse 2; www.stadt-oppenheim.de

The pride of Oppenheim , a centre of the wine trade 20 km (12 miles) south of Mainz, is its Gothic Katharinenkirche (St Katharine's Church) built of red sandstone in the 13th–14th centuries. The neighbouring hill and the ruins of Landskron castle provide stunning views over the Rhine valley. The Weinbaumuseum of viticulture is also worth visiting.

Worms' Dom St Peter is one of the largest late-Romanesque cathedrals in Germany. It was built in 1171-1230 as a two-choir basilica, with eastern transept.

↑ Cruise ships at Koblenz with Festung Ehrenbreit-stein in the background

9

Koblenz

 B5 🚉 ℹ Zentralplatz 1; www.koblenz-tourism.de

The name the Romans gave to their camp in 9 BC – *castellum apud confluentes*, meaning the "camp at the confluence" – reflects the town's strategic importance, for it is here that the Mosel flows into the Rhine. From the Middle Ages until the 19th century, Koblenz was the seat of the powerful archbishop-electors of Trier. It was also the birthplace of Prince von Metternich, the 19th-century Austrian statesman. Today it is a modern metropolis and the main centre of the region's cultural life.

Deutsches Eck, the "German Corner", is where the Mosel flows into the Rhine. Here stands an enormous equestrian statue of Emperor Wilhelm I designed by Bruno

> **At the highest point in Koblenz's old town is the Romanesque Liebfrauenkirche (Church of Our Dear Lady).**

Schmitz. It was erected in 1897, destroyed in World War II and replaced with a copy in 1993. The name Deutsches Eck refers to the complex of buildings known as Deutschherrenhaus belonging to the Order of Teutonic Knights. Only part of the three-wing residence of the order's commander, which was built in the early 14th century, has survived. The building now houses the **Ludwig-Museum**, with a collection of modern art.

The collegial **Basilika St Kastor** was built in 817–36 on the initiative of the Archbishop of Trier, on a site formerly occupied by an early Christian church. The present appearance of the church is the result of extensions from the 11th–13th centuries.

The modern Forum Confluentes building near the river houses the **Mittelrhein-Museum**, which covers 2,000 years of Central Rhine regional history. It houses a collection of archaeology and medieval art. One remarkable exhibit is the original head of the Emperor Wilhelm I statue, at the river's confluence.

In the Middle Ages, the powerful von Arken family had a fortified residence, Alte

Burg (Old Castle), built for themselves in the north-western section of the Roman fortifications. In 1277 the building was taken over by Heinrich von Finstingen, the Archbishop of Trier, who ordered its extension. The fortress was to protect him from the citizens of Koblenz, who were striving for independence. Successive archbishops continued with the conversion of the building, which acquired its final shape in the 17th century. The eastern Renaissance façade of the complex is particularly attractive. Today, at No. 1 Burgstrasse, it houses the municipal archives and parts of the library.

At the highest point in the old town is the Romanesque **Liebfrauenkirche** (church of Our Dear Lady). Its history dates back to early Christian times, but its present form is the result of remodelling work in 1182–1250. A triple-nave basilica with galleries, it has a twin-tower western façade. The beautiful Gothic choir was added in 1404–30.

Not far from the bridge across the Rhine, in Neustadt, stands the Electoral Palace, Kurfürstliches Schloss, an example of the Rhineland's early Neo-Classical architecture. It was built, and for a short time occupied, by Clemens Wenzeslaus von Sachsen, the last of Trier's electors. Construction of the castle began in 1777, designed by Michael d'Ixnard, and continued until 1786, overseen by Antoine François Peyère the Younger. Unfortunately it is closed to the public.

On the opposite side of the Rhine is the mighty **Festung Ehrenbreitstein**, one of the world's largest fortresses and barely changed since Prussian days. A smaller fortress was erected on this site in 1000 and extended in subsequent years by the archbishop-electors of Trier, who lived in it from 1648 to 1786. Trier's holiest relic, the Rock Christi (vestments of Christ) was kept here. The fortress offers splendid views over Koblenz, the Rhine and the Mosel. Today, it is home to the Landesmuseum Koblenz (regional museum) with an interesting collection on the development of technology, and to the Rhein-Museum, with hydrological collections.

Ludwig-Museum

◈ 🕙 🗋 Danziger Freiheit 1 🕙 10:30am–5pm Tue–Sat, 11am–6pm Sun 🖰 ludwig museum.org

Basilika St Kastor

🗋 Kastorstrasse 7 🕙 9am–6pm daily 🖰 sankt-kastor-koblenz.de

Mittelrhein-Museum

◈ 🗋 Zentralplatz 1 🕙 10am–6pm Tue–Sun 🖰 mittelrhein-museum.de

Liebfrauenkirche

🗋 An der Liebfrauenkirche 1 📞 (0261) 315 50 🕙 Apr–Oct: 8:15am–7pm daily; Nov–Mar: 8:15am–6pm Mon–Sat, 9am–5pm Sun

Festung Ehrenbreitstein

◈ 🕙 🗋 🕙 🗋 Festung Ehrenbreitstein 📞 (0261) 66 750 🕙 Apr–Oct: 10am–6pm daily (Nov–Mar: to 5pm daily)

HIDDEN GEM
History Column

On Josef-Görres-Platz in Koblenz, the unusual Historiensäule (History Column) tells the story of the city's past in ten scenes stacked in a pile. It commemorates 2,000 years of the Rhineland-Palatinate region.

Maria Laach

🗛 B5 🗋 Glees 🕙 5:30am–8pm daily 🖰 maria-laach.de

A true masterpiece of German and European Romanesque architecture, the Maria Laach Abbey stands next to the Laacher See, a lake formed in the crater of an extinct volcano. Construction began in 1093 at the behest of Heinrich II – who is also buried here – and finished in 1220. Until secularization in 1802, the Abbey was the home of the Benedictines. Since 1892 the church has resounded again with Gregorian chants, sung several times a day.

DRINK

Irish Pub Koblenz
This lively Irish pub offers quiz nights, karaoke parties and Guinness on draft.

🗛 B5 🗋 Burgstrasse 7 🖰 irishpubkoblenz.com

Cafe Einstein
Centrally located café, restaurant and bar that draws a broad mix of locals for its international food and live music.

🗛 B5 🗋 Firmung-strasse 30 🖰 einstein-koblenz.de

Daddy O's
American-themed cocktail bar with a menu of classic drinks, made with a collection of over 100 spirits from around the world.

🗛 B5 🗋 Eltzerhofstrasse 1 📞 (0176) 76 57 90 48

↑ The Maria Laach abbey and its surrounding grounds in full bloom

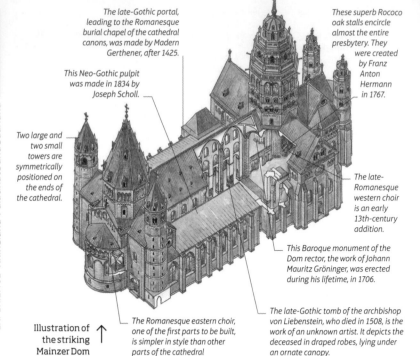

The late-Gothic portal, leading to the Romanesque burial chapel of the cathedral canons, was made by Madern Gerthener, after 1425.

These superb Rococo oak stalls encircle almost the entire presbytery. They were created by Franz Anton Hermann in 1767.

This Neo-Gothic pulpit was made in 1834 by Joseph Scholl.

Two large and two small towers are symmetrically positioned on the ends of the cathedral.

The late-Romanesque western choir is an early 13th-century addition.

This Baroque monument of the Dom rector, the work of Johann Mauritz Gröninger, was erected during his lifetime, in 1706.

Illustration of the striking Mainzer Dom

The Romanesque eastern choir, one of the first parts to be built, is simpler in style than other parts of the cathedral

The late-Gothic tomb of the archbishop von Liebenstein, who died in 1508, is the work of an unknown artist. It depicts the deceased in draped robes, lying under an ornate canopy.

EAT

El Chico
This rustic steak house offers a menu of quality meat cuts from Argentina and New Zealand.

◨ Kötherhofstrasse 1, Mainz ☎ (0613) 123 84 40

€€€

Weinstube zum Bacchus
Regional German cuisine supplemented by a menu of international dishes and a good range of European wines.

◨ Jakobsbergstrasse 7, Mainz ◷ Mon ◌ weinstube-zum-bacchus.de

€€€

Mainz

🅰C5 🚉 🛈 Brückenturm, Rheinstrasse 55; mainz-tourismus.com

This town, which grew out of the Roman military camp Moguntiacum, established in 39 BC, is today the capital of the Rhineland-Palatinate. Mainz is the home of an important German television station (ZDF). It is also the main centre of trade for the popular Rhine wines. Its late-Romanesque cathedral symbolizes the power of the Kurfürsten, the prince-electors, who used to crown German kings.

Construction of the Baroque Kurfürstliches Schloss (Electoral Palace) began in 1627 and was completed in 1776. Today the palace houses the fascinating **Römisch-Germanisches Zentralmuseum** (or RGZM), on the history of pre- and early German history.

Indisputably the town's most famous resident is Johannes Gutenberg (c 1400–68), the inventor of the printing press. He gained renown as the inventor of the printing process using movable metal type, and he prepared the Bible for printing and publication in 1454–5. From the original 200 copies, only 46 survive. The **Gutenberg Museum**, which opened in 1900, shows a reconstruction of the master's workshop from 1450 and includes priceless early books.

The greatest attraction of Mainz is the superb **Mainzer Dom**, or St Martin cathedral. It is one of the only three Romanesque imperial cathedrals to have survived almost intact to this day (the others are Worms and Speyer). Its oldest parts date from the early 11th century, with the Gothic side chapels added during the 13th and 14th centuries.

Near the Baroque hospital of St Roch, built in 1721 and now an old people's home, is a street called Kirschgarten (cherry orchard). The well-preserved houses here date from the 16th–18th centuries.

The Gothic parish church **St Stephan-Kirche** was built on the site of an edifice dating from the 10th century. Construction ran from the mid-13th century until the end of the 15th century. The resulting church is a triple-nave hall with eastern transept and a single-nave choir. The adjacent cloisters are a true gem of late-Gothic design. The original stained-glass windows in the presbytery, destroyed in World War II, were replaced by six new ones in 1978–81, designed and partly made by Marc Chagall. The church interior contains many other original features. The four large candelabra were cast in Mainz in 1509, and the polyptych of the Crucifixion dates from around 1400.

Southeast of the university campus are the Römersteine, the impressive remains of the Roman aqueduct dating from the 1st century AD.

Römisch-Germanisches Zentralmuseum

⌂ Kurfürstliches Schloss zu Mainz 🅲 (06131) 912 40 🆀 For renovations until mid-2021

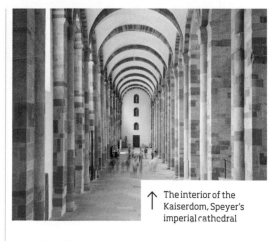

↑ The interior of the Kaiserdom, Speyer's imperial cathedral

Gutenberg-Museum

🄯 ⌂ Liebfrauenplatz 5 🕘 9am–5pm Tue–Sat, 11am–5pm Sun 🆆 gutenberg-museum.de

Mainzer Dom

⌂ Markt 10 🕘 Times vary, check website 🆆 mainzerdom.bistummainz.de

St Stephan-Kirche

⌂ Kleine Weissgasse 12 🅲 (06131) 23 16 40 🕘 Mar–Oct: 10am–5pm Mon–Sat, noon–5pm Sun; Nov–Feb: 10am–4:30pm Mon–Sat, noon–4:30pm Sun

---

Speyer

⌂ C6 🅡 🄸 Maximilianstrasse 13; (06232) 14 23 92

In the 7th century Speyer was the seat of a diocese. As a free city of the Holy Roman Empire from 1294 until 1779, it hosted 50 sessions of the imperial parliament. The most significant session took place in 1529, when the Protestant states of the Holy Roman Empire lodged a protest

← Rudolf von Habsburg, buried in the Dom in 1291

(hence "Protestant") against the decisions of the Catholic majority.

The most important historic building in Speyer is the Romanesque Kaiserdom (Cathedral of St Maria and St Stephan), a World Heritage site. The Dom, built in 1025–61 on the initiative of Conrad II, is a triple-nave, cross-vaulted basilica with transept, vestibule, choir, apse and several towers. Its triple-nave crypt, the burial place of Salian emperors, has stunning stone carvings. St Afra's, dating from around 1100, has some interesting sculptures, including Christ Bearing His Cross and Annunciation (around 1470). The Domnapf, a vast stone bowl seen in the cathedral forecourt, dates from 1490. It was used during enthroning ceremonies, when the newly anointed bishop would order it to be filled with wine right to the brim in order to win the hearts of his flock.

Another 11th-century building of interest is the Mikwe in Judenbadgasse, a ritual Jewish bath for women, near the remains of a synagogue. To the west of the Dom stand the remains of the medieval fortifications including the Altpörtel, a 14th- to 16th-century town gate. The late-Baroque Dreifaltigkeitskirche (church of the Holy Trinity), was built in 1701–17.

A DRIVING TOUR
DEUTSCHE WEINSTRASSE

Length: 83 km (51 miles) **Stopping-off points:** Landau has many cafés, bars and restaurants, and St Martin is a good place to stop for wine tasting. **Signs:** Look for signposts showing a bunch of grapes or a wine jug.

Travelling along the German Wine Route, Germany's second-oldest tourist route, visitors can see fascinating historic buildings and taste the different types of wine made by the numerous small vineyards scattered throughout the region. The German Wine Route starts in Bockenheim and ends in Schweigen; the tour suggested here includes the most interesting sections of this route. This is a delightful part of Germany, where visitors will encounter aspects of German and European cultural heritage at every step.

Enjoy the views on the way out of **Leinsweiler,** *as you peel away from the main road and head up into the hills.*

Frankenstein

Lambrecht

Hambacher Schloss

St Martin

RHEINLAND-PFALZ

Ramberg

Frankweiler

Siebeldingen

Annweiler

Trifels

Leinsweiler

Wilgartswiesen

Lug

Klingenmünster

Gleiszellen-Gleishorbach

Bad Bergzabern

Trifels Castle *once served as a prison for many important people, including the King of England, Richard the Lionheart.*

The village of **Leinsweiler** *houses a 13th-century Gothic church and an attractive town hall (1619). Hilltop Hof Neukastel was once the home of the Impressionist artist Max Slevogt.*

On the road from Bad Bergzabern to Leinsweiler keep an eye out for the imposing **Landeck Castle** *on the hillside near Klingenmünster.*

Bad Bergzabern *has some interesting Renaissance remains, including the Gasthaus zum Engel (Angel's Inn) and a royal castle. It is also home to a medical and wellness centre.*

Dörrenbach
START

Schweigen-Rechtenbach

The first stop on the route is **Dörrenbach.** *The star attractions in this small town are the half-timbered town hall and the Gothic church surrounded by fortifications.*

↑ Almond blossoms lining a road through Bad Bergzabern

Locator Map
For more detail see p336

RHINELAND-
PALATINATE
AND SAARLAND

Deutsche
Weinstrasse

Bad Dürkheim *is best known for its annual Wurstmarkt festival, held in September to celebrate the wine harvest. Also here is the world's biggest wine barrel, which can hold nearly 2 million hectolitres (44 million gallons) of wine.*

Deep in the heart of wine country, the road from Hambacher Schloss passes through a sea of grapevines on the way to your final stop.

Although it dates back to Roman times, **Hambacher Schloss's** *fame is based on the Hambacher Fest when, on 27 May 1832, students protested against the fragmentation of Germany.*

Nested in the hills and surrounded by vineyards, **St Martin**, *with its medieval centre and enchanting 16th- to 18th-century buildings, is one of the Wine Route's most picturesque villages.*

The little town of **Landau** *has the remains of the fortress built by Vauban, and an extraordinarily beautiful post-Augustinian church. With a good selection of cafés and wine bars, it's also an excellent place to stop before continuing northwards.*

Hambacher Schloss nestled ↑
amongst the green hills overlooking
the village of Hamback

0 kilometres   10

0 miles   10

N ↑

HESSE

For most of its history, Hesse was divided between Hesse-Darmstadt and Hesse-Kassel. The current boundaries, a post-World War II creation, roughly approximate those of its 13th-century forerunner. Scattered over the region are many reminders of its former glory: Roman camps, Carolingian buildings, Romanesque churches and Gothic cathedrals with lofty spires.

But Hesse is also a state of modern cities, international business and world-class culture. Today, when admiring the distinctive panorama of Frankfurt am Main – its towering banks and skyscrapers more reminiscent of New York's Manhattan than of a European metropolis – it is hard to believe that this was the birthplace of Goethe. The importance of this city extends far beyond Hesse: it is the financial centre of the European Union and its annual Book Fair is the largest event of its kind in the world. And lovers of modern art will know of Kassel – every five years it hosts the documenta, an exciting exhibition of artistic developments. The region also offers attractive countryside, from the Rhön mountains and Kellerwald-Edersee National Park – homeland of the Brothers Grimm – to the Waldecker Land near Kassel (which boasts the Eder lake and attractive health resorts).

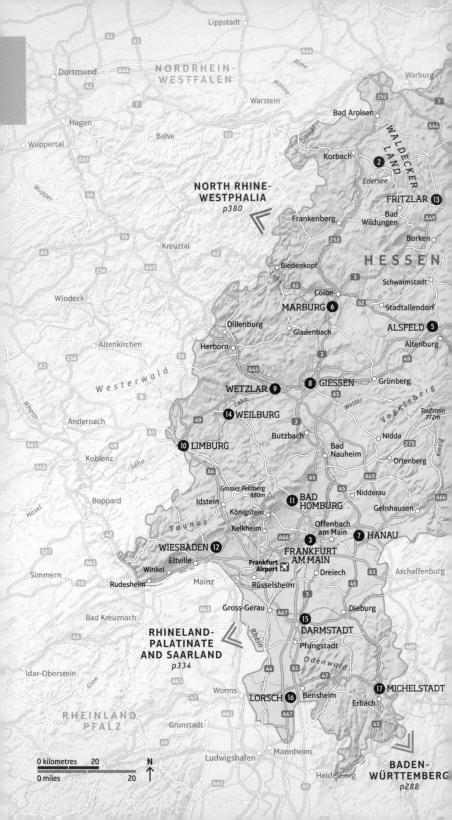

LOWER SAXONY,
HAMBURG AND BREMEN
p418

THURINGIA
p184

HESSE

BAVARIA
p242

HESSE

Must Sees

1 Kassel
2 Waldecker Land
3 Frankfurt am Main

Experience More

4 Fulda
5 Alsfeld
6 Marburg
7 Hanau
8 Giessen
9 Wetzlar
10 Limburg
11 Bad Homburg
12 Wiesbaden
13 Fritzlar
14 Weilburg
15 Darmstadt
16 Lorsch
17 Michelstadt

←

1 Frankfurt skyline.

2 Wiesbaden train station.

3 Marktkirche cathedral in Wiesbaden.

4 Frankfurt's Museum of Modern Art.

YELLOW AND GREEN

3 DAYS

In Hesse

Day 1

Morning Arrive in Frankfurt am Main *(p364)*. First stop is breakfast on Römerberg *(p367)*, a square that is home to impressive sights such as the Römer, St Nicholas' Church and City Hall.

Afternoon Cross the river and choose between a number of incredible institutions at the Museumsufer (Museum Embankment), including the Städelsches Kunstinstitut *(p369)* with its prodigious collection of contemporary art, the Deutches Filmmuseum *(p368)* and the Museum für Kommunikation.

Evening Enjoy a sophisticated menu and a 360-degree view of Frankfurt from the Main Tower Restaurant *(Neue Mainzer Strasse 52-58)*.

Day 2

Morning Take a train to the state capital of Wiesbaden *(p376)* and head to Schlossplatz, where you can admire the city's amazing sights, such as the Stadtschloss, the seat of the state parliament, the Neo-Gothic Marktkirche and the 17th-century Altes Rathaus.

Afternoon Stroll around the beautifully landscaped Kurpark before diving in to the Museum Wiesbaden, which has natural history and art exhibits. If you

have time, catch the funicular railway *(Nerobergbahn)* to the Neroberg hill for fabulous panoramic views.

Evening Return to Wiesbaden and dine at Lambertus *(Kurhausplatz 1)*, a spacious and busy bistro combining German portions and produce with French subtlety. There's a good variety of wines and a large terrace, too.

Day 3

Morning After breakfast, take a train to Lorsch *(p381)*, a small town in the south of Hesse.

Afternoon Spend the day exploring the fabulous UNESCO World Heritage Benedictine abbey, which was founded in 764 by Chrodegang of Metz. Fragments of the 13th-century nave, the towers and the gate-house, dating from around 790, are all that has survived. The Torhalle (gatehouse) is one of the most important architectural remains of the Carolingian period.

Evening Enjoy an early dinner at Hexenhaus *(Nibelungenstrasse 46)*, which has a good regional menu (wines included, alongside international varieties) and great service.

↑ The splendid Orangerie, with its lovely terrace, at the Karlsaue complex

 KASSEL

🄰 C4 ✈ Kassel, 13 km (8 miles) northwest of town
🛈 Wilhelmsstrasse 23; www.kassel.de

Largely rebuilt after World War II, the town of Kassel is synonymous today with one of the most important shows of contemporary art – documenta – held here every five years (the 13th documenta is scheduled for 2022). The town is also known for its outstanding collection of European art and its many parks.

①
Ottoneum

🄰 Steinweg 2 📞 (0561) 787 40 66 🕓 10am-5pm Tue-Sun (to 8pm Wed, 6pm Sun)

The Ottoneum (1604–5) was Germany's first permanent theatre. Designed by Wilhelm Vernukken and later remodelled by Paul du Ry, it was converted into a natural history museum in 1885.

②
Neue Galerie

🄰 Schöne Aussicht 1 🕓 10am-5pm Tue-Sun 🌐 museum-kassel.de

The New Gallery, founded in 1976 and devoted to 19th- and 20th-century art, occupies a Neo-Classicist building from 1871–74. The gallery's collection includes a number of canvases by artists such as Carl Schuch, Max Slevogt and Lovis Corinth.

The collection of 20th-century paintings focuses on German Expressionism and an entire room is devoted to the installations of the controversial sculptor and performance artist Joseph Beuys.

③
Orangerie

🄰 An der Karlsaue 20c 🕓 10am-5pm Tue-Sun 🌐 museum-kassel.de

The southern part of Kassel is home to Karlsaue, a vast palace and garden complex. In 1702–10 Pierre-Etienne Monnot built the large Orangerie, which now houses a fascinating museum of astronomy and technology. Monnot was also the creator of Marmorbad, a bath pavilion, while the kitchen pavilion was designed by Simon Louis du Ry in 1765.

↑ An exhibit at the documenta contemporary art show, Neue Galerie

← Marble bust (c 2nd or 3rd century AD), Hessisches Landesmuseum

④
Kunsthalle Fridericianum

🏠 Friedrichsplatz 18
🕐 11am–6pm Tue–Sun & hols (to 8pm Thu)
🌐 fridericianum.org

The Neo-Classical Fridericianum, built by Simon Louis du Ry in 1769–76, became the second public museum (after the British Museum in London) to be built in Europe. Since 1955 the Fridricianum has been the main venue for Kassel's contemporary art show – the documenta – which takes over the city every five years.

⑤
Hessisches Landesmuseum

🏠 Brüder-Grimm-Platz 5
🕐 10am–5pm Tue
🌐 museum-kassel.de

Outstanding items in the Neo-Baroque Hesse Regional Museum, built in 1910–13, are the astronomical instruments, originally installed in 1560 in a landgrave's castle, that no longer exists. The ethnographic section has Hessian folk costumes and

regional craft items. The Landesmuseum also houses the Tapeten-museum (Wallpaper Museum). Established in 1923, the museum presents the history of wallpaper and its production methods around the world.

⑥
Schloss Wilhelmshöhe

🏠 Schlosspark 1
🕐 10am–5pm Tue–Sun
🌐 museum-kassel.de

Wilhelmshöhe is a splendid palace set in a large, attractive park. The palace was designed by Simon Louis du Ry and Heinrich Christoph Jussow and built in 1793–1801 for the Elector Wilhelm. Now it houses

the Gemäldegalerie Alte Meister with its outstanding collection of European masters including paintings by Rubens, Titian, Rembrandt and Dürer.

⑦
GRIMMWELT Kassel

🏠 Weinbergstrasse 21
🕐 10am–6pm Tue–Sun (to 8pm Fri)
🌐 grimm welt.de

Although brothers Jacob and Wilhelm Grimm were born in Hanau, they lived in Kassel from 1798 until 1830, and this museum presents the lives and works of the prolific fairytale tellers and philologers using five themes, and many original first editions. There are art installations, films and hands-on activities, and the rooftop terrace has excellent views.

2

WALDECKER LAND

📍 C4 🌐 waldecker-land.de

The Waldecker countryside is a rich tapestry of thick forests, sparkling lakes (the Edersee, the Diemelsee), Baroque castles like that at Bad Arolsen, and charming, medieval towns such as Korbach, Frankenberg and Bad Wildungen.

The Waldecker Land, situated west of Kassel, was once an independent county and, up until 1929, was a free state within the German Reich. Today this region, with its Eder-Stausee (reservoir) and mountain railway, is one of the most attractive tourist regions in Germany.

Paths, Trails and Routes

The wooded hills and well-signed hiking paths provide a perfect setting for long rambles, the roads and tracks are ideally suited to cycling tours, and the rivers and lakes are perfect for visitors to enjoy a wide variety of watersports. As well as sights like the castles of Bad Wildungen and the historical mining town of Waldeck, the area is also part of the Deutsche Märchenstrasse (German Fairytale Route), along which visitors can discover places related largely to the tales of the Brothers Grimm.

↑ Hikers exploring one of the many walking routes through Waldecker Land's forests

EAT

Hotel Schloss Waldeck

Refined restaurant, overlooking the Edersee, serving both regional and seasonal dishes.

 Waldeck schloss-hotel-waldeck.com

€€€

Athen

This restaurant offers good quality seafood, Mediterranean dishes and outdoor dining in a pleasant garden.

Schulstrassee 4, Waldeck athen-waldeck.de

€€€

Brathähnchenfarm

Romantic mountain-top hotel and restaurant with alfresco dining.

Im Ohl 1, Steinau an der Strasse brathaenchenfarm.de

€€€

↑ Sunrise over the Edersee, on the southern border of Waldecker Land

FAIRYTALE ROUTE

The fact that Germany is famous for fairytales is thanks largely to the work of the Brothers Grimm, Jacob and Wilhelm, who collected and published stories based on local folklore. This 603-km (375-mile) route travels through charming villages and towns that have a connection to the brothers' work and their lives. Stops include their childhood hometown of Steinau and Alsfield *(p374)* – said to be the home of Little Red Riding Hood, as her outfit was inspired by regional clothing. The route also includes the forests and castles that provided the setting for such timeless tales as *Snow White* and *Sleeping Beauty*.

↑ The impressive Frankfurt skyline at sunset

3

FRANKFURT AM MAIN

🔲 C5 ✈ Frankfurt 🚇🚊🚉 ℹ Hauptbahnhof; www.frankfurt-tourismus.de

Frankfurt, nicknamed "Mainhattan" and "Chicago am Main" because of its skyscrapers, is one of the main economic and cultural centres of Germany. The city boasts magnificent art collections, a variety of interesting museums and impressive architecture.

Located on the Main river, Frankfurt is known as the smallest metropolis in the world. The headquarters of many major banks and newspaper publishers are to be found here, including those of the *Frankfurter Allgemeine Zeitung*, one of Europe's most influential newspapers. The city's International Book Fair, held annually in October, is the world's largest event of its kind. Goethe was born in Frankfurt, and the Johann-Wolfgang-Goethe-Universität is one of Germany's most prominent universities. The city now hosts a museum dedicated to his life and literary works.

①

Eschenheimer Turm

🏠 Grosse Eschenheimer Strasse

The Eschenheimer Turm, at the corner of Hochstrasse, presents a silhouette typical of old Frankfurt. A relic of the medieval town's fortifications, the tower was designed by the carpenter Klaus Mengoz; construction began in 1400 and was completed in 1428 by Madern Gerthener. The façade of the tower features many attractive bay windows; it also has two reliefs depicting eagles, the symbol of the German Empire and the city of Frankfurt.

②

Frankfurter Goethe-Haus

🏠 Grosser Hirschgraben 23
🕐 11am–5pm Mon, Wed & Thu; 10am–6pm Fri–Sun
🌐 goethehaus-frankfurt.de

Southwest of the Hauptwache is Johann Wolfgang Goethe's family home. The great German poet, novelist and dramatist was born here on 28 August 1749. The house, along with many other buildings in Frankfurt, was totally destroyed in World War II, but later lovingly restored, its interior reconstructed to represent the style typical of the mid- to late 18th century. Goethe lived in this house until 1775, when he moved to Weimar. The desk at which he wrote his early works, including the first versions of the plays *Götz von Berlichingen* (1771) and *Egmont* (1774), has been preserved.

The adjacent building now houses the grand Goethemuseum. Opened in 1997, the museum recreates the atmosphere of the 1750–1830 period, and holds a collection of items related to the writer. There is also an excellent library worth visiting, which contains a selection of his writings.

③
Alte Oper

🏛 Opernplatz 1
🌐 alteoper.de

The monumental old opera house was built in 1872–80, but completely burned down during World War II. Rebuilt nearly four decades later, it is today used as a concert hall and conference centre. It also offers visitors an outstanding program that features a wide range of music, from jazz to classical music. Its façade and interior decorations are a faithful imitation of the Italian Renaissance style.

④
St Leonhardskirche

🏛 Am Leonhardstor 25
📞 (069) 297 03 20 🕐 Times vary, call ahead

Close to the banks of the Main, the church of St Leonard is a fine example of Gothic and Romanesque architecture. A five-naved hall-church with an elongated choir, it was built in stages in the 13th and 15th centuries. Its many impressive treasures include a copy of Leonardo da Vinci's *Last Supper* by Hans Holbein the Elder, from 1501. Next to it is St Mary's altar, created by master craftsmen from Antwerp in 1515–20. On the north wall of the choir is a beautiful fresco depicting the *Tree of Life and the Apostles* (1536) by Hans Dietz.

↑ The Neo-Renaissance façade of the Alte Oper on Opernplatz

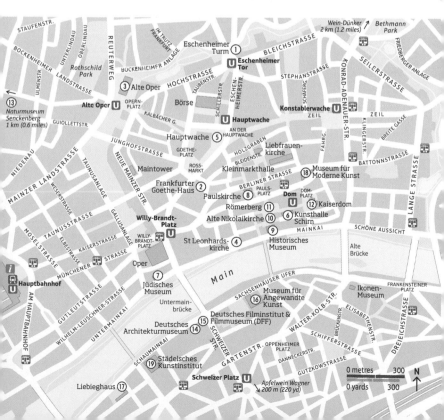

→
The old Hauptwache contrasted with modern skyscrapers

 ⑤

Hauptwache

 An der Hauptwache

Built in 1730, the Hauptwache was originally a guardhouse and was later turned into a prison. Dismantled stone by stone during the construction of the town's underground system, it was reassembled in its original form following the completion of the project. Since 1904 the Hauptwache has been a chic café and a popular meeting place.

 ⑥

Kunsthalle Schirn

Römerberg 6 **10am-7pm Tue-Sun (to 10pm Wed & Thu)** **schirn.de**

One of Europe's most prestigious exhibition buildings, the Kunsthalle Schirn opened in 1986. It hosts temporary art exhibitions dedicated to archaeological themes and the work of old masters and contemporary artists, from Henri Matisse to Yoko Ono.

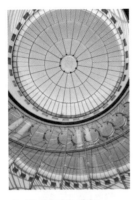

↑ Glass cupola of the Kunsthalle Schirn's rotunda

⑦

Jüdisches Museum

Untermainkai 14-15 **10am-6pm Tue-Sun (to 8pm Tue)** **juedisches museum.de**

The Jewish community of Frankfurt was the second largest in Germany after that of Berlin. This museum, in the former Rothschild Palace, documents their rich cultural heritage and holds the title of being the first Jewish museum in Germany.

⑧

Paulskirche

Paulsplatz 11 **(069) 21 27 06 58** **10am-5pm daily**

The distinctive Neo-Classical rotunda of the church was begun in 1786 but not completed until 1833, due to continuous hostilities with France. Today, however, this building is no longer thought of, or indeed used as, a church. After the first, albeit ill-fated, German National Assembly met here following the revolutionary upheavals of 1848–9, the church became a symbol of republican and liberal Germany. The Paulskirche now serves as a venue for many important events. Each year, for example, the awards ceremony for the prestigious German Publishers' Peace Prize takes place here.

⑨

Historisches Museum

Saalhof 1 **10am-6pm Tue-Fri, 11am-7pm Sat & Sun** **historisches-museum. frankfurt.de**

The building housing the history museum was finished in 1972. The museum has an interesting display of items relating to Frankfurt's history, including a fascinating model of the medieval town, a collection of local prehistoric finds and several decorative architectural fragments from buildings that were destroyed during World War II.

The adjacent building is the Saalhof, which dates back

(Fountain of Justice). Its highlight, however, is the Römer (literally "the Roman"). So called after the remains of ancient settlements, it is a complex of 15th- to 18th-century houses, including the Altes Rathaus (old town hall), which were rebuilt after World War II. Opposite is a group of beautiful half-timbered houses, commonly referred to as Ostzeile. The Steinernes Haus (Stone House) was originally built in 1464 for a Köln silk merchant. It has been reconstructed and is now the home of the Frankfurter Kunstverein (Artists' League).

⑫ Kaiserdom

🏠 Domplatz 14 🕐 Dom: 8am–8pm Mon–Thu, noon–8pm Fri, 9am–8pm Sat & Sun; Dommuseum: 10am–5pm Tue–Fri, 11am–5pm Sat & Sun 🌐 dommuseum-frankfurt.de

Near the archaeological park, where the ruins of a Carolingian fortress were unearthed in 1953, stands the Gothic Imperial Cathedral, built between the 13th and 15th centuries on the site of a Carolingian chapel. The Kaiserdom was used for the coronation of German kings from 1356, and of Holy Roman Emperors from 1562. The cathedral, dedicated to St Bartholomew and Charlemagne, has several priceless masterpieces of Gothic art, including the magnificent 15th-century Maria-Schlaf-Altar and a high altar dating from the second half of the 15th century. The choir has original 14th-century stalls; above these there is a fresco painted in 1427 which depicts scenes from the life of its patron saint, Bartholomew, one of the apostles of Jesus.

The Dom's huge tower affords some magnificent views of the town, while in the cloisters is the Dommuseum, which has an interesting collection of liturgical objects, sacred art and precious artifacts.

→ The Fountain of Justice, Römerberg

to the time of the Emperor Friedrich I Barbarossa (1122–90). A permanent exhibition room, "Frankfurt Now!", opened in 2017 and features a model of Frankfurt as described by the city's residents.

⑩ Alte Nikolaikirche

🏠 Römerberg 11 ☎ (069) 28 42 35 🕐 Apr–Oct: 10am–8pm daily (Nov–Mar: to 6pm)

This peaceful twin-naved church was consecrated in 1290. Used as a court church until the late 15th century, it now serves a Lutheran congregation. Its many statues of St Nicholas (Santa Claus) are a city landmark.

⑪ Römerberg

Located in the centre of Frankfurt's old town, this square contains the Gerechtigkeitsbrunnen

Naturmuseum Senckenberg

🅰 Senckenberganlage 25
🕐 Times vary, check website 🆆 museum frankfurt.senckenberg.de

This museum, situated near the university, is one of the best natural history museums in Germany. Besides a vast collection of plants and animals, including dinosaur skeletons, it contains human and animal mummies from Egypt.

Deutsches Architekturmuseum

🅰 Schaumainkai 43
🕐 10am-6pm Tue-Sun (to 8pm Wed) 🆆 dam-online.de

One of the most interesting museums in the Schaumainkai complex is undoubtedly the Museum of Architecture, in an avant-garde building designed by Oswald Mathias Ungers. The museum has a permanent collection as well as temporary exhibitions concentrating mainly on developments in 20th-century architecture.

→

The spacious exhibition area of the Deutsches Architekturmuseum

↑ Fashion exhibit at the Museum für Angewandte Kunst

Deutsches Filminstitut & Filmmuseum (DFF)

🅰 Schaumainkai 41
🕐 10am-6pm Tue-Sun 🆆 dff.film

Near the Deutsches Architekturmuseum is the Deutsches Filminstitut & Filmmuseum, which holds documents and objects relating to the art of film making and the development of film technology. The museum has its own cinema, which shows old and often long-forgotten films. The monthly film schedule can be found on their website.

Museum für Angewandte Kunst

🅰 Schaumainkai 17
🕐 10am-6pm Tue-Sun (to 8pm Wed) 🆆 museum angewandtekunst.de

The Museum of Applied Arts was opened in 1983, in a building designed by the American artist and architect Richard Meier. He used a Biedermeier house, the Villa Metzler, and added a modern wing. The museum has a collection of some 30,000 objects of applied art from Europe and Asia, and places a particular emphasis on design and fashion.

Nearby, in another villa in the Schaumainkai complex, is the small but fascinating Museum der Weltkulturen (ethnography museum), which has an impressive collection of photographs and films.

3,100

The number of paintings held in the Städelsches Kunstinstitut.

Liebieghaus

🏛 Schaumainkai 71
🕐 10am-6pm Tue-Sun (to 9pm Thu) 🌐 liebieghaus.de

Built for the Czech industrialist Baron Heinrich Liebieg in 1896, today this building houses a museum of sculpture, with works ranging from antiquity through to Mannerism, Baroque and Rococo. The museum also has superb examples of ancient Egyptian and Far Eastern art, as well as works from the Middle Ages and the Renaissance. Its highlights are the works of Neo-Classical masters such as Antonio Canova, Bertel Thorwaldsen and Johann Heinrich Dannecker.

Museum für Moderne Kunst (MMK)

🏛 Domstrasse 10
🕐 10am-6pm Tue (to 8pm Wed) 🌐 mmk.art

The modern art museum occupies a building that looks like a slice of cake. It was designed by Hans Hollein in 1989–92. The museum's collection represents all the major artistic trends from the 1960s until the present day, and includes works by Roy Lichtenstein, Andy Warhol and Claes Oldenburg. Temporary exhibitions focus on multi-media shows, incorporating photography and video art.

Städelsches Kunstinstitut

🏛 Schaumainkai 63
🕐 10am-6pm Tue-Sun (to 9pm Thu & Fri) 🌐 staedelmuseum.de

The founder of this excellent museum, banker Johann Friedrich Städel, left his art collection to the town in 1815. Since then, the museum has grown through acquisitions and donations, and now contains many masterpieces from seven centuries of European art, including Jan van Eyck's *Lucca Madonna* (1437) and Rembrandt's *Blinding of Samson* (1636). It moved to a Neo-Renaissance building in 1878, on the tree-lined "museum embankment" by the Main. In the 1920s it acquired the Hohenzollern collection from Sigmaringen. The museum has undergone renovation and new buildings have been constructed, including a subterranean exhibition hall for contemporary art.

Weihnachtsmarkt (Christmas market) in Frankfurt am Main

EXPERIENCE MORE

④ Fulda

🅐D5 🚉 ℹ️ Bonifatiusplatz 1; (0661) 10 21 814

Fulda's history began in AD 744, when Sturmius, a pupil of St Boniface, laid the foundation stone for the Benedictine abbey. Ten years later the body of St Boniface was laid to rest here. The town, which grew around the abbey, experienced its heyday during the Baroque period, and a new Baroque building, designed by Johann Dientzenhofer, was built in 1704–12 on the foundations of the old abbey. The Dom St Salvator und Bonifatius is a triple-nave basilica with a dome above the nave intersection, a monumental eastern façade and a shrine with the saint's relics under the high altar.

Opposite the cathedral stands the Stadtschloss (former episcopal palace), built by Johann Dientzenhofer and Andreas Gallasini, with richly decorated Baroque and Rococo interiors. Particularly noteworthy are the Kaisersaal (Imperial Hall) on the ground floor, the magnificent Fürstensaal (Hall of Princes) and the charming Rococo-style Spiegelsaal (Chamber of Mirrors) on the first floor.

To the north of the Dom stands the round Michaelskirche, a Carolingian chapel dating from 822, one of the oldest church buildings in Germany. Inside, the church has a ring of eight columns forming a rotunda and a crypt supported by a single column. The circular gallery, the side nave and the western tower are 11th-century additions.

Another interesting sight in Fulda is the late 18th-century parish church of St Blasius. In the 8th century, five abbeys were established on the hills surrounding the town. On Petersberg stands the former Benedictine abbey church of St Peter (Liobakirche), from the 9th–15th centuries, with a Carolingian crypt.

⑤ Alsfeld

🅐C4 🚉 ℹ️ Markt 3; www.alsfeld.de

The first historic records of Alsfeld date from the late 9th century. Today the town draws visitors with its pretty old town with numerous 16th- to 17th-century half-timbered buildings, including a grand late-Gothic Rathaus (town hall), built in 1512–16. Other interesting features in the market square are the stone Weinhaus, with its distinctive stepped gable (1538), and the Renaissance Hochzeitshaus (wedding house), dating from 1565. Opposite the town hall stands the Stumpfhaus (1609), named after a former mayor, its façade decorated with wood carvings and paintings. From the town hall runs the picturesque Fulder Gasse, with the Gothic parish church Walpurgiskirche (13th–15th centuries), which has 15th-century wall paintings. In Rossmarkt stands the former Augustian Dreifaltigkeitskirche (church of the Holy Trinity), from the 13th–15th centuries. It was from here that in 1522 the monk Tilemann Schnabel began to spread the Reformation in Alsfeld.

The Märchenhaus (Fairytale House) on Markt has several rooms devoted to the tales of the Brothers Grimm.

TOWNS IN THE RHEINGAU WINE REGION

There are several towns that visitors may want to use as base camps when setting out to explore Hesse's vineyards. Eltville boasts several mansions and the ruins of a 14th-century castle with original wall paintings and friezes. Rüdesheim, on the banks of the Rhine, features the Drosselgasse, a street lined with wine bars and shops. There are also the remains of two castles and several historic mansions.

⑥ Marburg

🅐C4 🚉 ℹ️ Biegenstrasse 15; www.marburg-tourismus.de

When in 1248 the county of Hesse broke away from Thuringia, Marburg became one of the most important seats of the landgraves. The first landgrave, Heinrich II,

↑ The handsome Baroque basilica of St Salvator und Bonifatius Fulda

→

The altar of
St Elisabeth, by
sculptor Ludwig
Juppe, in Marburg's
Elisabethkirche

lived in the castle that towers over the town. The town's history is inseparably linked with the 13th-century figure of Elisabeth of Thuringia, wife of Ludwig IV, who devoted her life to the poor and died here. In 1527, Philip the Magnanimous founded the first Protestant university in the Reich at Marburg. He also instigated the first Marburg Colloquy in 1529, to unify the Protestant faith. The "articles" presented by Martin Luther to Melanchthon and Zwingli later formed the basis for the Augsburg Creed.

Today Marburg is a picturesque university town. The Gothic **Elisabethkirche**, built in 1235–83, features a large set of Gothic altars from the early 16th century, including the altars of St Elisabeth (1513) and of the Holy Family (1511). Next to the north choir entrance stands the statue of St Elisabeth with a model of the

church (1480). The choir contains the tomb of the Saint, positioned under the baldachin (around 1280). The vestry houses the greatest treasure, the reliquary of St Elisabeth (1235–49). In the south choir is an interesting group of monuments to the Hessian landgraves, from the 13th–16th centuries.

The **Kunstmuseum Marburg** holds a collection of paintings produced after 1500, with a predominance of 19th- and 20th-century German artists. Around the market square stands a group of historic, half-timbered houses from the 14th–17th centuries. Particularly pretty are the Sonne (Sun, No. 14) and the Stiefel (Boot, No. 17). The Steinernes Haus (Stone House, No. 18), built in 1318, is the oldest in Marburg, along with that at No. 13 Hirschgasse. High above the town towers the **Landgrafenschloss**, the landgraves'

castle, dating from the 10th–16th centuries. The two-storey Fürstenbau (Dukes' Building) has a large ducal chamber, dating from 1330. The Wilhelmsbau was built in 1492–8.

Elisabethkirche
⌂ Elisabethstrasse
☏ (06421) 65 573 ◷ Apr-Oct: 9am-5pm; Nov-Mar: 10am-4pm daily

Kunstmuseum Marburg
♿ ⌂ Biegenstrasse 11
☏ (06421) 28 22 355
⊘ For renovations

Landgrafenschloss
♿ ⌂ Schloss 1 ☏ (06421) 282 23 55 ◷ 10am-6pm Tue-Sun (Nov-Mar: to 4pm)

7
Hanau

🅐C5 🅰 🅘 Am Markt 14–18;
www.hanau.de

Thanks to its trading in gold and silver, Hanau was once a wealthy port city. Although many of its architectural charms were destroyed during the war, the 18th-century Wilhelmsbad spa and Schloss Philippsruhe, a Baroque castle on the riverbank, survived, and they are attractive buildings to visit. There are also several museums and galleries.

However, Hanau's biggest draw is its link to the Brothers Grimm, who were born here in 1785 and 1786 respectively. Indeed, the town is sometimes referred to as "Brüder-Grimm-Stadt". Hanau marks the starting point of the German Fairytale Route *(p363)*; there's a bronze memorial to the brothers at the town market (Neustädter Markt), which dates back to 1896, and an annual theatre festival dedicated to them takes place each summer in Schloss Philippsruhe. An interactive Brothers

BROTHERS GRIMM

The two brothers are known around the world as collectors of German folk tales, which were first published in 1812 and later translated into many languages. Fairy-tales such as *Hansel and Gretel, Cinderella* and *Little Red Riding Hood* have been favourites for generations of children. Above all, however, the Grimm Brothers were scholars, and they also initiated the publication of the *Dictionary of the German Language*.

Brüder Grimm Märchen

Grimm museum for children was installed on the upper floors of the palace in 2019.

8
Giessen

🅐C4 🅰 🅘 Schulstrasse 4;
www.giessen-entdecken.de

Giessen was granted town status in 1248, and in 1607 it acquired its university. In Brandplatz stands the partially reconstructed Altes Schloss (Old Palace), dating from the 14th–15th centuries. Now the home of the Oberhessisches Museum, it holds a large collection of art dating from the Gothic period to today.

The Botanischer Garten (botanic garden) was estab-lished in 1609 for the purposes of scientific research. To the north of it stands the Neues Schloss (New Palace), built in 1533–9 for Landgrave Philip the Magnanimous. The Wallenfelssches

← Monument to the Brothers Grimm in their home town of Hanau

Haus nearby houses interesting ethnological collections. The only remaining part of the Gothic Pfarrkirche St Pankratius, which was almost completely destroyed in 1944, is its tower, dating from 1500.

At No. 2 Georg-Schlosser-Strasse is the half-timbered Burgmannenhaus, dating from the 14th century. Along with the old stable block in Dammstrasse, it is the only half-timbered building that has survived to this day.

9
Wetzlar

🅐C5 🅰 🅘 Domplatz 8;
www.wetzlar.de

Occupying a picturesque spot on the banks of the Lahn river, Wetzlar is overlooked by the ruins of the 12th-century Kalsmunt fortress. It was built for the Emperor Friedrich I Barbarossa (1122–90). Only parts of the tower remain intact. The Dom (collegiate church of St Mary) was begun in 897 but by the late 15th century had only been partly completed. The splendid western double portal has remained unusable for the last 500 years – although the iconography of the tympanum was finished, the stairs leading to the entrance were never built. Wetzlar's Dom is a rare surviving example of the typical appearance of most European churches in the mid-15th century. Inside are several artifacts, including the statue of the *Madonna on the Moon Crescent* (mid-15th century) and a late-Renaissance *Crucifixion*.

In 1772 the young Johann Wolfgang Goethe spent three months in Wetzlar working at the Imperial Court. During this time he fell in love with Charlotte (or Lotte) Buff. The Lottehaus, her former home, has a collection of items relating to Goethe and Lotte. It was the suicide of a friend, Karl Wilhelm Jerusalem, who lived in the 18th-century Jerusalemhaus at No. 5 Schillerplatz, that inspired Goethe to write his tragic novel, *The Sorrows of Young Werther* (1774). Jerusalem had suffered unrequited love. The novel, which was published two years later, made Goethe famous around Europe, but it also unwittingly led many young men to commit suicide.

---

⑩
Limburg

🄰 C5 🚉 🛈 Bahnhofsplatz 2; (06431) 61 66

Limburg's history dates back to the 8th century. The Dom (collegiate cathedral church of St George) towers high above the Lahn river. This monumental building, whose style combines late-Romanesque and early French-Gothic architecture, was erected in 1190–1250. Its well-proportioned interior contains a rich variety of historic artifacts, including some 13th-century wall paintings in the presbytery and the transept, a font dating from the same period and the tombstone of Konrad Kurzbold, who founded the first church on this site.

To the south of the Dom stands the Burg (castle), an irregular structure built in

PICTURE PERFECT
Schloss Philippsruhe

This palace in Hanau has one of the most architecturally significant façades in Hesse, with a perfectly symmetrical frontage enhanced by the fountain in front.

the 13th–16th centuries. Limburg has many original examples of half-timbered buildings. The houses at No. 1 Römerstrasse, No. 6 Kolpingstrasse, No. 4 Kleine Rütsche and No. 11 Kornmarkt date from the last decade of the 13th century. Near the 14th-century Alte Lahnbrücke (Old Lahn Bridge), with its defensive towers, stands a mansion belonging to the Cistercians of Eberbach. The post-Franciscan Sebastiankirche (church of St Sebastian) dates from the 14th and 18th centuries. In 1821 the town became the seat of a newly created diocese.

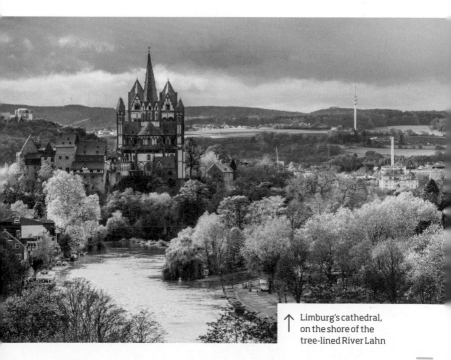

↑ Limburg's cathedral, on the shore of the tree-lined River Lahn

↑ Wiesbaden's Marktplatz still hosts a popular weekly market

⑪ Bad Homburg

🄰C5 🚉 𝒊 Kurhaus, Louisenstrasse 58; www. bad-homburg-tourismus.de

Bad Homburg grew up around a fortress whose earliest records date back to 1180. Friedrich II von Hessen-Homburg initiated the conversion of the medieval castle into the Schloss, a Baroque palace built in 1678–86. It features a lavish Festsaal (ballroom) and Spiegelkabinett (Hall of Mirrors). Following the annexation of Hesse-Homburg by Prussia in 1866, the palace became the favourite summer residence of the royal, then (from 1871) imperial family.

Homburg was one of the most fashionable spas in Germany, and today the town reflects its former splendour. The Kurpark, a landscaped park established in 1854–67, was designed by Peter Joseph Lenné. The Spielbank (1838), in Brunnenallee, claims to be the oldest casino in the world. Built in 1887–90, the Kaiser-Wilhelm-Bad is still used as the main bath complex for therapeutic treatments.

⑫ Wiesbaden

🄰C5 🚉 𝒊 Marktplatz 1; www.wiesbaden.de

Wiesbaden is the modern capital of Hesse. Highly valued as a spa by the Romans, the town grew from a small settlement known as aquae mattiacorum after the Germanic tribe of the Mattiacs. In 1774 the Nassau-Usingen family chose Wiesbaden as their residence. This, and the subsequent rapid growth of the town as a spa resort in the 19th century, laid the foundations for its lasting prosperity. Today the town is still dominated by large-scale developments carried out in the spirit and style of Classicism and Historicism.

The Stadtschloss (municipal castle), today the seat of the state parliament, was built in 1835–42. In Schlossplatz the Neo-Renaissance Marktkirche (market church), built in 1853–62, soars above the town's other buildings.

The oldest building in the town is the Altes Rathaus (old town hall), dating from 1610. In Wilhelmstrasse is the imposing Neo-Renaissance and Neo-Baroque Hessisches Staatstheater (state theatre). It was built in 1892–4 for Kaiser Wilhelm II to the designs of the theatre architects Fellner and Helmer. Adjacent to the Marktkirche is the attractive Kurhauskolonnade (spa house colonnade). It was erected in 1825 and is the longest colonnade in Europe. The early 20th-century Kurhaus (spa house) itself, with its grand façade and portico, is the work of Friedrich Thiersch. Inside is the original Spielbank (casino), where Fyodor Dostoyevsky and Richard Wagner tried their luck at the tables.

To the south of the town centre stands Schloss Biebrich, where the Counts von Nassau-Usingen resided until the early 19th century. The north pavilion was built first, in 1700, followed nine years later by the south

> **Inside is the original Spielbank (casino), where Fyodor Dostoyevsky and Richard Wagner tried their luck at the tables.**

pavilion. The wings, which join the two pavilions, and the central rotunda were added during the first two decades of the 18th century. The two external wings were added in 1734–44. The interior is richly furnished, predominantly in Baroque-Rococo style.

On the northern outskirts of the town is the Neroberg hill, whose summit can be reached by funicular railway. At the top is the Griechische Kapelle (Greek chapel). Built in 1847–55 by Philipp Hoffmann, it served as a mausoleum for Princess Elisabeth von Nassau, who died giving birth to her firstborn at the age of 19.

Fritzlar

C4 🏛 🚌 ℹ **Rathaus, Zwischen den Krämen 5; (05622) 98 86 43**

The pretty town of Fritzlar has preserved its nearly complete ring of medieval walls with watchtowers, bastions and over 450 half-timbered houses. In the early 8th century, St Boniface, the apostle of Germany, had the holy oak of the Germanic god Donar, which grew here, cut down to build a Christian chapel. In 724 he founded the Benedictine Dom (abbey church of St Peter). In 1118 the original church was replaced by a vaulted basilica with a triple-nave crypt, and this was remodelled in the 13th and 14th centuries. The east wall of the transept is decorated with wall paintings from around 1320, and the south nave includes a Pietà (1300). The 14th-century parish church of the Franciscan Order nearby has a lovely painting of the Madonna, on the northern wall of the choir.

→

Travelling down from Wiesbaden's Neroberg hill by funicular

In Fritzlar's picturesque old town stands the Rathaus (town hall). The exquisite Hochzeits-haus (wedding house), in the street of the same name, is a Renaissance half-timbered house, built in 1580–90, which now houses a museum.

Weilburg

C5 🏛 ℹ **Mauerstrasse 6; (06471) 314 67**

Weilburg enjoys a scenic location on the Lahn river. The town is dominated by the Renaissance-Baroque Schloss of the Nassau-Weilburg family. The monumental castle complex was created in stages. Its main section dates from the Renaissance era; the east wing was built in 1533–9; the south and west wings in 1540–48 and the west tower in 1567.

The northern part of the palace was completed in 1570–73. In the late 17th century various Baroque additions were made, mainly to the interior of the castle. The 16th-century furnishings show the rich ornamentation typical of the German Renaissance. The Obere Orangerie (Upper Orangery), built in 1703–5 and today used for temporary exhibitions, and the Hofkirche (castle church), dating from 1707–13, are the work of Ludwig Rothweil.

Did You Know?

The Freienfelser Ritterspiele is a historical re-enactment held every May in Weilburg.

The picture gallery in
Darmstadt's Hessisches
Landesmuseum

(1710), which houses the
**Grossherzoglich-Hessische
Porzellansammlung**, an
extensive porcelain collection.
The last Grand Duke of Hesse,
Ernst Ludwig, was a patron of
the Jugendstil, the German Art
Nouveau movement. He
initiated the building of an
exhibition and residential
complex, the Mathildenhöhe,
which was established in 1901
in the grounds of the former
ducal park, to serve the
existing artists' colony led by
Joseph Maria Olbrich. Olbrich
designed the Ernst-Ludwig-
Haus, which now houses the
Museum Künstlerkolonie,
an exhibition space for the
colony's artists, as well as
the Hochzeitsturm (wedding
tower), erected in 1907–8 to
celebrate the Grand Duke's
wedding. The Orthodox
church of St Mary Magdalene
was built in 1897–9 in honour
of Alix, wife of the last tsar
of Russia and sister of
Ernst Ludwig.

Schlossmuseum
◉◉ ◨Residenzschloss,
Marktplatz 15 ◷10am–5pm
Fri–Sun ◧schlossmuseum-
darmstadt.de

Hessisches
Landesmuseum
◉◉◉ ◨Friedensplatz 1
◷10am–6pm Tue, Thu & Fri,
10am–8pm Wed, 11am–5pm
Sat & Sun ◧hlmd.de

Grossherzoglich-
Hessische Porzellan-
sammlung
◉◉ ◨Schlossgarten-
strasse 10 ◖(06151) 71
32 33 ◷Apr–Oct: 10am–5pm
Fri–Sun

Museum Künstlerkolonie
◉◉ ◨Olbrichweg 15/
Mathildenhöhe
◷11am–6pm Tue–Sun
◧mathildenhoehe.eu

⓯
Darmstadt

C5 ◙ ✗Luisencenter,
Luisenplatz 5; www.
darmstadt-tourismus.de

The earliest historical records
of Darmstadt, which was
probably named after Dari-
mund, a Franconian settler,
date from the 12th century.
Until 1479 the castle and the
town belonged to the Counts
von Katzenelnbogen, and
later to Hessian landgraves.
In 1567 the Landgraves von
Hessen-Darmstadt chose
Darmstadt as their residence,
and they lived here until 1918.

To the north of the old town
stands the Residenzschloss,
initially a ducal palace, and
from 1806 residence of the
Landgraves von Hessen-
Darmstadt. The Renaissance-
Baroque complex is centred

around three courtyards. An
earlier medieval castle that
stood on the same site burned
down in 1546. The present
palace was created in stages,
with its earliest parts, the
Renaissance wings, dating
from 1567–97. The Glockenbau
has a 35-bell carillon which
can be heard every half hour;
it was completed in 1663. Two
Baroque wings, the so-called
Neubau or Neuschloss (New
Castle), surround older
buildings to the south and
west. Bombed in World War II,
the Schloss was later rebuilt.
Today it houses part of the
Technical University, while the
Glockenbau is home to the
fascinating **Schlossmuseum**
(castle museum). As well as a
splendid collection of coaches
and furniture, it contains the
masterly *Darmstädter
Madonna* (1526), by Holbein.

To the north of the Schloss
is the **Hessisches Landesmuseum** (one of Hesse's three
state museums), with artifacts
dating from the Roman era to
the 20th century. The museum
also has an excellent natural
history section, whose exhibits
include the skeleton of a
mammoth and birds native to
southern Hesse. In the park
behind the museum is the
Baroque Prinz-Georg-Palais

11

The number of
chemical elements
discovered in
Darmstadt.

Lorsch

🄰C5 🛈 Marktplatz 1; www. lorsch.de

This small town is mainly known for its Kloster, a Benedictine abbey first founded in 764 by Chrodegang of Metz and one of Europe's main cultural and intellectual centres in the Carolingian era. It reached the peak of its power in the 8th–13th centuries, before being sold to the Archbishop of Mainz in 1232. The Benedictines were forced to leave, and in their place the Cistercians arrived. The monastery was dissolved during the Reformation, and in 1621 the Spanish Army destroyed and plundered the greater part of the complex.

Fragments of the 13th century nave, the towers and the gatehouse, dating from around 790, are all that has survived. The original 8th-century church, a basilica without transept, burned down in 1090 and was rebuilt in the 12th century. The original crypt is the burial place of Ludwig II the German, the first ruler of the Eastern Franks. The Torhalle (gate-house) is one of the most

Lorsch's 18th-century town hall dominating the market square

important and best preserved architectural remains of the Carolingian period, and it was listed as a UNESCO World Heritage site in 1991. Its lower section is made up of three arcades, modelled on Roman triumphal arches. The first-floor quarters were likely used as a guest room or courtroom, and from the 14th century were used as a chapel. Remains of the original wall paintings are still visible here. The façade is decorated with red and white stone mosaics inspired by Franco-Merovingian art. The vertical divides, created by pilasters and entablature, are copies of ancient designs – an archi-tectural feature typical of the Carolingian Renaissance. The chapel's high roof and vaults date from the 14th century.

Michelstadt

🄰C5 🛈 Marktplatz 1; (06061) 979 41 10

Michelstadt, set among the hills of the Odenwald, is first mentioned in historical records in 741. From the 13th century the town belonged to the von Erbach family (the future Counts von Erbach). It has preserved many historic half-timbered houses and presents

a typical image of medieval Germany. The 16th-century Kellerei castle is built around the remains of an earlier castle dating from 970. It now houses a regional museum. The sight most popular with photographers is the half-timbered Rathaus (town hall), dating from 1484, with its three towers and an open ground-floor gallery. Nearby stands the late-Gothic, 15th-century Pfarrkirche (parish church) St Michael. Inside are some interesting epitaphs including the double tombstone of Philipp I and Georg I, dating from the late 15th century. A true rarity is the 18th-century synagogue, which escaped being burned by the National Socialists in 1938.

In the Steinbach district of Michelstadt stands the Einhardsbasilika, a church dating from around 821. The first church built on this site – at the initiative of Einhard, a courtier of Charlemagne – was a small, pillared and vaulted basilica with a short choir ending with a rounded apse. The parts that still remain include the nave, the north aisle with an apse and the crypt, which holds religious relics.

NORTH RHINE-WESTPHALIA

As a province, the North Rhineland goes back to Roman times. In the Middle Ages most of this area was ruled by the bishops of Köln. The North Rhineland cities grew and prospered thanks to their trade links, and in the 19th century they became major centres of mining and heavy industry. Westphalia forms the eastern part of the region. Once a Saxon territory, its history was often intertwined with that of the Rhineland. Only its western end has been heavily industrialized.

North Rhine-Westphalia is not the largest of the German regions, but is home to nearly 18 million people, it is the most highly populated one. It is often thought that the region – and in particular the heavily industrialized Ruhr valley – has little to offer to its visitors, but this is a mistaken belief. Its splendid past has left many priceless historic monuments and more recently, thanks to major investment, its industrial cities have transformed themselves into attractive cultural centres. The region is also an ideal base for outdoor adventures, with thousands of kilometres of tracks for walking in the Teutoburg Forest and in the Northern Eifel mountains, as well as splendid conditions for watersports and fishing in the Sauerland.

N

0 kilometres 20
0 miles 20

Mittellandkanal

Bramsche

Espelkamp

Weser

Stadthagen

A1

68

Lübbecke

65

MINDEN

27

Bückeburg

A2

65

Elze

3

A7

1

Hildesheim

Osnabrück

Porta Westfalica

Bad Oeynhausen

217

A30

Enger

Bad Salzuflen

**LOWER SAXONY,
HAMBURG AND BREMEN**
p418

51

BIELEFELD 26

A2

24 LEMGO

25

Detmold

1

Einbeck

A7

Warendorf

TEUTOBURGER WALD

Hermannsdenkmal

Northeim

Ems

Stukenbrock

Wiedenbrück

A33

64

Uslar

Beckum

64

PADERBORN 22

HÖXTER 23

Lippstadt

Bad
Driburg

SOEST 21

1

A44

55

68

Warburg

Göttingen

Alme

Möhnesee

Warstein

Diemel

252

Münden

Werra

rnsberg

A46

Brilon

Kassel

27

Meschede

A44

HESSE
p354

20

SÄUERLAND

Rothaargebirge

Winterberg

HESSEN

A44

55

Lennestadt

480

Bad Berleburg

Fritzlar

A7

Fulda

27

A4

Kreuztal

62

Bad Laasphe

252

3

19 SIEGEN

A45

54

Weilburg

54

Lahn

A3

NORTH RHINE-WESTPHALIA

Must Sees

1 Düsseldorf
2 Köln
3 Bonn

Experience More

4 Kleve
5 Xanten
6 Dortmund
7 Hagen
8 Essen
9 Wuppertal
10 Dormagen
11 Solingen
12 Altenberg
13 Northern Eifel

14 Aachen
15 Münster
16 Duisburg
17 Königswinter
18 Brühl
19 Siegen
20 Sauerland
21 Soest
22 Paderborn
23 Höxter
24 Lemgo
25 Teutoburger Wald
26 Bielefeld
27 Minden

⟶
1 The Gothic Köln Cathedral towering over the modern skyline.

2 Essen's Alte Synagoge.

3 Street in Aachen.

4 Louis Béroud work on display at Museum Folkwang in Essen.

3 DAYS

In North Rhine-Westphalia

Day 1

Morning Grab a coffee at the Marktplatz in Aachen *(p403)*, which bustles with market stalls on Tuesdays and Thursdays, then head south to visit the Pfalzkapelle, the only remaining legacy of the former palace of Charlemagne. The Pfalz is known for its palace chapel and shrine, as well as its treasury which holds one of Europe's most valuable collections of medieval liturgical art.

Afternoon Set in an historic 17th-century town house, the Couven Museum has an interesting collection of bourgeois furnishings and decor from the 18th and 19th centuries. If you feel like museum hopping, head to the Internationales Zeitungsmuseum, which is devoted to the history of the press, with over 200,000 newspapers from the 16th century up until today.

Evening Finish your day at Aachener Brauhaus *(Kapuzinergraben 4)*, near the city's iconic Elisenbrunnen pavilion, for traditional German dishes in a cosy atmosphere.

Day 2

Morning Take a short train trip to Köln *(p388)*. Once you've arrived, head out to climb the steps up the soaring cathedral *(p392)*, where you'll be rewarded with a beautiful view of the city and beyond. Afterwards admire the stunning interiors and treasury inside.

Afternoon Take a boat cruise or a short train ride to Bonn *(p396)*, where there's plenty to explore for the rest of the day: the Beethovenhaus, the city's striking university, the Rheinisches Landesmuseum and the Kunstmuseum Bonn to name a few. Whenever you feel yourself flagging, make time for lunch in between sights at Taj India *(Kölnstrasse 49)*.

Evening Return by train to Köln for a lovely evening riverside walk and delightful dinner at the traditional Bei Oma Kleinmann (Zülpicher Strasse 9).

Day 3

Morning Head to Essen *(p400)* and take a stroll to admire its architectural highlights, including the city's beautiful Alte Synagogue – the largest in Germany – and the Opera House designed by Finnish architect, Alvar Aalto.

Afternoon After lunch a visit to the Museum Folkwang is a must, not least for its collection of German Expressionism.

Evening Relax with a sundowner in the Grugapark, which has botanical gardens, a zoo and an Orangerie restaurant, as well as occasional concerts.

↑ Düsseldorf's modern buildings clustered along the Rhine

❶ DÜSSELDORF

🅰B4 ✈Düsseldorf 🚍 ℹImmermannstrasse 65B (am Hauptbahnhof), Marktstrasse; www.duesseldorf-tourismus.de

Düsseldorf was the capital of the Duchy of Berg from the late 14th century, and of the Palatine from 1614. An important industrial and cultural centre in the Rhine Valley, this metropolis has a renowned university, fine museums, wonderful theatres and, as the German capital of fashion, many excellent shops and boutiques.

①
Altstadt

The small old town area suffered severe damage in World War II. Among surviving monuments it is worth seeing some of the beautiful town houses and the late-Gothic Rathaus (town hall), built in 1570–73. Düsseldorf's castle, burned down in 1872, retains only the Schlossturm (castle tower). Another building worth visiting is the Baroque Pfarrkirche St Andreas, from 1622–9, and the medieval Lambertuskirche, the former collegiate church of St Lambertus, which took over a century to complete.

②
Kunstsammlung Nordrhein-Westfalen

🏛Grabbeplatz 5
🕐10am-6pm Tue-Fri, 11am-6pm Sat & Sun
🌐kunstsammlung.de

The art collection of the state of North Rhine-Westphalia is enormous. Particularly valuable are 88 paintings by Paul Klee. There are also works by Wassily Kandinsky, Marcel Duchamp, Piet Mondrian and Pablo Picasso. The gallery at Grabbeplatz is known as K20, and a second building at Ständehausstrasse 1, where contemporary art is exhibited, is known as K21.

Temporary exhibitions are held nearby, at Kunsthalle Düsseldorf, located at No. 4 Grabbeplatz.

③
Königsallee

The kings' avenue, often just referred to as Kö, was laid out at the beginning of the 19th century, along the old city moat. The Kö is lined with expensive shops, galleries, boutiques, department stores and many bars and restaurants.

④
Hofgarten

🏛Schloss Jägerhof
📞(0211) 89 96 262
🕐11am-5pm Tue-Fri & Sun, 1-5pm Sat

This charming park, originally laid out in 1769 for Elector Karl Theodor, was recreated in the English style at the beginning of the 19th century. The park is a marvellous setting for Schloss Jägerhof, a Baroque hunting lodge dating from the years 1752–63 and built according to a design by Johann Josef Couven and Nicolas de Pigage. The castle was rebuilt after World War II. It now houses the Goethe-Museum, holding memorabilia and documents related to the writer's life.

Schloss Benrath

 Benrather Schlossallee Apr-Oct: 11am-5pm Tue-Fri, 11am-6pm Sat & Sun; Nov-Mar: 11am-5pm Tue-Sun schloss-benrath.de

Part of Düsseldorf since 1929, Benrath is home to this beautiful Neo-Classical hunting palace, built for the electors of the Palatine in 1755–73 by Nicolas de Pigage. Decor, beautiful furnishings and an extensive park and gardens have survived.

Kunstpalast

 Ehrenhof 4-5 11am-6pm Tue-Sun (to 9pm Thu) kunstpalast.de

The Art Palace is one of the most interesting museums in Germany, with a collection of paintings dating from the 16th to the 20th centuries, including works by Dutch masters of the 17th century. It also holds a large collection of paintings by the Düsseldorf school of painting, who were a group of artists that showed at the Düsseldorf Academy in the 1830s and 1840s. Other highlights include Japanese woodblock prints and the outstanding Helmut Hentrich Glass Museum.

---

⑦

Neanderthal Museum

 Talstrasse 300, Mettmann 10 am-6pm Tue-Sun neanderthal.de

The Neanderthal Museum is located close to the site where the first recognized Neanderthal man was found in 1856. Through a mix of multimedia installations, audio presentations, texts and physical exhibits such as life-sized figures and fossils, the museum tells the story of humankind from its beginnings on the African savannah to the present day.

←
Fine paintings on display in the Museum Kunstpalast

Map

Nordstrasse Ⓤ
0 metres 300 N
0 yards 300

⑥ Kunstpalast
JOSEPH-BEUYS-UFER
FISCHERSTR
FREILIGRATHSTR
INSELSTRASSE
Sternstrasse
ROSENSTRASSE
KAISERSTRASSE
FELDSTR

Oberkasseler Brücke
Tonhalle
HOFGARTENRAMPE
④ Hofgarten
GARTENSTRASSE
JÄGERHOFSTRASSE

Rhein
HEINRICHE-
MAXIMILIAN WEYHE-ALLEE

REUTERKASERNE
RITTERSTRASSE
RATINGER STRASSE
Schauspiel-haus

Lambertus-kirche
Pfarrkirche St. Andreas
② Kunstsammlung Nordrhein-Westfalen
GRABBE-PLATZ
JAN-WELLEM-PLATZ
Schlossturm
MÜHLENSTR
MEERTENSTR
BURG-PLATZ ①
Deutsche Oper am Rhein
J.-ERWIN-PLATZ
Schadow-strasse Ⓤ
Rathaus Altstadt
NEUSTRASSE
CORNELIUS-PLATZ
SCHADOWSTR
MARKT-PLATZ
BOLKERSTRASSE
GASSE
Kaufhof-Galeria
RHEINWERFT
FLINGERSTRASSE
Ⓤ Heinrich-Heine-Allee
Hetjens-Museum
WALLSTRASSE
MITTELSTR
KASERNENSTR
BREITE STRASSE
Königsallee ③
Hauptbahnhof 1 km (0.6 miles)
CARLS-PLATZ
MAX-PLATZ
BENRATHERSTR
HOHE STRASSE
Ⓤ Benrather-strasse
KÖNIGSALLEE
BERLINER ALLEE
Ⓤ Steinstrasse
Neanderthal Museum ⑦ 13 km (8 miles)
Heinrich-Heine-Institut
Spee'scher Graben
BASTIONSTRASSE
Schloss Benrath ⑤ 11 km (7 miles)

↑ Köln's Gothic Dom
standing on the far
bank of the Rhine

2

KÖLN

 **B4** ✈ Cologne-Bonn Airport 🚌🚆 ℹ Kardinal-Höffnerplatz 1; www.koelntourismus.de

Founded by the Romans in 38 BC, Köln (known as Cologne in English) is one of the oldest towns in Germany. Since the 5th century it has been a powerful ecclesiastical centre, encompassing 12 Romanesque churches as well as its impressive Gothic cathedral (*p392*). Present-day Köln is known for its trade fairs and as an important centre for art and culture, with excellent museums, historic buildings and art galleries.

1 ✏️

Kolumba Museum

🏛 Kolumbastrasse 4
🕐 Noon-5pm Wed-Mon
🌐 kolumba.de

Designed by Swiss architect Peter Zumthor to much critical acclaim, this museum houses the archbishopric of Köln's collection of religious art. The building accommodates the ruins of St Kolumba – a chapel built in the 1950s to house a statue of the Madonna that miraculously escaped bombing during World War II – and a unique archaeological excavation from the 1970s.

 2 ✏️ 🎨

Farina Haus

🏛 Obenmarspforten 21
🕐 10am-7pm Mon-Sat, 11am-5pm Sun 🌐 farina.org

Located opposite the town hall, Farina Haus traces the history of fragrance. Tours lead down to the cellar, which is over 300 years old and is where the Italian perfumier Johann Maria Farina first began producing Eau de Cologne. Farina's invention spawned a huge number of imitations, and eau de cologne is now a generic term recognized worldwide.

 3 ✏️ 🏛

Wallraf-Richartz-Museum & Fondation Corboud

🏛 Obenmarspforten 40
🕐 10am-6pm Tue-Sun & hols (to 10pm 1st Thu of month) 🌐 wallraf.museum

This museum was named after Ferdinand Franz Wallraf, who bequeathed his art collection to the city in 1824, and Johann Heinrich Richartz, who funded the first building. Medieval and early modern paintings (1250–1550) form the core of the collection, though there are also examples from Impressionism, Realism and Symbolism. In 2001 the museum

↑ *Four Girls on the Bridge* (1905) by Edvard Munch, Wallraf-Richartz Museum

THE CHURCHES OF KÖLN

Köln became the seat of the archbishop in 795 and, as an important centre for the German Christian community, the city is bursting with an eclectic mix of stunning historical religious sights. Some highlights are the parish church of Pfarrkirche St Mariä Himmelfahrt on Marzellenstrasse - one of the few Baroque buildings in the city - and Gross St Martin on An Gross St Martin, built on top of a Roman sports arena whose remains were found under the crypt.

moved to this new building, incorporating works from the collection of Gérard Corboud.

④ ⑱
Rathaus

🏛 Alter Markt 📞 (0221) 34 64 30

The town hall is an irregular shape created by successive modifications. The first phase and main wing dates from around 1330. A vast Gothic tower was added in 1407–14, and in the 16th century the arcaded Renaissance Lions Courtyard and a magnificent front lodge were built.

From Kleine Budengasse you can enter the **Praetorium**, the remains of a Roman town hall that were uncovered beneath the Rathaus. A controversial "archaeology zone" is under

construction, to showcase the excavated Roman walls and items such as the remains of 12th-century ritual Jewish baths, destroyed after the expulsion of the Jews in 1424.

Praetorium
⊗ 🏛 Kleine Budengasse 📞 (0221) 223 94 🔒 For renovations

⑤
Gürzenich

🏛 Gürzenichstrasse

This Gothic building has a huge celebration hall (1437–44), occupying the entire first floor. Next to it are the ruins of the Romanesque church Alt St Alban. It has a copy of Käthe Kollwitz's *Parents* sculpture.

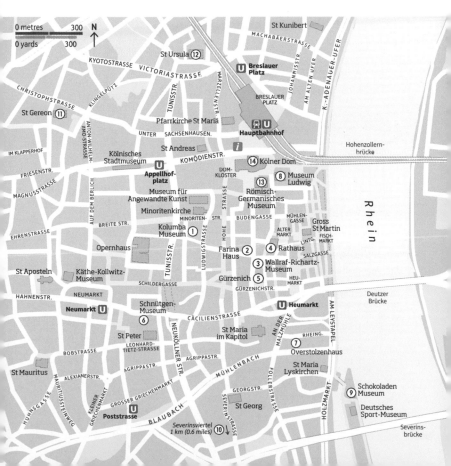

⑥ Schnütgen-Museum

🏛 Cäcilienstrasse 29
🕐 10am-6pm Tue-Sun
(to 8pm Thu) 🌐 museum-
schnuetgen.de

The Romanesque church of St Cecilia, built in 1130–60 as a nunnery, was taken over in 1479 by the Augustinian Sisters; today it houses the Schnütgen-Museum, the first pieces of which were given to the city by Alexander Schnütgen in 1906. Destroyed during World War II and subsequently rebuilt, this museum specializes in religious art, mainly from the Middle Ages. Its collection includes magnificent sculptures, gold and ivory items and sacral objects.

⑦ Overstolzenhaus

🏛 Rheingasse 8

World War II deprived Köln of many of its historic buildings, but this one has since been lovingly restored. Built for a prosperous patrician family in the 13th century, it is one of the city's finest Gothic houses.

---

⑧ Museum Ludwig

🏛 Heinrich-Böll-Platz
🕐 10am-6pm Tue-Sun (to 10pm 1st Thu of month)
🌐 museum-ludwig.de

Inaugurated in 1976, this museum houses one of

> **According to legend, the church shrines hold the remains of St Ursula and 11,000 virgins, all of whom were reputedly killed at the hands of the Huns.**

Europe's best collections of modern art. There are several hundred pieces by Picasso, paintings by German Expressionists, Surrealists, American Pop Artists and the Russian avant-garde, as well as many sculptures.

---

⑨ Schokoladen Museum

🏛 Rheinauhafen 1a
🕐 10am-6pm daily
🚫 Jan-Mar & Nov: Mon
🌐 schokoladenmuseum.de

Founded in 1993 by local businessman Hans Imhoff, this fantastic museum explains the history of cocoa bean cultivation as well as the cultural significance, use and marketing of chocolate. Nine exhibitions flow from Aztec and Maya traditions to the present day, after which visitors can also

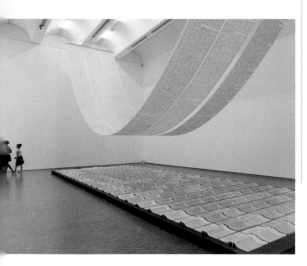

←

Book from the Sky (1987-91) by Xu Bing, Museum Ludwig

KÖLN'S ROMANESQUE CHURCHES

Although best known for its towering cathedral, Köln is also home to 12 surviving Romanesque churches, bearing testimony to the importance of the Church in the town's development. The churches are set in a semi-circle around the city centre, and were built between 1150 and 1250. Constructed on the graves of martyrs and early bishops of Köln, the forms of the churches influenced the development of Romanesque architecture well beyond the Rhineland. Almost all the churches were damaged in World War II; some, such as the church of St Kolumba, have not been restored, but most were returned to their former glory.

① The late-Romanesque basilica of St Andreas was founded in around 1200.

② Gross St Martin, with its attractive triangular presbytery and vast tower, dominates Fischmarkt.

③ The grand 12th-century basilica St Aposteln has a low tower at the junction of the naves and a tall front tower, with turrets flanking the presbytery apse.

view the production process, and, of course, sample and purchase the final product.

---

⑩
Severinsviertel

The Severin Quarter, a district located on the southern edge of the old town, owes its name to the 13th-century Romanesque church of St Severinus. The church, largely remodelled in the Gothic style in the 15th and 16th centuries, features many rich original furnishings and has a mid-10th-century crypt.

---

⑪
St Gereon

🏛 Gereonsdriesch 2-4 🕐 10am-6pm Mon-Fri, 10am-5pm Sat, 1-6pm Sun

Named after a Roman officer who was martyred in Köln, this church must be the most unusual edifice in all of Germany. Its oldest part, an oval building surrounded by small conchas, was built in the late 4th century on the graves of martyrs and – according to legend – founded by St Helen. The Romanesque presbytery is an 11th-century addition and, in 1219–27, the oval was

encircled with a ten-sided, four-storey structure in early-Gothic style. This is topped with a vast dome, 48 m (157 ft) in diameter, with ribbed vault.

---

⑫
St Ursula

🏛 Ursulaplatz 24 🕐 10am-noon, 3-5pm Mon-Sat (to 4:30pm Wed), 3-4:30pm Sun

This church was built in the 12th century, on the site of an earlier church that probably dated from around 400. In the late 13th century the presbytery was rebuilt in Gothic style.

The Baroque *Goldene Kammer* (Golden Chamber) at the southern end, added in the 17th century, is lined with many shrines. According to legend, these hold the remains of St Ursula and 11,000 virgins, all of whom were reportedly killed at the hands of the Huns in the 4th century. The chamber walls are covered with bones, arranged in elaborate designs or spelling out phrases in Latin. The city insignia of Köln also testify to the veneration of the virgins.

↑ A marble bust on display in the Römisch-Germanisches Museum

⑬ 🏛🏢💻🏛
Römisch-Germanisches Museum

🏛 Roncalliplatz 4 🕐 For renovations 🌐 roemisch-germanisches-museum.de

This building houses a number of Roman and pre-Roman archaeological finds that were unearthed in Köln and in the Rhine valley. On display are fascinating weapons, ornamental and artistic objects, and – probably the best-known exhibits – the superb Dionysus mosaic and the monument to Poblicius.

(14)

KÖLNER DOM

Domkloster 4 **May-Oct: 6am-9pm daily (Nov-Apr: to 7:30pm)**
koelner-dom.de

One of the finest examples of Gothic architecture anywhere in the world, Köln's cathedral is the city's main landmark and a UNESCO World Heritage Site. As well as the many treasures within, the views from the tower are peerless.

The greatest Gothic structure in Germany, the Dom is also unusually complex, whether in terms of its splendour, its size and even simply the date of its construction. The foundation stone was laid on 15 August 1248, the presbytery consecrated in 1322. The cathedral was built gradually until around 1520. It then remained unfinished until the 19th century, when Romanticists revived interest in it. The building was finally completed in 1842–80, according to the rediscovered, original Gothic designs. Like many of Köln's buildings, the cathedral was seriously damaged by fire and bombing during World War II, although the medieval windows and all major works of art had either been protected or removed, and escaped destruction. Minor examples of the war damage to the building remain visible to this day, but it was largely restored before its 700th anniversary in 1948. Today the cathedral is observable from almost every point in the city centre; conversely, it's possible to enjoy panoramic views of the city from its South Tower. Look out, too, for the cathedral treasury, the contents of which hark back to the 5th century.

GREAT VIEW
Towering Above

Climb the 533 steps of the cathedral's South Tower to find the wide observation deck. From here, at a height of about 100 m (303 ft), sweeping panoramic views take in the city, the Rhine and the Siebengebirge hills.

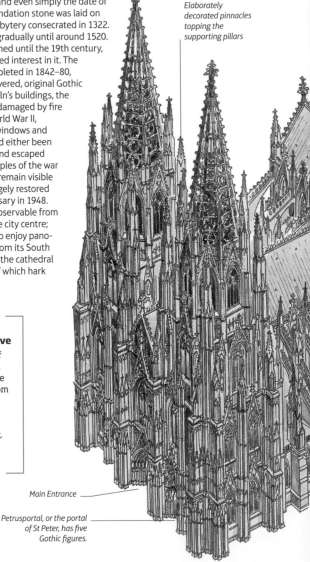

Elaborately decorated pinnacles topping the supporting pillars

Main Entrance

Petrusportal, or the portal of St Peter, has five Gothic figures.

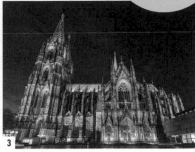

① Elaborate 19th-century decoration above the cathedral's main entrance.

② The church's wide middle nave and high arched roof, with elegant stained glass windows at the head of the aisle.

③ Night time illuminations keep this landmark cathedral visible all night long.

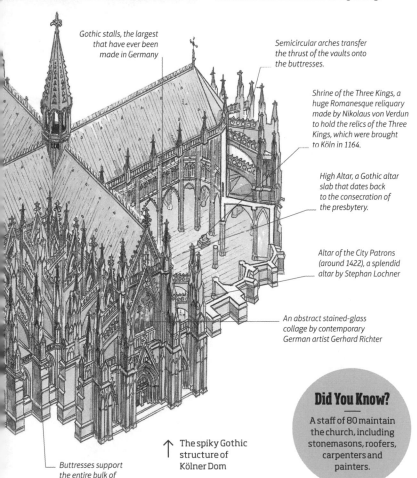

Gothic stalls, the largest that have ever been made in Germany

Semicircular arches transfer the thrust of the vaults onto the buttresses.

Shrine of the Three Kings, a huge Romanesque reliquary made by Nikolaus von Verdun to hold the relics of the Three Kings, which were brought to Köln in 1164.

High Altar, a Gothic altar slab that dates back to the consecration of the presbytery.

Altar of the City Patrons (around 1422), a splendid altar by Stephan Lochner

An abstract stained-glass collage by contemporary German artist Gerhard Richter

↑ The spiky Gothic structure of Kölner Dom

Buttresses support the entire bulk of the cathedral

Did You Know?

A staff of 80 maintain the church, including stonemasons, roofers, carpenters and painters.

Must See

Köln's Kranhäuser (crane houses) and Gothic Kölner Dom

↑ Bonn's handsome Romanesque cathedral, the Münster St Martin

③

BONN

B4 ✈ Cologne-Bonn, to the north 🚊 ℹ Windeckstrasse 1; www.bonn.de

Founded by the Romans in 11 BC, Bonn entered the world stage when, on 10 May 1949, it was elevated to the status of capital of the Federal Republic of Germany. When parliament decided in 1991 to make Berlin the capital, Bonn resumed its provincial role. With its scenic setting on the Rhine and pedestrianized old town, Bonn is a pleasure to visit.

Beethovenhaus

📍 Bonngasse 18-26
🕐 Apr-Oct: 10am-6pm daily; Nov-Mar: 10am-5pm Mon-Sat, 11am-5pm Sun
🌐 beethoven.de

The Beethoven museum is housed in the Baroque 18th-century house where the composer Ludwig van Beethoven was born in 1770 and lived until the age of 22. A new permanent exhibition features portraits, music instruments, original manuscripts and memorabilia from Beethoven's life. Regular chamber-music concerts are held at the museum.

②

Markt

The central market square is a mixture of modern and Baroque architecture. Its most outstanding feature is the Rathaus (town hall), built in 1737–8 by Michel Leveilly. The centre of the market square is decorated with a fountain in the shape of an obelisk.

③

Rheinufer

The Rhine embankment, which changes its name several times along its course,

runs along the western bank of the Rhine. To the north of Kennedybrücke lies the Beethovenhalle, a vast concert and congress hall, and to the south of the bridge is the Bonn opera house. Next to the opera is the Alter Zoll, the former customs house.

④

Universität

📍 Am Hofgarten

Founded in 1818, the university is based in an elegant, apricot-coloured Baroque castle, which was built in 1607–1705 to a design by Enrico Zuccalli, and extended after 1715 by Robert de Cotte.

⑤

Münster St Martin

📍 Münsterplatz

Bonn's cathedral is a magnificent example of Romanesque architecture in the Rhine valley. The cathedral was built around 1150–1230, on the site of an earlier 11th-century church.

⑥ 🔥 🏛 🍴 🛍

Rheinisches Landesmuseum

📍 Colmantstrasse 14-16
🕐 11am-5pm Tue-Sun
🌐 landesmuseum-bonn.lvr.de

This interesting regional museum has a vast collection of excavated items dating back to Roman times. It also features a selection of medieval and modern art.

---

⑦ Museumsmeile

One of the most impressive buildings on Bonn's Museum Mile is the excellent free **Haus der Geschicte der BR Deutschland**, which details the history of Germany after World War II. Nearby is the superb **Kunstmuseum**, which houses 20th-century art in an interesting building designed by Axel Schultes. It displays a fabulous collection of Expressionist paintings. Next

door stands the Kunst- und Ausstellungshalle, which opened in 1992 as a venue for temporary exhibitions.

Haus der Geschicte der BR Deutschland

🚇🚌 📍 Willy-Brandt-Allee 14
🕐 9am-7pm Tue-Fri, 10am-6pm Sat & Sun 🌐 hdg.de

Kunstmuseum

🚇🚌🛍 📍 Friedrich-Ebert-Allee 2 🕐 11am-6pm Tue-Sun (to 9pm Wed)
🌐 kunstmuseum-bonn.de

---

⑧ Poppelsdorf

This leafy southwestern suburb is home to the Baroque Schloss Clemensruhe (1715–18). Both the castle and its extensive park, with a botanical garden, belong to the university. The pilgrimage church on the Kreuzberg, a low hill, houses the chapel of the Holy Steps, which is attributed to Balthasar Neumann.

↑ The Beethoven Monument on the central Münsterplatz

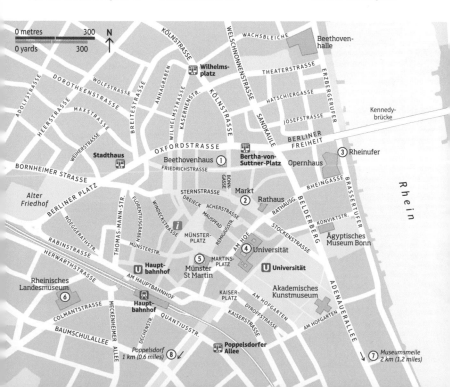

EXPERIENCE MORE

4

Kleve

B3 🚂🚌 ℹ️ Minoritenplatz 2; (02821) 848 06

The town of Kleve (known as Cleves in English) is named after the high cliff on which a castle was built in the 10th century. Around it a settlement developed, which became a town in 1242. It was ruled by the dukes of Kleve, whose ambitions reached their peak in 1539, when Anne of Cleves married the English king Henry VIII.

During World War II Kleve lost most of its historic buildings. One that has survived is the imposing Gothic church of the Assumption of the Virgin Mary, St Mariä Himmelfahrt (1341–1426). It has remains of the high altar, dating from 1510–13, with reliefs by Henrik Douvermann and Jakob Dericks, as well as beautiful monuments to the von Kleve dukes. The former Franciscan St Mariä Empfängnis (church of the Immaculate Conception), a Gothic twin-nave hall-church from the first half of the 15th

century, includes noteworthy features such as the Gothic stalls and a Baroque pulpit. The well-preserved ducal castle of **Schwanenburg** was remodelled twice: in Gothic style in the late 15th century, and in Baroque style in 1636–66. Testifying to former splendour are the parks established in the mid-17th century by Johann Moritz von Nassau. The most beautiful of these is the Neuer Tiergarten (wildlife park). Haus Koekkoek once belonged to the painter Barend Cornalis Koekkoek, after whom it was named. The **Museum Kurhaus Kleve – Ewald Mataré-Sammlung** presents interesting and diverse art exhibitions.

A suspension bridge across the Rhine – at 1,228 m (4,028 ft) the longest in Germany – connects Kleve with Emmerich. Worth a visit here is the Martinskirche (church of St Martin), with its exquisite, late-10th-century shrine of St Willibrod.

Lying 6 km (4 miles) southeast of Kleve is the moated castle of Moyland. It houses an art collection with over 4,000 works by Joseph Beuys. A further 12 km (7 miles) southeast is the town of Kalkar, which was once home to the Kalkar School, specializing in woodcarving.

Schwanenburg

⊘ 🏛️ Am Schlossberg
📞 (02821) 228 84 🕐 Apr-Oct: 11am-5pm daily; Nov-Mar: 11am-5pm Sat & Sun

Museum Kurhaus Kleve-Ewald Mataré-Sammlung

⊘ 🏛️ Tiergartenstrasse 41
🕐 11am-5pm Tue-Sun
🌐 museumkurhaus.de

5

Xanten

B3 🚂🚌 ℹ️ Kurfürstenstrasse 9; (02801) 77 22 00

The history of Xanten goes back to the Romans, who founded the settlement of Colonia Ulpia Traiana near the local garrison. The present town, however, did not rise out of the ruins of the Roman town. It was established nearby, around the memorial church (now the Dom). It was named Sanctos ("by the saints"), later changed to Xanten. A powerful town in the Middle Ages, Xanten also features in the Nibelung myth, and was said to be the birthplace of Siegfried.

The most important historic building in the town is the Dom St Viktor, which, according to legend, was built

The Hafentempel in the Archäologischer Park, Xanten

← A temple and waterfall in the pretty Neuer Tiergarten park, Kleve

Museum für Kunst- und Kulturgeschichte

 □ Hansastrasse 3
☎ (0231) 502 55 22
🕐 11am–6pm Tue–Wed & Sat–Sun, 11am–8pm Thu–Fri
🚫 Mon

Museum am Ostwall

□ Leonie-Reygers-Terrasse 2 🕐 11am–6pm Tue, Wed, Sat & Sun (to 8pm Thu & Fri) 🌐 museum ostwall.dortmund.de

---

 7

Hagen

🅰 B4 🚃 *i* Körnerstrasse 25; (02331) 809 99 80

Karl Ernst Osthaus brought fame to this town when he created an artists' colony here at the beginning of the 1900s, inviting Art Nouveau designers such as Peter Behrens and Henry van der Velde. The magnificent Hohenhof, Osthaus's home, was created by van der Velde. It houses the Karl-Ernst-Osthaus-Museum, with a collection of modern art. Behrens designed the crematorium in the suburb of Delstern and the beautiful villas Haus Cuno (Hassleyer Strasse 35) and Haus Goedeke (Amselgasse). In the south is the Westfälisches Freilicht-museum, an open-air museum that has many historic workshops and factories.

on the graves of St Viktor and members of the Thebian Legion. The surviving Gothic cathedral (1263–1517) holds the shrine of St Victor (1129), the early-Gothic stalls (1228) and, above all, the exquisite Marienaltar (St Mary's altar) by Henrik Douvermann.

Also worth visiting is the Klever Tor, a magnificent late-14th-century double town-gate, northwest of the town. The Archäologischer Park, on the site of the Roman town, and the Römer Museum display reconstructed Roman public buildings including the impressive Hafentempel (Harbour Temple).

 6

Dortmund

🅰 B4 🚃 *i* Kampstrasse 80; www.dortmund-tourismus.de

The large city of Dortmund is known not only for its excellent beer and highly developed industry, but also for its more than 1,000 years of history. In the Middle Ages the town grew rich through trade and joined the Hanseatic League; after a period of decline it flourished again in the 19th century.

A walk through the small old town will take visitors to the **Museum für Kunst- und Kulturgeschichte** (Museum for Art and Cultural History) with displays of interiors from various periods, including Secessionist designs by Joseph Maria Olbrich. A short distance from here is the Petrikirche, a Gothic 14th-century hall-church, whose greatest attraction is its high altar (1521), the work of Gilles, a master from Antwerp. A shortcut across the market square and along Ostenhellweg takes the visitor to two more churches: the Reinoldikirche and the Marienkirche. The former, dedicated to St Reinold, the patron saint of Dortmund, has an early-Gothic 13th-century main body and a late-Gothic 15th-century presbytery. The church of St Mary is a 12th-century Romanesque structure. It has a magnificent main altar, by Conrad von Soest (1415–20) and a statue of the Madonna (around 1230). Inside the Dortmunder U tower, the **Museum am Ostwall** has an excellent modern art collection.

> ## Did You Know?
>
> In 2005 a teapot designed by Henry van der Velde sold at auction for €170,000.

8

Essen

🅰B4 🔲📧 **i** Im Handelshof
(am Hauptbahnhof 2);
www.visitessen.de

It is hard to believe that this former industrial metropolis has grown from a monastery, established in 852. The town owes its development and pro-minence to the Krupp family, who, over several generations from the mid-19th century, created the powerful German steel and arms industry.

The most important historic building in the town is the Münster, the former collegiate church of the canonesses. This unusual edifice consists of the 15th-century Gothic church of St John, an 11th-century atrium and the main church, which in turn has a Romanesque 11th-century frontage and a Gothic 14th-century main body. The most precious object held by the church is the Goldene Madonna, a statue of the Virgin Mary with the Infant, made from sheet gold, probably around 980, by an unknown artist. The treasury has an outstanding collection of gold items from the Ottonian period.

Another important sight in Essen is the Synagogue built by Edmund Körner in 1911–13. One of the largest synagogues in Germany, it managed to outlast the Third Reich and is now the "House of Jewish Culture", which examines the contemporary

Jewish way of life. Visitors who are interested in 20th-century architecture should see the church of St Engelbert in Fischerstrasse, designed by Dominikus Böhm (1934–6), the garden city of Margarethenhöhe, built from 1909 to a design by Georg Metzendorf, and the opera house designed by the Finnish architect Alvar Aalto.

Essen has much to offer to modern art enthusiasts. The **Museum Folkwang** boasts an excellent collection of 20th-century paintings, mainly by French and German Expressionists. It is also home to the German Poster Museum.

The Grugapark is a large green area with botanical gardens, zoo and the Grugahalle, where major concerts are held. To the south of the centre, on the banks of the Baldeneysee, stands Villa Hügel, which belonged to the Krupp family until 1945. Today interesting art exhibitions are frequently hosted here. Farther south, in Werden, is the former Benedictine church of St Ludger, consisting of a 13th-century body fronted by a 10th-century imperial façade. The treasury holds many precious objects including a bronze crucifix from around 1060.

Museum Folkwang
😊🎨 🅰Goethestrasse 41
🕐10am–6pm Tue, Wed, Sat & Sun (to 8pm Thu & Fri)
🌐museum-folkwang.de

Did You Know?

The Schwebebahn monorail, with its famous hanging cars, is the only one of its kind in Germany.

9

Wuppertal

🅰B4 🔲 **i** Kirchstrasse 16, Elberfeld; Informations-zentrum am Döppersberg; www.wuppertal.de

Wuppertal, capital of the Bergisches Land area, was created in 1929 by combining six towns along a 20-km (12-mile) stretch of the Wupper river. The towns are joined by the Schwebebahn, a monorail constructed in 1900.

The most interesting of the former towns is Elberfeld, with a museum of clocks, and the **Von der Heydt-Museum** of 19th- and 20th-century German art. The museum in the Friedrich-Engels-Haus in Barmen (Engelsstrasse 10) is

One of the beautiful original interiors of Essen's Villa Hügel

↑ The Schwebebahn monorail connecting the Wuppertal towns

worth seeing, and Neviges has a Baroque pilgrimage church, with a much-visited miraculous picture of the Virgin Mary.

Von der Heydt-Museum

 🏠 Elberfeld Turmhof 8 📞 (0202) 563 62 31 🕐 11am–6pm Tue, Wed & Fri-Sun, 11am–8pm Thu

---

⑩ Dormagen

🅰B4 🚃🚍 *i* Schlossstrasse 2-4; (02133) 257 647

This medium-sized town, which principally relies on its chemical industry, is known for two remarkable historic monuments. On the banks of the Rhine lies the fortified customs town of Zons, established around 1373–1414 at the instigation of Archbishop Friedrich von Saarwerden. This small, four-sided fortress has survived in excellent condition. The buildings are mainly from a later time, but the walls, gates and ruined Schloss Friedestrom are among the most fascinating examples of medieval for-

tifications in the Rhine valley.

Equally interesting is Knechtsteden, to the west, where an amazing monastery was built for the Norbertines in the 12th century. Amid orchards, the twin-choired basilica has mighty towers and attractive cloisters. Impressive murals include a 12th-century depiction of Christ in the western apsis.

---

⑪ Solingen

🅰B4 🚃🚍 *i* Clemens-Galerien, Mummstrasse 10; (0212) 290 36 01

Solingen is synonymous with its factory, where scissors and knives are made. The main attraction in town is the Klingenmuseum, showing cutting tools from the Stone Age to the present. The **Kunstmuseum Solingen** (Centre for Persecuted Arts) displays works that were banned by the Nazi regime.

Remscheid, 7 km (4 miles) east of Solingen, has the Röntgen-Museum, dedicated to Nobel Prize winner Wilhelm Röntgen, who discovered the

X-ray. He was born here. One of the most beautiful buildings is the Heimatmuseum, with typical regional interiors.

A short drive from the town is the Müngstener Bridge, Germany's highest railway bridge and Schloss Burg, the 12th-century fortress of the von Berg family, which now houses a museum.

Kunstmuseum Solingen

 🏠 Wuppertaler Strasse 160 🕐 10am–5pm Tue-Sun 🌐 verfolgte-kuenste.de

---

⑫ Altenberg

🅰B4 🚃🚍 *i* Eugen Heinen Platz 2, Odenthal; www.altenberg-info.de

Altenberg near Odenthal has preserved its Bergischer Dom, a former Cistercian church and an important pilgrim destination. Built in 1259–1379, it is also one of the most beautiful Gothic buildings in Germany. In accordance with their rules, the Cistercians built the church without a tower. The interior has Gothic works of art and stunningly beautiful stained-glass windows, the altar piece of the *Coronation of the Blessed Virgin Mary* (late 15th century), a beautiful 14th-century *Annunciation* and a sacrarium (1490). After the dissolution of the order in 1803, the cathedral suffered a turbulent history. Children now enjoy Altenberg for its Märchenwald (fairytale wood), an enchanted forest with interactive scenes and statues representing popular fairytales.

> **The Museum Folkwang boasts an excellent collection of 20th-century paintings, mainly by German Expressionists.**

↑ Half-timbered houses along the River Rur at Monschau

⑬

Northern Eifel

🅰 B4/5 🅹 Bahnhofstraße 13; (02441) 994 57 11

About 20 per cent of the Eifel range is in North Rhine-Westphalia. Low, forested mountains line the valley of the Rur river, which has been dammed in several places. The resulting artificial lakes provide a perfect opportunity for relaxation and sports.

Blankenheim is famed for its picturesque half-timbered houses, the late-Gothic church and the frequently modified 12th-century castle of the Counts von Manderscheid-Blankenheim, which today is a youth hostel. The source of the Ahr river can also be seen here – a house was built over the top of it in 1726.

In Schleiden the castle, built in the 12th century and frequently rebuilt up until the 18th century, is worth visiting. There is also a late-Gothic church with valuable stained-glass windows and an impressive organ dating from 1770.

Probably the most beautiful town in this region is Monschau, which until 1919 was called Montjoie. It is known also for its Montjoier Düttchen (croissants) and an excellent mustard. The ruin of a 13th-century castle towers on a hill. At its foot, the Rur river runs through a narrow valley, with attractive small towns, narrow, steep streets and timber-frame houses from various eras.

In Hasenfeld visitors can see a dam dating from 1904, and an amazing hydroelectric building, decorated in a way that reflects its purpose. One of the most interesting monuments of this region is the Steinfeld monastery, with a history dating from the 10th century. In 1121 the Augustinians settled here; in 1126 they accepted the rule of St Norbert of Xanten, and this became one of the first monasteries on German territory. A beautiful Romanesque basilica was built in the second half of the 12th century. It has retained wall paintings from the 12th and 14th centuries, and vaulted ceilings from the 16th century.

The **Rheinisches Freilichtmuseum Kommern** is an open-air museum with examples of the building styles typical of the Northern Eifel. It is also worth visiting the town of Euskirchen, which has an attractive Gothic church with superb furnishings, and the moated castle of Veynau (14th–15th centuries). The spa town of Bad Münstereifel dates back to 830, when a Benedictine monastery was established here. The present church is a 12th-century Romanesque basilica with impressive 11th-century frontage. Also worth seeing are the Gothic town hall and a Romanesque house, now housing a museum.

Rheinisches Freilicht-museum Kommern

⊗ 🅰 Auf dem Kahlenbusch, Mechernich-Kommern
🕐 Apr–Oct: 9am–7pm daily; Nov–Mar: 10am–5pm daily
🆆 kommern.lvr.de

> Probably the most beautiful town in the northern Eifel region is Monschau, which until 1919 was called Montjoie. It is known also for its Montjoier Düttchen (croissants).

Aachen

⚠A4 🚉🚌 ℹ Friedrich-Wilhelm-Platz; (0241) 180 29 50

Aachen owes its fame to its hot springs, whose healing powers were already highly rated by the Romans when they established baths here in the 1st–2nd centuries AD. The name of the town, aquae grani or Aquisgrani, also relates to the source.

The settlement grew in the 8th century, when Charlemagne chose it as his principal residence in 768. He built a huge palace complex with chapel, cloistered courtyard and hall for himself.

When Charlemagne was crowned emperor in 800, Aachen became the capital of the Holy Roman Empire. Although the town soon lost this title, it remained an important destination for pilgrims because of the valuable relics brought here by Charlemagne. From the 10th to the 16th centuries, nearly all German kings were crowned in the palace chapel.

In the 18th and 19th centuries, Aachen gained great importance as a spa. Many buildings from this era have long since vanished. Further destruction was inflicted by World War II, yet some historic monuments have survived. The most important of these is the **Pfalz**, a complex of buildings belonging to Charlemagne's former palace. They include a cathedral with a palace chapel and a hall which was rebuilt as the Rathaus (town hall). The original palace of Charlemagne in Aachen did not survive; of his vast construction only the Palatine chapel (Pfalzkapelle) remains.

→

The octagonal Palatine chapel forms the central part of Aachen Cathedral

In the old town, near the cathedral complex, is the church of St Foillan, where a Gothic Madonna dating from 1411 has survived. A short distance south from here is the Elisenbrunnen fountain, an exceptionally beautiful building where mineral water can be taken. It was built in 1822–7 to designs by Johann Peter Cremer and Karl Friedrich Schinkel.

After admiring the houses around the central market square visitors can enjoy the **Couven-Museum**. Based in a historic middle-class town house, it has a collection dedicated to the life of the bourgeoisie in the 18th and 19th centuries.

The modern **Centre Charlemagne,** which opened in 2014, presents the city's history from the Neolithic age to the present day. The legend of Emperor Charlemagne and the history of his rule are crucial aspects of the permanent exhibition, which incorporates interactive displays and offers family-friendly activities. The centre also hosts various lectures and film screenings.

It is also worth visiting the **Suermondt-Ludwig-Museum,** not far beyond the town centre, which has a great collection of art from the Middle Ages up to the present day, including some sculptures and paintings from the 17th century. To the northeast of

GREAT VIEW
Lousberg Hill

The wooded hill of Lousberg rises 264 m (866 ft) above Aachen. Reach it via Kupferstrasse - then a 25-minute stroll will take you to the top. From the peak there are superb views of the city below.

the old town is the spa district of Aachen. Here, visitors can stroll through the park or spend an evening at the casino. Lovers of modern art will enjoy the Ludwig-Forum für Internationale Kunst, which hosts interesting exhibitions.

Pfalz
🕭 ⚐Münsterplatz ⏰7am-7pm daily (Jan-Mar: to 6pm) 🖳aachenerdom.de

Couven-Museum
♿ ⚐Hühnermarkt 17 ☎(0241) 432 44 21 ⏰10am-5pm Tue-Sun

Centre Charlemagne
♿🖭 ⚐Katschhof 1 ⏰10am-6pm Tue-Sun ☎(0241) 432-4994

Suermondt-Ludwig-Museum
♿🕭🖭🅟 ⚐Wilhelmstrasse 18 ☎(0241) 47 98 40 ⏰10am-5pm Tue-Sun

Münster

🛫 B3 ✈ Münster-Osnabrück to the north 🚌 ℹ Heinrich-Brüning-Strasse 7; www.tourismus.muenster.de

Münster and its surroundings were already inhabited in Roman times, but its history proper started in the 9th century, with the establishment of a bishopric. Town status was granted in 1137, and in the 13th century Münster joined the Hanseatic League. In 1648 the Westphalian peace treaty was signed here, ending the Thirty Years' War. Münster's Westfälische Wilhelms-Universität (1773) is one of Germany's largest universities. World War II saw 90 per cent of the old town laid to ruins, but most of it has now been rebuilt.

At No. 38 Salzstrasse the beautiful Erbdrostenhof mansion was skilfully positioned diagonally across a corner site. Designed by Johann Conrad Schlaun, it was built in 1753–7, and despite destruction in World War II it still enchants with its "wavy" late-Baroque façade.

The imposing Gothic **Rathaus** (town hall), the pride of Münster, was almost completely destroyed during World War II but has been beautifully restored. It was here that on 15 May 1648 part of the Treaty of Westphalia was signed.

In Prinzipalmarkt, Lambertikirche, or St Lamberti, is an excellent example of the hall-churches characteristic of Westphalia. It was built in 1375–1450, but the openwork finial of the tower dates from 1887.

The most precious historic relic in Münster is undeniably its massive cathedral, **Dom St Paulus**, built in 1225–65 and representing a transitional style between late Romanesque and early Gothic. Especially worth seeing are the two altars by Gerhard Gröninger (first half of the 17th century), the early-16th-century stained-glass windows brought here from Marienfeld, and monuments of many bishops. The cathedral's best-known treasure is the astronomical clock (1540), with paintings by Ludger tom Ring the Elder and sculptures by Johann Brabender. At noon figures show the Magi paying tribute to the infant Jesus to the sounds of the carillon.

Located in a sandstone building with increased exhibition space and facilities, the **LWL Museum für Kunst und Kultur** (Westphalian regional museum) specializes mainly in Gothic art, with a large collection of sculptures and altars rescued in World War II. Its most noteworthy exhibits include the works by Heinrich and Johann Brabender, Conrad von Soest and the tom Ring family.

The beautiful Baroque Residenzschloss was built in 1767–87 by Prince-Bishop Maximilian Friedrich. It was designed by Johann Conrad Schlaun, a local master of Baroque architecture. Maximilian Friedrich started the redevelopment of Münster in the northern Baroque style.

The **Mühlenhof** is an open-air museum on the banks of the Aasee, Münster's lake and recreation area. There are rural dwellings with authentic furnishings and two mills (17th and 18th centuries).

Southeast of the town, in Wolbeck, is an original Renaissance mansion from the mid-16th century called Drostenhof. Its exquisite gate-house leads into the courtyard of the mansion, which has original fireplaces and ceiling paintings.

↑ Lambertikirche on Prinzipalmarkt, lined with gabled houses

Rathaus

⊛ 🅰Prinzipalmarkt 📞(0251) 492 27 24 🕐10am-5pm Tue-Fri (to 4pm Sat & Sun)

Dom St Paulus

⊛ 🅰Domplatz 📞(0251) 448 93 🕐6:30am-7pm Mon-Sat (to 7:30pm Sun & hols)

LWL Museum für Kunst und Kultur

⊛ 🅰Domplatz 10 📞(0251) 590 72 01 🕐10am-6pm Tue-Sun

Mühlenhof

⊛ 🅰Theo-Breider-Weg 1 🕐 Mar-Oct: 10am-6pm daily; Nov-Feb: 11am-5:30pm Sat & Sun 🌐muehlenhof-muenster.org

---

Duisburg

🅰B4 🚉🚌 ℹ️Königstrasse 86; www.duisburg.de

Duisburg, on the edge of the Ruhr region, underwent a period of rapid development in the 19th and 20th centuries. Once a small town, it became the world's largest inland harbour thanks to its location

at the spot where the Ruhr flows into the Rhine.

The small old town was almost totally destroyed in World War II, but the 15th-century Gothic Salvatorkirche (church of St Saviour) has been rebuilt. Some of the town's greatest attractions are its museums. The **Wilhelm-Lehmbruck-Museum** focuses on the work of the sculptor Lehmbruck, who was born in Duisburg. The museum has an interesting collection of 20th-century sculptures, including works by artists such as Salvador Dali, Henry Moore and Max Ernst. In the 16th century, Duisburg was the home of the famous geographer and cartographer Gerhard Mercator, whose collection of globes, maps and charts can now be seen in the Kultur- und Stadthistorisches Museum.

Duisburg has repurposed some of its former industrial sites, notably, the Duisburg-Nord Landscape Park, which is now a popular recreational area. Another highlight is the roller-coaster style installation "Tiger & Turtle - Magic Mountain", which offers great views from the top.

Krefeld, 6 km (4 miles) southwest of Duisburg, has been a centre of silk fabric production since the 17th century, and the Deutsches Textilmuseum contains over 20,000 exhibits, ranging from antiquity to the present day.

Wilhelm-Lehmbruck-Museum

⊛ 🅰Friedrich-Wilhelm Strasse 40 🕐Noon-5pm Tue-Fri, 11am-5pm Sun 🌐lehmbruckmuseum.de

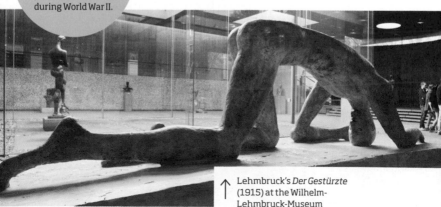

↑ Lehmbruck's *Der Gestürzte* (1915) at the Wilhelm-Lehmbruck-Museum

Königswinter

B4 🚗🚌 *i* Drachenfels-strasse 51 (02223) 91 77 11

Königswinter lies on the Rhine at the foot of the Siebengebirge, an attractive range of wooded hills. The name literally means "seven mountains", but there are far more. The hills are well suited for walking and the most popular is the Drachenfels (dragon's rock). The oldest mountain railway in Germany, built in 1883, takes visitors to the top (321 m/1,053 ft). During the ascent visitors can see the Neo-Gothic Drachenburg, a palace dating from 1879–84, and on the top are the ruins of the Gothic Drachenburg, dating from the 12th century. The "dragon" in the name relates to the myth of the Nibelungs. Königswinter itself has picturesque 17th-century half-timbered houses, town houses and late 19th-century hotels.

Bad Honnef, 6 km (4 miles) to the south, is a charming spa town known as "Nice on the Rhine", where the former chancellor Konrad Adenauer lived until his death.

Situated 15 km (9 miles) to the north is Siegburg, home to a Benedictine monastery from 1064 (closed to the public). The present church, a 17th-century building, was reconstructed after World War II.

The small spa town of Bad Godesberg was incorporated into Bonn in 1969. An elegant neighbourhood, its villas line the spa park. On top of the hill is the Godesburg, a ruined 13th-century castle.

Did You Know?

Phantasialand's Taron is the world's fastest and longest multi-launched roller coaster.

---

18 **Brühl**

B4 🚗🚌 *i* Uhlstrasse 1 (02232) 79 382

The small town of Brühl has one of the most beautiful palace complexes, since 1984 a UNESCO World Heritage site. As early as the 13th century, a palace was established here for the arch-bishops of nearby Köln, but this was destroyed in 1689. A Baroque palace, **Augustusburg**, was built on its foundations in 1725–8, according to a design by Johann Conrad Schlaun. It was named after the instigator of the building, Elector Clemens August. The building was almost immediately refurbished, with a new façade and furnishings, the work of François de Cuvilliés, and in the 1940s a new staircase was completed to a design by Balthasar Neumann. After devastation in World War II, the palace was carefully restored, and the magnificently furnished late-Baroque and Rococo interior, especially a stunning dining room designed by Cuvilliés, can now be seen again. A path leads from the orangery to a Gothic church built for the Franciscans in the 15th century. The *Annunciation* on the high altar is the work of Johann Wolfgang van der Auwer, while the magnificent canopy above was designed by Balthasar Neumann. The castle is surrounded by a Baroque park, designed by Dominique Girard.

About 2 km (1 mile) east of the main residence is another castle, **Falkenlust**, built in 1729–40 to a design by Cuvilliés. Its captivating interior includes a lacquered and a mirror cabinet. Nearby stands an octagonal chapel, its interior decoration modelled on a secluded grotto.

It is also worth visiting the small villa near Augustusburg where the great Surrealist artist Max Ernst was born. It now houses a small display commemorating his work.

Another attraction, which draws many visitors, is **Phantasialand**, Germany's second largest theme park. Several days are needed to see all the attractions of this vast fairground with its roller-coaster, water rides and merry-go-rounds.

 Rising above Königswinter, the Drachenfels is the epitome of Rhineland romanticism

Two moated houses can be seen at Kerpen, 27 km (17 miles) to the north: the 16th-century castle of Lörsfeld, and the Baroque palace of Türnich, built in 1756–66.

In Pulheim-Brauweiler, 30 km (19 miles) to the north, is a beautiful Benedictine monastery, founded in 1024. From here, travel 23 km (14 miles) west to Bedburg, where the moated castle is also worth seeing. This is a vast brick structure with four wings, which was established in stages over 300 years, starting in around 1300.

Augustusburg
 ⬤⬤⬤ ⬤ Parkplatz
⬤ Times vary, check website ⬤schlossbruehl.de

Falkenlust
⬤⬤⬤ ⬤ Parkplatz ⬤Feb-Nov: 9am-noon & 1:30-4pm Tue-Fri, 10am-5pm Sat & Sun ⬤ schlossbruehl.de

Phantasialand
⬤⬤⬤⬤
⬤Berggeiststrasse 31-41 ⬤Apr-Oct: 9am-6pm daily, later in summer ⬤phantasialand.de

⑲

Siegen

⬤C4 ⬤⬤ ⬤Markt 2 (0271) 404 13 16

Located amid the hills on the banks of the Sieg river, Siegen is the largest town in the Siegerland region. For centuries the city was the residence of the dukes of Nassau. Religious divisions in the family resulted in two castles being built. The Oberes Schloss (Upper Castle) is a medieval building, frequently refurbished in the 16th–18th centuries. The museum inside has some paintings by Peter Paul Rubens, who was born in Siegen. The lower Unteres Schloss is a Baroque palace, which replaced an earlier building. In the centre of Siegen is the Nikolaikirche, a 13th-century hexagonal church, which served as the ducal family mausoleum.

In Freudenberg, 10 km (6 miles) northwest, is the small settlement of Alter Flecken. Founded in 1666 at the instigation of Duke Johann Moritz von Nassau, the village consists of identical half-timbered houses.

↑ Identical half-timbered houses in Freudenberg, near Siegen

↑ The river Lenne running through Saalhausen in the Sauerland region

⑳ Sauerland

🅰C4 🛈 Sauerland-Touristik, Johannes-Hummel-Weg 1, Schmallenberg; www.sauerland.com

The Sauerland is the region to the south and east of the Ruhr coalfields, making an obvious holiday destination for the inhabitants of this large, industrialized conurbation. Embracing the northern part of the Rhenish slate massif, its densely wooded mountains

are not high – the highest peak is Hegekopf at 843 m (2,766 ft) – but crossed by rivers and full of artificial lakes, the area is perfect for walking, cycling and fishing.

Enjoyable days can be had on an excursion to one of the caves such as Attahöhle, Dechenhöhle or Heinrichshöhle near Iserlohn. There are charming towns, too. In Breckerfeld the Gothic parish church has preserved a superb altar, from around 1520. The main attraction in Altena is the gigantic Burg (castle), built in the 12th century and restored in the early 20th century. In 1910 the world's first youth hostel for tourists was created here. One of the greatest tourist draws in the Sauerland is the Möhnesee, a lake with a huge dam, built in 1908–12 and bombed by Allied "dambusters" in 1943 with catastrophic consequences. Arnsberg has a regional museum and the lovely Neo-Gothic moated castle Herdringen with assorted furnishings from other castles.

In the south are the Rothaargebirge (red-haired mountains). Their most beautiful town is the spa resort of Bad Berleburg, while the Kahler Asten (bare branch) mountain and the town of Winterberg are popular winter sports areas.

㉑ Soest

🅰C4 🚉🚌 🛈 Teichsmühlengasse 3; www.soest.de

The Westphalian town of Soest made its mark in history when, in about 1100, the town's civic rights were formulated and subsequently adopted by 65 other towns. Today the town captivates visitors with its well-preserved old town, its historic churches, and the almost

← A humanoid robot at the Heinz Nixdorf MuseumsForum, Paderborn

> 🔍 HIDDEN GEM
> ### Taking a Break
> The Paderquellgebiet in Paderborn is a relaxing place to head when you've seen the sights or are planning a picnic. An incredible 200 springs rise here to create the River Pader, Germany's shortest at just 4 km (2.5 miles).

completely intact walls that surround the town. The focus of the old town is the Romanesque Propsteikirche St Patrokli (provost church of St Patroclus), founded in 965 by Bruno, Archbishop of Köln, and built in stages until the 13th century. Further historic buildings are grouped around the church: the 18th-century Baroque Rathaus (town hall), the 12th-century Romanesque Petrikirche (St Peter's church) with its Gothic presbytery, and the 12th-century Nicolaikapelle, a chapel with 13th-century wall paintings and an altar painted by Konrad von Soest.

In the northern part of the old town, two churches are worth seeing: the Hohnekirche (St Kilian) with beautiful Gothic and early Baroque furnishings; and the Wiesenkirche, with a group of stained-glass windows from the 14th and 15th centuries. The window above the northern portal shows the Westphalian Last Supper, depicting a table laden with plentiful Westphalian smoked ham and pumpernickel bread.

In Lippstadt, 23 km (14 miles) east of Soest, visit the Gothic Marienkirche (St Mary's church). In the suburb of Bökenförde is the 18th-century Baroque moated palace Schwarzenraben, and there is an early-Baroque castle in Overhagen.

22
Paderborn
🅰C3 🚗🚌 ℹ️Marienplatz 2; www.paderborn.de

Paderborn has been on the map for over 1,000 years. In the 8th century Charlemagne built a palace here and, in about AD 800, a bishopric was established. The town's most

important monument is the Dom St Maria, St Kilian and St Liborius, a Romanesque-Gothic cathedral. This large hall-church with two transepts and tall front tower suffered during World War II, but it continues to captivate visitors with its superb decor, the great Romanesque crypt, interesting plaques and richly decorated bishops' tombs and epitaphs. The diocesan museum holds the Imad-Madonna, funded by Bishop Imad, an outstanding figure of the Madonna and Child dating from 1051–8. On the northern side of the cathedral, a section of the foundations of the emperor's palace can be seen, together with the Bartholomäuskapelle (chapel of St Bartholomew), the oldest hall-church in Germany, completed in 1017. To the south of the cathedral complex the **Heinz Nixdorf MuseumsForum** is dedicated to the history of computers.

Heinz Nixdorf MuseumsForum
🏠 Fürstenallee 7, 33102 Paderborn ⏰9am-6pm Tue-Fri, 10am-6pm Sat & Sun 🌐hnf.de/start.html

> **Enjoyable days can be had on an excursion to one of Sauerland's caves such as Attahöhle, Dechenhöhle or Heinrichshöhle near Iserlohn.**

23
Höxter
🅰C3 🚗🚌 ℹ️Weserstrasse 11; www.hoexter-tourismus.de

In a picturesque spot on the Weser river, Höxter has a beautiful old town with many timber-frame houses, fragments of the city walls, a Renaissance Rathaus (town hall) from 1610, and important churches. The history of Kilianikirche, in the centre of the old town, goes back to the late 8th century, but the current Romanesque building dates from the 11th–12th centuries. Also in the town is a Gothic church built for the Franciscans in 1248–1320.

The city's greatest attraction, however, is the magnificent Abtei Corvey, a monastery founded in 822. It was originally built as the church of St Stephen and St Vitus, but only the grandiose two-storey frontage completed in 885 survived. It became the model for several other churches built in Westphalia, while the main body of the church was rebuilt in the 17th century.

→
The interior of the ancient Corvey monastery, Höxter

An 18th-century oil mill at Schloss Brake in Lemgo, which also houses a museum

24

Lemgo

🅰C3 🏛💬 ℹKramerstrasse 1; (05261) 988 70

This exceptionally pretty town was founded in 1190 by Bernhard II von Lippe. It was a member of the Hanseatic League, and had its heyday during the witch hunts of the 17th century. Today Lemgo has numerous Renaissance monuments – it was spared during World War II, and the Gothic Nicolaikirche (St Nicholas') and Marienkirche (St Mary's), with Gothic wall paintings and a Renaissance organ by Georg Slegel, have survived. The pearl of the city is the beautiful Rathaus (town hall), built in the 15th–17th centuries. It contains an original pharmacy that is still in use. Many timber-frame houses have also survived, the best ones in Papen-, Mittel- and Echternstrasse. The most beautiful house in Lemgo is the Hexenbürger-meisterhaus. This "witches' mayor's house" (1571), an excellent example of Weser Renaissance, belonged to the mayor, Hermann Cothmann, who instigated the witch hunt. It now houses a town museum. Also worth visiting are the Junkerhaus (1891), the architect's home, and Schloss Brake (13th–16th centuries), a castle which now houses the **Weserrenaissance-Museum**.

Weserrenaissance-Museum

⊛ 🅰Schloss Brake 🕙10am–6pm Tue–Sun 🔳museum-schloss-brake.de

25

Teutoburger Wald

🅰C3 ℹRathaus Am Markt 5 Detmold; www.teuto burgerwald.de

A range of low mountains extending from Osnabrück through Bielefeld right up to Paderborn, the Teutoburg Forest is one of the most attractive tourist regions in Westphalia. The best base for walking and cycling holidays is the city of Detmold, which has a very attractive old town with well-preserved timber-frame buildings from various periods and the elegant Residenzschloss, the castle of the zur Lippe family. Originally medieval, the palace was rebuilt in the 16th century in the Weser-Renaissance style.

The interior is composed of 17th- and 19th-century furnishings. The star feature is a set of eight Gobelins tapestries, crafted in Brussels around 1670, showing scenes of Alexander the Great's triumphs. Furnishings from the 19th century include designs by notable French artist Charles Le Brun.

Just 3 km (2 miles) south of Detmold is the spot where in the year AD 9 Cherusko Arminius, known as Hermann, leader of the Germanic tribes, triumphed against the Roman army led by Varus. At the top of the mountain, the Hermannsdenkmal, a huge monument designed by Ernst von Bandel, was erected in 1838–75. It was supposed to symbolize the German struggle for unification.

Two additional fascinating attractions near Detmold are the Adlerwarte Berlebeck, an ornithological research station, where eagles and many other birds of prey can be observed, and the Vogelpark Heiligen-kirchen, a bird park with over 2,000 varieties of birds in all shapes and sizes from around the world.

→

Sandstone rock formations in the Teutoburger Wald

Bielefeld

🄰 C3 🚃🚌 ℹ️ Niederwall 23; (0521) 51 69 99

On the edge of the Teutoburg Forest, Bielefeld owes its evolution to the production of and trading in linen. The old town is dominated by the Sparrenburg castle, built in the 13th century for the von Ravensberg family. In the 1500s the castle was surrounded by new fortifications, including new bastions, and in the 19th century the residential part of the city was greatly extended.

The central feature of the old town is Alter Markt (old market), with the Nicolaikirche. This Gothic church suffered heavily in World War II, although the marvellous Antwerp altar (around 1524) was preserved. Nearby, on Obernstrasse, stands the Crüwell-Haus, an interesting late-Gothic town house from the early 16th century. The street leads to St Jodokus-Kirche, a late-Gothic church whose greatest treasure is the amazing figure of the Black Madonna (around 1220). Further south is the Kunsthalle, a modern building with a significant collection of 20th-century art. It is also worth visiting the Marienkirche in the new town. Built in 1280–1330, this Gothic church holds the tomb of one of the von Ravensberg dukes (around 1320) and a high altar (from around 1400) with a central Gothic section.

Picturesque Herford, 17 km (11 miles) north of Bielefeld, has timber-frame houses, beautiful Gothic churches and MARTa Herford, an art and design museum by Frank O Gehry. In Enger, 21 km (13 miles) to the north, in the former church of the canons, a tomb dating from 1100 holds the remains of the Saxon Duke Widukind, buried in 807.

Bad Salzuflen, with its pretty old town and spa, is the ideal place to visit for a little relaxation.

___

Minden

🄰 C3 🚃🚌 ℹ️ Domstrasse 2; www.minden.de

Charlemagne created a bishopric here as early as AD 798. The town then evolved thanks to its location on the Weser river. The city's most important monument is the cathedral, Dompfarrkirche St Petrus und St Gorgonius. It has a Romanesque presbytery, transept and monumental frontage built in the 11th–12th centuries, although the body of the church is an example of early-Gothic style from the 13th century. It is worth visiting the church treasury with its 11th-century crucifix.

The Rathaus (town hall), with 13th-century lower sections, is also well worth seeing, as are Minden's many charming houses, set around the market square. A great attraction is the Wasser-strassenkreuz (waterway junction), where a 375-m- (1,230-ft-) long bridge takes the Mittellandkanal (Midland Canal) across the Weser river.

A little further afield, on top of a hill in Porta Westfalica, 6 km (4 miles) south of Minden, is a giant monument to Kaiser Wilhelm (1892–6), created by Bruno Schmitz.

The Westfälische Mühlen-strasse, (Westphalian Mill Route), signposted around Minden, takes visitors past 42 different mills and windmills.

4,000
___
The total area in sq km of the Teutoburger Wald (1,544 sq miles).

NORTHERN GERMANY

Lower Saxony,
Hamburg and Bremen 418

Schleswig-Holstein 450

Mecklenburg-Vorpommern 464

Lighthouse on Amrum in the North Frisian islands

EXPLORE
NORTHERN
GERMANY

This section divides northern
Germany into three colour-coded
sightseeing areas, as shown on the
map below. Find out more about each
area on the following pages.

DENMARK

Fredericia

Esbjerg

Kolding

Odense

Haderslev

Faaborg

Flensburg

Schleswig

Husum

Kiel

Rendsburg

Neumünster

SCHLESWIG-
HOLSTEIN
p450

Meldorf

*North
Sea*

Itzehoe

Bad Segeberg

Cuxhaven

Elmshorn

Wilhelmshaven

Bremerhaven

Stade

Hamburg

Emden

Seevetal

Groningen

Leer

Oldenburg

Bremen

Rotenburg

Soltau

NETHERLANDS

Cloppenburg

LOWER SAXONY,
HAMBURG AND BREMEN
p418

Hoogeveen

Meppen

Diepholz

Nienburg

Celle

Lingen

Bramsche

Enschede

Osnabrück

Minden

Hanover

Hildesheim

Münster

Bielefeld

Einbeck

NORTH RHINE-
WESTPHALIA

Wesel

Paderborn

Göttingen

Duisburg

Essen

Dortmund

Soest

Brilon

HESSE

Kassel

Wuppertal

GETTING TO KNOW
NORTHERN
GERMANY

Nature lovers will be enchanted by northern Germany's varied landscapes, ranging from sandy coastal beaches to moraine hills and moorlands. History fans, meanwhile, can admire the Renaissance cathedrals and Gothic brick architecture in former Hanseatic towns.

LOWER SAXONY, HAMBURG AND BREMEN

PAGE 418

Characterized principally by lowlands, the southern part of the region gradually becomes more mountainous, culminating in the Harz area. Other scenic hotspots include the heather-clad Lüneburger Heide and the sandy beaches of the East Frisian Islands. The region's major cities, Hanover and Braunschweig, are both vibrant and cosmopolitan, offering plenty of commercial and cultural highlights.

Best for
Culture and dining

Home to
Bremen, Hamburg and Hanover

Experience
Taking a river cruise along the Elbe and enjoying a concert at the Hamburg Philharmonie

PAGE 450

SCHLESWIG HOLSTEIN

The northernmost state in Germany, Schleswig-Holstein belonged to neighbouring Denmark until 1864. Jutting north between the North and Baltic seas means it has a lot of coastline, fjords and beaches to explore, making it a popular summer hotspot. Its highlights include the preserved medieval city of Lübeck, with its 16th-century city gate and Gothic cathedral, the charming port city of Kiel, and lively, attractive Flensburg. Maritime fans will want to explore the North Frisian Islands off the western coast, as well as popular island destinations such as Amrum and Sylt.

Best for
Beaches and island-hopping

Home to
Lübeck

Experience
Enjoying a ride along the Kiel Canal, which links the North and Baltic seas, via a river cruise ship or an old-fashioned paddle steamer

PAGE 464

MECKLENBURG-VORPOMMERN

Thanks largely to its beach-dotted coastline and the rural Baltic destinations such as Darss, Usedom and Rügen – not to mention its alluring lake district and the natural charms of Müritz National Park – the region of Mecklenburg-Lower Pomerania has become a major summer hotspot.

Best for
Beaches, nature, hiking

Home to
Schwerin, Nationalpark-Müritz and Rügen

Experience
Exploring the Hanseatic town of Stralsund before crossing to the island of Rügen for sea, sun and sand

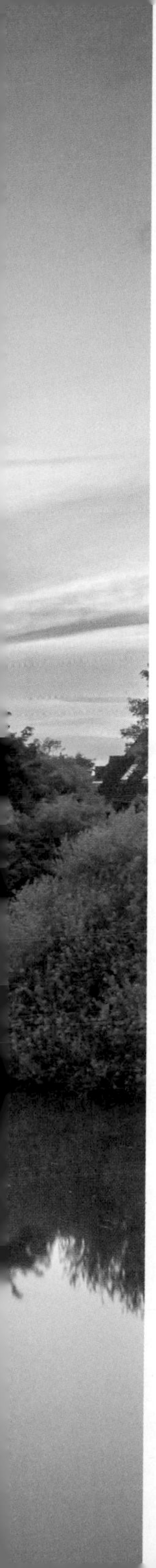

LOWER SAXONY, HAMBURG AND BREMEN

Three federal states – Lower Saxony and the independent city-states of Hamburg and Bremen – cover an enormous terrain, embracing the whole of northwestern Germany. For the visitor they provide a series of memorable snapshots: the mighty cosmopolitan port of Hamburg, enchanting towns and villages with half-timbered houses and the blooming heather of the Lüneburger Heide.

The second-largest German state after Bavaria, Lower Saxony only ranks fourth in terms of the number of its inhabitants, being less densely populated than other states. It is characterized by lowlands that become hillier in the south, culminating in the Harz Mountains. Nature lovers will enjoy excursions to the Lüneburger Heide or paddling in the endless expanses of mud flats in the North Sea. Tourists are also attracted by the sandy beaches of the East Frisian islands, as well as the solitary rock of the island of Heligoland.

The "free and Hanseatic" towns of Hamburg and Bremen have a different atmosphere – urban and urbane, tolerant and multicultural, based on centuries of trade with the world.

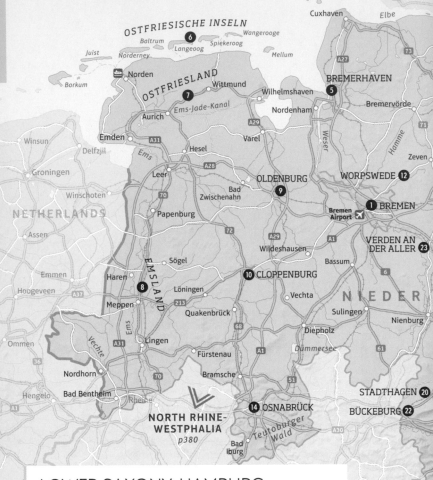

LOWER SAXONY, HAMBURG AND BREMEN

Must Sees

1 Bremen
2 Hamburg
3 Hanover

Experience More

4 Hildesheim
5 Bremerhaven
6 Ostfriesische Inseln (East Frisian Islands)
7 Ostfriesland (East Frisia)
8 Emsland
9 Oldenburg
10 Cloppenburg
11 Goslar
12 Worpswede
13 Wolfenbüttel
14 Osnabrück
15 Stade
16 Lüneburg
17 Lüneburger Heide
18 Soltau
19 Celle
20 Stadthagen
21 Wolfsburg
22 Bückeburg
23 Verden an der Aller
24 Braunschweig (Brunswick)
25 Göttingen
26 Einbeck
27 Duderstadt

0 kilometres 30
0 miles 30
N

SCHLESWIG-HOLSTEIN
p450

MECKLENBURG-
VORPOMMERN
p464

SAXONY-
ANHALT
p144

THURINGIA
p184

HESSE
p354

LOWER SAXONY,
HAMBURG AND BREMEN

15 STADE
Hamburg Airport
2 HAMBURG
16 LÜNEBURG
17 LÜNEBURGER HEIDE
18 SOLTAU
19 CELLE
Hannover Airport
3 HANOVER
21 WOLFSBURG
24 BRAUNSCHWEIG (BRUNSWICK)
4 HILDESHEIM
13 WOLFENBÜTTEL
11 GOSLAR
26 EINBECK
25 GÖTTINGEN
27 DUDERSTADT

SACHSEN

→

1 The Elbphilharmonie in Hamburg.

2 Hamburg's historic warehouse district.

3 Fischbrötchen.

4 Böttcherstrasse brewery in Bremen.

3 DAYS

In Hamburg and Bremen

Day 1

Morning Start with a stroll around Hamburg's Altstadt (Old Town; *p430*), where you can find the city's Neo-Renaissance Rathaus. Follow the elegant arcades to the Binnenalster lake; the Alsterpavilion (*Jungfernstieg 54*) is a nice spot to relax with a coffee and take in the lake views.

Afternoon The Hamburger Kunsthalle (*p431*) is an absolute must for art lovers, with a grand collection showcasing the works of European masters and 19th-century German Romantics. When you're ready for a break, meander south through the bustling shopping streets until you reach the canals and UNESCO-listed warehouses of the Speicherstadt (*p430*).

Evening Weave your way across the bridges and canals to nearby HafenCity (*p429*), a redevelopment project that's bringing life back to the old port. Although the project is ongoing, there are already several architectural highlights to see – not least Herzog & de Meuron's Elbphilharmonie concert hall, where you can catch a world-class performance after a canalside dinner.

Day 2

Morning Begin the day early with a Fischbrötchen (fish sandwich) at the legendary Fischmarkt (*p430*), where you can watch the fishermen returning with their catch and browse the many market stalls. Stroll along the harbour to the Landungsbrücken before heading north to visit the Baroque Michaeliskirche (*p431*) and the Museum of Hamburg History.

Afternoon At the beautifully landscaped Planten un Blomen gardens you can enjoy lunch on the terrace at the

Restaurant Rosenhof (*Tiergartenstrasse 10*). Stroll through the Sternschanze and Karolinenviertel neighbourhoods, enjoying indie boutiques and cafés such as Elbgold (*Lagerstrasse 34c*).

Evening For a fun family evening head to the Hamburger Dom – a huge funfair, where a cathedral once stood. Or, if your group is adults only, spend the evening exploring St Pauli (*p431*) and the Reeperbahn. Although it's Hamburg's red-light district, it's also a great place for regular nightlife – cool bars, good restaurants and homage to The Beatles.

Day 3

Morning Catch a train to Bremen (*p424*). To become acquainted with the town, head to the main square and take photos of the striking Rathaus (*p425*) and the equally magnificent Romanesque cathedral (*p425*). Down towards the Weser is the Böttcherstrasse, an ornate red-brick street that hosts several attractions including the Ludwig Roselius Museum, the Paula Modersohn-Becker Museum and the 16th-century Roseliushaus (*p427*).

Afternoon Next, explore the charming medieval character of the Schnoorviertel (*p426*), before heading to the Focke-Museum (*p426*), with its collection of Bremen-related art and culture from the Middle Ages to the present day.

Evening Take a stroll in the nearby Rhododendronpark (*p426*) before heading out to the Meierei im Bürgerpark (*Bürgerpark 1*) for an elegant dinner.

①

BREMEN

🅰C2 🚉 🛈 Hauptbahnhof & Böttcherstrasse 4; www.bremen.eu/tourism

Bremen is one of Germany's three city-states. Its origins date back to Charlemagne, and the town enjoyed prosperity from 1358 when it joined the Hanseatic League, its wealth based on the coffee and wool trades. Though Bremen still benefits from its bustling deep-water port, most of its attractions – such as the magnificent cathedral – are in the old town.

① Kunsthalle

🏛 Am Wall 207 🕙 10am–5pm Tue–Sun (to 9pm Tue) 🌐 kunsthalle-bremen.de/en

This art gallery on the edge of the old town lost most of its collection to Russia during World War II. The works that remained, however, as well as works subsequently acquired, make the collection of great importance. There are pieces by Dürer, Altdorfer, Rubens, Jan Breughel, van Dyck and Rembrandt. There is also an excellent French section, with works by Delacroix, Monet and Manet, as well as 19th- and 20th-century German painters such as Beckmann and Kirchner. At the heart of this section are about 40 paintings by Paula Modersohn-Becker (p439).

② Marktplatz

On the main square of medieval Bremen stand the town hall and the cathedral, with several gabled houses on the west side. This lovely view is slightly marred by the glass-fronted 1960s Haus der Bürgerschaft, the state parliament building.

Did You Know?

The European contribution to the International Space Station was built in Bremen.

↑ Bremen's Marktplatz, dominated by the striking town hall building

In front of the town hall stands a 10-m (32-ft) statue of Roland, dating from 1404. A nephew of Charlemagne, Roland came to symbolize the town's independence from the local nobility. The statue faces the cathedral, the residence of the bishop, who often sought to restrict Bremen's autonomy. Roland's sword of justice symbolizes the judiciary's independence, and the engraved motto confirms the emperor's edict, conferring town rights onto Bremen.

The second, more recent (1953) monument in the square is dedicated to the Bremen Town Musicians – a donkey, dog, cat and cockerel, who, according to the Grimm fairytale, trekked to Bremen.

③ 🚗 🏚

Rathaus

🏛 Marktplatz 📞 (0421) 30 80 00

This original Gothic building dates from 1405–10 and was clad with a magnificent façade, a fine example of Weser Renaissance architecture in

← Van Gogh's *Field with Poppies* (1889), on display in the Kunsthalle

northern Germany. It was designed by Lüder von Bentheim, who masterfully incorporated the Gothic figures of Charlemagne and seven electors, as well as four prophets and four wise men. In the Grosse Halle (Great Hall) new laws were passed, as symbolized by the fresco (1932) of Solomon's court. Other treasures include the Renaissance spiral staircase. On the western side of the town hall is the entrance to the "Ratskeller" where you can sample 600 different wines. Tours of the Rathaus take place daily.

④

St Petri Dom

🏛 Sandstrasse 10-12 🕐 Apr-Oct: 10am-5pm Mon-Fri, 10am-2pm Sat, 2-5pm Sun 🌐 stpetridom.de

This Romanesque cathedral, with its vast twin-towered

façade, dates from the 11th century and has been extensively refurbished. At the end of the 19th century, while the southern tower was rebuilt, the façade was also reconstructed and a tower was added. Inside, sandstone bas-reliefs divide the western choir stalls, and fragments of Gothic stalls that were destroyed in the 19th century can still be seen. There is also a Baroque pulpit paid for by Queen Christina of Sweden in 1638, and numerous multi-coloured memorials. The larger eastern crypt has interesting Romanesque capitals, while in the second eastern crypt visitors can admire the oldest Bremen sculpture of Christ the Omnipotent (1050) as well as the baptismal font. In the Bleikeller (lead cellar), beneath the former cloisters, eight perfectly preserved mummies are on show.

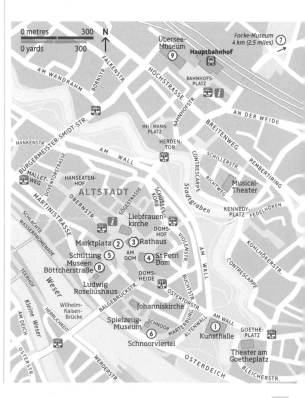

⑤ Schütting

 Marktplatz

On the southwestern side of Marktplatz (p424) stands this mansion used by the Merchants' Guild for their conventions. It was built in 1537–9 by the Antwerp architect Johann der Buschener in Dutch Mannerist style. The eastern gable, which is more classically Renaissance in design, is the work of the local builder Carsten Husmann. The motto of Bremen's merchants – "Outside and in, venture and win" – was added to the façade in 1899. Today the building is home to Bremen's chamber of commerce.

📷 PICTURE PERFECT
Floral Photos

Green-fingered visitors to Bremen should aim to arrive in late spring and head for the Rhododendronpark. You'll be able to snap a blaze of colours across one of the world's largest and most beautiful plant collections, laid out in themed areas including the rose and bonsai gardens.

---

⑥ Schnoorviertel

This historic district of small houses dates back to the 15th–18th centuries. One of Bremen's poorest areas before World War II – it was variously the fisherman's quarter and later a red-light district – Schnoorviertel miraculously escaped the destruction that affected so much of the rest of the city. It has been restored gradually since 1958 and now teems with restaurants, cafés, souvenir shops and tourists. In the centre of the district is the Gothic Johanniskirche, which once belonged to the Franciscans. In accordance with the order's rules it has no tower, although this is compensated for by a decorative gable on the western façade, three levels of arched alcoves and herringbone brickwork.

---

⑦

Focke-Museum

 Schwachhauser-Heerstrasse 240 ⏰ **10am–5pm Tue–Sat (to 9pm Tue, to 6pm Sun)** 🌐 **focke-museum.de**

The excellent collections of this museum make up for its inconvenient location at the edge of the city. Founded in 1918, when the history museum was amalgamated with the decorative arts museum, it presents Bremen's art and culture from the Middle Ages to the present day. Exhibits from patrician houses and original sculptures from the façade of the town hall testify to the wealth of the Hanseatic town. Other sections are devoted to the archaeology of the region as well as to whaling and emigration to the US in the 19th

↑ A visitor examining an early wagon at Bremen's Focke-Museum

↑ A charming alleyway in the historic district of Schnoorviertel

and 20th centuries. In summer, a series of concerts are held in the museum gardens.

The Rhododendronpark nearby offers a unique and pleasant respite from the museums. It includes 1,600 varieties of rhododendron, which become a sea of flowers from late April to June.

Museen Böttcherstraße

🏠 Böttcherstrasse 6-10
🕐 11am-6pm Tue-Sun
🌐 museen-boettcher strasse.de

This once-insignificant lane where coopers lived was transformed into Art Deco style in 1926–30 by Ludwig Roselius, a wealthy coffee merchant. The street was preserved by National Socialists as an example of degenerate art. At its entrance is a bas-relief by Bernhard Hoetger from 1920, of the Archangel Michael fighting a dragon.

The Böttcherstraße museums, including the Paula Modersohn-Becker Museum and the Ludwig Roseliushaus, are located here. The Paula Modersohn-Becker

Museum, built in the Expressionist style, was the first museum in the world to be dedicated to the work of a female painter.

Next door, inside the 16th-century Roseliushaus, the original period interiors can be admired. The street's other draw is a carillon that chimes tuneful melodies daily at noon, 3pm and 6pm.

Übersee-Museum

🏠 Bahnhofplatz 13
🕐 9am-6pm Tue-Fri,
10am-6pm Sat & Sun
🌐 uebersee-museum.de

This museum of overseas countries transports visitors to faraway places. Built in 1891, it was originally a museum of German colonialism and is now dedicated to the culture of non-European nations. Of special interest are exhibits on Pacific cultures, which include life-sized models of a house and a boat.

→

Detailed wooden carving on the Senate Bench in the Rathaus

Must See

STAY

Turmhotel Weserblick
When making a reservation here, make sure you get one of the tower suites, which come with their own kitchens and views of the River Weser.

🏠 Osterdeich 53
🌐 turmhotel-weserblick-bremen.de

Hotel Überfluss
A hotel with an angular design, bold decor, its own spa and pool. It also offers a very good breakfast buffet.

🏠 Langenstrasse 72
🌐 designhotel-ueberfluss.de

Parkhotel Bremen
One of Bremen's top addresses, this large palace hotel is surrounded by parkland and offers a long list of facilities including a heated outdoor pool.

🏠 Im Bürgerpark
🌐 hommage-hotels.com

↑ Hamburg's town hall, on the banks of the Alsterfleet canal

HAMBURG

⊞ **Hauptbahnhof, Kirchenallee; www.hamburg.com**

Germany's second largest city, Hamburg has both a diversity of outlook and a jumble of architectural styles that make it a fascinating place to visit. For many years Hamburg was a leading member of the Hanseatic League and an independent trading town, and in 1945 it became a city-state of the Federal Republic. Visitors are attracted by Hamburg's enormous port, situated right in the centre of the city; colourful entertainment in notorious St Pauli; many attractive parks and lakes; and the warm welcome extended by locals who, on first encounter, may seem a little cool.

① Rathausmarkt

This wide town hall square is enclosed on one side by Alsterfleet. Once a small river, it is now one of the many canals that earned Hamburg the nickname "Venice of the North". A monument by artist Ernst Barlach pays tribute to the victims of World War I.

The square is dominated by the enormous Neo-Renaissance town hall, the fifth in the city's history and now a symbol of Hamburg in

its own right. Previous town halls were destroyed by wars or catastrophic fire (in 1842). Similarly, little remains of Hamburg's old town; the city's current appearance is characterized by 19th-century style and Modernism.

② Binnenalster

Elegant arcades lead from the Rathausmarkt to the Binnenalster, a large lake in the middle of the city. Like the Aussenalster to the north, it was created by damming the Alster river. On a sunny day the elegant riverside boulevard of Jungfernstieg is a pleasant place for a walk. Great views of the city can be had from the café in the Alsterpavilion. From a small quay, boats depart for an Alsterrundfahrt – a cruise to the Aussenalster and to smaller canals offering views of the villas in the north of Hamburg and the cityscape of the centre.

③ St Petrikirche

 Mönckebergstrasse
☎ (040) 325 74 00 ⏰ 10am-6:30pm Mon-Fri (to 7pm Wed), 10am-5pm Sat, 9am-8pm Sun

The church of St Petri, originally Gothic, was extensively rebuilt in the Neo-Gothic style after the Great Fire of 1842. It is the city's oldest parish church, and its steeple marks the highest point of the Old Town. The Grabower Altar that once belonged to the church has been transferred to the Kunsthalle (p424), but visitors can still admire the sculpture of the Madonna (1470).

④
HafenCity

Still under construction, with completion projected in stages between 2025 and 2030, HafenCity is a huge project that involves redeveloping the old port, expanding the city by as much as 40 per cent. While parts of this new quarter are still to be finished, some landmarks are open to the public. Designed by Herzog & de Meuron, the Elbphilharmonie concert hall contains two auditoriums, a five-star hotel, apartments and a viewing platform. The 110-m- (354-ft-) tall building was constructed with acoustics in mind and is topped by a vast glass wave-like structure. Also in HafenCity is the Internationales Maritimes Museum, which covers more than 3,000 years of maritime history, including model ships, sextants, and a copy of the first nautical atlas ever printed. Traditional sailing ships line the Magellan Terraces in celebration of the area's

maritime history. This Traditions-schiffhafen (traditional ship harbour) is run by the Hamburg Maritime Foundation.

---

⑤
Kontorhausviertel

This district of commercial offices was built between Mönckebergstrasse, Messberg and Steinstrasse at the start

↑ HafenCity's skyline, including the striking Elbphilharmonie building

of the 20th century. Together with nearby Speicherstadt, this historic quarter is UNESCO World Heritage listed. Chilehaus, built by Fritz Höger in 1922–4, is a fine example of Brick Expressionism, with its pointed eastern façade resembling a ship's bow.

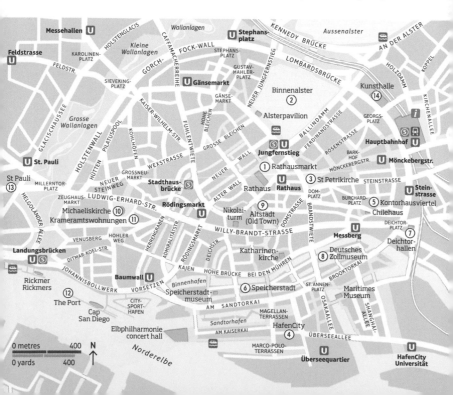

⑥ Speicherstadt

Located within the toll-free area of the port, this giant warehouse district is reached after crossing the customs post. It is the largest complex of warehouses in the world. The Neo-Gothic buildings, dating from the end of the 19th century, are separated by canals. Modern industries, such as multimedia companies, are slowly replacing the store-rooms packed with spices, coffee and carpets. Listed as one of the city's historic monuments, the area also houses the Speicherstadt Museum.

⑦ Deichtorhallen

🏠 Deichtorstrasse 1-2
🕐 11am-6pm Tue-Sun (during exhibitions)

The enormous market halls of the port, built in 1911–12, were turned into dramatic display halls in 1997 and are now used for major art exhibitions.

⑧ Deutches Zollmuseum

🏠 Alter Wandrahm 16, 20457 🕐 10am-5pm Tue-Sun 🌐 museum.zoll.de

Located by Kornhausbrücke, this museum tells the story of customs and excise from the Roman Empire to the present day.

⑨ Altstadt (Old Town)

Hamburg's old town extends to the south of the Rathaus (town hall) but, following the Great Fire of 1842 and bombing during World War II, only a few original buildings remain. Katharinenkirche (St Catherine's), with its characteristic tower, was begun in the 13th century and completed in the 17th century. It has been restored after damage in World War II.

Of the neighbouring Neo-Gothic Nikolaikirche (St Nicholas's) only a single tower remained after 1945, the Nikolaiturm, which is the third tallest in Germany. It serves as a monument to the tragic consequences of war.

Deichstrasse is one of a few surviving streets in the old town, with the original angular façades still visible from both the road and the canal (seek out the Hohe Brücke bridge for the best view). One of the more famous restaurants is the Zum Brandanfang, at No. 25. It was here that the Great Fire, which eventually destroyed much of the city, is said to have broken out.

HAMBURG'S FISCHMARKT

This is an attraction for early risers, or for those who never get to bed at all. From 5am (7am in winter) on Sundays the Auktionshalle (auction hall) and nearby waterside turn into a bustling marketplace. Fishermen proffering freshly caught fish compete with noisy greengrocers and bric-à-brac merchants; tourists mingle with sailors and ladies of the night, and snippets of Plattdeutsch, the northern patois, can be heard. The 10am morning Mass used to mark the end of this, but today's public lingers on before hurrying to bed instead of church.

→ Fisherman statue at the Market

The impressive Speicherstadt district, lit up at night

Michaeliskirche

🏠 Englische Planke 1
📞 (040) 37 67 80
🕐 Times vary, call ahead

The massive Baroque church of St Michael, visible from afar with its 132-m- (433-ft) tower (the "Michel"), is a renowned symbol of Hamburg. The observation platform offers splendid views of the city and its extensive harbour.

Krameramts-wohnungen

🏠 Krayenkamp 10 📞 (040) 37 50 19 88 🕐 Apr-Oct: 10am-5pm Wed-Fri (to 6pm Sat & Sun); Nov-Mar: 10am-5pm Sat & Sun 🌐 kramer-witwen-wohnung.de

Near the Michaeliskirche, the Krameramtswohnungen have miraculously survived – the last remaining example of a 17th-century residential complex. These half-timbered houses were funded by the merchants' guild and housed the widows of shopkeepers. Today they are home to shops, cafés and restaurants.

The Port

Ⓤ Baumwall

Situated 104 km (62 miles) inland along the Elbe river, Hamburg is Europe's second largest port after Rotterdam, and this dominates the city's panorama. Every year 12,000 ships dock here from 90 countries. From the U3 Baumwall metro station it is best to walk to Landungsbrücken, past the museum ships moored here: the freighter *Cap San Diego* and the sailing boat *Rickmer Rickmers* (1896). Landungs-brücken is a 200-m- (656-ft-) long building from where the passenger ferries depart. A tour of the harbour is highly recommended. Nearby is the entrance to the Alter Elbtunnel (the old tunnel under the Elbe), where people and cars are lowered in a giant lift.

St Pauli

Notorious around the world, this area is also known as Reeperbahn, after the main street. It is a world of night-clubs and bars, theatres and pubs, sex clubs and brothels. It was here, in Hamburg's red-light district, that some teenage seasonal workers from Liverpool, the Beatles, started their careers. On Herbertstrasse, scantily clad women offer their services behind a metal barrier; women and under 18s are forbidden entrance. St Pauli even has an Erotic Art Museum, where exhibits are curated to "prove" that everything revolves around the female posterior.

Kunsthalle

🏠 Glockengiesserwall
🕐 10am-6pm Tue-Sun (to 9pm Thu)
🌐 hamburger-kunsthalle.de

Northern Germany's most interesting art gallery, the Kunsthalle has a tradition dating back to 1817, when the Kunstverein (Friends of the Fine Arts) was established. It opened to the public in 1869. An extension was added in 1919 and together both buildings are called the Lichtwark Galerie, after Alfred Lichtwark, the first director of the Kunsthalle. The collection has a chronological review of European art movements, with an emphasis on 19th-century German Romantics. A second extension, the Galerie der Gegenwart (contemporary gallery), was built in 1996 to a design by the architect O M Ungers.

The Judgment of Paris (1870) by Feuerbach, in the Kunsthalle

St Pauli landing piers in the Port of Hamburg

↑ The sun setting over Hanover's striking skyline

❸

HANOVER

⚐ D2 🚌🚇🚋 ℹ Ernst-August-Platz 8 & Tramm platz 11; www.hannover.de

Hanover, the capital of Lower Saxony, may not seem immediately exciting, but appearances can be deceptive: the town offers interesting architecture, magnificent gardens and an unmissable modern art museum. Many historic monuments were rebuilt post-1945, and the old town's compact size makes it easy to explore on foot.

Niedersächsisches Landesmuseum

⚐ Willy-Brandt-Allee 5 ☎ (0511) 980 76 86 🕐 10am-6pm Tue-Sun

The most interesting part of Lower Saxony's state museum is the picture gallery, which houses excellent German medieval and Renaissance paintings (including works by Dürer, Spranger, Cranach) and a good section of Dutch and Flemish paintings (Rubens and Rembrandt are both featured). There are also 19th- and 20th-century German paintings, with fine examples of Romanticism and Impressionism.

Leineschloss

⚐ Hinrich-Wilhelm-Kopf-Platz

In the historic city centre stands this 17th-century palace completely rebuilt in 1817–42 by Hanover's most important architect, Georg Ludwig Friedrich Laves. It was rebuilt again after destruction in World War II, and now serves as headquarters for the Lower Saxony state parliament.

Opernhaus

⚐ Opernplatz 1 ☎ (0511) 99 99 11 11

The Neo-Classical opera house was built by Laves in 1845–57 to a fine Neo-Classical design. Particularly charming is the façade with portico columns.

Neues Rathaus

⚐ Trammplatz 2 ☎ (0511) 168 45 333 🕐 9:30am-6pm Mon-Fri, 10am-6pm Sat & Sun

This gigantic town hall was built from 1901–13, modelled on a Baroque palace with a central dome, and decorated with Secessionist and Neo-Gothic detail. A vast painting entitled *Einigkeit* (Unity) by the Swiss artist Ferdinand Hodler in the Debating Hall depicts the arrival of Protestantism to the town in 1533.

A unique oblique lift takes you up to the dome from where there are wonderful views of the town.

→
Picasso's *Femme au bouquet* (1909), on display in the Sprengel Museum

⑤

Sprengel Museum

📍 Kurt-Schwitters-Platz 1
📞 (0511) 16 84 38 75
🕐 10am–6pm Tue–Sun
(to 8pm Wed)

One of Europe's finest museums of modern art, the Sprengel Museum reflects the city's role as an artists' mecca in the 1920s, before the National Socialists destroyed works of art that they decreed to be degenerate. Funded by Bernhard Sprengel, a chocolate magnate who bequeathed his art collection to the city of Hanover in 1969, the museum was built in two phases –

one in 1979 and the other in 1992. It holds works by Munch, Chagall and Picasso, and installations from more recent artists like James Turrell. The museum also houses the Kurt Schwitters Archive, El Lissitzky's *Abstract Cabinet* – a small room designed to display constructivist paintings – and photography exhibitions.

⑥

Marktplatz

Although the houses on this square had to be almost completely rebuilt after World War II, this remains one of the town's best examples of 15th-century red-brick architecture. Nearby, the Marktkirche St Georg und St Jacobus (church of St George and St Jacob) features a 14th-century nave. The most valuable object among its furnishings is the Gothic altar, with scenes of the Passion, and copper engravings by Martin Schongauer.

⑦

Herrenhäuser Gärten

📍 Herrenhäuser Strasse 4

These fabulous gardens in Hanover's Herrenhausen district are among the most beautiful Baroque examples in Germany. They were established by Duchess Sophie von der Pfalz, mother of England's George I. The Grosser Garten, the most important of the four gardens, was modelled on 17th- and 18th-century Dutch parks and is home to the Grosse Fontäne – the tallest on the European mainland with a 72-m (236-ft) water spout. The gardens are immaculately laid out, with a maze, a grotto and sculptures, plus some 21 km (13 miles) of hedges.

EXPERIENCE MORE

4

Hildesheim

D3 **Rathausstrasssse 18-20; www.hildesheim.de**

The undisputed capital of Romanesque culture, the old town of Hildesheim was destroyed by heavy bombing on 22 March 1945. The most important monuments have now been recreated, with mixed results, surrounded by modern developments.

Since gaining civic rights in the 11th century, the heart of the bishopric town has been its market square, or Marktplatz. Every detail has been faithfully reconstructed. In 1987 the Knochen-haueramtshaus (Butchers' Guild Hall) was rebuilt, the largest and most famous half-timbered house in Germany, dating from 1529. Opposite are the Gothic town hall and the Tempelhaus, an original 15th-century building with round turrets and a half-timbered annexe, added in 1591. Reliefs depict the story of the prodigal son.

Built on the instructions of Bishop Bernward, the **Michaeliskirche** (St Michael's) church is a textbook example of what became known as the Ottonian style, the early Romanesque culture of the Otto dynasty. Its characteristic feature is the streamlined simplicity of interior and exterior, with square pillars intersecting with the naves. The sarcophagus of the founder, St Bernward, is in the crypt in the western part of the church. Luckily, a rare painted 12th century ceiling was removed during World War II and thus largely survived. It depicts the story of Redemption, from Adam and Eve through to Mary and the Saviour.

The pride of the **Roemer-Pelizaeus Museum** is the Ancient Egyptian collection, which includes the burial figures of Hem Om and the writer Heti from the Old Kingdom (around 2600 BC). It also has fine collections of Chinese porcelain and Inca artifacts, and it is famed for its temporary exhibitions on ancient cultures.

In 815, during a hunting expedition, Ludwig der Fromme (the Devout), son of Charlemagne, allegedly hung relics of the Virgin Mary on a wild rose bush. When he tried to remove them they would not budge – which he took to be a heavenly sign that a church should be founded on this site and a town alongside it. The Tausendjähriger Rosenstock (1,000-year-old rose) of this legend grows to this day outside the apse of the **Dom St Mariä**, and it even survived bombing. The cathedral was reconstructed after World War II, using a model of the church's 11th-century appearance. Original works of art bear witness to the cathedral's foundry, which flourished under bishop Bernward. Bronze double doors depict the Old Testament version of the Creation on one side, and the life of Christ according to the New Testament on the other. The Bernwardsäule, a huge bronze column from 1022, depicts scenes from the life of

7,000,0000

The number of people who emigrated from Bremerhaven's ports between 1830 and 1974.

←

Michaeliskirche, an early Romanesque church in the town of Hildesheim

Christ arranged as a spiralling picture story, recalling the column of Emperor Trajan in Rome. Two further important works of art are a chandelier from 1060, with a diameter of 3 m (10 ft), and a baptismal font (c 1225) based on the personifications of the four rivers of the Garden of Eden.

The **Godehardkirche** is a church dedicated to Bernward's successor, Bishop Godehard, who, like him, has been included in the canon of saints. Built in 1133–72, it is typical of local architecture, and also recalls the earlier Michaeliskirche. It has interesting carved capitals as well as a northern doorway with the Blessed Jesus Christ accompanied by St Godehard and St Epiphany.

Michaeliskirche

🅐 Michaelisplatz 🅒 (05121) 344 10 🕑 Apr–Oct: 8am–6pm daily; Nov–Mar: 9am–4pm daily

Roemer-Pelizaeus Museum

 🅐 Am Steine 1 🕑 10am–6pm Tue–Sun 🔳 rpmuseum.de

Dom St Mariä

🅐 Domhof 🕑 10am–6pm daily 🔳 domhildesheim.de

Godehardkirche

🅐 Godehardsplatz 🅒 (05121) 345 78 🕑 9am–6pm daily

---

⑤

Bremerhaven

🅐 C2 🚩 H.-H.-Meier-Strasse 6; www.erlebnis-bremerhaven.de

About 50 km (31 miles) to the north of Bremen lies its deep-sea harbour, Bremerhaven. The **Deutsches Schifffahrts-museum**, a marine museum designed by the architect Hans Scharoun, displays both originals and models of a wide range of ships, dating from the Roman Empire to the present day. A special hall displays the *Hanse Kogge*, a merchant ship dredged from the bottom of the Weser River in 1962. Displayed outside are the last great German sailing boat, *Seute Deern*, the polar ship *Grönland* and *Wilhelm Bauer*, a U-boat from World War II. The **Deutsches Auswandererhaus**

↑ The Bremerhaven waterfront with the Sail City hotel on the right

Bremerhaven traces the history of more than 7 million Germans who emigrated via Bremerhaven.

Deutsches Schifffahrtsmuseum

🏛 🅐 Hans-Scharoun-Platz 1 🅒 (0471) 482 070 🕑 10am–6pm daily (Nov–Feb: Tue–Sun)

Deutsches Auswandererhaus Bremerhaven

 🅐 Columbus-strasse 65 🕑 10am–6pm daily (Nov–Feb: to 5pm) 🔳 dah-bremerhaven.de

---

⚠ GREAT VIEW
City Panorama

The viewing platform (Aussichtsplattform) at Sail City hotel at Am Strom 1 offers 360-degree views of the city and the sea. Only €4, it is open from 9am to 9pm in summer, 10am to 5pm in winter.

↑ A flock of starlings flying over the marshes of the River Ems, in Petkum, Ostfriesland

 6

Ostfriesische Inseln (East Frisian Islands)

🅐 B2 🚉 Emden-Borkum, Norden-Norddeich to Juist and Norderney, Nessmersiel-Baltrum, Bensersiel-Langeoog, Neuharlingersiel-Spiekeroog, Harlesiel-Wangerooge 🛈 Ledastrasse 10, Leer; www.ostfriesland.de

Along the North Sea coast extends the belt of East Frisian Islands consisting of, from west to east: Borkum, Juist, Norderney, Baltrum, Langeoog, Spiekeroog and Wangerooge. All around them is the Nationalpark Niedersächsisches Wattenmeer, a large national park established to protect the unique ecosystem of the shallow seas. At low tide it turns into vast mud flats, extending to the horizon. This is the best time to tour the Watt, as it is known locally.

The islands themselves, with their beautiful sandy beaches, sand dunes and healthy climate, are among the most popular holiday destinations in Germany.

The car-free island Juist, a 17-km (11-mile) strip of land less than 500 m (1,640 ft) wide,

7

The number of islands in the East Frisian group.

and Norderney, with its main town of the same name, are the most interesting islands. Neo-Classical villas recall the days when such figures as Heinrich Heine and Otto von Bismarck spent their holidays here. It is also worth visiting Wangerooge, another island where cars are banned. Three lighthouses – Westturm, Alter Leuchtturm and Neuer Leuchtturm – indicate the island's role in the navigation of the Weser river estuary.

 7

Ostfriesland (East Frisia)

🅐 B/C2 🚉 Emden, Leer, Norden 🛈 Ledastrasse 10, Leer; www.ostfriesland.de

East Frisia is a peninsula near the border with the Netherlands and the Jadebusen bay, at

Wilhelmshaven. This is a land of flat meadows, grazing cows and windmills.

Emden, the region's main city, has an attractive town hall resembling that in Antwerp, and a town centre crossed by many canals. The **Kunsthalle Emden**, founded in the early 1990s by Henri Nannen, publisher of the magazine *Stern*, holds a remarkable collection of 19th-century paintings, including the works of many German Expressionists such as Emil Nolde, Max Beckmann and Oskar Kokoschka.

Another attraction is the **Moor- und Fehnmuseum** (Moor and Fen museum) in Elisabethfehn, which is dedicated to the extraction of peat. Its exhibits include the world's largest plough, as well as the story of Jever, the local beer. Also worth visiting are the Renaissance castle, whose reception hall has a ceiling with sunken panels, and next to the parish church the wood and stone tomb of the Frisian chief Edo Wiemken, made in 1561–4 by master craftsmen from Antwerp.

Kunsthalle Emden

⊛ 🅓 Hinter dem Rahmen 13 📞 (04921) 975 00 🕙 10am–5pm Tue–Fri (to 9pm 1st Tue of month), 11am–5pm Sat & Sun

Moor- und Fehnmuseum

⊛⊛ ◘ Oldenburger Strasse 1 🕐 Apr–Oct: 10am–5pm Tue–Sun 🌐 fehnmuseum.de

---

⑧

Emsland

🅰B2 🚗 ℹ Herzog-Arenberg-Strasse 12; www.emsland.com

Emsland, to the south of East Frisia, extends along the Dutch border, which was known as the "poor-house of Germany" until the "Emsland Plan" of 1950 helped develop the region's wastelands. Today, it offers moors and forests, the river courses of the Ems and Hase, and numerous megalithic tombs from the Stone Age. Emsland is also a popular destination for cycling and family holidays, and is a great base for exploring local sights like the Dankern Castle holiday centre in Haren, the Meyer Werft visitor centre in Papenburg, and the Emsflower adventure park in Emsbüren.

The municipality of Sögel, 33 km (21 miles) south of Papenburg, has the region's greatest attraction, the palatial hunting lodge

↑ The scattered pavilions at Schloss Clemens-werth, Emsland

Schloss Clemenswerth, built in 1737–49. Inside there is a museum of the region.

---

⑨

Oldenburg

🅰C2 🚗 ℹ Lange Strasse 3; www.oldenburg-tourismus.de

A thousand years old, and formerly part of Denmark, the town of Oldenburg remained the seat of a duchy until 1918.

The Lambertikirche, in the central market square, is a late-Gothic hall-church with a Neo-Classical rotunda added in 1797. The Schloss, the ducal residence, displays a similar marriage of styles, particularly Baroque and Neo-Classical. The **Landesmuseum für Kunst und Kulturgeschichte** (State Museum of Art and Culture), based in the castle, is known mainly for its collection of paintings assembled by Wilhelm Tischbein, who lived here for 25 years. The affiliated Augusteum, a Neo-Renaissance building in a picturesque spot, holds the Old Master's Gallery.

Landesmuseum für Kunst und Kulturgeschichte

⊛ ◘ Schloßplatz 1 📞 (0441) 4057 04 00 🕐 10am–6pm Tue–Sun

---

⑩

Cloppenburg

🅰C2 ℹ Eschstrasse 29; (04471) 152 56

The small market town of Cloppenburg boasts the **Museumsdorf**, the oldest open-air museum in Germany, established in 1934. On an expansive site, as many as 50 architectural monuments from all over Lower Saxony have been assembled. There are houses, including charming examples of the

half-timbered style of Wehlburg, windmills and a small 17th-century church from Klein-Escherde near Hildesheim.

To the east of Cloppenburg lies Visbek. Here the visitor is taken back to the Stone Age, with megalithic graves from 3,500 to 1,800 BC, including the 80-m- (262-ft-) long grave known as "Visbeker Bräutigam" (Bridegroom) and the even larger, 100-m- (321-ft-) long "Visbeker Braut" (Bride).

Museumsdorf Cloppenburg

⊛ ◘ Bether Strasse 6 📞 (04471) 948 40 🕐 Mar–Oct: 10am–6pm daily; Nov–Feb: 10am–4:30pm Sat & Sun

PAULA MODERSOHN-BECKER

A student of Fritz Mackensen and wife of Otto Modersohn, Paula Modersohn-Becker was Worpswede's most significant artistic figure. She learned about the Impressionist use of colour during visits to Paris, and her own unique sensibility made her a precursor of Expressionism. She won acclaim for her naturalistic paintings of poor, starving and dying country folk. She died in childbirth in 1907, aged only 31. The sculptor Bernhard Hoetger created the statue on her tombstone, in the village cemetery in Worpswede.

Goslar

A D30 **R** **i** Markt 7; (05321) 780 60

Goslar, at the foot of the Harz Mountains, is a captivating town with as many as 1,500 charming, half-timbered houses, the largest number in Germany. For 300 years the Holy Roman Emperors of Germany resided in Goslar, a member of the Hanseatic League also known as "the treasure chest of the North". Goslar's main source of wealth was the nearby mine in Rammelsberg, where zinc, copper and especially silver were mined. The townscape has remained largely unchanged, making it a great tourist attraction as well as a UNESCO World Heritage site.

Visitors should make sure to stop at the Siemenshaus, one of the most attractive half-timbered houses in town, which was once owned by the Siemens family – founders of the technology and tele-communications brand – who have their roots in Goslar.

Located on Frankenberger Platz, St Peter and Paul was one of 47 churches which once stood in the town. It was built in the 12th century, and the tympanum of the south portal dates from this period. Extensively refurbished, the church prides itself on its magnificent Baroque furnishings.

The present appearance of **St Jakobi**, the only Catholic church in Goslar, is the result of Gothic additions, although the structure of the walls remains Romanesque. The most important work of art in the church is a sculpture of the Pietà by Hans von Witten, but it is also worth looking at the wall paintings, the organ and the baptismal font.

With its impressive late-Romanesque architecture, the **Neuwerkkirche** was constructed in the 12th–13th centuries for the Cistercian Order, although the surviving monastic buildings date from the early 18th century. Inside, the wall paintings and the choir partition are of interest. The church is surrounded by a peaceful garden.

Some parts of the town's defensive system, dating mainly from around 1500, are well preserved. The Breites Tor (Wide Gate), which can be seen on Breite Strasse, on the eastern approach of the town, is the most imposing part of the structure.

Another historic sight is **St Annen-Stift**, a former hospice for orphans, the elderly and infirm, which was founded in 1494. It holds the impressive title of the oldest preserved half-timbered house in Germany. Behind its façade is a beautiful chapel with superb paintings on a wooden ceiling.

Goslar's mining museum, **Bergbaumuseum Rammelsberg,** is based in the 10th-century silver mine. One of the oldest industrial structures in the world, it is now a UNESCO World Heritage site. On display are mining tools and utensils used in various periods of Goslar's mining industry. Visitors can take a train ride through the mine and learn about the history of mining.

St Jakobi

A Jakobi-Kirchhof **C** (05321) 30 36 72 **O** 9:30am–4pm daily

Neuwerkkirche

A Rosentorstrasse 27a **C** (05321) 228 39 **O** Mar–Oct: 10am–noon & 2:30–4:30pm Mon–Sat; 2:30–4:30pm Sun

← Attractive half-timbered houses in the pedestrianized centre of Goslar

Heinrich Vogeler. However, the greatest artist in Worpswede was Paula Modersohn-Becker (p439), whose sad fairytale world of rustic subjects cannot be defined within one style. Work by the artists of the founding era is on display in the **Grosse Kunstschau** and the **Worpsweder Kunsthalle** as well as in the private Museum am Modersohn-Haus.

Grosse Kunstschau

◈ 🏠 Lindenallee 3 & 5 📞 (04792) 13 02 🕐 Mar–Oct: 10am–6pm daily (Nov–Mar: Tue–Sun)

Worpsweder Kunsthalle

◈ 🏠 Bergstrasse 17 🕐 Apr–Oct: 10am–6pm daily; Nov–Mar: 11am–6pm daily 🌐 worpswede-museen.de

---

🔟3️⃣

Wolfenbüttel

🅰️ D3 🚉 ℹ️ Löwenstrasse 1; (05331) 862 80

This small town has a turbulent past. From 1432 until 1753 the Welf dukes moved their seat here from Brunswick. In the 16th century, innovative town design introduced wide avenues and spacious squares. Left largely unscathed by World War II, the town has 500 historic half-timbered houses, and a magnificent library.

The Herzog-August-Bibliothek holds 130,000 volumes, including the most valuable book in the world, Henry the Lion's Gospel book. Associated with the town are the philosopher Gottfried Wilhelm Leibniz and writer Gotthold Ephraim Lessing. The **Lessinghaus** houses a literature museum.

The centre of the town is dominated by the **Schloss**, the largest castle in Lower Saxony It houses a museum with regional items such as furniture and tapestries. The Venussaal (Hall of Venus) has beautiful Baroque ceiling frescoes. Opposite the castle is the Zeughaus (armoury), built in 1613–19 to a design by Paul Francke.

Continuing eastwards the visitor will get to the Hauptkirche, the 16th-century church dedicated to Beatae Mariae Virginis, the ducal pantheon and the leading example of Protestant Mannerist architecture. Begun in 1608, the church's façade has delicate reliefs, while the interior has an unusual combination of styles.

Lessinghaus

🏠 Lessingplatz 1 📞 (05331) 80 82 14 🕐 11am–5pm Tue–Sun

Schloss

◈ 🕐 🏠 Schlossplatz 13 📞 (05331) 924 60 🕐 10am–5pm Tue–Sun

1,000

The number of years iron ore was mined near Goslar – the mines closed in 1988.

St Annen-Stift

🏠 Glockengiesserstrasse 65 📞 (05321) 39 87 00 🕐 10am–noon Mon, Thu & Fri

Bergbaumuseum Rammelsberg

◈ 🕐 🏠 Bergtal 19 🕐 9am–6pm daily 🌐 rammelsberg.de

1️⃣2️⃣

Worpswede

🅰️ C2 ℹ️ Bergstrasse 13

From 1889, this small village in the middle of the peat bogs northeast of Bremen has been known as a famous artists' colony. Apart from poets, such as Rainer Maria Rilke, and such archi-tects as Bernhard Hoetger, the fame of this village rested principally on the painters: Fritz Mackensen, Otto Modersohn, Hans am Ende, Fritz Overbeck and

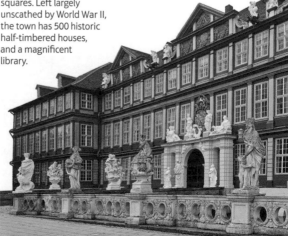

→ The elegant Baroque façade of the Schloss in Wolfenbüttel

14
Osnabrück

C3 <i>i</i> Bierstrasse 22–23; www.osnabrueck.de

This Westphalian town has been a bishop's see since the time of Charlemagne. In 1648 negotiations took place here between representatives of Sweden and the Protestant duchies of the Reich to end the Thirty Years' War. The signing of the resulting Treaty of Westphalia was announced from the town hall steps. The town was also the birthplace of the writer Erich Maria Remarque in 1899.

Dom St Peter, Osnabrück's 13th-century cathedral, has a bronze baptismal font and enormous triumphal cross, and the late-Gothic Snetlage-Altar of the Crucifixion. From here a short walk takes the visitor to the market square, Marienkirche (St Mary's Church) and the Gothic Rathaus (town hall).

South of town is the western part of the Teutoburger Wald (Teutoburg Forest, *p412*). The spa town of Bad Iburg, 12 km (8 miles) to the south of Osnabrück, has a monumental Benedictine monastery and bishop's palace. The Rittersaal (Knights' Hall) has a giant ceiling fresco depicting an architectural fantasy of foreshortened perspectives.

→
The old wooden crane in Stade's Alter Hafen

15
Stade

D2 <i>i</i> Hansestrasse 16; www.stade-tourismus.de

This medieval Hanseatic town has retained most of its half-timbered buildings, with the most attractive in the Alter Hafen (Old Harbour). There is also a quaint crane and the Schwedenspeicher (Swedish granary) dating from the Swedish occupation during the Thirty Years' War (1692–1705). The harbour is now home to the **Schwedenspeicher-Museum**, with exhibits on the town's history and defence system, including wheels from 700 BC that were part of a Bronze-Age cart. Nearby, No. 7 Am Wasser West houses the Kunsthaus, which exhibits prestigious 20th-century artists.

Other attractions are the Bürgermeister-Hintze-Haus at No. 23 Am Wasser West – a house built for the mayor, Hintze, in 1617–46 – and the exquisite Baroque Rathaus (town hall) from 1667, its design revealing the influence of Dutch architecture.

> Johanniskirche (St John's), one of Lüneburg's three Gothic churches, has a west tower that leans more than 2 m (6 ft) from the perpendicular.

The 14th-century Gothic church of St Wilhadi boasts an interesting hall and a leaning tower, while St Cosmas and Damiani, founded after the Great Fire of 1659, features Baroque furnishings.

Schwedenspeicher-Museum

 Am Wasser West 39 (04141) 79 77 30 10am–5pm Tue–Fri, 10am–6pm Sat & Sun

16
Lüneburg

D2 <i>i</i> Rathaus, Am Markt; www.lueneburg.de

This small, Hanseatic town was once one of the wealthiest in Germany. Its prosperity was founded on salt mines. First mentioned in 956, the mines provided work for more than 2,000 people by the late Middle Ages and were the largest industry in Europe.

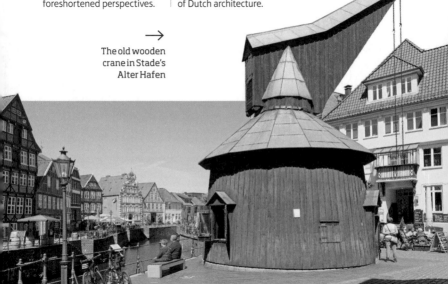

Lüneburg's most important monument is the **Rathaus** (town hall). The interior is intriguing, especially the Gerichtslaube (main hall), with its Gothic stained-glass windows and 15th-century frescoes of the Last Judgement, and the Grosse Ratsstube (council chamber), with Renaissance woodwork by Albert von Soest.

Johanniskirche (St John's), one of the town's three Gothic churches, has a west tower that leans more than 2 m (6 ft) from the perpendicular. In one of its five naves there is a panelled painting dating from 1482–5, the masterful work of the German painter Hinrik Funhof. Also interesting is the soaring basilica of Nicolaikirche (St Nicolas), consecrated in 1409.

Not far from here is the old port on the Ilmenau River. On Lüner Strasse stands the Altes Kaufhaus, a former herring warehouse with a Baroque façade. The 14th-century wooden crane was rebuilt in the 1700s. The decorative wavy brick lines (Taustäbe) on many of the old buildings are characteristic of the town.

Rathaus

 Am Markt
(04131) 30 92 30
Tours at 10am, noon & 3pm Tue–Sat

 17

Lüneburger Heide

D2 Wallstrasse 4, Lüneburg; www. lueneburger-heide.de

South of Hamburg, between the rivers Elbe and Aller, is a sprawling area of heathland, grazed by heifers and sheep and buzzing with bees. Until the Middle Ages, this area was covered by dense forests, but these were felled to satisfy demand for wood in the saltworks of Lüneburg. The heather moors are best seen at the Naturschutzpark

Lüneburger Heide, a nature reserve founded in 1921. From the village of Undeloh it is best to continue by foot, bike or carriage to the traditional village of Wilsede. From here it is not far to Wilseder Berg, the highest peak of this moraine region. The view of the surrounding countryside is particularly beautiful at the end of August, when the purple heather is blooming.

18

Soltau

D2 Am Alten Stadt-graben 3; www.soltau.de

The main attraction of the town of Soltau is **Heide Park Resort**, a huge leisure park with 40 attractions, as well as an adventure hotel and a holiday camp. For nature lovers, the Vogelpark Walsrode, 20 km (12 miles) southwest of Soltau, holds about 1,000 species of birds, from penguins to birds of paradise.

In grim contrast to both parks stands **Bergen-Belsen**, a concentration camp in the moorland of Osterheide, about 30 km (19 miles) south of Soltau. A monument and small museum commemorate the place where 50,000 people were murdered during World War II, among them Anne Frank.

↑ The Big Loop rollercoaster at the vast Heide Park Soltau

Heide Park Resort

Heide Park 1
Apr–Oct: 9am–6pm daily
heide-park.de

Vogelpark Walsrode

Am Vogelpark
Apr–Oct: 9am–7pm daily; Nov–Mar: 10am–4pm daily
weltvogelpark.de

Gedenkstätte Bergen-Belsen

Lohheide
10am–6pm daily (Oct–Mar: to 5pm) bergen-belsen. stiftung-ng.de

EAT

Romantik Restaurant Walhalla
This sophisticated restaurant is part of the beautiful Romantik Hotel Walhalla, a half-timbered building in the heart of Osnabrück's old town. The menu consists of European cuisines, including French, German and Italian dishes.

C3 Bierstrasse 24
hotel-walhalla.de

€€€

 The Car Tower at the Volkswagenwerk Autostadt, Wolfsburg

Byzantine-style image of Christ's Enthronement on a vaulted ceiling.

St Martini

🏠 Schulstrasse18 📞 (05721) 78070 🕐 9am-noon, 2-4pm Mon-Thu, 9am-noon Fri

㉑

Wolfsburg

🅰 D3 🚌 ℹ Willy-Brandt-Platz 3; www.wolfsburg.de

During the 1930s this small village began to develop into a sizeable town, based around the Volkswagen car works. Production of a "people's car" was conceived by Hitler – every German was to be able to afford this inexpensive car, the Beetle, designed by Ferdinand Porsche. The model reached its peak during the post-war economic boom years. The **Volkswagenwerk Autostadt** factory is open to visitors, offering unique attractions like an ascent

400

The number of new cars in each car tower at Volkswagenwerk Autostadt.

⑲

Celle

 🅰 D3 🚌 ℹ Markt 14-6; www.celle-tourismus.de

Between 1378 and 1705 Celle was the seat of distant relations of the Welf family, the reigning dynasty in the Duchy of Brunswick-Lüneburg. The **Schloss** (castle), rebuilt in Renaissance style after 1533, has a façade with octagonal towers, gables and bay windows. It is one of the main early-Renaissance buildings in Germany. The Gothic chapel was rebuilt in Mannerist style to a design by Martin de Vos, who created 76 of its paintings, including the *Crucifixion* triptych (late 1500s).

Celle prides itself on 500 half-timbered houses, with the most interesting ones found on the picturesque streets of Kalandgasse and Zöllnerstrasse. Hoppner Haus, at No. 8 Poststrasse, is richly decorated with reliefs of mythological beasts. Equally interesting is the painted decoration of the Rathaus (town hall), a great example of Weser Renaissance, which dates back to 1579. From the **Stadtkirche** church tower great views unfold. The Baroque **Synagoge**, beyond the old town, is the oldest half-timbered synagogue in Lower-Saxony.

Schloss

🎫 🎫 🕐 Times vary, check website 🌐 celle.travel/celle-palace.html

Stadtkirche

📞 (05141) 7735 🕐 Jan-Mar: 11am-5pm Tue-Sat; Apr-Dec 10am-6pm Tue-Sat; Tower: Apr-Oct: 11am-4pm Tue-Sat; Nov-Mar: noon-3pm Tue-Sat

Synagoge

🏠 Im Kreise24 📞 (05141) 9090 80 🕐 Times vary, call ahead

⑳

Stadthagen

 🅰 C3 🚌 ℹ Am Markt 1; www.stadthagen.de

The former counts of Schaumburg-Lippe used the Renaissance Schloss (castle) as their private residence. Apart from this and the town hall, the main attraction is the church of **St Martini**, featuring a Baroque mausoleum, and a masterful bronze monument by Adrian de Vries, court artist to Rudolf II in Prague.

A gem of Romanesque architecture can be found at Idensen near Wunsdorf, 22 km (14 miles) northeast of Stadthagen. The church interior of Alte Kirche (old church, 1120) is entirely painted with scenes from the Old and New testaments, and there is also a vast up one of the car towers. Wolfsburg also has some outstanding examples of modern architecture: a cultural centre designed by Alvar Aalto, a city theatre designed by Hans Scharoun and the "Phaeno" science center, designed by Zaha Hadid.

Volkswagenwerk Autostadt
🕸🕙🚻⛲ ⬛ Stadtbrücke
🕐 9am-6pm daily
🌐 autostadt.de

22
Bückeburg

🗺 C3 🚉 🛈 Schlossplatz 5; (05722) 89 31 81

In the 16th century this town became the capital of the principality of Schaumburg-Lippe. The philosopher Johann Gottfried von Herder was the preacher here. The **Stadtkirche**, one of the first Protestant churches in Germany, is a pinnacle of Mannerism with its fantasy façade. Another attraction in Bückeburg is the **Schloss** with its enchanting chapel. The Goldener Saal (Golden Hall), from 1605, has a Götterpforte (portal of the divinities) and a beautiful panelled ceiling.

Stadtkirche
🏛 Lange Strasse
🕐 Times vary, check website
🌐 stadtkirchengemeinde-bueckeburg.de

Schloss
🏛 Schlossplatz 1
📞 (05722) 50 39
🕐 Apr-Sep: 9:30am-6pm; Oct-Mar: 9:30am-5pm

23
Verden an der Aller

🗺 C2 🚉 🛈 Grosse Strasse 40; www.verden.de

Verden an der Aller, once a free town of the Reich, is well known to sports enthusiasts thanks to its horseracing track, training centre and stadium. The **Deutsches Pferdemuseum** (German Horse Museum) houses a large collection of artifacts dedicated to the animal's history. Seven horse auctions are held in the town each year, the main ones being in April and October.

Above the town rises the Dom, with a large, steep roof. The hall, a modification of earlier basilicas, is architecturally interesting, with a multi-sided presbytery, a passageway dating from 1268–1311, Romanesque cloisters and a tower.

North of the cathedral is the Domherrenhaus, housing the Historisches Museum, with exhibits on regional history as well as archaeological and ethnographic departments.

Deutsches Pferdemuseum
🕸🕙 🏛 Holzmarkt 9
🕐 10am-5pm Tue-Sun
🌐 dpm-verden.info

↑ The two bronze horses in Verden's pedestrianized centre

The Phaeno Science Centre in Wolfsburg ↓

Braunschweig (Brunswick)

A D3 **R** **i** Kleine Burg 14; (0531) 47 02 040

An important commercial and political centre from the early Middle Ages, Braunschweig (Brunswick) was chosen as town of residence by Heinrich der Löwe (Henry the Lion), ruler of Saxony and Bavaria. A member of the Welf family, he eventually lost in his struggle against the German emperor.

Very different in character was Till Eulenspiegel, an ordinary man who was born in Braunschweig and poked fun at dim-witted citizens, the aristocracy and the clergy. His exploits were fictionalized in the 16th century, and he was immortalized with a fountain on Bäckerklint square.

Braunschweig's continued decline culminated in the almost total destruction of the town in 1944. During reconstruction, the concept of the "Traditionsinsel" was developed: small islands of rebuilt historic monuments adrift in a sea of modernism.

A tour of the town is best started from Burgplatz (castle square). Here is the Burglöwe,

Braunschweig's Burglöwe, Henry the Lion's symbolic statue

Did You Know?

In 1806, Brünswick was captured by the French and became part of the Napoleonic Kingdom of Westphalia in 1807.

the monument of a lion funded by Heinrich in 1166 (the original is in a museum). Symbolizing Heinrich's rule, it was the first such sculpture to be erected since Roman days. The **Dom** (cathedral) on Burgplatz is well worth seeing. In the north nave, an extension, are unusual turned pillars, and in the transept and presbytery are some 13th-century frescoes. Its marvellous treasures include a gigantic seven-armed bronze candlestick, the tomb of Duke Heinrich and his wife Mathilde, the Crucifix of Imerward and a wooden cross with the figure of Christ modelled on the *Volto Santo* (Holy Face) in Lucca. Visitors can also see the column of the Passion with the figure of Christ, the work of Hans Witten.

To the west of the cathedral lies the Altstadtmarkt (old town market). Here are the L-shaped Rathaus (town hall), with a cloister, and the Gothic church of **St Martini**. The beautiful Gewandhaus (cloth hall) is also worth seeing.

To the east of the cathedral is the **Herzog Anton Ulrich Museum**, which is one of the oldest museums in Europe. It was opened to the public as a gallery by Duke Anton Ulrich and holds a variety of gems such as Rembrandt's *Family Portrait*, a Giorgioni self-portrait and Vermeer van Delft's renowned *Girl with a Glass of Wine*.

In the town of Königslutter, 35 km (22 miles) east of Braunschweig, Emperor Lothar initiated the building of the Benedictine **Kaiserdom**, a monastery church. The portal with figures of lions, a frieze with figures of fishermen, and the cloisters reflect the taste of the times and the northern Italian origin of architects and sculptors; only the frescoes are late 19th-century additions.

The town of Helmstedt, 45 km (28 miles) to the east, is unjustifiably only associated with the former border crossing between East and West Germany during the Cold War. The town actually has a rich cultural history: it was here in 1576 Duke Julius of Braunschweig founded the Julius Academy, one of Germany's most popular Protestant universities, where Italian philosopher Giordano Bruno taught. Juleum (1592–7), the main building, has a central tower and two decorative gables. It is now home to the **Kreis- und Universitätsmuseum**, a regional museum and library.

Dom

A Burgplatz **C** (0531) 24 33 50 **O** 10am–5pm daily

St Martini

A Altstadtmarkt **C** (0531) 161 21 **O** 10am–noon Mon, Tue, Thu & Fri; 4–6pm Wed

Herzog Anton Ulrich Museum

A Museumsstrasse 1 **C** (0531) 122 50 **O** 11am–6pm Tue–Sun

Kaiserdom

A Königslutter **C** (05353) 91 21 29 **O** 9am–6pm daily, (to 5pm in winter)

Kreis- und Universitätsmuseum

A Collegienplatz 1 **C** (05351) 121 11 32 **O** 10am–noon & 3–5pm Tue–Fri; 3–5pm Sat & Sun

→ An alfresco café in front of an old half-timbered building in Duderstadt

 25

Göttingen

△D4 🚊 ℹ️ Altes Rathaus, Markt 9; www.goettingen.de

Along with Tübingen, Marburg and Heidelberg, Göttingen is one of the most renowned German university towns. Established in 1737 by the English king George II, who was also the ruler of Hanover, the university taught the sons of wealthy German, English and Russian aristocrats. Important cultural figures worked here, including the writer Heinrich Heine, the brothers Grimm and the explorer Alexander von Humboldt. The city's reputation as an educational centre continues today, partly due to the establishment of the Max Planck Institute, named after the Göttingen-born scientist who developed quantum theory.

Göttingen is a lively town thanks to its student population, with dozens of cafés, cosmopolitan restaurants and bars. University buildings are scattered all over town, and the Aula, a Neo-Classical assembly hall, is worth a visit. On the Marktplatz in the town centre stands the Rathaus (town hall) with a Gothic stone façade. The town's iconic Gänselieselbrunnen (Goose Girl Fountain), in front dates from 1901. It is kissed by students who have completed a doctorate, and is much loved by tourists.

From the southeastern end of the market square, Göttingen's main churches can be seen: St Michael to the south, St Jakobi to the north, St Johannis to the west and St Albani to the east. The latter two have late-Gothic altars worth visiting. Together,

they testify to Göttingen's early importance during the Middle Ages.

 26

Einbeck

△D3 🚊 ℹ️ Eickeschen Haus, Marktstrasse 13; www.einbeck.de

In the Middle Ages this town had 600 breweries and today it is still known for its beers; Bockbier, the famous German strong beer, was invented here. Burned down in 1540 and 1549, the town was subsequently rebuilt in a uniformly Renaissance style. The historic centre is enclosed by the city walls. More than 100 half-timbered houses have survived to this day. Eickesches Haus (No. 13 Marktstrasse) is particularly eye-catching, with a sculpted façade based on biblical and classical stories. Other picturesque houses can be found in Tiedexer Strasse and in Marktplatz. The latter boasts the Rathaus (town hall) and the Ratswaage (municipal weigh house).

Another big attraction here is the PS.SPEICHER, an interactive exhibition on the subject of mobility, with Europe's largest freely accessible collection of classic cars.

 27

Duderstadt

△D4 🚊 ℹ️ Marktstrasse 66; (05527) 84 12 00

To the south of the Harz Mountains lies this medieval gem. On Obermarkt (upper market) stands the half-timbered Rathaus (town hall), with an interesting façade and spiky towers. Inside it has exhibition halls and a cultural centre. East of the town hall rises the Catholic church of St Cyriakus with its rich interior of altars and 15 Baroque statues. St Servatius, its Protestant counterpart, combines Gothic architecture with a Secessionist interior. Nearby is the Westertorturm, the only surviving town gate. Its strangely spiralling finial is the consequence of a construction error.

 PICTURE PERFECT
Braunschweig's Altstadtmarkt

This old marketplace, the former epicentre of the town, provides the perfect historical backdrop for some memorable holiday snaps, particularly of the Gewandhaus.

Evening in old town Hameln, the setting for the fairy tale *The Pied Piper of Hamelin* ↑

A DRIVING TOUR
THE WESER RENAISSANCE

Locator Map
For more detail see p420

LOWER SAXONY, HAMBURG AND BREMEN

The Weser Renaissance

Length 112 km (70 miles) **Stopping-off points** The stunning view from the Weser-Skywalk scenic outlook in Bad Karlshafen is well worth the short hike to the clifftop

This route takes drivers on a tour of architectural highlights of the Weser Renaissance style. Dating from the mid-16th- to the mid-17th-century, the style takes its inspiration from the tall roofs and gables of Dutch architecture, although it has many original features: the Zwerchhäuser (bay windows, one or more storeys high), the Utlucht (protruding sections of the façade), lavish decorations and multiwing castles.

Hameln's most striking Weser Renaissance structures are the Rattenfängerhaus (rat-catcher's house), Hochzeitshaus (wedding house) and Demptersches Haus (Dempsters' house).

Schloss Hämelschenburg has an impressive exterior with towers and decorative gables; its original interiors are also preserved.

Another gem of the Weser Renaissance style, the castle in **Bevern** has four wings as well as two towers in the corners of its courtyard.

The town of **Höxter** has several notable Weser Renaissance structures, including the Adam-und-Eva-Haus.

Bad Karlshafen is a great place to stay if you want more time in the area, with many spas and the lovely Reinhardswald nearby.

In **Münden**, the town hall and Welfenschloss castle exemplify the medieval Weser Renaissance style.

START Hameln

FINISH Münden

0 kilometres 15
0 miles 15

N

SCHLESWIG-HOLSTEIN

Originally this state comprised two territories: Schleswig in the north, which was inhabited by Germanic tribes (Angles, Saxons, Vikings and Danes) in the Middle Ages, and Holstein in the south, mainly populated by Slavs. Its more recent history was characterized by struggles between the Hanseatic towns and the rulers of Denmark. In the 18th century the entire region belonged to Denmark, but in 1866 it was annexed to Bismarck's Prussia. The political borders that exist today were established in 1920, when Denmark regained the northern part of Schleswig after a plebiscite, leaving a significant Danish minority on the German side.

Schleswig-Holstein is principally an agricultural region, and less densely populated than any other state in Germany, but the wide sandy beaches, impressive lakes, and magnificent countryside more than compensates for the lack of major cultural monuments.

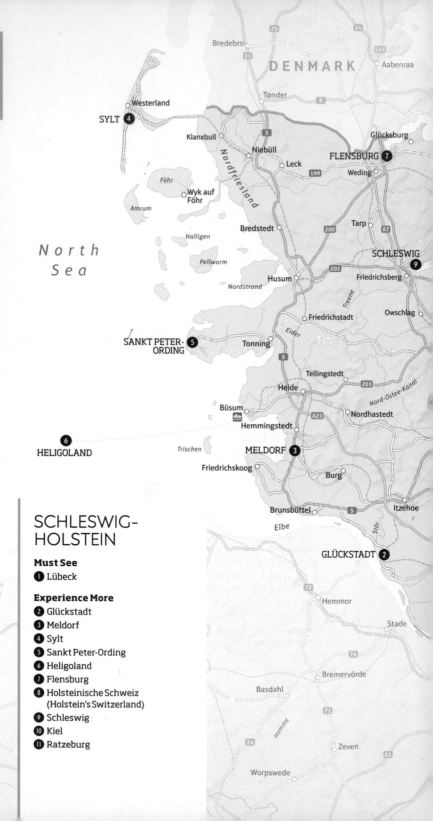

North
Sea

DENMARK

SYLT 4

FLENSBURG 7

SCHLESWIG 9

SANKT PETER-
ORDING 5

HELIGOLAND 6

MELDORF 3

GLÜCKSTADT 2

SCHLESWIG-
HOLSTEIN

Must See
1 Lübeck

Experience More
2 Glückstadt
3 Meldorf
4 Sylt
5 Sankt Peter-Ording
6 Heligoland
7 Flensburg
8 Holsteinische Schweiz
(Holstein's Switzerland)
9 Schleswig
10 Kiel
11 Ratzeburg

❶
LÜBECK

Ⓐ D2 🚆🚌 ℹ Holstentorplatz 1; www.luebeck-tourism.de

This beautifully restored medieval town, located in Germany's northernmost state, was listed as a UNESCO World Heritage Site in 1987. Visitors flock here to admire its iconic Holstentor and wander the cobbled streets of its rich historic centre.

Described as a "specific nest" by Thomas Mann, the town's most famous resident, Lübeck is well worth a visit. An important town in the Baltic basin by the end of the Middle Ages, it is now a magnet for fans of *Backsteingotik*, Gothic brick architecture, which has been elevated to a national style. After just a short stay in Lübeck it is easy to see why: church interiors, the façades of buildings, the city gates, the unique town hall and even the medieval hospital all resemble pictures from an illustrated history of architecture brought to life. The city was beautifully rebuilt after the destruction of World War II and enjoys a thriving tourist industry.

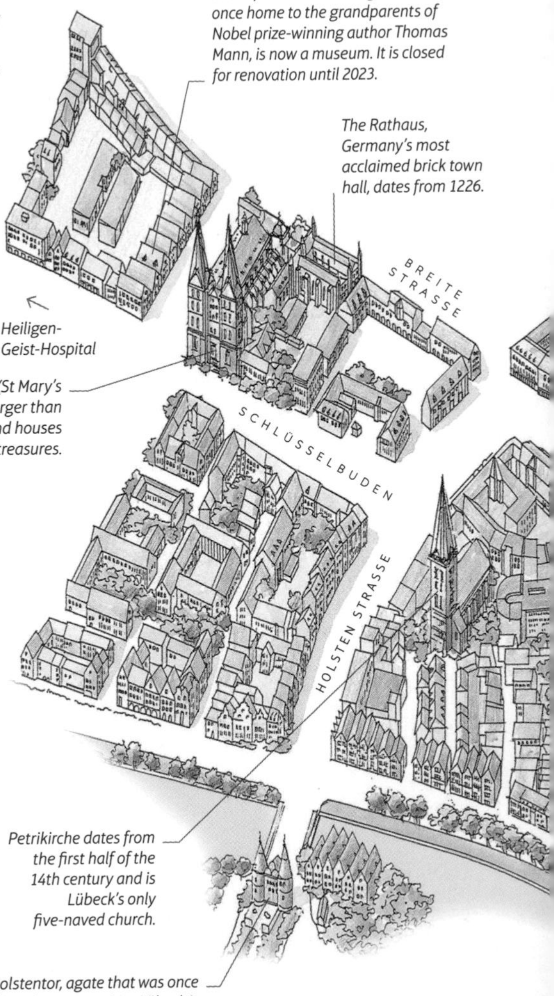

Buddenbrookhaus (p456), a beautiful Gothic building that was once home to the grandparents of Nobel prize-winning author Thomas Mann, is now a museum. It is closed for renovation until 2023.

The Rathaus, Germany's most acclaimed brick town hall, dates from 1226.

BREITE STRASSE

← Heiligen-Geist-Hospital

SCHLÜSSELBUDEN

Marienkirche (St Mary's church; p456) is larger than the cathedral and houses great art treasures.

HOLSTEN STRASSE

↑ Lübeck's medieval Holstentor (Holstein Gate)

Petrikirche dates from the first half of the 14th century and is Lübeck's only five-naved church.

Holstentor, a gate that was once the only entrance into Lübeck is now an emblem of the town.

MARZIPAN FROM LÜBECK

A favourite present from Lübeck is marzipan, which has been popular throughout Europe since the 19th century. Its name was recorded as *Martzapaen* for the first time in Lübeck in 1530. It is made from two-thirds sweet almonds imported from Venice and one-third sugar and aromatic oils. In 1806 the Niederegger patisserie perfected the recipe, and their Breite Strasse premises still operate today.

Did You Know?

Lübeck was home to three Nobel Laureates: Thomas Mann, Günter Grass and Willy Brandt.

Aegidienkirche, the smallest church in the town centre

St Annen-Museum (p457), housed in an Augustinian convent, portrays life and culture in 13th- to 18th-century Lübeck.

→ *Freilichtbühne*

The Dom (p457), the cathedral, was begun in 1173 and completed in 1230.

Herz-Jesu-Kirche, a 19th-century Catholic church

↑ Lübeck's old town, enclosed by the River Trave and presided over by seven towers

Lübeck's picturesque buildings lining the banks of the River Trave ↑

①

Marienkirche

 Marienkirchhof 1
☎ (0451) 39 77 00 ⏰ 10am–6pm daily (winter: to 4pm)

The twin-towered basilica of St Mary's Church is the brick modification of a Neo-Classical French cathedral.

Its vast interior boasts the highest vaulted brick ceiling in the world, which dominates the other interior features. In one of the towers, the

← Bronze sculpture of a devil outside the Marienkirche

shattered fragments of the church bells lie embedded in the floor, where they fell during the bombing in 1942.

②

Buddenbrookhaus

 Mengstrasse ↺ For renovations ⎄ budden brookhaus.de

Behind the 1758 Rococo façade of the Buddenbrook House is a museum devoted to the Mann family, writers who lived here in 1841–91. It was here that Thomas Mann wrote the saga of the Buddenbrooks, for which he was awarded the Nobel Prize in 1929. The centre exhibits an array of documents relating to this distinguished family.

③

Schabbelhaus

 Mengstrasse 48 & 52

Many of Lübeck's wealthy, patrician houses were

damaged in the bombing raids of March 1942, but carefully restored after the war. The most interesting buildings survived in Mengstrasse – especially the Schabbelhaus at No. 48. Today a restaurant, this house dates from 1558 and features an 18th-century Baroque hall.

④

Haus der Schiffergesellschaft

 Breite Strasse 2

The house of the Marine Guild, which dates from 1535, has a splendid interior and now houses one of the city's most elegant restaurants. The façade has the stepped gables that are typical of Lübeck.

⑤

Füchtingshof

 Glockengiesserstrasse 23

The eastern part of the town is very different to the west; here, narrow streets link charming *Höfe* (courtyards) and modest houses. Füchtingshof can be found at number 23, where a Baroque portal leads to 17th-century residences.

⑥
Günter-Grass-Haus

📍 Glockengiesserstr 21
🕐 Jan-Mar: 11am-5pm Tue-Sun; Apr-Dec: 10am-5pm daily 🌐 grass-haus.de

More than 1,100 exhibits (including drawings and manuscripts) here give an insight into the life and work of Nobel Prize-winning author and artist Günter Grass.

⑦
Burgtor

📍 Grosse Burgstrasse

On the northern limits of the old town stands the castle gate, a second surviving gate of the historic fortifications. A Baroque finial was added to the gate in 1685.

⑧
Jakobikirche

📍 Jakobikirchhof 3

This 15th-century church has preserved its original, mainly Baroque features. Of particular note are the main altar and the side altar in the south chapel. The latter was established around 1500

by the mayor, Heinrich Brömbse, and depicts a scene of the Crucifixion carved in sandstone.

⑨
Heiligen-Geist-Hospital

📍 Am Koberg 11 ☎ (0451) 79 07 841 🕐 Apr-Sep: 10am-5pm Tue-Sun; Oct-Mar: 10am-4pm Tue-Sun

The Holy Ghost hospital is the best-preserved medieval building of its type in central Europe. Built in the shape of the letter T, it has a shorter western section with a twin-aisled hall-church (c 1286).

⑩
Katharinenkirche

📍 Königstrasse ☎ (0451) 12 24 137 🕐 10am-5pm Fri-Sun (Nov-Mar: to 4pm)

St Catherine's, the town's only surviving monastic church, was built by the Franciscans, as is apparent from the lack of a tower and its monastic gallery in the presbytery of the main nave. In the 20th century, sculptures carved by Ernst Barlach were added.

⑪
St Annen-Museum

📍 St-Annen-Strasse 15
🕐 Jan-May: 11am-5pm Tue-Sun; Apr-Dec: 10am-5pm Tue-Sun 🌐 st-annen-museum.de

This Augustinian convent houses unusual Lübeck art treasures. There is an impressive number of wooden Gothic altars, commissioned by wealthy families for their private chapels in one of the five churches. Gems of the collection are the Hans Memling altar and the side wings of the Schonenfahrer Altar by Bernt Notke, a celebrated local artist.

⑫
Dom

📍 Mühlendamm 2-6
☎ (0451) 747 04
🕐 10am-6pm daily (Nov-Mar: to 4pm)

The most precious possession at Lübeck's cathedral is the Triumphal Cross sculpted from a 17-m (55-ft) oak tree by Bernt Notke. The giant figures, resplendent with emotion, include Adam and Eve, as well as the founder, Bishop Albert Krummedick. The 1455 bronze baptismal font by Lorenz Grove is also of note.

⑬
Travemünde

📍 Bertlingstrasse 21; www.travemuende-tourism.de

Taking its name from its location at the mouth of the River Trave, this popular seaside resort also functions as a harbour, with daily ferries leaving for places like Malmö, Helsinki and Riga. Those who stick around rather than passing through can experience the town's pristine white-sand beach and breezy Hanseatic charm.

Strandkörben beach chairs dotting the sand in Travemünde ↓

EXPERIENCE MORE

Glückstadt

D2 | **Grosse Nübelstrasse 31; www.glueckstadt-tourismus.de**

The Danish king Christian IV founded this little town in 1617. Although less impressive than Hamburg, it is worth a visit for its layout – roads radiate out from the hexagonal market square, once surrounded by fortifications. On the square stands the reconstructed 17th-century town hall as well as the Baroque Stadtkirche (town church). In 1648 parts of the duchy of Holstein were transferred to Glückstadt. Most of the palaces built to house the dukes survived, for example the Wasmer Palais, with its amazing ballroom. The **Detlefsen-Museum** is now in Brockdorff-Palais, another palace from 1632.

Detlefsen-Museum

Am Fleth 43 | **(04124) 93 76 30** | Jun-Aug: 2-6pm Wed-Sun; Sep-May: 2-5pm Wed & Sun, 2-6pm Thu-Sat

Meldorf

C1 | **Nordermarkt 10; www.meldorf-nordsee.de**

Meldorf has successfully preserved the Dithmarscher Dom, its cathedral, a 13th-century basilica with an exterior rebuilt in the 19th century. The vaulting in the transept is decorated with Gothic frescoes, depicting the legends of saints Catherine, Christopher and Nicholas. There is a richly decorated dividing wall (1603) and a grand triptych of the Crucifixion (around 1520).

Sylt

C1 | **Stephanstrasse 6, Westerland; www.sylt.de**

The island of Sylt, the largest of the North Frisian islands, has long attracted wealthy German visitors. The 50-km- (31-mile-) long island offers a rich variety of landscapes: white, sandy beaches; shifting sand dunes near List, towering up to 25 m (82ft) high; steep shorelines; the Rotes Kliff (Red Cliff) near Kampen; and the Watt, the endless expanse of mud flats in the national park, Schleswig-Holsteinisches Wattenmeer. Westerland is Sylt's main town, and its promenade, Friedrichstrasse, is "the" place to be seen. There is also a casino in a former Secessionist spa building.

Sankt Peter-Ording

C1 | **Altes Rathaus, Badallee 1; (04863) 99 90**

At the western edge of the Eiderstedt peninsula, Sankt Peter-Ording is a firm tourist favourite on the North Sea Coast, especially for nearby

Did You Know?

Sylt was a bombing range for the British Royal Air Force until it was returned to West Germany in 1952.

Hamburgers. A beach resort since the 19th century, its main draws are the scenic dunes, salt meadows and pine forests, as well as an extensive beach. Recreational opportunities range from beach strolls and hikes and horseback riding. Thanks to its exposed location and occasional high winds, it's also a popular spot for surfers and kite-surfers, while its long-standing reputation as an area of wellness means it offers lots of spa packages and services, such as sea-salt treatments. Local sights include the Westerhever lighthouse and the enjoyable West Coast Park & Sealarium.

Heligoland

🅰C1 ℹ️Lung Wai 28; www.heligoland.de

The archipelago of Heligoland lies around 50 km (31 miles) off the German coast. A former Danish and British colony, it was handed back to Germany in the 19th century in exchange for German interests in Zanzibar and parts of East Africa. Its isolated yet

strategic position has held a fascination for visitors for centuries. The main island has a fairly good infrastructure, with colourful residential houses blending with cute cafés, restaurants and the occasional spa hotel. Most people come for the sweeping sandstone cliffs, birdwatching possibilities and the feeling of remoteness. Themed trails offer insights into the island's flora and fauna, while the Heligoland Museum presents the island's fascinating history and culture. Other sights include Düne, a designated nature reserve, and the Lummenfelsen (guillemot cliffs), one of the world's smallest nature conservation area.

Flensburg

🅰D1 🚉 ℹ️Rathausstrasse 1; (0461) 90 90 920

The most northerly town in Germany, Flensburg was an important trading centre in the 16th century with 200 ships, although at times it belonged to Denmark. The Nordertor (Northern Gate),

←

Vibrantly coloured huts lining the harbour on Helgoland's main island

↑ Cone seals on a beach on the island of Düne, in the Heligoland archipelago

dating from 1595, is an emblem of the city. The shipping museum is fascinating while the Marien-kirche (St Mary's church)has a Renaissance altar, sculptures and a Last Supper painting (1598). Nearby is the Heilig-Geist-Kirche (church of the Holy Ghost), which has belonged to the town's Danish community since 1588. Other interesting churches are Nikolaikirche (St Nicholas), which boasts a magnificent Renaissance organ, and Johanniskirche (St John's), with a vaulted ceiling dating from around 1500. Its painted scenes show people disguised as animals, a covert way of criticizing the church and the system of indulgences.

Schloss Glücksburg, 9 km (6 miles) northeast of Flensburg, is a square castle with massive corner towers built in 1582–7. Visit its captivating castle chapel, the Roter Saal (Red Hall) with its low vaulting, and the valuable collection of 18th-century tapestries from Brussels. The artist Emil Nolde lived and worked in Seebüll, west of Flensburg, from the age of 20 until his death in 1956.

→ Pier stretching into the calm water at Bosau on the Grosser Plöner See

8

Holsteinische Schweiz (Holstein's Switzerland)

 D1 🚉 *i* Bahnhofstrasse 3, Malente; (04523) 984 27 30

The moraine hills, which reach a height of 164 m (538 ft), and 140 lakes are the reasons this area has been known as Holstein's Switzerland since the 19th century. The best means of transport here is the bicycle, which allows visitors to appreciate the beauty of nature and the wealth of the fauna – ornithologists have counted as many as 200 species of birds. The main centre of this holiday area is Plön on the Grosser Plöner See (lake). Nearby is Preetz, an old shoemakers' town, which has a towerless Gothic church that belonged to a former Benedictine monastery. Older still is the Romanesque church in Bosau, a small town in a picturesque location on the Grosser Plöner See. It was the first bishopric in this area, and home to Vizelin – the apostle of the Slavs.

It is also worth visiting Eutin, a small town full of picturesque buildings, which is sometimes referred to as the "Weimar of the north". The original Schloss, a brick

structure with four wings, was built in the Middle Ages as the residence of the Lübeck bishops. Worth seeing inside are the palace chapel, the Blauer Salon (Blue Salon) with Rococo stucco work, as well as paintings by Johann Heinrich Wilhelm Tischbein, which were inspired by Homer's epic *Iliad* and *Odyssey*. The castle's landscaped park is also worth strolling around.

9

Schleswig

 D1 🚉 *i* Plessenstrasse 7; www.schleswig.de

The main seat of the Vikings, the town of Schleswig became a bishop's see as early as 947, and from 1544 to 1713 it was the residence of the dukes of Schleswig-Holstein-Gottorf, once related to the rulers of Denmark and Russia. They resided in **Schloss Gottorf**, a castle that now houses the **Schleswig-Holsteinisches Landesmuseum** (regional museum) as well as northern Germany's most popular archaeological museum,

the **Archäologisches Landesmuseum**, exhibiting the *Moorleichen*, prehistoric corpses preserved in peat. It is also worth seeing the two-storey chapel (1590).

The Dom (cathedral) was built in stages between the 12th and 15th centuries. Its largest treasure is the Bordesholmer Altar, a triptych altar carved by Hans Brüggemann in 1514–21. A masterpiece of Gothic carving, it is 12 m (39 ft) high and comprises 392 figures; the only one to look straight at the visitor is the sculptor himself, bearded and hat askew (in the house of Abraham and Melchisede).

Visitors can also walk around the historic fishermen's district of Holm, and visit the **Wikinger-Museum Haithabu**,

→ *Geistkämpfer*, a statue by Ernst Barlach in front of the Nikolaikirche in Kiel

→ Lombard-Romanesque brick interior of the cathedral in Ratzeburg

about 4 km (2 miles) from the town centre. The fortifications have survived in the grounds of this ancient Viking settlement. The museum is housed in a modern building that looks like an upturned boat. Exhibits include scenes of Viking life, models of boats, jewellery and everyday items.

Schloss Gottorf, Schleswig-Holsteinisches Landesmuseum and Archäologisches Landesmuseum

🏛 🏛 🏛 ⬛ Schlossinsel 1 ☎ (04621) 81 30 ⬛ Apr–Oct: 10am–6pm daily; Nov–Mar: 10am–4pm Tue–Fri, 10am–5pm Sat & Sun

Wikinger-Museum Haithabu

🏛 ⬛ Am Haddebyer Noor 3, Busdorf ⬛ 9am–5pm daily

Kiel

⬛ D1 🚉 ℹ Andreas-Gayk-Strasse 31; www.kiel-sailing-city.de

Located at the end of the Kieler Förde inlet, Kiel marks the beginning of the Nord-Ostsee-Kanal (Kiel Canal), which has been in service since 1895, with two giant locks. Ferries depart from Kiel for Scandinavia, and in the summer the "Kieler Woche" (Kiel Week) turns the town into a mecca for yachtsmen from around the world.

A walk along the busy Schweden-Kai (embankment) and surroundings will take visitors to the vast **Rathaus** (town hall), dating from the beginning of the 20th century, and the Nikolaikirche (church of St Nicholas), which was rebuilt after the devastation of World War II, with its baptismal font and Gothic altar. Ernst Barlach created *Geistkämpfer*, the sculpture outside the church, which symbolizes the triumph of mind over matter. Pieces of the sculpture, which had been cut up by the National Socialists, were found and reassembled after the war.

The most interesting of Kiel's many museums is the **Schleswig-Holsteinisches Freilichtmuseum**, an open-air museum in Molfsee, 6 km (4 miles) from the centre of Kiel, where German rural architecture from the 16th–19th centuries is on show. Pottery, basket-making and baking are demonstrated, and the products are sold here.

Rathaus

⬛ Rathausplatz ⬛ 9am–6pm Mon–Fri, 9am–1pm Sat

Schleswig-Holsteinisches Freilichtmuseum

🏛 ⬛ Hamburger Landstrasse 97, Molfsee ☎ (0431) 65 96 60 ⬛ Apr–Oct: 10am–6pm daily; Nov–Mar: 11am–4pm Sun

---

Ratzeburg

⬛ D2 🚉 ℹ Unter den Linden 1; (04541) 800 08 86

Ratzeburg, situated on an island in the Grosser Ratzeburger See, is linked with the mainland by three causeways. The town was named after Ratibor, the duke of the Elbe river area. Henry the Lion established a missionary bishopric here in 1154, and later it became the residence of the Lauenburg dukes.

The Dom (cathedral) is one of the earliest examples of brick architecture, a style that was imported from Lombardy. The southern vestibule of the Romanesque basilica is particularly impressive – with herringbone-pattern brickwork and lines of black tiles as interior decoration. The Romanesque stalls, a 13th-century crucifix in a rainbow arch, the ducal gallery above the nave and the Baroque altar in the southern transept are some of its treasures.

A SHORT WALK
HELIGOLAND

Distance 1.5 km (1 mile) **Walking time** 20 minutes
Terrain Some uphill walking as visitors head up the cliffs
Nearest ferry terminal katamaran from Hamburg

Heligoland (*p459*) is an archipelago in the North Sea, the German islands furthest out in the open sea at 50 km (31 miles) from the mainland. What it lacks in tourist attractions, Heligoland makes up for with natural beauty – notably its rugged red cliffs contrasting against the clear blue sea – and the sense of peace that comes from an island with no traffic to remind visitors of the busy world back on the mainland.

Locator Map
For more detail see p452

Jutting alone on the north end of the island, **Lange Anna** (Tall Anna) is Helgoland's distinctive red sandstone stack.

A crater marks the spot where the British detonated a huge bomb in 1947.

In the town of **Unterland**, fishermen store their nets in the colourful houses called Hummerbuden (lobster huts).

In the upper town of Oberland stands the **Nikolaikirche**, dating from 1959. Close by, and worth a visit, are 16th-century tombs.

↑ A grey seal lounging on the beach

0 metres 300
0 yards 300
N ↑

↑ Boats moored near Helgoland's traditional *Hummerbuden* (lobster huts).

MECKLENBURG-VORPOMMERN

Mecklenburg-Vorpommern (Lower Pomerania) is a mosaic of regions with an eventful history. In the 12th century indigenous Slav tribes were colonized and converted to Christianity. In the Middle Ages several towns became rich trading centres and joined the Hanseatic League. From the 18th century, the Swedish Empire was the most powerful political force in this part of Europe, ruling Wismar until 1903, and Rügen and Stralsund until when the territories became part of Prussia, and later the German Reich. The Baltic towns suffered terrible destruction during World War II, followed by decades of neglect under the German Democratic Republic.

Although still one of the poorest states in Germany, Mecklenburg-Vorpommern has become an idyllic holiday destination. The medieval towns of Schwerin, Wismar, Rostock and Stralsund, as well as several magnificent architectural monuments, provide reason enough to visit this part of Germany, and it also offers a largely untouched landscape of forests and lakes. Along the Baltic (Ostsee) coastline, tourists delight in the beautiful sandy beaches of Darss or Usedom, but above all they head for the island of Rügen, with its distinctive white cliffs.

↗ Trelleborg

Kap Arkona

Hiddensee

0 kilometres 20
0 miles 20

N ↑

Sassnitz

NATIONALPARK VORPOMMERSCHE
BODDENLANDSCHAFT

8

RÜGEN

3

Trelleborg,
Bornholm, Baltijsk →

Prerow

Darß

Zingst

Waase

Bergen

Sellin

Barth

Putbus

Göhren

STRALSUND 17

Franzburg

Greifswalder
Bodden

105

194

96

15 PEENEMÜNDE

Grimmen

A20

11 GREIFSWALD

14 WOLGAST

109

Gnoien

MECKLENBURG-
VORPOMMERN

111

Heringsdorf
Ahlbeck

USEDOM

13

Swinoujście

Recknitz

Peene

Demmin

110

Wolin

Kummerower
See

ANKLAM 12

Usedom

Oderhaff

Teterow

Zarow

Malchin

Malchiner
See

Reuterstadt

104

Friedland

Ueckermünde

Dobieszczyn

108

Basedow

197

Torgelow

Uecker

NATIONALPARK MÜRITZ

NEUBRANDENBURG

7

A20

109

Pasewalk

Waren 2

192

Tollensesee

Stargard

Strasburg

Locknitz

Szczecin

Müritzsee

Röbel

Neustrelitz

Woldegk

198

198

Prenzlau

A11

Seenplatte

96

Mirow

Wesenberg

Strom

Penkun

Rheinsberg

MECKLENBURG-VORPOMMERN

Must Sees

1 Schwerin
2 Nationalpark Müritz
3 Rügen

Experience More

4 Ludwigslust
5 Gadebusch
6 Wismar
7 Neubrandenburg
8 Nationalpark Vorpommersche
Boddenlandschaft

9 Güstrow
10 Bad Doberan
11 Greifswald
12 Anklam
13 Usedom
14 Wolgast
15 Peenemünde
16 Rostock
17 Stralsund

A24

Neuruppin

Rhinkanal

5

The sun setting over the sandy seaside resort of Binz →

MECKLENBURG-VORPOMMERN'S
AMAZING BEACHES

Temperatures may be a little lower than in the Mediterranean but the stunning stretch of coastline in north Germany attracts locals in their droves – and is fast-becoming one of the country's best-known secrets. Here we pick some of our favourite places to enjoy its sandy shores.

A Haven at Hiddensee

Just 17 sq km (25 sq miles), the island of Hiddensee (p475) is located just off Rügen's west coast and makes for a charming and tranquil retreat – not least because it's completely car-free. Instead, you can hike, bike, ride a horse or take the Bimmelbahn toy train – or simply enjoy the scenery. The island has a long, sandy beach and rugged sand dunes to explore. Head for the sections at Vitte, Kloster and Neuendorf – these are arguably the best maintained and certainly the most popular with visitors.

→

The picturesque shoreline at Vitte, on Hiddensee

The German Riviera

Breathtaking white-sand beaches that stretch for miles, attractive promenades and piers with splendid sea views, historic towns dotted with superb Art Nouveau architecture – you've reached Rügen, Germany's largest island and quintessential slice of seaside splendour *(p474)*.

Kap Arkona, with its steep rugged cliffs, is the northernmost point of the island, while the no-less-beautiful pebble beaches at Jasmund National Park are wilder and have wonderful views out to the sea and of the surrounding cliffs and beech forest. The island also has a well-developed network of hiking and biking trails, making it the ideal place to venture off road and explore the beauty of Germany's coastline.

← Wicker beach chairs sit beneath a beautiful blue sky at Binz

↑ Fishing boat docked on the clear sea at Bansin, on the island of Usedom

Sunshine in Usedom

One of the sunniest regions in all of Germany, Usedom *(p481)* offers a 48-km- (30-mile-) long coast studded with attractive bays and long, sandy beaches. The three main villages – Heringsdorf, Ahlbeck and Bansin – all have popular beaches, as do the resorts of Drei Kaiserbäder, Bernsteinbäder and the Ostseebäder. The island is also home to wellness complexes including the Ostseetherme and luxurious Puria Spa, perfect for a spot of relaxation. Usedom is also a popular place for Polish holidaymakers – the eastern corner of the island is actually part of Poland.

↑ The colourful buildings of Schwerin's old town market square

SCHWERIN

🅰E2 🚉 🅸 Am Markt 14 🆆 schwerin.de/urlaub

The state capital is picturesquely situated amid several lakes, with a fairytale castle on an island, an enchanting old town and many historic buildings that survived World War II largely unscathed. Intellectual life flourished here in the 16th century and so the city is known as "Florence of the North".

① Schloss

🅰Schlossinsel ☎(0385) 588 415 72 🕐Mid-Apr-mid-Oct: 10am-6pm daily; mid-Oct-mid-Apr: 10am-5pm Tue-Sun

Situated on Burg island, this castle is often referred to as the Neuschwanstein of Mecklenburg, after the famous Bavarian castle. It was, in fact, largely built earlier (1843–57) to an eclectic design by Georg Adolph Demmler and Friedrich August Stüler, who were inspired by the turrets of Château Chambord in France. Major refurbishment tried to re-create some of the castle's original Renaissance features, of which some of the ceramic decorations have remained. Inside, the castle chapel built by Johann Baptist Parr in 1560–63 has survived. The elegant rooms in the castle are decorated with gilded stucco work.

② Burggarten Schlossgarten

The remaining part of the island is occupied by the Burggarten (fortress garden), which has an orangery and an artificial grotto, built from granite around 1850. A bridge leads to the larger Schlossgarten (castle garden), a favourite place for the town's inhabitants to relax. The Kreuzkanal, a canal built in 1748–56 and one of the garden's axes, is lined with copies of Baroque statues, including the *Four Seasons*, created by the renowned sculptor of the Dresden Zwinger, Balthasar Permoser.

③ Rathausplatz

The town hall square is surrounded by the homes of wealthy citizens, often with 19th-century façades concealing older walls. This is true of the Gothic town hall, which is hidden under an

> **Did You Know?**
>
> The Neo-Gothic tower of Dom St Maria und St Johannes affords a marvellous view of the entire town.

English mock-Tudor-style façade. Demmler was the architect responsible for numerous Neo-Renaissance and Neo-Gothic buildings, the showpieces of Schwerin. One of the outstanding buildings in the market square is Neues Gebäude (New Building) on the north side. This is actually a covered market from 1783, with a showpiece façade comprising 12 Doric columns.

Freilichtmuseum Schwerin-Muess

Alte Crivitzer Landstrasse 13 (0385) 20 84 10 **May-Oct: 10am-6pm Tue-Sun (Oct: to 5pm)**

The museum contains a collection of Mecklenburg folk architecture, including 17 houses of the 17th–19th centuries, which strive to recreate the look of an original village. Combine a visit with a leisurely day on the beach in Zippendorf.

Dom St Maria und St Johannes

Am Dom 4 (0385) 56 50 14 **Tower: Apr-Oct: 10am-5pm Mon-Sat, noon-5pm Sun; Nov-Mar: 11am-2pm Mon-Fri, 11am-4pm Sat, noon-3pm Sun**

This cathedral is regarded as the most important work of Gothic brick architecture in the Baltic region. The basilica, dating from 1240–1416, with its wide transept and passageway around the presbytery and its wreath of chapels, is reminiscent of the design of French cathedrals. Some of its most outstanding original features include the wooden late-Gothic multi-panelled Crucifixion, worked in sandstone; the 14th-century baptismal font; a memorial to Duchess

Helene of Mecklenburg created by the Vischer workshop in Nürnberg; and the tombstones of Duke Christoph and his wife.

Staatliches Museum

Am Alten Garten 3 **10am-6pm Tue-Sun (Nov-Mar: to 5pm)** **museum-schwerin.de**

The state art museum stands in Alter Garten, one of the most attractive squares in Germany, where the waters reflect the castle and Neo-Renaissance theatre. The museum houses an art collection based on that of Duke Christian Ludwig II, a testimony to his taste and erudition. As well as works by German and Dutch painters Hals and Fabritius, it holds

↑ *Family Recital* (1658) by Frans van Mieris the Elder, Staatliches Museum

works by many French artists. This includes 34 paintings by Jean-Baptiste Oudry, who was court painter to Louis XV, as well as paintings by Dadaist artist Marcel Duchamp and sculptures by Expressionist artist Ernst Barlach.

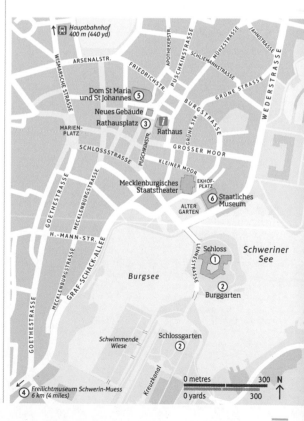

2

NATIONALPARK MÜRITZ

🄰 E2 🄰 Schlossplatz 3, 17237 Hohenzieritz 𝒊 Neuer Markt 21, Waren; Neustrelitz, Strelitzerstraße 1; www.mueritz-nationalpark.de

This scenic national park sprawls across 322 sq km (124 sq miles) and offers visitors a unique landscape in the heart of Germany's farmland. Part of the Pomerania Lake District, Nationalpark Müritz is a diverse patchwork of ancient beech forests and endless expanses of water. The park is also a great spot to take part in outdoor activities, from sailing to hiking.

This region, between Neubrandenburg and Schwerin, is commonly referred to as "the land of a thousand lakes", with more than 100 dotting the area. The largest of these is Müritzsee, and a national park was established to the east of this in 1990. Müritz, which translates as "small sea", is the second largest lake in Germany after Lake Constance, and perhaps the most popular attraction in the park. Tourists flock here for the breathtaking scenery, which can be easily explored via an impressive network of trails. The area similarly draws fans of watersports, as kayaks and canoes are permitted on certain lakes. There are also good opportunities for wildlife spotting, and the Müritzeum visitor centre, featuring 50 species of fish, aquatic plants and crustaceans, shouldn't be missed.

1 A boat skimming across Kolpinsee, one of the region's lakes, at sunset.

2 The irregular, three-winged palace in Basedow, one of the historic castles that dot the national park.

3 Stargard castle in the Mecklenburgische Schweiz (Swiss Mecklenburg), a particularly attractive area of the lake district.

Did You Know?

White-tailed eagles, which have the largest wingspan of the species, can be spotted in the park.

↑ An aerial view of the national park's wide lakes and lush greenery

A HIKERS' PARADISE

As well as being a nature reserve, National Park Müritz also serves as a recreation area for visitors who want to take advantage of the area's abundant opportunities for outdoor sports. The park is criss-crossed with an extensive network of foot- and cycle paths, with options for seasoned hikers and cyclists as well as those with less experience who just want to enjoy the fresh air. Occasional viewing points offer wonderful vistas of the country-side, and make for rewarding places to stop and rest on your outdoor adventures. There are also two waterside walks which present a particularly pleasant stroll, and guided nature walks led by experienced tour guides.

↑ White-sand beach outside the lovely Binz resort

3

RÜGEN

🅰 F1 🚊 *i* Markt 23, Bergen; Heinrich-Heine-Strasse 7, Binz; Achtern Diek 18, Hiddensee and Alleestrasse 2, Putbus; www.ruegen.de

The largest of Germany's islands, Rügen is also the most beautiful and diverse, featuring steep cliffs, sandy beaches, a hilly, forest-covered hinterland and rugged coastline that extends for hundreds of miles. Variously ruled by the Huns, Slavs, Danes and Swedes, Rügen came under Prussian rule in 1815. In 1936 it was linked to the mainland by the 1-km- (half-a-mile-) long Rügendamm bridge.

①

Ostseebad Binz

🌐 ostseebad-binz.de

Rügen's most popular seaside resort, Binz has a beautiful white beach, grand early 20th-century villas and a pier. Enjoy a stroll along its elegant promenade or take in great vistas from the viewing platform of Jagdschloss Granitz, the town's hunting lodge. Just north of this are the ruins of Prora, a Nazi-era holiday resort that now houses a modern hotel and group of apartments.

②

Waase

The small but charming village of Waase is situated just before the bridge that links Ummanz to Rügen, and is an ideal place to break for some sightseeing. In many ways a typical fishing village, offering low-key activities such as pedal boating and a number of top-notch seafood restaurants, Waase is also home to an unusual work of art: a beautiful carved altarpiece from Antwerp, which dates from around 1520.

③

Jasmund Peninsula

Situated in the northeast of Rügen, the Jasmund peninsula is characterized by its wonderful forests (especially those in Stubnitz, a UNESCO natural World Heritage site), its coastal atmosphere and dramatic white cliffs – as depicted by Romantic artist Caspar David Friedrich. The port town of Sassnitz serves as the primary gateway to the peninsula.

④

Nationalpark Jasmund

🅰 Stubbenkammer 2a, Sassnitz 🌐 nationalpark-jasmund.de

The Jasmund National Park – Germany's smallest at just 30 sq km (12 sq miles) – is a stunning nature reserve on the Jasmund peninsula. Founded in 1990, the park possesses the largest chalk cliffs in Germany, the so-called Königsstuhl ("King's Chair"), which rise up to 118 m (387 ft) above the Baltic Sea.

Behind the cliffs lie undisturbed beech forests that date back over 700 years. There is also an abundance of flora and fauna in the park, including a number of protected orchid varieties, such as the striking lady's slipper. Numerous hiking trails and cycle paths allow visitors to explore the park and wider peninsula. One of the most attractive walks begins at the Königsstuhl, continuing along the cliff-top path past a number of other viewpoints to end at Sassnitz.

⑤ Hiddensee

This tranquil, car-free island, which is just under 19 sq km (7 sq miles), is a must-visit for those in the area. It's accessible via ferry from Stralsund or Schaprode on Rügen, and horse-drawn carts and bikes replace motors on the streets. The scenery, too, makes it a wonderful place to unwind: here you'll find white sandy beaches, rugged cliffs and pristine pine forests. The island is also part of the Boddenlandschaft National Park (p478) and a protected breeding ground for many bird species, including terns, cranes, ducks, and waders. Guided walks are available in summer and there are places to stay and eat on the island.

⑥ Kap Arkona

🌐 kap-arkona.de

The rugged cliffs of Kap Arkona, which rise 45 m (148 ft) above the crashing waves below, are at Rügen's northern tip. Famed for its two lighthouses – a smaller one built in 1827 that is now a museum, and a larger one that was built in 1902 and is still in use – the cape is also home to a number of military bunker complexes, which can still be viewed today. Other attractions include a temple fortress, as well as a few inns and restaurants.

⑦ Putbus

This elegant late Neo-Classical town, on Rügen's southeastern coast, was modelled on Bad Doberan in 1807. Its centre-piece is the theatre, which was built in 1819 to a design by Wilhelm Steinbach, but its plaza – "the Circus" – is its social hub.

↑ Kap Arkona's Peilturm, a brick-built marine navigation tower

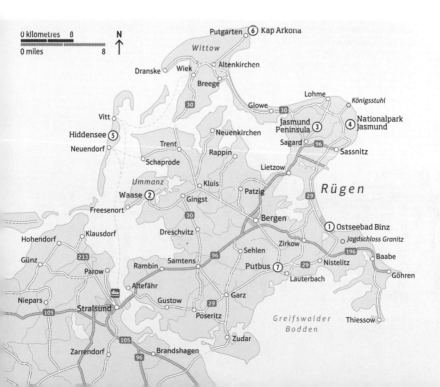

4

Ludwigslust

🅰 E2 🚌 ℹ Schlossstrasse 36; www.stadtludwigslust.de

At the beginning of the 18th century, the small village of Klenow was founded here; from 1765 it grew into a town, which was laid out around the opulent **Schloss**, residence of the dukes of Mecklenburg-Schwerin until 1837. Although known as the "Versailles of Mecklenburg" it is quite different from its French namesake. The Baroque palace was built entirely in brick, concealed beneath sandstone from the Ruda hills. The ornate interior, particularly the elegant Goldener Saal (Gold Hall), was decorated in Ludwigsluster Carton, a type of papier-mâché, to cut costs.

In the mid-19th century, the vast Schlosspark was redesigned by Peter Joseph Lenné as an English-style landscaped garden. On a scenic walk round the large grounds, the visitor can discover some 24 waterfalls, a canal, artificial ruins, a stone bridge and the mausoleum of Helena Pavlovna, daughter of Tsar Peter I. In the town stands the Protestant **Stadtkirche** (town church), built in 1765–70 to look like an antique temple.

Schloss

 📞 (03874) 571 90 🕐 10am–6pm Tue–Sun (mid-Oct–mid-Apr: to 5pm)

Stadtkirche

🏠 Kirchenplatz 📞 (03874) 219 68 🕐 Times vary, scall ahead

5

Gadebusch

🅰 D2 🚌 ℹ Mühlenstrasse 19; www.gadebusch.de

This small town, next to the former East–West border, has two interesting historic monuments. The Stadtkirche (1220) is the oldest brick church in Mecklenburg. Its cross vaulting, chunky pillars and goblet-shaped capitals are Romanesque in style. One of its most precious pieces is the bronze baptismal font (1450). In the 16th and 17th centuries, the Schloss was the residence of distant relations of the dukes of Mecklenburg. It is not open to visitors.

6

Wismar

🅰 E2 🚌 ℹ Lübsche Strasse 23a; (03841) 194 33

Wismar is undoubtedly one of the most attractive towns in Mecklenburg. During the Middle Ages it was an important Hanseatic centre, as evidenced by the monumental brick church, which is completely out of proportion with the provincial town of today. After the Thirty Years' War, in 1648, the Swedes were established in the town, and rebuilt it as the strongest fortress in Europe. In 1803 they leased Wismar to Mecklenburg, but never claimed it back. The town's centrepiece is its grand market

→ Market square in Wismar, with the wellhouse in the foreground

square, in the middle of which is the Wasserspiele (wellhouse), a Dutch-Renaissance pavilion from 1602. Until 1897 water was piped here from a source 4 km (2 miles) away to supply 220 private and 16 public buildings. The most beautiful house on the square is the Alter Schwede (Old Swede), built about 1380, with a protruding Gothic brick gable. To the west of the market there are two churches which act as sad examples of the GDR's neglect of its historical legacy. The reconstruction of the Georgenkirche, damaged in World War II, was begun in

> To the west of the market there are two churches, which act as sad examples of the GDR's neglect of its historical legacy.

The Schloss at Ludwigslust, commonly known as the "Versailles of Mecklenburg"

1989, and it will soon be returned to its former glory. The Marienkirche has only one surviving tower – the ruined nave was blown up in 1960.

Nearby lies the Fürstenhof, the former residence of the dukes of Wismar. The north wing is the most interesting – its Mannerist style was inspired by the Italian town of Ferrari and north European ceramic traditions (such as Lübeck workshop). The magnificent sandstone portal is flanked by pairs of inter-twined fauns. Nikolaikirche (church of St Nicholas) is a gem of Wismar architecture. Spared in World War II, the façade of this late-Gothic basilica from the 14th and 15th centuries is decorated with glazed friezes of mythological creatures, saints and, at the peak of the transept, a huge rose window. The proportions of the interior and the height of the vaulted main nave, measuring 37 m (121 ft), are captivating. Some of the interior fixtures and fittings came from other churches in the city, which were either ruined or no longer exist, including the Krämeraltar with a sculpture of the Beautiful Madonna and Child (around 1420). The room by the tower has the most complete cycle of frescoes in the region (around 1450).

← The Schloss at Ludwigslust, commonly known as the "Versailles of Mecklenburg"

7

Neubrandenburg

F2 i Marktplatz 1; www.neubrandenburg-touristinfo.de

Founded in 1248 as a sister town to Brandenburg on the Havel, Neubrandenburg prospered as a trading centre until the Thirty Years' War, following which it fell into disrepair. It now has probably the only example of post-World War II concrete tower blocks surrounded by medieval town walls. The walls are interspersed with half-timbered houses, known as *Wiekhäuser*. Of the four city gates the most interesting are Friedländer Tor (begun in 1300), as well as Neues and Stargarder Tor.

EAT

Wiekhaus 45
This cute tavern in the town walls serves delicious regional dishes. It has a good range of wines and outdoor seating in the warmer months.

F2 Ringstrasse 4, Neubrandenburg
w wiekhaus45.de

€€€

---

8 Nationalpark Vorpommersche Boddenlandschaft

🅰 E/F1 🅰 Nationalparkamt Vorpommern, Im Forst 5 Born am Darss 🆆 nationalpark-vorpommersche-boddenlandschaft.de

The Western Pomerania Lagoon Area National Park stretches from the Darss-Zingst peninsula towards the west coast of Rügen and offers an alluring and diverse landscape of cliffs, dunes, beaches lagoons and spits. The name in German refers to the park's *Bodden*, shallow lagoons, cut off from the Baltic, that contain a briny, brackish mix of salt and fresh water and can be explored via boat tours. The park also contains woodlands such as the Osterwald and Darss forests, which have walking trails. Known as a meeting point for cranes, the park sees around 86,000 of them arrive every autumn, but visitors might also spot red deer and wild boar among the array of flora and fauna. Related attractions include the lighthouse at Darsser Ort on the northern tip of the peninsula and the car-free island of Hiddensee (p475).

Did You Know?

Vorpommersche Boddenlandschaft is the largest national park on the Baltic coast.

9 Güstrow

🅰 E2 🅰 🆔 Franz-Parr-Platz 10; www.guestrow.de

Güstrow is one of the most architecrually harmonious towns of the former German Democratic Republic, with an attractive old town, unmarred by prefabricated tower blocks. All the most important monuments are within easy reach. The town is dominated by the Schloss, built from 1558 by Franz Parr, a member of a renowned family of sculptors and architects from northern Italy. German, Italian and Dutch elements come together here, including fantastical chimneys and two-storey arcades in the courtyards. The architect's brother decorated the Festsaal (ballroom) with a hunting frieze – the stucco heads of the deer have real antlers.

In the nearby Dom, a brick cathedral of the 13th and 14th centuries, there is a fascinating Gothic altar (around 1500). Look for the vast figures of the apostles on the pillars of the nave and the 16th-century tomb of Duke Ulrich and his two wives, with a large genealogical family tree of all three of them. In the north nave hangs the burly *Schwebende* (Hovering Angel), a remarkable work by Ernst Barlach, who lived here from 1910 until his death in 1938. He described his works to Bertolt Brecht as: "beautiful without beautifying, sizeable without enlarging, harmonious without smoothness, and full of vitality without brutality". Barlach's work bore the brunt of National Socialist condemnation – the original *Schwebende* was melted down and made into cannons but the artistic impression that replaced it was made from the original plaster cast. Other works by Barlach are in the museum dedicated to him.

→ Darsser Ort lighthouse and a red fox *(inset)* in the National Park

↑ A steam train on the narrow-gauge "Molli" railway, Bad Doberan

It is worth concluding a visit in the market, near which stands the Pfarrkirche St Marien (parish church of St Mary). This has a magnificent high altar, a panelled work of art with painted wings by Belgian artists (around 1522).

The **Archäologisches Freilichtmuseum** in Gross-Raden, near Sternberg, is popular with tourists as well as archaeology students.

Archäologisches Freilichtmuseum

 🏛 Gross-Raden
🕿 (03847) 22 52 🕐 Apr-Oct: 10am-5:30pm daily; Nov-Mar: 10am-4:30pm Tue-Sun

---

🔟
Bad Doberan

🅰 E1 🚉 🛈 Severinstrasse 6; (038203) 770 52

When Duke Heinrich Borwin was hunting deer, a passing swan reportedly shouted "*Dobr Dobr*" (a good location) as the deer fell. Borwin duly founded the most important Cistercian monastery of the Baltic region here. The **Doberaner Münster** was built in 1295–1368, with a severe interior and a small bell, in accordance with the order's rules which stipulate that no tower should be built. The interior is fascinating, its walls surfaced in red, with white plasterwork and colourful ribbing. Most of the original fixtures and fittings have survived almost intact. Among the treasures are a vast, gilded panelled painting, produced in Lübeck in 1310, a 12-m (39-ft) Holy Sacrament made from oak, a small cupboard holding the chalice and relics from an earlier Romanesque building, as well as a statue of the Virgin Mary. Beautiful tombs mark the resting places of the rulers of Mecklenburg, of the Danish Queen Margaret, and Albrecht, King of Sweden, who died in 1412. Visitors can walk around the outside of the church, which has a pleasant lawn. Beyond, you can find a small octagonal building, decorated with glazed brickwork – this lovely piece of 13th-century architecture is the morgue.

A stroll around the health spa is also recommended. Right in its centre it has two early 19th-century pavilions with Chinese features – an ideal place for a coffee break. Another adventure is a trip on the "Molli", a narrow-gauge railway that links Bad Doberan with Heiligendamm and Kühlungsborn, where there is a 4-km- (2-mile-) long beach. On the way, a little gem of 13th-century country architecture, the church in Steffenshagen, calls for a visit. On its south portal are terracotta figures of the apostles, while across the presbytery runs a brickwork relief with mythological creatures.

Doberaner Münster

🕥 🏛 Klosterstrasse 2
🕐 May-Sep: 9am-6pm daily (from 11am Sun); Mar, Apr & Oct: 10am-5pm daily (from 11am Sun); Nov-Feb: 10am-4pm daily (from 11am Sun)
🔲 muenster-doberan.de

 PICTURE PERFECT
Birdwatching

Birdwatchers have a lot to look forward to in the Western Pomerania Lagoon Area National Park. A host of gulls, ducks and other water-dwelling birds can be easily spotted across the park.

The ruined monastery of Eldena, just outside Greifswald

Greifswald

🅰F1 🚉 ℹ Rathaus Am Markt; www.greifswald. info

This former Hanseatic town is situated 5 km (3 miles) from the Bay of Greifswald. From afar the picturesque silhouette of the town with its three church towers, nicknamed Fat Mary, Little Jakob and Long Michael, appears like a painting by Caspar David Friedrich – the town's most famous resident – come to life. Charm pervades the old town, its architectural mix resulting from 40 years of East German rule. Greifswald, an important academic centre and market town, has geared up more for tourism since 1989. It is certainly worth a visit –

INSIDER TIP
Trip to Poland

Around a quarter of Usedom island belongs to Poland. The main Polish settlement is Świnoujście (known as Swinemünde in German), a lovely day trip. Many ferries leave from the port here for Scandinavia.

---

a short walk from east to west enables visitors to see all the most important monuments in town.

The 14th-century Marienkirche has a vast square tower, giving it a rather squat appearance and its nickname, Fat Mary. Inside, the church contains the remains of frescoes and an amazing Renaissance pulpit depicting the Reformation figures of Luther, Bugenhagen and Melanchthon. The Gemäldegalerie has a collection of paintings by Caspar David Friedrich, including his remarkable landscapes of the ruined monastery of Eldena, *Ruined Eldena in the Riesengebirge*, which he transposed to the mountains of present-day Poland and Czech Republic.

The market square with its Baroque town hall is surrounded by handsome patrician houses, with exemplary rich brickwork façades (particularly Nos. 11 and 13). Nearby rises the vast Dom St Nikolai. The cathedral's octagonal tower, topped with a Baroque helm, affords extensive views of

the town. The Rubenow-Bild (1460), one of the paintings inside, depicts the founding professor of Greifswald's university in front of Mary, Mother of God.

Wieck, an attractive working fishing village, is now incorporated into Greifswald. It has a drawbridge dating from 1887, reminiscent of typical Dutch bridges. The Cistercian monastery of Eldena, just 1 km (half a mile) south of Wieck district, was immortalized by the Romantic paintings of Caspar David Friedrich. The monastery was founded in 1199 and plundered by the Swedes in 1637. Its ruined red walls amid the green grass and trees look wildly romantic.

Anklam

🅰F2 🚉 ℹ Rathaus, Markt 3; www.anklam.de

A former Hanseatic town, Anklam's erstwhile importance is revealed by its vast defensive walls, in which is set the mid-15th-century city gate, Steintor. It is worth visiting

The beach at Ahlbeck, Usedom, with the pier in the background

the Gothic Marienkirche. Inside, the church's octagonal pillars and the arches of its arcades are painted with graceful figures, which reveal a Lübeck influence. The **Otto-Lilienthal-Museum** recalls the life and work of this inventor, born here in 1848. After observing storks, he built a flying machine and completed his first flight in 1891. He created 2,000 machines, none of which flew further than 350 m (1,150 ft).

Otto-Lilienthal-Museum
⊗ 🎨 🖼 📍 Ellbogenstrasse 1
🕐 Jun–Sep: 10am–5pm daily; Oct & May: 10am–5pm Tue–Fri, 1pm–5pm Sat & Sun; Nov–Apr: 11am–3:30pm Wed–Fri, 1pm–3:30pm Sun
🌐 lilienthal-museum.de

Usedom

🅰️ F2 🖼 📍 Delbrückstrasse 69, Heringsdorf; Dünenstrasse 45, Ahlbeck; www.kaiserbaeder-auf-usedom.de

The island, named after the town of Usedom and separated from the mainland by the Peenestrom, is the second largest in Germany at 445 sq km (172 sq miles). A small corner in the east was incorporated into Poland after 1945. Usedom is as attractive as Rügen, possessing white beaches, forests, peat bogs and bays overgrown with rushes in the south. It is linked with the mainland by two drawbridges (near Anklam and Wolgast). The resorts follow one after the other like pearls on a string: Bansin, Heringsdorf and Ahlbeck – known as the "three sisters" – are connected by a wide beach. At the beginning of the 20th century they evolved into elegant holiday resorts, with white villas, hotels and boarding houses, as typical of seaside towns of that era. Worth a visit is the industrialist Oechsler's house in Heringsdorf (Delbrückstrasse 5), which has an antique appearance with mosaics on its façade. During the past few years, the early 20th-century piers in all three spas have been rebuilt and restored. The longest, in Heringsdorf, is also the second largest in Europe, after one in Poland. The Marienkirche (St Mary's church), one of the island's main attractions, was erected in the 19th century.

> **Wolgast castle was destroyed in 1713, when Peter the Great ordered the town to be burned. A notable surviving building is the 12-sided cemetery chapel.**

Wolgast

🅰️ F1 🖼 📍 Rathausplatz 10; www.stadt-wolgast.de

Originally the seat of the Pomeranian-Wolgast dukes, Wolgast Castle was destroyed in 1713, when Peter the Great ordered the town to be burned. A notable surviving building is the 12-sided cemetery chapel. The most valuable work of art can now be seen in Pfarrkirche St Petri, a 14th-century parish church. Dating from the turn of the 18th century, the *Totentanz* frieze is an imitation of the *Dance of Death* by Hans Holbein in Basle. The city's other main attraction is the **Philipp-Otto-Runge-Gedenkstätte**, the family home of the painter and adopted son of Hamburg, Philipp Otto Runge. The house hosts performances for the town's annual cultural event.

Philipp-Otto-Runge-Gedenkstätte
⊗ 📍 Kronwieckstrasse 45
☎ (03836) 20 30 41 🕐 May–Oct: 11am–6pm Tue–Fri, 11am–4pm Sat & Sun

Peenemünde

A F1 **ℹ** Peeneplatz 6; (038371) 216 56

Historically, the most interesting spot on the island of Usedom is the **Historisch-Technisches Museum** at Peenemünde, located on former military territory. It shows the evolution of space travel, pioneered at this research station since 1936. During World War II, long-distance rockets, powered by liquid fuel and known as V-2 (*Vergeltungswaffe*; retaliatory weapon), were produced here, which inflicted heavy damage on the cities of London and Antwerp in 1944.

Historisch-Technisches Museum

⊛⊜⊕ **A** Im Kraftwerk **C** Apr–Sep: 10am–6pm daily (Oct–Mar: to 4pm) **N** Nov–Mar: Mon **w** museum-peenemuende.de

---

 Rostock

A E1 **🚌** **ℹ** Universitätsplatz 6, Warnemünde, Am Strom 59; www.rostock.de

The history of the most important German port in the Baltic has been turbulent. This prosperous Hanseatic town had established trade links with distant ports such as Bergen (Norway), Riga (Latvia) and Bruges (Belgium) as early as the 15th century. In 1419 the first university in northern Europe was founded here, and the town flourished again in the 19th century. After it suffered heavy damage in the Allied air raids of 1942, Rostock was rebuilt as the GDR's showpiece.

Kröpelinerstrasse, the most popular street in the city, is lined by 17th- to 19th-century houses. In summer students gather around the "Brunnen der Lebensfreude" (Fountain of Happiness) on Universitätsplatz (university square).

The main university building, dating from 1867–70, is in Neo-Renaissance style. The southern part of the square is occupied by a palace with a beautiful Baroque hall where concerts are hosted. A Neo-Classical annexe with a Doric colonnade (1823) stands nearby. A statue on the square commemorates the town's most famous resident, Field Marshal Blücher, who helped defeat Napoleon at Waterloo.

Between Rostock and Stralsund lies a delightful coastal area. The peninsula attracts visitors to its quiet, beautiful beaches and splendid natural scenery. Particularly attractive are the villages of Ahrenshoop, which was an artists' colony; Prerow, which has traditional fishermen's houses; and Wieck, with its charming thatched houses. A national park has been established here.

←

The brightly coloured houses in Rostock's old town

 Educational displays
in the OZEANEUM
building in Stralsund

Did You Know?

In 2010, the OZEANEUM received the European Museum of the Year Award.

17

Stralsund

 F1 🚇 🚇 Universitäts-
platz 6 and Am Strom 59,
Warnemünde; www.
stralsundtourismus.de

The town centre of Stralsund
is surrounded by water on all
sides, but all the most interesting historic monuments
are easily accessible on foot.

Alter Markt, the old market
square, affords the best view
of the filigree façade of the
Rathaus (town hall), beyond
which stands the vast edifice
of the Nikolaikirche (church of
St Nicholas). It is surrounded
by houses from various eras,
of which the two most
important are the Gothic
Wulflamhaus, and the
Commandantenhaus,
Baroque headquarters of
the town's former Swedish
commandant. The Rathaus
dates from the 13th century
with a 14th-century façade
and ground-floor arcades, and
resembles the one in Lübeck.
In 1370 the Hanseatic League

and the defeated Danish king
signed a peace treaty here.
The Nikolaikirche, built from
1270–1360, was inspired by
French Gothic cathedrals as
well as the Marienkirche in
Lübeck. Its free-standing
flying buttresses are in brick
rather than the more usual
stone. Inside there are several
intriguing furnishings, such as
the statue of St Anna (around
1290) and fragments of the
Novgorod stall with various
fascinating scenes, including
one of hunting for sables.
The Baroque main altar
was designed in 1798 by
Andreas Schlüter.

The Katharinen kloster,
a former 15th-century
Dominican abbey, now houses
the **Kulturhistorisches
Museum**, with its historic
exhibitions, including copies
of the extraordinary Viking
treasure from Hiddensee.

The **Deutsches Meeres-
museum** (German Oceano-
graphic Museum), based in a
former Dominican convent and
the Ozeanum building, has

almost 100 aquariums with
sharks, marine turtles, and a
16-m- (52-ft-) long skeleton of
a fin whale. It is also a scientific establishment researching
the life of sea organisms.

Dominating the Neuer Mark
is the town's largest church,
Marienkirche (St Mary's),
built in 1383–1473, with an
octagonal tower (with good
views of Stralsund).

Kulturhistorisches
Museum

♿ 🏛 📍 Mönchstrasse 25/27
📞 (0381) 12 87 90 🕐 Feb-
Nov: 10am-5pm daily

Deutsches
Meeresmuseum

♿ 🏛 📍 Katharinenberg 14
📞 (03831) 265 210 🕐 10am-
6pm daily (Oct-May: to 5pm)

> 💬 INSIDER TIP
> ### Medieval Walls
>
> Only two gates and a
> section of wall survive
> from Rostock's medieval
> defences. It's a pleasant
> walk between the
> 55-m- (180-ft-) tall
> Kröpeliner Tor and the
> Steintor following the
> line of the old ramparts.

NEED TO KNOW

Sylvenstein Lake in the Bavarian Alps

Before You Go.............................486

Getting Around.........................488

Practical Information...........................492

BEFORE YOU GO

Things change, so plan ahead to make the most of your trip. Be prepared for all eventualities by considering the following points before you travel.

AT A GLANCE

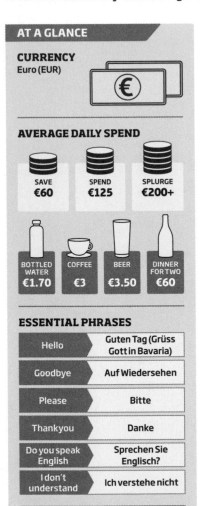

CURRENCY
Euro (EUR)

AVERAGE DAILY SPEND

SAVE	SPEND	SPLURGE
€60	€125	€200+

BOTTLED WATER	COFFEE	BEER	DINNER FOR TWO
€1.70	€3	€3.50	€60

ESSENTIAL PHRASES

Hello	Guten Tag (Grüss Gott in Bavaria)
Goodbye	Auf Wiedersehen
Please	Bitte
Thankyou	Danke
Do you speak English	Sprechen Sie Englisch?
I don't understand	Ich verstehe nicht

ELECTRICITY SUPPLY

Power sockets are type C and F, both fitting two-pronged plugs. Standard voltage is 230 volts.

Passports and Visas

For entry requirements, including visas, consult your nearest German embassy or check the **German Federal Foreign Office** website. EU nationals and citizens of the UK, US, Canada, Australia and New Zealand do not need visas for stays of up to three months.
German Federal Foreign Office
w auswaertiges-amt.de

Government Advice

Now more than ever, it is important to consult both your and the German government's advice before travelling. The **UK Foreign and Commonwealth Office**, the **US State Department**, the **Australian Department of Foreign Affairs and Trade** and the German Federal Foreign Office offer the latest information on security, health and local regulations.
Australian Department of Foreign Affairs and Trade
w smartraveller.gov.au
UK Foreign and Commonwealth Office
w gov.uk/foreign-travel-advice
US State Department
w travel.state.gov

Customs Information

You can find information on the laws relating to goods and currency taken in or out of Germany on the Federal Customs Service (**Zoll**) website.
Zoll
w zoll.de

Insurance

We strongly recommend taking out a comprehensive insurance policy covering theft, loss of belongings, medical care, cancellations and delays, and make sure you read the small print very carefully.

UK citizens are eligible for free emergency medical care in Germany provided they have a valid European Health Insurance Card (**EHIC**) or UK Global Health Insurance Card (**GHIC**).

EHIC
ec.europa.eu
GHIC
ghic.org.uk

Vaccinations

No inoculations are needed for Germany.

Booking Accommodation

Germany offers a variety of accommodation to suit any budget, ranging from luxury five-star hotels to family run B&Bs and budget hostels.

Lodgings can fill up during the busy summer months (or winter months in the Alps), and prices are inflated during these peak seasons, so it's worth booking in advance. Keep an eye out for major events in your chosen destinations, as these can also push hotel prices higher. This can include trade fairs in big cities like Frankfurt or regional festivals such as Oktoberfest in Munich.

Individual city tourism websites usually have lists of inspected accommodation, but popular booking websites tend to offer a greater variety.

Money

Major credit, debit and prepaid currency cards are accepted in most shops and establishments. Contactless payments have become the norm since the COVID-19 pandemic, though they are not generally used on public transport. It is always worth carrying cash, as some smaller businesses don't accept card. A tip of 5–10 per cent is customary if service is particularly good.

Travellers with Specific Requirements

Germany is ahead of the curve when it comes to barrier-free travel. Most public transport, tourist sights and accommodation facilities cater for those with mobility issues. Request airport assistance through your airline in advance. The **Travel for All** project reviews and certifies places of tourist interest for accessibility. Stations have grooved platform borders to assist the visually impaired, and guide dogs are allowed on all public transport.
Travel for All
reisen-fuer-alle.de

Language

German is the official language, but in large, international cities like Berlin and Frankfurt am Main the use of English is almost as prevalent as German. You can generally get by without knowing a word of German, but a few niceties in the local language are usually appreciated before continuing in English. English is commonly spoken throughout the tourist industry but outside large towns you may still encounter people who speak only German.

Opening Hours

> **COVID-19** The pandemic continues to affect Germany. Some sights and hospitality venues are operating on reduced or temporary opening hours, and require visitors to make advance bookings. Always check ahead before visiting.

Monday Some museums and tourist attractions are closed for the day.
Sunday Most shops and small businesses close early or for the entire day.
Public holidays Post offices and banks are closed for the entire day; shops normally close, museums and attractions are usually open.

PUBLIC HOLIDAYS	
1 Jan	New Year's Day
Mar/Apr	Good Friday
Mar/Apr	Easter Sunday
Mar/Apr	Easter Monday
1 May	Labour Day
30 May	Ascension Day
10 Jun	Whit Monday
3 Oct	Day of German Unity
25 Dec	Christmas Day
26 Dec	St Stephen's Day

GETTING
AROUND

Whether you are visiting for a city break or a rural country retreat, discover how best to reach your destination and travel like a pro.

AT A GLANCE

PUBLIC TRANSPORT COSTS

BERLIN

€3.80

Single journey

MUNICH

€3.30

Single journey

FRANKFURT

€2.90

Single journey

SPEED LIMIT

REGIONAL ROADS

100 km/h (60mph)

RURAL ROADS

70 km/h (43mph)

MOTORWAY

130 km/h (80mph)

URBAN AREAS

50 km/h (30mph)

Arriving by Air

Germany's major airports are Frankfurt am Main, Munich, Berlin-Brandenburg and Düsseldorf. These airports are outside the city centres, but are well-connected by public transport or coaches that can take you from the airport right into the heart of the city centre.

The country's national carrier, Lufthansa, operates regular, scheduled flights to most of the world's major cities. Other airlines such as British Airways and Ryanair also offer regular flights to Germany from London as well as from a handful of regional airports in the United Kingdom. The US is well served, with flights to German cities, particularly to Frankfurt am Main, which is Germany's largest airport and one of the busiest in Europe.

Train Travel

Train is the best way to get around Germany, which has an efficient high-speed network and a reliable local service.

International Train Travel

There are regular rail services into Germany from many European cities. A common route into Germany from the UK is to take the Eurostar to Brussels or Paris, where there are regular connecting services into Germany.

Domestic Train Travel

Deutsche Bahn (**DB**) operates the vast majority of services in Germany. The fastest trains – InterCity Express (ICE) – connect the largest cities, and can travel at more than 200 km/h (125 mph). This means that crossing almost the entire country on a journey from Hamburg to Munich takes only 6 hours.

Somewhat slower but less expensive are the InterCity (IC) trains. When travelling over shorter distances it is often quicker to take the Regional Express (RE) trains. Many other companies operate lines that connect the smaller or less-frequented towns.

DB

w www.bahn.de

GETTING TO AND FROM THE AIRPORT

Airport	Distance to City	Time by Taxi	Public Transport	Journey Time
Berlin-Brandeburg	27 km (16.8 miles)	45 mins	Airport Express (FEX)	25 mins
			S-Bahn	30 mins
Köln-Bonn	Bonn: 28 km (17.5 miles)	Bonn: 15 mins	Bonn: Bus	35 mins
	Köln: 17 km (10.5 miles)	Köln: 10 mins	Köln: bus	45 mins
Dresden	9 km (5.5 miles)	25 mins	Bus	30 mins
Düsseldorf	8 km (5 miles)	25 mis	S-Bahn	13 mins
Frankfurt	10 km (6 miles)	20 mins	Train	11 mins
			S-Bahn	10 mins
Hamburg	13 km (8 miles)	30 mins	Bus	30 mins
Hanover	12 km (7.5 miles)	20 mins	S-Bahn	13 mins
Leipzig-Halle	Leipzig: 20 km (12 miles)	Leipzig: 30 mins	Leipzig: S-Bahn	15 mins
	Halle: 24 km (15 miles)	Halle: 40 mins	Halle: S-Bahn	12 mins
Munich	40 km (25 miles)	45 mins	S-Bahn	40 mins
			Bus	45 mins
Nürnberg	6 km (4 miles)	20 mins	Bus	45 mins
			U-Bahn	12 mins

RAIL JOURNEY PLANNER

Plotting Germany's major train routes according to journey time, this map is a handy reference for inter-city rail travel. Times given are for the fastest available service.

Berlin to Potsdam	30 mins
Berlin to Dresden	2 hrs
Munich to Berchtesgaden	3 hrs
Munich to Berlin	4 hrs
Munich to Stuttgart	2.5 hrs
Stuttgart to Heidelberg	1 hr
Heidelberg to Frankfurt	1 hr
Frankfurt to Köln	1.5 hrs
Köln to Bremen	3 hrs
Bremen to Hamburg	1 hr
Hamburg to Berlin	2 hrs

Long-Distance Bus Travel

Flixbus operates a dense network of national bus services linking all major cities as well as many minor ones. Tickets are cheapest when bought in advance. Flixbus also runs many international services across Europe.

Other companies you might encounter are **Eurolines**, **Ecolines** and **Student Agency Bus**. Bus travel is cheaper than high-speed trains but journeys can be longer and less comfortable.

Ecolines
W ecolines.net

Eurolines
W eurolines.de

Flixbus
W flixbus.de

Student Agency Bus
W studentagencybus.com

Public Transport

Germany has some of the best public transport in the world, with every town and city operating an efficient and relatively inexpensive network of bus, tram, urban rail and metro lines. These are inevitably better than attempting to drive around German cities, where parking can be limited and expensive.

You can plan ahead by visiting the website of the transport company for the town or city in which you want to travel. Safety and hygiene measures, timetables, ticket information, transport maps and more can be obtained online from regional transport providers.

Berlin
W bvg.de

Frankfurt am Main
W rmv.de

Munich
W mvv-muenchen.de

Tickets

Large cities are generally divided into public transport zones; the cost of a ticket depends on which zones you are visiting. In addition to standard tickets, there are also cheaper tickets (*Kurzstrecke*) that limit you to short distances. In many cities you can buy tickets in the form of a strip, which is punched according to the length of your journey. Contactless payments are generally not accepted on public transport.

Children under 14 travel at a reduced rate, while those under the age of six go free. Other types of tickets include a one-day ticket (*Tageskarte*), a one-day group ticket (*Gruppen-tageskarte*) and a weekly ticket (*7-Tage-Karte*).

S-Bahn and U-Bahn

Most German cities have a network of fast connections by S-Bahn (commuter rail) and U-Bahn (underground railway). The S-Bahn offers services every 10–20 minutes and connects city centres with the suburbs. The U-Bahn offers a more frequent service – trains run every 3–5 minutes in peak hours – and individual stations are close to each other.

Generally, the S- and U-Bahn use the same tickets as buses and trams within a city. Tickets can be bought from machines at the entrance to stations or on platforms; the tickets often need to be validated in timestamp machines nearby. €40 fines are imposed on the spot for those not holding a valid ticket.

S-Bahn stations have round signs with a white "S" on a green background, while U-Bahn stations use square signs with a white "U" on a dark blue background.

On maps of the network, each line of the S- and U-Bahn is marked in a different colour and has its own number. The direction of the route is indicated by the name of the terminus station. On every platform a display shows the destination of the next incoming train. A white circle or oval on the map indicates an interchange station. Carriage doors on S- and U-Bahn trains are sometimes opened manually, but they close automatically. Passengers are not allowed to board the train after an operator's call of "*Zurückbleiben!*" ("Stay back!").

Tram

Trams can be seen in almost all large cities as well as countless smaller ones. They are comfortable, air-conditioned in summer and do not get stuck in traffic jams, making them a great option for travelling around busy cities. They run as frequently as buses and have similar operating hours and fares.

Bus

Bus operating hours vary from city to city and are more limited in rural areas. Timetables can be found online or in ticket or tourist offices at your destination. In rural areas tickets can be purchased from the driver but this is not the case in large cities, where tickets must be purchased in advance of your journey.

On city buses a screen shows the next stop. Buses normally stop at every bus stop. They are a slower alternative to trams and U-Bahn, especially during rush hour, but can be a great way to experience the city if you're not in a rush.

Ferry

Ferries form part of the public transport system in some areas, most notably on the Bodensee (p304). Ferries are also a good way to get around the lakes of Bavaria (p242).

Germany is linked to several other European countries by ferry, most notably Denmark, Sweden and Poland.

Taxis

Taxis are a comfortable though very expensive way of getting around. Even if several people share a cab it can still be more expensive than using the public transport system.

Most taxis are cream coloured and have a "TAXI" sign on the roof; this is illuminated if the taxi is free. Taxis can be booked by telephone or picked up at taxi ranks.

Ride sharing apps such as Uber and Lyft also operate in many German cities.

Driving

Driving licences issued by any of the European Union member states are valid throughout the EU. If visiting from outside the EU, you may need to apply for an International Driving Permit. Check with your local automobile association before you travel.

Motorways and regional roads are well-maintained and easy to navigate, but driving in large cities can be difficult. Watch out for bus lanes marked by round blue signs; these can only be used by buses, taxis and cyclists.

Many cities have introduced **Environmental Green Zones** (*Umweltzonen*) which only allow access to vehicles with an *Umweltplakette* (environmental badge). You will need to obtain this permit prior to travelling to these zones in your car. It can be bought online or from any participating garage in Germany.
Environmental Green Zones
ⓦ umwelt-plakette.de

Car Rental

Car-hire firms can be found at airports and railway stations. Drivers need to produce their passport, driving licence and a credit card with enough capacity to cover the excess. Most rental agencies require drivers to be over the age of 21 and to have an international licence.

Parking

Parking is normally free and easy in small towns and villages, but can be expensive and hard to find in big cities. The best option is to find a *Parkhaus* (car park) or metered parking spot. Cars left in a controlled parking zone must display a ticket bought from a machine nearby. Most hotels have some form of parking on offer, but this can come at an additional cost. Another alternative are the "park and ride" facilities which can be found near some S-Bahn stations.

Illegally parked cars can be towed; retrieving them is expensive and difficult.

Rules of the Road

Drive on the right. Unless otherwise signposted, vehicles coming from the right have priority.

At all times, drivers must carry a valid driver's licence, registration and insurance documents. The wearing of seat belts is compulsory for drivers and passengers, lights must be used in tunnels and the use of a mobile phone while driving is prohibited, with the exception of a hands-free system.

All drivers must have third-party insurance (*Haftpflichtversicherung*) – it is the minimum insurance requirement in Germany. Drivers will be fined for speeding, tailgating and for committing parking offences. The drink-drive limit (*p493*) is strictly enforced.

Cycling

German cities are criss-crossed with cycle lanes, making it safe and quick to get around on two wheels. Pedestrians should always make sure they don't wander onto high-speed cycle lanes.

Outside of the cities, cycle trails abound and these can be a convenient, fun and eco-friendly way of reaching out-of-the-way locations. Local tourist offices have the details of cycle trails in their respective areas.

Bicycle Hire

Bikes can be hired from a number of locations including railway stations, bike repair shops, tourist offices and hotels. Rates start at around €15-20 per day.

Bicycle Safety

Like drivers, cyclists must travel on the right. If you are unsure or unsteady, practise in one of the inner-city parks first. If in doubt, dismount: many novices cross busy junctions on foot; if you do so, switch to the pedestrian section of the crossing. Beware of tram tracks; cross them at an angle to avoid getting stuck. For your own safety do not walk with your bike in a bike lane or cycle on pavements, on the side of the road, in pedestrian zones or in the dark without lights. Wearing a helmet is recommended, but it is not a legal requirement.

Walking and Hiking

With a vast network of clearly way-marked footpaths, Germany is a fantastic destination for walkers and hikers. Rural areas are easy to reach but bad weather can strike at any time, so planning and good preparation are essential. Ensure you have good hiking boots, warm waterproof clothing, a map and a compass. Tell someone where you're going and when you plan to return.

Walking is also an enjoyable way to explore compact city centres such as Berlin, Frankfurt am Main and Munich, where most of the key sites are within walking distance of one another.

PRACTICAL
INFORMATION

A little local know-how goes a long way in Germany. Here you will find all the essential advice and information you will need during your stay.

AT A GLANCE

EMERGENCY NUMBERS

GENERAL EMERGENCY

112

AMBULANCE

112

FIRE SERVICE

112

POLICE

110

TIME ZONE
CET/CEST
Central European Summer Time runs from late March to late October.

TAP WATER
Unless otherwise stated, tap water in Germany is safe to drink.

WEBSITES AND APPS

BVG FahrInfo Plus
Live departures and travel updates from Berlin's local transport operator BVG

www.apotheken.de
Find your nearest chemist

www.handbookgermany.de
A complete A–Z of life in Germany, available in multiple languages

www.germany.travel
National Tourist Board website

Personal Security

Germany is generally a safe place for visitors, but it is always a good idea to take sensible precautions and be aware of your surroundings. Pickpockets are known to operate in busy tourist areas, particularly on public transport.

If you have anything stolen, report the crime as soon as possible to the nearest police station. Get a copy of the crime report in order to claim on your insurance. Contact your embassy if you have your passport stolen, or in the event of a serious crime or accident.

Germans are generally accepting of all people, regardless of their race, gender or sexuality. Although long celebrated as a liberal and tolerant country, homosexuality was only officially legalized in Germany in 1994. Despite all the freedoms that the LGBT+ community enjoy, acceptance is not always a given. If you do at any point feel unsafe, the **Safe Space Alliance** pinpoints your nearest place of refuge. In Berlin The **Maneo** emergency hotline run by **Mann-O-Meter** supports victims of homophobic behaviour, while **Lesbenberatung** is a lesbian safe space that offers help and advice for women, girls and transgender people.

Lesbenberatung
W esbenberatung-berlin.de
Maneo
C (030) 216 33 36
W maneo.de
Mann-O-Meter
W mann-o-meter.de
Safe Space Alliance
W safespacealliance.com

Health

Germany has a world-class health service. EU citizens are eligible to receive emergency medical treatment in Germany free of charge. If you have an EHIC or GHIC *(p487)* present this as soon as possible.

For visitors from outside the EU, payment of medical expenses is the patient's responsibility. It is important to arrange comprehensive medical insurance before travelling *(p486)*.

Pharmacies (*Apotheke*) are indicated by a red stylized letter "A" and can be used for help with minor ailments or prescriptions. You may need a doctor's prescription to obtain certain pharmaceuticals, and the pharmacist can inform you of the closest doctor's practice.

Pharmacies are usually open 8am–6pm, and details of the nearest 24-hour service are posted in all pharmacy windows or can be found online.

For a serious illness or injury, visit a hospital (*Krankenhaus*) or call an ambulance. All emergency rooms are part of the public health system, so your EHIC, GHIC or insurance will cover you.

Smoking, Alcohol and Drugs

Germany has a smoking ban in all public places, including bars, cafés, restaurants and hotels. However, many establishments circumvent these laws by naming themselves a *Raucherkneipe*, or smoking pub.

The possession of narcotics is prohibited and could result in prosecution and a prison sentence.

Unless stated otherwise, it is permitted to drink alcohol on the streets and in public parks and gardens. Germany has a strict limit of 0.05 per cent BAC (blood alcohol content) for drivers.

ID

There is no requirement for visitors to carry ID, but in the event of a routine check you may be asked to show your passport. If you don't have it with you, the police may escort you to wherever your passport is being kept.

Local Customs

Germany has strict laws on hate speech and symbols linked to the Nazis. Disrespectful behaviour in public places can warrant a fine, or even prosecution. Pay close attention to signage indicating when photos aren't allowed and think carefully about how you compose your shots. Visitors have come under serious criticism for posting inappropriate photos taken at sites of national significance on social media.

Visiting Places of Worship

Dress respectfully: cover your torso and upper arms; ensure shorts and skirts cover your knees.

Mobile Phones and Wi-Fi

Visitors travelling to Germany with EU tariffs can use their mobile phones abroad without being affected by data roaming charges; instead they will be charged the same rates for data, SMS and voice calls as they would pay at home. Visitors from other countries should check their contracts before using their phone in Germany in order to avoid unexpected charges.

Free Wi-Fi hotspots are widely available in big cities like Berlin, Munich and Frankfurt am Main. Hotels usually offer free Wi-Fi to their guests; cafés and restaurants are often happy to permit the use of their Wi-Fi on the condition that you make a purchase.

Post

German post offices and post boxes are easy to spot with their distinctive yellow *Deutsche Post* signs. Stamps (*Briefmarke*) can be bought in post offices, newsagents, tobacconists and most major supermarkets. There are usually self-service stamp machines conveniently placed outside post offices.

Taxes and Refunds

VAT is 19 per cent in Germany. Non-EU residents are entitled to a tax refund subject to certain conditions. In order to obtain this, you must request a tax receipt and export papers (*Ausfuhrbescheinigung*) when you purchase your goods. When leaving the country, present these papers, along with the receipt and your ID, at customs to receive your refund.

Discount Cards

Many cities have a discount card giving unlimited access to public transport plus free or discounted admission to local attractions for a short period of time. The **Berlin Welcome Card** and **Munich City Tour Card** offer free entry to numerous tourist attractions and discounted entry for many more. They also cover the cost of public transport for a specified duration.
Berlin Welcome Card
W berlin-welcomecard.de
Munich CityTour Card
W mvv-muenchen.de

INDEX

Page numbers in **bold** refer to main entries

A

Aachen **403**
Aalto, Alvar 400
Accommodation
    booking 487
    see also Camping; Hostels;
    Hotels
Adenauer, Konrad 406
Ahlbeck (Usedom) 469, 481
Ahr wine region 338
Ahrenshoop 482
Air travel 488, 489
Airports 489
Akademie der Kunst (Berlin) 62
Albert, Prince 197
Albertinum (Dresden) **171**
Albrecht der Bär 125, 161
Albrecht-Dürer-Haus
    (Nürnberg) **255**
Alexander I, Tsar 81
Alexanderplatz (Berlin) **81**
Alexandrowska (Potsdam) **132-3**
Alsfeld 35, **372**
Altdorfer, Albrecht 256, 424
    Battle of Alexander at Issus
    219
Alte Brücke (Heidelberg) 326
Alte Hofhaltung Historisches
    Museum (Bamberg) **252**
Alte Mainbrücke (Würzburg) **263**
Alte Nationalgalerie (Berlin) 64,
    73, 75
Alte Nikolaikirche (Frankfurt am
    Main) **367**
Alte Oper (Frankfurt am Main)
    365
Alte Pinakothek (Munich) 214,
    218-19
Alte Universität (Heidelberg) 327
Altena 408
Altenberg **401**
Altenburg **201**
Alter Markt (Potsdam) **135**
Altes Museum (Berlin) **74-5**
Altes Rathaus (Bamberg) **252-3**
Altes Rathaus (Leipzig) **167**
Altes Rathaus (Munich) 230, 241
Altes Rathaus (Potsdam) **134**
Altes Rathaus (Regensburg)
    282, 283
Altes Schloss (Stuttgart) **296**
Altmark 145
Altötting **278**
Altstadt (Düsseldorf) **386**
Altstadt (Hamburg) **430**

Altstadtmarkt (Braunschweig)
    447
Amberg 271
Ammersee 275
Amphitheater (Trier) **345**
Andechs **277**
Anger (Erfurt) **189**
Angermuseum (Erfurt) **189**
Anklam **480-81**
Anna Amalia, Duchess 190, 191,
    192
Anne-Frank-Zentrum (Berlin) **84**
Apps 492
Archäologische Staatsammlung
    (Munich) **235**
Archäologischer Park
    Cambodunum (Kempten) 269
Archäologisches
    Freilichtmuseum (Güstrow)
    479
Archäologischer
    Landesmuseum (Schleswig)
    460, 461
Archenhold Sternwarte (Berlin)
    117
Architecture **20-21**
Arnsberg 408
Art 24
    Berlin **64-5**
    Artist's Studio at the
    Brandenburg Gate in Berlin
    (Liebermann) 24
Asam, Cosmas Damian and Egid
    Quirin 229
Asamkirche (Munich) **229**
Asisi, Yadegar 45
Auer Mühlbach (Munich) **226**
Augsburg **284**, 286-7
Augustinerbräu (Munich) 240
Augustinerkloster-
    Augustinerkirche (Erfurt)
    188-9
Augustus the Strong 169, 171,
    177, 180
Augustusburg **180**
Aula Palatina (Konstantin-
    Basilika) (Trier) **342-3**
Auto- und Spielzeugmuseum
    (Tübingen) 323
Automobile Welt Eisenach 195

B

Bach, J S 25
    Bacharchive und
        Bachmuseum (Leipzig) **167**
    Bachhaus (Eisenach) 195
Bad Bergzabern 352
Bad Berleburg 408

Bad Cannstatt (Stuttgart) **299**
Bad Doberan **479**
Bad Dürkheim 353
Bad Frankenhausen 196
Bad Godesburg 406
Bad Homburg **376**
Bad Honnef 406
Bad Hönningen 340
Bad Marienburg 340
Bad Mergentheim **311**
Bad Muskau **178**
Bad Salzuflen 411
Bad Schandau 183
Bad Wilsnack 138
Bad Wimpfen **315**
Baden-Baden **314-15**
Baden-Württemberg 207,
    288-327
    bars and pubs 297
    hotels 317
    itinerary 292-3
    map 290-91
    restaurants 311
    walk 326-7
Ballenstedt **161**
Baltic coast 28
Balve 408
Bamberg **252-3**
Bansin (Usedom) 469, 481
Barbarathermen (Trier) **345**
Barlach, Ernst 160, 201, 428,
    457, 478
    Geistkämpfer 460, 461
Baroque architecture 20
Bars and pubs
    Berlin 83, 121
    Brandenburg 133
    Frankfurt am Main 369
    Koblenz 349
    live music bars 27
    Munich 216, 231
    Stuttgart 297
Basedow 473
Basilika St Kastor (Koblenz) 348,
    349
Basquiat, Jean-Michel 236
Bastei (Sächsische Schweiz)
    182
Battle of Alexander at Issus, The
    (Altdorfer) 219
Battle of Nations 166
bauhaus museum weimar **192**
Bauhaus-Archiv (Berlin) **95**
Bauhausmuseum (Dessau)
    158-9
Bautzen **178**
Bavaria 29, 207, **242-87**
    castles 250-51
    hotels 281

itinerary 246-7
map 244-5
medieval towns 271
natural wonders 248-9
restaurants 273
shopping 264
walk 286-7
Bavaria-Filmstadt (Munich) **239**
Bavarian Alps 249, 250-0, 278-9
Bavarian Forest 249
Bayerische Staatsbibliothek
(Munich) **235**
Daycrisches Armeemuseum
(Ingolstadt) 275
Bayerisches Nationalmuseum
(Munich) **234**
Bayreuth **280-81**
Beaches 15, 28
Mecklenburg-Vorpommern
468-9
Beatles Museum (Halle) 158
Bebelplatz (Berlin) **76-7**
Beckmann, Max 226, 438
Beer 14
Munich 216-17, 231, 232, 240
Beethoven, Ludwig van,
Beethovenhaus (Bonn) **396**
Belvedere (Schlosspark, Berlin)
113
Bendlerblock (Gedenkstätte
Deutscher Wilderstand)
(Berlin) **96**
Berching 271
Berchtesgaden **258**
Berchtesgadener Land **258-9**
Bergbaumuseum Rammelsberg
(Goslar) 440, 441
Bergen-Belsen 443
Bergischer Dom (Altenberg) 401
Berlin 14, **54-123**
art **64-5**
bars and pubs 83, 121
Beyond the Centre 59,
104-23
budget travel **62-3**
Eastern Centre 58, **68-87**
hostels 63
hotels 79, 95
itineraries **60-61**
map 56-7
map: Beyond the Centre
106-7
map: Eastern Centre 70-71
map: Western Centre 90-91
music **66-7**
restaurants 84, 93, 119
walks 86-7, 102-3
Western Centre 59, **88-103**
Berlin Airlift 115

Berlin Wall 44, 45
East Side Gallery 63, 65,
110-11
Gedenkstätte Berliner Mauer
123
Berliner Dom **75**
Berlinisches Galerie 65
Bernburg **156-7**
Reuron **302-3**
Beuys, Joseph 236, 405
Bevern 449
Bicycle hire 491
Bielefeld **411**
Binnenalster (Hamburg) **428**
Binz (Rügen) 469, **474**
Bismarck, Otto von 42, 438
Black Death 40
Black Forest see Schwarzwald
Blockhaus Nikolskoe (Berlin)
122
BMW Museum + Welt (Munich)
214, **237**
Boat trips
Spreewald 142
Böcklin, Arnold 215, 235
Bode-Museum (Berlin) 65, **75**
Bodensee 289, **304-5**
Bonn **396-7**
Book from the Sky (Bing), 390
Bormann, Martin 259
Bosau 460
Brahms, Johannes 15, 25, 315
Brahmshaus (Baden-Baden)
315
Brandenburg 52, **124-43**
bars and pubs 133
hotels 139
itinerary 128-9
map 126-7
restaurants 142
spas 130-31
Brandenburg/Havel **139**
Brandenburger Tor (Berlin) 21,
62, **76**
Brandenburgisches
Apothekenmuseum (Cottbus)
141
Brandt, Willy 454
Braque, Georges 226
Braunschweig **446**, 447
Brecht, Bertolt 25, 101, 286, 478
Brecht-Weigel-Gedenkstätte
(Berlin) **101**
Breckerfeld 408
Bremen 419, **424-7**
Bremerhaven **437**
Breughel, Jan 424
Brodowin **139**
Bröhan Museum (Berlin) **112**

Brothers Grimm 360-61, 363,
374, 447
Bruchsal **313**
Brücke Museum (Berlin) 64, **120**
GRIMMWELT Kassel **360-61**
Brühische Terrasse (Dresden)
170
Brühl **406-7**
Brunswick see Braunschweig
Buchenwald **193**
Bückeburg **445**
Buddenbrookhaus (Lübeck)
454, **456**
Budget travel, Berlin **62-3**
Burckhardt, Johann Ludwig 73
Burg Hohenzollern **302**
Burg Lichtenstein **303**
Burg- und Schlossgarten
(Schwerin) **470**
Bürgersaal (Munich) 226, 240
Burggarten (Rothenburg ob der
Tauber) **264**
Burghausen **278**
Burgtor (Lübeck) **457**
Bus travel 490
Berlin 62
Munich 237

C

Calder, Alexander 103, 296
Calendar of events **36-7**
Camping 23
Canigiani Holy Family, The
(Raphael) 219
Car rental 491
Carolingian Empire 39
Cash 487
Castles and fortifications 12
Albrechtsburg (Meissen)
177
Altes Schloss (Stuttgart) **296**
Bavarian **250-51**
Bernburg Schloss 157
Burg Drachenfels 406
Burg Hohenzollern **302**
Burg Hohnstein 183
Burg Lichtenstein **303**
Burg Trausnitz (Landshut)
275
Burghausen Castle 251, 278,
279
Burgtor (Lübeck) **457**
Colditz Castle 174
Eschenheimer Turm
(Frankfurt am Main) **364**
Falkenlust (Brühl) 406, 407
Festung Ehrenbreitstein
(Koblenz) 349

Castles and fortifications (cont.)
 Festung Königstein 183
 Festung Marienberg
  (Würzburg) **263**
 Frauentor (Nürnberg) **254**
 Fürstenzug (Dresden) **168–9**
 Haigerloch castle **302**
 Hambacher Schloss 353
 Hämelschenburg 449
 Heidelberg Castle **308–9**
 Hexenturm (Heidelberg) 327
 Hohenneuffen castle **303**
 Holstentor (Lübeck) 454
 Kaiserburg (Nürnberg) **256–7**
 Karlstor (Munich) 240
 Landeck Castle 352
 Landgrafenschloss (Marburg)
  373
 Neustädter Tor
  (Tangermünde) 161
 Plattenburg Castle 138
 Porta Nigra (Trier) **344**
 Querfurt Schloss 157
 Rödertor (Rothenburg ob der
  Tauber) **265**
 Schloss (Bückeburg) 445
 Schloss (Celle) 444
 Schloss (Schwerin) **470**
 Schloss (Wolfenbüttel) 441
 Schloss Saalfeld 200, 201
 Schloss Altenburg 201
 Schloss Babelsberg
  (Potsdam) **134**
 Schloss Ehrenburg (Coburg)
  271
 Schloss Gottorf (Schleswig)
  460, 461
 Schloss Hartenfels (Torgau)
  174
 Schloss Hohenschwangau
  251, **268**
 Schloss Hohentübingen 322,
  323
 Schloss Johannisburg
  (Aschaffenburg) 270
 Schloss Neuburg 276
 Schloss Neuschwanstein
  250, **266–7**
 Schloss Wernigerode 155
 Wittenberg Castle
  (Lutherstadt Wittenberg)
  150
 Schwanenburg (Kleve) 398
 Stadtschloss (Weimar) **191**
 Stargard hill castle
  (Nationalpark Müritz) 473
 Steintor (Anklam) 480
 Stolpen Castle 182
 Stralsund medieval walls
  483
 Trifels Castle 352
 Veste Coburg 270–71
 Wartburg (Eisenach) **194–5**

Castles and fortifications (cont.)
 Zitadelle Spandau (Berlin)
  114
Caves
 Feengrotten Grottoneum
  (Saalfeld) 201
 Sauerland 408, 409
Cecilienhof (Potsdam) **134**,
  135
Celle **444**
Ceramics, Kannenbäcker 340
Chagall, Marc 435
Charlemagne 39, 403, 409
Charles IV 159
Checkpoint Charlie (Berlin) **82**
Chemnitz **175**
Chiemsee 248, **285**
Children **28–9**
Chinesisches Teehaus
 (Potsdam) **137**
Christmas Museum
 (Rothenburg ob der Tauber)
 264
Christo 435
Church of St Anna (Augsburg)
  286
Churches and cathedrals
 visiting 493
 see individual entries
Classical music 25, 66, 215
 Wörlitzer Park concerts 149
Cloppenburg **439**
Closures 487
Coast 22, 28
Coburg **270–71**
Cold War 44, 82, 97, 123
 see also Berlin Wall
Colditz 174
Concert halls *see* Entertainment
Congress of Vienna 163
Contemporary architecture 21
Corinth, Lovis 171
Cottbus **141**
Couven-Museum (Aachen) 403
COVID-19 **487**
Cranach, Lucas (the Elder) 151,
  152, 159, 194, 197
 Cranachhaus (Lutherstadt
  Wittenberg) **150**
 *Portrait of Christiane of
  Eulenau* 253
Cranach, Lucas (the Younger)
  270
Cuckoo clocks 306, 307
Currency 486
Customs information 486
Cycling 491
 biking trails 33

D

Dachau **274**
Dachau Gemäldegalerie 274

Daimler Contemporary (Berlin)
  62
Dalí, Salvador 98, 405
 Dalí Museum (Berlin) **97**
Darmstadt **378**
Darsser Ort 478
DDR Museum (Berlin) 24, **82**
De Chirico, Giorgio 226
Degas, Edgar 171
Deichtorhallen (Hamburg) **430**
Delacroix, Eugène 424
Der Gestürzte (Lehmbruck) 405
Dessau 145, **158–9**
Detlefsen-Museum (Glückstadt)
  458
Deutsche Weinstrasse **352–3**
Deutscher Dom (Berlin) **78**
Deutsches Architekturmuseum
 (Frankfurt am Main) **368**
Deutsches Auswandererhaus
 Bremerhaven 437
Deutsches Buch- und
 Schriftmuseum (Leipzig) **166**
Deutsches Filmmuseum
 (Frankfurt am Main) **368**
Deutsches Historisches
 Museum (Berlin) 79
Deutsches Jagd- und
 Fischereimuseum (Munich)
  241
Deutsches Medizinhistorisches
 Museum (Ingolstadt) 275
Deutsches Meeresmuseum
 (Stralsund) 483
Deutsches Museum (Munich)
  24, 214, **222–3**
Deutsches Musikautomaten
 Museum (Bruchsal) 313
Deutsches Pferdemuseum
 (Verden an der Aller) 445
Deutsches Schifffahrtsmuseum
 (Bremerhaven) 437
Deutsches Technikmuseum
 Berlin 29, **82**
Deutschordensmuseum (Bad
 Mergentheim) 311
Die Brücke 64
Dietrich, Marlene 135
Dinkelsbühl 271
Diözesanmuseum (Freising)
  277
Disabled travellers 487
Discount cards 493
 Berlin 65, 74
Dix, Otto 24, 98
 Otto-Dix-Haus (Gera) 197
 The Poet Iwar von Lücken 65
Doberaner Münster (Bad
 Doberan) 479
Documentation Centre of
 Everyday Culture of the GDR
 (Frankfurt an der Oder) 140,
  141

Dokumentationszentrum Obersalzberg (Berchtesgaden) **258**
Dokumentationszentrum Reichsparteitagsgelände (Nürnberg) **257**
Dom (Bamberg) **252**
Dom (Braunschweig) 446
Dom (Limburg)377
Dom (Lübeck) 455, **457**
Dom St Kilian (Würzburg) **262**
Dom St Mariä (Hildesheim) 436, 437
Dom St Maria (Paderborn) 409
Dom St Maria und St Johannes (Schwerin) **471**
Dom St Marien (Erfurt) **188**
Dom St Marien (Freiberg) 176
Dom St Marien (Havelberg) 161
Dom St Mauritius und St Katharina (Magdeburg) 160, 161
Dom St Paulus (Münster) 404, 405
Dom St Peter (Regensburg) 282, 283
Dom St Peter (Trier) 343
Dom St Peter (Worms) 347
Dom Unserer Lieben Frau (Augsburg) 284, 285
Domburg (Merseburg) 157
Dominikanermuseum (Rottweil) 321
Dommuseum (Brandenburg/ Havel) 139
Domschatz (Halberstadt) 154
Domschatzmuseum (Regensburg) 282, 283
Donatello, *Pazzi Madonna* 65
Donaubergland **303**
Dormagen **401**
Dörrenbach 352
Dortmund **399**
Dreifaltigkeitskirche (Munich) **226**
Dresden 163, **168–73**
Driving 491
Driving tours
  Deutsche Weinstrasse **352–3**
  Sächsische Schweiz **182–3**
  Weser Renaissance Trail **449**
Duchamp, Marcel 386, 471
Duderstadt **447**
Duisburg **405**
Düne 459
Dunkel beer 217
Dürer, Albrecht **255**, 257, 424
  Albrecht-Dürer-Haus (Nürnberg) 24, **255**
  Four Apostles 218

Dürer, Albrecht (cont.), *Self-Portrait with Fur-trimmed Robe* 219
Düsseldorf **386–7**

E

East Germany *see* German Democratic Republic
East Side Gallery (Berlin) 63, 65, **110–11**
Eastern Germany **48–201**
  Berlin **54–123**
  Brandenburg 52, **124–43**
  map 50–51
  Saxony 53, **162–83**
  Saxony Anhalt 52, **144–61**
  Thuringia 53, **184–201**
Egapark (Erfurt) **189**
Eifel Mountains 402
Einbeck **447**
Einstein, Albert 117
Einsteinturm (Potsdam) **135**
Eisbock 217
Eisenach 194, **195**
Elbtalaue **138**
Electricity supply 486
Elisabethkirche (Marburg) 373
Eltville 372
Emden 438
Emergency numbers 492
Emsland **439**
Englischer Garten (Munich) **238–9**
Entertainment
  Alte Oper (Frankfurt am Main) **365**
  Cuvilliés Theater (Residenz, Munich) 225
  Deutsches Nationaltheater (Weimar) **193**
  Konzerthaus (Berlin) 66, **79**
  Live Events **26–7**
  Opernhaus (Hanover) **434**
  Philharmonie and Kammermusiksaal (Berlin) 66, **98–9**, 103
  Sächsische Staatsoper (Dresden) **168**
  Staatsoper Unter Den Linden (Berlin) 78, **79**
Erfurt **188–9**
Ernst, Max 98, 405
Erzgebirge Mountains 163
Eschenheimer Turm (Frankfurt am Main) **364**
Essen **400**
Esslingen **318**
Europa Park **318–19**
European Route of Historic Theatres 295
European Union 355

Eutin 460
Events *see* Festivals and events

F

Fairy Tale Route 363
Family Recital (van Mieris) 471
Farina Haus (Köln) **388**
Federal Republic of Germany 44–5
Feengrotten Grottoneum (Saalfeld) 201
Felderrnhalle (Munich) **233**
Femme au bouquet (Picasso) 435
Fernmeldeturm (Mannheim) 313
Fernsehturm (Berlin) **81**
Fernsehturm (Stuttgart) **298**
Ferries 490
Festivals and events
  A Year in Germany **36–7**
  beer festivals 217
  cultural festivals 27
  Festival of Lights (Berlin) 93
  music festivals 26
  Passion Play (Oberammergau) 279
Festung Marienberg (Würzburg) **263**
Feuerbach, Anselm 215, 235, 257
Field with Poppies (Van Gogh) 424
Film studios 25
Filmpark Babelsberg **134–5**
Fischmarkt (Erfurt) **188**
Fischmarkt (Hamburg) **430**
Flavin, Dan 100
Flensburg **459**
Flughafen Tempelhof (Berlin) 114, **115**
Focke-Museum (Bremen) **426–7**
Food and drink
  Berlin 62
  for children 28
  Germany for Foodies **30–31**
  Lübeck marzipan 455
  traditional 12
  Wurstküche (Regensburg) 282, 283
  see also Bars and pubs; Beer; Restaurants; Wine
Forests 23
Fortuna (Scheibe) 108
Foster, Norman 92, 93
Four Apostles, The (Dürer) 218
Fra Angelico 201
Frank, Anne 84
Frankfurt am Main 355, **364–9**
  bars and pubs 369
Frankfurt an der Oder **140**
Fränkische Schweiz **272**
Französischer Dom (Berlin) **78**
Frauenkirche (Dresden) 20, **170**

Frauenkirche (Munich) **228**, 241
Frauentor (Nürnberg) **254**
Frederick I Barbarossa 315
Frederick II the Great 41, 108, 136
Freiberg **176**
Freiburg im Breisgau **325**
Freilichtmuseum Schwerin-
    Muess **471**
Freising **276-7**
Freudenberg 407
Friedrich, Caspar David 73, 113,
    181, 480
Friedrich IV, Elector Palatine 308
Friedrich Wilhelm II 109, 113
Friedrich Wilhelm III 72
Friedrich Wilhelm IV 108
Fritzlar **377**
Füchtingshof (Lübeck) **456**
Fuggerei-Museum (Augsburg)
    284
Fuggerhäuser (Augsburg) 287
Fulda **372**
Fünfseenland **274-5**
Fürstenzug (Dresden) **168-9**
Fürst-Pückler-Museum (Cottbus)
    141
Füssen **269**

G

Gadebusch **476**
Gaertner, Eduard 113
Gallery of Beauties (Schloss
    Nymphenburg) 220, 221
Garden Kingdom of Dessau-
    Wörlitz 145, 148
Garmisch-Partenkirchen **278-9**
Gäubodenmuseum (Straubing)
    273
Gedenkstätte Bergen-Belsen
    443
Gedenkstätte Berliner Mauer **123**
Gedenkstätte Plötzensee
    (Berlin) **115**
Gedenkstätte Stille Heiden
    (Berlin) **84**
Gedenktätte der Deutschen
    Arbeiterbewegung (Gotha)
    197
Gehry, Frank O 411
Geistkämpfer (Barlach) 460, 461
Gemäldegalerie (Berlin) **96**
Gemäldegalerie (Zwinger,
    Dresden) 172, 173
Gera **197**
German Democratic Republic
    (GDR) 44
    DDR Museum (Berlin) 24, **82**
    Documentation Centre of
        Everyday Culture of the
        GDR (Frankfurt an der
        Oder) 140, 141
    see also Stasi

German Empire 42
German Enlightenment 185
German Spy Museum (Berlin) **97**
Germanic tribes 38
Germanisches Nationalmuseum
    (Nürnberg) 24, **256**
Gestapo 83
Giessen **374**
Glasmuseum (Wertheim) 310
Glückstadt **458**
Glyptothek (Munich) 21
Godehardkirche (Hildesheim)
    437
Goethe, Johann Wolfgang von
    194, 295, 375, 387
    Frankfurter Goethe-haus
        364
    Goethes Gartenhaus
        (Weimar) **192**
    Goethes Wohnhaus and
        National Museum (Weimar)
        24, **193**
Gorgione 173
Görlitz **179**
Goslar **440-41**
Gotha **197**
Gotisches Haus (Wörlitzer Park)
    148, 149
Gotischer Dom am Wasser
    (Schinkel) 64
Göttingen **447**
Grafschaftsmuseum
    (Wertheim) 310
Grass, Günther 454
    Günter-Grass-Haus (Lübeck)
        457
Grassimuseum (Leipzig) **166**
Great Famine 40
Greifswald **480**
Gropius, Walter 95, 158, 192
Gross St Martin (Köln) 390-91
Grosse Kunstschau
    (Worpswede) 441
Grosser Garten (Dresden) **171**
Grosser Plöner See 460
Grossherzoglich-Hessische
    Porzellansammlung
    (Darmstadt) 378
Grüner Markt (Bamberg) **253**
Gürzenich (Köln) **389**
Güstrow **478-9**
Gutenberg, Johannes 350, 351
Gutenberg Museum (Mainz)
    350, 351

H

Hachenburg 340
Hackesche Höfe (Berlin) **85**
HafenCity (Hamburg) 21, **429**
Hagen **399**
Haigerloch **302**
Halberstadt **154**

Halle **158**
Halle an der Buttergasse
    (Magdeburg) 160
Hals, Frans 159, 197, 471
Hamburg 419, **428-31**
Hamburger Bahnhof (Berlin) **100**
Hameln 449
Hanau 35, **374**
Hanover **434-5**
Hanseatic League 40
Harz Mountain Trail **154**
Harz Mountains 145, 154, 161,
    419
Hasenfeld 402
Hauptmarkt (Nürnberg) **257**
Hauptmarkt (Trier) **342**
Hauptwache (Frankfurt am
    Main) **366**
Haus der Kulturen der Welt
    (Berlin) **101**
Haus der Kunst (Munich) **233**
Haus der Schiffergesellschaft
    (Lübeck) **456**
Haus Schwarzenberg Museums
    (Berlin) **84**
Haus zum Ritter (Heidelberg)
    327
Havel, River 139
Havelberg 161
Health 492
Hechingen **302**
Hegel, Georg Wilhelm Friedrich
    200
    Hegel-Haus (Stuttgart) **298**
Heidelberg 289, **308-9**
    walk 326-7
Heilbronn **316**
Heilig-Geist-Spital (Nürnberg)
    255
Heiligen-Geist-Hospital
    (Lübeck) 454, **457**
Heiligenstadt **196**
Heiliggeistkirche (Heidelberg)
    326
Heiligkreuzkapelle (Trier) **345**
Heine, Heinrich 196, 438, 447
Heligoland 419, **459**
    walk 462
Helles beer 217
Hemp Museum (Berlin) 87
Henry V, Emperor 156
Herford 411
Heringsdorf (Usedom) 469, 481
Herrenhäuser Gärten (Hanover)
    435
Herrmann, Curt, *Schloss
    Belvedere* 193
Herzogin-Anna-Amalia
    Bibliothek (Weimar) **192**
Hess, Rudolf 114
Hesse 333, **354-79**
    bars and pubs 369
    itinerary 358-9

Hesse (cont.)
  map 356–7
  restaurants 363, 373
Hessisches Landesmuseum
  (Darmstadt) 378
Hessisches Landesmuseum
  (Kassel) 360
Hidden gems 34
Hiddensee 468, **475**, 478
Hiking
  and walking 491
  Herrsching to Andechs 277
  King Ludwig Path 249
  Sächsische Schweiz 182
  Schwarzwald 307
  trails 32
  Waldecker Land 362
  Westerwald Trail 340
Hildesheim **436–7**
Hintersee **259**
Hirst, Damien 236
Historic buildings
  see individual entries
Historiengewölbe
  (Rothenburg ob der Tauber)
  265
Historiensäule (Koblenz) **349**
Historisches Museum
  (Frankfurt am Main) **366–7**
Historisch-technisches Museum
  (Peenemünde) 482
History 12, **38–45**
Hitler, Adolf 43, 444
  assassination attempt 96, 115
  Felderrnhalle (Munich) **233**
  Kehlsteinhaus **259**
Hofbräuhaus (Munich) 216, **232**
Hofkirche (Dresden) **168**
Hohenneuffen **303**
Hohenschwangau 251, **268**
Hohenstaufen dynasty 289
Hohenzollern dynasty 125, 289,
  302
Hölderlin, Friedrich 322
Hölderlinturm (Tübingen) 322,
  323
Holländisches Viertel (Potsdam)
  135
Holocaust Denkmal (Berlin)
  76
Holsteinische Schweiz
  (Holstein's Switzerland) **460**
Holy Roman Empire 39, 403
Homburg **346**
Homeopathy 131
Hospitals 492–3
Hostels, Berlin 63
Hotels
  Baden-Württemberg 317
  Bavaria 281
  Berlin 79, 95
  booking 487
  Brandenburg 139

Hotels (cont.)
  Lower Saxony, Hamburg and
    Bremen 427
  Mecklenburg-Vorpommern
    469
  Munich 239
  North Rhine-Westphalia 405
  Saxony Anhalt 153
Höxter **409**
Humboldt, Alexander von 447

I

ID 493
Industrial style 21
Ingolstadt **275**
Insurance 486
Internationales Zeitungs-
  museum (Aachen) 403
Internet access 493
Isozaki, Arata 97
Itineraries
  1 Day in Munich 212–13
  2 Days in Berlin 60–61
  2 Days in Brandenburg 128–9
  2 Weeks in Germany 16–19
  3 Days in Baden-
    Württemberg 292–3
  3 Days in Hesse 358–9
  3 Days in Hamburg and
    Bremen 422–3
  3 Days in North Rhine-
    Westphalia 384–5
  7 Days in Bavaria 246–7
  see also Driving tours; Walks

J

Jagdschloss Grunewald (Berlin)
  120
Jahn, Helmut 97
Jakobikirche (Lübeck) **457**
Japanisches Palais (Dresden) **171**
Jasmund Peninsula (Rügen) **474**
Jazz 66, 215
Jena **200**
Jesuitenkirche (Heidelberg) 327
Jesuitenkirche (Trier) **344**
Judaism
  Holocaust Denkmal (Berlin)
    76
  Jüdisches Museum Berlin **83**
  Jüdisches Museum (Frankfurt
    am Main) **366**
  Jüdisches Zentrum
    Jakobsplatz (Munich)
    228–9
  Neue Synagogue and
    Centrum Judaicum (Berlin)
    84–5
  see also Synagogues
Juist 438
Jüterbog **142**

K

Kaiser-Wilhelm-Gedächtnis-
  Kirche (Berlin) **99**
Kaiserburg (Nürnberg) **256–7**
Kaiserdom (Braunschweig) 446
Kaiserdom (Frankfurt am Main)
  367
Kaiserdom (Speyer) 20, 351
Kaiserthermen (Trier) **344**
Kamenz **181**
Kandinsky, Wassily 95, 159, 238,
  386
Kannenhäcker **340**
Kap Arkona (Rügen) 469, **475**
Käppele (Würzburg) **263**
Karl Marx Monument (Chemnitz)
  174
Karl-Marx-Allee (Berlin) **116**
Karl-May-Museum 171
Karlsruhe **316–17**
Kassel 355, **361–2**
Katharinenkirche (Lübeck) **457**
Kehlsteinhaus **259**
Kelley, Mike 236
Kempten **269**
Kennedy, John F 119
Kepler, Johannes **319**
  Kepler-Museum (Weil der
    Stadt) 319
Kiel **461**
Kindercafes (Berlin) 28
Kirms-Krackow-Haus (Weimar)
  190
Klee, Paul 95, 159, 386
Klein Glienicke (Berlin) **122–3**
Klein-Venedig (Bamberg) **253**
Kleist, Heinrich von 140
Klenze, Leo von 21, 235, 237, 271
Kleve **398**
Kloster Chorin **140**
Kloster Michelsberg (Bamberg)
  253
Kneipp spas 130
Koblenz **348–9**
Kokoschka, Oskar 438
Kollwitz, Käthe 77, 177, 389
Köln **388–93**
  Romanesque churches
    390–91
Kölner Dom **392–3**
Kölpinsee 473
Kolumba Museum (Köln) **388**
Königsalle (Düsseldorf) **386**
Königsee **259**
Königswinter **406**
Konstanz **304**
Kontorhausviertel (Hamburg)
  429
Konzerthaus (Berlin) 66, **79**
Köpenick (Berlin) **118**
Krameramtswohnungen
  (Hamburg) **431**

Krämerbrücke (Erfurt) **188**
Kraszewski-Museum (Dresden) 171
Kreis- und Universitätsmuseum (Braunschweig) 446
Kreuzkirche (Dresden) **169**
Kulturbrauerei (Berlin) 116-17
Kulturforum (Berlin) **102-3**
Kulturhistorisches Museum (Magdeburg) 160, 161
Kulturhistorisches Museum (Stralsund) 483
Kunst- und Wunderkammer (Landshut) 275
Kunstbau (Munich) 238
Kunstbibliothek (Berlin) 102
Kunstgewerbemuseum (Berlin) **98**, 102
Kunsthalle (Bremen) **424**
Kunsthalle Emden 438
Kunsthalle (Hamburg) **431**
Kunsthalle (Munich) 215
Kunsthalle (Tübingen) 323
Kunsthalle Fridericianum (Kassel) **361**
Kunsthalle Mannheim 312, 313
Kunsthalle Schirn (Frankfurt am Main) **366**
Kunstmuseum Marburg 373
Kunstmuseum Solingen 401
Kunstmuseum Stuttgart **296**
Kunstsammlung (Gera) 197
Kunstsammlung Nordrhein-Westfalen (Düsseldorf) **386**
Museen Böttcherstrasse (Bremen) **427**
Kunstsammlungen Chemnitz 175
Kunststiftung des Landes Sachsen-Anhalt (Halle) 158
Kupferstichkabinett (Berlin) 102
Kurpfälzisches Museum (Heidelberg) 309
Kurfürstendamm (Berlin) **94**
Kurfürstliches Palais (Trier) **345**
Kyffhäuser Mountains **196**, 197
KZ-Gedenkstätte (Dachau) 274

L

Lake Dwelling Museum (Bodensee) **305**
Lakes 23
Landau 353
Landesmuseum für Kunst und Kulturgeschichte (Oldenburg) 439
Landesmuseum für Vorgeschichte (Halle) 158
Landsberg am Lech **277**
Landscape 15, **22-3**

Landschaftsmuseum (Tauberbischofsheim) 311
Landshut **275**
Lang, Fritz 25, 135
Lange Anna (Heligoland) 462
Langhansbau (Schloss Charlottenburg, Berlin) **113**
Language 487
  essential phrases 486
  phrasebook 508-10
Last Judgement (Rubens) 219
Lehde 142
Lehmbruck, Wilhelm, *Der Gestürzte* 405
Leibniz, Gottfried Wilhelm 441
Leineschloss (Hanover) **434**
Leinsweiler 352
Leipzig **166-7**
Leipziger Platz (Berlin) **97**
Lemgo **410**
Lenbach, Franz von 235, 276
  Lenbachhaus (Munich) **238**
Leonardo da Vinci, *Virgin with Child* 219
Lepsius, Carl Richard 72, 73
Lessing, Ephraim 181
  Lessinghaus (Wolfenbüttel) 441
  Lessingmuseum (Kamenz) 181
LGBT+
  Berlin 43
  events 27
Libeskind, Daniel 83
Liebermann, Max 24, 116, 171, 197, 201
  Artist's Studio at the Brandenburg Gate in Berlin 24
Liebfrauenkirche (Koblenz) 348, 349
Liebfrauenkirche (Trier) 343
Liebighaus (Frankfurt am Main) **369**
Liebknecht, Karl 117
Liederhalle (Stuttgart) **298**
Lilienstein (Sächsische Schweiz) 183
Lilienthal, Otto 481
Limburg **375**
Lindau **283**
Linden-Museum and Staatlisches Museum für Völkerkunde (Stuttgart) **299**
Lindenau-Museum (Altenburg) 201
Lippstadt 409
Liszt, Franz 161, 281
  Liszt Museum (Weimar) **192**
Literature 24
Live Events **26-7**
Local customs 493
Lohse, Carl, "Ludwig Renn" 171
Lorenzer Platz (Nürnberg) **254-5**

Lorsch **379**
Loschwitz (Dresden) **170-71**
Lousberg Hill (Aachen) **403**
Lower Saxony, Hamburg and Bremen 416, **418-49**
  driving tour 449
  hotels 427
  itinerary 422-3
  map 420-21
Lübben 142
Lübbenau 142
Lübeck **454-7**
Luckau 142
Ludwig I of Bavaria 235, 237
Ludwig II of Bavaria 221, 235, **250**, **267**, 274
  Schloss Hohenschwangau 251
  Schloss Linderhof 251, 285
  Schloss Neuschwanstein 250, **266-7**
  and Wagner 280
Ludwig-Museum (Koblenz) 348, 349
"Ludwig Renn" (Lohse) 171
Ludwigskirche (Munich) **235**
Ludwigslust **476**
Lüneburg **442-3**
Lüneburger Heide 419, **443**
Luther, Martin 40, 145, 150-51, 195, 270
  Lutherhaus Eisenach **194**
  Lutherhaus (Lutherstadt Wittenberg) **151**
Lutherstadt Eisleben **155**
Lutherstadt Wittenberg 145, **150-51**
Luxemburg, Rosa 117
LWL Museum für Kunst und Kultur (Münster) 404, 405

M

Magdeburg **160-61**
Magritte, René 98
Maibock 217
Mainau **305**
Mainz **350-51**
Mainzer Dom 350, 351
Manet, Eduard 424
Mann, Thomas 454, 456
Mannheim **312-13**
Mao (Warhol) 100
Maps
  Baden-Württemberg 290-91
  Bamberg 253
  Bavaria 244-5
  Berchtesgadener Land 259
  Berlin 56-7
  Berlin: Beyond the Centre 106-7
  Berlin: Eastern Centre 70-71
  Berlin: Western Centre 90-91

Maps (cont.)
Bodensee 305
Bonn 397
Brandenburg 126-7
Bremen 425
Dresden 169
Düsseldorf 387
Eastern Germany 50-51
Erfurt 189
Frankfurt am Main 365
Germany 10-11
Hamburg 429
Hanover 435
Heligoland 462
Hesse 356-7
Kassel 361
Köln 389
Leipzig 167
Lower Saxony, Hamburg and
    Bremen 420-21
Lübeck 454-5
Lutherstadt Wittenberg 151
Mecklenburg-Vorpommern
    466-7
Munich 210-11
North Rhine-Westphalia
    382-3
Northern Germany 414-15
Nürnberg 255
Potsdam 133
Rail Journey Planner 489
Rhineland-Palatinate and
    Saarland 336-7
Rothenburg ob der Tauber 265
Rügen 475
Sächsische Schweiz 182-3
Saxony 164-5
Saxony Anhalt 146-7
Schleswig-Holstein 452-3
Schwäbische Alb 303
Schwerin 471
Southern Germany 204-5
Stuttgart 297
Thuringia 186-7
Trier 343
Weimar 191
Western Germany 330-31
Würzburg 263
Marbach **318**
Marburg **372-3**
Maria Laach **349**
Marienkirche (Berlin) 62, **80**
Marienkirche (Lübeck) 454, **456**
Marienkirche (Lutherstadt
    Wittenberg) **151**
Marienplatz (Munich) **240-41**
Märkisches Museum (Berlin) **81**
Markt (Bonn) **396**
Markthalle (Stuttgart) **297**
Marktplatz (Bremen) **424-5**
Marktplatz (Hanover) **435**
Marktplatz (Heidelberg) 326
Marble House (Potsdam) **132**

Marstall (Potsdam) **133**
Martini, Simone 201
Marx, Erich 100
Marx, Karl **344**
    monument (Chemnitz) 174
Matisse, Henri 226
Maulbronn **323**
Mausoleum (Schlosspark, Berlin)
    113
Mauthalle (Nürnberg) **254**
Maximilian II of Bavaria 251, 268,
    284
Maximilianmuseum (Augsburg)
    286
Maximilianstrasse (Augsburg)
    287
Mecklenburg-Vorpommern 417,
    464-83
    beaches 468-9
    hotels 469
    map 466-7
    restaurants 477
Mecklenburgische Schweiz 473
Medieval towns 14
Meersburg 35, **305**
Meissen **176-7**
Melanchthonhaus (Lutherstadt
    Wittenberg) **151**
Meldorf **458**
Menzel, Adolph 73
Mercedes-Benz Museum
    (Stuttgart) **299**
Merkel, Angela 45
Merseburg **157**
Messegelände (Berlin) **113**
Michaeliskirche (Hamburg) **431**
Michaeliskirche (Hildesheim)
    436, 437
Michaelskirche (Munich) **236**, 240
Michelstadt **379**
Mielke, Erich 117
Mies van der Rohe, Ludwig 95,
    98, 102, 103
Minden **411**
Mineral spas 130
Mineralien- und
    Lagerstättensammlung der
    Bergakademie (Freiberg) 176
Mittelalterliches
    Kriminalmuseum
    (Rothenburg ob der Tauber)
    265
Mittelrhein-Museum (Koblenz)
    348
Mittelrhein wine region 338
Mobile phones 493
Modersohn-Becker, Paula 427,
    439
Möhnesee 408
Moltke, Count Helmut James von
    115
Monasteries and convents
    Abtei Corvey (Höxter) 409

Monasteries and convents (cont.)
    Augustinerkloster (Erfurt)
        188-9
    Gothic abbey (Oybin) 181
    Kloster (Lorsch) 379
    Kloster Chorin **140**
    Kloster Lichtenthal (Baden-
        Baden) 315
    Kloster Maulbronn 323
    Kloster Michelsberg
        (Bamberg) **253**
    Kloster Unser Lieben Frauen
        (Magdeburg) 160, 161
    Maria Laach abbey **349**
    Ottobeuren abbey 280
    Pulheim-Brauweiler
        monastery 407
    St Marienthal (Ostritz) 179
    Steinfeld monastery 402
Mondrian, Piet 386
Monet, Claude 171, 424
Money 487
Monschau 402
Monsterkabinett (Berlin) **84**
Moor- und Fehnmuseum
    (Emden) 438, 439
Moore, Henry 103, 405
Moritzburg **177**
Mosel wine region 339
Mountain climbing 33
Mountains 23
Mozart, Wolfgang Amadeus 225
Müggelberge hills 118
Mühlenhof (Münster) 404, 405
Mulde Valley **174-5**
Munch, Edvard 98, 388, 435
Münden 449
Munich 206, **208-41**
    bars and pubs 216, 231, 232,
        240
    beer 216-17, 231, 232, 240
    culture 214-15
    hotels 239
    itinerary 212-13
    map 210-11
    restaurants 232
    shopping 228
    walk 240-41
Munich Secession **215**
Münster **404-5**
Münster St Martin (Bonn) **396**
Müritz, Nationalpark **472-3**
Museum Mile (Bonn) **397**
Museuminsel (Berlin) **72-5**
Museums and galleries
    see individual entries
Museum am Dom Trier **342**
Museum am Ostwall
    (Dortmund) 399
Museum Barberini (Potsdam)
    137
Museum Blindenwerkstatt Otto
    Weidt (Berlin) **84**

Museum Brandhorst (Munich) **236**

Museum der Bayerischen Geschichte (Regensburg) 282-3

Museum der Bildenden Künste (Leipzig) **167**

Museum der Brot und Kunst (Ulm) 324

Museum in der Kulturbrauerei (Berlin) 116-17

Museum Europäischer Kulturen (Berlin) **119**

Museum Folkwang (Essen) 400

Museum Fünf Kontinente (Munich) **231**

Museum für Angewandte Kunst (Frankfurt am Main) **368**

Museum für Film und Fernsehen (Berlin) **97**

Museum für Kunst- und Kulturgeschichte (Dortmund) 399

Museum für Moderne Kunst (MMK) (Frankfurt am Main) **369**

Museum für Naturkunde (Berlin) **100**, 101

Museum für Sächsische Volkskunst (Jägerhof) (Dresden) **171**

Museum Kunst Palast (Düsseldorf) **387**

Museum Künstlerkolonie (Darmstadt) 378

Museum Kurhaus Kleve-Ewald Mataré-Sammlung (Kleve) 398

Museum Ludwig (Köln) **390**

Museum Mile (Bonn) **397**

Museum Schloss Hohentübingen 323

Museum Schlösschen im Hofgarten (Wertheim) 310

Museumsdorf Cloppenburg 439

Museum Ulm (Ulm) 324

Music 15, 25

   Berlin **66-7**

   live events 26

   see also Entertainment

Musikinstrumenten-Museum (Berlin) **99**, 103

My God, Help Me to Survive This Deadly Love (Vrubel) 111

N

Nahe wine region 339

Napoleon I, Emperor 42, 163

National parks

   Nationalpark Jasmund 469, **474-5**

National parks (cont.)

   Nationalpark Müritz **472-3**

   Nationalpark Neidersächsisches Wattenmeer 438

   Western Pomerania Lagoon Area National Park **478**

Nature reserves

   Gegensteine-Schierberg 161

   Pfaueninsel (Berlin) **120-21**

   Schorfheide-Chorin biosphere reserve 139, 140

   Spreewald **142**

Naturmuseum Senckenberg (Frankfurt am Main) **368**

Naumburg **153**

Naumburg Dom **152-3**

Naumburg Master 152

Nazi Party 43

   Dokumentationszentrum Reichsparteitagsgelände (Nürnberg) **257**

   NS-Dokumentationszentrum (Munich) **236-7**

Neanderthal Museum (Düsseldorf) **387**

Neo-Classical architecture 21

Neuberg an der Donau **276**

Neubrandenburg **477**

Neue Galerie (Kassel) **360**

Neue Nationalgalerie (Berlin) **98**, 103

Neue Residenz und Staatsgalerie (Bamberg) **253**

Neue Schatzkammer and Wallfahrtsmuseum (Altötting) 278

Neue Synagoge and Centrum Judaicum (Berlin) **84-5**

Neue Wache (Berlin) 21, **77**

Neuer Landtag (Potsdam) **133**

Neuer Pavilion (Schlosspark, Berlin) 113

Neues Museum (Berlin) **73**

Neues Museum Weimar **190**

Neues Rathaus (Dresden) **168**

Neues Rathaus (Hanover) **434**

Neues Rathaus (Munich) **230-31**, 241

Neues Stadtmuseum (Landsberg am Lech) 277

Neukölln (Berlin) **123**

Neumünster (Würzburg) **262-3**

Neuruppin **138-9**

Neuschwanstein 250, **266-7**

Neuwerkirche (Goslar) 440

New Objectivity (*Neue Sachlichkeit*) 65

Newman, Barnett 98

Nicholas I, Tsar 122, 136

Niedersächsisches Landesmuseum (Hanover) **434**

Nightlife 26-7

   Berlin 67

Nikolaikirche (Berlin) 86

Nikolaikirche (Leipzig) **166**

Nikolaikirche (Potsdam) **135**

Nikolaikirche (Wismar) 477

Nikolaiviertel (Berlin) **86-7**

Nikolskoe (Berlin) **122**

Nolde, Emil 405, 438, 459

Norderney 438

Nordhausen 197

North Rhine-Westphalia 353, **380-411**

   hotels 405

   itinerary 384-5

   map 382-3

   restaurants 407

Northern Eifel 381, **402**

Northern Germany **412-83**

   Lower Saxony, Hamburg and Bremen 416, **418-49**

   map 414-15

   Mecklenburg-Vorpommern 417, **464-83**

   Schleswig-Holstein 417, **450-63**

NS-Dokumentationszentrum (Muncih) **236-7**

Nürnberg **254-7**

O

Oberammergau **279**

Oberland (Heligoland) 462

Obersee Lake 35

Oberstdorf **268**, 269

Oktoberfest (Munich) 216, 217

Oldenburg **439**

Olympiapark (Munich) **238**

Olympiastadion (Berlin) **114**

Olympic Games 278, 279

Opernhaus (Hanover) **434**

Oppenheim **347**

Orangerie (Kassel) **361**

Orangerieschloss (Potsdam) **136**

Oranienburg **142**

Osnabrück **442**

Ostfriesische Inseln (East Frisian Islands) 419, **438**

Ostfriesland (East Frisia) **438-9**

Ostritz 179

Ostseebad Binz (Rügen) **474**

Otto I of Bavaria 237

Otto I, Emperor 39, 156, 160

Ottobeuren **280**

Otto-Dix-Haus (Gera) 197

Otto-Lilienthal-Museum (Anklam) 481

Ottoneum (Kassel) **361**

Ottweiler **346-7**

Outdoor activities 32
Overstolzenhaus (Köln) **390**
Oybin **181**

P

Paderborn **409**
Palaces
　Altes Schloss (Schleissheim)
　　274
　Augustusburg (Brühl) 406,
　　407
　Cecilienhof (Potsdam) **134**,
　　135
　Dornburg Palaces (near Jena)
　　200
　Ephraim-Palais (Berlin) 86
　Eremitage (Bayreuth) 281
　Fasanenschlösschen
　　(Moritzburg) 177
　Jagdschloss Grunewald
　　(Berlin) **120**
　Japanisches Palais (Dresden)
　　171
　Kempten Residenz 269
　Klein Glienicke (Berlin) **122-3**
　Kurfürstliches Palais (Trier) **345**
　Leineschloss (Hanover) **434**
　Marble House (Potsdam) **132**
　Neue Residenz (Bamberg)
　　253
　Neues Palais (Potsdam) **136-7**
　Neues Schloss (Bayreuth) 281
　Neues Schloss (Schleissheim)
　　274
　Orangerieschloss (Potsdam)
　　136
　Palais Schwerin (Berlin) 87
　Pfalz (Aachen) 403
　Residenz (Munich) 214, **224-5**
　Residenz (Würzburg) 250,
　　262
　Residenzschloss
　　Ludwigsburg **294-5**
　Schloss (Ludwigslust) 476
　Schloss Augustusburg 180
　Schloss Belvedere (Weimar)
　　192-3
　Schloss Benrath (Düsseldorf)
　　387
　Schloss Branitz (Cottbus) 141
　Schloss Bruchsal 313
　Schloss Charlottenburg
　　(Berlin) **108-9**, 112-13
　Schloss Charlottenhof
　　(Potsdam) **136**
　Schloss Dachau 274
　Schloss Friedenstein (Gotha)
　　197
　Schloss Georgium (Dessau)
　　159
　Schloss Heidecksburg **200**
　Schloss Köpenick (Berlin) 118

Palaces (cont.)
　Schloss Linderhof 251,
　　284-5
　Schloss Lustheim
　　(Schleissheim) 274
　Schloss Moritzburg 177
　Schloss Mosigkau (Dessau)
　　159
　Schloss Muskau (Bad Muskau)
　　178
　Schloss Neue Kammern
　　(Potsdam) **134**
　Schloss Nymphenburg
　　(Munich) **220-21**
　Schloss Oranienburg 142
　Schloss Pfaueninsel (Berlin)
　　121
　Schloss Philippsruhe (Hanau)
　　375
　Schloss Pillnitz (near Pirna)
　　180
　Schloss Sanssouci (Potsdam)
　　132, 136
　Schloss Schwetzingen 312
　Schloss Seehof (Bamberg)
　　253
　Schloss Solitude (Stuttgart)
　　297
　Schloss Sonderhausen 196
　Schloss Tegel (Berlin) **115**
　Schloss Thurn und Taxis
　　(Regensburg) 282, 283
　Schloss Weesenstein (near
　　Pirna) 180
　Schloss Weikersheim 320
　Schloss Weissenstein
　　(Pommersfelden) 270
　Stadtresidenz (Landshut)
　　275
　Wasserschloss Concordia
　　(Bamberg) **252**
　Wilhelmshöhe (Kassel) **361**
　Wittumspalais (Weimar) **191**
　Zwinger (Dresden) **172-3**
Palatinate/Pfalz wine region
　339
Panoramapunkt (Berlin) **97**
Paragliding 33
Parking 491
Parks and gardens
　Brühische Terrasse (Dresden)
　　170
　Burg- und Schlossgarten
　　(Schwerin) **470**
　Burggarten (Rothenburg ob
　　der Tauber) **264**
　Egapark (Erfurt) **189**
　Englischer Garten (Munich)
　　238-9
　Grosser Garten (Dresden) **171**
　Grosssedlitz 182
　Herrenhäuser Gärten
　　(Hanover) **435**

Parks and gardens (cont.)
　Hofgarten (Düsseldorf)
　　386-7
　Klein Glienicke (Berlin) **122-3**
　Mauerpark (Berlin) 63
　Paderquellgebiet (Paderborn)
　　408
　Park Sanssouci (Potsdam) **136**
　Residenzschloss
　　Ludwigsburg **294-5**
　Rhododendronpark (Bremen)
　　426, 427
　Schloss Muskau (Bad Muskau)
　　178
　Schloss Nymphenburg) 220
　Schlossgarten (Stuttgart)
　　297
　Schlosspark (Berlin) 108,
　　112-13
　Tempelhofer Feld (Berlin) 63,
　　115
　Tiergarten (Berlin) **94-5**
　Treptower Park (Berlin) **117**
　Viktoriapark (Berlin)
　　118-19
　Wörlitzer Park **148-9**
　see also National parks;
　　Nature reserves; Theme
　　parks
Passau 248, **285**
Passports 486
Paula-Modersohn-Becker-
　Museum (Bremen) **427**
Paulskirche (Frankfurt am Main)
　366
Pazzi Madonna (Donatello) 65
Peasants' War 196
Peenemünde **482**
Pergamonmuseum (Berlin) **74**, 75
Perleberg 138
Personal security 492
Peter the Great, Tsar 41
Petrikirche (Lübeck) 454
Pfarrkirche (Bad Mergentheim)
　311
Pfarrkirche St Johannis
　(Magdeburg) 161
Pfarrkirche St Mariä
　Himmelfahrt (Köln) 389
　Pfaueninsel (Berlin) **120-21**
Pfunds Molkerei (Dresden)
　171
Pharmacies 492-3
Philharmonie and
　Kammermusiksaal (Berlin)
　66, **98-9**, 103
Philipp-Otto-Runge
　Gedenkstätte (Wolgast) 481
Phrasebook 508-10
Piano, Renzo 97
Picasso, Pablo 98, 112, 126, 386,
　390
　Femme au bouquet 435

Pieck, Wilhelm 117
Pilsensee 275
Pinakothek der Moderne (Munich) **226-7**
Pirna **180**
Plön 460
Poland, day trips to 480
Polke, Sigmar 236
Pommersfelden **270**
Pop and rock music 66, 215
Poppelsdorf (Bonn) **397**
Porcelain
    Grossherzoglich-Hessische Porzellansammlung (Darmstadt) 378
    Staatliche Porzellan-Manufaktur (Meissen) 176-7
Port, The (Hamburg) **431**
Porta Nigra (Trier) **344**
Portrait of Christiane of Eulenau (Cranach) 253
Postal services 493
Potsdam 125, **132-7**
Potsdam Conference 44, 134, **135**
Potsdamer Platz (Berlin) **96-7**
Praetorium (Köln) 389
Predigerkirche (Eisenach) 195
Preetz 460
Prenzlauer Berg (Berlin) **116**
Prerow 482
Prices
    average daily spend 486
    public transport 488
Pritzwalk 138
Propyläen (Munich) **237**
Prora (Rügen) 474
Prussia 41, 42
Prusso-Danish War 95
Public holidays 487
Public transport **490**
    prices 488
Puppen- und Spielzeugmuseum (Rottweil) 321
Putbus (Rügen) **475**

Q

Quedlinburg **156**
Querfurt **157**

R

Racing cars 33
Rail travel 488, 489
    Black Forest Railway 307
    Brockenbahn 155
    "Molli" narrow-gauge railway 479
Ramsau an der Ache **259**
Raphael
    Canigiani Holy Family 219
    Sistine Madonna 173

Rathaus (Augsburg) 287
Rathaus (Bremen) **425**
Rathaus (Kiel) 461
Rathaus (Köln) **389**
Rathaus (Lübeck) 454
Rathaus (Lüneburg) 443
Rathaus (Lutherstadt Wittenberg) **150-51**
Rathaus (Münster) 404, 405
Rathaus (Nürnberg) **256**
Rathaus (Rothenburg ob der Tauber) **264**
Rathaus Schöneberg (Berlin) **119**
Rathaus (Tangermünde) 159
Rathausmarkt (Hamburg) **428**
Rathausplatz (Schwerin) **470-71**
Ratzeburg **461**
Ravensburg **324-5**
Reasons to Love Germany **12-15**
Reformation 40
    Lutherhaus (Lutherstadt Wittenberg) **151**
    Lutherstadt Eisleben **155**
Regensburg (Ratisbon) **282**
Regierungsviertel (Berlin) **100**
Reichenau **304**
Reichstag (Berlin) 43, 63, **92-3**
Reiss-Engelhorn-Museum (Mannheim) 312, 313
Rembrandt 369, 424
Renaissance art 65
Residenz (Munich) 214, **224-5**
Residenz (Würzburg) 250, **262**
Residenzschloss (Dresden) **170**
Residenzschloss Ludwigsburg **294-5**
Restaurants
    Baden-Württemberg 311
    Bavaria 273
    Berlin 84, 93, 119
    Brandenburg 142
    Hesse 363, 373
    Mecklenburg-Vorpommern 477
    Munich 232
    North Rhine-Westphalia 407
    Rhineland-Palatinate and Saarland 350
    Saxony 179
    Saxony Anhalt 157
    Schleswig-Holstein 461
    Thuringia 192
Reunification 44-5
Rheingau wine region **372**
Rheinhessen wine region 339
Rheinisches Freilichtmuseum Kommern **402**
Rheinisches Landesmuseum (Bonn) **397**
Rheinisches Landesmuseum (Trier) **343**

Rheinufer (Bonn) **396**
Rhineland-Palatinate and Saarland 332, **334-53**
    bars and pubs 349
    driving tour 352-3
    map 336-7
    restaurants 350
    wine regions 338-9
Richard Wagner Museum (Bayreuth) 281
Riemenschneider, Tilman 194, 196
Rivers 23
Road travel 491
Rock climbing 33
Rödertor (Rothenburg ob der Tauber) **265**
Rodin, Auguste 201
Roemer-Pelizaeus Museum (Hildesheim) 436, 437
Romanesque architecture 20
Romanesque Route 148, 152, **160**, 161
Romans 38
    Aachen 403
    Hechingen 302
    Kempten 269
    Köln 389, 391
    Mainz 350
    Teutoburger Wald 410
    Trier 342-5
    Xanten 398-9
Romanticism 64
Römerberg (Frankfurt am Main) **367**
Römisch-Germanisches Museum (Köln) **391**
Römisch-Germanisches Zentralmuseum (Mainz) 350, 351
Römischer Bäder (Potsdam) **137**
Roseliushaus (Bremen) **427**
Rostock 465, **482**
Rotes Rathaus (Berlin) **80-81**, 87
Rothaargebirge 381, 408
Rothenburg Museum **265**
Rothenburg ob der Tauber **264-5**
    shopping 264
Rottweil **320-21**
Rubens, Peter Paul 159, 197, 424
    Last Judgement 219
Rüdesheim 372
Rügen 465, 468, 469, **474-5**
Rules of the road 488, 491
Russische Kirche (Leipzig) **167**

S

S-Bahn 490
Saalfeld **200-201**
Saarbrücken **346**
Saarland see Rhineland-Palatinate and Saarland

Sababurg 35
Sachsenhausen 142
Sächsische Schweiz 163, **182-3**
Sächsische Staatsoper
  (Dresden) **168**
Safety
  cycling 491
  government advice 486
  personal security 492
SAIL City (Bremerhaven)
  437
Saint Luke Drawing the Virgin
  (van der Weyden) 218
Saint Phalle, Niki de 435
Sammlung Berggruen (Berlin)
  112
Sammlung Schack (Munich) 215,
  234-5
Sankt Peter-Ording **458-9**
Sanssouci (Potsdam) 132, 136-7
Sauerland 381, **408**
Sausages 30, 31
Saxony 53, **162-83**
  driving tour 182-3
  map 164-5
  restaurants 179
Saxony Anhalt 52, **144-61**
  hotels 153
  map 146-7
  restaurants 157
Schabbelhaus (Lübeck) **456**
Schadow, Johann Gottfried 73, 76
Scharoun, Hans 98-9, 102, 103
Scheibe, Ricard, *Fortuna* 108
Schiller, Friedrich 78, 79, 193,
  200
  Schiller-Geburtshaus
    (Marbach) 318
  Schiller-Nationalmuseum
    (Marbach) 318
  Schillerhaus (Weimar) **191**
Schillerplatz (Stuttgart) **298**,
  299
Schinkel, Karl Friedrich **20**, 21,
  77, 139
  Alte Nationalgalerie (Berlin)
    73
  Altes Museum (Berlin) 74
  Gotischer Dom am Wasser 64
  Klein Glienicke (Berlin) 122
  Konzerthaus (Berlin) 79
  Neue Wache (Berlin) 77
  Nikolaikirche (Potsdam) 135
  Römischer Bäder (Potsdam)
    137
  Schloss Babelsberg
    (Potsdam) 136
  Schloss Charlottenhof
    (Potsdam) 136
  Schloss Tegel (Berlin) 115
  Schlosspark (Berlin) 113
  Viktoriapark (Berlin) 118
  Zittau 179

Schleiden 402
Schleissheim **274**
Schleswig **460-61**
Schleswig-Holstein 417, **450-63**
  map 452-3
  restaurants 461
Schleswig-Holsteinisches
  Freilichtmuseum (Kiel) 461
Schleswig-Holsteinisches
  Landesmuseum (Schleswig)
  460, 461
Schliemann, Heinrich 72
Schloss (Schwerin) **470**
Schloss Babelsberg (Potsdam)
  134
Schloss Belvedere (Weimar)
  192-3
Schloss Benrath (Düsseldorf)
  387
Schloss Charlottenburg (Berlin)
  108-9, 112-13
Schloss Charlottenhof
  (Potsdam) **136**
Schloss Heidecksburg **200**
Schloss Hohenschwangau 251,
  268
Schloss Linderhof 251, **284-5**
Schloss Neue Kammern
  (Potsdam) **134**
Schloss Neuschwanstein 250,
  266-7
Schloss Nymphenburg (Munich)
  220-21
Schloss Sanssouci (Potsdam)
  132, 136
Schloss Seehof (Bamberg) **253**
Schloss Solitude (Stuttgart) **297**
Schloss Tegel (Berlin) **115**
Schlossgarten (Stuttgart) **297**
Schlosskirche (Lutherstadt
  Wittenberg) **150**
Schlossmuseum (Darmstadt)
  378
Schlosspark (Berlin) 108, **112-13**
Schlossplatz (Stuttgart) **296**
Schmidt-Rottluff, Karl 65
Schnoorviertel (Bremen) **426**
Schnütgen-Museum (Köln) **390**
Schokoladen Museum (Köln)
  390-91
Schütting (Bremen) **426**
Schwäbisch Gmünd **316**
Schwäbisch Hall **313**
Schwäbische Alb **302-3**
Schwarzwald 29, 289, **306-7**
Schwedenspeicher-Museum
  (Stade) 442
Schwerin 465, **470-71**
Schwetzingen **312**
Schwind, Moritz von 215, 235,
  268
Semper Gallery (Zwinger,
  Dresden) 173

Seven Years' War 163
Severinsviertel (Köln) **391**
Shopping
  Bavaria 264
  Munich 228
  opening hours 487
Siebengebirge 392, 406
Sieburg 406
Siegen **407**
Siegessäule (Berlin) **95**
Sigmaringen **302**
Sistine Madonna (Raphael) 173
Smoking 493
Soest **408-9**
Sögel 439
Solingen **401**
Soltau **443**
Sonderhausen **196-7**
Sorbisches Museum (Bautzen)
  178
Sorbs (Lusatians/Wends) 178,
  181
Southern Germany **202-327**
  Baden-Württemberg 207,
    288-327
  Bavaria 207, **242-87**
  map 204-5
  Munich 206, **208-41**
Spandau **114**
Spas 13
  Aachen **403**
  Bad Berleburg 408
  Bad Cannstatt (Stuttgart)
    299
  Bad Frankenhausen 196
  Bad Godesburg 406
  Bad Homburg **376**
  Bad Iburg 442
  Bad Muskau **178**
  Bad Salzuflen 411
  Bad Schandau 183
  Baden-Baden **314-15**
  Brandenburg **130-31**
  Fontane Therme (Neuruppin)
    138-9
  Oybin **181**
  Usedom 469
  Wiesbaden **376-7**
Specific requirements,
  travellers with 487
Speed limit 480
Speicherstadt (Hamburg)
  430
Speyer **351**
Spielkartenmuseum (Altenburg)
  201
Spielzeugmuseum (Munich) 230
Spielzeugmuseum (Nürnberg)
  29, **256**
Spitzweg, Carl 235
Sport 13
Spree, River 72, 110
Spreewald **142**

Sprengel Museum (Hanover) **435**
Staatliche Antikensammlungen (Munich) **237**
Staatliche Kunsthalle Baden-Baden 315
Staatliche Kunsthalle (Karlsruhe) 317
Staatliches Museum (Schwerin) **471**
Staatsbibliothek (Berlin) 103
Staatsgalerie (Stuttgart) **298**
Staatsoper Unter Den Linden (Berlin) 78, **79**
Stade **442**
Städelsches Kunstinstitut (Franfurt am Main) **369**
Stadt- und Bergbaumuseum (Freiberg) 176
Stadtbibliothek (Trier) **343**
Stadtgeschichtliches Museum (Tangermünde) 159
Stadthagen **444**
Stadthaus (Berlin) 87
Stadtkirche (Bückeburg) 445
Stadtkirche (Celle) 444
Stadtkirche (Ludwigslust) 476
Stadtkirche St Wenzel (Naumburg) 153
Stadtmuseum (Baden-Baden) 315
Stadtmuseum (Brandenburg/Havel) 139
Stadtmuseum (Erfurt) **189**
Stadtmuseum (Lindau) 283
Stadtmuseum (Munich) **229**
Stadtmuseum (Rottweil) 321
Stadtmuseum (Tübingen) 323
Stadtmuseum (Weimar) **190**
Stadtmuseum im Prinz-Max-Palais (Karlsruhe) 317
Stadtschloss (Weimar) **191**
St Andreas (Köln) 390–91
St Annen-Museum (Lübeck) 455, **457**
St Annen-Stift (Goslar) 440, 441
St Apostein (Köln) 390–91
Starnberger See 267, 274–5
Stasi 44, 83, **117**
    Stasi-Museum (Berlin) **117**
    Stasi-Prison (Berlin) **117**
Stauffenberg, Claus Schenk von 96, 115
Stella, Frank 98
Stendal 161
Stephanskirche (Tangermünde) 161
St Gereon (Köln) 389, **391**
Stiftskirche (Hl. Kreuz) (Stuttgart) **298**
Stiftskirche St Georg (Tübingen) 322, 323

Stiftskirche St Servatius (Quedlinburg) 156
St Jakobi (Goslar) 440
St Jakob's Kirche (Rothenburg ob der Tauber) **264**
St-Johannis-Friedhof (Nürnberg) **257**
St Kajetan (Munich) **232–3**
St Kolumba 388, 390
St Leonhardskirche (Frankfurt am Main) **365**
St Martin (Mainz) 352
St Martini (Braunschweig) 446
St Martini (Stadthagen) 444
St-Matthäus-Kirche (Berlin) 103
St Nikolai (Stendal) 161
St Pauli (Hamburg) **431**
St Peter und St Paul (Weimar) **190**
St Petri Dom (Bremen) **425**
St Petrikirche (Hamburg) **428**
Stralsund 465, **483**
Strandbad Wannsee (Berlin) **120**
Straubing **273**
Street art 65
Street food 62
St Severi-Kirche (Erfurt) **188**
St Stephan-Kirche (Mainz) 350–51
St Stephans Dom (Halberstadt) 154
St Ursula (Köln) **391**
Stuttgart **296–9**
    bars and pubs 297
Suermondt-Ludwig-Museum (Aachen) 403
Świnoujście (Poland) 480
Sylt **458**
Synagogues
    Neue Synagogue and Centrum Judaicum (Berlin) **84–5**
    Synagogue (Celle) 444

T

Tangermünde **159**, 161
Tap water 492
Tauberbischofsheim **310–11**
Tauberländer Dorfmuseum (Weikersheim) 320
Taxes 493
Taxis 491
TECHNOSEUM (Mannheim) 312–13
Telephone services 493
Tempelhofer Feld (Berlin) 63, **115**
Teutoburger Wald 381, **410**, 411, 442
Teutonic Knights **310**, 311
The Poet Iwar von Lücken, The (Dix) 65

Theatre 25
    see also Entertainment
Theme and amusement parks
    Europa Park **318–19**
    Heidepark Soltau 443
    Movie Park Germany 409
    Phantasialand 406-7
Therme 130, 131
Thirty Years' War 41
    Brandenburg 125
    Magdeburg 160
    Oberammergau 279
Thuringia 53, **184–201**
    map 186–7
    restaurants 192
Thuringian War of Secession 185
Tickets, public transport 490
Tiergarten (Berlin) **94–5**
Time zone 492
Tipping 487
Titian 218
    Tribute Money 173
Topographie des Terrors (Berlin) 63, **82–3**
Torgau **174**
Tours *see* Driving tours; Itineraries
Trains *see* Rail travel
Trams 490
Travel
    getting around **488–91**
    government advice 486
Travemünde 457
Treptower Park (Berlin) **117**
Tribute Money (Titian) 173
Trier **342–5**
Tübingen 289, **322–3**
Twombly, Cy 236

U

U-Bahn 490
Übersee-Museum (Bremen) **427**
Ulm **324**
Ulm Münster 324
Universistät (Bonn) **396**
Universitätmuseum (Heidelberg) 309
Unter den Linden (Berlin) **77**
Unterland (Heligoland) 462
Usedom 469, 480, **481–2**

V

Vaccinations 487
Van der Velde, Henry 399
Van Dyck, Anthony 197, 424
Van Eyck, Jan 102, 369
Van Gogh, Vincent 171
    Field with Poppies 424
Van Goyen, Jan 197

Van Mieris, Frans, *Family Recital* 471
VAT refunds 493
Verden an der Aller **445**
Verkehrsmuseum (Johanneum) (Dresden) **169**
Vermeer, Jan 102, 173
Victoria, Queen 197
Viehmarktthermen (Trier) **344**
Vierzehnheiligen **272**
Vikings 460
Viktoriapark (Berlin) **118-19**
Viktualienmarkt (Munich) **230**, 231
Vinache, Jean Joseph 169
Virgin with Child (Leonardo da Vinci) 219
Visas 486
Visbek 439
Vitte 468
Völkerschlachtdenkmal (Leipzig) **166**
Völklingen **346**
Volkswagenwerk Autostadt (Wolfsburg) 444-5
Von der Heydt-Museum (Wuppertal) 400
Vrubel, Dmitri 65
My God, Help Me to Survive This Deadly Love 111

W

Waase (Rügen) **474**
Wagner, Richard 194, 266, **280**, 295
   Richard Wagner Museum (Bayreuth) 281
Waldecker Land 355, **362-3**
Walhalla **271**
Walking and hiking **491**
Walks
   A Short Walk: Around Marienplatz (Munich) **240-41**
   A Short Walk: Around the Kulturforum (Berlin) **102-3**
   A Short Walk: Augsburg **286-7**
   A Short Walk: Heidelberg **326-7**
   A Short Walk: Heligoland **462**
   A Short Walk: Nikolaiviertel (Berlin) **86-7**
Wallfahrtskirche Maria Gern **258-9**
Wallraf-Richartz-Museum & Fondation Corboud (Köln) **388-9**
Wannsee (Berlin) **120-21**

Warhol, Andy 236, 369
   Big Torn Campbell's Soup Can (Black Bean) 19
   Mao 100
Wasserburg **304**
Watersports 32
Websites 492
Weidt, Otto 84
Weigel, Helene 101
Weikersheim **320**
Weil der Stadt **319**
Weilburg **377**
Weimar 185, **190-93**
   Weimar years 43
Weissbier 217
Wendisches Museum (Cottbus) 141
Werdenfels Museum (Garmisch-Partenkirchen) 279
Werder 139
Wernigerode **154-5**
Wertheim **310**
Weser Renaissance Trail **449**
Weserrenaissance-Museum (Lemgo) 410
Wesslingersee 275
West Germany *see* Federal Republic of Germany
Western Germany **328-411**
   Hesse 333, **354-79**
   map 330-31
   North Rhine-Westphalia 353, **380-411**
   Rhineland-Palatinate and Saarland 332, **334-53**
Western Pomerania Lagoon Area National Park **478**
Westerwald, The **340-41**
Wetzlar **374-5**
Weyden, Rogier van der, *Saint Luke Drawing the Virgin* 218
Wi-Fi 493
Wieck (Greifswald) 480
Wieck (near Rostock) 482
Wiesbaden **376-7**
Wikinger-Museum Haithabu (Schleswig) 460-61
Wildlife
   birdwatching (Western Pomerania Lagoon Area National Park) 479
   Schloss Nymphenburg (Munich) 220
Wilhelm I, Kaiser 113, 411
Wilhelm-Lehmbruck-Museum (Duisburg) 405
Wilhelmshöhe (Kassel) **361**
Wine 14
   Deutsche Weinstrasse **352-3**
   red wines 338
   Rheingau wine region 372
   Rhineland-Palatinate and Saarland **338-9**

Winterberg 408
Wismar 465, **476-7**
Wittelsbach dynasty 220, 224, 274, 308
Wittenberg *see* Lutherstadt Wittenberg
Wittenberg Castle (Lutherstadt Wittenberg) **150**
Wittumspalais (Weimar) **191**
Wolfenbüttel **441**
Wolfsburg **444-5**
Wolgast **481**
World War I 42
   Neue Wache (Berlin) **77**
World War II 43
   Bendlerblock (Gedenkstätte Deutscher Wilderstand) (Berlin) **96**
   Buchenwald **193**
   Gedenkstätte Bergen-Belsen 443
   Gedenkstätte Plötzensee (Berlin) **115**
   Gedenkstätte Stille Heiden (Berlin) **84**
   Holocaust Denkmal (Berlin) 63, **76**
   Kaiser-Wilhelm-Gedächtnis-Kirche (Berlin) **99**
   KZ-Gedenkstätte (Dachau) 274
   Peenemünde 482
   Potsdam Conference **135**
   Sachsenhausen 142
   Topographie des Terrors (Berlin) 63, **82-3**
Wörlitzer Park **148-9**
Worms **347**
Worpswede **441**
Worpsweder Kunsthalle 441
Wörthsee 275
Wuppertal **400-401**
Würzburg 250, **262-3**

X

Xanten **398-9**

Z

Zeughaus (Augsburg) 286
Zeughaus (Berlin) **78-9**
Zitadelle Spandau (Berlin) **114**
Zittau **179**
Zoo Berlin (Berlin) **94-5**
Zugspitze 279
Zwickau **175**
Zwinger (Dresden) **172-3**

PHRASE BOOK

IN AN EMERGENCY

Where is the telephone?	Wo ist das telefon?	voh ist duss tele-fon?
Help!	Hilfe!	hilf-uh
Please call a doctor	Bitte rufen Sie einen Arzt	bitt-uh roof'n zee ine-en artst
Please call the police	Bitte rufen Sie die Polizei	bitt-uh roof'n zee dee poli-tsy
Please call the fire brigade	Bitte rufen Sie die Feuerwehr	bitt-uh roof'n zee dee foyer-vayr
Stop!	Halt!	hult

COMMUNICATION ESSENTIALS

Yes	Ja	yah
No	Nein	nine
Please	Bitte	bitt-uh
Thank you	Danke	dunk-uh
Excuse me	Verzeihung	fair-tsy-hoong
Hello (good day)	Guten Tag	goot-en tahk
Goodbye	Auf Wiedersehen	owf-veed-er-zay-ern
Good evening	Guten Abend	goot'n ahb'nt
Good night	Gute Nacht	goot-uh nukht
Until tomorrow	Bis morgen	biss morg'n
See you	Tschüss	chooss
What is that?	Was ist das?	voss ist duss
Why?	Warum?	var-room
Where?	Wo?	voh
When?	Wann?	vunn
today	heute	hoyt-uh
tomorrow	morgen	morg'n
month	Monat	mohn-aht
night	Nacht	nukht
afternoon	Nachmittag	nahkh-mit-tahk
morning	Morgen	morg'n
year	Jahr	yar
there	dort	dort
here	hier	hear
week	Woche	vokh-uh
yesterday	gestern	gest'n
evening	Abend	ahb'nt

USEFUL PHRASES

How are you? (informal)	Wie geht's?	vee gayts
Fine, thanks	Danke, es geht mir gut	dunk-uh, es gayt meer goot
Until later	Bis später	biss shpay-ter
Where is/are?	Wo ist/sind...?	voh ist/sind
How far is it to...?	Wie weit ist es...?	vee vite ist ess
Do you speak English?	Sprechen Sie Englisch?	shpresh'n zee eng-glish
I don't understand	Ich verstehe nicht	ish fair-shtay-uh nisht
Could you speak more slowly?	Könnten Sie langsamer sprechen?	kurnt-en zee lung-zam-er shpresh'n

USEFUL WORDS

large	gross	grohss
small	klein	kline
hot	heiss	hyce
cold	kalt	kult
good	gut	goot
bad	böse/schlecht	burss-uh/shlesht
open	geöffnet	g'urff-nett
closed	geschlossen	g'shloss'n
left	links	links
right	rechts	reshts
straight ahead	geradeaus	g'rah-der-owss

MAKING A TELEPHONE CALL

I would like to make a phone call	Ich möchte telefonieren	ish mer-shtuh tel-e-fon-eer'n
I'll try again later	Ich versuche es später noch einmal	ish fair-zookh-uh es shpay-ter nokh ine-mull
Can I leave a message?	Kann ich eine Nachricht hinterlassen?	kan ish ine-uh nakh-risht hinter-lahss-en
answer phone	Anrufbeantworter	an-roof-be-ahnt-vort-er
telephone card	Telefonkarte	tel-e-fohn-kart-uh
receiver	Hörer	hur-er
mobile	Handy	han-dee
engaged (busy)	besetzt	b'zetst
wrong number	Falsche Verbindung	falsh-uh fair-bin-doong

SIGHTSEEING

library	Bibliothek	bib-leo-tek
entrance ticket	Eintrittskarte	ine-tritz-kart-uh
cemetery	Friedhof	freed-hofe
train station	Bahnhof	barn-hofe
gallery	Galerie	gall-er-ree
information	Auskunft	owss-koonft
church	Kirche	keersh-uh
garden	Garten	gart'n
palace/castle	Palast/Schloss	pallast/shloss
place (square)	Platz	plats
bus stop	Haltestelle	hal-te-shtel-uh
national holiday	Nationalfeiertag	nats-yon-ahl-fire-tahk
theatre	Theater	tay-aht-er
free admission	Eintritt frei	ine-tritt fry

SHOPPING

Do you have/ Is there...?	Gibt es...?	geept ess
How much does it cost?	Was kostet das?	voss kost't duss?
When do you open?	Wann öffnen Sie?	vunn off'n zee
close?	schliessen Sie?	shlees'n zee
this	das	duss
expensive	teuer	toy-er
cheap	preiswert	price-vurt
size	Grösse	gruhs-uh
number	Nummer	noom-er
colour	Farbe	farb-uh
brown	braun	brown
black	schwarz	shvarts
red	rot	roht
blue	blau	blau
green	grün	groon
yellow	gelb	gelp

TYPES OF SHOP

antique shop	Antiquariat	antik-var-yat
chemist (pharmacy)	Apotheke	appo-tay-kuh
bank	Bank	bunk
market	Markt	markt
travel agency	Reisebüro	rye-zer-boo-roe
department store	Warenhaus	vahr'n-hows
chemist's/ drugstore	Drogerie	droog-er-ree
hairdresser	Friseur	freezz-er
newspaper kiosk	Zeitungskiosk	tsytoongs-kee-osk
bookshop	Buchhandlung	bookh-hant-loong
bakery	Bäckerei	beck-er-eye
post office	Post	posst
shop/store	Geschäft/Laden	gush-eft/lard'n

film processing shop	**Fotogeschäft**	fo-to-gush-**eft**
self-service shop	**Selbstbedienungs- laden**	selpst-bed-**ee**-nungs-lard'n
shoe shop	**Schuhladen**	shoo-lard'n
clothes shop	**Kleiderladen/ Boutique**	klyder-lard'n boo-**teek**-uh
food shop	**Lebensmittel- geschäft**	lay-bens-mittel-gush-eft
glass, porcelain	**Glas, Porzellan**	glars, port-sell-ahn

STAYING IN A HOTEL

Do you have any vacancies?	**Haben Sie noch Zimmer frei?**	harb'n zee nokh tsimm-er-fry
with twin beds?	**mit zwei Betten?**	mitt tsvy bett'n
with a	**mit einem**	mitt ine'm
double bed?	**Doppelbett?**	dopp'l-bet
with a bath?	**mit Bad?**	mitt bart
with a shower?	**mit Dusche?**	mitt doosh-uh
I have a reservation	**Ich habe eine Reservierung**	ish harb-uh ine-uh rez-er-veer-oong
key	**Schlüssel**	shlooss'l
porter	**Pförtner**	pfert-ner

EATING OUT

Do you have a table for...?	**Haben Sie einen Tisch für...?**	harb'n zee tish foor
I would like to reserve a table	**Ich möchte eine Reservierung machen**	ish mer-shtuh ine-uh rezer-veer-oong makh'n
I'm a vegetarian	**Ich bin Vegetarier**	ish bin vegg-er-tah-ree-er
Waiter!	**Herr Ober!**	hair oh-barel
The bill (check), please	**Die Rechnung, bitte**	dee resh-noong bitt-uh
breakfast	**Frühstück**	froo-shtock
lunch	**Mittagessen**	mit-targ-ess'n
dinner	**Abendessen**	arb'nt-ess'n
bottle	**Flasche**	flush-uh
dish of the day	**Tagesgericht**	tahg-es-gur-isht
main dish	**Hauptgericht**	howpt-gur-isht
dessert	**Nachtisch**	nahkh-tish
cup	**Tasse**	tass-uh
wine list	**Weinkarte**	vine-kart-uh
tankard	**Krug**	khroog
glass	**Glas**	glars
spoon	**Löffel**	lerff'l
teaspoon	**Teelöffel**	tay-lerff'l
tip	**Trinkgeld**	trink-gelt
knife	**Messer**	mess-er
starter (appetizer)	**Vorspeise**	for-shpize-uh
the bill	**Rechnung**	resh-noong
plate	**Teller**	tell-er
fork	**Gabel**	gahb'l

MENU DECODER

Aal	arl	eel
Apfel	upf'l	apple
Apfelschorle	upf'l-shoorl-uh	apple juice with sparkling mineral water
Apfelsine	upf'l-seen-uh	orange
Aprikose	upri-kawz-uh	apricot
Artischocke	arti-shokh-uh-	artichoke
Aubergine	or-ber-jeen-uh	aubergine (eggplant)
Banane	bar-narn-uh	banana
Beefsteak	beef-stayk	steak
Bier	beer	beer
Bockwurst	bokh-voorst	a type of sausage
Bohnensuppe	burn-en-zoop-uh	bean soup
Branntwein	brant-vine	spirits
Bratkartoffeln	brat-kar-toff'ln	fried potatoes
Bratwurst	brat-voorst	fried sausage
Brot	brot	bread
Brötchen	bret-tchen	bread roll
Brühe	bruh-uh	broth
Butter	boot-ter	butter
Champignon	shum-pin-yong	mushroom
Currywurst	kha-ree-voorst	sausage with curry sauce
Dill	dill	dill
Ei	eye	egg
Eis	ice	ice/ice cream
Ente	ent-uh	duck
Erdbeeren	ayrt-beer'n	strawberries
Fisch	fish	fish
Forelle	for-ell-uh	trout
Frikadelle	Frika-dayl-uh	rissole/ hamburger
Gans	ganns	goose
Garnele	gar-nayl-uh	prawn/shrimp
gebraten	g'braat'n	fried
gegrillt	g'grilt	grilled
gekocht	g'kokht	boiled
geräuchert	g'rowk-ert	smoked
Geflügel	g'floog'l	poultry
Gemüse	g'mooz-uh	vegetables
Grütze	grurt-ser	groats, gruel
Gulasch	goo-lush	goulash
Gurke	goork-uh	gherkin
Hammelbraten	hamm'l-braat'n	roast mutton
Hähnchen	haynsh'n	chicken
Hering	hair-ing	herring
Himbeeren	him-beer'n	raspberries
Honig	hoe-nikh	honey
Kaffee	kaf-fay	coffee
Kalbfleisch	kalp-flysh	veal
Kaninchen	ka-neensh'n	rabbit
Karpfen	karpf'n	carp
Kartoffelpüree	kar-toff'l-poor-ay	mashed potatoes
Käse	kayz-uh	cheese
Kaviar	kar-vee-ar	caviar
Knoblauch	k'nob-lowkh	garlic
Knödel	k'nerd'l	noodle
Kohl	koal	cabbage
Kopfsalat	kopf-zal-aat	lettuce
Krebs	krayps	crab
Kuchen	kookh'n	cake
Lachs	lahkhs	salmon
Leber	lay-ber	liver
mariniert	mari-neert	marinated
Marmelade	marmer-lard-uh	marmalade, jam
Meerrettich	may-re-tish	horseradish
Milch	milsh	milk
Mineralwasser	minn-er-arl-vuss-er	mineral water
Möhre	mer-uh	carrot
Nuss	nooss	nut
Öl	erl	oil
Olive	o-leev-uh	olive
Petersilie	payt-er-zee-li-uh	parsley
Pfeffer	pfeff-er	pepper
Pfirsich	pfir-zish	peach
Pflaumen	pflow-men	plum
Pommes frites	pomm-fritt	chips/ French fries
Quark	kvark	soft cheese
Radieschen	ra-deesh'n	radish
Rinderbraten	rind-er-brat'n	joint of beef
Rinderroulade	rind-er-roo-lard-uh	beef olive
Rindfleisch	rint-flysh	beef
Rippchen	rip-sh'n	cured pork rib
Rotkohl	raht-koal	red cabbage
Rüben	rhoob'n	turnip
Rührei	rhoo-er-eye	scrambled eggs

Saft	**zuft**	*juice*
Salat	*zal-aat*	*salad*
Salz	**zults**	*salt*
Salzkartoffeln	*zults-kar-toff'l*	*boiled potatoes*
Sauerkirschen	*zow-er-***keersh'n**	*cherries*
Sauerkraut	*zow-er-krowt*	*sauerkraut*
Sekt	**zekt**	*sparkling wine*
Senf	**zenf**	*mustard*
scharf	*sharf*	*spicy*
Schaschlik	*shash-lik*	*kebab*
Schlagsahne	*shlahgg-zarn-uh*	*whipped cream*
Schnittlauch	*shnit-lowhkh*	*chives*
Schnitzel	**shnitz'l**	*veal or pork cutlet*
Schweinefleisch	*shvine-flysh*	*pork*
Spargel	**shparg'l**	*asparagus*
Spiegelei	*shpeeg'l-eye*	*fried egg*
Spinat	*shpin-art*	*spinach*
Tee	*tay*	*tea*
Tomate	*tom-art-uh*	*tomato*
Wassermelone	*vuss-er-me-lohn-uh*	*watermelon*
Wein	*vine*	*wine*
Weintrauben	*vine-trowb'n*	*grapes*
Wiener Würstchen	*veen-er voorst-sh'n*	*frankfurter*
Zander	**tsan-der**	*pike-perch*
Zitrone	*tsi-trohn-uh*	*lemon*
Zucker	**tsook-er**	*sugar*
Zwieback	*tsvee-bak*	*rusk*
Zwiebel	**tsveeb'l**	*onion*

NUMBERS

0	**null**	*nool*
1	**eins**	*eye'ns*
2	**zwei**	*tsvy*
3	**drei**	*dry*
4	**vier**	*feer*
5	**fünf**	*foonf*
6	**sechs**	*zex*
7	**sieben**	*zeeb'n*
8	**acht**	*uhkht*
9	**neun**	*noyn*
10	**zehn**	*tsayn*
11	**elf**	*elf*
12	**zwölf**	*tserlf*
13	**dreizehn**	*dry-tsayn*
14	**vierzehn**	*feer-tsayn*
15	**fünfzehn**	*foonf-tsayn*
16	**sechzehn**	*zex-tsayn*
17	**siebzehn**	*zeep-tsayn*
18	**achtzehn**	*uhkht-tsayn*
19	**neunzehn**	*noyn-tsayn*
20	**zwanzig**	*tsvunn-tsig*
21	**einundzwanzig**	*ine-oont-tsvunn-tsig*
30	**dreissig**	*dry-sig*
40	**vierzig**	*feer-sig*
50	**fünfzig**	*foonf-tsig*
60	**sechzig**	*zex-tsig*
70	**siebzig**	*zeep-tsig*
80	**achtzig**	*uhkht-tsig*
90	**neunzig**	*noyn-tsig*
100	**hundert**	*hoond't*
1,000	**tausend**	*towz'nt*
1,000,000	**eine Million**	*ine-uh mill-yon*

TIME

one minute	**eine Minute**	*ine-uh min-oot-uh*
one hour	**eine Stunde**	*ine-uh shtoond-uh*
half an hour	**eine halbe Stunde**	*ine-uh hullb-uh shtoond-uh*
Monday	**Montag**	*mohn-targ*
Tuesday	**Dienstag**	*deens-targ*
Wednesday	**Mittwoch**	*mitt-vokh*
Thursday	**Donnerstag**	*donn-ers-targ*
Friday	**Freitag**	*fry-targ*
Saturday	**Samstag/**	*zums-targ*
	Sonnabend	*zonn-ah-bent*
Sunday	**Sonntag**	*zon-targ*
January	**Januar**	*yan-ooar*
February	**Februar**	*fay-brooar*
March	**März**	*mairts*
April	**April**	*april*
May	**Mai**	*my*
June	**Juni**	*yoo-ni*
July	**Juli**	*yoo-lee*
August	**August**	*ow-goost*
September	**September**	*zep-tem-ber*
October	**Oktober**	*ok-toh-ber*
November	**November**	*no-vem-ber*
December	**Dezember**	*day-tsem-ber*
spring	**Frühling**	*froo-ling*
summer	**Sommer**	*zomm-er*
autumn (fall)	**Herbst**	*hairpst*
winter	**Winter**	*vint-er*

ACKNOWLEDGMENTS

DK would like to thank the following for their contribution to the previous edition: Paul Sullivan, Marc Di Duca, Joanna Egert-Romanowska, Małgorzata Omilanowska, Helen Peters

The publisher would like to thank the following for their kind permission to reproduce their photographs:

Key: a-above; b-below/bottom; c-centre; f-far; l-left; r-right; t-top

123RF.com: Nikolay Antonov 366-7t; avtg 40br; preve beatrice 238-9b; Thanawat Chawpetthai 292t; Anton Ivanov 128t; jovannig 60t; Bernd Keller 320-1b; lianem 148-9b; William Perry 150br; Łukasz Stefański 34-5b.

4Corners: Martin Brunner 271t; Francesco Carovillano 328-9; Cornelia Dörr 143; Sabine Lubenow 469cl, 482-3t; Douglas Pearson 314-5b; Maurizio Rellini 52bl, 144; Luca Da Ros 474t; Reinhard Schmid 13crb, 52cl, 124, 276-7b.

akg-images: 388br, 471tr; Book cover of the Brother Grimm's "Kindermärchen": Edited by Paul Moritz, published in Stuttgart (K.Thienemann), undated (c. 1920). With cover vignette "Cinderella" after illustration by Paul Hey 374tr.

Alamy Stock Photo: A Media Press 74crb; AA World Travel Library 267cr; Michael Abid 230-1t; age fotostock 12-3b, 235br; Agencja Fotograficzna Caro 21cl, 384br, / Andreas Teich 67br; ALLTRAVEL 28-9t; Arcaid Images 444tl; Archivart 173cr; Archive PL 361tl; GL Archive 319br; Arco Images GmbH 118bl, 195br, 311br, 400-1t; The Archives 439cr; Arterra Picture Library 456bl; ASK Images 30-1t, 221br; Aurelian Images 346tr; B.O'Kane 246tr, 287cr; Peter Baum 153bc; Berlin-Zeitgeist 75bl; Bildagentur-online / Exß 178b, / Schoening 113tr; Bildarchiv Monheim GmbH 122br, 140-1b, 141cr, 316tl, 441br; Kerstin Bittner 462bl; Blickwinkel 249c, 398b, 408t, 463; Hans Blossey 406bl; Sergey Borisov 370-1; Eden Breitz 83br; Michael Brooks 93br; Chronicle 42cla, 93bc; Classic Image 42-3t; Cultura RM 287tr; Simon Curtis 341cra; Ian G Dagnall 40tl, 218-9t, 342t, 393cla, 342; Design Pics Inc 295cra; Diadem Images / Jonathan Larsen 193br, 444-5b; dieKleinert 215cr; Alesia Dmitrienko 285bl; doc-stock 130-1b; DPA picture alliance archive 14clb, 15cr, 42tl, 45bc, 62br, 62-3t, 128cr, 181br, 192b, 217tl, 426b, © DACS 2018 435tr, / Marijan Murat 298tl, / Armin Weigel 131cl; dpa-Zentralbild / Martin Schutt 53bl, 184-5; dpict 377br; Eva Agata Draze 63cl; Sergey Dzyuba 156t, 283b, 325t; Adam Eastland 75cb; Edpics 318bl; Andreas von Einsiedel 358crb; Eye Ubiquitous 87tl, 151ca; F1online digitale Bildagentur GmbH 269bl, 476-7b, 479t; Falkensteinfoto 39tr, 142tc; Flintsquare Photography 295cb; FocusTechnology 237tr; Peter Forsberg 236-7b; Eddy Galeotti 93cr; Bildagentur Geduldig 321tr; Manfred Gottschalk 45tr; Tim Graham 455tr; Uwe Grün 20tr; Ezio Gutzemberg 44cr; Hemis 60bl, 116tc; 313br; 431br; Heritage Image Partnership Ltd 25cl, 267clb; Julian Herzog 296t; Arnulf Hettrich 298-9b; Johann Hinrichs 221tr, 228t; Historic Images 40cb, 299tr; Historical image collection by Bildagentur-online 38bl; Heinz Tschanz-Hofmann 268t; Peter Horree 41bc, 193cla; HTHphoto 309br, 327br; Ulf Huebner 283crb; imageBROKER 23crb, 29cl, 44-5t, 77tr, 84-5t, 149bc, 159tr, 166br, 174b, 191cra, 196tl, 201br, 238tl, 240bl, 256bl, 259tr, 274bl, 276tr, 307c, 310t, 338cla, 363br, 366bl, 373tl, 373br, 374bl, 379b, 399tl, 410tl, 458-9b, 472-3b, 473cla; Incamerastock 247cla; IndustryAndTravel 384cr; Interfoto 39cb, 218clb, 219cb, 219bc, 234bl, 352bl, 353br, 217 cr; iWebbtravel 267cra; Jam World Images 281tr; Jean 312tl; Kim Kaminski 292cl; John Kellerman 97tl; Gunter Kirsch 478b; Indranil Kishor 292cr; Sergii Koval 16crb; Kraftfoto 360br; Daniel Kühne 161b; Maris Kurme 402t; Kuttig - Travel 442b; Victor Lacken 324bl; Lanmas 39cra, 41tr; LH Images 226bl; LOOK Die Bildagentur der Fotografen GmbH 29crb, 100-1br, 138-9t, 160cl, 230br, 233tr, 368-9b, 460t; Lumi Imagel 54cl; Cro Magnon 195tl; Iain Masterton; 75crb, 82tr, 94t, 96b, 98b, 114cra, 128br, 158t, 172bl, 173br, 387bl, / © DACS 2018100tl, 171br; mauritius images GmbH 36br, 123br, 200br, 212cr, 292bl, 362-3t, 468-9b; Michel Meijer 115br; Bernd Mellmann 407t; Katho Menden 340-1; MJ Photography 140tl; Novarc Images 149cra, 154-5t, 189tr, 194t, 201t, 270bl, 280-1b, 447tr; Rupert Oberhäuser 344bc; Werner Otto 120tl, 445tr; PAINTING 454br; Panther Media GmbH 180-1b, 478crb, 480tl; Sean Pavone 286bl, 482bl; Philipus 422br; Pictorial Press Ltd 135tr; Jenny Pohl 181tr; Vladimir Pomortzeff 219clb; The Print Collector 173cra; Prisma Archivo 218clb, 218br, 391tr; Prisma by Dukas Presseagentur GmbH 120clb, 111crb; 351bl; Simon Reddy 430br; Dirk Renckhoff 422clb; Ricardo Ribas 108-9; robertharding 170tl, 282tl, 367br, / Markus Lange 37bl;

McPhoto / Rolfes 459tr; A Room With Views 247tr; Rudi1976 247tl, 284-5t; Paul Rushton 78tl; Peter Schickert 225cr, 404t, 461tr; Sculpies 318-9t; ShootingCompany 410-1b; Shotshop GmbH 149cr, 151tc; Roman Sigaev 232b, 436bl; Michal Sikorski 152bl; Witold Skrypczak 175t; Friedrich Stark 408bl; Focke Strangmann 427br; Boris Stroujko 251br; Sueddeutsche Zeitung Photo 79b; Jochen Tack 338clb; Geoffrey Taunton 219br; The History Collection 39bc; The Picture Art Collection 38cb; travelbild-germany 112-3b; travelbild.com 180ca; TravelCollection 346-7b, 360t, 362br; Travelstock44 216cr, 246cra, 256-7tc; Trinity Mirror / Mirrorpix 42crb, 43br, 44tl; Igor Tumarkin 340cla; Jorge Tutor 393tl; Urbanmyth 13br, / © DACS 2018 18tr; UtCon Collection 112tr; Lucas Vallecillos 66-7t; Ivan Vdovin 218bc; velislava 136bl; Steve Vidler 212bl, 265cr; Volkerpreusser 138bc, 248tl, 278bl, 345br; Dieter Wanke 473tl; Alexander Weickart 128cl; Westend61 GmbH 30tc; 158b, 300-1, 348t, 349br, / Michael Runkel 338-9b; Scott Wilson 264t, 266-7; Julie g Woodhouse 103br, 134 5b, 190t; World History Archive 24 5b, 93clb, 111cr; Ernst Wrba 378tl; Zoonar GmbH 149tl, 218cra, 384cl, 400bl, 405b, 409br, 454clb, 477tr.

AWL Images: Peter Adams 484-5; Marco Bottigelli 202-3; Sabine Lubenow 33cl, 59tl, 88-9, 417bl, 464-5; Travel Pix Collection 217clb.

Bleiche Resort & Spa: Nikolaj Georgiew 131cb.

Bridgeman Images: Alte Pinakothek, Munich215cla.

Depositphotos Inc: jovannig 177br; S_Kohl 108br; konrad. kerker 59cb, 104; sepavone 364t; Toyechkina 136-7t.

Deutsches Museum: 28-9b, 214-5b, 222cb, 222-23c 223cra, 223cr, 223br.

Dorling Kindersley: Peter Wilson 295br.

Dreamstime.com: Rostislav Ageev 232clb; Aldorado10 120-1b; Aragami12345 446bl; Balipadma 175br; Biathlonua 473tr; Kirill Bobrov 21br; Boggy 230tl; Boris Breytman 250-1t, 263tr, 272tl; Daliu80 8-9b; Dirk E. Ellmer 280tr; Alexandre Fagundes De Fagundes 108cl; Evgeniy Fesenko 27br; Peter Fuchs 344-5t; Klaus Hoffmann 365tr; Ildipapp 31br; Irisz 240t; Jamiemaio 315tr; Bernd Juergens 271cla; Sergey Kelin 64-5b; Vassiliy Kochetkov 117tr; Ivan Kravtsov 403br; Laurentiuq 294-5t; Mikhail Markovskiy 229bl; Mijeshots 196cla; Minnystock 22t, 258; Christian Mueringer 372clb; Nellmac 80tl; Oleks2ds 60cr; Felix Pergande 197b; Patrick Poendl 339cl; Jan Schneckenhaus 416c, 418-9; Siempreverde22 440-1t; Vof Vermeulen Perdaen & Steyaert 284clb; Tarawa 157tc; Anibal Trejo 95bl; Val_th 27cb; Venemama 341tl; Wibaimages 8clb; Xantana 274-5; Yorgy67 108clb; Andreas Zerndl 272-3b.

Getty Images: AFP / Odd Andersen 45clb; Ulrich Baumgarten 44crb; Adam Berry 60crb; Buyenlarge 25br; Ventura Carmona 333tl, 354; Cultura Exclusive / Stephen Lux 207t, 242-3; De Agostini / Biblioteca Ambrosiana 42bc, / A. Dagli Orti 267bc; Werner Dieterich 132t; DigitalVision / Walter Bibikow 26tr; EyeEm / Johannes Hulsch 249tl, / Karsten Müller 176-7t, / Ole Spata 30-1b; Sean Gallup 114t; Gerdtromm 438t; Alexander Hassenstein 13t; Historic Map Works LLC and Osher Map Library 38t; Hulton Deutsch / Corbis 43cb; Keystone-France / Gamma-Keystone 44bl; Joerg Koch 216-7b; LightRocket / Olaf Protze 179tr; Hans Lippert 4; LOOK-foto / Florian Werner 217cla; Sabine Lubenow 54-5, 73tr, 417t, 450-1; Harald Nachtmann 248b; NATO 110crb; Kristian Peetz 460br; Photolibrary / Hans-Peter Merten 156-7b; PPAMPicture 412-3; Redferns / Frank Hoensch 19cl; Matthias Rietschel 26-7b; Stocktrek Images / Jinn Parrot 41crb; Jochen Tack 375b; TASS 43tr; Ullstein Bild / Chronos Media GmbH 110bc, / Rolf Schulten 92br, / Anke Thomass 214-5t, / XAMAX 19tr; Ron Watts 74-5t; Westend61 249tl, 448, 468-9t; Valentin Wolf 2-3.

Haus der Kunst: Markus Tretter 233br.

iStockphoto.com: 77studio 393tr, 397tr; Acnakelsy 457bl; 470t; Altmodern 279t; AM-C 339cra; AnkNet 309cla; bbsferrari 332c, 334-5; Benedek 65tr; Bluejayphoto 34t, 35cla, 54-5, 58c, 68-9, 80-1b, 250bl, 254t, 262t, 302t,428t; bpperry 150t; Andrey Danilovich 37br, 116-7b; Simon Dannhauer 32-3t; DaveLongMedia 260-1; DawidMarkiewicz 110cr; DerLue 475cr; DieterMeyrl 15br, 23cl, 33cb, 48-9; DimaBerkut 14t; duncan1890 39tl; E+ / Kerrick 198-9, / Juergen Sack 188t; ewg3D 32br; freie-kreation 18cr; Georgeclerk 422cl; GeorgHanf 35cr; graphia76 27tr; Grafissimo 16cr, 212cl; mf-guddyx 429tr, 430-1t; holgs 63br; Horstgerlach 351tr, 394-5; hsvrs 66bl; Igmarx 434t; imagemanufaktur 76ca; instamatics 327tl; Xu Jian 307cra; Jotily 19tl, 386t, 432-3; justhavealook 333cb, 380-1; JWackenhut 307br, 314cl; lesart777 86bl; LianeM 183cra; LiliGraphie 339tl; LordRunar 110-1t; MarekKijevsky 53t, 162;

A NOTE FROM DK EYEWITNESS

The rapid rate at which the world is changing is
constantly keeping the DK Eyewitness team on our
toes. While we've worked hard to ensure that this
edition of Germany is accurate and up-to-date, we know
that opening hours alter, standards shift, prices
fluctuate, places close and new ones pop up in their
stead. So, if you notice we've got something wrong
or left something out, we want to hear about it.
Please get in touch at travelguides@dk.com

Penguin Random House

This edition updated by

Contributors Petra Falkenberg,
Paul Sullivan

Senior Editor Alison McGill

Senior Designer Vinita Venugopal

Project Editors Parnika Bagla, Danielle Watt

Project Art Editor Bharti Karakoti

Editors Avanika, Arushi Mathur,
Chhavi Nagpal, Lucy Sara-Kelly, Mark Silas

Picture Research Coordinator
Sumita Khatwani

Assistant Picture Research Administrator
Vagisha Pushp

Jacket Coordinator Bella Talbot

Jacket Designer Laura O'Brien

Senior Cartographic Editor Subhashree Bharati

Cartography Manager Suresh Kumar

DTP Designer Tanveer Zaidi

Senior Production Editor Jason Little

Production Controller Kariss Ainsworth

Managing Editors Shikha Kulkarni,
Hollie Teague

Deputy Managing Editor Beverly Smart

Managing Art Editors Bess Daly,
Priyanka Thakur

Art Director Maxine Pedliham

Publishing Director Georgina Dee

First edition 2001

Published in Great Britain by Dorling Kindersley Limited,
One Embassy Gardens, 8 Viaduct Gardens, London SW11 7BW

Published in the United States by DK Publishing,
1450 Broadway, Suite 801, New York, NY 10018

Copyright © 2001, 2021 Dorling Kindersley Limited
A Penguin Random House Company
21 22 23 24 10 9 8 7 6 5 4 3 2 1

A CIP catalogue record for this book
is available from the British Library.

A catalogue record for this book is available
from the Library of Congress.

ISSN: 1542 1554
ISBN: 978 0 2414 6278 2

Printed and bound in China.

www.dk.com